Y0-AGT-806

Preface

How is food digested? What is DNA fingerprinting? How do anesthetics work?

For all of these questions, chemistry provides an answer. Chemistry, the study of matter, is essential for understanding the physical world, from acid rain to gene therapy to the ozone layer. Chemical laboratory tests are a routine part of medical care. The functioning of our bodies is a result of thousands of biochemical reactions. To study life, you must first study chemistry.

Both the textbook and this *Study Guide and Solutions Manual* are designed to be as helpful as possible to you in your chemistry course. The textbook contains numerous solved problems that show you techniques for solving specific types of chemistry problems. In addition, the text includes applications of the material in each chapter to contemporary science problems. This Study Guide consists of several types of study aids: detailed solutions to all textbook problems, outlines of the chapters, and self-tests.

The following suggestions may help you:

1. *Attend all classes.* Although it's possible to learn chemistry just by reading the textbook and study guide, a lecturer makes difficult topics much easier to understand and ties together seemingly unrelated topics.

2. *Read the textbook.* The best way to study is to skim the chapter to be covered before class, and then to read it more thoroughly after the lecturer has discussed the material. Use the textbook to help you understand subjects you find especially difficult. It is also helpful to use the chapter outlines in the *Study Guide* after reading the textbook.

3. *Work the problems.* Start by reading carefully the Solved Problems in the textbook. Next, try to work the Practice Problems, using the steps outlined in the Solved Problems. Finally, attempt the Additional Problems at the end of the chapter. Although this *Study Guide and Solutions Manual* has detailed solutions to all text problems, it's better to use the solutions in this book as a last resort. You will learn more if you first struggle a bit with a problem before checking its answer, than if you look up the answer right away.

4. Use the supplementary material in the *Study Guide* to help you review each chapter. The chapter outlines organize and restate both the major themes of each chapter and the detailed contents. Go over the list of key terms in the textbook to make sure that you know the meaning of each important term. Test yourself with the self-tests, which include multiple choice, sentence completions, matching, and true/false questions.

Acknowledgments

I would like to thank the following people for their assistance with this book: John McMurry (of course), David Ballantine, Virginia Peterson, Carl Hoeger, Donna Young, Kristen Kaiser, Jennifer Hart, and Edward Tisko. I am grateful to my entire family for their patience and support.

STUDY GUIDE AND SELECTED SOLUTIONS MANUAL

SUSAN E. McMURRY

Fundamentals of GENERAL, ORGANIC, and BIOLOGICAL CHEMISTRY

Fifth Edition

McMURRY CASTELLION BALLANTINE

PEARSON Prentice Hall

Upper Saddle River, NJ 07458

Assistant Editor: Jennifer Hart
Senior Editor: Kent Porter Hamann
Editor-in-Chief, Science: Dan Kaveney
Executive Managing Editor: Kathleen Schiaparelli
Senior Managing Editor: Nicole M. Jackson
Assistant Managing Editor: Karen Bosch
Production Editor: Debbie Ryan
Supplement Cover Mgmt/Design: Paul Gourhan/Christopher Kossa
Manufacturing Buyer: Ilene Kahn
Manufacturing Manager: Alexis Heydt-Long
Cover Photo Credit: Denis Anthony Valentine/CORBIS

PEARSON Prentice Hall

© 2007 Pearson Education, Inc.
Pearson Prentice Hall
Pearson Education, Inc.
Upper Saddle River, NJ 07458

All rights reserved. No part of this book may be reproduced in any form or by any means, without permission in writing from the publisher.

Pearson Prentice Hall™ is a trademark of Pearson Education, Inc.

The author and publisher of this book have used their best efforts in preparing this book. These efforts include the development, research, and testing of the theories and programs to determine their effectiveness. The author and publisher make no warranty of any kind, expressed or implied, with regard to these programs or the documentation contained in this book. The author and publisher shall not be liable in any event for incidental or consequential damages in connection with, or arising out of, the furnishing, performance, or use of these programs.

This work is protected by United States copyright laws and is provided solely for teaching courses and assessing student learning. Dissemination or sale of any part of this work (including on the World Wide Web) will destroy the integrity of the work and is not permitted. The work and materials from it should never be made available except by instructors using the accompanying text in their classes. All recipients of this work are expected to abide by these restrictions and to honor the intended pedagogical purposes and the needs of other instructors who rely on these materials.

Printed in the United States of America

10 9 8 7 6 5 4 3 2 1

ISBN 0-13-187749-6

Pearson Education Ltd., *London*
Pearson Education Australia Pty. Ltd., *Sydney*
Pearson Education Singapore, Pte. Ltd.
Pearson Education North Asia Ltd., *Hong Kong*
Pearson Education Canada, Inc., *Toronto*
Pearson Educación de Mexico, S.A. de C.V.
Pearson Education—Japan, *Tokyo*
Pearson Education Malaysia, Pte. Ltd.

Contents

Chapter 1 Matter, Energy, and Life 1
Chapter 2 Measurements in Chemistry 7
Chapter 3 Atoms and the Periodic Table 21
Chapter 4 Ionic Compounds 33
Chapter 5 Molecular Compounds 43
Chapter 6 Chemical Reactions: Classification and Mass Relationships 58
Chapter 7 Chemical Reactions: Energy, Rates, and Equilibrium 75
Chapter 8 Gases, Liquids, and Solids 88
Chapter 9 Solutions 106
Chapter 10 Acids and Bases 121
Chapter 11 Nuclear Chemistry 136
Chapter 12 Introduction to Organic Chemistry: Alkanes 147
Chapter 13 Alkenes, Alkynes, and Aromatic Compounds 164
Chapter 14 Some Compounds with Oxygen, Sulfur, or Halogens 185
Chapter 15 Amines 202
Chapter 16 Aldehydes and Ketones 216
Chapter 17 Carboxylic Acids and Their Derivatives 232
Chapter 18 Amino Acids and Proteins 254
Chapter 19 Enzymes and Vitamins 276
Chapter 20 Chemical Messengers 287
Chapter 21 The Generation of Biochemical Energy 300
Chapter 22 Carbohydrates 312
Chapter 23 Carbohydrate Metabolism 332
Chapter 24 Lipids 344
Chapter 25 Lipid Metabolism 360
Chapter 26 Nucleic Acids and Protein Synthesis 371
Chapter 27 Genomics 386
Chapter 28 Protein and Amino Acid Metabolism 394
Chapter 29 Body Fluids 406

Answers to Self Tests 415

Chapter 1 – Matter, Energy, and Life

Chapter Outline

I. Matter and its properties (Sections 1.1–1.2).
  A. Matter is anything that is physically real (Section 1.1).
  B. Properties are the characteristics of matter.
    1. Physical properties are those properties that can be measured without altering the identity of a substance. Examples include mass, melting point, boiling point, color.
    2. Chemical properties must be determined by changing the identity of the substance. Examples include rusting, combustion, and chemical reactivity.
    3. A physical change does not alter the identity of a substance.
    4. A chemical change is a process in which one or more substances undergoes a change in identity.
  C. States of matter (Section 1.2).
    1. The states of matter are solid, liquid, and gas.
      a. Solids have definite volume and definite shape.
      b. Liquids have definite volume and indefinite shape.
      c. Gases have indefinite volume and indefinite shape.
    2. Changes of state are melting, boiling, condensing, freezing.

II. Classification of matter (Sections 1.3–1.6).
  A. Mixtures (Section 1.3).
    1. Mixtures vary in composition and properties.
    2. Mixtures can be separated by physical methods.
  B. Pure substances.
    1. Pure substances include chemical compounds and chemical elements.
    2. Pure substances don't vary in composition and properties.
    3. Chemical compounds can be broken down to elements by chemical change.
      a. A chemical reaction represents a chemical change between pure substances (Section 1.4).
      b. In a chemical reaction, the reactants are written on the left, the products are written on the right, and an arrow connects them
    4. Chemical elements can't be broken down.
  C. Elements (Sections 1.5-1.6).
    1. There are 114 elements; 90 of them occur naturally.
    2. Elements are represented by one or two-letter symbols.
    3. The symbols for elements can be combined to produce chemical formulas.
    4. Elements are presented in a table – the periodic table.
    5. Elements can be classified as metals, nonmetals or metalloids.
      a. Metals are solids that are lustrous, brittle, malleable, and good conductors of heat and electricity.
      b. Nonmetals may be solid, liquid, or gas and are poor conductors.
      c. Metalloids have characteristics intermediate between metals and nonmetals.

Solutions to Chapter 1 Problems

1.1 All of the listed items are made of chemicals. A goldfish (b) and a watermelon (d) consist of "natural" chemicals; hairspray (a) and paint (c) consist of "synthetic" chemicals.

1.2 *Change in physical properties*: (a) grinding a metal surface; (d) a puddle evaporating
Change in chemical properties: (b) fruit ripening (c) wood burning

1.3 Formaldehyde is a gas at room temperature (25°C).

1.4 At 10°C, acetic acid is a solid.

1.5 *Mixtures*: (a) concrete; (d) wood
Pure substances: (b) helium; (c) a lead weight

1.6 *Physical changes*: (a) separation by filtration; (c) mixing alcohol and water
Chemical changes: (b) production of carbon dioxide by heating limestone

1.7 (a) U = uranium; (b) Ti = titanium; (c) W = tungsten; (d) Nd = neodymium;
(e) I = iodine; (f) H = hydrogen

1.8 (a) Na = sodium; (b) Ca = calcium; (c) Pd = palladium; (d) K = potassium
(e) Sr = strontium; (f) Sn = tin

1.9 (a) Ammonia (NH_3) contains one nitrogen atom and three hydrogen atoms.
(b) Sodium bicarbonate ($NaHCO_3$) contains one sodium atom, one hydrogen atom, one carbon atom, and three oxygen atoms.
(c) Octane (C_8H_{18}) contains eight carbon atoms and eighteen hydrogen atoms.
(d) Vitamin C ($C_6H_8O_6$) contains six carbon atoms, eight hydrogen atoms, and six oxygen atoms.

1.10

Element	*Name*	*Number in Periodic Table*
(a) Cr	chromium	24
(b) Na	sodium	11
(c) P	phosphorus	15
(d) Rn	radon	86

1.11

(a) B	boron	5
(b) Si	silicon	14
(c) Ge	germanium	32
(d) As	arsenic	33
(e) Sb	antimony	51
(f) Te	tellurium	52
(g) At	astatine	85

The metalloids occur at the boundary between metals and nonmetals.

Understanding Key Concepts

1.12 From top to bottom: helium (He), neon (Ne), argon (Ar), krypton (Kr), xenon (Xe), radon (Rn).

1.13 From top to bottom: copper (Cu), silver (Ag), gold (Au)

1.14 Blue: argon (Ar) – nonmetal
Green: arsenic (As) – metalloid
Red: yttrium (Y) – metal

1.15 The element, americium (Am), is a metal.

Chemistry and the Properties of Matter

1.16 Chemistry is the study of matter – its nature, properties and transformations.

1.18 *Physical changes:* (a) boiling water; (c) dissolving sugar in water; (e) breaking of glass
Chemical changes: (b) decomposing water by passing a current through it; (d) exploding of potassium when placed in water

States and Classification of Matter

1.20 A *gas* is a substance that has no definite shape or volume.
A *liquid* has no definite shape but has a definite volume.
A *solid* has a definite volume and a definite shape.

1.22 Sulfur dioxide is a gas at 25°C.

1.24 *Mixtures:* (a) pea soup; (b) seawater; (d) urine; (f) multivitamin tablet
Pure substances: (c) C_3H_8; (e) lead

1.26 *Element:* (a) aluminum foil
Compounds: (b) table salt; (c) water
Mixtures: (d) air; (e) banana; (f) notebook paper

1.28

Reactant		*Products*		
Hydrogen peroxide	⟶	water	+	oxygen
chemical compound		*chemical compound*		*element*

Elements and Their Symbols

1.30 114 elements are presently known; 90 elements occur naturally.

1.32 *Metals* are elements that are solids at room temperature (except for Hg), are lustrous and malleable, and are good conductors of heat and electricity.

Nonmetals are elements that are gases or brittle solids (except for Br) and are poor conductors.

Metalloids are elements that have properties intermediate between those of metals and nonmetals.

1.34 (a) Gadolinium (Gd); (b) Germanium (Ge); (c) Technetium (Tc); (d) Arsenic (As); (e) Cadmium (Cd)

1.36 (a) nitrogen; (b) potassium; (c) chlorine; (d) calcium; (e) phosphorus; (f) manganese

1.38 The first letter of a chemical symbol is always capitalized; the second letter, if any, is never capitalized. Thus, Co stands for cobalt, and CO stands for carbon monoxide, a compound composed of carbon (C) and oxygen (O).

1.40 (a) The symbol for bromine is Br (the second letter in a symbol is never capitalized).
(b) The symbol for manganese is Mn (Mg is the symbol for magnesium).
(c) The symbol for carbon is C (Ca is the symbol for calcium).
(d) The symbol for potassium is K; the first letter of an element is always capitalized.

1.42 (a) "Fool's gold" is a compound with the formula CuS; the symbol for copper is Cu.
(b) The formula for "laughing gas" is N_2O; the symbol for nitrogen is N.

1.44 (a) $MgSO_4$: magnesium, sulfur, oxygen
(b) $FeBr_2$: iron, bromine
(c) CoP: cobalt, phosphorus
(d) AsH_3: arsenic, hydrogen
(e) $CaCr_2O_7$: calcium, chromium, oxygen

1.46 Carbon, hydrogen, nitrogen, and oxygen are present in glycine. The formula $C_2H_5NO_2$ represents 10 atoms.

1.48 Ibuprofen: $C_{13}H_{18}O_2$

1.50 (a) Osmium (Os) is a metal.
(b) Xenon (Xe) is a nonmetal.

Applications

1.52 (no answer)

General Questions and Problems

1.54 (a) A *physical change* is a change in the property of a substance that doesn't alter its chemical makeup. A *chemical change* alters a substance's chemical makeup.
(b) *Melting point* is the temperature at which a change of state from solid to liquid occurs. *Boiling point* is the temperature at which a change of state from liquid to gas occurs.
(c) An *element* is a pure substance that can't be broken down chemically into simpler substances. A *compound* is a pure substance that has a definite composition and that can be broken down chemically to yield elements. A *mixture* can vary in both composition and properties, and its components can be separated by physical methods.
(d) A *chemical symbol* is composed of one or two letters and represents an element. A *chemical formula* is a grouping of chemical symbols that gives the number of atoms for each element in a chemical compound.
(e) A *reactant* is a substance that undergoes change in a chemical reaction. A *product* is a substance formed as a result of a chemical reaction.
(f) A *metal* is a lustrous malleable element that is a good conductor of heat and electricity; a *nonmetal* is an element that is a poor conductor.

1.56 *Chemical compounds:* (a) H_2O_2; (d) NO; (e) $NaHCO_3$
Elements: (b) Mo; (c) C

1.58 The liquid is a mixture.

1.60 (a) Fe; (b) Cu; (c) Co; (d) Mo; (e) Cr; (f) F; (g) S

1.62 If the undiscovered elements follow the pattern of the periodic table, element 115 would be placed below bismuth and would be a metal. Element 117 would be placed below astatine and might be either a metal or a metalloid. Element 119 would be placed below francium and would be a metal.

Self-Test for Chapter 1

Multiple Choice

1. Which of the following is a chemical property?
(a) melting point (b) reaction with acid (c) hardness (d) transparency

2. The change of state that occurs when a gas is cooled to a liquid is called:
(a) boiling (b) melting (c) evaporation (d) condensation

3. Which of the following is not an element?
(a) fluorine (b) freon (c) neon (d) radon

4. The chemical formula for fructose is $C_6H_{12}O_6$. How many different elements does fructose contain?
(a) 24 (b) 18 (c) 6 (d) 3

5. How many atoms does the formula for fructose represent?
(a) 24 (b) 18 (c) 6 (d) 3

6. A solution of fructose in water is a:
(a) mixture (b) pure substance (c) chemical compound (d) element

7. Which of the following is not a characteristic of a metal?
(a) electrical conductivity (b) malleability (c) brittleness (d) luster

8. All of the following have uniform composition except: (a) element (b) solution (c) pure substance (d) chemical compound

Sentence Completion

1. Sulfur is a _________element.

2. Color is a ____________ property.

3. ____ is the symbol for the element bismuth.

4. When a substance ________, it changes from gas to liquid.

5. Matter is anything that has _______ and _______.

6. A _______ has definite volume but indefinite shape.

7. A ______ ______ doesn't vary in its properties or composition.

8. Symbols of elements are combined to produce _______ _______.

9. A ________ substance can be beaten or rolled into different shapes.

10. ____, ____, ____, and ____ are four elements present in all living organisms.

True or False

1. Cobalt is an element essential for human life.

2. Rust formation is a chemical change.

3. A chemical compound is a pure substance.

4. The components of a solution are separable by chemical methods.

5. The formula C_2H_4O represents three atoms.

6. A metalloid has properties intermediate between metals and nonmetals.

7. The chemical symbol for silver is Si.

8. In the chemical reaction carbon + oxygen —> carbon dioxide, the reactants are elements.

9. Methyl bromide, a compound formerly used for fumigation, has a melting point of –93.7 °C and a boiling point of 3.6 °C and is a liquid at room temperature.

10. Nonmetals may be solids, liquids or gases.

Chapter 2 – Measurements in Chemistry

Chapter Outline

I. Measurements (Sections 2.1–2.3).
  A. Physical quantities (Section 2.1).
    1. All physical quantities consist of a number plus a unit.
      a. SI units, the standard units for scientists, are the kilogram, the meter, and the Kelvin.
      b. Metric units are the gram, the meter, the liter and the degree Celsius.
      c. Other units, such as those for speed and concentration, can be derived from SI and metric units.
    2. Prefixes are used with units to indicate multiples of 10.
  B. Measuring mass (Section 2.2).
    1. Mass is the amount of matter in a substance.
    2. Mass differs from weight (a measure of the gravitational pull exerted on an object).
    3. The SI unit of mass is the kilogram, but in chemistry the gram and milligram are more often used.
  C. Measuring length (Section 2.3).
    The meter is the standard unit for length.
  D. Measuring volume.
    1. Volume is the amount of space that a substance occupies.
    2. Units for volume are the liter (L) and the cubic meter (m^3) — the SI unit.

II. Numbers in measurement (Sections 2.4–2.6).
  A. Significant figures (Section 2.4).
    1. All measurements have a degree of uncertainty.
    2. For any measurement, the number of digits known with certainty, plus one digit considered uncertain, is known as the number of significant figures.
    3. Rules for significant figures:
      a. Zeroes in the middle of a number are always significant.
      b. Zeroes at the beginning of a number are never significant.
      c. Zeroes at the end of a number but after a decimal point are significant.
      d. Zeroes at the end of a number but before an implied decimal point may or may not be significant.
    4. Some numbers are exact and have an unlimited number of significant figures,
  B. Scientific notation (Section 2.5).
    1. In scientific notation, a number is written as the product of a number between 1 and 10 times 10 raised to a power.
      a. For numbers greater than 10, the power of 10 is positive.
      b. For numbers less than 1, the power of 10 is negative.
    2. Scientific notation is helpful in indicating the number of significant figures in a number.
  C. Rounding off numbers (Section 2.6).
    1. Numbers must be rounded off if they contain more digits than are significant.
    2. Rounding in calculations.
      a. In multiplication or division, the result can't have more significant figures than any of the original numbers.
      b. In addition or subtraction, the result can't have more digits to the right of the decimal point than any of the original numbers.

3. Rules of rounding:
   a. If the digit to be removed is 4 or less, drop it and remove all following digits.
   b. If the digit to be removed is 5 or greater, add 1 to the digit to the left of the digit you drop.

III. Calculations (Sections 2.7–2.8).
  A. Converting a quantity from one unit to another (Section 2.7).
    1. In the *factor-label* method:
       (quantity in old units) x (conversion factor) = (quantity in new units)
       a. The conversion factor is a fraction that converts one unit to another.
       b. All conversion factors are equal to 1.
    2. In the factor-label method, units are treated as numbers.
    3. In the factor-label method, all unwanted units cancel.
  B. Problem solving (Section 2.8).
    1. Identify the information known.
    2. Identify the information needed in the answer.
    3. Use conversion factors to convert the given information to the answer.
    4. Make a "ballpark" estimate of the answer and compare it to the calculated answer.

IV. Heat (Sections 2.9–2.10).
  A. Measuring temperature (Section 2.9).
    1. Units of temperature are the degree Fahrenheit, the degree Celsius, and the Kelvin.
    2. Temperature in °C = Temperature in K – 273.15°.
    3. $°F = \left(\frac{9°F}{5°C} \times °C\right) + 32°F$.
    4. $°C = \frac{5°C}{9°F} \times (°F - 32°F)$.
  B. Heat and energy (Section 2.10).
    1. All chemical reactions are accompanied by a change in energy.
       a. Potential energy is stored energy.
       b. Kinetic energy is the energy of motion.
    2. Heat is the energy transferred from a hotter object to a cooler object when the two are in contact.
    3. Units of energy are the joule and the calorie.
    4. $\text{Specific heat} = \frac{\text{calories}}{\text{grams} \times °C}$.

V. Density and specific gravity (Sections 2.11–2.12).
  A. Density (Section 2.11).
    1. Density = mass (g) / volume (mL or cm^3).
    2. Density is temperature dependent.
  B. Specific gravity (Section 2.12).
    1. $\text{Specific gravity} = \frac{\text{density of substance (g/mL)}}{\text{density of water (1 g/mL)}}$.
    2. Specific gravity has no units.

Solutions to Chapter 2 Problems

2.1 (a) mL = milliliter (b) kg = kilogram (c) cm = centimeter
(d) km = kilometer (e) μg = microgram

2.2 (a) liter = L (b) microliter = μL (c) nanometer = nm
(d) megameter = Mm

2.3 (a) 1 nm = 0.000 000 001 m (b) 1 dg = 0.1 g (c) 1 km = 1000 m
(d) 1 mL = 0.001 L (e) 1 ng = 0.000 000 001 g

2.4

Number	*Significant Figures*	*Reason*
(a) 3.45 m	3	
(b) 0.1400 kg	4	Rule 3
(c) 10.003 L	5	Rule 1
(d) 35 cents	Exact	

2.5 32.6°C. The answer has three significant figures.

2.6 In scientific notation, a number is written as the product of a number between one and ten times ten raised to a power. In (a), 58 g = 5.8×10^1 g.

Value	*Scientific Notation*
(a) 58 g	5.8×10^1 g
(b) 46,792 m	4.6792×10^4 m
(c) 0.000 672 0 cm	6.720×10^{-4} cm
(d) 345.3 kg	3.453×10^2 kg

2.7

Value in Scientific Notation	*Value in Normal Notation*
(a) 4.885×10^4 mg	48,850 mg
(b) 8.3×10^{-6} m	0.000 008 3 m
(c) 4.00×10^{-2} m	0.0400 m

2.8 (a) 6.0×10^5 (b) 1.300×10^3 (c) 7.942×10^{11}

2.9 0.000 000 000 278 m = 2.78×10^{-10} m. (The decimal point must be moved 10 places to the right.)

$$2.78 \times 10^{-10}\ \text{m} \times \frac{1\ \text{pm}}{10^{-12}\ \text{m}} = 2.78 \times 10^2\ \text{pm}$$

2.10 (a) 2.30 g (b) 188.38 mL (c) 0.009 L (d) 1.000 kg

2.11 Remember:
(1) The sum or difference of two numbers can't have more digits to the right of the decimal point than either of the two numbers.
(2) The product or quotient of two numbers can't have more significant figures than either of the two numbers.

Calculation	*Rounded to:*
(a) 4.87 mL + 46.0 mL = 50.87 mL	50.9 mL
(b) 3.4 x 0.023 g = 0.0782 g	0.078 g
(c) 19.333 m − 7.4 m = 11.933 m	11.9 m
(d) 55 mg − 4.671 mg + 0.894 mg = 51.223 mg	51 mg
(e) 62,911 ÷ 611 = 102.96399	103

2.12

(a) $\dfrac{1\text{ L}}{1000\text{ mL}}, \dfrac{1000\text{ mL}}{1\text{ L}}; \dfrac{1\text{ mL}}{0.001\text{ L}}, \dfrac{0.001\text{ L}}{1\text{ mL}}$

(b) $\dfrac{1\text{ g}}{0.03527\text{ oz}}, \dfrac{0.03527\text{ oz}}{1\text{ g}}; \dfrac{1\text{ oz}}{28.35\text{ g}}, \dfrac{28.35\text{ g}}{1\text{ oz}}$

(c) $\dfrac{1\text{ L}}{1.057\text{ qt}}, \dfrac{1.057\text{ qt}}{1\text{ L}}; \dfrac{1\text{ qt}}{0.9461\text{ L}}, \dfrac{0.9461\text{ L}}{1\text{ qt}}$

2.13

(a) $16.0\text{ oz} \times \dfrac{28.35\text{ g}}{1\text{ oz}} = 454\text{ g}$ (b) $2500\text{ mL} \times \dfrac{1\text{ L}}{1000\text{ mL}} = 2.5\text{ L}$

(c) $99.0\text{ L} \times \dfrac{1\text{ qt}}{0.9461\text{ L}} = 105\text{ qt}$

2.14

$$0.840\text{ quart} \times \frac{1\text{ L}}{1.057\text{ quart}} \times \frac{1000\text{ mL}}{1\text{ L}} = 795\text{ mL}$$

2.15 This is a *long* unit conversion! Remember that all units must cancel at the end, except for the units needed in the final answer (meters and seconds). Nautical miles must be converted to meters, and hours must be converted to seconds. Also remember the definition of a knot – one nautical mile per hour.

$$\frac{14.3\text{ naut. mi}}{1\text{ hr}} \times \frac{6076.1155\text{ ft}}{1\text{ naut. mi}} \times \frac{0.3048\text{ m}}{1\text{ ft}} \times \frac{1\text{ hr}}{60\text{ min}} \times \frac{1\text{ min}}{60\text{ s}} = 7.36\text{ m/s}$$

2.16

(a) $7.5\text{ lb} \times \dfrac{1\text{ kg}}{2.205\text{ lb}} = 3.4\text{ kg}$

Ballpark check: Since a kilogram is approximately 2 pounds, the infant is expected to weigh about 3.5 lb. The ballpark check is close to the exact solution.

(b) $4.0 \text{ oz} \times \dfrac{29.57 \text{ mL}}{1 \text{ oz}} = 120 \text{ mL}$

Ballpark check: There are approximately 30 mL in an ounce, and the ballpark check thus gives an answer of 120 mL, which agrees with the exact solution.
Remember: The answers must have the correct number of significant figures.

2.17

$$2 \times 0.324 \text{ g} \times \frac{1000 \text{ mg}}{1 \text{ g}} \times \frac{1}{135 \text{ lb}} \times \frac{2.205 \text{ lb}}{1 \text{ kg}} = 10.6 \frac{\text{mg}}{\text{kg}}$$

$$2 \times 0.324 \text{ g} \times \frac{1000 \text{ mg}}{1 \text{ g}} \times \frac{1}{40 \text{ lb}} \times \frac{2.205 \text{ lb}}{1 \text{ kg}} = 36 \frac{\text{mg}}{\text{kg}}$$

2.18 From Section 2.9, we find the formula:

$$(°\text{F} - 32°\text{F}) \times \frac{5°\text{C}}{9°\text{F}} = °\text{C}$$

Substituting 136°F into the preceding formula:

$$(136°\text{F} - 32°\text{F}) \times \frac{5°\text{C}}{9°\text{F}} = 57.8°\text{C}$$

Ballpark check: The numerator in the preceding expression is approximately 500°C. Dividing by 9°F gives the answer 55.5°C, which approximates the exact solution.

2.19

$$°\text{F} = \left(\frac{9°\text{F}}{5°\text{C}} \times °\text{C}\right) + 32°\text{F}; \text{ In this problem, } °\text{C} = -38.9°.$$

$$= (1.8°\text{F} \times -38.9°) + 32°\text{F} = -38.0°\text{F}$$

$$= (273.15 - 38.9)\text{K} = 234.3 \text{ K}$$

2.20

$$\text{Heat (cal)} = \text{mass (g)} \times \text{temperature change (°C)} \times \text{specific heat}\left(\frac{\text{cal}}{\text{g} \cdot °\text{C}}\right)$$

$$= 350 \text{ g} \times (25°\text{C} - 3°\text{C}) \times \frac{1.0 \text{ cal}}{\text{g} \cdot °\text{C}}$$

$$= 7700 \text{ cal} = 7.7 \times 10^3 \text{ cal}$$

Ballpark check: The temperature change is approximately 20°C. The mass of Coca-Cola, times the temperature change equals 7000, a number close to the exact solution.

2.21

$$\text{Specific heat} = \frac{\text{calories}}{\text{grams} \times °\text{C}}$$

$$\text{Specific heat} = \frac{161 \text{ cal}}{75 \text{ g} \times 10°\text{C}} = 0.21 \frac{\text{cal}}{\text{g} \cdot °\text{C}}$$

2.22 Solids with densities greater than water will sink; solids with densities less than water will float.
Solids that float: ice, human fat, cork, balsa wood
Solids that sink: gold, table sugar, earth

2.23

$$12.37 \text{ g} \times \frac{1 \text{ mL}}{1.474 \text{ g}} = 8.392 \text{ mL}$$

Ballpark check: Since the density of chloroform is approximately 1.5, the volume needed is about 2/3 of the mass needed.

2.24

$$\text{Density} = \frac{\text{Mass}}{\text{Volume}} = \frac{16.8 \text{ g}}{7.60 \text{ cm}^3} = 2.21 \frac{\text{g}}{\text{cm}^3}$$

2.25 Battery acid is more dense than water.

Understanding Key Concepts

2.26 The graduated cylinder contains 34 mL; the paper clip is 2.7 cm long. Both answers have two significant figures.

2.27 (no answer)

2.28 The specific gravity is found by reading the liquid level on the scale of the hydrometer. The specific gravity of this solution is 0.978.
(a) The answer has three significant figures.
(b) The solution is less dense than water.

2.29

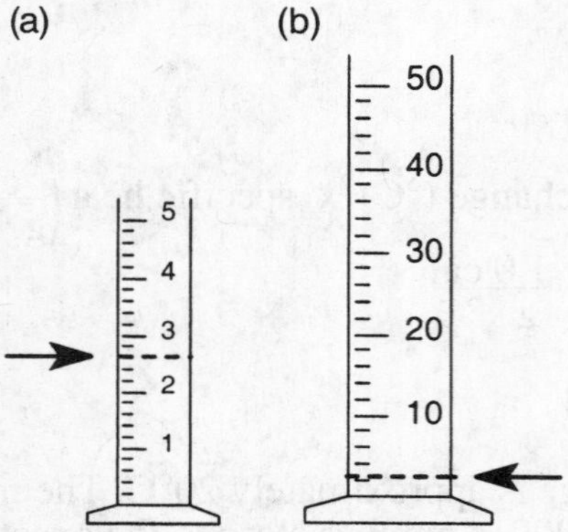

(a)
(b)
5
4
3
2
1
50
40
30
20
10

The smaller graduated cylinder is more accurate for two reasons. (1) The distance between two gradations represents a smaller volume, making it easier to measure volumes more accurately. (2) The percent error is greater when a small volume is measured in a large graduated cylinder.

2.30 The length of the pencil is either 8.0 cm or 3 1/8 in.

2.31 The liquid level is 0.11 mL before dispensing the sample and 0.25 mL after dispensing, indicating a sample size of 0.14 mL.

2.32 (a) Both are equally precise.
(b) The volume is approximately 360 mL; the exact value is 355 mL.

2.33 If two identical hydrometers are placed in ethanol and in chloroform, the hydrometer in chloroform will float higher. Since a hydrometer bulb sinks until it displaces a volume of liquid equal to its mass, it displaces a smaller volume of chloroform, the denser liquid, and the bulb floats higher.

Definitions and Units

2.34 A *physical quantity* is a physical property that can be measured; it consists of a number plus a unit.

2.36

Quantity	*SI Unit*	*Metric Unit*
Mass	kilogram (kg)	gram (g)
Volume	cubic meter (m^3)	liter (L)
Length	meter (m)	meter (m)
Temperature	kelvin (K)	degree Celsius (°C)

2.38 A cubic decimeter and a liter represent the same volume expressed in two different systems of units.

2.40 (a) centiliter (b) decimeter (c) millimeter (d) nanoliter
(e) milligram (f) cubic meter (g) cubic centimeter

2.42

$$1 \text{ mg} \times \frac{10^{-3} \text{ g}}{1 \text{ mg}} \times \frac{10^{12} \text{ pg}}{1 \text{ g}} = 10^{9} \text{ pg}$$

$$35 \text{ ng} \times \frac{10^{-9} \text{ g}}{1 \text{ ng}} \times \frac{10^{12} \text{ pg}}{1 \text{ g}} = 3.5 \times 10^{4} \text{ pg}$$

Scientific Notation and Significant Figures

2.44 (a) 9.457×10^3 (b) 7×10^{-5} (c) 2.000×10^{10}
(d) 1.2345×10^{-2} (e) 6.5238×10^2

2.46 (a) six (b) three (c) three (d) four
(e) 1–5 (f) 2–3

2.48 (a) 7,926 mi; 7,900 mi; 7,926.38 mi
(b) $7.926\,381 \times 10^3$ mi

2.50 (a) 12.1 g (b) 96.19 cm (c) 263 mL (d) 20.9 mg

Unit Conversions and Problem Solving

2.52 (a) 0.3614 cg (b) 0.0120 ML (c) 0.0144 mm (d) 60.3 ng (e) 1.745 dL (f) 1.5×10^3 cm

2.54 (a) 97.8 kg (b) 0.133 mL (c) 0.46 ng (d) 2.99 Mm

2.56

$$\frac{100\text{ km}}{1\text{ hr}} \times \frac{0.6214\text{ mi}}{1\text{ km}} = 62.1\ \frac{\text{mi}}{\text{hr}}$$

$$\frac{62.1\text{ mi}}{1\text{ hr}} \times \frac{5280\text{ ft}}{1\text{ mi}} \times \frac{1\text{ hr}}{60\text{ min}} \times \frac{1\text{ min}}{60\text{ s}} = 91.1\ \frac{\text{ft}}{\text{s}}$$

2.58

$$\frac{1\text{ cell}}{6 \times 10^{-6}\text{ m}} \times \frac{1\text{ m}}{39.37\text{ in}} = 4 \times 10^3\ \frac{\text{cells}}{\text{in}}$$

2.60

$$\frac{200\text{ mg}}{1\text{ dL}} \times \frac{10\text{ dL}}{1\text{ L}} \times 5\text{ L} = 10^4\text{ mg};\ 10^4\text{ mg} \times \frac{1\text{ g}}{10^3\text{ mg}} = 10\text{ g cholesterol}$$

2.62

$$\frac{1.2 \times 10^4\text{ cells}}{1\text{ mm}^3} \times \frac{10^6\text{ mm}^3}{1\text{ L}} \times 5\text{ L} = 6 \times 10^{10}\text{ cells}$$

Temperature and Heat

2.64

$$°\text{C} = \frac{5°\text{C}}{9°\text{F}} \times (°\text{F} - 32°\text{F}) = \frac{5°\text{C}}{9°\text{F}} \times (98.6°\text{F} - 32°\text{F}) = \frac{66.6°\text{C}}{1.8} = 37.0°\text{C, or } 310.2\text{ K}$$

2.66

$$\text{Heat (cal)} = \text{mass (g)} \times \text{temperature change (°C)} \times \text{specific heat}\left(\frac{\text{cal}}{\text{g}\cdot°\text{C}}\right)$$

$$= 30.0\text{ g} \times (30.0\text{ °C} - 10.0°\text{C}) \times \frac{0.895\text{ cal}}{\text{g}\cdot°\text{C}} = 537\text{ cal}$$

$$= 0.537\text{ kcal}$$

2.68

$$\text{Specific heat} = \frac{\text{cal}}{\text{g}\cdot°\text{C}} = \frac{23\text{ cal}}{5.0\text{ g} \times 50°\text{C}} = 0.092\ \frac{\text{cal}}{\text{g}\cdot°\text{C}}$$

2.70 See Problem 2.69 for help in solving this problem.

For mercury: Temperature change (°C) = $\dfrac{250\text{ cal}}{150\text{ g} \times 0.033\dfrac{\text{cal}}{\text{g}\cdot{}^\circ\text{C}}} = 51^\circ\text{C}$

Final temp = 25°C + 51°C = 76°C

For iron: Temperature change (°C) = $\dfrac{250\text{ cal}}{150\text{ g} \times 0.106\dfrac{\text{cal}}{\text{g}\cdot{}^\circ\text{C}}} = 15.7^\circ\text{C}$

Final temp = 25.0°C + 15.7°C = 40.7°C

Density and Specific Gravity

2.72

$$250\text{ mg} \times \frac{1\text{ g}}{10^3\text{ mg}} \times \frac{1\text{ cm}^3}{1.40\text{ g}} = 0.179\text{ cm}^3$$

2.74 To find the density of lead, divide the mass of lead by the volume of the bar in cm^3. 0.500 cm x 1.55 cm x 25.00 cm = 19.38 cm^3.

$$\frac{220.9\text{ g}}{19.38\text{ cm}^3} = 11.4\frac{\text{g}}{\text{cm}^3}$$

2.76

$$\frac{3.928\text{ g}}{5.000\text{ mL}} = 0.7856\frac{\text{g}}{\text{mL}};\ \text{specific gravity} = 0.7856$$

Applications

2.78

(a) $\dfrac{1\text{ grain}}{64.8\text{ mg}} = \dfrac{0.0154\text{ grain}}{1\text{ mg}}$ (b) $\dfrac{1\text{ fluid oz}}{8\text{ fluidram}} = \dfrac{0.125\text{ fluid oz}}{1\text{ fluidram}}$

(c) $\dfrac{1\text{ fluidram}}{3.72\text{ mL}} = \dfrac{0.269\text{ fluidram}}{1\text{ mL}}$ (d) $\dfrac{1\text{ minim}}{0.062\text{ mL}} = \dfrac{16\text{ minim}}{1\text{ mL}}$

(e) $\dfrac{1\text{ fluid oz}}{480\text{ minim}} = \dfrac{2.08 \times 10^{-3}\text{ fluid oz}}{1\text{ minim}}$

2.80 BMI is defined as a person's weight in kilograms divided by the square of height in meters. Alternatively, a person's weight in pounds divided by the square of height in inches and multiplied by 703, also gives the same value for BMI. A value of BMI between 25 and 29 indicates overweight, and a value of BMI over 30 indicates obesity.

2.82 Body fat acts as a shock absorber, a thermal insulator, and as an energy storehouse.

General Questions and Problems

2.84

$$3.12 \text{ in.} \times \frac{2.54 \text{ cm}}{1 \text{ in.}} = 7.92 \text{ cm}$$

The difference in the calculated length (7.92 cm) and the measured length (8.0 cm) is due to the lack of precision of the ruler and to rounding.

2.86

$$°\text{C} = \frac{5°\text{C}}{9°\text{F}}(°\text{F} - 32°\text{F}) = \frac{5°\text{C}}{9°\text{F}}(350°\text{F} - 32°\text{F}) = \frac{5°\text{C}}{9°\text{F}}(318°\text{F}) = 177°\text{C}$$

2.88 3.9×10^{-2} g/dL iron, 8.3×10^{-3} g/dL calcium, 2.24×10^{-1} g/dL cholesterol

2.90

$$75\,\frac{\text{mL}}{\text{beat}} \times 72\,\frac{\text{beats}}{\text{min}} \times 60\,\frac{\text{min}}{\text{hr}} \times 24\,\frac{\text{hr}}{\text{day}} = 7.8 \times 10^{6}\,\frac{\text{mL}}{\text{day}}$$

2.92

$$0.14 \text{ mL} \times \frac{0.963 \text{ g}}{1 \text{ mL}} = 0.13 \text{ g}$$

2.94

$$\frac{85 \text{ mg}}{100 \text{ mL}} \times \frac{10^3 \text{ mL}}{1 \text{ L}} \times \frac{0.9464 \text{ L}}{1 \text{ qt}} \times \frac{1 \text{ qt}}{2 \text{ pt}} \times 11 \text{ pt} = 4.4 \text{ g}$$

$$4.4 \text{ g} \times \frac{1 \text{ lb}}{454 \text{ g}} = 0.0097 \text{ lb}$$

2.96

$$\left(\frac{100 \text{ mL}}{1 \text{ kg}} \times 10 \text{ kg}\right) + \left(\frac{50 \text{ mL}}{1 \text{ kg}} \times 10 \text{ kg}\right) + \left(\frac{20 \text{ mL}}{1 \text{ kg}} \times 35 \text{ kg}\right) = 2200 \text{ mL}$$

2.98

$$\text{Heat (cal)} = \text{mass (g)} \times \text{temperature change (°C)} \times \text{specific heat}\left(\frac{\text{cal}}{\text{g} \cdot °\text{C}}\right)$$

For water: specific heat = 1.00 cal /(g·°C);

$$\text{mass} = 3.00 \text{ L} \times \frac{10^3 \text{ mL}}{1 \text{ L}} \times \frac{1.00 \text{ g}}{1 \text{ mL}} = 3.00 \times 10^3 \text{ g};$$

$$\text{temperature change} = 90.0°\text{C} - 18.0°\text{C} = 72.0°\text{C}$$

$$\text{calories needed} = 3.00 \times 10^3 \text{ g} \times 72.0°\text{C} \times \frac{1.00 \text{ cal}}{\text{g} \cdot °\text{C}} = 2.16 \times 10^5 \text{ cal} = 216 \text{ kcal}$$

$$216 \text{ kcal} \times \frac{1.0 \text{ tbsp}}{100 \text{ kcal}} = 2.2 \text{ tbsp butter}$$

The calculated specific heat, 0.107, is closer to the value for iron than for gold.

2.100

$$\frac{1620 \text{ g}}{205 \text{ mL}} = 7.90 \frac{\text{g}}{\text{mL}}$$

The value calculated for density very nearly agrees with the density of iron (7.86 g/mL).

2.102

$$2.01 \times 10^{10} \text{ lb} \times \frac{1 \text{ gal}}{15.28 \text{ lb}} \times \frac{3.7856 \text{ L}}{1 \text{ gal}} = 4.98 \times 10^{10} \text{ L}$$

2.104 (a)

$$\frac{200 \text{ mg}}{100 \text{ mL}} \times \frac{1000 \text{ mL}}{1 \text{ L}} = 2 \times 10^3 \frac{\text{mg}}{\text{L}}$$

(b)

$$\frac{200 \text{ mg}}{100 \text{ mL}} \times \frac{10^3 \text{ µg}}{\text{mg}} = 2 \times 10^3 \frac{\text{µg}}{\text{mL}}$$

(c)

$$\frac{200 \text{ mg}}{100 \text{ mL}} \times \frac{1 \text{ g}}{1000 \text{ mg}} \times \frac{1000 \text{ mL}}{1 \text{ L}} = 2 \frac{\text{g}}{\text{L}}$$

(d)

$$\frac{200 \text{ mg}}{100 \text{ mL}} \times \frac{10^6 \text{ ng}}{1 \text{ mg}} \times \frac{1 \text{ mL}}{10^3 \text{µL}} = 2 \times 10^3 \frac{\text{ng}}{\text{µL}}$$

2.106 The initial temperature: 293.2 K – 273.2 K = 20.0 K = 20.0°C
The temperature change: 3.0°F/min x 8.42 min = 25.3°F = 14.1°C (since a Celsius degree is 1.8 times larger than a Fahrenheit degree)
The final temperature: 20.0°C + 14.1°C = 34.1°C

2.108 Strategy: Use the dimensions of the cork and of the lead to find their respective volumes. Multiply the volume of each substance by its density to arrive at the mass of each.
Volume of cork: 1.30 cm x 5.50 cm x 3.00 cm = 21.45 cm^3
Volume of lead: $(1.15 \text{ cm})^3 = 1.521 \text{ cm}^3$

Mass of cork:

$$21.45 \text{ cm}^3 \times \frac{0.235 \text{ g}}{1 \text{ cm}^3} = 5.04 \text{ g cork}$$

Mass of lead:

$$1.521 \text{ cm}^3 \times \frac{11.35 \text{ g}}{1 \text{ cm}^3} = 17.26 \text{ g lead}$$

Add the two masses, and divide by the sum of the two volumes to find the density of the combination.

$$\text{Density} = \frac{5.04\text{g} + 17.26 \text{ g}}{21.45 \text{ cm}^3 + 1.521 \text{ cm}^3} = \frac{22.30 \text{ g}}{22.97 \text{ cm}^3} = 0.971 \text{ g/cm}^3$$

The combination will float because its density is less than the density of water.

Self-Test for Chapter 2

1. Write the full name of these units:
(a) μm (b) dL (c) Mg (d) L (e) ng

2. Write the abbreviation for each of the following units:
(a) kiloliter (b) picogram (c) centimeter (d) hectoliter

3.

Quantity	*Significant Figures?*
(a) 1.0037 g	
(b) 0.0080 L	
(c) 0.008 L	
(d) 2 aspirin	
(e) 273,000 mi	

4. Express the following in scientific notation:
(a) 0.000 070 3 g (b) 137,100 m (c) 0.011 L (d) 18,371,008 mm
How many significant figures do each of these quantities have?

5. Round the following to three significant figures:
(a) 807.3 L (b) 4,773,112 people (c) 0.00127 g (d) 10370 μm
Express each of these quantities in scientific notation.

6. Convert the following quantities:
(a) 256 g = _____ lb (b) 417 mm = _____ m
(c) 2.0 gallons = _____ L (d) 2.17 m = _____ inches
(e) 35°C = _____ °F (f) 298 K = _____ °C
(g) 175 mL = _____ fl oz (h) 175 mg = _____ oz

7. If the specific heat of gold is 0.031 cal/g °C, how many calories does it take to heat 10 g of gold from 0°C to 100°C?

8. If the density of ethanol is 0.7893 g/mL, how many grams does 275 mL of ethanol weigh?

Multiple Choice

1. Which of the following is not an SI unit?
(a) kg (b) L (c) m (d) K

2. How many significant figures does the number 4500 have?
(a) 2 (b) 3 (c) 4 (d) any of the above

3. Which of the following quantities is larger than a gram?
(a) 1 nanogram (b) 1 dekagram (c) 1 centigram (d) 1 microgram

4. Which of the following conversion factors do you need for converting 3.2 lb/qt to kg/L?
(a) $\frac{1\ \text{kg}}{2.2\ \text{lb}} \times \frac{1\ \text{qt}}{0.95\ \text{L}}$ (b) $\frac{2.2\ \text{lb}}{1\ \text{kg}} \times \frac{1\ \text{qt}}{0.95\ \text{L}}$ (c) $\frac{2.2\ \text{lb}}{1\ \text{kg}} \times \frac{0.95\ \text{L}}{1\ \text{qt}}$ (d) $\frac{1\ \text{kg}}{2.2\ \text{lb}} \times \frac{0.95\ \text{L}}{1\ \text{qt}}$

5. When written in scientific notation, the exponent in the number 0.000 007 316 is
(a) 10^{-6} (b) 6 (c) –6 (d) 10^{6}

6. Which of the following is more dense than water?
(a) ice (b) human fat (c) ethyl alcohol (d) urine

7. How many zeros are significant in the number 0.007 006?
(a) 1 (b) 2 (c) 3 (d) 4

8. Which of the following temperatures doesn't equal the other two?
(a) 100°F (b) 37.8°C (c) 297.8 K

9. To measure the amount of heat needed to raise the temperature of a given substance, you need to know all of the following except
(a) the mass of the substance (b) the specific heat of the substance (c) the density of the substance (d) the initial and final temperature

10. For which of the following is specific gravity a useful measure?
(a) to describe the amount of solids in urine (b) to indicate the amount of heat necessary to raise the temperature of one gram of a substance by 1°C (c) to determine if an object will float on water

Sentence Completion

1. The fundamental SI units are _____, _____, _____, and _____.

2. Physical quantities are described by a _____ and a _____.

3. The amount of heat necessary to raise the temperature of one gram of a substance by one degree is the substance's _____ _____.

4. The prefix _____ indicates 10^{-9}.

5. The number 0.003 06 has _____ significant figures.

6. To convert from grams to pounds, use the conversion factor _____.

7. Two units for measuring energy are _____ and _____.

8. The method used for converting units is called the _____ _____ method.

9. _____ _____ is the density of a substance divided by the density of water at the same temperature.

10. The size of a degree is the same in both _____ and _____ units.

True or False

1. The units of specific gravity are g/mL.
2. The number 0.07350 has four significant figures.
3. The sum of 57.35 and 1.3 has four significant figures.
4. The conversion factor 1.057 quarts/liter is used to convert quarts into liters.
5. Some SI units are the same as metric units.
6. The temperature in °C is always a larger number than the temperature in K.
7. Raising the temperature of 10 g of water by 10°C takes less heat than raising the temperature of 10 g of gold by 10°C.
8. Mass measures the amount of matter in an object.
9. Ice is more dense than water.
10. A nanogram is larger than a picogram.

Match each entry on the left with its partner on the right.

1.	5003	(a) Converts pounds to kilograms
2.	1 centimeter	(b) 0.1 grams
3.	$\frac{2.205\text{ lb}}{1\text{ kg}}$	(c) Larger than one inch
4.	263 K	(d) –17.8°C
5.	1 dekagram	(e) Four significant figures
6.	0.0486	(f) SI unit of volume measure
7.	1 m^3	(g) Converts kilograms to pounds
8.	1 liter	(h) 10 grams
9.	1 decimeter	(i) –10°C
10.	$\frac{1\text{ kg}}{2.205\text{ lb}}$	(j) Smaller than one inch
11.	0°F	(k) Metric unit of volume measure
12.	1 decigram	(l) Three significant figures

Chapter 3 – Atoms and the Periodic Table

Chapter Outline

I. Atomic Theory (Sections 3.1–3.3).
   A. Fundamental assumptions about atoms (Section 3.1).
      1. All matter is composed of atoms.
      2. The atoms of each element are different from the atoms of all other elements.
      3. Chemical compounds consist of elements combined in definite proportions.
      4. Chemical reactions only change the way that atoms are combined in compounds; the atoms themselves are unchanged.
   B. Nature of the atom (Sections 3.1).
      1. Atoms are very small (~10^{-11} m in diameter).
      2. Atoms consist of subatomic particles.
         a. A proton is positively charged and has a mass of 1.6726×10^{-24} g.
         b. A neutron has no charge and has a mass of 1.6749×10^{-24} g.
         c. An electron is negatively charged and has a mass of 9.1093×10^{-28} g.
      3. The masses of atoms are expressed in relative terms.
         a. Under this system, a carbon atom with 6 protons and 6 neutrons is given a mass of 12 atomic mass units (amu).
         b. Consequently, a proton and a neutron each have a mass of approximately 1 amu.
      4. Atoms are held together by the interplay of attractive and repulsive forces of positively charged protons and negatively charged electrons.
      5. Protons and neutrons are located in the nucleus of an atom, and electrons move around the nucleus.
      6. The size of the nucleus is small compared to the size of the atom.
   C. Composition of atoms (Section 3.2).
      1. Atoms of different elements differ from each other according to how many protons they contain.
      2. Z stands for the number of protons an atom has and is known as the atomic number.
      3. The number of electrons in an atom is the same as the number of protons.
      4. The mass number A stands for the number of protons plus the number of neutrons.
   D. Isotopes and atomic weight (Section 3.3).
      1. Isotopes are atoms of the same element that differ only in the number of neutrons.
      2. Isotopes are represented by showing the mass number as a superscript on the left side of the symbol for the chemical element; the atomic number is shown as a subscript on the left side.
      3. Most elements occur in nature as a mixture of isotopes.
      4. The atomic weight of an element can be calculated if the percent of contributing isotopes is known.

II. The Periodic Table (Sections 3.4–3.5).
   A. The periodic table is a classification of elements according to their properties (Section 3.4).
      1. Elements are arranged by increasing atomic number in seven rows called periods.
      2. Elements are also arranged in 18 vertical columns called groups.
         a. Main group elements occur on the left and right of the periodic table.
         b. Transition-metal groups occur in the middle of the periodic table.
         c. Inner transition-metal groups are shown separately at the bottom.
      3. The elements in each group have similar chemical properties.

B. Chemical characteristics of groups of elements (Section 3.5).
  1. Group 1A – Alkali metals (Li, Na, K, Rb, Cs, Fr).
    a. Shiny, soft, low-melting.
    b. React violently with water.
  2. Group 2A – Alkaline earth metals (Be, Mg, Ca, Sr, Ba, Ra).
    a. Lustrous, shiny metals.
    b. Less reactive than metals in group 1A.
  3. Group 7A – Halogens (F, Cl, Br, I, At).
    a. Corrosive, nonmetals.
    b. Found in nature only in combination with other elements.
  4. Group 8A – Noble gases (He, Ne, Ar, Kr, Xe, Rn). Extremely unreactive.

C. Neighboring groups have similar behaviors.
  1. Metals.
    a. Found on the left side of the periodic table.
    b. Silvery, ductile, good conductors.
  2. Nonmetals.
    a. Found on the right side of the periodic table.
    b. Eleven of the seventeen nonmetals are gases.
    c. Solid nonmetals are brittle and are poor conductors of electricity.
  3. Metalloids.
    a. Occur on the boundary between metals and nonmetals.
    b. Have intermediate chemical behavior.

III. Electrons (Sections 3.6–3.8).

A. The properties of the elements are due to the distribution of electrons in their atoms (Section 3.6).

B. Location of electrons.
  1. Electrons are located in specific regions about the nucleus.
  2. The energies of electrons are quantized.
  3. The locations of electrons are described by shells, subshells, and orbitals.
    a. Shells.
      i. Shells describe the energy level of an electron.
      ii. Shells are related to an electron's distance from the nucleus.
    b. Subshells.
      i. Subshells describe the energy levels of electrons within each shell.
      ii. The four types of subshell are *s, p, d,* and *f*.
    c. Orbitals.
      i. Orbitals are the regions of subshells in which electrons of a specific energy can be found.
      ii. An *s* subshell contains one orbital, a *p* subshell contains three orbitals, a *d* subshell contains five orbitals, and an *f* subshell contains seven orbitals.
      iii. Each orbital can hold two electrons, and they must be of opposite spin.
      iv. An *s* orbital is spherical, and a *p* orbital is dumbbell-shaped.
  4. Since the exact position of electrons can't be specified, orbitals are often referred to as electron clouds.

C. Electron configurations (Section 3.7)
  1. The specific arrangement of electrons in an atom's shells and subshells is known as its electron configuration.
  2. This arrangement can be predicted by using three rules.
    a. Electrons occupy the lowest orbitals available within each subshell
       Within each shell, the subshell energy levels increase in the order *s, p, d, f.*
    b. If two or more orbitals have the same energy, each orbital is half filled before any orbital is completely filled.
    c. Each orbital can hold only two electrons, and they must be of opposite spin.
  3. The number of electrons in each subshell is given by a superscript.

D. Electron configuration and the periodic table (Section 3.8).
  1. Properties of elements are determined by their location in the periodic table.
  2. The periodic table is divided into four regions.
     a. Elements in groups 1A and 2A are *s*-block elements because they result from filling *s* orbitals.
     b. Groups 3A–8A are *p*-block elements.
     c. Transition metals are *d*-block elements.
     d. Inner transition metals are *f*-block elements.
  3. The periodic table can be used as a reminder of the order of orbital filling.
  4. Elements within a group of the periodic table have similar electronic configurations of their valence electronic shells and thus similar chemical behavior.

Solutions to Chapter 3 Problems

3.1 Use the conversion factor that relates mass and amu.

$$2.33 \times 10^{-23}\ \text{g} \times \frac{1\ \text{amu}}{1.660\ 539 \times 10^{-24}\ \text{g}} = 14.0\ \text{amu}$$

3.2

$$10^5\ \text{atoms} \times \frac{197\ \text{amu}}{1\ \text{atom}} \times \frac{1.660\ 539 \times 10^{-24}\ \text{g}}{1\ \text{amu}} = 3.27 \times 10^{-17}\ \text{g}$$

3.3

(a) $$1.0\ \text{g} \times \frac{1\ \text{amu}}{1.660\ 539 \times 10^{-24}\ \text{g}} \times \frac{1\ \text{atom}}{1.0\ \text{amu}} = 6.0 \times 10^{23}\ \text{atoms}$$

(b) $$12.0\ \text{g} \times \frac{1\ \text{amu}}{1.660\ 539 \times 10^{-24}\ \text{g}} \times \frac{1\ \text{atom}}{12.0\ \text{amu}} = 6.02 \times 10^{23}\ \text{atoms}$$

(c) $$23.0\ \text{g} \times \frac{1\ \text{amu}}{1.660\ 539 \times 10^{-24}\ \text{g}} \times \frac{1\ \text{atom}}{23.0\ \text{amu}} = 6.02 \times 10^{23}\ \text{atoms}$$

3.4 In each of the preceding examples, the mass in grams equals the mass in amu, and the number of atoms in all three samples is identical.

3.5 (a) Re (b) Ca (c) Te

3.6 Recall that the *atomic number* (*Z*) shows how many protons an atom contains. Uranium, with an atomic number of 92, thus contains 92 protons.
Uranium also contains 92 electrons, since the number of protons equals the number of electrons.
The *mass number* (*A*) shows the number of protons plus the number of neutrons. To find the number of neutrons in an atom, subtract the atomic number from the mass number.
For uranium: Mass number – atomic number = 235 – 92 = 143.
The uranium atom has 143 neutrons.

3.7 From Problem 3.6, we know that $A - Z$ = number of neutrons.
In this problem, $A = 52$, and the number of neutrons = 28. Thus $Z = 24$. The table of elements in the front of the book shows that chromium is the element with $Z = 24$.

3.8 Contribution from ^{39}K: 93.1% of 38.96 amu = 36.27 amu
Contribution from ^{41}K: 6.88% of 40.96 amu = 2.82 amu

Atomic weight = 39.1 amu

The calculated value agrees exactly with the reported value.

3.9 Both chlorine isotopes have 17 protons. The chlorine isotope with mass number 35 has 18 neutrons, and the isotope with mass number 37 has 20 neutrons.
The atomic number is written at the lower left of the element symbol, and the mass number is written at the upper left.

$^{35}_{17}\text{Cl}$ and $^{37}_{17}\text{Cl}$

3.10 (a) $^{11}_{5}\text{B}$ (b) $^{56}_{26}\text{Fe}$

3.11 Aluminum is in group 3A (or 13) and period 3.

3.12 The group 1B element in period 5 is silver (Ag).
The group 2A element in period 4 is calcium (Ca).

3.13

Group 5A Element	*Period*
Nitrogen (N)	2
Phosphorus (P)	3
Arsenic (As)	4
Antimony (Sb)	5
Bismuth (Bi)	6

3.14 Metals: titanium (Ti), scandium (Sc)
Nonmetals: selenium (Se), argon (Ar)
Metalloids: tellurium (Te), astatine (At)

3.15 (a) Krypton – (ii) nonmetal, (iv) main group element, (v) noble gas
(b) Strontium – (i) metal, (iv) main group element
(c) Nitrogen – (ii) nonmetal, (iv) main group element
(d) Cobalt – (i) metal, (iii) transition element

3.16 The element zinc (Zn) is a metal found in period 4, group 2B (or 12).

3.17 (a) A maximum of six electrons can occupy a 3*p* subshell.
(b) A maximum of two electrons can occupy a 2*s* subshell.
(c) A maximum of six electrons can occupy a 2*p* subshell.

3.18 Ten electrons are present in this atom, which is neon.

3.19 Twelve electrons are present in this atom, which is magnesium.

3.20 To find the electron configuration of an atom, first find its atomic number. For C (carbon), the atomic number is 6; thus, carbon has 6 protons and 6 electrons. Then, assign electrons to the proper orbitals. For carbon, the electron configuration is $1s^2\ 2s^2\ 2p^2$.

Element	*Atomic Number*	*Electron Configuration*
(a) C (carbon)	6	$1s^2\ 2s^2\ 2p^2$
(b) Na (sodium)	11	$1s^2\ 2s^2\ 2p^6\ 3s^1$
(c) Cl (chlorine)	17	$1s^2\ 2s^2\ 2p^6\ 3s^2\ 3p^5$
(d) Ca (calcium)	20	$1s^2\ 2s^2\ 2p^6\ 3s^2\ 3p^6\ 4s^2$

3.21 Element 14 (Si): $1s^2\ 2s^2\ 2p^6\ 3s^2\ 3p^2$
Element 36 (Kr): $1s^2\ 2s^2\ 2p^6\ 3s^2\ 3p^6\ 4s^2\ 3d^{10}\ 4p^6$

3.22 Element 33 (As): $1s^2\ 2s^2\ 2p^6\ 3s^2\ 3p^6\ 4s^2\ 3d^{10}\ 4p^3$. The $4p$ subshell is incompletely filled. Notice that only one electron occupies each orbital of the $4p$ subshell.

$\underline{\uparrow}\ \underline{\uparrow}\ \underline{\uparrow}\ \ 4p^3$

3.23 The atom has 31 electrons (and 31 protons) and can be identified as gallium.

3.24 (a) F: $1s^2\ 2s^2\ 2p^5$; [He] $\mathbf{2s^2\ 2p^5}$ (b) Al: $1s^2\ 2s^2\ 2p^6\ 3s^2\ 3p^1$; [Ne] $\mathbf{3s^2\ 3p^1}$
(c) As: $1s^2\ 2s^2\ 2p^6\ 3s^2\ 3p^6\ 4s^2\ 3d^{10}\ 4p^3$; [Ar] $\mathbf{4s^2}\ 3d^{10}\ \mathbf{4p^3}$
(Valence electrons are bold.)

3.25 In group 2A, all elements have the outer-shell configuration ns^2.

3.26 Chlorine, in group 7A (17), has seventeen electrons. Its electron configuration is $1s^2\ 2s^2\ 2p^6\ 3s^2\ 3p^5$. Two electrons are in shell 1, eight electrons are in shell 2, and seven electrons are in shell 3. The outer shell configuration is $3s^2\ 3p^5$.

3.27 The elements form group 6A (16) and have the general configuration ns^2np^4.

Understanding Key Concepts

3.28 Drawing (a) represents a p orbital (dumbbell-shaped), and drawing (b) represents an s orbital (spherical).

3.29

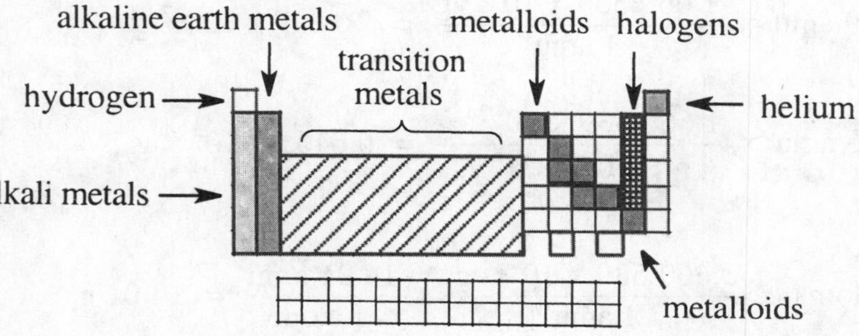
alkaline earth metals
metalloids
halogens
transition metals
hydrogen
helium
alkali metals
metalloids

3.30 The element marked in red is a gas (argon – a group 8A noble gas)
The element marked in blue has atomic number 42 (molybdenum).
All elements in group 1A have chemical behavior similar to the element marked in green (cesium). These include lithium, sodium, potassium and rubidium.

3.31

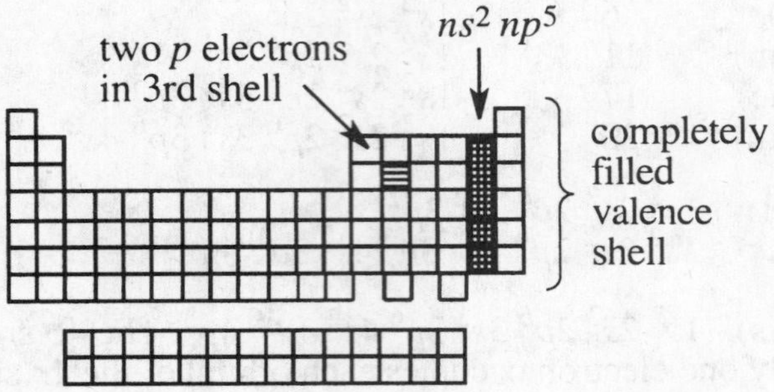
$ns^2\ np^5$
two *p* electrons in 3rd shell
completely filled valence shell

3.32 Nickel (Z = 28) is the element whose orbital-filling diagram is shown. Notice that it is possible to identify the element by counting its electrons, which equal the number of protons and give the value of Z.

3.33 Se: $1s^2\ 2s^2\ 2p^6\ 3s^2\ 3p^6$ ↑↓ (4*s*) ↑↓ ↑↓ ↑↓ ↑↓ ↑↓ (3*d*) ↑↓ ↑ ↑ (4*p*)

Atomic Theory and the Composition of Atoms

3.34 (1) All matter is composed of atoms.
(2) The atoms of a given element differ from the atoms of all other elements.
(3) Chemical compounds consist of atoms combined in specific proportions.
(4) Chemical reactions change only the way that atoms are combined in compounds; the atoms themselves are unchanged.

3.36

(a) Bi: $208.9804 \text{ amu} \times \dfrac{1.660\,539 \times 10^{-24}\text{ g}}{1 \text{ amu}} = 3.470201 \times 10^{-22}\text{ g}$

(b) Xe: $131.29 \text{ amu} \times \dfrac{1.660\,539 \times 10^{-24}\text{ g}}{1 \text{ amu}} = 2.1801 \times 10^{-22}\text{ g}$

(c) He: $4.0026 \text{ amu} \times \dfrac{1.660\,539 \times 10^{-24}\text{ g}}{1 \text{ amu}} = 6.6465 \times 10^{-24}\text{ g}$

3.38

$$6.022 \times 10^{23} \text{ atoms} \times \frac{1.660\,539 \times 10^{-24}\text{ g}}{1 \text{ amu}} \times \frac{14.01 \text{ amu}}{1 \text{ atom}} = 14.01 \text{ g}$$

3.40

$$15.99 \text{ g} \times \frac{1 \text{ amu}}{1.660\ 539 \times 10^{-24} \text{ g}} \times \frac{1 \text{ atom}}{15.99 \text{ amu}} = 6.022 \times 10^{23} \text{ atoms}$$

3.42

Particle	*Mass in amu*	*Charge*
Proton	1.007 276	+1
Neutron	1.008 665	0
Electron	$5.485\ 799 \times 10^{-4}$	−1

3.44 (a) Potassium (K) (b) Tin (Sn) (c) Zinc (Zn)

3.46

Isotope	*Argon-36*	*Argon-38*	*Argon-40*
Number of neutrons	18	20	22

3.48 Symbols (a) and (c) represent isotopes because they have the same atomic number but different mass numbers.

3.50 (a) fluorine-19 (b) neon-19 (c) fluorine-21 (d) magnesium-21

3.52

(a) ${}^{14}_{6}\text{C}$ (b) ${}^{39}_{19}\text{K}$ (c) ${}^{20}_{10}\text{Ne}$

3.54

${}^{12}_{6}\text{C}$ – six neutrons ${}^{13}_{6}\text{C}$ – seven neutrons ${}^{14}_{6}\text{C}$ – eight neutrons

3.56 Contribution from ${}^{63}\text{Cu}$: 69.17% of 62.93 amu = 43.53 amu
Contribution from ${}^{65}\text{Cu}$: 30.83% of 64.93 amu = 20.02 amu

Average atomic weight = 63.55 amu

The Periodic Table

3.58 The third period in the periodic table contains eight elements because eight electrons are needed to fill the *s* subshell (two electrons)and *p* subshell (six electrons) of the third shell.

3.60 Americium (Am; atomic number 95) is a metal.

3.62 (a) They are metals.
(b) They are transition metals.
(c) The 3*d* subshell is being filled.

3.64 (a) Rubidium: (i) metal (v) main group element (vii) alkali metal
(b) Tungsten: (i) metal (iv) transition element
(c) Germanium: (iii) metalloid (v) main group element
(d) Krypton: (ii) nonmetal (v) main group element (vi) noble gas

3.66 Selenium is chemically similar to sulfur.

3.68 The alkali metal family is composed of lithium, sodium, potassium, rubidium, cesium, and francium.

Electron Configuration

3.70 A maximum of two electrons can go into an orbital.

3.72 First shell – 2 electrons
Second shell – 8 electrons
Third shell – 18 electrons

3.74 The third shell contains three subshells: 3*s*, 3*p*, 3*d*. The fourth shell contains four subshells: 4*s*, 4*p*, 4*d*, 4*f*. The fifth shell also contains four subshells: 5*s*, 5*p*, 5*d*, 5*f*.

3.76 Ten electrons are present; the element is neon.

3.78

(a) Sulfur	(b) Bromine	(c) Silicon
↑↓ ↑ ↑	↑↓ ↑↓ ↑	↑ ↑ __
$3p^4$	$4p^5$	$3p^2$

3.80

Element:	Sulfur	Bromine	Silicon	Calcium	Vanadium	Iron
Number of unpaired electrons	2	1	2	0	3	4

3.82 The element with atomic number 20 (Ca) has two electrons in its outer shell.

3.84 Beryllium: 2*s* Arsenic: 4*p*

3.86

Element:	(a) Kr	(b) C	(c) Ca	(d) K	(e) B	(f) Cl
Number of valence-shell electrons:	8	4	2	1	3	7

Applications

3.88 A normal light microscope can't reach the degree of precision of a scanning tunneling microscope.

3.90 Hydrogen and helium are the first two elements made in stars.

3.92

	Higher energy	*Lower energy*
(a)	ultraviolet	infrared
(b)	gamma waves	microwaves
(c)	X rays	visible light

General Questions and Problems

3.94 Helium, neon, argon, krypton, xenon, and radon make up the noble gas family.

3.96 Tellurium has a greater atomic weight because its nuclei contain, on the average, more neutrons than an iodine nucleus.

3.98 Pb: $1s^2\ 2s^2\ 2p^6\ 3s^2\ 3p^6\ 4s^2\ 3d^{10}\ 4p^6\ 5s^2\ 4d^{10}\ 5p^6\ 6s^2\ 4f^{14}\ 5d^{10}\ 6p^2$

Shell 1: 2 electrons	Shell 2: 8 electrons	Shell 3: 18 electrons
Shell 4: 32 electrons	Shell 5: 18 electrons	Shell 6: 4 electrons

3.100 Contribution from ^{79}Br: 50.69% of 78.92 amu = 40.00 amu
Contribution from ^{81}Br: 49.31% of 80.91 amu = 39.90 amu

Average atomic weight = 79.90 amu

3.102 One atom of carbon weighs more than one atom of hydrogen because the mass of carbon (12 amu) is greater than the mass of hydrogen (1 amu).

3.104 If 10^{23} hydrogen atoms weigh about 1 g, then 10^{23} carbon atoms will weigh about 12 g.

3.106 The unidentified element is strontium, which occurs directly below calcium in group 2A and thus has similar chemical behavior. Strontium is a metal, has 38 protons, and is in the fifth period.

3.108 Zirconium, a metal, has an electron configuration by shell of 2 8 18 10 2.

3.110 (a) Electrons must fill the 4*s* subshell before entering the 3*d* subshell. The correct configuration:

$$1s^2\ 2s^2\ 2p^6\ 3s^2\ 3p^6\ 4s^2\ 3d^8$$

(b) Electrons must fill the 2*s* subshell before entering the 2*p* subshell. The correct configuration:

$$1s^2\ 2s^2\ 2p^3$$

(c) Silicon has 14 electrons. The *p* orbitals must be half-filled before any one orbital is completely filled. The correct configuration:

$$1s^2\ 2s^2\ 2p^6\ 3s^2\ \underbrace{\uparrow\ \uparrow\ \_}_{3p}$$

(d) The 3*s* electrons must have opposite spins. The correct configuration:

$$1s^2\ 2s^2\ 2p^6\ \underbrace{\uparrow\downarrow}_{3s}$$

3.112 An electron will fill or half-fill a *d* subshell instead of filling an *s* subshell of a higher shell.

Self-Test for Chapter 3

Multiple Choice

1. Which of the following is a metalloid?
(a) carbon (b) aluminum (c) silicon (d) phosphorus

2. Which of the following has a partially filled *d* subshell?
(a) calcium (b) vanadium (c) zinc (d) arsenic

3. Which of the following is not a part of atomic theory?
(a) All metal is composed of atoms. (b) The atoms of each element are different from the atoms of other elements. (c) In chemical compounds, atoms are combined in specific proportions. (d) Chemical reactions only change the way that atoms are combined.

4. How many isotopes of hydrogen are there?
(a) one (b) two (c) three (d) can't be determined

5. What holds protons and neutrons together in the nucleus?
(a) attraction (b) repulsion (c) electrons (d) internuclear forces

6. Which of the following has a mass number of 33?
(a) $^{74}_{33}As$ (b) $^{35}_{17}Cl$ (c) $^{32}_{16}S$ (d) $^{33}_{16}S$

7. In which order are subshells usually filled?
(a) *s, p, d, f* (b) *d, f, p, s* (c) *s, p, f, d* (d) *s, d, p, f*

8. An element with atomic number 38 is likely to be
(a) an alkali metal (b) an alkaline earth metal (c) a transition metal (d) a metalloid

9. The element that has atomic weight = 91 and has 40 electrons is
(a) protactinium (b) niobium (c) antimony (d) zirconium

10. The element that has electron configuration $1s^2\ 2s^2\ 2p^6\ 3s^2\ 3p^6\ 4s^2\ 3d^7$ is:
(a) copper (b) rhodium (c) arsenic (d) cobalt

11. An element that has electrons in its *f* subshell is:
(a) europium (b) technetium (c) antimony (d) xenon

12. $^{195}_{78}X$ is the symbol for
(a) gold (b) platinum (c) iridium (d) iron

Sentence Completion

1. A _____ orbital is dumbbell-shaped.

2. An atomic mass unit is also known as a ________.

3. The nucleus of an atom is made up of _____ and _____.

4. The _____ _____ indicates the number of protons in an atom.

5. The electrons in an atom are grouped by energy into _____.

6. Elements belonging to the same _____ have similar chemical properties.

7. The atomic number of aluminum is _____.

8. Protons, neutrons, and electrons are known as _____ _____.

9. Atoms having the same number of protons but different numbers of neutrons are called _____.

10. The third shell contains _____ electrons.

11. The word _____ means that electrons can have certain energy values and no others.

True or False

1. Bismuth is a metal.

2. The mass of an electron is approximately 1 amu.

3. A 4*s* electron is higher in energy than a 3*d* electron.

4. Isotopes have the same number of protons but different numbers of neutrons.

5. An atom's atomic number indicates the number of protons and neutrons the atom has.

6. Elements in group 2A are more reactive than elements in group 1A.

7. Elements in the same period have similar chemical properties.

8. More elements are metals than are nonmetals.

9. All compounds consist of atoms combined in specific proportions.

10. A subshell contains only two electrons.

11. An element can have the same number of protons, neutrons, and electrons.

12. Atomic weight always increases with atomic number.

Match each entry on the left with its partner on the right.

1. $1s^2\ 2s^2$	(a) Mendeleev
2. Group	(b) Number of protons in an element
3. Atomic mass unit	(c) Reactive metals
4. Formulated the periodic table	(d) Average mass of a large number of an element's atoms
5. Neutron	(e) Column in the periodic table
6. $^{28}_{14}Si$	(f) Row in the periodic table
7. Group 1A	(g) Element with atomic mass of 14 amu
8. Atomic number	(h) Electron configuration of beryllium
9. $^{29}_{14}Si$	(i) Element having 15 neutrons
10. Atomic weight	(j) Subatomic particle with zero charge
11. $^{14}_{7}N$	(k) Dalton
12. Period	(l) Element with atomic number 14

Chapter 4 – Ionic Compounds

Chapter Outline

I. Ions (Sections 4.1–4.2).
  A. Ions are formed when a neutral atom either gains an electron (to form an anion) or loses an electron (to form a cation).
    1. Ionization energy measures the ease with which an atom gives up an electron.
      a. Energy must be supplied in order to remove an electron.
      b. Elements on the far left of the periodic table have smaller ionization energies and lose electrons more easily.
      c. Elements on the far right of the periodic table have larger ionization energies and lose electrons with difficulty.
    2. Electron affinity measures the ease with which an atom gains an electron.
      a. Energy is released when an atom gains an electron.
      b. Elements on the far right of the periodic table have larger electron affinities and gain electrons easily.
      c. Elements on the far left of the periodic table have smaller electron affinities and gain electrons less easily.
  B. Main group elements in the middle of the periodic table neither lose or gain electrons easily.

II. Formation of ionic compounds (Sections 4.3–4.6).
  A. Compounds formed between an element on the far left side of the periodic table and an element on the far right of the periodic table are electronically neutral (Section 4.3).
    1. These compounds consist of a large number of cations and anions packed together in a regular arrangement in a crystal.
    2. The bonds between ions in the crystal are known as ionic bonds.
    3. The crystal is known as an ionic solid.
  B. Properties of ionic compounds (Section 4.4)
    1. Ionic compounds are crystalline.
    2. Solutions of ionic compounds conduct electricity.
    3. Ionic compounds are high-melting.
    4. Many, but not all, ionic compounds are water-soluble.
  C. The octet rule (Sections 4.5–4.6).
    1. Main group elements undergo reactions that leave them with eight valence electrons – an octet (Section 4.5).
    2. The valence electrons in an ionic compound can be represented by electron dots (Section 4.6).

III. Ions of some common elements (Sections 4.7–4.9).
  A. Cations (Section 4.7)
    1. Group 1A $\quad M\cdot \longrightarrow M^{+} + e^{-}$
    2. Group 2A $\quad \cdot M\cdot \longrightarrow M^{2+} + 2e^{-}$
    3. Group 3A $\quad Al^{3+}$ is the only common cation.
    4. Transition metals often form more than one cation.

B. Anions.

1. Group 6A $\quad :\dot{\underset{\cdot}{X}}: + 2e^- \longrightarrow :\ddot{\underset{\cdot\cdot}{X}}:^{2-}$

2. Group 7A $\quad :\dot{\underset{\cdot\cdot}{X}}: + e^- \longrightarrow :\ddot{\underset{\cdot\cdot}{X}}:^-$

C. Group 4A, group 5A and group 8A elements don't usually form cations or anions.

D. Naming ions (Section 4.8).

1. Main group cations are named by identifying the metal and then adding the word "ion."
2. Transition metal cations are named by identifying the metal, specifying the charge and adding the word "ion."
3. Anions are named by replacing the end of the name of the element with *-ide* and adding the word "ion."
4. Polyatomic ions (Section 4.9).
   a. Polyatomic ions are composed of more than one atom.
   b. Subscripts in polyatomic ions indicate how many of each ion are present in the formula unit (no subscripts are necessary if only one ion is present).
   c. The names of polyatomic ions should be memorized.

IV. Ionic compounds (Sections 4.10–4.12).

A. Formulas of ionic compounds (Section 4.10).

1. Formulas are written so that the number of positive charges equals the number of negative charges.
   a. Cations are listed first, anions second.
   b. It is not necessary to write the charges of the ions.
   c. Use parentheses around a polyatomic ion if it has a subscript.
2. A formula unit shows the simplest neutral unit of an ionic compound.

B. Naming ionic compounds (Section 4.11).

Ionic compounds are named by citing the cation and then the anion, with a space between the two words.

C. Acids and bases (Section 4.12).

1. Acids are compounds that provide H^+ ions in solution.
2. Bases are compounds that provide OH^- ions in solution.
3. Acids and bases can each provide more than one H^+ or OH^- ion in solution.

Solutions to Chapter 4 Problems

4.1 The Mg^{2+} ion is a cation.

4.2 The O^{2-} ion is an anion.

4.3 Figure 4.1 shows approximate ionization energies for argon and krypton. In line with this trend, it is predicted that the ionization energy of xenon should be somewhat less than that of krypton but greater than the ionization energy of most other elements.

4.4 (a) According to Figure 4.1, B ($Z = 5$) loses an electron more easily than Be ($Z = 4$).
(b) Ca ($Z = 20$) loses an electron more easily than Co ($Z = 27$).
(c) Sc ($Z = 21$) loses an electron more easily than Se($Z = 34$).

4.5 (a) According to Figure 4.1, H gains an electron more easily than He. Because the electron affinity for He is zero, it does not accept an electron.
(b) S gains an electron more easily than Si.
(c) Cr gains an electron more easily than Mn.

4.6 Potassium (atomic number 19): $1s^2\ 2s^2\ 2p^6\ 3s^2\ 3p^6\ 4s^1$
Argon (atomic number 18): $1s^2\ 2s^2\ 2p^6\ 3s^2\ 3p^6$
Potassium can attain the noble-gas configuration of argon by losing an electron from its 4*s* subshell, forming the K^+ cation.

4.7 Aluminum (atomic number 13): $1s^2\ 2s^2\ 2p^6\ 3s^2\ 3p^1$
Neon (atomic number 10): $1s^2\ 2s^2\ 2p^6$
Aluminum can attain the noble-gas configuration of neon by losing three electrons, two from its 3*s* subshell and one from its 3*p* subshell, resulting in the formation of the Al^{3+} ion.

4.8 Oxygen atom (atomic number 8): $1s^2\ 2s^2\ 2p^4$
Neon atom (atomic number 10): $1s^2\ 2s^2\ 2p^6$
Oxygen can attain the noble-gas configuration of neon by gaining two electrons in its 2*p* subshell.

4.9

·Ẋ·

4.10

:R̈n: ·Ṗb· :Ẍe: ·Ra·

4.11

(a) :Ṡe· + 2 e⁻ ⟶ :S̈e:$^{2-}$; Se + 2 e⁻ ⟶ Se^{2-}

(b) ·Ba· ⟶ Ba^{2+} + 2e⁻; Ba ⟶ Ba^{2+} + 2 e⁻

(c) :B̈r· + e⁻ ⟶ :B̈r:⁻ ; Br + e⁻ ⟶ Br^-

4.12 Molybdenum, a transition metal, is more likely to form a cation than an anion.

4.13 Strontium loses two electrons to form the Sr^{2+} cation, and bromine gains an electron to form the Br^- anion. Only chromium, a transition metal, can form more than one cation.

4.14 (a) Al^{+2} is not likely to form because loss of two electrons doesn't give a cation with a noble-gas configuration. Al^{+3} is the cation that forms from the loss of three electrons from the outermost subshells of aluminum.
(b) O^- doesn't form because it is one electron short of having a noble-gas configuration. O^{2-} is the ion that is formed from oxygen.
(c) Se^{2-} has a noble-gas configuration and is produced by the gain of two electrons by selenium.

4.15 (a) Cu^{2+} copper(II) ion (cupric ion) (b) F^- fluoride ion
(c) Mg^{2+} magnesium ion (d) S^{2-} sulfide ion

4.16 (a) Ag^+ (b) Fe^{2+} (c) Cu^+ (d) Te^{2-}

4.17 Na^+ sodium ion K^+ potassium ion
Ca^{2+} calcium ion Cl^- chloride ion

4.18 (a) NO_3^- nitrate ion (b) CN^- cyanide ion
(c) OH^- hydroxide ion (d) HPO_4^{2-} hydrogen phosphate ion

4.19 (a) HCO_3^- bicarbonate ion (b) NH_4^+ ammonium ion
(c) PO_4^{3-} phosphate ion (d) MnO_4^- permanganate ion

4.20 (a) The two ions are Ag^+ and I^-. Since they have the same charge, only one of each ion is needed. The formula is AgI.
(b) Ions: Ag^+, O^{2-}. Two Ag^+ ions will balance the O^{2-} ion. The formula is Ag_2O.
(c) The ions are Ag^+ and PO_4^{3-}. Three Ag^+ ions are needed to balance the PO_4^{3-} anion. The formula is Ag_3PO_4.

4.21 (a) Na_2SO_4 (b) $FeSO_4$ (c) $Cr_2(SO_4)_3$

4.22 $(NH_4)_2CO_3$

4.23 $Al_2(SO_4)_3$, $Al(CH_3CO_2)_3$

4.24 Use the periodic table to identify the elements present, and use the rules described in Section 4.10 to write the formulas. The formulas are K_2S (blue), $BaBr_2$ (red), and Al_2O_3 (green).

4.25 $BaSO_4$. One barium ion is present for each sulfate ion.

4.26 Ag_2S – silver(I) sulfide. The charge on silver is +1.

4.27 (a) SnO_2 tin(IV) oxide (b) $Ca(CN)_2$ calcium cyanide
(c) Na_2CO_3 sodium carbonate (d) Cu_2SO_4 copper(I) sulfate
(e) $Ba(OH)_2$ barium hydroxide (f) $Fe(NO_3)_2$ iron(II) nitrate

4.28 (a) Li_3PO_4 (b) $CuCO_3$ (c) $Al_2(SO_3)_3$ (d) CuF (e) $Fe_2(SO_4)_3$ (f) NH_4Cl

4.29 Acids provide H^+ ions when dissolved in water.
Bases provide OH^- ions when dissolved in water.

Acids: $HF \xrightarrow{\text{dissolve in water}} H^+ + F^-$

$HCN \xrightarrow{\text{dissolve in water}} H^+ + CN^-$

Bases: $Ca(OH)_2 \xrightarrow{\text{dissolve in water}} Ca^{2+} + 2\ OH^-$

$LiOH \xrightarrow{\text{dissolve in water}} Li^+ + OH^-$

4.30 Solution (a) represents HCl; the drawing shows that there are equal numbers of cations and anions in solution. Solution (b) represents H_2SO_4; two cations are present for each anion.

Understanding Key Concepts

4.31

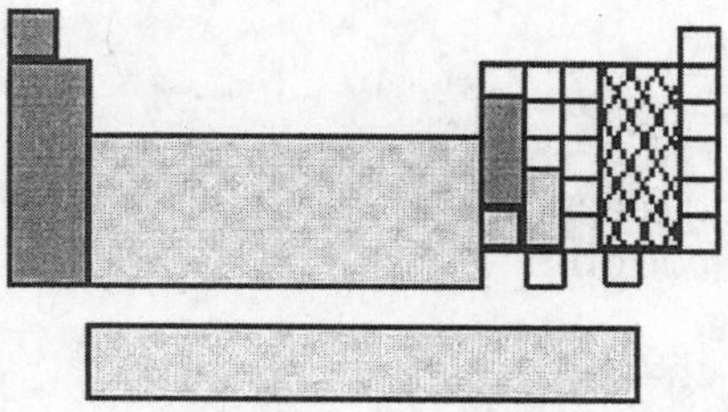

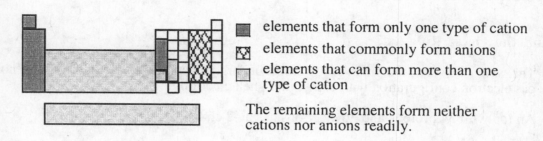

elements that form only one type of cation

elements that commonly form anions

elements that can form more than one type of cation

The remaining elements form neither cations nor anions readily.

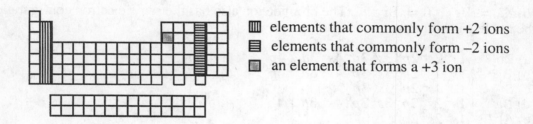

4.32

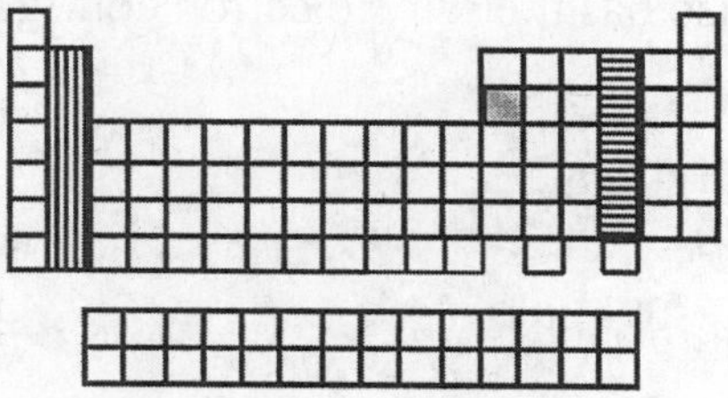

elements that commonly form +2 ions

elements that commonly form –2 ions

an element that forms a +3 ion

4.33 Drawing (a) shows an ion that has two more electrons than protons and thus represents an O^{2-} ion.
Drawing (b) represents Na^+, an ion with one more proton than electron.
Drawing (c) represents calcium, a neutral atom.

4.34 Drawing (a) represents a sodium atom, and drawing (b) represents an Na^+ ion. The Na atom is larger because its 3*s* electron lies in an orbital that is farther from the nucleus.

4.35 Drawing (a) represents a chlorine atom, and drawing (b) represents a Cl^- anion. The anion is larger because its extra electron is not as tightly held by the positively charged nucleus as are the electrons of the atom.

4.36 red – MgO (magnesium oxide) blue – LiCl (lithium chloride)
green – $AlBr_3$ (aluminum bromide)

4.37 Use the ratios of atoms to assign answers. Picture (a) represents ZnS, because one cation is present for each anion. Picture (b) represents $PbBr_2$, (c) represents CrF_3, and (d) represents Al_2O_3.

Ions and Ionic Bonding

4.38

(a) ·Be· (b) :Ne: (c) ·Sr· (d) ·Al·

4.40 (a) $Ca \rightarrow Ca^{2+} + 2\,e^-$ (b) $Au \rightarrow Au^+ + e^-$
(c) $F + e^- \rightarrow F^-$ (d) $Cr \rightarrow Cr^{3+} + 3\,e^-$

4.42 (a) False. A cation is formed by *loss* of one or more electrons from an atom. (b), (c) False. Group 4A elements rarely form ions. (d) True.

Ions and the Octet Rule

4.44 The *octet rule* states that main group atoms undergo reactions in order to achieve a noble-gas electron configuration with eight outer-shell electrons.

4.46 An ion with 34 protons and 36 electrons has a –2 charge.

4.48 (a) $X^{2+} = Sr^{2+}$; X = Sr The strontium ion has the same electron configuration as the noble gas krypton.
(b) $X^- = Br^-$; X = Br The bromide ion also has the same electron configuration as the noble gas krypton.

4.50 (a) Rb^+ $1s^2\,2s^2\,2p^6\,3s^2\,3p^6\,4s^2\,3d^{10}\,4p^6$
(b) Br^- $1s^2\,2s^2\,2p^6\,3s^2\,3p^6\,4s^2\,3d^{10}\,4p^6$
(c) S^{2-} $1s^2\,2s^2\,2p^6\,3s^2\,3p^6$
(d) Ba^{2+} $1s^2\,2s^2\,2p^6\,3s^2\,3p^6\,4s^2\,3d^{10}\,4p^6\,5s^2\,4d^{10}\,5p^6$
(e) Al^{3+} $1s^2\,2s^2\,2p^6$

Periodic Properties and Ion Formation

4.52 (a) O (b) Li (c) Zn (d) N

4.54 None of the ions are stable because all lack eight outer-shell electrons.

4.56 Cr^{2+}: $1s^2\,2s^2\,2p^6\,3s^2\,3p^6\,3d^4$
Cr^{3+}: $1s^2\,2s^2\,2p^6\,3s^2\,3p^6\,3d^3$

4.58 The ionization energy of Li^+ is much greater than that of Li. Li readily loses an electron to form an ion with eight outer-shell electrons, but Li^+ would need to lose one electron from a stable octet in order to form the Li^{2+} cation.

Symbols, Formulas, and Names for Ions

4.60 (a) S^{2-} sulfide ion (b) Sn^{2+} tin(II) ion (c) Sr^{2+} strontium ion
(d) Mg^{2+} magnesium ion (e) Au^+ gold(I) ion

4.62 (a) Se^{2-} (b) O^{2-} (c) Ag^+

4.64 (a) OH^- (b) HSO_4^- (c) $CH_3CO_2^-$ (d) MnO_4^- (e) OCl^- (f) NO_3^-
(g) CO_3^{2-} (h) $Cr_2O_7^{2-}$

Names and Formulas for Ionic Compounds

4.66 (a) $Al_2(SO_4)_3$ (b) Ag_2SO_4 (c) $ZnSO_4$ (d) $BaSO_4$

4.68 (a) $NaHCO_3$ (b) KNO_3 (c) $CaCO_3$ (d) NH_4NO_3

4.70

	S^{2-}	Cl^-	PO_4^{3-}	CO_3^{2-}
Copper(II)	CuS	$CuCl_2$	$Cu_3(PO_4)_2$	$CuCO_3$
Ca^{2+}	CaS	$CaCl_2$	$Ca_3(PO_4)_2$	$CaCO_3$
NH_4^+	$(NH_4)_2S$	NH_4Cl	$(NH_4)_3PO_4$	$(NH_4)_2CO_3$
Ferric ion	Fe_2S_3	$FeCl_3$	$FePO_4$	$Fe_2(CO_3)_3$

4.72

copper(II) sulfide	copper(II) chloride	copper(II) phosphate	copper(II) carbonate
calcium sulfide	calcium chloride	calcium phosphate	calcium carbonate
ammonium sulfide	ammonium chloride	ammonium phosphate	ammonium carbonate
ferric sulfide	ferric chloride	ferric phosphate	ferric carbonate

4.74 (a) $MgCO_3$ magnesium carbonate (b) $Ca(CH_3CO_2)_2$ calcium acetate
(c) $AgCN$ silver(I) cyanide (d) $Na_2Cr_2O_7$ sodium dichromate

4.76 $Ca_3(PO_4)_2$ (d) is the correct formula because the six positive charges from the three Ca^{2+} ions are balanced by the six negative charges of the two PO_4^{3-} ions.

Acids and Bases

4.78 An acid provides H^+ ions when dissolved in water. A base provides OH^- ions when dissolved in water.

4.80

(a) $HNO_2 \xrightarrow{\text{dissolve in water}} H^+ + NO_2^-$

(b) $HCN \xrightarrow{\text{dissolve in water}} H^+ + CN^-$

(c) $Ca(OH)_2 \xrightarrow{\text{dissolve in water}} Ca^{2+} + 2\ OH^-$

(d) $CH_3CO_2H \xrightarrow{\text{dissolve in water}} H^+ + CH_3CO_2^-$

Applications

4.82 To a geologist, a mineral is a naturally occurring crystalline compound. To a nutritionist, a mineral is a metal ion essential for human health.

4.84 For most people, the effect of salt consumption on blood pressure elevation is slight, but a small proportion of people may suffer high blood pressure as a result of excessive salt consumption.

4.86 Sodium protects against fluid loss and is necessary for muscle contraction and transmission of nerve impulses.

4.88

Ion	*Name*	*Charge*	*Total Charge*
Ca^{2+}	calcium ion	2+	10 x (2+) = 20+
PO_4^{3-}	phosphate ion	3–	6 x (3–) = 18–
OH^-	hydroxide ion	1–	2 x (1–) = 2–

The formula correctly represents a neutral compound because the number of positive charges equals the number of negative charges.

General Questions and Problems

4.90 The hydride ion has the same electron configuration ($1s^2$) as the noble gas helium.

4.92 (a) CrO_3 (b) VCl_5 (c) MnO_2 (d) MoS_2

4.94 (a) A gluconate ion has one negative charge.
(b) Three gluconate ions are in one formula unit of iron(III) gluconate, and the formula is $Fe(gluconate)_3$.

4.96 (a) $Co(CN)_2$ (b) UO_3 (c) $SnSO_4$ (d) MnO_2 (e) K_3PO_4 (f) Ca_3P_2
(g) $LiHSO_4$ (h) $Al(OH)_3$

4.98 (a) X is likely to be a metal, because metals are more likely to form cations.
(b) Y is likely to be a nonmetal.
(c) The formula for the product is X_2Y_3.
(d) X is likely to be in group 3A or group 3B (or to be a transition metal) and Y is likely to be in Group 6A.

Self-Test for Chapter 4

Multiple Choice

1. How many atoms does a formula unit of Li_2CO_3 contain?
(a) 3 (b) 4 (c) 5 (d) 6

2. How many ions are produced when a formula unit of Li_2CO_3 is dissolved in water?
(a) 3 (b) 4 (c) 5 (d) 6

3. Which of the following is not a property of ionic compounds?
(a) crystalline (b) conductor of electricity (c) high melting (d) 1:1 ratio of cations to anions

4. Which of the following is the correct name for $Fe(NO_3)_3$?
(a) ferrous nitrate (b) iron nitrate (c) iron(III) nitrate (d) iron(II) nitrate

5. Bromine has a
(a) large ionization energy and large electron affinity (b) large ionization energy and small electron affinity (c) small ionization energy and large electron affinity (d) small ionization energy and small electron affinity

6. H_2CrO_4 is an acid that
   (a) provides one H^+ ion when dissolved (b) provides two H^+ ions when dissolved
   (c) provides one OH^- when dissolved (d) H_2CrO_4 is not an acid.

7. An element that loses three electrons to attain the electron configuration of argon is
   (a) titanium (b) scandium (c) calcium (d) potassium

8. The formula for gold(III) chloride is
   (a) Au_3Cl (b) $AuCl$ (c) $AuCl_2$ (d) $AuCl_3$

9. Which of the following anions is not biologically important?
   (a) Cl^- (b) Br^- (c) HCO_3^- (d) HPO_4^-

10. The redness of rubies is due to which ion?
    (a) iron (b) titanium (c) aluminum (d) chromium

Sentence Completion

1. ______ ______ measures the ease with which an atom gives up an electron.

2. The name of K_3PO_4 is _______ _______.

3. Radium (atomic number 88) loses ______ electrons to achieve a noble gas configuration.

4. NO_3^- is an example of a _______ ion.

5. The formulas of ionic compounds are _______ formulas.

6. Atoms of main-group elements tend to combine in chemical compounds so that they attain ______ outer-shell electrons.

7. A _____ provides OH^- ions in water.

8. ___________ is the principal mineral component of bone.

9. Ionic compounds are usually ______ solids.

10. The first three elements in group ____A form neither cations nor anions.

True or False

1. Zinc can form ions with different charges.

2. Na^+ and F^- have the same electron configuration.

3. Ionization energy measures the amount of energy released when an ion is formed from a neutral atom.

4. $Co(CO_3)_2$ is a possible compound.

5. A solution of H_3PO_4 contains only H^+ and $H_2PO_4^-$ ions.

6. Ionic crystals conduct electricity.

7. Cuprous ion is the same as copper(II) ion.

8. Many ionic compounds are not water-soluble.

9. Group 5A consists of metals and nonmetals.

10. Elements in group 7A have the largest ionization energies.

11. The octet rule is limited to main-group elements.

12. Both men and women suffer the same percent bone loss over their lifetimes.

Match each entry on the left with its partner on the right.

1. $FeBr_2$	(a) Sulfite anion
2. S^{2-}	(b) Electron-dot symbol
3. NH_4^+	(c) Alkali metal
4. SO_3^{2-}	(d) Has the same electron configuration as Na^+
5. Ca	(e) Iron(II) bromide
6. $FeBr_3$	(f) Transition metal
7. Ar	(g) Sulfate anion
8. ·Be·	(h) Alkaline earth metal
9. Co	(i) Has the same electron configuration as Cl^-
10. SO_4^{2-}	(j) Iron(III) bromide
11. Ne	(k) Polyatomic cation
12. K	(l) Sulfide anion

Chapter 5 – Molecular Compounds

Chapter Outline

I. Covalent bonds (Sections 5.1–5.4).
  A Formation of covalent bonds (Section 5.1).
    1. Covalent bonds occur when two atoms share electrons.
    2. Electron sharing results from the overlap of orbitals of two atoms.
    3. The optimum distance between nuclei of two atoms is the bond length.
    4. Seven elements exist as diatomic molecules: H_2, N_2, O_2, F_2, Cl_2, Br_2, I_2.
  B. Covalent bonds and the periodic table (Section 5.2).
    1. Molecular compounds result when atoms form covalent bonds to another atom or to more than one atom.
    2 The octet rule states that each atom in a molecular compound shares the number of electrons necessary to achieve a noble-gas configuration.
    3 Most main group elements form from one to four covalent bonds and obey the octet rule.
      a. Boron forms only three bonds because it has only three valence electrons.
      b. Sulfur and phosphorus may form five or six bonds if they use *d* orbitals.
  C. Multiple covalent bonds (Section 5.3).
    1. Some atoms can share more than one electron pair to form multiple bonds.
      a. A double bond is formed when two pairs are shared.
      b. A triple bond is formed when three pairs are shared.
    2. Even when multiple bonds occur, the atoms still obey the octet rule.
  D. Coordinate bonds occur when one atom donates both of the shared electrons (Section 5.4).

II. Formulas, structures and shapes (Sections 5.5–5.7).
  A. Formulas (Section 5.5).
    1. Molecular formulas show the numbers and kinds of atoms in one molecule of a compound.
    2. Structural formulas show how atoms are connected.
    3. Lewis structures are structural formulas that show electron lone pairs (Section 5.6).
      a. One approach to drawing Lewis structures involves knowing common bonding patterns.
      b. The other approach is a general method.
        i. Find the number of valence electrons for all atoms.
        ii. Draw a line between each pair of connected atoms to represent an electron pair.
        iii. Place lone pairs around all peripheral atoms to give them octets.
        iv. Place remaining electrons around the central atom.
        v. If the central atom doesn't have an octet, use an electron pair from a neighboring atom to form a multiple bond to the central atom.
    4. Some larger organic molecules are written as condensed structures.
  B. Molecular shapes can be predicted by using the VSEPR model (Section 5.7).
    1. Draw a Lewis structure of the molecule, and identify the atom whose geometry you want to know.
    2. Count the number of charge clouds around the atom.
    3. Predict shape by assuming that the charge clouds orient in space so that they are as far apart as possible.
      a. If there are two charge clouds, the geometry is linear.
      b. If there are three charge clouds, the geometry is linear or bent.
      c. If there are four charge clouds, the geometry is tetrahedral, trigonal pyramidal or bent.

III. Polar covalent bonds (Sections 5.8–5.9).
   A. Polar covalent bonds occur when the electrons in a covalent bond are attracted more to one atom than another (Section 5.8).
      1. The ability of an atom to attract electrons is called electronegativity.
      2. Atoms with electronegativity differences < 1.9 form polar covalent bonds.
      3. Atoms with electronegativity differences > 1.9 form ionic bonds.
   B. Molecules containing polar covalent bonds can be polar (Section 5.9).
      1. Molecular polarity depends on both the presence of polar covalent bonds and on molecular shape.
      2. Polarity has a dramatic effect on molecular properties.

IV. Molecular compounds (Sections 5.10–5.11).
   A. Naming binary molecular compounds (Section 5.10).
      1. Name the first element in the compound, using a prefix if necessary.
      2. Name the second element, using an *-ide* ending and using a prefix if necessary.
   B. Properties of molecular compounds (Section 5.11).
      1. Molecular compounds are electrically neutral.
      2. Molecular compounds have low melting and boiling points.
      3. Molecular compounds may be solids, liquids, or gases.

Solutions to Chapter 5 Problems

5.1

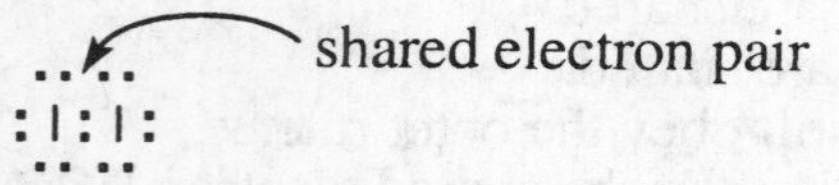
shared electron pair

Each iodine atom achieves the noble-gas configuration of xenon.

5.2

(a) PH_3	hydrogen – one covalent bond;	phosphorus – three covalent bonds
(b) H_2Se	hydrogen – one covalent bond;	selenium – two covalent bonds
(c) HCl	hydrogen – one covalent bond;	chlorine – one covalent bond
(d) SiF_4	fluorine – one covalent bond;	silicon – four covalent bonds

5.3 Lead is a member of group 4A and should form four covalent bonds, as do carbon and silicon. $PbCl_4$ is thus a more likely formula for a compound containing lead and chlorine than is $PbCl_5$.

5.4 (a) CH_2Cl_2. Carbon forms four covalent bonds. Two bonds form between carbon and hydrogen, and the other two form between carbon and chlorine.
(b) BH_3. Boron forms three covalent bonds.
(c) NI_3
(d) $SiCl_4$

5.5 In acetic acid, all hydrogen atoms have two outer-shell electrons and all carbon and oxygen atoms have eight outer-shell electrons.

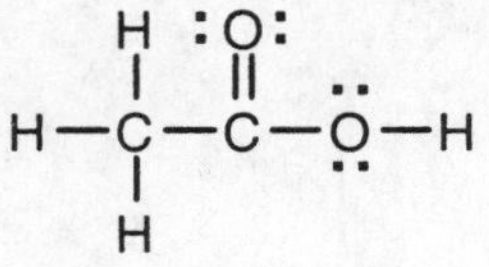

Acetic acid

5.6

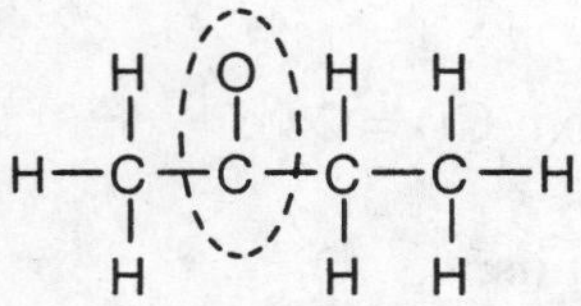

Methyl ethyl ketone

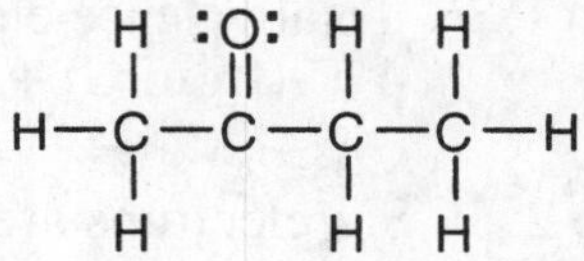

Neither of the two circled atoms in the structure on the left has a complete octet, even when electrons not involved in bonding are considered. A double bond between carbon and oxygen allows all atoms to have electron octets.

5.7 C and N must be bonded to each other. After drawing the C—N bond and all bonds to hydrogens, two electrons remain; they are a lone pair on nitrogen. All atoms now have a noble-gas configuration.

CH_5N: 14 valence electrons

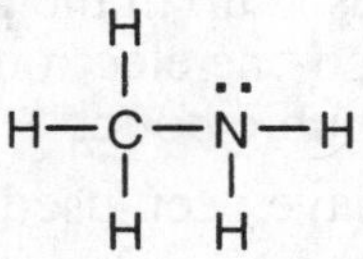

5.8

C_3H_8: 20 valence electrons

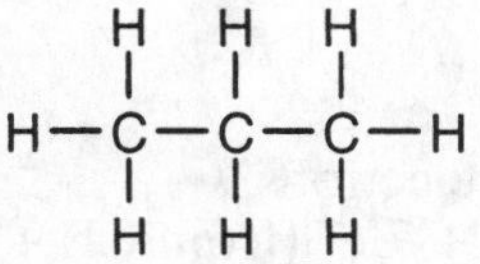

5.9

CH_2O: 12 valence electrons

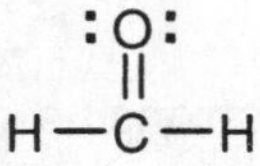

5.10

(a)

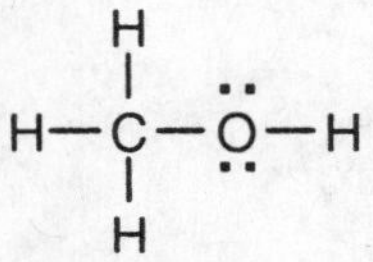

(b)

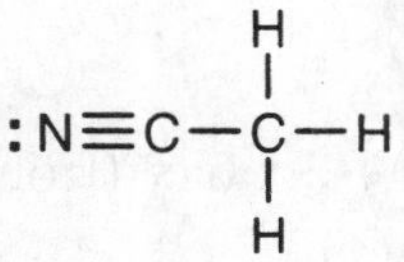

(c)

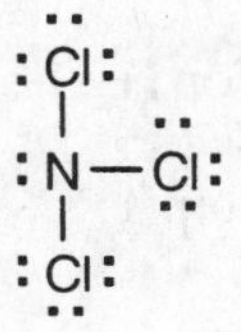

5.11 (a) The molecular formula for methyl methacrylate is $C_6H_{10}O_2$.
(b) Methyl methacrylate has two double bonds and four electron lone pairs.

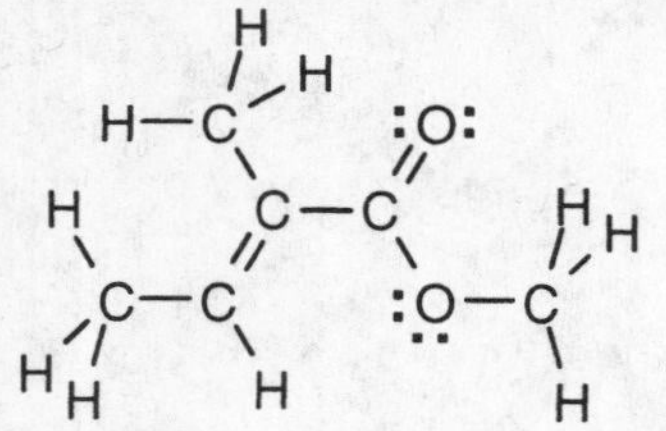

Methyl methacrylate

5.12 (a) For phosgene, $COCl_2$:

Step 1: Total valence electrons
$4\ e^-$ (from C) + $6\ e^-$ (from O) + $2 \times 7\ e^-$ (from Cl) = $24\ e^-$

Step 2: Six electrons are involved in the covalent bonds.

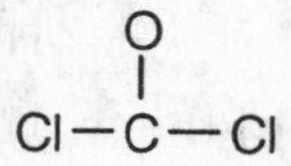

Step 3: The other 18 electrons are placed in nine lone pairs.

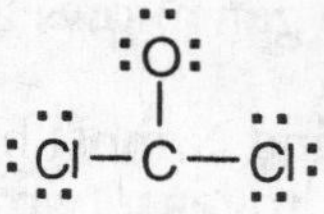

Step 4: All electrons are used up in the preceding structure, but carbon doesn't have an electron octet, so one electron pair must be moved from oxygen to form a carbon–oxygen double bond.

Step 5: The 24 electrons have been used up, and all atoms have a complete octet.

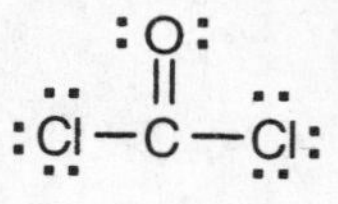

(b) For OCl^-:

Step 1: Total valence electrons
$6\ e^-$ (from O) + $7\ e^-$ (from Cl) + $1\ e^-$ (negative charge) = $14\ e^-$

Step 2: Two electrons used. O—Cl

Step 3: Twelve additional electrons used. 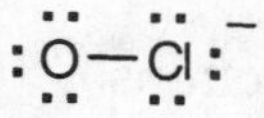

Step 4: The preceding structure uses fourteen valence electrons, and all atoms have complete octets.

(c) For H_2O_2:

Step 1: $2\ e^-$ (from 2 H) + $2 \times 6\ e^-$ (from O) = 14 electrons

Step 2: Six electrons are involved in covalent bonds. H—O—O—H

Step 3: The other eight electrons are placed in four lone pairs. 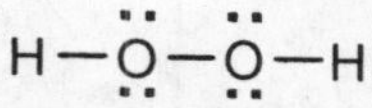

Step 4: The 14 electrons have been used up, and all atoms have complete octets.

(d) SCl_2 : 20 electrons

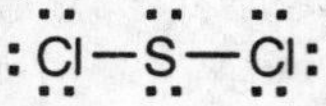

5.13

HNO_3 : 24 electrons

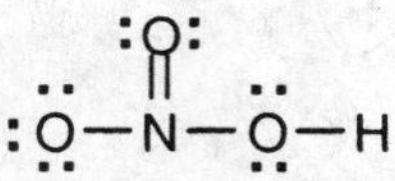

5.14

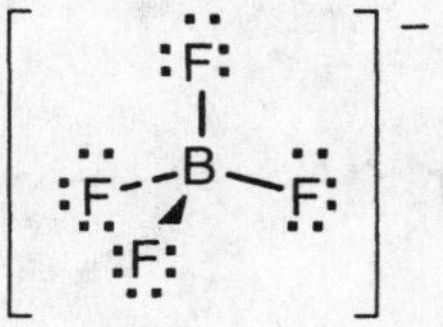

tetrahedral

5.15 Carbon, the central atom, is surrounded by four bonds. Referring to Table 5.1, we see that chloroform has tetrahedral geometry.

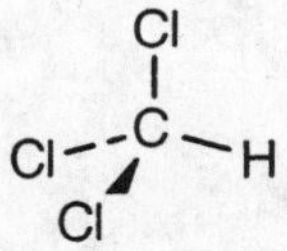

Chloroform

Each carbon of dichloroethylene is surrounded by three charge clouds. Dichloroethylene is planar, with 120° bond angles.

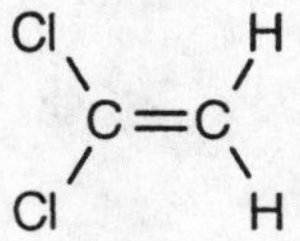

Dichloroethylene

5.16 Both ammonium ion and sulfate ion are tetrahedral.

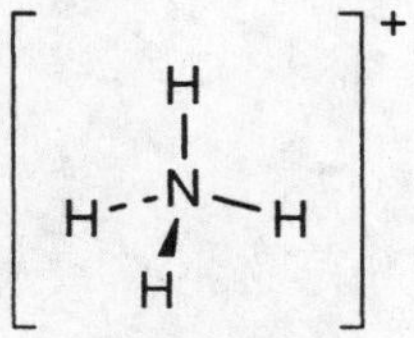

Ammonium ion

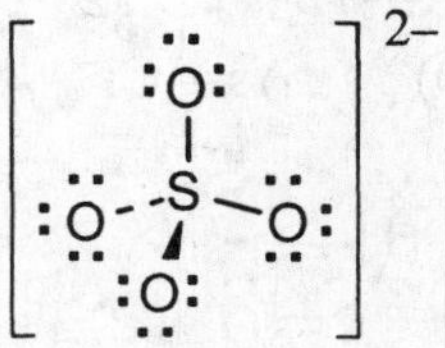

Sulfate ion

5.17 Both molecules are bent and have bond angles of approximately 105°.

5.18

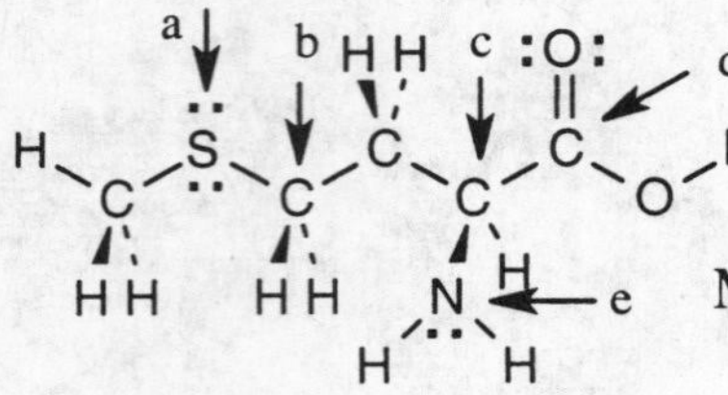

Methionine

a. bent
b. tetrahedral
c. tetrahedral
d. planar triangular
e. pyramidal

5.19 Use Figure 5.7 to predict electronegativity:

Least electronegative ——————> *Most electronegative*

H (2.1), P (2.1) < S (2.5) < N (3.0) < O (3.5)

5.20

Electronegativity		*Difference*	*Type of Bond*
(a) I (2.5),	Cl (3.0)	0.5	polar covalent
(b) Li (1.0),	O (3.5)	2.5	ionic
(c) Br (2.8),	Br (2.8)	0	covalent
(d) P (2.1),	Br (2.8)	0.7	polar covalent

5.21

Electronegativity	*Bond polarity*
(a) F (4.0), S (2.5)	$\overset{\delta-}{F}$—$\overset{\delta+}{S}$
(b) P (2.1), O (3.5)	$\overset{\delta+}{P}$—$\overset{\delta-}{O}$
(c) As (2.0), Cl (3.0)	$\overset{\delta+}{As}$—$\overset{\delta-}{Cl}$

5.22

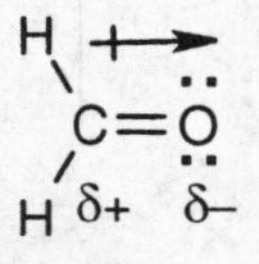

Formaldehyde is polar because of the polarity of the carbon–oxygen bond and because of the two electron lone pairs.

5.23 The —CH_3 portions of diethyl ether are tetrahedral. The C–O–C portion is bent, and has a bond angle of 112°. The molecule has the indicated polarity because of the polar C–O bonds and because of the two lone pairs of electrons.

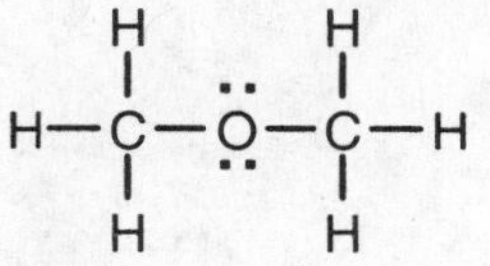

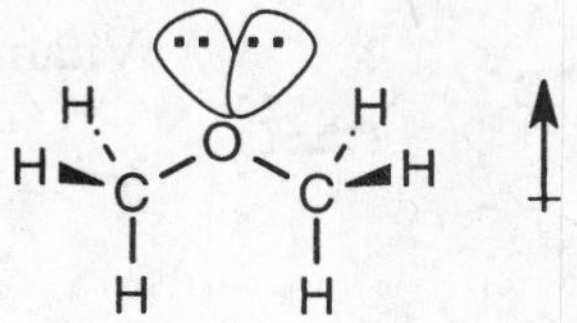

5.24

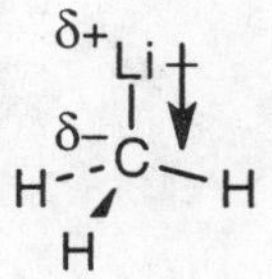

The difference in electronegativity between Li (1.0) and C (2.5) indicates that the bond between them is polar covalent, with carbon the more electronegative atom. The electrostatic potential map shows that carbon is electron-rich (red) and lithium is electron-poor (blue).

5.25 (a) S_2Cl_2 Disulfur dichloride (b) ICl Iodine chloride
(c) ICl_3 Iodine trichloride

5.26 (a) SeF_4 Selenium tetrafluoride (b) P_2O_5 Diphosphorus pentoxide
(c) BrF_3 Bromine trifluoride

Understanding Key Concepts

5.27 Drawing (a) represents an ionic compound because ions are held together by strong attractive forces in all directions. Drawing (b) represents a covalent compound because the covalent bonds that hold atoms together in a molecule are much stronger than the forces between molecules.

5.28 Drawing (a), which shows molecules composed of one sulfur atom and two oxygen atoms, depicts SO_2.

5.29 (a) tetrahedral geometry (b) pyramidal geometry (c) planar triangular geometry

5.30 All models except (c) represent a molecule with a tetrahedral central atom. In models (b) and (d), some atoms are hidden.

5.31

(a) (b)

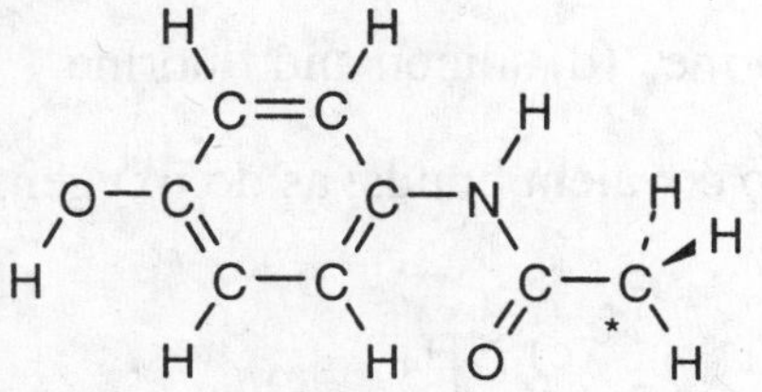

Acetaminophen $C_8H_9NO_2$

(c) All carbons except for the starred carbon have planar triangular geometry.
The starred carbon has tetrahedral geometry.
Nitrogen has pyramidal geometry.

5.32

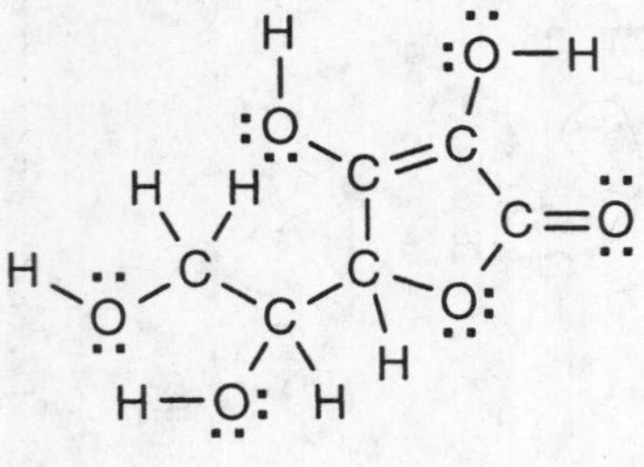

Vitamin C

5.33

(a) (b)

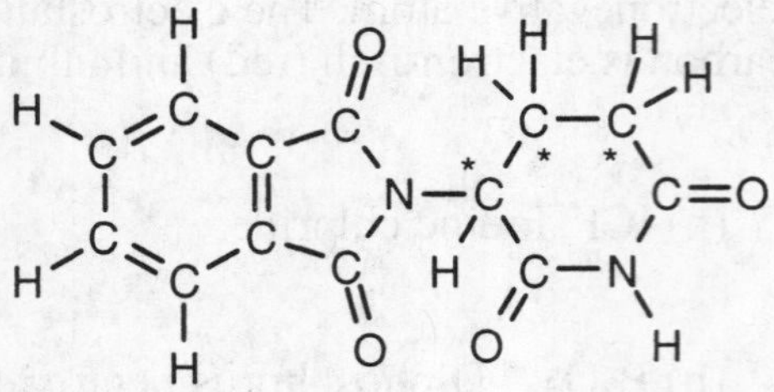

Thalidomide $C_{13}H_{10}N_2O_4$

(c) All carbons except for the starred carbons have planar triangular geometry.
The starred carbons have tetrahedral geometry.
The nitrogens have pyramidal geometry.

5.34

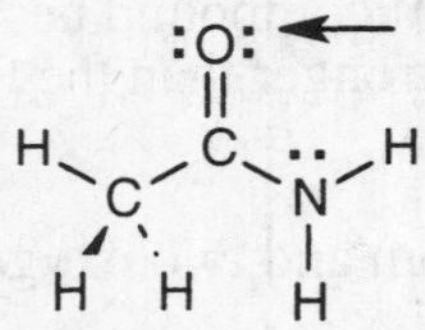
electron-rich

Acetamide

The electrostatic potential maps show that oxygen is the most electron-rich atom (red) in acetamide. The hydrogens are most electron-poor (blue).

Covalent Bonds

5.36 In a covalent bond, each atom donates an electron to the bond. Both electrons in a coordinate covalent bond come from the same atom.

5.38 Form covalent bonds: (b) carbon and fluorine, (d) silicon and fluorine

5.40 Tellurium, a group 6A element, forms two covalent bonds, as do oxygen, sulfur, and other members of group 6A.

5.42 Coordinate covalent bonds: (b) $Cu(NH_3)_4^{2+}$ (c) NH_4^+

5.44 Since tin is a member of group 4A, it forms four covalent bonds. $SnCl_4$ is the most likely formula for a molecular compound of tin and chlorine.

5.46 The indicated bond is coordinate covalent because both electrons in the bond come from nitrogen.

 coordinate covalent

Structural Formulas

5.48 (a) A *molecular formula* shows the numbers and kinds of atoms in a molecule; a *structural formula* shows how the atoms in a molecule are bonded to one another.
(b) A *structural formula* shows the bonds between atoms; a *condensed structure* shows central atoms and the atoms connected to them written as groups but does not show bonds.
(c) A *lone pair* of valence electrons is a pair that is not shared; a *shared pair* of electrons is shared between two atoms as a covalent bond.

5.50 (a) N_2 10 valence electrons (b) CO 10 valence electrons
(c) CH_3CH_2CHO 24 valence electrons (d) OF_2 20 valence electrons

5.52 A compound with the formula C_2H_8 can't exist because any structure drawn would violate the rules of valence.

5.54

(a) 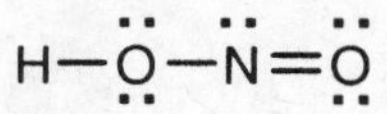

(b) 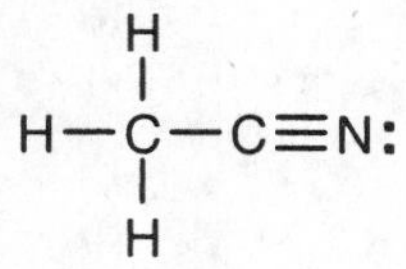

(c) 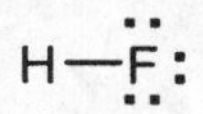

5.56 (a) $CH_3CH_2CH_3$ (b) $H_2C{=}CHCH_3$ (c) CH_3CH_2Cl

5.58 CH_3CO_2H

Drawing Lewis Structures

5.60

(a) 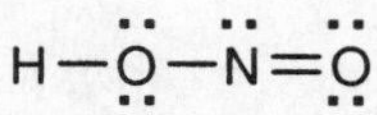

(b) 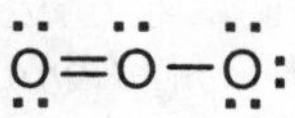

(c) 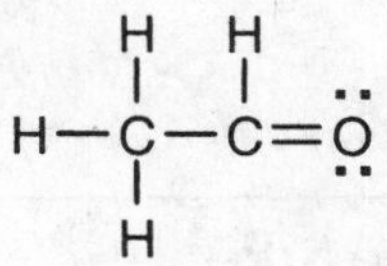

5.62

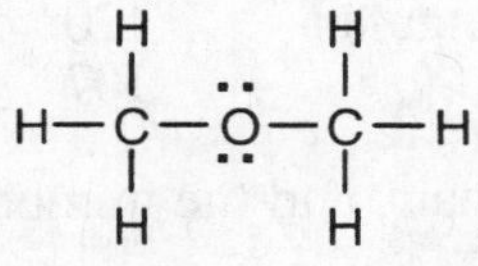 Dimethyl ether

5.64

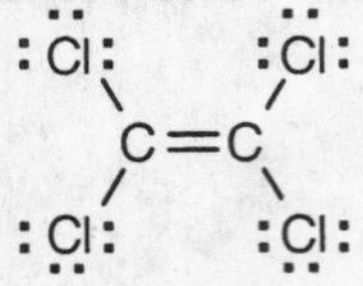

Tetrachloroethylene contains a double bond.

5.66

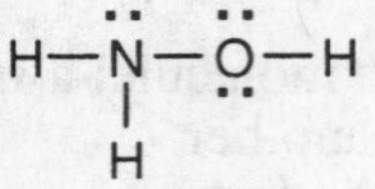

Hydroxylamine

5.68

(a) 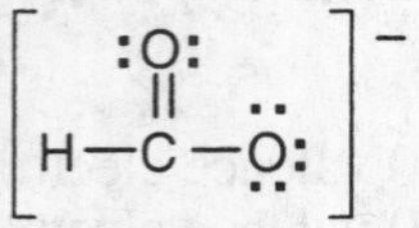

(b) 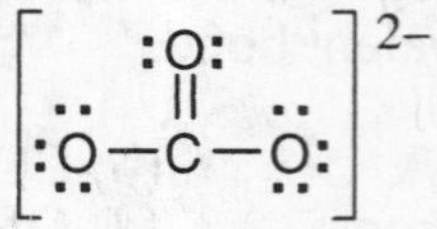

(c) 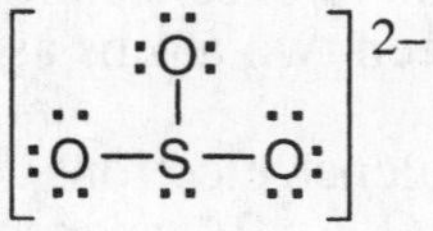

(d) 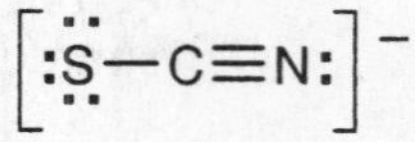

(e) 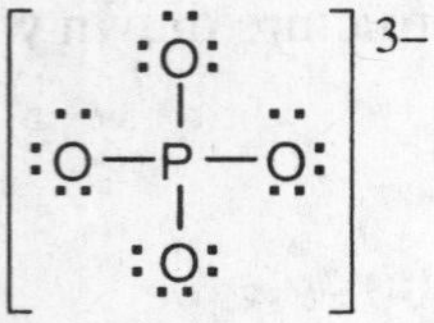

(f) 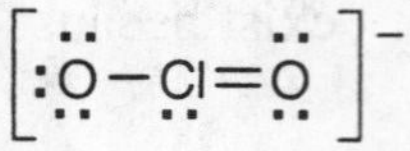

Molecular Geometry

5.70 As in the previous problem, use Table 5.1.

Molecule	*Number of Bonds*	*Number of Lone Pairs*	*Shape*	*Bond Angle*
(a) AB_4	4	0	tetrahedral	109°
(b) AB_3E	3	1	pyramidal	109°
(c) AB_2E_2	2	2	bent	109°

5.72

Molecule	*Number of Bonding Pairs Around Central Atom*	*Number of Lone Pairs*	*Shape*	*Bond Angle*
(a) SiF_4	4	0	tetrahedral	109°
(b) CF_2Cl_2	4	0	tetrahedral	109°
(c) SO_3	3*	0	planar triangular	120°
(d) BBr_3	3	0	planar triangular	120°
(e) NF_3	3	1	pyramidal	107°

* For determining shape, the double bond counts as one bond pair, and the number of bonds is three.

5.74

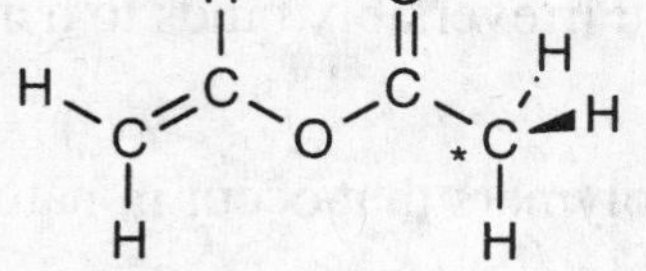

Vinyl acetate

All carbons are planar triangular, except for the starred carbon, which is tetrahedral.

Polarity of Bonds and Molecules

5.76 Using the periodic table, count up from element 114. Element 119 should occur under francium and accordingly should be one of the least electronegative elements, with an electronegativity of 0.8.

5.78 *More electronegative* ———> *Less electronegative*

Cl > C > Cu > Ca > Cs

5.80

(a) $\overset{\delta-}{O}$—$\overset{\delta+}{Br}$ (b) $\overset{\delta-}{N}$—$\overset{\delta+}{H}$ (c) $\overset{\delta+}{P}$—$\overset{\delta-}{O}$ (d) nonpolar (e) $\overset{\delta-}{C}$—$\overset{\delta+}{Li}$

5.82 Use Figure 5.5 to determine bond polarities

Least polar bonds ———> *Most polar bonds*

$PH_3 < HCl < H_2O < CF_4$

5.84

(a)

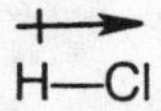

polar

(b)

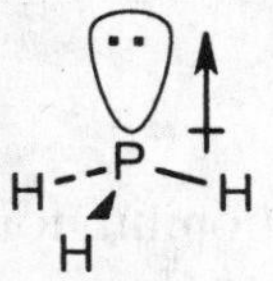

polar

(c)

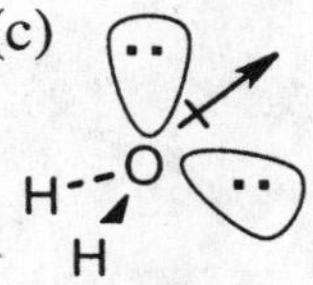

polar

(d) nonpolar

5.86 The bonds between oxygen and hydrogen are polar covalent, but the bonds between sulfur and hydrogen are nonpolar.

Names and Formulas of Molecular Compounds

5.88 (a) $SiCl_4$ silicon tetrachloride (b) NaH sodium hydride
(c) SbF_5 antimony pentafluoride (d) OsO_4 osmium tetroxide

5.90 (a) SeO_2 (b) XeO_4 (c) N_2S_5 (d) P_3Se_4

Applications

5.92 Carbon monoxide is toxic in high concentration because it irreversibly binds to hemoglobin and thus prevents transfer of oxygen to tissues.

5.94 Carbohydrates, proteins, and DNA are all examples of polymers that occur in nature.

5.96 The name of a chemical gives no clue as to whether the chemical is natural or synthetic, although certain chemicals are unlikely to occur in nature.

General Questions and Problems

5.98

(a)

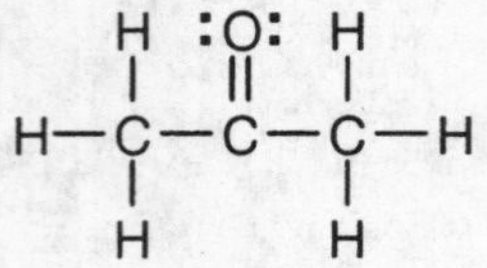

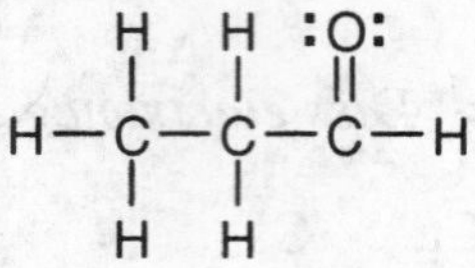

(b) The C=O carbon atoms have planar triangular geometry, and the other carbons have tetrahedral geometry.
(c) The C=O bonds are polar.

5.100 Consult Figure 5.4 for help.

(a) Carbon forms four bonds. The correct formula is CCl_4.
(b) Nitrogen forms three bonds. The correct formula is N_2H_4.
(c) Sulfur forms two bonds. The correct formula is H_2S.
(d) C_2OS *could* actually be correct (S=C=C=O), but compounds with such adjacent double bonds are rare. More likely is the formula COS, a structural relative of carbon dioxide (S=C=O).

5.102

(a)

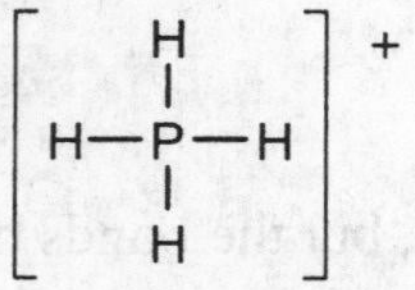

(b) Phosphonium ion is tetrahedral.

(c) Phosphorus donates its lone pair of electrons to H^+ to form a coordinate covalent bond.
(d) Number of electrons: 15 (from P) + 3 (from 3 H) = 18
Number of protons: 15 (from P) + 4 (from 4 H) = 19
PH_4^+ is positive because the number of protons exceeds the number of electrons by one.

5.104

Compound	*Name*
(a) $CaCl_2$	calcium chloride
(b) $TeCl_2$	tellurium dichloride
(c) BF_3	boron trifluoride
(d) $MgSO_4$	magnesium sulfate
(e) K_2O	potassium oxide
(f) FeF_3	iron(III) fluoride
(g) PF_3	phosphorus trifluoride

5.106

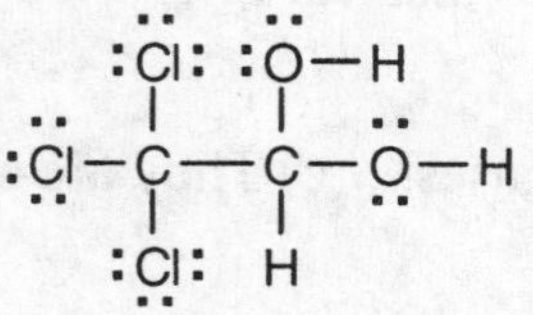

Chloral hydrate

5.108

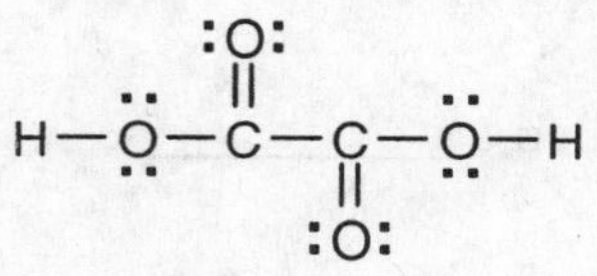

Oxalic acid

5.110

(a)

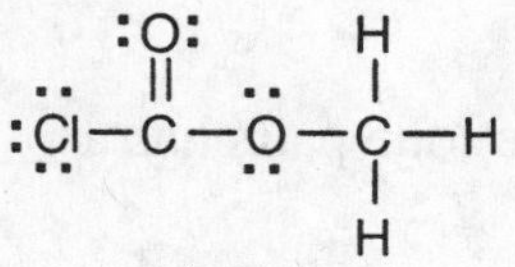

(b)

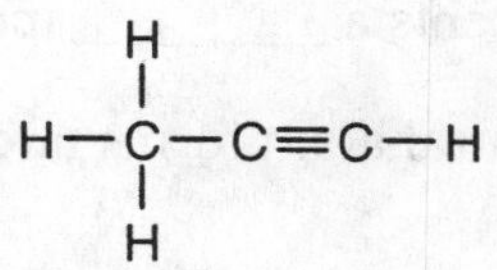

Self-Test for Chapter 5

Multiple Choice

1. Which of these diatomic molecules contains a double bond?
(a) H_2 (b) I_2 (c) O_2 (d) N_2

2. Which of these molecules is pyramidal?
(a) CBr_4 (b) $AlCl_3$ (c) SF_6 (d) PH_3

3. Choose the element that forms three covalent bonds and has one lone pair of electrons.
(a) C (b) N (c) O (d) F

4. How many charge clouds does the molecule H_2S have?
(a) 2 (b) 3 (c) 4 (d) can't tell

5. Which of the following double bonds is not likely to be found in organic molecules?
(a) O=O (b) C=C (c) C=O (d) C=N

6. All of the following are true about the polyatomic ion BF_4^- except
(a) All atoms don't have electron octets. (b) It has polar covalent bonds. (c) It contains a coordinate covalent bond. (d) It has a tetrahedral shape.

7. One of these molecules doesn't contain a polar covalent bond. Which is it?
(a) $BeBr_2$ (b) PCl_3 (c) CO_2 (d) CS_2

8. Which of the following compounds is polar?
(a) $BeBr_2$ (b) PCl_3 (c) CO_2 (d) CS_2

9. A name for S_2F_2 is
(a) sulfur fluoride (b) sulfur difluoride (c) disulfur fluoride (d) disulfur difluoride

10. Which of the following is not true for molecular compounds?
(a) They are water-soluble. (b) They can be solids, liquids, or gases. (c) They are composed of nonmetals. (d) They have low melting points.

Sentence Completion

1. An _______ element strongly attracts electrons.

2. A molecular compound that occurs in living organisms is called a __________.

3. In Lewis structures, a line represents a _______ bond.

4. _____ and _____ are the most common triple bonds in chemical compounds.

5. The formula X_2 represents a ________ molecule.

6. A molecule whose central atom forms three bonds and has no lone pairs has a ____________ shape.

7. _____ orbitals in sulfur and phosphorus can be used for covalent bonds.

8. N_2 contains a _______ bond.

9. _______ molecular compounds are formed from only two elements.

10. Many molecular compounds are soluble in _______ liquids.

11. Large organic molecules are often written as _______ structures.

True or False

1. Br_2 is a molecular compound.
2. Six electrons are used to form a triple bond.
3. Coordinate covalent bonds occur only in cations or anions, not in neutral compounds.
4. The first step in drawing a Lewis structure is to find the total number of electrons in the combined atoms.
5. $AlCl_3$ is a pyramidal molecule.
6. The shape of ionic compounds can be predicted by the VSEPR model.
7. Electronegativity decreases in going down the periodic table.
8. CI_4 contains polar covalent bonds.
9. Both planar and bent molecules have bond angles of 120°.
10. Group 7A elements can form more than one covalent bond.
11. Bent compounds may have either one or two lone pairs.

Match each entry on the left with its partner on the right.

1.	BCl_3	(a) Contains a pure covalent bond
2.	Planar molecule	(b) $BeCl_2$
3.	Bent molecule	(c) Exception to the octet rule
4.	Cl_2	(d) NH_3
5.	BCl_4^-	(e) Contains a triple bond
6.	NaI	(f) H_2O
7.	C≡O	(g) Contains a double bond
8.	SF_6	(h) Central atom doesn't have an electron octet
9.	Linear molecule	(i) Contains an ionic bond
10.	O=C=O	(j) $AlCl_3$
11.	Pyramidal molecule	(k) Contains a coordinate covalent bond
12.	CH_3Cl	(l) Contains a polar covalent bond

Chapter 6 – Chemical Reactions: Classification and Mass Relationships

Chapter Outline

I. Chemical equations (Sections 6.1–6.2).
  A. Writing chemical equations (Section 6.1).
    1. A chemical equation describes a chemical reaction.
      a. The reactants are written on the left.
      b. The products are written on the right.
      c. An arrow goes between them.
    2. The number and kinds of atoms must be the same on both sides of the equation. This is known as the law of conservation of mass.
    3. Numbers that are placed in front of formulas are called coefficients.
    4. States of matter (*s*), (*g*), (*l*) are often placed after chemical formulas.
  B. Balancing chemical equations (Section 6.2).
    1. Write an unbalanced equation using the correct formulas for all substances.
    2. Add appropriate coefficients to balance the atoms of each type, one at a time.
    3. Check to make sure that the numbers and kinds of atoms are balanced.
    4. Make sure all coefficients are reduced to their lowest whole-number values.

II. Molar relationships (Sections 6.3–6.7).
  A. The mole (Section 6.3).
    1. Molecular weight is the sum of the atomic weights of atoms in a molecule.
    2. Formula weight is the sum of the atomic weights of atoms in a formula unit.
    3. One mole of any pure substance has a mass equal to its molecular or formula weight in grams.
      Avogadro's number (6.022×10^{23}), known as the mole, represents the number of formula units that has a mass in grams equal to its weight in amu.
  B. Mole–mass relationships (Section 6.4–6.6).
    1. Gram–mole conversions (Section 6.4).
      a. Molar mass is the mass in grams of one mole of any substance.
      b. Molar mass is a conversion factor that allows calculation of moles from grams and vice versa.
    2. Molar relationships from chemical equations (Section 6.5).
      a. The coefficients in an equation tell how many moles of reactant or product are involved in the reaction.
      b. The coefficients can be put in a mole ratio, which can be used as a conversion factor.
    3. Mass relationships (Section 6.6).
      a. Mole–mole conversions are made by using mole ratios.
      b. Mole–mass conversions are made by using molar mass as a conversion factor.
      c. Mass–mass conversions can be made by a mass–mole conversion of one substance, using mole ratios, and making a mole–mass conversion of the other substance.
    4. A summary of calculations using mole–mass relationships:
      a. Write the balanced equation.
      b. Choose mole–mass relationships and mole ratios to calculate the desired quantity.
      c. Set up the factor-label method to calculate the answer.
      d. Check the answer with a ballpark solution.
  C. Percent yield (Section 6.7).
    1. Percent yield = actual yield / theoretical yield x 100%
    2. Theoretical yield is found by using a mass–mass calculation.

III. Chemical reactions (Sections 6.8–6.13).
  A. Classes of chemical reactions (Section 6.8).
    1. Precipitation reactions occur when an insoluble solid is formed.
    2. Acid–base reactions occur when an acid and a base react to yield water and a salt.
    3. Redox reactions occur when electrons are transferred between reaction partners.
  B. Precipitation reactions (Section 6.9).
    1. To predict whether a precipitation reaction occurs, you must know the solubilities of the products.
    2. Table 6.1 gives general solubility rules to predict if a precipitation reaction will occur.
  C. Acid–base reactions (Section 6.10).
    1. Acid–base reactions are known as neutralization reactions because when the reaction is complete the solution is neither acidic nor basic.
    2. An example: $HA(aq) + MOH(aq) \longrightarrow H_2O(l) + MA(aq)$
    3. When a carbonate or bicarbonate is one of the reactants, CO_2 is also produced.
  D. Redox reactions (Sections 6.11–6.12).
    1. Definition of redox reactions (Section 6.11).
      a. A redox reaction occurs when electrons are transferred from one atom to another.
      b. The substance that loses electrons is oxidized and is known as the reducing agent.
      c. The substance that gains electrons is reduced and is known as the oxidizing agent.
      d. Redox reactions occur during corrosion, combustion, respiration, and photography.
    2. Recognizing redox reactions (Section 6.12).
      a. With some substances, it isn't obvious if a redox reaction has occurred.
      b. In a neutral compound, oxidation numbers are assigned to each element to indicate electron ownership.
      c. To assign oxidation numbers:
        i. An atom in its elemental state has an oxidation number of zero.
        ii. A monatomic ion has an oxidation number equal to its charge.
        iii. In a molecular compound, an atom usually has the same oxidation number that it would have if it were a monatomic ion.
        iv. The sum of the oxidation numbers in a neutral compound is zero.
        v. The oxidation number of oxygen is usually –2; the oxidation number of hydrogen is usually +1.
  E. Net ionic equations (Section 6.13).
    1. A molecular equation shows reactants and products as molecules and doesn't indicate if they are ions.
    2. An ionic equation is written if ions are involved and shows all ionic reactants and products.
    3. A net ionic equation includes only the ions that undergo change and deletes spectator ions.

Solutions to Chapter 6 Problems

6.1 (a) Solid cobalt(II) chloride plus gaseous hydrogen fluoride yield solid cobalt(II) fluoride plus gaseous hydrogen chloride.

(b) Aqueous lead(II) nitrate plus aqueous potassium iodide yield solid lead(II) iodide plus aqueous potassium nitrate.

6.2 An equation is balanced if the number and types of atoms on the left side equals the number and types of atoms on the right side.

(a) On the left: 2 H + Cl + K + O
On the right: 2 H + Cl + K + O The equation is balanced.

(b) On the left: 1 C + 4 H + 2 Cl
On the right: 1 C + 3 H + 3 Cl The equation is not balanced.
(c) Balanced
(d) Not balanced in H, O.

6.3 *Step 1.* Write the unbalanced equation.

$$O_2 \longrightarrow O_3$$

Step 2. Balance the atoms of each type, one by one.

$$3\ O_2 \longrightarrow 2\ O_3$$ The equation is balanced.

6.4 (a) $Ca(OH)_2 + 2\ HCl \longrightarrow CaCl_2 + 2\ H_2O$

(b) $4\ Al + 3\ O_2 \longrightarrow 2\ Al_2O_3$

(c) $2\ CH_3CH_3 + 7\ O_2 \longrightarrow 4\ CO_2 + 6\ H_2O$

(d) $2\ AgNO_3 + MgCl_2 \longrightarrow 2\ AgCl + Mg(NO_3)_2$

6.5 *Step 1.* $A + B_2 \longrightarrow A_2B_2$

Step 2. $2\ A + B_2 \longrightarrow A_2B_2$ The equation is balanced.

6.6 (a) For ibuprofen, $C_{13}H_{18}O_2$:

At. wt of 13 C = 13 x 12.0 amu = 156.0 amu
At. wt of 18 H = 18 x 1.0 amu = 18.0 amu
At. wt of 2 O = 2 x 16.0 amu = 32.0 amu

MW of $C_{13}H_{18}O_2$ = 206.0 amu

(b) For phenobarbital, $C_{12}H_{12}N_2O_3$:

At. wt of 12 C = 12 x 12.0 amu = 144.0 amu
At. wt of 12 H = 12 x 1.0 amu = 12.0 amu
At. wt of 2 N = 2 x 14.0 amu = 28.0 amu
At. wt of 3 O = 3 x 16.0 amu = 48.0 amu

MW of $C_{12}H_{12}N_2O_3$ = 232.0 amu

6.7 At. wt of 6 C = 6 x 12.0 amu = 72.0 amu
At. wt of 8 H = 8 x 1.0 amu = 8.0 amu
At. wt of 6 O = 6 x 16.0 amu = 96.0 amu

MW of $C_6H_8O_6$ = 176.0 amu

Since the molecular weight of ascorbic acid is 176.0 amu, 6.022×10^{23} molecules have a mass of 176 g.

$$500 \text{ mg ascorbic acid} \times \frac{1 \text{ g}}{10^3 \text{ mg}} \times \frac{6.022 \times 10^{23} \text{ molecules}}{176 \text{ g}} = 1.71 \times 10^{21} \text{ molecules}$$

A 500 mg tablet contains 1.71×10^{21} molecules of ascorbic acid.

6.8 At. wt of 9 C = 9 x 12.0 amu = 108.0 amu
At. wt of 8 H = 8 x 1.0 amu = 8.0 amu
At. wt of 4 O = 4 x 16.0 amu = 64.0 amu

MW of $C_9H_8O_4$ = 180.0 amu

$$5.0 \times 10^{20} \text{ molecules} \times \frac{180.0 \text{ g}}{1 \text{ mol}} \times \frac{1 \text{ mol}}{6.022 \times 10^{23} \text{molecules}} = 0.15 \text{ g}$$

5.0×10^{20} molecules of aspirin weigh 0.15 g

6.9

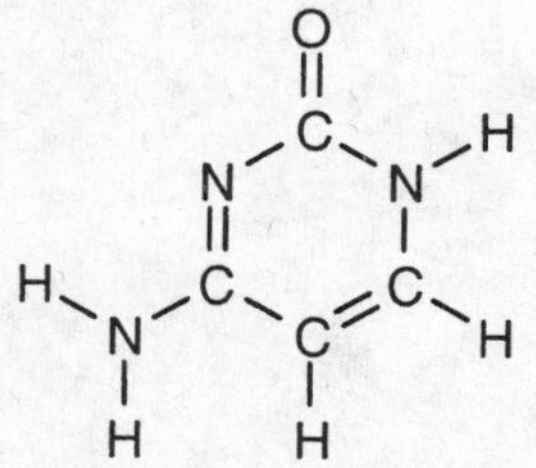

Cytosine $C_4H_5N_3O$

At. wt of 4 C = 4 x 12.0 amu = 48.0 amu
At. wt of 5 H = 5 x 1.0 amu = 5.0 amu
At. wt of 3 N = 3 x 14.0 amu = 42.0 amu
At. wt of 1 O = 1 x 16.0 amu = 16.0 amu

MW of $C_4H_5N_3O$ = 111.0 amu

6.10 Molar mass of C_2H_6O = 46.0 g/mol

$$10.0 \text{ g} \times \frac{1 \text{ mol}}{46.0 \text{ g}} = 0.217 \text{ mol in a 10.0 g sample}$$

Ballpark check: The sample size, 10.0 g, is about 1/5 mol, or about 0.2 mol.

$$0.10 \text{ mol} \times \frac{46.0 \text{ g}}{1 \text{ mol}} = 4.6 \text{ g in a 0.10 mol sample}$$

6.11 Molar mass of acetaminophen = 151 g

$$0.0225 \text{ mol} \times \frac{151 \text{ g}}{1 \text{ mol}} = 3.40 \text{ g}$$

5.00 g acetaminophen weighs more than 0.0225 mol.

6.12 (a) $Ni(s) + 2\,HCl(aq) \longrightarrow NiCl_2(aq) + H_2(g)$

$$9.81 \text{ mol HCl} \times \frac{1 \text{ mol Ni}}{2 \text{ mol HCl}} = 4.90 \text{ mol Ni}$$

(b) $$6.00 \text{ mol Ni} \times \frac{1 \text{ mol } NiCl_2}{1 \text{ mol Ni}} = 6.00 \text{ mol } NiCl_2 \text{ from } 6.00 \text{ mol Ni}$$

$$12.00 \text{ mol HCl} \times \frac{1 \text{ mol } NiCl_2}{2 \text{ mol HCl}} = 6.00 \text{ mol } NiCl_2 \text{ from } 12.00 \text{ mol HCl}$$

6.00 mol $NiCl_2$ can be formed from 6.00 mol Ni and 12.00 mol HCl.

6.13 $6\,CO_2 + 6\,H_2O \longrightarrow C_6H_{12}O_6 + 6\,O_2$

$$15.0 \text{ mol glucose} \times \frac{6 \text{ mol } CO_2}{1 \text{ mol glucose}} = 90.0 \text{ mol } CO_2$$

6.14 (a) This is a mole-to-mole problem.

$$9.90 \text{ mol } SiO_2 \times \frac{4 \text{ mol HF}}{1 \text{ mol } SiO_2} = 39.6 \text{ mol HF}$$

(b) This is a mass-to-mass problem.

$$23.0 \text{ g } SiO_2 \times \frac{1 \text{ mol } SiO_2}{60.1 \text{ g } SiO_2} \times \frac{2 \text{ mol } H_2O}{1 \text{ mol } SiO_2} \times \frac{18.0 \text{ g } H_2O}{1 \text{ mol } H_2O} = 13.8 \text{ g } H_2O$$

Ballpark check: About 1/3 mol SiO_2 is used to produce 2/3 mol H_2O. Since the molar mass of H_2O is 18 g, we expect about 12 g H_2O, which is reasonably close to the calculated answer.

6.15 For WO_3:

$$5.00 \text{ g W} \times \frac{1 \text{ mol W}}{183.8 \text{ g W}} \times \frac{1 \text{ mol } WO_3}{1 \text{ mol W}} \times \frac{231.8 \text{ g } WO_3}{1 \text{ mol } WO_3} = 6.31 \text{ g } WO_3$$

For H_2:

$$5.00 \text{ g W} \times \frac{1 \text{ mol W}}{183.8 \text{ g W}} \times \frac{3 \text{ mol } H_2}{1 \text{ mol W}} \times \frac{2.02 \text{ g } H_2}{1 \text{ mol } H_2} = 0.165 \text{ g } H_2$$

6.31 g WO_3 and 0.165 g H_2 are needed to produce 5.00 g W.

Ballpark check: About 3/4 of the mass of WO_3 is composed of W. Thus, 5.00 g W comes from about 4/3 x 5.00 g W = 6.33 g WO_3, a result almost identical to the calculated result.

6.16 The molar mass of ethylene is 28.0 g/mol; the molar mass of ethyl chloride is 64.5 g/mol.

$$19.4 \text{ g ethylene} \times \frac{1 \text{ mol ethylene}}{28.0 \text{ g ethylene}} \times \frac{1 \text{ mol ethyl chloride}}{1 \text{ mol ethylene}} \times \frac{64.5 \text{ g ethyl chloride}}{1 \text{ mol ethyl chloride}}$$

$$= 44.7 \text{ g ethyl chloride}$$

$$\frac{25.5 \text{ g ethyl chloride actually formed}}{44.7 \text{ g theoretical yield of ethyl chloride}} \times 100\% = 57.0\%$$

Ballpark check: The amount of ethylene reactant corresponds to about 2/3 mol.The theoretical yield of product is about 2/3 mol ethyl chloride (somewhat more than 40 g). Since the actual yield is 25.5 g, the percent yield should be around 60%.

6.17 Note: to save space, ethylene oxide will be represented as EO, and ethylene glycol as EG.

$$35.0 \text{ g EO} \times \frac{1 \text{ mol EO}}{44.0 \text{ g EO}} \times \frac{1 \text{ mol EG}}{1 \text{ mol EO}} \times \frac{62.0 \text{ g EG}}{1 \text{ mol EG}} = 49.3 \text{ g ethylene glycol}$$

This quantity represents the maximum possible amount of ethylene glycol that can be produced. If the reaction occurs in 96.0% yield, then 49.3 g EG x 0.960 = 47.3 g EG is actually formed.

Ballpark check: A bit less than 3/4 mol EO is used to produce the same number of mol of EG, corresponding to about 45 g EG, close to the calculated result. The percent yield is also in close agreement.

6.18 (a) $AgNO_3(aq) + KCl(aq) \longrightarrow AgCl(s) + KNO_3(aq)$
Precipitation: Solid AgCl is formed.

(b) $2\ Al(s) + 3\ Br_2(l) \longrightarrow 2\ AlBr_3(s)$
Redox reaction: Al^{+3} is formed from Al, and Br^- is formed from Br_2.

(c) $Ca(OH)_2(aq) + 2\ HNO_3(aq) \longrightarrow 2\ H_2O(l) + Ca(NO_3)_2(aq)$
Acid–base neutralization

6.19 Use Table 6.1 for solubility guidelines.

Insoluble	*Soluble*
(a) $CdCO_3$ (most carbonates are insoluble)	(b) Na_2S
(c) $PbSO_4$ (exception to the rule that sulfates are soluble)	(d) $(NH_4)_3PO_4$
(e) Hg_2Cl_2 (exception to the rule that chlorides are soluble)	

6.20 As in Worked Example 6.13, identify the products, and use Table 6.1 to predict their solubility. If the products are insoluble, a precipitation reaction will occur.

(a) $NiCl_2(aq) + (NH_4)_2S(aq) \longrightarrow 2\ NH_4Cl(aq) + NiS(s)$
A precipitation reaction will occur.

(b) $2\ AgNO_3(aq) + CaBr_2(aq) \longrightarrow Ca(NO_3)_2(aq) + 2\ AgBr(s)$
A precipitation reaction will occur.

6.21 (a) $2\ CsOH(aq) + H_2SO_4(aq) \longrightarrow Cs_2SO_4(aq) + 2\ H_2O(l)$

(b) $Ca(OH)_2(aq) + 2\ CH_3CO_2H(aq) \longrightarrow Ca(CH_3CO_2)_2(aq) + 2\ H_2O(l)$

(c) $NaHCO_3(aq) + HBr(aq) \longrightarrow NaBr(aq) + CO_2(g) + H_2O(l)$

6.22

	Oxidized Reactant/ Reducing Agent	*Reduced Reactant/ Oxidizing Agent*
(a)	Fe	Cu^{2+}
(b)	Mg	Cl_2
(c)	Al	Cr_2O_3

The oxidizing agent is the reduced reactant, and the reducing agent is the oxidized reactant.

6.23 $2\ K(s) + Br_2(l) \longrightarrow 2\ KBr(s)$

Reducing agent (K), *Oxidizing agent* (Br_2)

6.24

Compound	*Oxidation Number of Metal*	*Name*
(a) VCl_3	+3	vanadium(III) chloride
(b) $SnCl_4$	+4	tin(IV) chloride
(c) CrO_3	+6	chromium(VI) oxide
(d) $Cu(NO_3)_2$	+2	copper(II) nitrate
(e) $NiSO_4$	+2	nickel(II) sulfate

6.25

Compound	*Atom*	*Oxidation Number*
(a) N_2O_4	N	+4
	O	−2
(b) $HClO_4$	H	+1
	Cl	+7
	O	−2
(c) MnO_4^-	Mn	+7
	O	−2
(d) H_2SO_4	H	+1
	S	+6
	O	−2

6.26 Oxidation numbers are written above the atoms.

(a) $\overset{+1-2}{Na_2S}(aq) + \overset{+2-1}{NiCl_2}(aq) \longrightarrow 2\,\overset{+1-1}{NaCl}(aq) + \overset{+2-2}{NiS}(s)$

This reaction is not a redox reaction because no atoms change oxidation numbers.

(b) $2\,\overset{0}{Na}(s) + 2\,\overset{+1-2}{H_2O}(l) \longrightarrow 2\,\overset{+1-2+1}{NaOH}(aq) + \overset{0}{H_2}(g)$

Sodium is oxidized and hydrogen is reduced in this reaction.

(c) $\overset{0}{C}(s) + \overset{0}{O_2}(g) \longrightarrow \overset{+4-2}{CO_2}(g)$

Carbon is oxidized and oxygen is reduced in this redox reaction.

(d) $\overset{+2-2}{CuO}(s) + 2\,\overset{+1-1}{HCl}(aq) \longrightarrow \overset{+2-1}{CuCl_2}(aq) + \overset{+1-2}{H_2O}(l)$

This is not a redox reaction because no atoms change oxidation number.

(e) $2\,\overset{+7-2}{MnO_4^-}(aq) + 5\,\overset{+4-2}{SO_2}(g) + 2\,\overset{+1-2}{H_2O}(l) \longrightarrow 2\,\overset{+2}{Mn^{2+}}(aq) + \overset{+6-2}{SO_4^{2-}}(aq) + 4\,\overset{+1}{H^+}(aq)$

In this redox reaction, the oxidation number of Mn changes from +7 to +2 and the oxidation number of S changes from +4 to +6.

6.27 (a) Write the equation, including all ions.

$2\,Li(s) + Pb^{2+} + 2\,NO_3^- \longrightarrow 2\,Li^+ + 2\,NO_3^- + Pb(s)$

The nitrate ions on each side cancel.

$2\,Li(s) + Pb^{2+}(aq) \longrightarrow 2\,Li^+(aq) + Pb(s)$

(b) $OH^-(aq) + H^+(aq) \longrightarrow H_2O(l)$

K^+ and SO_4^{2-} cancel, and coefficients are reduced.

(c) $2\,Fe^{3+}(aq) + Sn^{2+}(aq) \longrightarrow 2\,Fe^{2+}(aq) + Sn^{4+}(aq)$

The chloride ions cancel.

Understanding Key Concepts

6.28 Product mixture (d) is the only mixture that contains the same number of atoms as (a).

6.29 (c) $2\,A + B_2 \longrightarrow A_2B_2$

6.30 (d) $\longrightarrow$ (c)
reactants products

6.31 Methionine: $C_5H_{11}NO_2S$

At. wt of 5 C	= 5 x 12.0 amu	=	60.0 amu
At. wt of 11 H	= 11 x 1.0 amu	=	11.0 amu
At. wt of N	=	=	14.0 amu
At. wt of 2 O	= 2 x 16.0 amu	=	32.0 amu
At. wt of S	=	=	32.1 amu
MW of $C_5H_{11}NO_2S$		=	149.1 amu

6.32 (a) $A_2 + 3\ B_2 \longrightarrow 2\ AB_3$

(b) $1.0 \text{ mol } A_2 \times \dfrac{2 \text{ mol } AB_3}{1 \text{ mol } A_2} = 2.0 \text{ mol } AB_3$

$1.0 \text{ mol } B_2 \times \dfrac{2 \text{ mol } AB_3}{3 \text{ mol } B_2} = 0.67 \text{ mol } AB_3$

6.33 (a) Mixing of sodium and carbonate ions produces outcome (1). No insoluble product is formed, and sodium and carbonate ions remain in solution.
(b) Mixing barium and chromate ions produces outcome (2). $BaCrO_4$ precipitate forms (one barium ion for each chromate ion), and the excess barium ions remain in solution.
(c) Mixing silver and sulfite ions yields outcome (3). Ag_2SO_3 precipitate forms (two silver ions for each sulfite ion), and no Ag^+ or SO_3^{2-} ions remain in solution.

6.34 The observed product is a precipitate that contains two cations per anion. From the list of cations, Ag^+ is the only one that forms precipitates and has a 2:1 cation/anion ratio with the anions listed. The anion can be either CO_3^{2-} or CrO_4^{2-}, since both form precipitates with Ag^+. Thus, the possible products are Ag_2CO_3 and Ag_2CrO_4.

6.35 Note: to save space, ethylene oxide will be represented as EO, and ethylene glycol as EG.

$$9.0 \text{ g } H_2O \times \frac{1 \text{ mol } H_2O}{18.0 \text{ g } H_2O} \times \frac{1 \text{ mol EO}}{1 \text{ mol } H_2O} \times \frac{44.0 \text{ g EO}}{1 \text{ mol EO}} = 22 \text{ g ethylene oxide}$$

$$9.0 \text{ g } H_2O \times \frac{1 \text{ mol } H_2O}{18.0 \text{ g } H_2O} \times \frac{1 \text{ mol EG}}{1 \text{ mol } H_2O} \times \frac{62.0 \text{ g EG}}{1 \text{ mol EG}} = 31 \text{ g ethylene glycol}$$

Balancing Chemical Equations

6.36 A balanced equation is an equation in which the number of atoms of each kind is the same on both sides of the reaction arrow.

6.38 (a) $SO_2(g) + H_2O(g) \longrightarrow H_2SO_3(aq)$

(b) $2\ K(s) + Br_2(l) \longrightarrow 2\ KBr(s)$

(c) $C_3H_8(g) + 5\ O_2(g) \longrightarrow 3\ CO_2(g) + 4\ H_2O(g)$

6.40 (a) $2\ C_2H_6(g) + 7\ O_2(g) \longrightarrow 4\ CO_2(g) + 6\ H_2O(l)$

(b) balanced

(c) $2\ Mg(s) + O_2(g) \longrightarrow 2\ MgO(s)$

(d) $2\ K(s) + 2\ H_2O(l) \longrightarrow 2\ KOH(aq) + H_2(g)$

6.42 (a) $Hg(NO_3)_2(aq) + 2\ LiI(aq) \longrightarrow 2\ LiNO_3(aq) + HgI_2(s)$

(b) $I_2(s) + 5\ Cl_2(g) \longrightarrow 2\ ICl_5(s)$

(c) $4\ Al(s) + 3\ O_2(g) \longrightarrow 2\ Al_2O_3(s)$

(d) $CuSO_4(aq) + 2\ AgNO_3(aq) \longrightarrow Ag_2SO_4(s) + Cu(NO_3)_2(aq)$

(e) $2\ Mn(NO_3)_3(aq) + 3\ Na_2S(aq) \longrightarrow Mn_2S_3(s) + 6\ NaNO_3(aq)$

(f) $4\ NO_2(g) + O_2(g) \longrightarrow 2\ N_2O_5(g)$

(g) $P_4O_{10}(s) + 6\ H_2O(l) \longrightarrow 4\ H_3PO_4(aq)$

6.44 (a) $2\ C_4H_{10}(g) + 13\ O_2(g) \longrightarrow 8\ CO_2(g) + 10\ H_2O(l)$

(b) $C_2H_6O(g) + 3\ O_2(g) \longrightarrow 2\ CO_2(g) + 3\ H_2O(l)$

(c) $2\ C_8H_{18}(g) + 25\ O_2(g) \longrightarrow 16\ CO_2(g) + 18\ H_2O(l)$

Molar Masses and Moles

6.46 Molecular weight is the sum of the atomic weights of the individual atoms in a molecule. Formula weight is the sum of the atomic weights of the individual atoms in a formula unit of any compound, whether molecular or ionic.
Molar mass is the mass in grams of 6.022×10^{23} molecules or formula units of any substance.

6.48 Each formula unit of K_2SO_4 contains three ions — two K^+ ions and one SO_4^{2-} ion. Thus, one mole of K_2SO_4 contains three moles of ions, and:

$$1.75\ \text{mol}\ K_2SO_4 \times \frac{3\ \text{mol ions}}{1\ \text{mol}\ K_2SO_4} = 5.25\ \text{mol ions}$$

6.50

$$2.68 \times 10^{22}\ \text{atoms} \times \frac{1\ \text{mol}}{6.022 \times 10^{23}\ \text{atoms}} \times \frac{238.0\ \text{g}}{1\ \text{mol}} = 10.6\ \text{g uranium}$$

6.52

Compound	*Molar Mass*	*Moles O_2*
(a) $CaCO_3$	100.1 g	3
(b) $CO(NH_2)_2$	60.05	1
(c) $Al_2(SO_4)_3$	342.1	12

6.54 Molar mass of caffeine = 194 g

$$125\ \text{mg caffeine} \times \frac{1\ \text{g}}{10^3\ \text{mg}} \times \frac{1\ \text{mol caffeine}}{194\ \text{g caffeine}} = 6.44 \times 10^{-4}\ \text{mol caffeine}$$

6.56 Molar mass of $C_{16}H_{13}ClN_2O$:
$(16 \times 12.0\ g) + (13 \times 1.0\ g) + (35.5\ g) + (2 \times 14.0\ g) + 16.0\ g = 284.5$ g/ mol Valium

6.58

Compound	*Molar Mass*	*Number of Moles in 5.00 g*
(a) C_6H_6	78.0 g	0.0641 mol
(b) $NaHCO_3$	84.0 g	0.0595 mol
(c) $CHCl_3$	119.5 g	0.0418 mol
(d) $C_{16}H_{18}N_2O_5S$	350.1 g	0.0143 mol

Note: Slightly different values for molar mass result when exact atomic weights are used.

6.60 Molar mass of aspirin = 180 g

$$0.0015 \text{ mol aspirin} \times \frac{180 \text{ g aspirin}}{1 \text{ mol aspirin}} = 0.27 \text{ g aspirin}$$

6.62

$$8.5 \times 10^{20} \text{ formula units} \times \frac{1 \text{ mol}}{6.022 \times 10^{23} \text{ formula units}} = 1.4 \times 10^{-3} \text{ mol}$$

$$0.0014 \text{ mol } CaC_2O_4 \times \frac{128 \text{ g } CaC_2O_4}{1 \text{ mol } CaC_2O_4} = 0.18 \text{ g } CaC_2O_4$$

Mole and Mass Relationships from Chemical Equations

6.64 (a) $C_4H_8O_2(l) + 2\ H_2(g) \longrightarrow 2\ C_2H_6O(l)$

(b) 3.0 mol of ethyl alcohol are produced from 1.5 mol of ethyl acetate.

(c) $$1.5 \text{ mol } C_4H_8O_2 \times \frac{2 \text{ mol } C_2H_6O}{1 \text{ mol } C_4H_8O_2} \times \frac{46.0 \text{ g } C_2H_6O}{1 \text{ mol } C_2H_6O} = 138 \text{ g } C_2H_6O$$

(d) $$12.0 \text{ g } C_4H_8O_2 \times \frac{1 \text{ mol } C_4H_8O_2}{88.0 \text{ g } C_4H_8O_2} \times \frac{2 \text{ mol } C_2H_6O}{1 \text{ mol } C_4H_8O_2} \times \frac{46.0 \text{ g } C_2H_6O}{1 \text{ mol } C_2H_6O}$$
$= 12.5$ g C_2H_6O

(e) $$12.0 \text{ g } C_4H_8O_2 \times \frac{1 \text{ mol } C_4H_8O_2}{88.0 \text{ g } C_4H_8O_2} \times \frac{2 \text{ mol } H_2}{1 \text{ mol } C_4H_8O_2} \times \frac{2.0 \text{ g } H_2}{1 \text{ mol } H_2} = 0.55 \text{ g } H_2$$

6.66 (a) $N_2(g) + 3\ H_2(g) \longrightarrow 2\ NH_3(g)$

(b) $$16.0 \text{ g } NH_3 \times \frac{1 \text{ mol } NH_3}{17.0 \text{ g } NH_3} \times \frac{1 \text{ mol } N_2}{2 \text{ mol } NH_3} = 0.471 \text{ mol } N_2$$

(c) $$75.0 \text{ g } N_2 \times \frac{1 \text{ mol } N_2}{28.0 \text{ g } N_2} \times \frac{3 \text{ mol } H_2}{1 \text{ mol } N_2} \times \frac{2.0 \text{ g } H_2}{1 \text{ mol } H_2} = 16.1 \text{ g } H_2$$

6.68 (a) $Fe_2O_3(s) + 3\,CO(g) \longrightarrow 2\,Fe(s) + 3\,CO_2(g)$

(b) $3.02\text{ g }Fe_2O_3 \times \dfrac{1\text{ mol }Fe_2O_3}{159.6\text{ g }Fe_2O_3} \times \dfrac{3\text{ mol CO}}{1\text{ mol }Fe_2O_3} \times \dfrac{28.0\text{ g CO}}{1\text{ mol CO}} = 1.59\text{ g CO}$

(c) $1.68\text{ mol }Fe_2O_3 \times \dfrac{3\text{ mol CO}}{1\text{ mol }Fe_2O_3} \times \dfrac{28.0\text{ g CO}}{1\text{ mol CO}} = 141\text{ g CO}$

6.70 $TiO_2(s) \longrightarrow Ti(s) + O_2(g)$

$95\text{ kg Ti} \times \dfrac{1\text{ mol Ti}}{47.9\text{ g Ti}} \times \dfrac{1\text{ mol }TiO_2}{1\text{ mol Ti}} \times \dfrac{79.9\text{ g }TiO_2}{1\text{ mol }TiO_2} = 158\text{ kg }TiO_2$

Percent Yield

6.72

(a) $10.0\text{ g CO} \times \dfrac{1\text{ mol CO}}{28.0\text{ g CO}} \times \dfrac{1\text{ mol }CH_3OH}{1\text{ mol CO}} \times \dfrac{32.0\text{ g }CH_3OH}{1\text{ mol }CH_3OH} = 11.4\text{ g }CH_3OH$

(b) $\dfrac{9.55\text{ g}}{11.4\text{ g}} \times 100\% = 83.8\%$ yield

6.74 (a) $CH_4(g) + 2\,Cl_2(g) \longrightarrow CH_2Cl_2(l) + 2\,HCl(g)$

(b) $50.0\text{ g }CH_4 \times \dfrac{1\text{ mol }CH_4}{16.0\text{ g }CH_4} \times \dfrac{2\text{ mol }Cl_2}{1\text{ mol }CH_4} \times \dfrac{71.0\text{ g }Cl_2}{1\text{ mol }Cl_2} = 444\text{ g }Cl_2$

(c) If the reaction occurred in 100% yield:

$50.0\text{ g }CH_4 \times \dfrac{1\text{ mol }CH_4}{16.0\text{ g }CH_4} \times \dfrac{1\text{ mol }CH_2Cl_2}{1\text{ mol }CH_4} \times \dfrac{85.0\text{ g }CH_2Cl_2}{1\text{ mol }CH_2Cl_2} = 266\text{ g }CH_2Cl_2$

Since the reaction occurs in 76% yield:

$266\text{ g} \times 0.76 = 202\text{ g }CH_2Cl_2$ are actually formed.

Types of Chemical Reactions

6.76 (a) $Mg(s) + 2\,HCl(aq) \longrightarrow MgCl_2(aq) + H_2(g)$ redox reaction

(b) $KOH(aq) + HNO_3(aq) \longrightarrow KNO_3(aq) + H_2O(l)$ neutralization reaction

(c) $Pb(NO_3)_2(aq) + 2\,HBr(aq) \longrightarrow PbBr_2(s) + 2\,HNO_3(aq)$ precipitation reaction

(d) $Ca(OH)_2(aq) + 2\,H_2SO_4(aq) \longrightarrow 2\,H_2O(l) + CaSO_4(aq)$ neutralization reaction

6.78

(a) $Ba^{2+}(aq) + 2\ NO_3^-(aq) + 2\ K^+(aq) + SO_4^{2-}(aq) \rightarrow BaSO_4(s) + 2\ K^+(aq) + 2\ NO_3^-(aq)$

$Ba^{2+}(aq) + SO_4^{2-}(aq) \rightarrow BaSO_4(s)$

(b) $Zn(s) + 2\ H^+(aq) + SO_4^{2-}(aq) \rightarrow Zn^{2+}(aq) + H_2(g) + SO_4^{2-}(aq)$

$Zn(s) + 2\ H^+(aq) \rightarrow Zn^{2+}(aq) + H_2(g)$

6.80 Use Section 6.9 as a guide.
Only $Ba(NO_3)_2$ is soluble in water.

6.82 If the products consist of soluble ions, no reaction will occur. No reaction occurs in (b) and (c).

(a) $2\ NaBr(aq) + Hg_2(NO_3)_2(aq) \longrightarrow Hg_2Br_2(s) + 2\ NaNO_3(aq)$

(d) $(NH_4)_2CO_3(aq) + CaCl_2(aq) \longrightarrow CaCO_3(s) + 2\ NH_4Cl(aq)$

(e) $2\ KOH(aq) + MnBr_2(aq) \longrightarrow Mn(OH)_2(s) + 2\ KBr(aq)$

(f) $3\ Na_2S(aq) + 2\ Al(NO_3)_3(aq) \longrightarrow Al_2S_3(s) + 6\ NaNO_3(aq)$

6.84 (a) $2\ Au^{3+}(aq) + 3\ Sn(s) \longrightarrow 3\ Sn^{2+}(aq) + 2\ Au(s)$

(b) $2\ I^-(aq) + Br_2(l) \longrightarrow 2\ Br^-(aq) + I_2(s)$

(c) $2\ Ag^+(aq) + Fe(s) \longrightarrow Fe^{2+}(aq) + 2\ Ag(s)$

Redox Reactions and Oxidation Numbers

6.86 The most easily reduced elements are found in groups 6A and 7A. The most easily oxidized elements are in groups 1A and 2A.

6.88 Oxidation number increases: (b) reducing agent, (c) substance undergoing oxidation
Oxidation number decreases: (a) oxidizing agent, (d) substance undergoing reduction

6.90 (a) Co: +3 (b) Fe: +2 (c) U: +6 (d) Cu: +2 (e) Ti: +4 (f) Sn: +2

6.92

	(a)	(b)	(c)	(d)
Oxidized	S	Na	Zn	Cl
Reduced	O	Cl	Cu	F

Applications

6.94

$$\frac{0.067\text{ g}}{1\text{ L}} \times \frac{1\text{ mol}}{190\text{ g}} = \frac{3.5 \times 10^{-4}\text{ mol}}{1\text{ L}}$$

3.5×10^{-4} mol of sodium urate dissolve in 1.00 L of water.

6.96 Light is passed through the negative image onto special paper coated with AgBr. The layer that is darkest has been exposed to the most light. The paper is developed with hydroquinone to amplify the image and fixed with sodium thiosulfate to remove the remaining AgBr, producing a positive image — the "negative of a negative."

General Questions and Problems

6.98

$$80.0\text{ kg } H_2O \times \frac{1\text{ mol } H_2O}{18.0\text{ g } H_2O} \times \frac{1\text{ mol } Li_2O}{1\text{ mol } H_2O} \times \frac{29.8\text{ g } Li_2O}{1\text{ mol } Li_2O} = 132\text{ kg } Li_2O$$

This is not a redox reaction because the oxidation numbers of reactant and product atoms remain the same.

6.100 Molar mass of batrachotoxin ($C_{31}H_{42}N_2O_6$) = 538 g/mol

$$0.05\ \mu\text{g} \times \frac{1\text{ g}}{10^6\ \mu\text{g}} \times \frac{1\text{ mol}}{538\text{ g}} \times \left[6.022 \times 10^{23}\frac{\text{molecules}}{\text{mol}}\right] = 6 \times 10^{13}\text{ molecules}$$

6.102 (a) $C_{12}H_{22}O_{11}(s) \longrightarrow 12\ C(s) + 11\ H_2O(l)$

(b) $$60.0\text{ g sucrose} \times \frac{1\text{ mol sucrose}}{342\text{ g sucrose}} \times \frac{12\text{ mol C}}{1\text{ mol sucrose}} \times \frac{12.0\text{ g C}}{1\text{ mol C}} = 25.3\text{ g carbon}$$

(c) $$6.50\text{ g C} \times \frac{1\text{ mol C}}{12.0\text{ g C}} \times \frac{11\text{ mol } H_2O}{12\text{ mol C}} \times \frac{18.0\text{ g } H_2O}{1\text{ mol } H_2O} = 8.94\text{ g } H_2O$$

6.104

(a) $$1.50\text{ g } C_2H_6O \times \frac{1\text{ mol } C_2H_6O}{46.0\text{ g } C_2H_6O} \times \frac{2\text{ mol } K_2Cr_2O_7}{3\text{ mol } C_2H_6O} \times \frac{294.2\text{ g } K_2Cr_2O_7}{1\text{ mol } K_2Cr_2O_7}$$

$= 6.40\text{ g } K_2Cr_2O_7$

(b) $$80.0\text{ g } C_2H_6O \times \frac{1\text{ mol } C_2H_6O}{46.0\text{ g } C_2H_6O} \times \frac{3\text{ mol } C_2H_4O_2}{3\text{ mol } C_2H_6O} \times \frac{60.0\text{ g } C_2H_4O_2}{1\text{ mol } C_2H_4O_2}$$

$= 104\text{ g } C_2H_4O_2$

6.106 (a) $Al(OH)_3(aq) + 3\ HNO_3(aq) \longrightarrow Al(NO_3)_3(aq) + 3\ H_2O(l)$

(b) $3\ AgNO_3(aq) + FeCl_3(aq) \longrightarrow 3\ AgCl(s) + Fe(NO_3)_3(aq)$

(c) $(NH_4)_2Cr_2O_7(s) \longrightarrow Cr_2O_3(s) + 4\ H_2O(g) + N_2(g)$

(d) $Mn_2(CO_3)_3(s) \longrightarrow Mn_2O_3(s) + 3\ CO_2(g)$

6.108 (a) $2\ SO_2(g) + O_2(g) \longrightarrow 2\ SO_3(g)$

(b) $SO_3(g) + H_2O(g) \longrightarrow H_2SO_4(l)$

(c) The oxidation number of sulfur is +4 in SO_2 and is +6 in both SO_3 and H_2SO_4.

Self-Test for Chapter 6

Multiple Choice

1. Which of the following salts is soluble in water?
(a) $FeSO_4$ (b) $BaSO_4$ (c) $SrSO_4$ (d) $PbSO_4$

2. Which of the following compounds has sulfur in a +1 oxidation state?
(a) S_2F_2 (b) H_2SO_4 (c) SO_2 (d) Na_2S

3. What mass of $CaCO_3$ has the same number of atoms as 21 g of NaF?
(a) 10 g (b) 20 g (c) 50 g (d) 100 g

4. In the equation $P_2O_5 + 3\ H_2O \longrightarrow 2\ H_3PO_4$ the mole ratio of product to H_2O is:
(a) 2:1 (b) 2:3 (c) 3:2 (d) 1:2

5. When the equation $SiCl_4 + H_2O \longrightarrow SiO_2 + HCl$ is balanced, the coefficients are:
(a) 1,1,1,1 (b) 1,1,1,2 (c) 1,2,1,2 (d) 1,2,1,4

6. Which of the following is not a redox process?
(a) respiration (b) corrosion (c) neutralization (d) combustion

7. If you wanted to remove Ba^{2+} from solution, which reagent would you add?
(a) CH_3CO_2H (b) NaOH (c) H_2SO_4 (d) HCl

8. In the reaction $2\ Ca + O_2 \longrightarrow 2\ CaO$, how many grams of CaO can be produced from 20 g of Ca? (a) 20 g (b) 28 g (c) 40 g (d) 56 g

9. When HCl is added to a solution, bubbles of gas appear. Which compound is probably present in the solution?
(a) $SrCO_3$ (b) $Ca(OH)_2$ (c) AgBr (d) K_2SO_4

10. $3\ NO_2 + H_2O \longrightarrow 2\ HNO_3 + NO$

All the following statements about this reaction are true except
(a) The starting material is both oxidized and reduced.
(b) NO_2 in the atmosphere might contribute to acid rain.
(c) At least 6 g of H_2O are needed to react completely with 46 g of NO_2.
(d) 92 g of NO_2 produces 28 g of NO.

Sentence Completion

1. The numbers placed in front of formulas to balance equations are called _______.
2. A _______ is a solid that forms during a reaction.
3. Ions that appear on both sides of the reaction arrow are _______ ions.
4. The substances in a reaction can be solids, liquids, or gases, or they can be in _______ solution.
5. Grams and moles can be converted by using ______ ______ as a conversion factor.
6. The amount of a substance produced in a reaction, divided by the amount that could theoretically be produced, is the ______ ______.
7. In a chemical equation, _______ are shown on the left of the reaction arrow.
8. The oxidation state of gold in $AuCl_3$ is _____.
9. In the reaction $2\ Mg + O_2 \longrightarrow 2\ MgO$, Mg is the _______ agent.
10. A reaction between an acid and a base is a _______ reaction.

True or False

1. A mole of oxygen atoms has the same mass as a mole of nitrogen atoms.
2. The coefficients in chemical reactions show the relative numbers of moles of reactants and products.
3. Limestone ($CaCO_3$) can be dissolved by treatment with HNO_3.
4. In a redox equation, the oxidizing agent is oxidized and the reducing agent is reduced.
5. If all coefficients in a chemical equation are even numbers, the equation is not completely balanced.
6. Mole ratios are used to convert between moles and grams of a compound.
7. In the reaction between K and Cl_2, K is the oxidizing agent.
8. In the reaction $4\ Al + 3\ O_2 \longrightarrow 2\ Al_2O_3$, the mole ratio of product to Al is 2.
9. Most sodium salts are soluble in water.
10. The same compound can be both oxidized and reduced in a reaction.

Match each entry on the left with its partner on the right.

1.	Zn	(a) Converts moles Na to grams Na
2.	$C_3H_8O + O_2 \longrightarrow C_3H_6O + H_2O$	(b) Molar mass of NaF
3.	42.0 amu	(c) Redox reaction
4.	23.0 g sodium / 1 mol	(d) Precipitation reaction
5.	$CoCO_3$	(e) Salt soluble in water
6.	$S + O_2 \longrightarrow SO_2$	(f) Unbalanced equation
7.	$HCl + NaOH \longrightarrow NaCl + H_2O$	(g) Converts grams Na to moles Na
8.	42.0 g	(h) Oxidized in a battery
9.	1 mol / 23.0 g sodium	(i) Salt insoluble in water
10.	MnO_2	(j) Neutralization reaction
11.	$AgNO_3 + NaCl \longrightarrow AgCl + NaNO_3$	(k) Formula weight of NaF
12.	$CoCl_2$	(l) Reduced in a battery

Chapter 7 – Chemical Reactions: Energy, Rates, and Equilibrium

Chapter Outline

I. Energy (Sections 7.1–7.4).
  A. Energy and chemical bonds (Section 7.1).
    1. There are two kinds of energy.
      a. Potential energy is stored energy.
      b. Kinetic energy is the energy of motion.
    2. Chemical bonds are a form of potential energy.
    3. Whether a reaction occurs, and how much heat is associated, depends on the potential energy of reactants and products.
  B. Heat changes during chemical reactions (Section 7.2).
    1. Bond dissociation energies measure the strength of covalent bonds.
      a. Bond breaking requires heat and is endothermic.
      b. Bond formation releases heat and is exothermic.
    2. The reverse of an endothermic process is exothermic, and the reverse of an exothermic process is endothermic.
    3. The law of conservation of energy states that energy can neither be created nor destroyed during any physical or chemical change.
    4. The difference between the energy needed for breaking bonds and the energy released in forming bonds is the heat of reaction, also known as enthalpy (ΔH).
  C. Exothermic and endothermic reactions: ΔH (Section 7.3).
    1. In exothermic reactions, the bond dissociation energies of the products are greater than the bond dissociation energies of the reactants, and ΔH is negative.
    2. In endothermic reactions, the bond dissociation energies of the products are smaller than the bond dissociation energies of the reactants, and ΔH is positive.
    3. The amount of heat absorbed or released in the reverse of a reaction is equal to that absorbed in the forward reaction, but ΔH has the opposite sign.
  D. Free energy: ΔG (Section 7.4).
    1. Spontaneous processes.
      a. A spontaneous process proceeds without any external influence.
      b. A nonspontaneous process needs a constant external source of energy.
    2. Entropy (ΔS) measures the amount of disorder in a system.
      a. If disorder increases, ΔS is positive.
      b. If disorder decreases, ΔS is negative.
    3. The absorption of heat and the increase or decrease in disorder determine if a reaction will be spontaneous.
      a. $\Delta G = \Delta H - T\Delta S$.
      b. If ΔG is negative, the process is spontaneous, and the reaction is exergonic.
      c. If ΔG is positive, the process isn't spontaneous, and the reaction is endergonic.
    4. ΔG for the reverse of a reaction is equal in value to ΔG for the forward reaction, but the sign is changed.
    5. Some nonspontaneous processes become spontaneous when temperature increases.

II. Reaction rates (Sections 7.5–7.6).
  A. How reactions occur (Section 7.5).
    1. In addition to the value of ΔG, other factors determine if a reaction will occur.
      a. Reactants must collide in the correct orientation.
      b. The energy of collision must be great enough to cause bond breaking.

   c. Many reactions with a favorable free energy don't occur at room temperature, and heat must be added to get them started
  2. The energy changes during a reaction can be graphed on a reaction energy diagram.
  3. The amount of energy needed to produce favorable collisions is the activation energy E_{act}.
   a. E_{act} determines the reaction rate.
   b. The size of E_{act} is unrelated to the size of ΔH.
 B. Factors that affect reaction rate (Section 7.6).
  1. Increasing temperature increases reaction rate.
  2. Increasing the concentration of reactants increases reaction rate.
  3. Catalysts increase the reaction rate by lowering E_{act}.
III. Chemical equilibrium (Sections 7.7–7.9).
 A. Reversible reactions (Section 7.7).
  1. Some reactions proceed to virtual completion.
  2. Other reactions go to partial completion, at which point products begin to reform starting material.
   a. These reactions are reversible.
   b. The reaction from left to right is the forward reaction.
   c. The reaction from right to left is the reverse reaction.
  3. At some point the rate of the forward reaction equals the rate of the reverse reaction, and equilibrium is established.
  4. It is not necessary for the concentrations of products and reactants to be equal at equilibrium.
 B. Equilibrium (Section 7.8).
  1. Equilibrium equations.
   a. For the reaction $a\,A + b\,B \longrightarrow c\,C + d\,D$,

$$K = \frac{[C]^c[D]^d}{[A]^a[B]^b}$$

   b. K = equilibrium constant.
   c. Expression on the right = equilibrium constant expression.
  2. The value of K determines the position of equilibrium.
   a. When $K >> 1$, reaction goes to completion.
   b. When $K > 1$, the forward reaction is favored.
   c. When K is of intermediate value, significant amounts of reactants and products are present at equilibrium.
   d. When $K < 1$, the reverse reaction is favored.
   e. When $K << 1$, there is essentially no reaction.
 C. Effect of changing reaction conditions (Section 7.9).
  1. Le Châtelier's principle: When a stress is applied to a system, the equilibrium shifts to remove the stress.
  2. Effect of changing concentration.
   a. Increasing the concentration of reactants favors the forward reaction.
   b. Increasing the concentration of products favors the reverse reaction.
  3. Effect of changing temperature.
   a. Decreasing temperature favors an exothermic reaction.
   b. Increasing temperature favors an endothermic reaction.
  4. Effect of changing pressure.
   a. No effect unless one of the reactants or products is a gas.
   b. Increasing pressure shifts the equilibrium in the direction that produces fewer gas molecules.

Solutions to Chapter 7 Problems

7.1 (a) The reaction is endothermic because heat appears on the left side of the equation and is absorbed in the reaction.
(b) $\Delta H = +678$ kcal
(c) $C_6H_{12}O_6(aq) + 6\ O_2(g) \longrightarrow 6\ CO_2(g) + 6\ H_2O(l) + 678$ kcal

7.2 (a) The reaction is endothermic because ΔH is positive.

(b) $\dfrac{801 \text{ kcal}}{4 \text{ mol Al}} \times 1.00 \text{ mol Al} = 200$ kcal required.

(c) $10.0 \text{ g Al} \times \dfrac{1 \text{ mol Al}}{27.0 \text{ g Al}} \times \dfrac{801 \text{ kcal}}{4 \text{ mol Al}} = 74.2$ kcal required

7.3

$127 \text{ g NO} \times \dfrac{1 \text{ mol}}{30.0 \text{ g NO}} \times \dfrac{43 \text{ kcal}}{2 \text{ mol NO}} = 91$ kcal absorbed

7.4 (a) Entropy increases.
(b) Entropy increases because disorder increases when liquids vaporize.
(c) Entropy decreases because one mole of product is formed for each two moles of reactant and because a gaseous reactant is converted into a solid product.

7.5 (a) Formation of lime from limestone doesn't occur at 25°C because ΔG is positive.
(b) Entropy increases because a gas is formed from a solid.
(c) The reaction is spontaneous at higher temperatures. In the expression $\Delta G = \Delta H - T\Delta S$, the term $T\Delta S$ becomes larger at high temperature and causes ΔG to become negative.

7.6 $\Delta G = \Delta H - T\Delta S$: $\Delta H = +1.44$ kcal/mol $\Delta S = +5.26$ cal/(mol · K)
(a) If $T = 263$ K,

$$T\Delta S = 263 \text{ K} \times \frac{5.26 \text{ cal}}{\text{mol K}} \times \frac{1 \text{ kcal}}{10^3 \text{ cal}} = \frac{1.38 \text{ kcal}}{\text{mol}}$$

$\Delta G = 1.44$ kcal/mol $- 1.38$ kcal/mol $= +0.06$ kcal/mol
At 263 K, melting is not spontaneous because ΔG is positive.

(b) If $T = 273$ K,

$$T\Delta S = 273 \text{ K} \times \frac{5.26 \text{ cal}}{\text{mol K}} \times \frac{1 \text{ kcal}}{10^3 \text{ cal}} = \frac{1.44 \text{ kcal}}{\text{mol}}$$

$\Delta G = 1.44$ kcal/mol $- 1.44$ kcal/mol $= +0.00$ kcal/mol
At 273 K, $\Delta G = 0$, and melting and freezing are in equilibrium.

(c) If $T = 283$ K,

$$T\Delta S = 283 \text{ K} \times \frac{5.26 \text{ cal}}{\text{mol K}} \times \frac{1 \text{ kcal}}{10^3 \text{ cal}} = \frac{1.49 \text{ kcal}}{\text{mol}}$$

$\Delta G = 1.44$ kcal/mol $- 1.49$ kcal/mol $= -0.05$ kcal/mol
At 283 K, melting is spontaneous because ΔG is negative.

7.7 (a) The sign of ΔS is positive because disorder increases from reactant to products.
(b) In the expression $\Delta G = \Delta H - T\Delta S$, ΔH is a negative number. Because ΔS is positive, $(-T\Delta S)$ is negative at all temperatures. Thus, ΔG is negative at all temperatures, and the reaction is spontaneous at all temperatures.

7.8

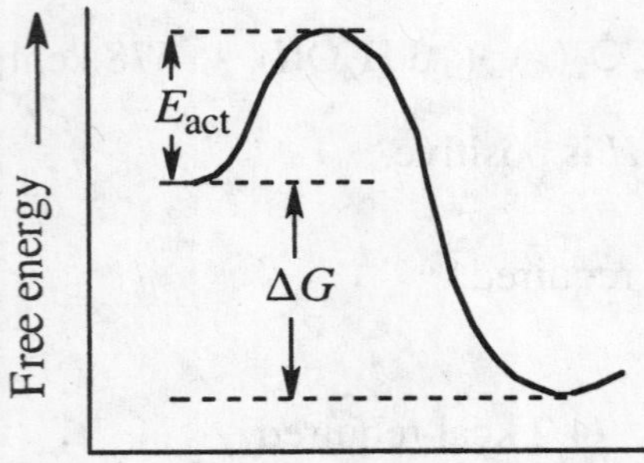

Free energy
E act
ΔG
Reaction

In this reaction, E_{act} is large, the reaction is slow, and the free-energy change is large and negative.

7.9

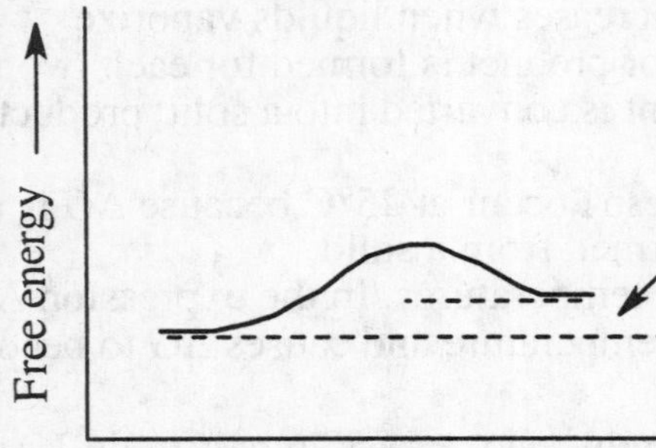

Free energy
ΔG
Reaction

In this reaction, ΔG is small and positive. E_{act} can be small or large, but it is always larger than ΔG.

7.10 (a) If the temperature is increased, the reaction rate increases.
(b) Removal of the catalyst decreases the reaction rate.
(c) Halving the concentration of H_2 decreases the rate.

7.11

$$K = \frac{[\text{products}]}{[\text{reactants}]}$$

(a) $K = \dfrac{[NO_2]^2}{[N_2O_4]}$ (b) $K = \dfrac{[CH_3Cl][HCl]}{[CH_4][Cl_2]}$ (c) $K = \dfrac{[Br_2][F_2]^5}{[BrF_5]^2}$

Don't forget that the coefficients of the reactants and products appear as exponents in the equilibrium expression.

7.12 If K is greater than 1, the reaction favors products. If K is less than 1, the reaction favors reactants.
(a) Products are strongly favored.
(b) Reactants are strongly favored.
(c) Products are somewhat favored.

7.13 In the expression for the equilibrium constant, the concentration of the product HI is squared in the numerator. The concentrations of the reactants appear in the denominator. Substitute the given concentrations into the expression.The equilibrium favors products.

$$K = \frac{[HI]^2}{[H_2][I_2]} = \frac{[0.507]^2}{[0.0510][0.174]} = 29.0$$

7.14 The reaction that forms CD has a larger equilibrium constant because it has a greater ratio of product to reactant than does the reaction that forms AB.

7.15 High pressure favors the production of SO_3 because increasing the pressure shifts the equilibrium in the direction that decreases the number of molecules in the gas phase. Low temperature favors the production of SO_3 because exothermic reactions are favored by lower temperatures.

7.16 (a) Increasing the temperature shifts the equilibrium to the left, favoring reactants.
(b) Increasing the pressure shifts the equilibrium to the right, favoring product.
(b) Removing CH_4 from the reaction vessel causes more CH_4 to be formed and shifts the equilibrium toward the right, favoring product.

Understanding Key Concepts

7.17 ΔH is positive because energy must be supplied in order to break the attractive forces between molecules of the crystal. ΔS is also positive because the molecules of gas are more disordered than the molecules of solid. ΔG is negative because it is stated in the problem that the reaction is spontaneous.

7.18 ΔH is negative because energy is released when a liquid condenses. ΔS is negative because disorder decreases when a gas condenses. ΔG is negative because it is stated in the problem that the reaction is spontaneous.

7.19 (a) $2\ A_2 + B_2 \longrightarrow 2\ A_2B$

(b) ΔG is negative because the reaction is spontaneous. ΔS is negative because the product mixture has fewer gas molecules and less disorder than the reactant mixture. ΔH must be negative in order for ΔG to be negative since $(-T\,\Delta S)$ is positive.

7.20 (a) The red curve represents the slower reaction, since more energy is needed to surmount the energy barrier leading to formation of products.
(b) The red curve represents a spontaneous reaction since the energy of its products is less than the energy of its reactants : ΔG is negative.

7.21 The red curve represents the catalyzed reaction, since a catalyst lowers the energy barrier of a reaction.

7.22

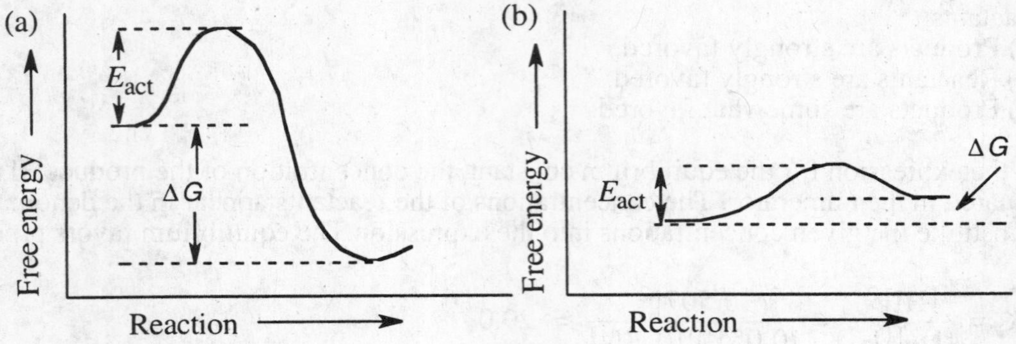
(a)
(b)
E_{act}
ΔG
Free energy
Reaction
ΔG
E_{act}
Free energy
Reaction

7.23 (a) ΔS is positive because the product has more disorder than the reactants.
(b) At low temperatures, the reaction is nonspontaneous because ΔH is positive and $T\Delta S$ is small. As the temperature rises, a certain temperature is reached at which $\Delta H = T\Delta S$. At this temperature, $\Delta G = 0$. Above this temperature, ΔG is negative and the reaction is spontaneous.

Enthalpy and Heat of Reaction

7.24 In an endothermic reaction, the total enthalpy of the products is greater than the total enthalpy of the reactants. In other words, the reactants have stronger bonds and are more stable, while the products have weaker bonds and are less stable. Energy must therefore be supplied for the reaction to take place.

7.26 (a) ΔH is positive.

(b) $5.8 \text{ mol } Br_2 \times \dfrac{7.4 \text{ kcal}}{1 \text{ mol } Br_2} = 43 \text{ kcal needed}$

(c) $82 \text{ g } Br_2 \times \dfrac{1 \text{ mol } Br_2}{159.8 \text{ g } Br_2} \times \dfrac{7.4 \text{ kcal}}{1 \text{ mol } Br_2} = 3.8 \text{ kcal needed}$

7.28 (a) $C_6H_{12}O_6 + 6\ O_2 \longrightarrow 6\ CO_2 + 6\ H_2O$

(b) $\dfrac{-3.8 \text{ kcal}}{1 \text{ g glucose}} \times \dfrac{180 \text{ g glucose}}{1 \text{ mol glucose}} \times 1.50 \text{ mol glucose} = -1.0 \times 10^3 \text{ kcal}$

(c) The production of glucose from CO_2 and H_2O is an endothermic process.

$$\frac{3.8 \text{ kcal}}{1 \text{ g glucose}} \times 15.0 \text{ g glucose} = 57 \text{ kcal needed to produce 15 g glucose}$$

Entropy and Free Energy

7.30 Increased disorder: (a)
Decreased disorder: (b) (c)

7.32 A spontaneous process is one that, once started, proceeds without any external influence.

7.34 The two factors that influence the spontaneity of a reaction are (1) the release or absorption of heat, and (2) the increase or decrease in entropy.

7.36 The free-energy change (ΔG) of a chemical reaction shows whether or not a reaction is spontaneous. If the sign of ΔG is negative, the reaction is spontaneous. Of the two factors that contribute to ΔG (ΔH and ΔS), ΔH is usually larger at low temperatures. Thus if a reaction is spontaneous (negative ΔG) it is usually exothermic (negative ΔH).

7.38 (a) Dissolution of NaCl is endothermic since ΔH is positive.
(b Entropy increases because disorder increases.
(c) Since the dissolution of NaCl is spontaneous, ΔG for the reaction must be negative. Because we already know that ΔH is positive, it must be true that $T\Delta S$ is the major contributor to ΔG.

7.40 (a) $H_2(g) + Br_2(l) \longrightarrow 2\ HBr(g)$
(b) Entropy increases because the number of gaseous product molecules is greater than the number of gaseous reactant molecules.
(c) The process is spontaneous at all temperatures because ΔH is negative and ΔS is positive.
(d) $\Delta G = \Delta H - T\Delta S$; $\Delta H = -17.4$ kcal/mol; $\Delta S = 27.2$ cal/(mol · K); $T = 300$ K

$$T\Delta S = 300\text{ K} \times \frac{27.2\text{ cal}}{\text{mol K}} \times \frac{1\text{ kcal}}{10^3\text{ cal}} = \frac{8.16\text{ kcal}}{\text{mol}}$$

$$\Delta G = -17.4\text{ kcal/mol} - 8.16\text{ kcal/mol} = -25.6\text{ kcal/mol}$$

Rates of Chemical Reactions

7.42 The *activation energy* of a reaction is the amount of energy needed for reactants to surmount the energy barrier to reaction.

7.44

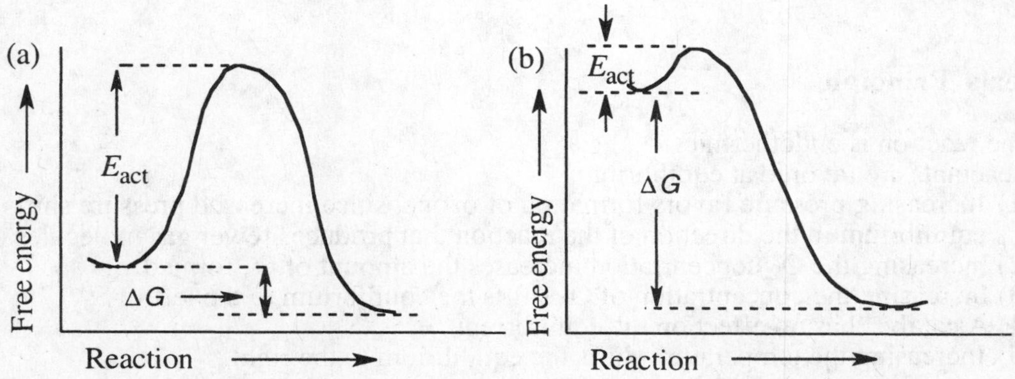
(a)
E_{act}
ΔG
Free energy
Reaction
(b)
E_{act}
ΔG
Free energy
Reaction

7.46 Increasing temperature increases reaction rate for two reasons:
1. Particles move faster and are more likely to collide.
2. Collisions occur with more energy.

7.48 A catalyst is a substance that increases reaction rate by lowering the activation energy barrier, yet remains unchanged when the reaction is completed.

7.50 (a) The negative value of ΔG indicates that diamonds spontaneously turn into graphite at 25°C.
(b) Because this behavior is not observed, the activation energy of the preceding reaction must be extremely high and the reaction rate must be extremely slow.

Chemical Equilibria

7.52 In a reversible reaction, chemical equilibrium is a state in which the rates of the forward reaction and the reverse reaction are equal. The amounts of reactants and products need not be equal at equilibrium.

7.54

(a) $K = \dfrac{[CO_2]^2}{[CO]^2[O_2]}$ (b) $K = \dfrac{[C_2H_4Cl_2][HCl]^2}{[C_2H_6][Cl_2]^2}$

(c) $K = \dfrac{[H_3O^+][F^-]}{[HF][H_2O]}$ (d) $K = \dfrac{[O_3]^2}{[O_2]^3}$

7.56

$$K = \frac{[NO_2]^2}{[N_2O_4]} = \frac{(0.0325\text{ mol/L})^2}{(0.147\text{ mol/L})} = 7.19 \times 10^{-3}$$

7.58

(a) $K = 7.19 \times 10^{-3} = \dfrac{(0.0250\text{ mol/L})^2}{[N_2O_4]}$; $[N_2O_4] = 0.0869\text{ mol/L}$

(b) $K = 7.19 \times 10^{-3} = \dfrac{[NO_2]^2}{(0.0750\text{ mol/L})}$; $[NO_2] = 0.0232\text{ mol/L}$

7.60 If the pressure is raised, relatively more reactants than products are found at equilibrium, because high pressure favors the reaction that produces fewer gas molecules.

Le Châtelier's Principle

7.62 (a) The reaction is endothermic.
(b) Reactants are favored at equilibrium.
(c) (1) Increasing pressure favors formation of ozone, since increased pressure shifts the equilibrium in the direction of the reaction that produces fewer gas molecules.
(2) Increasing the O_2 concentration increases the amount of O_3 formed.
(3) Increasing the concentration of O_3 shifts the equilibrium to the left.
(4) A catalyst has no effect on the equilibrium.
(5) Increasing the temperature shifts the equilibrium to the right.

7.64 According to Le Châtelier's principle, an increase in pressure shifts the equilibrium in the direction that decreases the number of molecules in the gas phase.
(a) The concentration of products decreases.
(b) The concentration of products remains the same.
(c) The concentration of products increases.

7.66 $$CO(g) + H_2O(g) \rightleftharpoons CO_2(g) + H_2(g) \quad \Delta H = -9.8 \text{ kcal/mol}$$
Because it has a negative value of ΔH, the reaction is exothermic, and the equilibrium favors products. Decreasing the temperature increases the amount of H_2.

7.68 $$H_2(g) + I_2(g) \rightleftharpoons 2\,HI(g) \quad \Delta H = -2.2 \text{ kcal/mol}$$
(a) Adding I_2 to the reaction mix increases the equilibrium concentration of HI.
(b) Removing H_2 causes the equilibrium concentration of HI to decrease.
(c) Addition of a catalyst does not change the equilibrium concentration of HI.
(d) Increasing the temperature decreases the concentration of HI.

Applications

7.70 A gram of fat contains more energy (9 kcal/g) than a gram of carbohydrate (4 kcal/g).

7.72 Dilation of the blood vessels cools the body by allowing more blood to flow close to the surface of the body.

General Questions and Problems

7.74 (a) $C_2H_5OH + 3\,O_2 \longrightarrow 2\,CO_2 + 3\,H_2O + \text{heat}$
(b) ΔH is negative, because energy is released.

(c) Calories needed = specific heat of H_2O x mass (g) x temperature change (°C)

Specific heat of water = 1.00 cal /(g · °C); mass of 500 mL H_2O = 500 g;
Temperature change = 80.0°C

$$\text{Calories} = \frac{1.00 \text{ cal}}{\text{g} \cdot °\text{C}} \times 500.0 \text{ g} \times 80.0°\text{C} = 4.00 \times 10^4 \text{ cal} = 40.0 \text{ kcal}$$

$$40.0 \text{ kcal} \times \frac{5.00 \text{ g } C_2H_5OH}{35.5 \text{ kcal}} = 5.63 \text{ g } C_2H_5OH$$

(d) $$\frac{35.5 \text{ kcal}}{5.00 \text{ g } C_2H_5OH} \times \frac{0.789 \text{ g } C_2H_5OH}{1 \text{ ml } C_2H_5OH} = 5.60 \text{ kcal/mL}$$

7.76 (a) $Fe_3O_4(s) + 4\,H_2(g) \longrightarrow 3\,Fe(s) + 4\,H_2O(g)$ $\Delta H = +36$ kcal/mol

(b) $55\text{ g Fe} \times \dfrac{1\text{ mol Fe}}{55.8\text{ g Fe}} \times \dfrac{36\text{ kcal}}{1\text{ mol Fe}_3\text{O}_4} \times \dfrac{1\text{ mol Fe}_3\text{O}_4}{3\text{ mol Fe}} = 12\text{ kcal required}$

(c) $75\text{ g Fe} \times \dfrac{1\text{ mol Fe}}{55.8\text{ g Fe}} \times \dfrac{4\text{ mol H}_2}{3\text{ mol Fe}} \times \dfrac{2.0\text{ g H}_2}{1\text{ mol H}_2} = 3.6\text{ g H}_2$

(d) Reactants are favored in this reaction.

7.78

$1700\text{ kcal} \times \dfrac{1\text{ g}}{3.8\text{ kcal}} = 450\text{ g glucose}$

7.80 (a) $4\,NH_3(g) + 5\,O_2(g) \rightleftharpoons 4\,NO(g) + 6\,H_2O(g) + \text{heat}$

(b) $K = \dfrac{[NO]^4[H_2O]^6}{[NH_3]^4[O_2]^5}$

(c) (1) Raising the pressure shifts the equilibrium to the left and increases reactants.
(2) Adding $NO(g)$ shifts the equilibrium to the left and increases reactants.
(3) Decreasing NH_3 shifts the equilibrium to the left and increases reactants.
(4) Lowering the temperature shifts the equilibrium to the right and increases products.

7.82

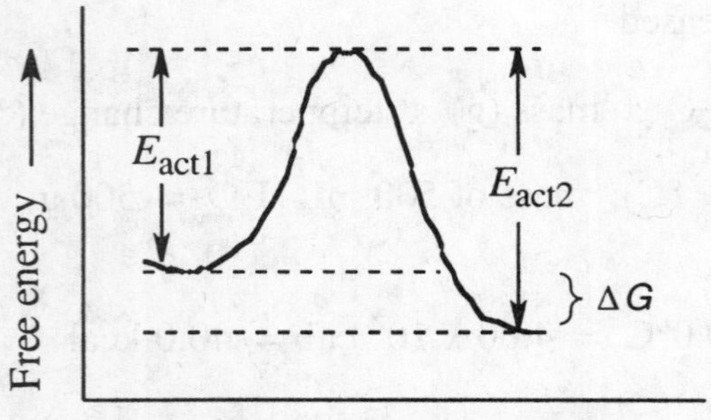

E_{act1}
E_{act2}
ΔG
Free energy
Reaction

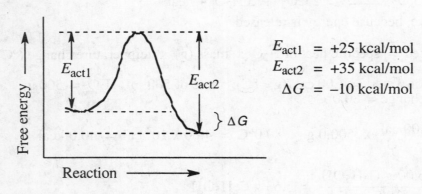

$E_{act1} = +25$ kcal/mol
$E_{act2} = +35$ kcal/mol
$\Delta G = -10$ kcal/mol

(a) The forward process is exergonic.
(b) $\Delta G = -10$ kcal/mol

7.84

$1.00\text{ g} \times \dfrac{1\text{ mol Na}}{23.0\text{ g}} \times \dfrac{-88.0\text{ kcal}}{2\text{ mol Na}} = -1.91\text{ kcal}$

1.91 kcal of heat is evolved. The reaction is exothermic.

Self-Test for Chapter 7

Multiple Choice

1. In which of the following processes does entropy decrease?
(a) $C_6H_{12}O_6(s) + 6\ O_2(g) \longrightarrow 6\ CO_2(g) + 6\ H_2O(l)$
(b) $2\ Na(s) + 2\ H_2O(l) \longrightarrow 2\ NaOH(aq) + H_2(g)$
(c) $2\ Mg(s) + O_2(g) \longrightarrow 2\ MgO(s)$
(d) $Zn(s) + CuSO_4(aq) \longrightarrow Cu(s) + ZnSO_4(aq)$

2. The reaction that will proceed at any temperature has
(a) negative ΔH, negative ΔS (b) negative ΔH, positive ΔS (c) positive ΔH, positive ΔS
(d) positive ΔH, negative ΔS

3. Which of the conditions in Problem 2 indicates the reaction with the largest positive value of ΔG?

4. In the reaction $CH_3CO_2H + CH_3OH \rightleftharpoons CH_3CO_2CH_3 + H_2O$, the yield of $CH_3CO_2CH_3$ can be improved by
(a) distilling off the $CH_3CO_2CH_3$ (b) removing the water (c) using more CH_3CO_2H and CH_3OH (d) all of the above

5. The equilibrium expression for the reaction $C_6H_6 + 3\ H_2 \longrightarrow C_6H_{12}$ is

(a) $\dfrac{[C_6H_{12}]}{[C_6H_6]\,[H_2]}$ (b) $\dfrac{[C_6H_{12}]}{[C_6H_6]\,[H_2]^3}$ (c) $\dfrac{[C_6H_{12}]}{[C_6H_6]\,[3\ H_2]}$ (d) $\dfrac{[C_6H_6]\,[H_2]^3}{[C_6H_{12}]}$

6. A reaction with which of the following K values is most likely to go to completion at room temperature?
(a) $K = 10^5$ (b) $K = 10^2$ (c) $K = 10^{-1}$ (d) $K = 10^{-4}$

7. In which of the following reactions will increasing the pressure decrease the yield of product?
(a) $2\ Mg(s) + O_2(g) \longrightarrow 2\ MgO(s)$
(b) $H_2C{=}CH_2(g) + H_2(g) \longrightarrow CH_3CH_3(g)$
(c) $C(s) + H_2O(g) \longrightarrow CO(g) + H_2(g)$
(d) $3\ O_2(g) \longrightarrow 2\ O_3(g)$

8. According to Le Châtelier's principle, which of the following changes also changes the value of K?
(a) changing temperature (b) changing concentration (c) changing pressure (d) all of the above

9. All of the following statements are true about the reaction $3\ O_2(g) \longrightarrow 2\ O_3(g)$ (heat of formation = +34 kcal/mol at 25°C) except
(a) The reaction is endothermic. (b) ΔS is negative. (c) ΔG is positive. (d) The rate of the reverse reaction increases with temperature.

10. In the reaction $Si + O_2 \longrightarrow SiO_2$ ($\Delta H = -218$ kcal/mol at 25°C), what is ΔH in kcal when 80 g of O_2 reacts with 70 g of Si?
(a) 218 kcal (b) –218 kcal (c) –436 kcal (d) –545 kcal

Sentence Completion

1. A reaction that has equal amounts of reactants and products at equilibrium has $K =$ ____.
2. The Law of _______ _______ states that energy can be neither created nor destroyed.
3. Addition of a _______ increases the rate of a reaction.
4. A reaction that easily proceeds in either direction is _______.
5. A reaction that absorbs heat from the surroundings is an _____ reaction.
6. An _______ _____ _____ gives the relationship between the concentrations of products and reactants at equilibrium.
7. The rate of a reaction can be increased by increasing _____ or _____ or by adding a _____.
8. The reactions that continually take place in the body are known as ______.
9. _____ ___ is unrelated to reaction spontaneity.
10. For a chemical reaction to occur, reactant molecules must _____.

Match each entry on the left with its partner on the right.

1. Enzyme	(a) Shows energy relationships in a reaction
2. Exergonic reaction	(b) A reaction that gives off heat
3. *K*	(c) Reduces the size of E_{act}
4. Enthalpy	(d) Energy needed for a reaction to occur
5. Reaction energy diagram	(e) Measure of the amount of disorder in a reaction
6. Free energy	(f) Reaction that is not spontaneous
7. Exothermic reaction	(g) Reaction that can go in either direction
8. Endergonic reaction	(h) Reaction that absorbs heat
9. E_{act}	(i) Difference in energy of products and reactants
10. Entropy	(j) Reaction that is spontaneous
11. Reversible reaction	(k) Determines if a reaction is spontaneous
12. Endothermic reaction	(l) Measures the ratio of products to reactants

True or False

1. The caloric value of food tells how much energy is absorbed when food is burned in oxygen.

2. In a chemical equilibrium, both product and reactant concentrations remain constant.

3. According to Le Châtelier's principle, changing pressure only affects equilibrium if gaseous reactants or products are involved.

4. In an exothermic reaction, the bond dissociation energies of the products are greater than the bond dissociation energies of the reactants.

5. A reaction with a large E_{act} will probably have a large heat of reaction.

6. Raising the temperature of a reaction always increases the rate of reaction.

7. A very unfavorable reaction may take place if the temperature is high enough.

8. Catalysts increase the rate of a reaction by increasing the number of collisions between reactants.

9. At chemical equilibrium, all chemical reaction stops.

10. At low temperatures, the spontaneity of a reaction is determined by ΔH.

Chapter 8 – Gases, Liquids, and Solids

Chapter Outline

I. Introduction to gases, liquids and solids (Section 8.1).
  A. Phases of matter are determined by the attractive forces between molecules.
    1. In gases, attractive forces are very weak.
    2. In liquids, attractive forces are strong.
    3. In solids, forces are so strong that atoms are held in place.
  B. During changes of phase, also known as changes of state, heat is either absorbed or released.
    1. Every change of state is characterized by a free-energy change, ΔG.
      a. ΔG consists of an enthalpy term and an entropy term.
      b. The enthalpy term is a measure of the heat absorbed or released during a phase change.
      c. The entropy change is a measure of the change in molecular disorder.
    2. At the temperature where a change of phase occurs, two states are in equilibrium.
    3. At the change from solid to liquid, two phases are at equilibrium at the melting point.
    4. At the change from liquid to gas, two phases are at equilibrium at the boiling point.

II. Gases (Sections 8.2–8.10).
  A. The kinetic-molecular theory explains the behavior of gases (Section 8.2).
    1. A gas consists of a great many molecules moving about with no attractive forces.
    2. The amount of space that molecules occupy is much smaller than the space between molecules.
    3. The energy of the molecules is related to Kelvin temperature.
    4. When molecules collide, their total kinetic energy is conserved.
    5. A gas that obeys all these behaviors is an ideal gas.
  B. Pressure (Sections 8.3).
    1. Pressure is defined as force per unit area.
    2. Units of pressure are mm Hg, Pascal (in the SI system), atmosphere and pounds per square inch.
    3. Gas pressure can be measured by using a barometer or a manometer.
  C. Gas laws (Sections 8.4–8.10).
    1. Boyle's law (for a fixed amount of gas at constant *T*) (Section 8.4):
      a. The pressure of a gas is inversely proportional to its volume.
      b. $P_1V_1 = P_2V_2$.
    2. Charles's law (for a fixed amount of gas at constant *P*) (Section 8.5):
      a. The volume of a gas is directly proportional to its temperature in K.
      b. $V_1/T_1 = V_2/T_2$.
    3. Gay-Lussac's law (for a fixed amount of gas at constant *V*) (Section 8.6):
      a. Pressure is directly proportional to temperature in K.
      b. $P_1/T_1 = P_2/T_2$.
    4. Combined gas law (Section 8.7).
      $P_1V_1/T_1 = P_2V_2/T_2$ for a fixed amount of gas.
    5. Avogadro's law (at constant *T* and *P*) (Section 8.8):
      a. The volume of a gas is directly proportional to its molar amount at constant *T* and *P*.
      b. $V_1/n_1 = V_2/n_2$.
      c. Standard temperature and pressure = 273.16 K and 1 atm.
      d. Standard molar volume of a gas = 22.4 L.

6. Ideal gas law (Section 8.9).
   $PV = nRT$, where R is a gas constant.
7. Dalton's law of partial pressure (Section 8.10).
   a. Mixtures of gases behave the same as a pure gas.
   b. The partial pressure of a gas in a mixture is the same as the gas would have if it were alone.

III. Intermolecular forces (Section 8.11).
   A. Intermolecular forces are the forces that act between molecules.
   B. In an ideal gas, intermolecular forces are unimportant.
   C. Three types of intermolecular forces are important in liquids and solids.
      1. Dipole–dipole forces occur when the positive end of a polar molecule is attracted to the negative end of a second molecule.
      2. London forces.
         a. Short-lived polarity in molecules causes a temporary attraction between molecules.
         b. London forces increase with increasing molecular weight and vary with molecular shape.
      3. Hydrogen bonding.
         a. Hydrogen bonds occur between a hydrogen atom bonded to an electronegative atom and an unshared electron pair of a second electronegative atom.
         b. In hydrogen bonds, the hydrogen atom is partially bonded to two different electronegative atoms.
         c. Hydrogen bonds can be quite strong, and hydrogen bonding is responsible for elevated boiling points.

IV. Liquids and solids (Sections 8.12–8.15).
   A. Liquids (Section 8.12–8.13).
      1. Evaporation occurs when molecules near the surface of a liquid escape into the gaseous state.
         When molecules are in the gaseous state, they obey gas laws.
      2. The contribution of the partial pressure of the escaped gas to the total pressure is known as vapor pressure.
         Vapor pressure rises with increasing temperature.
      3. The normal boiling point of a liquid is at 760 mm Hg.
         The boiling point rises or falls with atmospheric pressure.
      4. Viscosity and surface tension are properties of liquids.
         a. Viscosity is a liquid's resistance to flow.
         b. Surface tension is the resistance of a liquid to spread out.
      5. Water is a unique liquid (Section 8.13).
         a. Water has very high specific heat, high heat of vaporization, and strong hydrogen bonding.
         b. Solid water is less dense than liquid water.
   B. Solids (Section 8.14).
      1. A crystalline solid has atoms, molecules or ions rigidly held in an orderly arrangement.
         Categories of crystalline solids include ionic solids, molecular solids, covalent network solids and metallic solids.
      2. Particles in an amorphous solid do not have an orderly arrangement.
   C. Changes of phase (Section 8.15).
      1. The heat needed to completely melt a solid is the heat of fusion.
      2. The heat needed to completely vaporize a liquid is the heat of vaporization.

Solutions to Chapter 8 Problems

8.1 (a) The change of state from liquid to gas is disfavored by ΔH (positive sign) but is favored by ΔS (large positive value).

(b) $\Delta G = \Delta H - T\Delta S$: $\Delta H = +9.72$ kcal/mol; $\Delta S = +26.1$ cal/(mol · K); $T = 373$ K

$$T\Delta S = 373\text{ K} \times \frac{26.1\text{ cal}}{\text{mol K}} \times \frac{1\text{ kcal}}{10^3\text{ cal}} = \frac{9.74\text{ kcal}}{\text{mol}}$$

$$\Delta G = 9.72\text{ kcal/mol} - 9.74\text{ kcal/mol} = +0.02\text{ kcal/mol}$$

(c) For the change from gas to liquid, $\Delta H = -9.72$ kcal/mol and $\Delta S = -26.1$ cal/(mol·K)

8.2 Use the appropriate conversion factor from Section 8.3

$$220\text{ mm Hg} \times \frac{1\text{ atm}}{760\text{ mm Hg}} = 0.29\text{ atm}$$

$$220\text{ mm Hg} \times \frac{14.7\text{ psi}}{760\text{ mm Hg}} = 4.3\text{ psi}$$

$$220\text{ mm Hg} \times \frac{101{,}325\text{ Pa}}{760\text{ mm Hg}} = 29{,}000\text{ Pa}$$

8.3 The pressure of the gas inside the manometer is greater than atmospheric pressure because the mercury level is higher in the open arm of the manometer than in the closed end. Since atmospheric pressure is 750 mm Hg and since the difference in mercury levels in the manometer arm is 250 mm Hg, the pressure of the gas inside the manometer is 750 mm + 250 mm = 1000 mm Hg.

8.4 If the variables in the problem are pressure and volume, Boyle's law must be used.

Solution: $P_1 \times V_1 = P_2 \times V_2$

$$V_2 = \frac{P_1 \times V_1}{P_2} = \frac{(90\text{ atm})(5.0\text{ L})}{(1.0\text{ atm})} = 450\text{ L}$$

Ballpark check: Since the pressure is reduced by almost 100 times, the volume must increase by almost 100 times, from 5 L to 500 L.

The ballpark solution and the detailed solution agree.

8.5 *Solution*: $P_1 \times V_1 = P_2 \times V_2$

$$P_2 = \frac{P_1 \times V_1}{V_2} = \frac{(4.0\text{ atm})(3.2\text{ L})}{(10.0\text{ L})} = 1.3\text{ atm}$$

Ballpark Check: Since the volume increases by three times, the pressure must decrease by the same amount, from 4.0 atm to 1.3 atm.

At a volume of 0.20 L: $$P_2 = \frac{P_1 \times V_1}{V_2} = \frac{(4.0\text{ atm})(3.2\text{ L})}{(0.20\text{ L})} = 64\text{ atm}$$

8.6 Charles's Law is used to calculate volume or temperature changes when pressure and quantity remain constant.

Solution:

$$\frac{V_1}{T_1} = \frac{V_2}{T_2}$$

$$V_2 = \frac{V_1 \text{ x } T_2}{T_1} = \frac{(0.30 \text{ L})(250 \text{ K})}{273 \text{ K}} = 0.27 \text{ L}$$

Ballpark check: Since the temperature decreases by about 10%, the volume must also decrease by about 10%, from 0.30 L to around 0.27 L.

At 525°C (798 K): $V_2 = \frac{V_1 \text{ x } T_2}{T_1} = \frac{(0.30 \text{ L})(798 \text{ K})}{273 \text{ K}} = 0.88 \text{ L}$

8.7 Use Gay-Lussac's Law when pressure and temperature vary, and volume and quantity are unchanged.

Solution:

$$\frac{P_1}{T_1} = \frac{P_2}{T_2}$$

$$P_2 = \frac{P_1 \text{ x } T_2}{T_1} = 30 \text{ psi x } \frac{318 \text{ K}}{288 \text{ K}} = 33 \text{ psi}$$

Ballpark check: Since the temperature increase is about 10%, the pressure increase is also expected to be approximately 10%.

8.8 In this problem, P, V, and T vary. Don't forget to change temperature from °C to K.

$$\frac{P_1V_1}{T_1} = \frac{P_2V_2}{T_2}; \quad P_1 = 752 \text{ mm Hg}; \ T_1 = 295 \text{ K}; \ V_1 = 275 \text{ L}$$

$$P_2 = 480 \text{ mm Hg}; \ T_2 = 241 \text{ K}; \ V_2 = ?$$

$$V_2 = \frac{P_1V_1T_2}{P_2T_1} = \frac{(752 \text{ mm Hg})\,(275 \text{ L})(241 \text{ K})}{(480 \text{ mm Hg})(295 \text{ K})} = 352 \text{ L}$$

8.9

$$\frac{P_1V_1}{T_1} = \frac{P_2V_2}{T_2}; \quad T_1 = 291 \text{ K}; \ V_1 = 225 \text{ L}; \ P_1 = 763 \text{ mm Hg};$$

$$T_2 = 218 \text{ K}; \ V_2 = 1365 \text{ L}; \ P_2 = ?$$

$$P_2 = \frac{P_1V_1T_2}{V_2T_1} = \frac{(763 \text{ mm Hg})\,(225 \text{ L})(291 \text{ K})}{(1365 \text{ L})(218 \text{ K})} = 168 \text{ mm Hg}$$

Ballpark check: Although temperature varies from low to high altitude, the major change is the approximately fivefold increase in volume. The predicted pressure is about 1/5 the original pressure.

8.10 Use Avogadro's Law; the quantity on the left side of the equation is the standard molar volume of a gas, 22.4 L/mol.

$$\frac{V_1}{n_1} = \frac{V_2}{n_2}$$

$$n_2 = \frac{V_2 \text{ x } n_1}{V_1} = 1.00 \text{ x } 10^5 \text{ L } CH_4 \text{ x } \frac{1.0 \text{ mol}}{22.4 \text{ L}} = 4.46 \text{ x } 10^3 \text{ mol } CH_4$$

The same container could also hold 4.46 x 10^3 moles of CO_2.

$$4.46 \text{ x } 10^3 \text{ mol } CH_4 \text{ x } \frac{16.0 \text{ g } CH_4}{1 \text{ mol } CH_4} = 7.14 \text{ x } 10^4 \text{ g } CH_4$$

$$4.46 \text{ x } 10^3 \text{ mol } CO_2 \text{ x } \frac{44.0 \text{ g } CO_2}{1 \text{ mol } CO_2} = 1.96 \text{ x } 10^5 \text{ g } CO_2$$

Ballpark Check: Since one mole of a gas occupies 22.4 L at STP, a 100,000 L container holds 100,000/22.4 moles, or about 4500 moles. Thus, the ballpark solution and the exact solution agree.

8.11 $PV = nRT$; $P = nRT/V$

$$n = 3.2 \text{ g x } \frac{1 \text{ mol}}{44.0 \text{ g}} = 0.073 \text{ mol}; \quad R = 0.0821 \frac{\text{L} \cdot \text{atm}}{\text{mol} \cdot \text{K}}$$

$$T = 20 \text{ °C} = 293 \text{ K}; \quad V = 350 \text{ mL} = 0.35 \text{ L}$$

$$P = \frac{0.073 \text{ mol x } \dfrac{0.0821 \text{ L} \cdot \text{atm}}{\text{mol} \cdot \text{K}} \text{ x } 293 \text{ K}}{0.35 \text{ L}} = 5.0 \text{ atm}$$

8.12 $PV = nRT$; $n = PV/RT$

$$P = 150 \text{ atm}; \quad V = 180 \text{ L He}; \quad R = 0.0821 \frac{\text{L} \cdot \text{atm}}{\text{mol} \cdot \text{K}}; \quad T = 25\text{°C} = 298 \text{ K}$$

$$n = \frac{150 \text{ atm x } 180 \text{ L He}}{0.0821 \dfrac{\text{L} \cdot \text{atm}}{\text{mol} \cdot \text{K}} \text{ x } 298 \text{ K}} = 1.1 \text{ x } 10^3 \text{ mol He}$$

$$1.1 \text{ x } 10^3 \text{ mol He x } \frac{4.0 \text{ g}}{1 \text{ mol He}} = 4.4 \text{ x } 10^3 \text{ g He}$$

8.13 We can use the ideal gas law to compare the volumes of two gases: Since the piston is moveable, P = 1 atm in all cases.

(a) The increase in temperature increases the volume to 450/300 = 3/2 of the original volume, and the decrease in amount decreases the volume to 0.200/0.300 = 2/3 of the original value. Since 3/2 x 2/3 = 1, the two changes exactly cancel, and the final volume is the same as the original volume.

T_1 = 300 K; n_1 = 0.300 mol; T_2 = 450 K; n_2 = 0.200 mol; V_1/V_2 = ?

$$\frac{V_1}{V_2} = \frac{n_1T_1P_2}{n_2T_2P_1} = \frac{n_1T_1}{n_2T_2};\quad \frac{V_1}{V_2} = \frac{(0.300\text{ mol})(300\text{ K})}{((0.200\text{ mol})((450\text{ K})} = 1$$

(b) The decrease in temperature decreases the volume to 200/300 = 2/3 of the original, and the increase in amount increases the volume to 0.400/0.300 = 4/3 of the original volume. Since 2/3 x 4/3 = 8/9, the final volume is a bit less than the original volume.

T_1 = 300 K; n_1 = 0.300 mol; T_2 = 200 K; n_2 = 0.400 mol; V_1/V_2 = ?

$$\frac{V_1}{V_2} = \frac{(0.300\text{ mol})(300\text{ K})}{((0.400\text{ mol})((200\text{ K})} = \frac{9}{8}$$ The volume in (b) is 8/9 of the original volume.

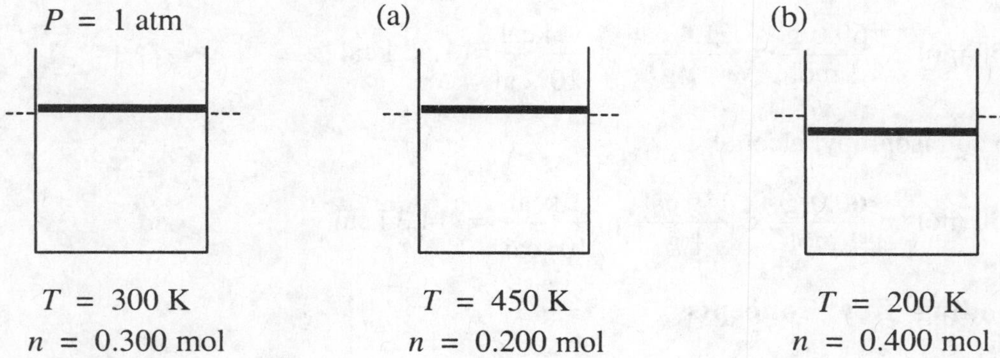
P = 1 atm
(a)
(b)
T = 300 K
n = 0.300 mol
T = 450 K
n = 0.200 mol
T = 200 K
n = 0.400 mol

8.14 0.98 x 9.5 atm = 9.3 atm He
0.020 x 9.5 atm = 0.19 atm O_2

The partial pressure of oxygen in diving gas (0.19 atm) is approximately equal to the partial pressure of oxygen in air (0.21 atm).

8.15

$$\frac{573\text{ mm Hg}}{760\text{ mm Hg}} \times 100\% = 75.4\%\ N_2;\qquad \frac{100\text{ mm Hg}}{760\text{ mm Hg}} \times 100\% = 13.2\%\ O_2$$

$$\frac{40\text{ mm Hg}}{760\text{ mm Hg}} \times 100\% = 5.3\%\ CO_2;\qquad \frac{47\text{ mm Hg}}{760\text{ mm Hg}} \times 100\% = 6.2\%\ H_2O$$

8.16 We know from the previous problem that the partial pressure of O_2 in the lungs at atmospheric pressure is 13.2%. Thus, at 265 mm Hg

265 mm x 0.132 = 35.0 mm Hg

8.17 Drawing (c) best represents the mixture. In (c), the particles act independently of each other, in accordance with kinetic–molecular theory, and the mixture is homogeneous.

8.18 Boiling points generally increase with increasing molecular (or atomic) weight because of London dispersion forces.

(a) Kr, Ar, Ne. This series is arranged in order of decreasing boiling point.
(b) Cl_2, Br_2, I_2. This series is arranged in order of increasing boiling point.

8.19 Methyl alcohol (a) and methylamine (c) are capable of hydrogen bonding because each contains a hydrogen atom bonded to an electronegative atom. Ethylene (b) does not form hydrogen bonds.

8.20 (a) *London forces* are the only intermolecular forces between nonpolar ethane molecules, and thus ethane has a low boiling point.
(b) The major intermolecular force between ethyl alcohol molecules is *hydrogen bonding*, which causes ethyl alcohol to be high boiling. Dipole–dipole interactions and London forces are also present but are weaker than hydrogen bonding.
(c) *Dipole–dipole* interactions are the principal forces between ethyl chloride molecules and cause the boiling point of ethyl chloride to be higher than that of ethane. London forces are also present.

8.21 To melt isopropyl alcohol:

$$1.50 \text{ mol} \times \frac{60.0 \text{ g}}{1 \text{ mol}} \times \frac{21.4 \text{ cal}}{1 \text{ g}} \times \frac{1 \text{ kcal}}{10^3 \text{ cal}} = 1.93 \text{ kcal}$$

To boil isopropyl alcohol:

$$1.50 \text{ mol} \times \frac{60.0 \text{ g}}{1 \text{ mol}} \times \frac{159 \text{ cal}}{1 \text{ g}} \times \frac{1 \text{ kcal}}{10^3 \text{ cal}} = 14.3 \text{ kcal}$$

Understanding Key Concepts

8.22

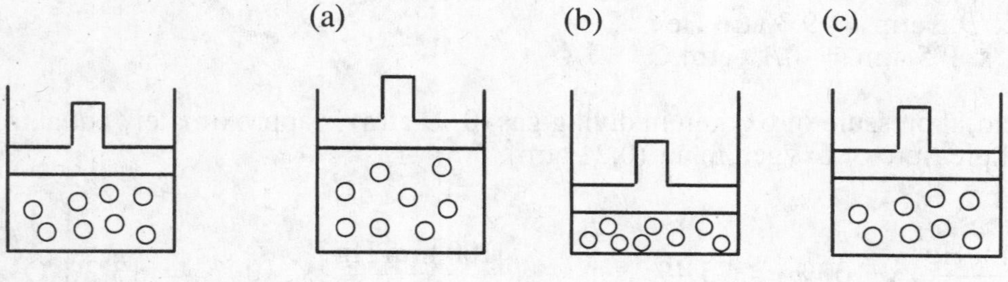
(a)
(b)
(c)

(a) According to Charles's Law, the volume of a gas at fixed pressure is directly proportional to its temperature. Since the temperature increases by 50% (from 300 K to 450 K), volume also increases by 50%.
(b) Boyle's Law states that the volume of a gas is inversely proportional to its pressure. Doubling the pressure halves the volume.
(c) For changes in both pressure and temperature, the combined gas law states that *PV/T* is constant. Thus, reducing both the pressure and the temperature by one-third leaves the volume unchanged.

8.23 Drawing (c) represents the gas in a sealed container after the temperature has been lowered from 350 K to 150 K. The gas remains a gas, and its volume is unchanged; only pressure is reduced.

8.24 Drawing (a) shows the sample of water as a solid, its state at 200 K. At 300 K, water is a liquid with a very low vapor pressure (as shown in Figure 8.20), represented by drawing (c).

8.25 At equilibrium, the gases are totally mixed.

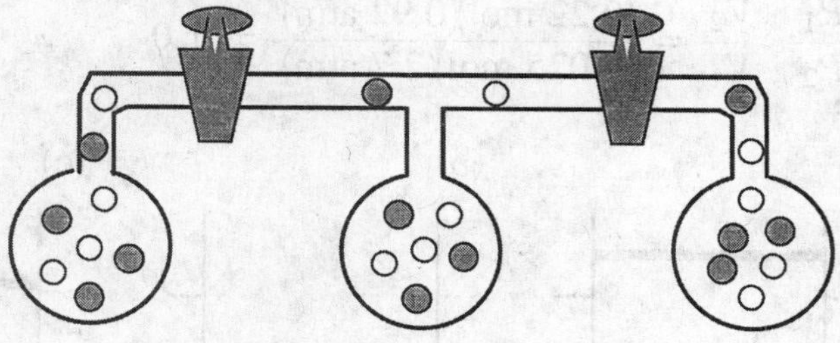

8.26

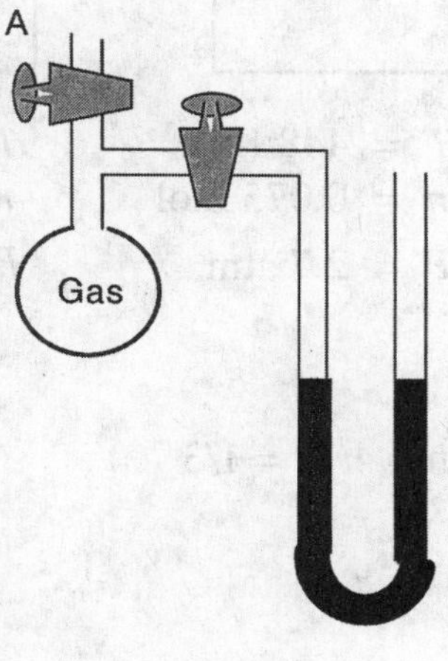
A
Gas

8.27 The horizontal parts of the curve represent phase changes.
(a) Melting point: 10°C
(b) Boiling point: 75°C
(c) Heat of fusion: 1 kcal/mol (the distance between the two points of the curve at the melting point)
(d) Heat of vaporization: 7.5 kcal/mol (the distance between the two points of the curve at the boiling point)

8.28 Refer to Problem 8.13 for an approach to solving this problem. Note the quantities that change and those that remain constant; these differ in each part of the problem. Be sure to convert temperature to Kelvins.

(a) $\dfrac{V_2}{V_1} = \dfrac{n_2T_2P_1}{n_1T_1P_2} = \dfrac{T_2}{T_1}; \quad \dfrac{V_2}{V_1} = \dfrac{(323\text{ K})}{((298\text{ K})} = 1.08$

(b) $\dfrac{V_2}{V_1} = \dfrac{n_2T_2P_1}{n_1T_1P_2} = \dfrac{T_2P_1}{T_1P_2}; \quad \dfrac{V_2}{V_1} = \dfrac{(448\text{ K})(0.92\text{ atm})}{((298\text{ K})(2.7\text{ atm})} = 0.51$

(c) $\dfrac{V_2}{V_1} = \dfrac{n_2T_2P_1}{n_1T_1P_2} = \dfrac{n_2P_1}{n_1P_2}; \quad \dfrac{V_2}{V_1} = \dfrac{(0.22\text{ mol})(0.92\text{ atm})}{(0.075\text{ mol})(2.7\text{ atm})} = 1.0$

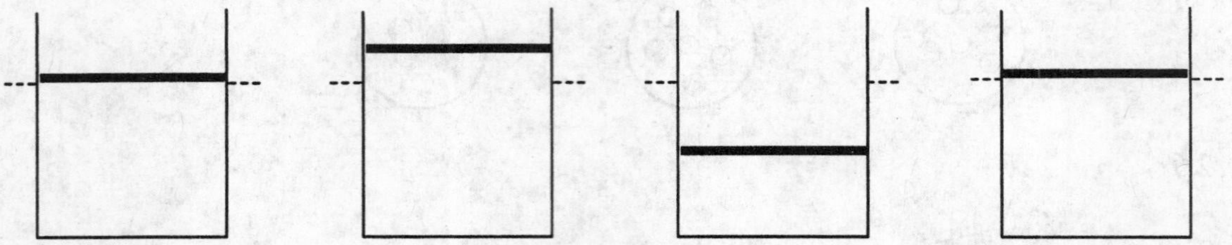

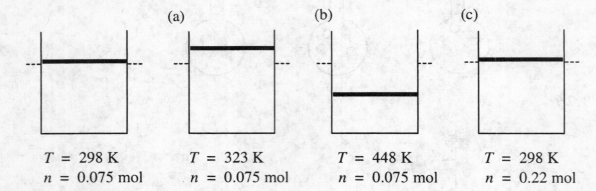

	(a)	(b)	(c)
T = 298 K	T = 323 K	T = 448 K	T = 298 K
n = 0.075 mol	n = 0.075 mol	n = 0.075 mol	n = 0.22 mol
P = 0.92 atm	P = 0.92 atm	P = 2.7 atm	P = 2.7 atm

8.29 The proportions of each gas in the container:
$P_{red} + P_{yellow} + P_{green} = 600$ mm:
red = 6/12 = 1/2; yellow = 2/12 = 1/6; green = 4/12 = 1/3
P_{red} = 1/2 x 600 mm Hg = 300 mm Hg;
P_{yellow} = 1/6 x 600 mm Hg = 100 mm Hg;
P_{green} = 1/3 x 600 mm Hg = 200 mm Hg

Gases and Pressure

8.30 One atmosphere is the amount of pressure needed to hold a column of mercury 760 mm high.

8.32 (1) A gas consists of many tiny particles moving about at random with no attractive forces between particles.
(2) The amount of space occupied by gas molecules is much smaller than the amount of space between molecules.
(3) The average kinetic energy of gas particles is proportional to Kelvin temperature.
(4) When molecules collide, they spring apart elastically, and their total energy is constant.

8.34

(a) $1 \text{ atm} \times \dfrac{760 \text{ mm Hg}}{1 \text{ atm}} = 760 \text{ mm Hg}$

(b) $25.3 \text{ psi} \times \dfrac{760 \text{ mm Hg}}{14.7 \text{ psi}} = 1310 \text{ mm Hg}$

(c) $7.5 \text{ atm} \times \dfrac{760 \text{ mm Hg}}{1 \text{ atm}} = 5.7 \times 10^3 \text{ mm Hg}$

(d) $28.0 \text{ in. Hg} \times \dfrac{25.4 \text{ mm}}{1 \text{ in.}} = 711 \text{ mm Hg}$

(e) $41.8 \text{ Pa} \times \dfrac{760 \text{ mm Hg}}{101{,}325 \text{ Pa}} = 0.314 \text{ mm Hg}$

8.36 When the level in the arm connected to the container is 176 mm (17.6 cm) lower than the level open to the atmosphere, the pressure in the gas container is greater than atmospheric pressure.

754.3 mm Hg + 176 mm Hg = 930 mm Hg

Boyle's Law

8.38 Boyle's law: Volume varies inversely with pressure at constant temperature and number of moles; that is, $P_1V_1 = P_2V_2$.

8.40 $P_1V_1 = P_2V_2$; $P_1 = 65.0$ mm Hg; $P_2 = 385$ mm Hg; $V_1 = 600.0$ mL $= 0.600$ L; $V_2 = ?$

$$V_2 = \frac{P_1V_1}{P_2} = \frac{65.0 \text{ mm Hg} \times 0.600 \text{ L}}{385 \text{ mm Hg}} = 0.101 \text{ L} = 101 \text{ mL}$$

8.42 $P_1V_1 = P_2V_2$; $P_1 = 150$ atm; $P_2 = 1.00$ atm; $V_1 = 50.0$ L; $V_2 = ?$

$$V_2 = \frac{P_1V_1}{P_2} = \frac{150 \text{ atm} \times 50.0 \text{ L}}{1.00 \text{ atm}} = 7500 \text{ L} = 7.5 \times 10^3 \text{ L}$$

Charles's Law

8.44 Charles's law: Volume varies directly with temperature at constant pressure and number of moles; that is, $V_1/T_1 = V_2/T_2$.

8.46

$\dfrac{V_1}{T_1} = \dfrac{V_2}{T_2}$; $V_1 = 960$ L; $V_2 = 1200$ L; $T_1 = 18°C = 291$ K; $T_2 = ?$

$$T_2 = \frac{V_2T_1}{V_1} = \frac{1200 \text{ L} \times 291 \text{ K}}{960 \text{ L}} = 364 \text{ K} = 91°\text{C}$$

8.48

$$\frac{V_1}{T_1} = \frac{V_2}{T_2}; \qquad V_1 = 147 \text{ mL};\ V_2 = ?;\ T_1 = 28°\text{C} = 301 \text{ K};\ T_2 = 37°\text{C} = 330 \text{ K}$$

$$V_2 = \frac{V_1T_2}{T_1} = \frac{147 \text{ mL x } 330 \text{ K}}{301 \text{ K}} = 161 \text{ mL}$$

Gay-Lussac's Law

8.50 Gay-Lussac's law: Pressure varies directly with temperature at constant volume and number of moles; that is, $P_1/T_1 = P_2/T_2$.

8.52

$$\frac{P_1}{T_1} = \frac{P_2}{T_2}; \qquad P_1 = 0.95 \text{ atm};\ P_2 = ?;\ T_1 = 25°\text{C} = 298 \text{ K};\ T_2 = 117°\text{C} = 390 \text{ K}$$

$$P_2 = \frac{P_1T_2}{T_1} = \frac{0.95 \text{ atm x } 390 \text{ K}}{298 \text{ K}} = 1.2 \text{ atm}$$

Combined Gas Law

8.54

$$\frac{P_1V_1}{T_1} = \frac{P_2V_2}{T_2}; \qquad P_1 = 760 \text{ mm Hg};\ V_1 = 2.84 \text{ L};\ T_1 = 273 \text{ K}$$

$$P_2 = 520 \text{ mm Hg};\ V_2 = 7.50 \text{ L};\ T_2 = ?$$

$$T_2 = \frac{P_2V_2T_1}{P_1V_1} = \frac{520 \text{ mm Hg x } 7.50 \text{ L x } 273 \text{ K}}{760 \text{ mm Hg x } 2.84 \text{ L}} = 493 \text{ K} = 220°\text{C}$$

8.56

$$\frac{P_1V_1}{T_1} = \frac{P_2V_2}{T_2}; \qquad P_1 = 752 \text{ mm Hg};\ V_1 = 62.4 \text{ mL};\ T_1 = 26°\text{C} = 299 \text{ K}$$

$$P_2 = 760 \text{ mm Hg};\ V_2 = ?;\ T_2 = 0\ °\text{C} = 273 \text{ K}$$

$$V_2 = \frac{P_1V_1T_2}{T_1P_2} = \frac{752 \text{ mm Hg x } 62.4 \text{ mL x } 273 \text{ K}}{299 \text{ K x } 760 \text{ mm Hg}} = 56.4 \text{ mL}$$

8.58 (a) For one mole of gas, the combined gas law states that P is proportional to T/V, or $P \propto T/V$. Thus, if the temperature doubles and the volume is halved, the new pressure is four times greater than the original pressure:

$$\frac{P_1V_1}{T_1} = \frac{P_2V_2}{T_2}; \qquad V_2 = 0.5\ V_1;\ T_2 = 2\ T_1;\ P_2 = ?$$

$$P_2 = \frac{P_1V_1T_2}{T_1V_2} = \frac{P_1V_1 \text{ x } 2T_1}{T_1 \text{ x } 0.5V_1} = 4\ P_1$$

(b) If the temperature is halved and the volume is doubled, the new pressure is one fourth the original pressure:

$$\frac{P_1V_1}{T_1} = \frac{P_2V_2}{T_2}; \qquad V_2 = 0.5V_1;\ T_2 = 2T_1;\ P_2 = ?$$

$$P_2 = \frac{P_1V_1T_2}{T_1V_2} = \frac{P_1V_1 \text{ x } 0.5T_1}{T_1 \text{ x } 2V_1} = 0.25\ P_1$$

8.60

$$\frac{P_1V_1}{T_1} = \frac{P_2V_2}{T_2}; \qquad P_1 = 775 \text{ mm Hg};\ V_1 = 590 \text{ mL};\ T_1 = 352 \text{ K}$$

$$P_2 = 800.0 \text{ mm Hg};\ V_2 = ?;\ T_2 = 298 \text{ K}$$

$$V_2 = \frac{P_1V_1T_2}{P_2T_1} = \frac{775 \text{ mm Hg x } 590 \text{ mL x } 298 \text{ K}}{800.0 \text{ mm Hg x } 352 \text{ K}} = 484 \text{ mL}$$

Avogadro's Law and Standard Molar Volume

8.62 Avogadro's law states that equal volumes of gases at the same temperature and pressure contain equal numbers of molecules. Since the volume of space taken up by gas molecules is so much smaller than the amount of space between molecules, Avogadro's law is true regardless of the chemical identity of the gas.

8.64 A mole of gas at STP occupies 22.4 L.

8.66 The samples contain equal numbers of molecules. 1.0 L of O_2 weighs more than 1.0 L of H_2 because the molar mass of O_2 is greater than the molar mass of H_2, and equal numbers of moles of both are present.

8.68

$$16.5 \text{ L x } \frac{1 \text{ mol}}{22.4 \text{ L}} \text{ x } \frac{16.0 \text{ g } CH_4}{1 \text{ mol } CH_4} = 11.8 \text{ g } CH_4$$

8.70

$$V = 4.0 \text{ m x } 5.0 \text{ m x } 2.5 \text{ m} = 50 \text{ m}^3;\ 50 \text{ m}^3 \text{ x } \frac{10^3 \text{ L}}{1 \text{ m}^3} = 5.0 \text{ x } 10^4 \text{ L}$$

$$\frac{1 \text{ mol}}{22.4 \text{ L}} \text{ x } 5.0 \text{ x } 10^4 \text{ L} = 2230 \text{ mol gas}$$

$$\frac{0.21 \text{ mol } O_2}{1 \text{ mol gas}} \text{ x } 2230 \text{ mol gas} = 470 \text{ mol } O_2$$

$$470 \text{ mol } O_2 \text{ x } \frac{32.0 \text{ g } O_2}{1 \text{ mol } O_2} = 15{,}000 \text{ g } O_2 = 15 \text{ kg } O_2$$

The Ideal Gas Law

8.72 The ideal gas law : $PV = nRT$

8.74 $PV = nRT;$ $n = PV/RT;$

For Cl_2: $P = 1.0$ atm; $V = 2.0$ L; $R = 0.082 \frac{L \cdot atm}{mol \cdot K}$; $T = 273$ K

$$n = \frac{1.0 \text{ atm} \times 2.0 \text{ L}}{0.082 \frac{L \cdot atm}{mol \cdot K} \times 273 \text{ K}} = 0.089 \text{ mol } Cl_2$$

$$0.089 \text{ mol } Cl_2 \times \frac{71 \text{ g}}{1 \text{ mol } Cl_2} = 6.3 \text{ g } Cl_2$$

For CH_4: $P = 1.5$ atm; $V = 3.0$ L; $R = 0.082 \frac{L \cdot atm}{mol \cdot K}$; $T = 300$ K

$$n = \frac{1.5 \text{ atm} \times 3.0 \text{ L}}{0.082 \frac{L \cdot atm}{mol \cdot K} \times 300 \text{ K}} = 0.18 \text{ mol } CH_4$$

$$0.18 \text{ mol } CH_4 \times \frac{16 \text{ g}}{1 \text{ mol } CH_4} = 2.9 \text{ g } CH_4$$

There are more molecules in the CH_4 sample than in the Cl_2 sample. The Cl_2 sample, however, weighs more because the molar mass of Cl_2 is much greater than the molar mass of CH_4.

8.76

$n = 2.3$ mol He; $T = 294$ K; $V = 1.5$ L

$$P = \frac{nRT}{V} = \frac{2.3 \text{ mol He} \times 0.082 \frac{L \cdot atm}{mol \cdot K} \times 294 \text{ K}}{1.5 \text{ L}} = 37 \text{ atm}$$

8.78

$n = 15.0 \text{ g } CO_2 \times \frac{1 \text{ mol}}{44 \text{ g}} = 0.341 \text{ mol } CO_2$; $T = 310$ K ; $V = 0.30$ L

$$P = \frac{nRT}{V} = \frac{0.341 \text{ mol } CO_2 \times 62.4 \frac{mm\ Hg \cdot L}{mol \cdot K} \times 310 \text{ K}}{0.30 \text{ L}} = 2.2 \times 10^4 \text{ mm Hg}$$

8.80

$n = 18.0 \text{ g } O_2 \times \frac{1 \text{ mol}}{32.0 \text{ g}} = 0.562 \text{ mol } O_2$; $T = 350$ K; $P = 550$ mm Hg

$$V = \frac{nRT}{P} = \frac{0.562 \text{ mol } O_2 \times 62.4 \frac{mm\ Hg \cdot L}{mol \cdot K} \times 350 \text{ K}}{550 \text{ mm Hg}} = 22.3 \text{ L } O_2$$

Dalton's Law and Partial Pressure

8.82 Partial pressure is the pressure contribution of one component of a mixture of gases to the total pressure.

8.84

$$440 \text{ mm Hg} \times \frac{1 \text{ atm}}{760 \text{ mm Hg}} \times \frac{160 \text{ mm Hg}}{1.0 \text{ atm}} = 93 \text{ mm Hg}$$

Liquids and Intermolecular Forces

8.86 The vapor pressure of a liquid is the partial pressure of the vapor above the liquid.

8.88 Increased pressure raises a liquid's boiling point; decreased pressure lowers a liquid's boiling point.

8.90 (a) All molecules exhibit London forces, which increase in strength with increasing molecular weight.
(b) Dipole–dipole interactions are important for molecules that have polar covalent bonds.
(c) Hydrogen bonding occurs between an unshared electron pair on an electronegative atom (O, N, or F) and a hydrogen atom bonded to a second electronegative atom (O, N, F).

8.92 Ethanol is higher boiling than dimethyl ether because of hydrogen bonding. Since molecules of ethanol are strongly attracted to each other, the boiling point of ethanol is higher than that of dimethyl ether, whose molecules are held together by weaker dipole–dipole interactions.

8.94

(a) $$\frac{9.72 \text{ kcal}}{1 \text{ mol } H_2O} \times 3.00 \text{ mol } H_2O = 29.2 \text{ kcal of heat required}$$

(b) $$\frac{9.72 \text{ kcal}}{1 \text{ mol } H_2O} \times \frac{1 \text{ mol } H_2O}{18.0 \text{ g}} \times 320 \text{ g} = 173 \text{ kcal of heat is released}$$

Solids

8.96 The atoms in a crystalline solid are arranged in a regular, orderly network. The atoms in an amorphous solid have no regular arrangement.

8.98

$$\frac{45.9 \text{ cal}}{1 \text{ g}} \times \frac{1 \text{ kcal}}{1000 \text{ cal}} \times \frac{60.0 \text{ g}}{1 \text{ mol}} \times 1.75 \text{ mol} = 4.82 \text{ kcal}$$

Applications

8.100 *Systolic pressure* (the higher number) is the maximum blood pressure developed in the artery just after contraction. *Diastolic pressure* (the lower number) is the minimum pressure that occurs at the end of the heartbeat cycle. A blood pressure reading of 180/110 is an indication of high blood pressure.

8.102 Normally, a large portion of solar radiation is reflected back into space. Greenhouse gases such as CO_2 trap some of this radiation, which warms the atmosphere. The larger the amount of greenhouse gas, the greater the amount of radiation absorbed, and the greater the warming.

8.104 The supercritical state of matter is a situation intermediate between liquid and gas, in which there is some space between molecules yet they are too close together to be truly a gas.

General Questions and Problems

8.106 As the temperature increases, the kinetic energy of gas molecules increases, and the force per unit area that they exert in colliding against the walls of a container increases, thus increasing pressure.

8.108 3.0 L of H_2 and 1.5 L of O_2 react completely. At STP, one mole of H_2 occupies 22.4 L. Thus, 3.0 L of hydrogen = 3.0/22.4 or 0.13 mol. This is also the number of moles of H_2O formed.

$n = 0.13 \text{ mol } H_2O; \quad T = 373 \text{ K}; \quad P = 1.0 \text{ atm}$

$$V = \frac{nRT}{P} = \frac{0.13 \text{ mol } H_2O \times 0.0821 \frac{\text{L} \cdot \text{atm}}{\text{mol} \cdot \text{K}} \times 373 \text{ K}}{1.0 \text{ atm}} = 4.0 \text{ L } H_2O$$

8.110

$$0.0094 \text{ mol } CO_2 \times \frac{44.0 \text{ g } CO_2}{1 \text{ mol } CO_2} = 0.41 \text{ g } CO_2$$

$$\frac{0.41 \text{ g } CO_2}{1 \text{ min}} \times \frac{60 \text{ min}}{1 \text{ hr}} \times \frac{24 \text{ hr}}{1 \text{ day}} = \frac{590 \text{ g } CO_2}{\text{day}}$$

8.112 $P = 0.975 \text{ atm}; \; V = 1.6 \times 10^5 \text{ L}; \; T = 375 \text{ K}$

$$n = \frac{PV}{RT} = \frac{0.975 \text{ atm} \times 1.6 \times 10^5 \text{ L}}{0.0821 \frac{\text{L} \cdot \text{atm}}{\text{mol} \cdot \text{K}} \times 375 \text{ K}} = 5.07 \times 10^3 \text{ mol}$$

$$\text{Density} = \frac{5.07 \times 10^3 \text{ mol}}{1.6 \times 10^5 \text{ L}} \times \frac{29 \text{ g}}{\text{mol}} = \frac{0.92 \text{ g}}{\text{L}}$$

The air in the balloon is less dense than air at STP (density = 1.3 g/L).

8.114 Divide the molar mass (molecular weight in grams) by 22.4 L to find the density in grams per liter.

Gas	*Molecular Weight*	*Density (g/L) at STP*
(a) CH_4	16.0 amu	0.714
(b) CO_2	44.0 amu	1.96
(c) O_2	32.0 amu	1.43

8.116

(a)

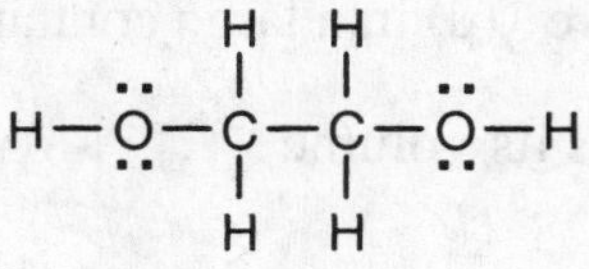

Ethylene glycol

(b)

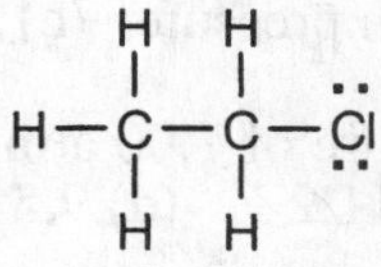

Chloroethane

(c) Ethylene glycol has a higher boiling point than chloroethane because it forms hydrogen bonds.

8.118 (a) Since the size of a Rankine degree is the same as a Fahrenheit degree, we can use the same conversion factor as we use for °F/°C conversions.

$$\frac{9°R}{5°C} \times 273.15°C = 492°R$$

(b) To calculate the gas constant R, use the ideal gas law at standard temperature and pressure.

$$R = \frac{PV}{nT};\quad P = 1 \text{ atm};\quad V = 22.4 \text{ L};\quad n = 1 \text{ mol};\quad T = 491.67°R$$

$$R = \frac{1 \text{ atm} \times 22.4 \text{ L}}{1 \text{ mol} \times 492°R} = 0.0455 \frac{\text{L} \cdot \text{atm}}{\text{mol} \cdot °R}$$

Self-Test for Chapter 8

Multiple Choice

1. Which of the following units would you be least likely to use in a chemical laboratory?
(a) Pascal (b) pounds per square inch (c) mm Hg (d) atmosphere

2. A fixed amount of a gas has its temperature and volume doubled. What happens to its pressure?
(a) increases fourfold (b) doubles (c) stays the same (d) is halved

3. In which of the gas laws is the amount of gas not fixed?
(a) Boyle's law (b) Charles's law (c) Gay-Lussac's law (d) Avogadro's law

4. Which of the following compounds does not exhibit hydrogen bonding?
(a) CH_3OCH_3 (b) CH_3OH (c) HF (d) CH_3NH_2

5. Which of the following compounds is the lowest melting?
(a) NaI (b) Au (c) SiO_2 (d) sugar

6. Which term describes the change of state that occurs when a gas changes to a solid?
(a) fusion (b) condensation (c) deposition (d) sublimation

7. When does a gas obey ideal behavior?
(a) at low density (b) at high pressure (c) at low temperature (d) in a large container

8. If 22.0 g of CO_2 has a pressure of 1.00 atm at 300 K, what is its volume?
(a) 22.4 L (b) 12.3 L (c) 11.2 L (d) 9.5 L

9. What volume does the amount of gas in Problem 8 occupy at STP?
(a) 22.4 L (b) 12.3 L (c) 11.2 L (d) 9.5 L

10. What is the density of CO_2 gas in g/L at STP if one mole of gas has a volume of 22.4 L?
(a) 44.0 g/L (b) 11.0 g/L (c) 6.4 g/L (d) 1.96 g/L

Sentence Completion

1. In Boyle's law, the _____ of a gas is inversely proportional to its _____.

2. A liquid has _____ volume and _____ shape.

3. _____ law states that the total pressure of a gas mixture is the sum of the individual pressure of the components in the mixture.

4. A pressure of 760 mm Hg and a temperature of 273 K are known as _____.

5. _____ law says that equal volumes of gases at the same temperature and pressure contain equal numbers of molecules.

6. In a closed container, liquid and vapor are at _____.

7. Units for measuring pressure include _____, _____, _____, and _____.

8. The _____ __ _____ is the heat necessary to melt one gram of a solid at its melting point.

9. In Charles's law, _____ and _____ are kept constant.

10. Gas particles move in straight lines, with energy proportional to _____.

11. The transformation of a substance from one phase to another is known as a __________ ________.

12. A liquid that evaporates readily is said to be ________.

True or False

1. Molecules of ethyl alcohol exhibit hydrogen bonding.
2. All gases are similar in their physical behavior.
3. Molecules of CH_3Cl experience both dipole–dipole interactions and London forces.
4. Doubling the pressure of a gas at constant temperature doubles the volume.
5. $R = 0.082$ L atm/(mol · K) is a value for the gas constant.
6. Atoms in solids have an orderly arrangement.
7. Standard temperature and pressure are 760 mm Hg and 273°C.
8. All substances become solids if the temperature is low enough.
9. The atmospheric pressure in Death Valley (282 ft below sea level) is lower than the atmospheric pressure at sea level.
10. The more liquid there is in a closed container, the higher the vapor pressure.
11. Surface tension is a liquid's resistance to flow.

Match each entry on the left with its partner on the right. Use each answer once.

1. $P_1V_1 = P_2V_2$	(a) Avogadro's law
2. Dipole–dipole attraction	(b) Gas constant
3. $P_{total} = P_{gas\ 1} + P_{gas\ 2} + \ldots$	(c) Force per unit area
4. 760 mm Hg at 273 K	(d) Charles's law
5. Hydrogen bonding	(e) Occurs between molecules of CH_3Br
6. $V_1/n_1 = V_2/n_2$	(f) STP
7. 0.007500 mm Hg	(g) Boyle's law
8. London forces	(h) Occurs between molecules of CH_3OH
9. 62.3 mm Hg L/mol K	(i) Ideal gas law
10. $V_1/T_1 = V_2/T_2$	(j) Pascal
11. Pressure	(k) Dalton's law of partial pressure
12. $PV = nRT$	(l) Occurs between molecules of N_2

Chapter 9 – Solutions

Chapter Outline

I. Characteristics of solutions (Sections 9.1–9.6).
  A. Mixtures and solutions (Section 9.1).
    1. Mixtures are either heterogeneous or homogeneous.
      a. Heterogeneous mixtures have non-uniform mixing.
      b. Homogeneous mixtures have uniform mixing.
    2. Homogeneous mixtures can be classified by particle size.
      a. In solutions, particles range in size from 0.1 to 2 nm.
      b. In colloids, particles range in size from 2 to 1000 nm.
    3. When a solid is dissolved in a liquid, the liquid is the solvent and the solid is the solute.
  B. The solution process (Sections 9.2–9.3).
    1. Solubility depends on the strength of attraction between solute particles and solvent relative to the attractions in the pure substances.
    2. In predicting solubility, polar solvents dissolve polar substances, and nonpolar solvents dissolve nonpolar substances.
    3. Solution can be either an exothermic or an endothermic process.
    4. Some ionic compounds attract water to form solid hydrates (Section 9.3).
  C. Solubility (Sections 9.4–9.6).
    1. Solubility is a dynamic process (Section 9.4).
      a. When no more of an added solute will dissolve, the solution is said to be saturated.
      b. In a saturated solution, an equilibrium is established between dissolving and crystallizing.
      c. Two liquids are miscible if they are mutually soluble in all proportions.
    2. The solubility of a substance is the maximum amount of the substance that will dissolve in a solvent.
    3. Effect of temperature on solubility (Section 9.5).
      a. The effect of temperature on the solubility of a solid solute is unpredictable.
      b. A gas is always less soluble as temperature increases.
      c. A solid that is more soluble at high temperature than at low may form a supersaturated solution.
    4. Effect of pressure on solubility (Section 9.6).
      a. Increased pressure makes gas molecules more soluble in a liquid.
      b. Henry's law: $P_{gas} = kC$.
         The solubility of a gas in a liquid is proportional to its partial pressure over the liquid at constant T.
      c. When the partial pressure of a gas changes:
$$\frac{C_1}{P_1} = \frac{C_2}{P_2} = k \text{ (at constant T)}$$

II. Quantitative relationships in solutions (Sections 9.7–9.10).
  A. Concentration (Section 9.7).
    1. $\text{Molarity} = \dfrac{\text{moles of solute}}{\text{volume of solution (L)}}$.
       Molarity can be used as a conversion factor.
    2. $\text{weight/volume \% concentration [(w/v)\%]} = \dfrac{\text{grams of solute}}{\text{mL of solution}} \times 100\%$.

3. volume/volume % concentration [(v/v)%] = $\dfrac{\text{volume of solute (mL)}}{\text{volume of solution (mL)}}$ x 100%.

4. parts per million (ppm) = $\dfrac{\text{mass of solute (g)}}{\text{mass of solution (g)}}$ x 10^6.

= $\dfrac{\text{volume of solute (mL)}}{\text{volume of solution (mL)}}$ x 10^6.

B. Dilution (Section 9.8).
1. During dilution, the number of moles of solute remains constant, while volume changes.
2. $M_1 \times V_1 = M_2 \times V_2$.
3. V_1 / V_2 is known as a dilution factor.

C. Equivalents and milliequivalents (Sections 9.9–9.10).
1. Electrolytes (Section 9.9).
a. Substances that dissociate completely are strong electrolytes.
b. Substances that dissociate partially are weak electrolytes.
c. Molecular substances that don't produce ions are nonelectrolytes.
2. The concentration of electrolytes is expressed in equivalents (Section 9.10).
a. 1 equivalent of an ion = $\dfrac{\text{molar mass of the ion}}{\text{number of charges on the ion}}$.
b. Milliequivalents are useful when measuring ion concentrations in body fluids.

III. Properties of solutions (Sections 9.11–9.13).
A. Effects of particles in solution - colligative properties (Section 9.11).
1. Lowering of vapor pressure.
2. Boiling point elevation.
3. Freezing point depression.
4. These effects don't depend on the identity of the particles.

B. Osmosis (Section 9.12–9.13).
1. When two solutions of different concentrations are separated by a semipermeable membrane, water passes through to the more concentrated side. This is known as osmosis.
2. Osmotic pressure can be applied to establish an equilibrium between the rates of forward and reverse passage of water across the membrane.
3. The osmotic pressure of a solution depends only on the number of particles in solution.
4. Osmolarity = molarity x number of particles per formula unit.
5. Two solutions that are isotonic have the same osmolarity.
a. In cells, a hypotonic solution causes hemolysis.
b. A hypertonic solution causes crenation.
6. Dialysis is a process similar to osmosis except that the pores in the membrane allow small solute molecules to pass (Section 9.13).
a. Hemodialysis is used to cleanse the blood of people whose kidneys malfunction.
b. Colloidal particles are too large to pass through semipermeable membranes.

Solutions to Chapter 9 Problems

9.1 Orange juice is heterogeneous, and all of the other mixtures are homogeneous, although hand lotion might be heterogeneous in some cases. Apple juice and tea are solutions because they are nonfilterable and transparent to light. Hand lotion is a colloid.

9.2 Remember the rule "like dissolves like."
(a) CCl_4 and H_2O don't form solutions because CCl_4 is nonpolar and H_2O is polar.
(b) Gasoline and $MgSO_4$ don't form solutions because $MgSO_4$ is ionic and gasoline is nonpolar.
(c)(d) These two pairs of substances form solutions because they are chemically similar.

9.3 Glauber's salt: $Na_2SO_4{\cdot}10H_2O$

9.4 Molar mass of Glauber's salt: 322 g/mol. 322 g of Glauber's salt provides 1.00 mol of sodium sulfate.

9.5 The solubility of KBr at 50°C is approximately 80 g/100 mL.

9.6

$$\frac{C_1}{P_1} = \frac{C_2}{P_2};\ P_1 = 760 \text{ mm Hg};\ C_1 = 0.169 \text{ g/100 mL};\ P_2 = 2.5 \times 10^4 \text{ mm Hg};\ C_2 = ?$$

$$C_2 = \frac{C_1P_2}{P_1} = \frac{\left(\frac{0.169 \text{ g}}{100 \text{ mL}}\right) \times 2.5 \times 10^4 \text{ mm Hg}}{760 \text{ mm Hg}} = 5.6 \text{ g } CO_2\text{/100 mL}$$

9.7

$$\frac{C_1}{P_1} = \frac{C_2}{P_2};\ P_1 = 1.00 \text{ atm};\ C_1 = 0.169 \text{ g/100 mL};\ P_2 = 4.0 \times 10^{-4} \text{ atm};\ C_2 = ?$$

$$C_2 = \frac{C_1P_2}{P_1} = \frac{\left(\frac{0.169 \text{ g}}{100 \text{ mL}}\right) \times 4.0 \times 10^{-4} \text{ atm}}{1.00 \text{ atm}} = 6.8 \times 10^{-5} \text{ g } CO_2\text{/100 mL}$$

9.8

$$50.0 \text{ g} \times \frac{1 \text{ mol}}{337 \text{ g}} = 0.148 \text{ mol};\quad \frac{0.148 \text{ mol}}{0.160 \text{ L}} = 0.925 \text{ M}$$

9.9

$$\text{moles of solute} = \text{molarity (M)} \times \text{volume} = \frac{\text{mol}}{\text{L}} \times \text{L}$$

(a) $M = \dfrac{0.35 \text{ mol } NaNO_3}{1 \text{ L}};\quad V = 175 \text{ mL} = 0.175 \text{ L}$

$$\text{\# moles} = \frac{0.35 \text{ mol}}{1 \text{ L}} \times 0.175 \text{ L} = 0.061 \text{ mol } NaNO_3$$

(b) $M = \dfrac{1.4 \text{ mol } HNO_3}{1 \text{ L}};\quad V = 480 \text{ mL} = 0.48 \text{ L}$

$$\text{\# moles} = \frac{1.4 \text{ mol}}{1 \text{ L}} \times 0.48 \text{ L} = 0.67 \text{ mol } HNO_3$$

9.10 First, find the number of moles of cholesterol in 250 mL of blood:

$$250 \text{ mL} \times \frac{0.0050 \text{ mol cholesterol}}{1000 \text{ mL}} = 0.001\ 25 \text{ mol cholesterol}$$

Next, find the molar mass of cholesterol:

$$(27 \times 12.0 \text{ g/mol C}) + (46 \times 1.0 \text{ g/mol H}) + (16.0 \text{ g/mol O}) = 386.0 \text{ g/mol}$$

Now, convert moles into grams:

$$0.001\ 25 \text{ mol cholesterol} \times \frac{386.0 \text{ g}}{1 \text{ mol}} = 0.48 \text{ g cholesterol}$$

9.11 Molar mass of $CaCO_3$ = 100.0 g

$$0.065 \text{ L} \times \frac{0.12 \text{ mol HCl}}{1 \text{ L}} \times \frac{1 \text{ mol } CaCO_3}{2 \text{ mol HCl}} \times \frac{100.0 \text{ g } CaCO_3}{1 \text{ mol } CaCO_3} = 0.39 \text{ g } CaCO_3$$

9.12 1 dL = 100 mL

$$\frac{8.6 \text{ mg}}{100 \text{ mL}} \times \frac{1 \text{ g}}{1000 \text{ mg}} \times 100\% = 0.0086\% \text{ (w/v) } Ca^{2+}$$

Remember: [(w/v)%] specifies that the weight of solute be expressed in grams.

9.13

$$\frac{23 \text{ g KI}}{350 \text{ mL}} \times 100\% = 6.6\% \text{ (w/v) KI}$$

9.14 (a) A 16% (w/v) solution contains 16 g of solute per 100 mL of solution.

$$125 \text{ mL} \times \frac{16 \text{ g glucose}}{100 \text{ mL}} = 20 \text{ g glucose}$$

(b) A 1.8% (w/v) solution contains 1.8 g of solute per 100 mL of solution.

$$65 \text{ mL} \times \frac{1.8 \text{ g KCl}}{100 \text{ mL}} = 1.2 \text{ g KCl}$$

9.15 A 7.5% (v/v) solution contains 7.5 mL of solute per 100 mL of solution.

$$500 \text{ mL solution} \times \frac{7.5 \text{ mL acetic acid}}{100 \text{ mL solution}} = 38 \text{ mL acetic acid}$$

To prepare the desired solution, measure 38 mL of acetic acid into a 500.0 mL volumetric flask and add water to the 500.0 mL mark.

9.16 (a) 22 mL of ethyl alcohol are needed.

(b) $150 \text{ mL solution} \times \frac{12 \text{ mL acetic acid}}{100 \text{ mL solution}} = 18 \text{ mL acetic acid}$

9.17

$$\frac{32\text{ mg NaF}}{20\text{ kg solution}} \times \frac{1\text{ kg}}{10^6\text{ mg}} \times 10^6 = 1.6\text{ ppm}$$

9.18 For lead:

$$\frac{0.015\text{ mg Pb}}{1\text{ kg solution}} \times \frac{1\text{ kg}}{10^6\text{ mg}} \times 10^6 = 0.015\text{ ppm}$$

$$\frac{0.015\text{ mg Pb}}{1\text{ kg solution}} \times \frac{1\text{ kg}}{10^3\text{ g}} \times 100\text{ g} = 0.0015\text{ mg Pb}$$

For copper:

$$\frac{1.3\text{ mg Cu}}{1\text{ kg solution}} \times \frac{1\text{ kg}}{10^6\text{ mg}} \times 10^6 = 1.3\text{ ppm}$$

$$\frac{1.3\text{ mg Cu}}{1\text{ kg solution}} \times \frac{1\text{ kg}}{10^3\text{ g}} \times 100\text{ g} = 0.13\text{ mg Cu}$$

9.19 $M_1 = 12.0\text{ M}$; $V_1 = 100.0\text{ mL}$; $V_2 = 500.0\text{ mL}$; $M_2 = ?$

$$M_2 = M_1 \times \frac{V_1}{V_2} = 12.0\text{ M} \times \frac{100.0\text{ mL}}{500.0\text{ mL}} = 2.40\text{ M}$$

Ballpark check: Since there is a fivefold dilution, the final molarity is 1/5 of the initial molarity.

9.20 $V_2 = 500.0\text{ mL}$; $M_2 = 1.25\text{ M}$; $M_1 = 16.0\text{ M}$; $V_1 = ?$

$$V_1 = V_2 \times \frac{M_2}{M_1} = 500.0\text{ mL} \times \frac{1.25\text{ M}}{16.0\text{ M}} = 39.1\text{ mL}$$

Ballpark check: Since the final molarity is about 1/12 the initial molarity, the initial volume is about 1/12 the final volume, or about 40 mL.

9.21 – 9.22

One equivalent = molar mass of ion (g) ÷ number of charges on ion

Ion	*Molar Mass*	*Charge*	*Equivalent Weight*	*Milliequivalent Weight*
(a) K^+	39.1 g	+1	39.1 g	39.1 mg, or 3.91×10^{-2} g
(b) Br^-	79.9 g	−1	79.9 g	79.9 mg, or 7.99×10^{-2} g
(c) Mg^{2+}	24.3 g	+2	12.2 g	12.2 mg, or 1.22×10^{-2} g
(d) SO_4^{2-}	96.0 g	−2	48.0 g	48.0 mg, or 4.80×10^{-2} g
(e) Al^{3+}	27.0 g	+3	9.0 g	9.0 mg, or 9.0×10^{-3} g
(f) PO_4^{3-}	95.0 g	−3	31.7 g	31.7 mg, or 31.7×10^{-2} g

9.23 One equivalent of Mg^{2+} = 12.2 g [Problem 9.21(c)].

$$\frac{g\ Mg^{2+}}{1\ L} = \frac{12\ g\ Mg^{2+}}{1\ Eq} \times \frac{1\ Eq}{1000\ mEq} \times \frac{3.0\ mEq}{1\ L} = \frac{0.036\ g\ Mg^{2+}}{1\ L}$$

$$\frac{0.036\ g\ Mg^{2+}}{L} \times \frac{1000\ mg}{1\ g} \times \frac{1\ L}{1000\ mL} \times 250\ mL = 9.0\ mg\ Mg^{2+}$$

9.24 0.67 mol of $MgCl_2$ in 0.5 kg H_2O yields 2.0 mol solute particles. This is equivalent to 4.0 mol particles in 1.0 kg H_2O, which raise the boiling point by 4.0 x 0.51°C = 2.0°C.

Boiling point = 100°C + 2.0°C = 102.0°C

9.25 If HF were a strong electrolyte it would dissociate completely, and a solution of 1.0 mol HF would yield 2.0 mol particles, which would elevate the boiling point of water by 2.0 x 0.51°C = 1.02°C. Since the observed boiling point elevation is only 0.5°C, HF must be a weak electrolyte that is only slightly dissociated.

9.26 (a) The red curve represents the pure solvent, because the solvent boils at a lower temperature than the solution.
(b) A liquid boils when its vapor pressure equals atmospheric pressure. The solvent boils at 62°C, and the solution boils at 69°C.
(c) One mole of solute raises the boiling point approximately 3.5°C, and the observed boiling point elevation is approximately 7°C. Thus, the concentration of the solute is about 2 M.

9.27 Glucose is not an electrolyte. Thus 1.0 mol glucose lowers the freezing point of 1.0 kg H_2O by 1.9°C.

Freezing point = 0°C – 1.9°C = –1.9°C

9.28 A freezing point depression of 1.86°C is produced by 1 mol of ions in 1 kg of water. Thus, a freezing point depression of 2.8°C must be produced by 2.8 ÷ 1.86 = 1.5 mol of ions. Since 0.5 mol of the ionic substance produces the freezing point depression expected for 1.5 mol ions, the substance gives three ions when it dissolves.

9.29 Osmolarity = molarity x number of particles

(a) For 0.35 M KBr, osmolarity = 0.35 M x 2 = 0.70 osmol, since KBr yields two particles (K^+ and Br^-) in solution.

(b) For 0.15 M glucose, osmolarity = 0.15 M x 1 = 0.15 osmol, since glucose yields only one particle in solution. For K_2SO_4, osmolarity = 0.05 M x 3 = 0.15 osmol, since K_2SO_4 provides three particles per mole in solution. Total osmolarity = 0.30 osmol.

9.30 For the oral rehydration solution, osmolarity is equal to the sum of the osmolarities of the individual components. For each of the ionic components, the number of millimoles = the number of mEq, since each ion has one charge. Thus,

$$90 \text{ mM Na}^+ + 20 \text{ mM K}^+ + 110 \text{ mM Cl}^- = 220 \text{ mM ions} = 0.22 \text{ M ions}$$

For glucose:

$$\frac{2.0 \text{ g glucose}}{100 \text{ mL}} \times \frac{1000 \text{ mL}}{1 \text{ L}} \times \frac{1 \text{ mol}}{180 \text{ g glucose}} = 0.11 \text{ M glucose}$$

Osmolarity = molarity x number of particles. In this problem, all components yield 1 particle in solution.
Osmolarity = 0.22 M + 0.11 M = 0.33 osmol

Understanding Key Concepts

9.31

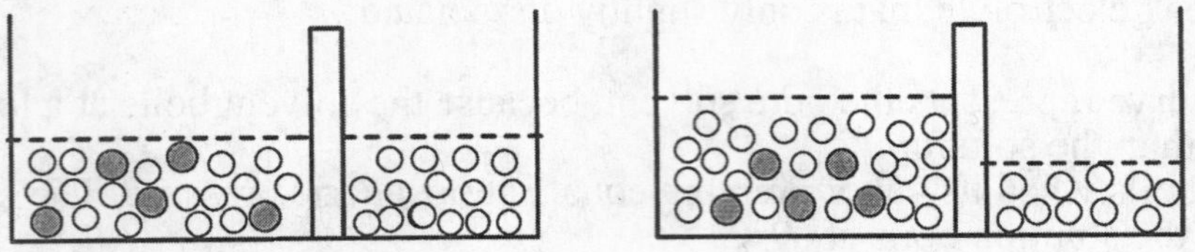

before equilibrium   at equilibrium

The membrane is permeable to the unshaded spheres but impermeable to the shaded spheres. Solvent (unshaded spheres) passes through the membrane until equilibrium is reached.

9.32 The boiling point of water is elevated by 0.5°C for every mole of dissolved particles. 1 mol HCl dissolves to form 2 mol particles, which elevate the boiling point of water by 1°C. Acetic acid exists in solution almost completely as CH_3COOH, and 1 mol acetic acid dissolves to form 1 mol particles, which elevate the boiling point of water by only 0.5°C.

9.33 The same reasoning used in the previous problem applies here. The freezing point of water is depressed by 1.9°C for every mole of dissolved particles. 1 mol HBr dissociates to form 2 mol ions, which lower the freezing point of water by 3.7°C, but 1 mol HF is only slightly dissociated and lowers the freezing point by 1.9°C.

9.34 The lower line on the graph (green) represents the solubility of a gas as a function of temperature. The solubility of a solid may increase or decrease with increasing temperature, but the solubility of a gas *always* decreases when temperature is raised.

9.35

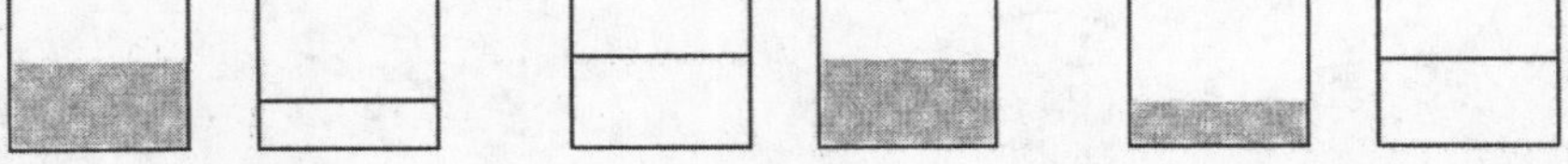

(a)   (b)   (c)

When a beaker of glucose solution (shaded) and a beaker of pure water (unshaded) stand for several days, the liquid levels appear as those pictured in (a). The dissolved glucose particles lower the vapor pressure of water and slow evaporation.

9.36 Drawing (d) represents the solution that results when 50.0 mL of (a) is withdrawn and diluted by a factor of 4.

9.37 At a given temperature, the vapor pressure of the solution is lower than that of the pure solvent because the dissolved particles in the solution slow evaporation of its solvent. The green curve represents the vapor pressure curve of the solution, and the red curve represents the vapor pressure of a solvent.

Solutions and Solubility

9.38 In a homogeneous mixture (such as tea), mixing is uniform throughout because the particle size is small. In a heterogeneous mixture (such as chicken soup), mixing is nonuniform because particle size is larger.

9.40 The polarity of water enables it to dissolve many ionic solids.

9.42 Rubbing alcohol (b) and black coffee (d) are solutions.

9.44

$$C_2 = \frac{C_1P_2}{P_1};\ C_1 = 51.8\text{ g/100 mL};\ P_1 = 760.0\text{ mm Hg};\ P_2 = 225.0\text{ mm Hg}$$

$$= \frac{(51.8\text{ g/100 mL})\ \text{x}\ 225.0\text{ mm Hg}}{760.0\text{ mm Hg}} = 15.3\text{ g/100 mL}$$

Concentration and Dilution of Solutions

9.46 Depending on the solubility of the solute in the solvent, a saturated solution may be either dilute or concentrated. If a solute is only slightly soluble in a solvent, a saturated solution will be dilute. If the solute is very soluble in the solvent, a saturated solution will be concentrated. For a highly soluble solute, even a highly concentrated solution may be unsaturated.

9.48 Molarity (M) is defined as the number of moles of solute per liter of solution.

9.50

$$\frac{6.0\text{ mL ethyl alcohol}}{100.0\text{ mL solution}}\ \text{x}\ 750.0\text{ mL solution} = 45.0\text{ mL ethyl alcohol}$$

Add water to 45.0 mL of ethyl alcohol to make a final volume of 750.0 mL.

9.52

$$250\text{ mL solution}\ \text{x}\ \frac{0.10\text{ mol NaCl}}{1000\text{ mL solution}} = 0.025\text{ mol NaCl}$$

$$0.025\text{ mol NaCl}\ \text{x}\ \frac{58.5\text{ g}}{1\text{ mol}} = 1.5\text{ g NaCl}$$

Dissolve 1.5 g NaCl in water to a final volume of 250 mL.

9.54

(a) $\dfrac{5.8\text{ g KCl}}{75\text{ mL}} \times 100\text{ mL} = 7.7\text{ g KCl};\ \dfrac{7.7\text{ g KCl}}{100\text{ mL}} \times 100\% = 7.7\%\text{ (w/v) KCl}$

(b) $\dfrac{15\text{ g sucrose}}{380\text{ mL}} \times 100\text{ mL} = 3.9\text{ g sucrose};\ \dfrac{3.9\text{ g}}{100\text{ mL}} \times 100\% = 3.9\%\text{ (w/v) sucrose}$

9.56

(a) $50.0\text{ mL} \times \dfrac{8.0\text{ g KCl}}{100\text{ mL}} = 4.0\text{ g KCl}$

(b) $200.0\text{ mL} \times \dfrac{7.5\text{ g acetic acid}}{100\text{ mL}} = 15\text{ g acetic acid}$

9.58

$23\text{ g KOH} \times \dfrac{100\text{ mL}}{10.0\text{ g KOH}} = 230\text{ mL of a }10.0\%\text{ (w/v) solution}$

$23\text{ g KOH} \times \dfrac{1\text{ mol}}{56.1\text{ g KOH}} = 0.41\text{ mol KOH}$

$0.41\text{ mol KOH} \times \dfrac{1000\text{ mL}}{0.25\text{ mol KOH}} = 1600\text{ mL of }0.25\text{ M solution}$

9.60

$\dfrac{10\text{ mg KCN}}{1\text{ kg body weight}} \times \dfrac{1\text{ kg}}{10^6\text{ mg}} \times 10^6 = 10\text{ ppm}$

9.62

(a) $12.5\text{ g NaHCO}_3 \times \dfrac{1\text{ mol}}{84.0\text{ g}} = 0.149\text{ mol NaHCO}_3;\ \dfrac{0.149\text{ mol}}{0.350\text{ L}} = 0.425\text{ M}$

(b) $45.0\text{ g H}_2\text{SO}_4 \times \dfrac{1\text{ mol}}{98.0\text{ g}} = 0.459\text{ mol H}_2\text{SO}_4;\ \dfrac{0.459\text{ mol}}{0.300\text{ L}} = 1.53\text{ M}$

(c) $30.0\text{ g NaCl} \times \dfrac{1\text{ mol}}{58.5\text{ g}} = 0.512\text{ mol NaCl};\ \dfrac{0.512\text{ mol}}{0.500\text{ L}} = 1.03\text{ M}$

9.64

$0.0040\text{ mol HCl} \times \dfrac{1000\text{ mL}}{0.75\text{ mol}} = 5.3\text{ mL HCl}$

9.66 First, calculate the number of moles of H_2SO_4 spilled:

$$0.450 \text{ L} \times \frac{0.50 \text{ mol } H_2SO_4}{1 \text{ L}} = 0.22 \text{ mol } H_2SO_4$$

According to the equation given in the problem, each mole of H_2SO_4 reacts with two moles of $NaHCO_3$. Thus, the 0.22 mol of H_2SO_4 spilled needs to be neutralized with 0.44 mol of $NaHCO_3$.

$$0.44 \text{ mol } NaHCO_3 \times \frac{84 \text{ g}}{1 \text{ mol}} = 37 \text{ g } NaHCO_3$$

9.68

20.0% (v/v) means $\frac{20.0 \text{ mL concentrate}}{100.0 \text{ mL juice}}$

Thus, $100.0 \text{ mL concentrate} \times \frac{100.0 \text{ mL juice}}{20.0 \text{ mL concentrate}} = 500.0 \text{ mL juice}$

Since the final volume of the diluted juice is 500.0 mL, you would have to add 400.0 mL water to the original 100.0 mL of concentrate.

9.70

$$V_1 = V_2 \times \frac{C_2}{C_1}; \; V_2 = 2.0 \text{ L}; \; C_2 = 75 \text{ ppm}; \; C_1 = 285 \text{ ppm}$$

$$= 2.0 \text{ L} \times \frac{75 \text{ ppm}}{285 \text{ ppm}} = 0.53 \text{ L of } 285 \text{ ppm } KNO_3 \text{ solution}$$

9.72

$$V_2 = V_1 \times \frac{M_1}{M_2}; \; V_1 = 25.0 \text{ mL}; \; M_1 = 12.0 \text{ M}; \; M_2 = 0.500 \text{ M}$$

$$= 25.0 \text{ mL} \times \frac{12.0 \text{ M}}{0.500 \text{ M}} = 600 \text{ mL of } 0.500 \text{ M HCl solution}$$

Electrolytes

9.74 An electrolyte is a substance that conducts electricity when dissolved in water.

9.76 If the concentration of Ca^{2+} is 3.0 mEq/L, there are 3.0 mmol of charges due to calcium per liter of blood. Since calcium has a charge of +2, there are 1.5 mmol of calcium per liter of blood.

9.78

$$10\% \text{ (w/v)} = \frac{10 \text{ g KCl}}{100 \text{ mL}}; \quad 30 \text{ mL} \times \frac{10 \text{ g KCl}}{100 \text{ mL}} = 3.0 \text{ g KCl}$$

The molar mass of KCl is 74.6 g/mol. Thus

$$3.0 \text{ g KCl} \times \frac{1 \text{ mol}}{74.6 \text{ g}} = 0.040 \text{ mol KCl}$$

Since one equivalent equals one mole when an ion has only one charge, there are 0.040 Eq, or 40 mEq, of K^+ in a 30 mL dose.

9.80 Use the value 100 mEq/L for the concentration of Cl^- in blood:
For Cl^- ion, 100 mEq = 100 mmol = 0.100 mol.

$$\frac{0.100 \text{ mol } Cl^-}{1 \text{ L}} \times 0.100 \text{ L} = 0.0100 \text{ mol } Cl^- \text{ in 100.0 mL blood}$$

$$0.0100 \text{ mol } Cl^- \times \frac{35.5 \text{ g}}{1 \text{ mol}} = 0.355 \text{ g } Cl^- \text{ in 100.0 mL blood}$$

Properties of Solutions

9.82 0.20 mol NaOH contains 0.40 mol solute particles, and 0.20 mol $Ba(OH)_2$ contains 0.60 mol solute particles. Since $Ba(OH)_2$ produces more solute particles, it produces greater lowering of the freezing point when dissolved in 2.0 kg of water.

9.84 Methanol has a molar mass of 32.0 g and provides one mole of solute particles per mole of methanol.

$$10.0°\text{C} \times \frac{1 \text{ mol}}{1.86°\text{C} \times 1 \text{ kg}} \times 5.00 \text{ kg} = 26.9 \text{ mol methanol}$$

$$26.9 \text{ mol} \times \frac{32.0 \text{ g}}{1 \text{ mol}} = 861 \text{ g of methanol needed}$$

Osmosis

9.86 The inside of a red blood cell contains dissolved substances and therefore has a higher osmolarity than pure water. Water thus passes through the cell membrane to dilute the cell contents until pressure builds up and the cell eventually bursts.

9.88

Solution	Molarity	Number of Particles	Osmolarity
(a) 0.25 M KBr	0.25 M	2	0.50 osmol
0.20 M Na_2SO_4	0.20 M	3	0.60 osmol (greater)
(b) 0.30 M NaOH	0.30 M	2	0.60 osmol
3% (w/v) NaOH	0.75 M	2	1.5 osmol (greater)

9.90 The molar mass of NaCl is 58.5 g, and each mole of NaCl yields two moles of particles.

$$\frac{270\text{ g}}{3.8\text{ L}} \times \frac{1\text{ mol}}{58.5\text{ g}} \times 2\text{ particles} = 2.4\text{ osmol}$$

Applications

9.92 At high altitude, P_{O2} is low, and not enough oxygen is available to cause 100% saturation of hemoglobin. In order to deliver enough oxygen to body tissues, the body compensates by manufacturing more hemoglobin, which drives the hemoglobin equilibrium to the right.

9.94 In addition to fluid replacement, sports drinks provide electrolytes to replenish those lost during exercise, they furnish soluble complex carbohydrates for slow-release energy, and they may contain vitamins to protect cells from damage.

General Questions and Problems

9.96 Molar mass of uric acid ($C_5H_4N_4O_3$) = 168 g.

(a) (w/v)%: $\frac{0.067\text{ g}}{1\text{ L}} = \frac{0.0067\text{ g}}{100\text{ mL}}$; $\frac{0.0067\text{ g}}{100\text{ mL}} \times 100\% = 0.0067\%\text{ (w/v)}$

(b) ppm: One L of water weighs 1 kg. Thus

$$\frac{0.067\text{ g}}{1\text{ L}} = \frac{0.067\text{ g}}{1\text{ kg}} \times \frac{1\text{ kg}}{1000\text{ g}};\ \frac{0.067\text{ g}}{1000\text{ g}} \times 10^6 = 67\text{ ppm}$$

(c) $\frac{0.067\text{ g}}{1\text{ L}} \times \frac{1\text{ mol}}{168\text{ g}} = 0.000\,40\text{ M} = 4.0 \times 10^{-4}\text{ M}$

9.98 $M_1 = 16$ M, $M_2 = 0.20$ M, $V_2 = 750$ mL

$$V_1 = V_2 \times \frac{M_2}{M_1} = 750\text{ mL} \times \frac{0.20\text{ M}}{16\text{ M}} = 9.4\text{ mL } HNO_3$$

9.100 $M_1 = 12.0$ M, $V_1 = 25$ mL, $V_2 = 525$ mL; $M_2 = ?$

$$M_2 = M_1 \times \frac{V_1}{V_2} = 12.0\text{ M} \times \frac{25\text{ mL}}{525\text{ mL}} = 0.57\text{ M}$$

9.102

Component	*Mass*	*Molar Mass*	*Molarity*
(a) NaCl	8.6 g	58.5 g	0.147 M
(b) KCl	0.30 g	74.6 g	0.0040 M
(c) $CaCl_2$	0.33 g	111 g	0.0030 M

9.104

$$\frac{10 \text{ mg}}{5.0 \text{ L}} \times \frac{1 \text{ L}}{1000 \text{ mL}} \times \frac{1 \text{ g}}{1000 \text{ mg}} \times 100\% = 0.0002\% \text{ (w/v)}$$

9.106

$$0.080\% \text{ (v/v)} = \frac{0.080 \text{ mL}}{100 \text{ mL}} = \frac{0.80 \text{ mL}}{1 \text{ L}}; \frac{0.80 \text{ mL}}{1 \text{ L}} \times 5.0 \text{ L} = 4.0 \text{ mL alcohol}$$

9.108 (a) $CoCl_2(s) + 6\ H_2O(g) \rightleftharpoons CoCl_2 \cdot 6H_2O(s)$

(b) Molar mass of $CoCl_2 \cdot 6H_2O$ = 238 g

$$2.50 \text{ g } CoCl_2 \times \frac{1 \text{ mol } CoCl_2 \cdot 6\ H_2O}{238 \text{ g}} \times \frac{6 \text{ mol } H_2O}{1 \text{ mol } CoCl_2 \cdot 6\ H_2O} \times \frac{18.0 \text{ g } H_2O}{1 \text{ mol } H_2O} = 1.13 \text{ g } H_2O$$

9.110 0.100 mol trichloroacetic acid (TCA) dissolved in 100.0 g water is equivalent to 1.00 mol TCA dissolved in 1000 g water. A freezing point depression of 1.86°C is produced by 1 mol of ions, so a freezing point depression of 2.53°C must be produced by 2.53 ÷ 1.86 = 1.36 mol of ions. Since 1.00 mol TCA behaves as 1.36 mol solute, the dissociated TCA is 1.36 mol/2 = 0.680 mol. Therefore, TCA is 68% dissociated.

Self-Test for Chapter 9

Multiple Choice

1. 50 mL of a 1.0 M NaOH solution is diluted to 1.0 L. What is the dilution factor?
(a) 1/50 (b) 1/20 (c) 1/10 (d) 1/2

2. Which of the following will not speed up the rate of solution of a solid?
(a) stirring (b) heating (c) grinding the solid into powder (d) increasing pressure on the solution

3. To make up 500 mL of a 5% (v/v) solution of methanol (CH_3OH ; molar mass = 32 g) in water:
(a) Dilute 25 mL of CH_3OH with water to a volume of 500 mL
(b) Dilute 5 mL of CH_3OH with water to a volume of 500 mL
(c) Add 32 g of CH_3OH to 500 g of water
(d) Add 25 mL of CH_3OH to 500 mL of water

4. Which solution has the greatest osmolarity?
(a) 0.2 M $CaCl_2$ (b) 0.3 M Na_3PO_4 (c) 0.5 M NaCl (d) 0.8 M glucose

5. Which of the following is a colloid?
(a) wine (b) maple syrup (c) milkshake (d) salad oil

6. How many mL of a 12.0 M HCl solution are needed to make 1.0 L of 0.10 M HCl?
(a) 120 mL (b) 83 mL (c) 50 mL (d) 8.3 mL

7. Which of the following properties do not depend on the number of particles in solution?
(a) boiling point elevation (b) osmotic pressure (c) heat of solution (d) freezing point depression

8. How many grams of NaOH are needed to make 300 mL of a 0.3 M solution?
(a) 40 g (b) 12 g (c) 3.6 g (d) 1.0 g

9. How many moles of glucose are present in 250 mL of a 0.25 M solution?
(a) 0.0625 mol (b) 0.1 mol (c) 0.25 mol (d) 1.0 mol

10. How many mL of a 0.20 M solution of NaF contain 2.1 g of NaF?
(a) 500 mL (b) 250 mL (c) 100 mL (d) 50 mL

Sentence Completion

1. Two liquids soluble in each other are said to be _____.

2. An _____ is the amount of an ion in grams that contains Avogadro's number of charges.

3. A weight/volume solution can be made up in a piece of glassware called a _____ _____.

4. According to Henry's law, the _____ of a gas varies with its _____ _____.

5. Two solutions that have the same osmolarity are ______.

6. Compounds that attract water from the atmosphere are called _____.

7. The formula used for calculating dilutions is __________.

8. Milk is an example of a _____.

9. _____ and _____ _____ _____ can pass through a dialysis membrane.

10. A solution that has reached its solubility limit is said to be _____.

11. An example of a nonelectrolyte is _____.

12. A solution that is hypotonic with respect to blood has a _____ osmolarity than blood plasma.

True or False

1. A solute is the liquid used to dissolve a substance.
2. It is possible to have a solution of a solid in a solid.
3. In making a volume/volume percent solution, one liquid is added to 100 mL of the other liquid.
4. All ionic compounds are soluble in water.
5. A solution of 0.10 M Na_3PO_4 has a greater osmolarity than a solution of 0.15 M NaCl.
6. Weight/weight percent is a useful way to express concentration.
7. In carrying out a dilution, the number of moles of solute remains constant.
8. The solubility of most substances increases with temperature.
9. A colloid differs from a solution in its ability to transmit light.
10. A blood cell undergoes crenation when placed in distilled water.
11. Particles dissolved in water lower the boiling point of water.
12. The amount of gas dissolved in a liquid increases with increasing pressure.

Match each entry on the left with its partner on the right.

1. Osmotic membrane	(a) Muddy water
2. V_1/V_2	(b) Molarity x number of particles
3. Solution	(c) Conducts electricity in water
4. Equivalent	(d) Vinegar
5. Suspension	(e) Crystalline compound that holds water
6. Dialysis membrane	(f) Dilution factor
7. Osmolarity	(g) Butter
8. Hypotonic	(h) Permeable only to water
9. Colloid	(i) A solution of lower osmolarity than another
10. Crenation	(j) Formula weight/number of charges
11. Hydrate	(k) Permeable to water and small molecules
12. Electrolyte	(l) Happens to cell in hypertonic solution

Chapter 10 – Acids and Bases

Chapter Outline

I. Introduction to acids and bases (Sections 10.1–10.5).
  A. Definition of acids and bases (Sections 10.1, 10.3).
    1. Arrhenius definition (Section 10.1).
      a. Acids donate H^+ ions in solution.
      b. Bases donate OH^- ions in solution.
      c. Acid + base —> salt + H_2O.
    2. Brønsted–Lowry definition (Section 10.3).
      a. A Brønsted–Lowry acid is a proton donor (an H_3O^+ donor).
      Some acids can donate more than one proton.
      b. A Brønsted–Lowry base is a proton acceptor.
      The base may be negatively charged or neutral.
      c. An acid–base reaction is one in which a proton is transferred.
      d. Products of acid–base reactions are also acids and bases.
      In the reaction HA + B: —> A^- + BH^+
        i. HA and A^- are an acid–conjugate base pair.
        ii. B: and BH^+ are a base–conjugate acid pair.
  B. Many common substances are acids or bases (Section 10.2).
  C. Water as acid and a base (Section 10.4).
    1. Water can act both as an acid and a base.
    2. Substances that can act as both acids and bases are amphoteric.
  D. Common acid–base reactions (Section 10.5).
    1. Acid + hydroxide ion —> water + salt.
    2. Acid + carbonate or bicarbonate —> water + salt + CO_2.
    3. Acid + ammonia —> ammonium salt.

II. Acid/base strength (Sections 10.6–10.11).
  A. Strong/weak acids and bases (Section 10.6).
    1. Strong acids and bases are 100% dissociated in water.
    2. Weak acids and bases are less than 100% dissociated in solution.
    3. The stronger the acid, the weaker the conjugate base.
    The weaker the acid, the stronger the conjugate base.
    4. An acid–base proton transfer always favors formation of the weaker acid.
  B. Acid dissociation constants (Section 10.7).
    1. K_a is a measure of the degree to which an acid HA dissociates to H_3O^+ and A^-.
    2. K_a values for weak acids are much less than 1.
    3. Donation of each successive H^+ ion from a polyprotic acid becomes successively more difficult.
    4. Most organic acids have K_a near 10^{-5}.
  C Dissociation of H_2O (Section 10.8).
    1. $K_w = [H_3O^+][OH^-] = 1.00 \times 10^{-14}$ at 25°C.
    2. This relationship is true for any aqueous solution.
    3. Thus, we can calculate $[H_3O^+]$ or $[OH^-]$ for any aqueous solution.

D. Measuring acidity (Sections 10.9–10.11).
   1. pH (Sections 10.9–10.10).
      a. A pH of < 7 indicates acidity; a pH of > 7 indicates basicity.
      b. pH is the negative logarithm of $[H_3O^+]$.
      c. The pH scale is logarithmic.
      d. pH can be computed with a calculator.
   2. In the laboratory, pH can be measured with indicators or a pH meter (Section 10.11).

III. Buffers (Sections 10.12–10.13).
   A. Characteristics of buffers (Section 10.12).
      1. A buffer is the solution of a weak acid and its salt (or a weak base and its salt) at similar concentration.
      2. When a small amount of acid or base is added to a buffered solution, pH changes very little.
      3. The effective pH range of a buffer solution is determined by the K_a of the acid or base.
         a. A buffer solution works best when [HA] is close in value to $[A^-]$.
         b. A buffer solution works best when [HA] and $[A^-]$ are approximately ten times greater than the amount of acid or base added.
   B. Buffers in the body (Section 10.13).
      1. The carbonate/bicarbonate buffer system is the major regulator of the pH of body fluids.
         a. An increase of $[CO_2]$ makes blood more acidic.
         b. A decrease in $[CO_2]$ makes blood less acidic.
         c. The acidity of blood is regulated by
            i. A reservoir of excess HCO_3^- that keeps pH fluctuations small.
            ii Change of breathing rate.
            iii. The kidneys.
         d. This regulation prevents alkalosis (pH greater than 7.45) and acidosis (pH lower than 7.35).
      2. The phosphate system and proteins are two other buffer systems in the body.

IV. Equivalents of acids and bases (Sections 10.14–10.15).
   A. Normality (Section 10.14).
      1. An equivalent of acid or base $= \dfrac{\text{molar mass}}{\text{number of H}^+ \text{ or OH}^- \text{ produced}}$.
      2. One equivalent of acid neutralizes one equivalent of base.
      3. Normality $= \dfrac{\text{equivalents of acid or base}}{\text{liters of solution}}$.
      4. Normality = (molarity of acid or base) x (number of H^+ or OH^- produced).
   B. Titration (Section 10.15).
      1. Titration is used to determine the acid or base concentration of a solution.
      2. In titration, a known volume of a solution of unknown acid or base concentration completely reacts with a solution of known concentration.
      3. The volume of solution of known concentration is measured, and the concentration of the unknown is calculated.

V. Acidity and basicity of salt solutions (Section 10.16).
   A. The salt of a strong base and a strong acid is neutral in solution.
   B. The salt of a strong base and a weak acid is basic in solution.
   C. The salt of a weak base and a strong acid is acidic in solution.
   D. The pH of the salt of a weak base and a weak acid can be predicted only if K_a values are known.

Solutions to Chapter 10 Problems

10.1 HCO_2H (a) and H_2S (b) are Brønsted–Lowry acids because they have protons to donate.

10.2 SO_3^{2-} (a) and F^- (c) are Brønsted–Lowry bases because they can be proton acceptors.

10.3 (a) The conjugate acid of HS^- is H_2S.
(b) The conjugate acid of PO_4^{3-} is HPO_4^{2-}.
(c) The conjugate base of H_2CO_3 is HCO_3^-.
(d) The conjugate base of NH_4^+ is NH_3.

10.4

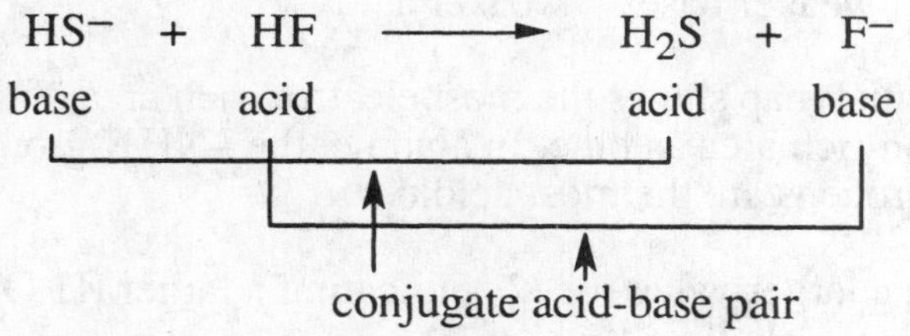
HS⁻ + HF → H₂S + F⁻
base
acid
acid
base
conjugate acid-base pair

10.5 Water acts as an acid when it reacts to form OH^-; water acts as a base when it reacts to form H_3O^+.

Water as an acid: (b) $F^-(aq) + H_2O(l) \rightleftharpoons HF(aq) + OH^-(aq)$

Water as a base: (a) $H_3PO_4(aq) + H_2O(l) \rightleftharpoons H_2PO_4^-(aq) + H_3O^+(aq)$

(c) $NH_4^+(aq) + H_2O(l) \rightleftharpoons H_3O^+(aq) + NH_3(aq)$

10.6 $3\ HCl(aq) + Al(OH)_3(aq) \longrightarrow 3\ H_2O(l) + AlCl_3(aq)$

$2\ HCl(aq) + Mg(OH)_2(aq) \longrightarrow 2\ H_2O(l) + MgCl_2(aq)$

10.7 (a) $2\ KHCO_3(aq) + H_2SO_4(aq) \longrightarrow 2\ H_2O(l) + 2\ CO_2(g) + K_2SO_4(aq)$

(b) $MgCO_3(aq) + 2\ HNO_3(aq) \longrightarrow H_2O(l) + CO_2(g) + Mg(NO_3)_2(aq)$

10.8 $H_2SO_4(aq) + 2\ NH_3(aq) \longrightarrow (NH_4)_2SO_4(aq)$

10.9

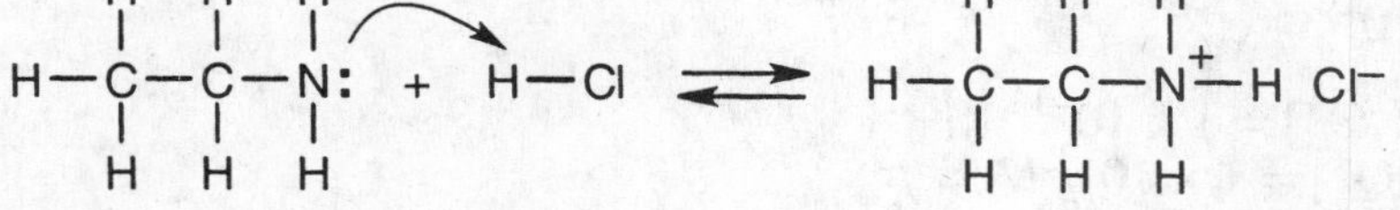

10.10 In Table 10.1, the stronger acid is listed *higher* in the table than the weaker acid.

Stronger acids: (a) NH_4^+ (b) H_2SO_4 (c) H_2CO_3

10.11 In Table 10.1, the stronger base is listed *lower* in the table than the weaker base.

Stronger bases: (a) F^- (b) OH^-

10.12

$$HPO_4^{2-}(aq) + OH^-(aq) \rightleftharpoons PO_4^{3-}(aq) + H_2O(l)$$

acid base base acid

conjugate acid–base pair

From Table 10.1, we see that OH^- is a stronger base than PO_4^{3-} and that HPO_4^{2-} is a stronger acid than H_2O. Thus, the forward direction of the equilibrium is favored.

$$HPO_4^{2-}(aq) + OH^-(aq) \rightleftharpoons PO_4^{3-}(aq) + H_2O(l)$$

stronger acid stronger base weaker base weaker acid

10.13 Remember that an electrostatic potential map shows the most electron-rich area of the molecule as red and the least electron-rich area as blue. In alanine, the $-NH_3^+$ group is the most electron-poor, and thus its hydrogens are the most acidic.

10.14 Citric acid is stronger because it has a larger value for K_a, indicating a larger $[H_3O^+]$.

10.15 (a) Beer is slightly acidic. Since $10^{-14} = [H_3O^+][OH^-]$,

$$[OH^-] = \frac{K_w}{[H_3O^+]} = \frac{1.0 \times 10^{-14}}{3.2 \times 10^{-5}} = 3.1 \times 10^{-10}\text{ M}$$

(b) Ammonia is basic.

$$[OH^-] = \frac{K_w}{[H_3O^+]} = \frac{1.0 \times 10^{-14}}{3.1 \times 10^{-12}} = 3.2 \times 10^{-3}\text{ M}$$

10.16 A solution with pH = 5 has a greater $[H_3O^+]$ because its pH is a smaller number, indicating a greater concentration of $[H_3O^+]$. The solution with pH = 9 has a greater $[OH^-]$.

10.17 (a) If $[H_3O^+] = 1 \times 10^{-5}$ M, then pH = 5.

(b) If $[OH^-] = 1 \times 10^{-9}$ M, then

$$[H_3O^+] = \frac{1 \times 10^{-14}}{1 \times 10^{-9}} = 1 \times 10^{-5}\text{ M; pH} = 5$$

10.18 (a) For pH = 13, $[H_3O^+] = 1 \times 10^{-13}$ M
(b) For pH = 3, $[H_3O^+] = 1 \times 10^{-3}$ M
(c) For pH = 8, $[H_3O^+] = 1 \times 10^{-8}$ M

The solution of pH = 3 is most acidic, and the solution of pH = 13 is most basic.

10.19 pH = $-\log [H_3O^+]$; $[H_3O^+] = 1 \times 10^{-4}$; $\log [H_3O^+] = -4$; $-\log [H_3O^+] = -(-4) = 4$

The pH of a 1×10^{-4} M solution of HNO_3 is 4.

10.20

Solution	*pH*	*Acidic/Basic*	$[H_3O^+]$
(a) Saliva	6.5	acidic	3×10^{-7} M
(b) Pancreatic juice	7.9	basic	1×10^{-8} M
(c) Orange juice	3.7	acidic	2×10^{-4} M
(d) Wine	3.5	acidic	3×10^{-4} M

Least acidic → Pancreatic juice, Saliva, Orange juice, Wine → Most acidic

10.21 Use a calculator to determine pH.

(a) $[H_3O^+] = 5.3 \times 10^{-9}$ mol/L: pH = 8.28
(b) $[H_3O^+] = 8.9 \times 10^{-6}$ mol/L: pH = 5.05

10.22 $[H_3O^+] = 2.5 \times 10^{-3}$, since HCl is a strong acid. As in the previous problem, use the EE key and the log key on your calculator, and take the negative value of the log.

$$[H_3O^+] = 2.5 \times 10^{-3};\ pH = -\log(2.5 \times 10^{-3}) = -(-2.60) = 2.60$$

10.23 Refer to Worked Examples 10.11 and 10.12 in the text.
When 0.020 mol of HNO_3 is added, the HF concentration increases from 0.100 M to 0.120 M, and the F^- decreases from 0.100 M to 0.080 M because of the reaction:

$$F^-(aq) + HNO_3(aq) \longrightarrow HF(aq) + NO_3^-(aq)$$

$$[H_3O^+] = K_a \frac{[HA]}{[A^-]} = (3.5 \times 10^{-4}) \frac{[0.120]}{[0.080]} = 5.2 \times 10^{-4}\ M$$

$$pH = -\log(5.2 \times 10^{-4}) = 3.28$$

10.24

$$NH_4^+(aq) + H_2O(aq) \rightleftharpoons H_3O^+(aq) + NH_3(aq)$$

$$[H_3O^+] = K_a \frac{[NH_4^+]}{[NH_3]} = (5.6 \times 10^{-10}) \frac{[0.050]}{[0.080]} = 3.5 \times 10^{-10}\ M$$

$$pH = -\log(3.5 \times 10^{-10}) = 9.46$$

10.25 You can see that there are nine HCN molecules and six CN^- molecules in the figure.

$$[H_3O^+] = K_a \frac{[HCN]}{[CN^-]} = (4.9 \times 10^{-10}) \frac{9}{6} = 7.4 \times 10^{-10}\ M$$

$$pH = -\log(7.4 \times 10^{-10}) = 9.13$$

10.26–10.27

Sample	*Mass*	*Molar Mass*	*# of ions**	*Equivalent Mass*	*# of Eq*	*Normality of 300.0 mL*
(a) HNO_3	5.0 g	63.0 g	1	63.0 g	0.079	0.26 N
(b) $Ca(OH)_2$	12.5 g	74.1 g	2	37.0 g	0.338	1.13 N
(c) H_3PO_4	4.5 g	98.0 g	3	32.7 g	0.14	0.47 N

*The "number of ions" refers to the number of H^+ or OH^- ions produced for each mole of acid or base in solution.

10.28 First, write the balanced equation for the neutralization reaction:

$$HCl(aq) + NaOH(aq) \longrightarrow H_2O(l) + NaCl(aq)$$

We see from this equation that one mole of base is needed to neutralize each mole of acid.

$$\text{Moles HCl} = 58.4 \text{ mL} \times \frac{0.250 \text{ mol NaOH}}{1 \text{ L}} \times \frac{1 \text{ L}}{1000 \text{ mL}} \times \frac{1 \text{ mol HCl}}{1 \text{ mol NaOH}}$$

$$= 0.0146 \text{ mol HCl}$$

$$\frac{0.0146 \text{ mol HCl}}{20.0 \text{ mL}} \times \frac{1000 \text{ mL}}{1 \text{ L}} = 0.730 \text{ M HCl}$$

10.29 $2\,NaOH(aq) + H_2SO_4(aq) \longrightarrow 2\,H_2O(l) + Na_2SO_4(aq)$

Notice that two moles of base are needed to neutralize one mole of acid.

$$\text{Moles NaOH} = 50.0 \text{ mL} \times \frac{0.200 \text{ mol } H_2SO_4}{1 \text{ L}} \times \frac{1 \text{ L}}{1000 \text{ mL}} \times \frac{2 \text{ mol NaOH}}{1 \text{ mol } H_2SO_4}$$

$$= 0.0200 \text{ mol NaOH}$$

$$0.0200 \text{ mol NaOH} \times \frac{1 \text{ L}}{0.150 \text{ mol}} = 0.133 \text{ L NaOH} = 133 \text{ mL NaOH}$$

10.30 $2\,KOH(aq) + H_2SO_4(aq) \longrightarrow 2\,H_2O(l) + Na_2SO_4(aq)$

$$\text{Moles KOH} = 16.1 \text{ mL} \times \frac{0.150 \text{ mol } H_2SO_4}{1 \text{ L}} \times \frac{1 \text{ L}}{1000 \text{ mL}} \times \frac{2 \text{ mol KOH}}{1 \text{ mol } H_2SO_4}$$

$$= 0.004\ 83 \text{ mol KOH}$$

$$\frac{0.004\ 83 \text{ mol}}{0.0215 \text{ L}} = 0.225 \text{ M KOH}$$

10.31 The salt of a weak acid and a strong base produces a basic solution, the salt of a strong acid and a weak base produces an acidic solution, and the salt of a strong acid and a strong base is neutral.

Salt	*Cation is from:*	*Anion is from:*	*Solution is:*
(a) K_2SO_4	strong base (KOH)	strong acid(H_2SO_4)	neutral
(b) Na_2HPO_4	strong base (NaOH)	weak acid ($H_2PO_4^-$)	basic
(c) MgF_2	strong base ($Mg(OH)_2$)	weak acid (HF)	basic
(d) NH_4Br	weak base (NH_3)	strong acid (HBr)	acidic

Understanding Key Concepts

10.32

(a)

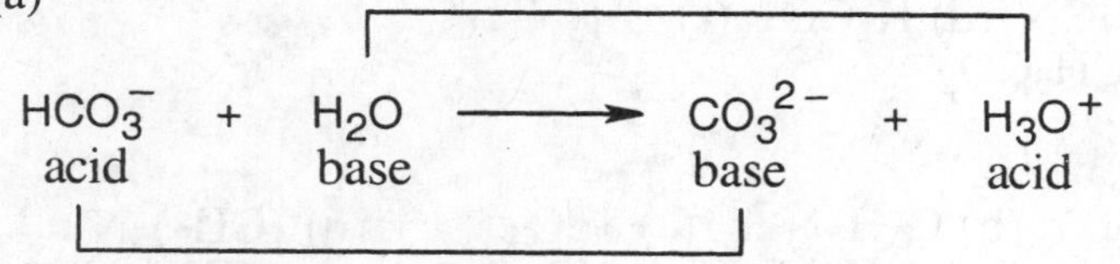
HCO3−
+
H2O
CO3 2−
+
H3O+
acid
base
base
acid

(b)

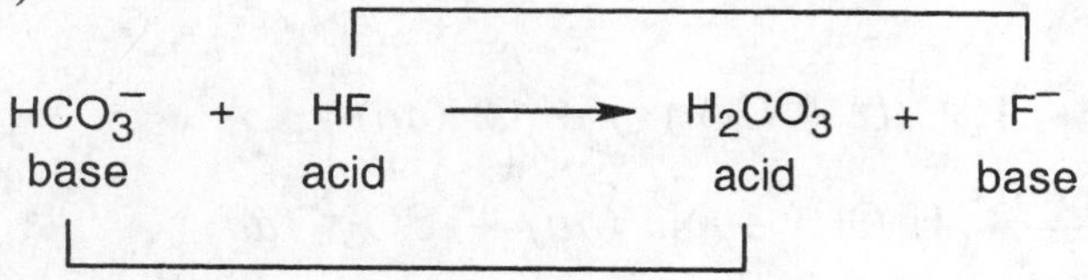
HCO3−
+
HF
H2CO3
+
F−
base
acid
acid
base

10.33 (a) The reaction of HF with OH^- is represented by outcome (2). One OH^- reacts with each HF to produce three F^- anions, and nine OH^- anions are left over.
(b) The reaction of H_2SO_3 with OH^- is represented by outcome (3). Two OH^- ions react with each H_2SO_3 molecule to produce three SO_3^{2-} anions, and six OH^- anions are left over.
(c) The reaction of H_3PO_4 with OH^- is represented by outcome (1). Three OH^- anions react with each H_3PO_4 molecule to produce three PO_4^{3-} anions, and three OH^- anions are left over.

10.34 In both molecules, the most acidic hydrogen (deepest blue) is bonded to oxygen. Acetic acid is more acidic because its hydrogen is more positively polarized and less tightly held.

10.35 (a) The acid in the first picture (1) is the weakest because it is the least dissociated.
(b) The acid in the second picture (2) is the strongest acid because all molecules of the acid are dissociated
(c) The acid in the first picture (1) has the smallest value of K_a because it is the weakest acid.

10.36 (a) Picture (3) represents a weak diprotic acid, which has dissociated slightly to form the HA^- anion.
(b) Picture (1) represents an impossible situation. H_2A dissociates stepwise to form HA^-. Only when virtually all H_2A has dissociated to form HA^- is A^{2-} formed by dissociation of HA^-.

10.37 The titration reaction uses up 2/3 of the 1.0 M solution in the buret. Since the solution in the buret is 1.0 M, the solution in the flask must be 0.67 M.

Acids and Bases

10.38 In water, HBr dissociates almost completely. Water acts as a base to accept a proton, and a solution of H_3O^+ and Br^- results.

10.40 In water, KOH dissociates completely to yield K^+ and OH^- ions.

10.42 A monoprotic acid, such as HCl, has only one proton to donate, whereas a diprotic acid, such as H_2SO_4, has two protons to donate.

10.44 Strong acids: (a) $HClO_4$ (e) HI

Brønsted–Lowry Acids and Bases

10.46 Brønsted–Lowry acids: (a) HCN (d) H_2CO_3 (f) $CH_3NH_3^+$
Brønsted–Lowry bases: (b) $CH_3CO_2^-$
Neither: (c) $AlCl_3$ (e) Mg^{2+}

10.48

	(a)	(b)	(c)	(d)
Base	$ClCH_2CO_2^-$	C_5H_5N	SeO_4^{2-}	$(CH_3)_3N$
Conjugate acid	$ClCH_2CO_2H$	$C_5H_5NH^+$	$HSeO_4^-$	$(CH_3)_3NH^+$

10.50 $HCO_3^-(aq) + HCl(aq) \longrightarrow H_2O(l) + CO_2(g) + Cl^-(aq)$

$HCO_3^-(aq) + NaOH(aq) \longrightarrow H_2O(l) + Na^+(aq) + CO_3^{2-}(aq)$

$H_2PO_4^-(aq) + HCl(aq) \longrightarrow H_3PO_4(aq) + Cl^-(aq)$

$H_2PO_4^-(aq) + NaOH(aq) \longrightarrow HPO_4^{2-}(aq) + H_2O(l) + Na^+(aq)$

10.52 $2\,HCl(aq) + CaCO_3(s) \longrightarrow H_2O(l) + CO_2(g) + CaCl_2(aq)$

Acid and Base Strength: K_a and pH

10.54 For the reaction: $HA(aq) + H_2O(l) \rightleftharpoons H_3O^+(l) + A^-(aq)$

$$K = \frac{[H_3O^+][A^-]}{[HA][H_2O]}$$

Since $[H_2O]$ is constant, we define a new constant:

$$K_a = K[H_2O] = \frac{[H_3O^+][A^-]}{[HA]}$$

10.56 K_w is the product of the molar concentrations of H_3O^+ and OH^- in any aqueous solution and is numerically equal to 1.0×10^{-14} at 25°C.

$$K_a = \frac{[H_3O^+][OH^-]}{[H_2O]};\ K_a[H_2O] = K_w = [H_3O^+][OH^-]$$

10.58 A solution of 0.10 M HCl is 100% dissociated; $[H^+] = [HCl] = 0.10$, and pH = 1. A solution of 0.10 M CH_3COOH is only partially dissociated, and its pH is expected to be higher than 1.0.

10.60 $H_3PO_4(aq) + H_2O(l) \rightleftharpoons H_2PO_4^-(aq) + H_3O^+(aq)$

$$K_a = \frac{[H_2PO_4^-][H_3O^+]}{[H_3PO_4]}$$

$H_2PO_4^-(aq) + H_2O(l) \rightleftharpoons HPO_4^{2-}(aq) + H_3O^+(aq)$

$$K_a = \frac{[HPO_4^{2-}][H_3O^+]}{[H_2PO_4^-]}$$

$HPO_4^{2-}(aq) + H_2O(l) \rightleftharpoons PO_4^{3-}(aq) + H_3O^+(aq)$

$$K_a = \frac{[PO_4^{3-}][H_3O^+]}{[HPO_4^{2-}]}$$

10.62 The stronger base appears lower in the "Base" column of Table 10.1.
(a) OH^- (b) NO_2^- (c) OH^- (d) CN^- (e) HPO_4^{2-}

10.64 Urine (pH = 7.9) is weakly basic, since solutions with pH greater than 7.0 are basic.

10.66 The concentration of HCl in gastric juice is approximately 1×10^{-2} M.

10.68 $[H_3O^+] = 10^{-pH}$. Since, in this problem, $[H_3O^+] = 0.10$ M $= 1.0 \times 10^{-1}$ M, the pH = 1.00.

10.70

	$[H_3O^+]$	pH
(a) Egg white	2.5×10^{-8} M	7.60
(b) Apple cider	5.0×10^{-4} M	3.30
(c) Ammonia	2.3×10^{-12} M	11.64

Ammonia is least acidic and apple cider is most acidic.

10.72 (a) $[OH^-] = 1 \times 10^{-10}$ M (b) $[OH^-] = 1 \times 10^{-3}$ M
(c) $[OH^-] = 1 \times 10^{-14}$ M (d) $[OH^-] = 2.4 \times 10^{-13}$ M
(e) $[OH^-] = 9.1 \times 10^{-7}$ M

Buffers

10.74 A buffer is composed of a weak acid and its conjugate base. Any added H_3O^+ can react with the conjugate base and be neutralized, and any added OH^- can react with the acid. In either case, the ratio of acid to conjugate base changes only slightly, and the pH of a buffered solution remains nearly constant.

10.76 $CH_3CO_2^-\,Na^+(aq) + HNO_3(aq) \longrightarrow CH_3CO_2H(aq) + NaNO_3(aq)$.
The added acid is neutralized by sodium acetate.

$CH_3CO_2H(aq) + OH^-(aq) \longrightarrow CH_3CO_2^-(aq) + H_2O(l)$
The added base is neutralized by acetic acid.

10.78

$$[H_3O^+] = \frac{K_a[HA]}{[A^-]};\ K_a = 4.9 \times 10^{-10}, [HCN] = 0.200\ M, [CN^-] = 0.150\ M$$

$$[H_3O^+] = \frac{4.9 \times 10^{-10}[0.200\ M]}{[0.150\ M]} = 6.5 \times 10^{-10}\ M;\ pH = 9.19$$

10.80

$$[H_3O^+] = \frac{K_a[HA]}{[A^-]};\ K_a = 5.6 \times 10^{-10}, [NH_4^+] = 0.15\ M, [NH_3] = 0.10\ M$$

$$[H_3O^+] = \frac{5.6 \times 10^{-10}[0.15\ M]}{[0.10\ M]} = 8.4 \times 10^{-10}\ M;\ pH = 9.08$$

Concentrations of Acid and Base Solutions

10.82 An equivalent of an acid or base is its formula weight in grams divided by the number of H_3O^+ or OH^- ions it produces.

10.84 The number of equivalents is equal to the number of moles times the number of H^+ or OH^- ions produced. In this problem, we first find the number of moles of each acid and then multiply by the number of H^+ ions produced.

$$\text{For } HNO_3\text{:}\ 0.500\ L \times \frac{0.50\ mol\ HNO_3}{1\ L} \times \frac{1\ Eq}{1\ mol} = 0.25\ Eq\ H^+$$

$$\text{For } H_3PO_4\text{:}\ 0.500\ L \times \frac{0.50\ mol\ H_3PO_4}{1\ L} \times \frac{3\ Eq}{1\ mol} = 0.75\ Eq\ H^+$$

10.86 Since a 0.0050 N solution of any acid has 0.0050 equivalents per liter, 25 mL of a 0.0050 N KOH solution is needed to neutralize 25 mL of either 0.0050 N H_2SO_4 or 0.0050 N HCl.

10.88 (a) 0.25 mol $Mg(OH)_2$ x 2 Eq/mol = 0.50 Eq $Mg(OH)_2$

(b) Molar mass of $Mg(OH)_2$ = 58.3 g; 1 Eq $Mg(OH)_2$ = 29.6 g

$$2.5\text{ g }Mg(OH)_2 \times \frac{1\text{ Eq}}{29.6\text{ g}} = 0.084\text{ Eq }Mg(OH)_2$$

(c) Molar mass of CH_3CO_2H = 60.0 g; 1 Eq CH_3CO_2H = 60.0 g

$$15\text{ g }CH_3CO_2H \times \frac{1\text{ Eq}}{60\text{ g}} = 0.25\text{ Eq }CH_3CO_2H$$

10.90 Molar mass of $Ca(OH)_2$ = 74.1 g; 1 Eq $Ca(OH)_2$ = 37.0 g

$$\frac{5.0\text{ g}}{0.500\text{ L}} \times \frac{1\text{ mol}}{74.1\text{ g}} = 0.13\text{ M};\ \frac{0.13\text{ mol}}{1\text{ L}} \times \frac{2\text{ Eq}}{1\text{ mol}} = \frac{0.26\text{ Eq}}{1\text{ L}} = 0.26\text{ N}$$

10.92 $HCl(aq) + NaOH(aq) \longrightarrow H_2O(l) + NaCl(aq)$

One mole of HCl is needed to neutralize one mole of NaOH.

$$\text{Moles HCl} = 22.4\text{ mL} \times \frac{0.12\text{ mol NaOH}}{1\text{ L}} \times \frac{1\text{ L}}{1000\text{ mL}} \times \frac{1\text{ mol HCl}}{1\text{ mol NaOH}}$$

$$= 0.0027\text{ mol HCl}$$

$$\frac{0.0027\text{ mol HCl}}{12\text{ mL}} \times \frac{1000\text{ mL}}{1\text{ L}} = 0.22\text{ M HCl}$$

10.94 $2\ KOH(aq) + H_2SO_4(aq) \longrightarrow 2\ H_2O(l) + K_2SO_4(aq)$

$$0.0150\text{ L }H_2SO_4 \times \frac{0.0250\text{ mol }H_2SO_4}{1\text{ L }H_2SO_4} \times \frac{2\text{ mol KOH}}{1\text{ mol }H_2SO_4} = 0.00075\text{ mol KOH}$$

$$\frac{0.00075\text{ mol NaOH}}{0.010\text{ L NaOH}} = 0.075\text{ M}$$

Applications

10.96 (a) $NaAl(OH)_2CO_3(aq) + 4\ HCl(aq) \longrightarrow$
$CO_2(g) + 3\ H_2O(l) + NaCl(aq) + AlCl_3(aq)$

(b) Molar mass of $NaAl(OH)_2CO_3(aq)$ = 144 g/mol

$$\frac{0.0955\text{ mol HCl}}{1\text{ L}} \times 0.0150\text{ L} = 0.001\ 43\text{ mol HCl}$$

$$0.001\ 43\text{ mol HCl} \times \frac{1\text{ mol antacid}}{4\text{ mol HCl}} \times \frac{144\text{ g}}{1\text{ mol antacid}} = 0.0515\text{ g} = 51.5\text{ mg}$$

10.98 Bicarbonate reacts with excess H_3O^+ to form H_2CO_3, which goes on to produce H_2O and CO_2 (which is exhaled). This reaction removes H_3O^+ from the bloodstream and lowers the serum pH.

10.100 pH of rain = 5.6; $[H_3O^+] = 2 \times 10^{-6}$ M

General Questions and Problems

10.102 Citric acid reacts with sodium bicarbonate to release CO_2 bubbles:

$$C_6H_5O_7H_3(aq) + 3\ NaHCO_3(aq) \longrightarrow C_6H_5O_7Na_3(aq) + 3\ H_2O(l) + 3\ CO_2(g)$$

Sodium bicarbonate is the antacid.

10.104

Both 50 mL of a 0.20 N HCl solution and 50 mL of a 0.20 acetic acid solution contain the same number of moles of acid — 0.010 moles. Because HCl is a strong acid, it is almost completely dissociated in water, and the H_3O^+ concentration approaches 0.20 M. Acetic acid, however, is a weak acid that is only slightly dissociated, and the H_3O^+ concentration is much lower – around 0.002 M. Since the HCl solution has a higher H_3O^+ concentration, it has a lower pH.

10.106

$$2\ HCl(aq) + Ca(OH)_2(aq) \longrightarrow 2\ H_2O(l) + CaCl_2(aq)$$

$$0.140\text{ L HCl} \times \frac{0.150\text{ mol HCl}}{1\text{ L HCl}} \times \frac{1\text{ mol Ca(OH)}_2}{2\text{ mol HCl}} = 0.0105\text{ mol Ca(OH)}_2$$

$$\frac{0.0105\text{ mol Ca(OH)}_2}{30.0\text{ mL Ca(OH)}_2} \times \frac{1000\text{mL}}{1\text{ L}} = 0.35\text{ M Ca(OH)}_2$$

10.108

(a) $NH_4^+(aq) + OH^-(aq) \longrightarrow NH_3(g) + H_2O(l)$

acid — base — conjugate base — conjugate acid

(b) $PV = nRT$; $P = 755$ mm Hg; $V = 2.86$ L; $T = 333$ K; $R = \dfrac{62.3\text{ mm Hg}\cdot\text{L}}{\text{mol}\cdot\text{K}}$

$$n = \frac{PV}{RT} = \frac{755\text{ mm} \times 2.86\text{ L}}{\dfrac{62.3\text{ mm Hg}\cdot\text{L}}{\text{mol}\cdot\text{K}} \times 333\text{ K}} = 0.104\text{ mol NH}_3$$

$$0.104\text{ mol} \times \frac{53.5\text{ g}}{1\text{ mol}} = 5.56\text{ g NH}_4\text{Cl}$$

10.110

(a) $Na_2O(aq) + H_2O(l) \longrightarrow 2\ NaOH(aq)$

(b) $1.55\text{ g } Na_2O \times \frac{1\text{ mol } Na_2O}{62.0\text{ g } Na_2O} \times \frac{2\text{ mol NaOH}}{1\text{ mol } Na_2O} = 0.0500\text{ mol NaOH}$

$\frac{0.0500\text{ mol NaOH}}{500.0\text{ mL}} \times \frac{1000\text{ mL}}{1\text{ L}} = 0.100\text{ M NaOH; pH} = 13.00$

(c) $0.0500\text{ mol NaOH} \times \frac{1\text{ mol HCl}}{1\text{ mol NaOH}} \times \frac{1\text{ L}}{0.0100\text{ mol HCl}} = 5.00\text{ L HCl}$

Self-Test for Chapter 10

Multiple Choice

1. What volume of 0.10 M H_2SO_4 will neutralize 30 mL of 0.05 M $Ca(OH)_2$?
(a) 30 mL (b) 15 mL (c) 10 mL (d) 6.0 mL

2. Which of the following salts is acidic in solution?
(a) NH_4Br (b) NaBr (c) NH_4CN (d) NaCN

3. KCN is the salt of a
(a) strong acid and strong base (b) strong acid and weak base (c) weak acid and strong base
(d) weak acid and weak base

4. A solution has a pH of 9. What is the value of $[OH^-]$?
(a) 5 (b) 10^{-9} (c) 9 (d) 10^{-5}

5. Which of the following is a diprotic acid?
(a) CH_3CO_2H (b) $Ba(OH)_2$ (c) H_2SO_3 (d) H_3PO_4

6. Look at Table 10.2 and decide which base is a weaker base than F^-:
(a) $H_2PO_4^-$ (b) HCO_3^- (c) CN^- (d) NH_3

7. Which of the following substances turns phenolphthalein red?
(a) urine (b) milk of magnesia (c) blood (d) coffee

8. Which of the following bases is an Arrhenius base?
(a) NaOH (b) $Ca_3(PO_4)_2$ (c) NH_3 (d) LiF

9. In the reaction $Mg(OH)_2(aq) + 2\ HBr(aq) \longrightarrow 2\ H_2O(l) + MgBr_2(aq)$, what is the conjugate acid of $Mg(OH)_2$?
(a) HBr (b) H_2O (c) $MgBr_2$ (d) can't tell

10. How many water molecules are produced in the balanced neutralization reaction of $H_3PO_4 + Mg(OH)_2$?
(a) 2 (b) 3 (c) 4 (d) 6

Sentence Completion

1. One _____ of an acid reacts with one _____ of a base.
2. Phenolphthalein turns _____ in basic solution.
3. H_2CO_3 is a _____ acid.
4. The anion of a weak acid is a _____ base.
5. _____ is the splitting apart of an acid into a proton and an anion.
6. An Arrhenius base yields _____ when dissolved in water.
7. _____ is the reaction of an acid with a base.
8. _____ is the measure of a solution's acidity.
9. To completely neutralize 10.0 mL of 1.0 M H_3PO_4, you need _____ mL of 1.0 M NaOH.
10. CH_3CO_2H and $CH_3CO_2^-$ are known as a _____ acid–base pair.
11. The buffer system of blood is the _____ / _____ system.
12. Substances that can act as either acids or bases are _______.

True or False

1. 30.0 mL of 0.10 M H_2SO_4 is neutralized by 30.0 mL of 0.10 M NaOH.
2. A change of one pH unit is a tenfold change in $[H_3O^+]$.
3. H_2SO_4 / HSO_4^- is a good buffer system.
4. All bases are negatively charged.
5. Bicarbonate ion neutralizes more acid than carbonate ion.
6. If the pH of a solution is 7.0, $[OH^-] = 10^{-7}$.
7. Water can act as both an acid and a base.
8. According to the Brønsted definition, an acid is a substance that dissolves in water to give H_3O^+ ions.
9. Ammonia reacts with an acid to yield ammonium hydroxide.
10. Whether an acid or a base is strong or weak depends on its percent dissociation in water.
11. The reaction $H_2O + H_2PO_4^- \longrightarrow H_3O^+ + HPO_4^{2-}$ proceeds in the direction written.
12. One equivalent of $Ca(OH)_2$ equals 37 g.

Match each entry on the left with its partner on the right.

1.	Strong acid	(a) $[H_3O^+]\,[OH^-]$
2.	1 M HCl	(b) Cl^-
3.	$[H_3O^+] = 10^{-8}$	(c) pH = 6
4.	Alkalosis	(d) HCl
5.	K_w	(e) 1 N acid
6.	Weak base	(f) CH_3CO_2H
7.	Strong base	(g) $[OH^-] = 10^{-6}$
8.	Salt	(h) Blood pH lower than 7.35
9.	$[H_3O^+] = 10^{-6}$	(i) $CH_3CO_2^-$
10.	Weak acid	(j) Na_2SO_4
11.	1 M H_3PO_4	(k) 3 N acid
12.	Acidosis	(l) Blood pH higher than 7.35

Chapter 11 – Nuclear Chemistry

Chapter Outline

I. Introduction to radioactivity (Sections 11.1–11.3)
  A Nuclear reactions (Section 11.1).
    1. A nuclear reaction occurs when a nuclide spontaneously changes to a different nuclide.
    2. Nuclear reactions differ from chemical reactions in several ways.
      a. Nuclear reactions produce different elements.
      b. Different isotopes have the same behavior in chemical reactions but different behavior in nuclear reactions.
      c. The rate of a nuclear reaction is unaffected by a change in temperature.
      d. A nuclear reaction is the same whether an atom is in a compound or is elemental.
      e. The energy change in a nuclear reaction is immense.
  B. The discovery and nature of radioactivity (Section 11.2).
    1. Radioactivity was discovered by Becquerel and the Curies.
    2. Three types of radiation may be emitted:
      a. α radiation: He^{2+} nuclei with low penetrating power.
      b. β radiation: electrons (e^-) with medium penetrating power.
      c γ radiation: high-energy light waves with very high penetrating power.
  C. Stable and unstable isotopes (Section 11.3).
    1. All elements have radioactive isotopes.
    2. Most radioisotopes are made in particle accelerators: These are known as artificial radioisotopes.
    3. Radioisotopes have the same chemical properties as their nonradioactive isotopes.

II. Nuclear decay (Sections 11.4–11.7).
  A. Nuclear emissions (Section 11.4).
    1. Alpha emission.
      After α emission, the atomic number of the resulting isotope decreases by 2, and the mass number decreases by 4.
    2. Beta emission.
      a. In β emission, a neutron decomposes to a proton and an electron.
      b. The electron is emitted, and the proton is retained.
      c. The atomic number of the resulting isotope increases by 1, and the mass number is unchanged.
    3. Gamma (γ) emission.
      Gamma (γ) emission usually accompanies α or β emission and doesn't affect either mass number or atomic number.
    4. Positron emission.
      a. Positron emission occurs when a proton is converted to a neutron and an ejected positron (positive electron).
      b. The mass number of the nucleus is unchanged, but the atomic number decreases by 1
    5. Electron capture (EC).
      a. EC occurs when a nucleus captures an electron from the surrounding electron cloud, converting a proton into a neutron.
      b. The mass number of the nucleus is unchanged, but the atomic number decreases by 1.

B. Half-life (Section 11.5).
   1. Half-life is the amount of time it takes for half of a sample of a radioisotope to decay.
   2. Half-life doesn't depend on the amount of sample or on temperature.
   3. Each half-life sees the decay of half of what remains of the sample.
C. Radioactive decay series (Section 11.6).
   Some heavy radioisotopes undergo a series of disintegrations until a nonradioactive product is reached.
D. Ionizing radiation (Section 11.7).
   1. Ionizing radiation is any high-energy radiation that can create reactive ions when it collides with a chemical compound.
   2. Ionizing radiation converts molecules into highly reactive ions.
   3. Ionizing radiation can injure the body.
      a. Gamma and X radiation are more harmful when radiation comes from outside the body.
      b. Alpha and β radiation are more dangerous when emitted from within the body.
   4. The intensity of radiation decreases with the square of the distance from the source.

III. Detecting radiation (Sections 11.8–11.9).
A. Devices for detecting radiation (Section 11.8).
   1. Photographic film badges.
   2. Geiger counter.
   3. Scintillation counter.
B. Units of radiation (Section 11.9).
   1. The *curie* measures the number of disintegrations per second.
   2. The *roentgen* measures the intensity of radiation.
   3. The *rad* measures the energy absorbed per gram tissue.
   4. The *rem* and the *sievert* measure tissue damage.

IV. Artificial transmutation (Section 11.10).
A. Artificial transmutation occurs when nuclei are bombarded with high-energy particles.
B. After bombardment, a new nucleus is produced.
C. The transuranium elements were all produced via artificial transmutation.

V. Nuclear fission and nuclear fusion (Section 11.11).
A. Nuclear fission.
   1. Nuclear fission occurs when a heavy nucleus fragments after bombardment by a small particle, such as a neutron.
   2. Many different fission products can result from one bombardment.
   3. In some cases, bombardment with one neutron can cause production of more than one neutron, in addition to fragmentation.
      a. This is called a chain reaction.
      b. If the bombarded sample weighs more than a critical mass, a nuclear explosion can result.
      c. A controlled fission reaction can be used to produce energy.
B. Nuclear fusion.
   1. If two light nuclei are made to collide, a nuclear fusion reaction occurs that produces a combined nucleus plus energy.
   2. Nuclear fusion reactions occur in stars.

Solutions to Chapter 11 Problems

11.1 For α emission, subtract 2 from the atomic number of radon and 4 from the mass number:

$$^{222}_{86}Rn \rightarrow {}^{4}_{2}He + {}^{218}_{84}?$$

Then look in the periodic table for the element with atomic number 84:

$$^{222}_{86}Rn \rightarrow {}^{4}_{2}He + {}^{218}_{84}Po$$

11.2 Add 4 to the mass number of radon-222 to calculate the isotope of radium:

$$^{226}_{88}Ra \rightarrow {}^{4}_{2}He + {}^{222}_{86}Rn$$

11.3

$$^{14}_{6}C \rightarrow {}^{0}_{-1}e + ?$$

The mass number of the product element stays the same, but the atomic number increases by 1, to 7. Looking in the periodic table, we find that ^{14}N is the element formed:

$$^{14}_{6}C \rightarrow {}^{0}_{-1}e + {}^{14}_{7}N$$

11.4

(a) $^{3}_{1}H \rightarrow {}^{0}_{-1}e + {}^{3}_{2}He$ (b) $^{210}_{82}Pb \rightarrow {}^{0}_{-1}e + {}^{210}_{83}Bi$ (c) $^{20}_{9}F \rightarrow {}^{0}_{-1}e + {}^{20}_{10}Ne$

11.5 For positron emission, the atomic number decreases by 1, but the mass number stays the same.

(a) $^{38}_{20}Ca \rightarrow {}^{0}_{1}e + {}^{38}_{19}K$ (b) $^{118}_{54}Xe \rightarrow {}^{0}_{1}e + {}^{118}_{53}I$ (c) $^{79}_{37}Rb \rightarrow {}^{0}_{1}e + {}^{79}_{36}Kr$

11.6 As in positron emission, the atomic number decreases by one and the mass number stays unchanged in electron capture.

(a) $^{62}_{30}Zn + {}^{0}_{-1}e \rightarrow {}^{62}_{29}Cu$ (b) $^{110}_{50}Sn + {}^{0}_{-1}e \rightarrow {}^{110}_{49}In$ (c) $^{81}_{36}Kr + {}^{0}_{-1}e \rightarrow {}^{81}_{35}Br$

11.7 Table 11.2 shows the changes brought about by various radioactive decay patterns. Only β emission produces a change of +1 to the atomic number and a decrease in the number of neutrons. The original element was indium ($Z = 49$), and tin ($Z = 50$) is the decay product.

$$^{120}_{49}In \rightarrow {}^{0}_{-1}e + {}^{120}_{50}Sn$$

11.8 17,000 ÷ 5730 = 2.97, or approximately 3 half-lives.
The percentage of $^{14}_{6}C$ is (1/2) x (1/2) x (1/2) x 100% = 12.5% of the original sample.

11.9 Find the point on the graph that represents 50% of the sample remaining. Locate the time that corresponds to this point; this is the half-life – 3 days.

11.10

$$\frac{I_1}{I_2} = \frac{d_2^2}{d_1^2} : I_1 = 250 \text{ units}; I_2 = 25 \text{ units}; d_1^2 = (4.0 \text{ m})^2 = 16 \text{ m}^2; d_2^2 = ?$$

$$d_2^2 = \frac{d_1^2 \text{ x } I_1}{I_2} = \frac{16 \text{ m}^2 \text{ x } 250 \text{ units}}{25 \text{ units}} = 160 \text{ m}^2$$

$d_2 = 13$ m

11.11

$$\frac{5 \text{ mrem}}{270 \text{ mrem}} \text{ x } 100\% = 1.9\%$$

The annual dose of radiation for most people will increase by approximately 2%.

11.12

$$\frac{175\ \mu\text{Ci}}{\text{dose}} \text{ x } \frac{1 \text{ mL}}{44\ \mu\text{Ci}} = \frac{4.0 \text{ mL}}{\text{dose}}$$

11.13

$${}^{241}_{95}\text{Am} \rightarrow {}^{4}_{2}\text{He} + {}^{237}_{93}\text{Np}$$

11.14

$${}^{241}_{95}\text{Am} + {}^{4}_{2}\text{He} \rightarrow 2\ {}^{1}_{0}\text{n} + {}^{243}_{97}\text{Bk}$$

11.15

$${}^{40}_{18}\text{Ar} + {}^{1}_{1}\text{H} \rightarrow {}^{1}_{0}\text{n} + {}^{40}_{19}\text{K}$$

11.16

$${}^{235}_{92}\text{U} + {}^{1}_{0}\text{n} \rightarrow 2\ {}^{1}_{0}\text{n} + {}^{137}_{52}\text{Te} + {}^{97}_{40}\text{Zr}$$

Understanding Key Concepts

11.17 After one half-life, the sample would consist of eight ${}^{28}_{13}\text{Al}$ atoms and eight ${}^{28}_{12}\text{Mg}$ atoms. After two half-lives, the remaining eight ${}^{28}_{12}\text{Mg}$ atoms would have decayed to four ${}^{28}_{13}\text{Al}$ atoms, producing the outcome shown in the picture.

11.18

$${}^{28}_{12}\text{Mg} \rightarrow {}^{0}_{-1}\text{e} + {}^{28}_{13}\text{Al}$$

11.19

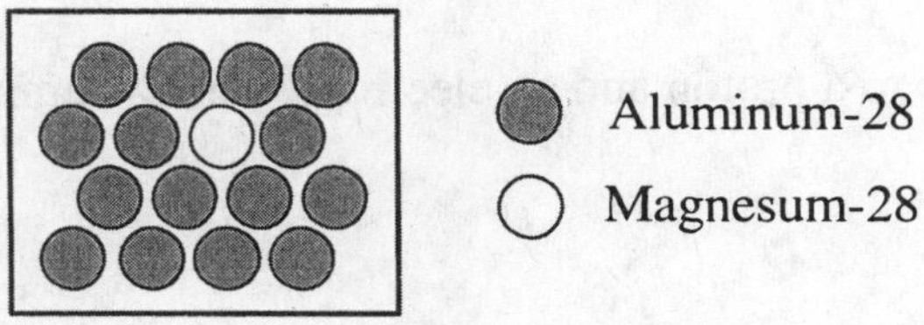
Aluminum-28
Magnesum-28

11.20 The illustrated isotope, with six protons and eight neutrons, is ${}^{14}_{6}\text{C}$.

11.21 The shorter arrows represent β emission because they show the decomposition of a neutron with an accompanying one-unit increase in atomic number.
The longer arrows represent α emission because they indicate a decay that results in the loss of two protons and two neutrons (α particle).

11.22

$$^{241}_{94}\text{Pu} \rightarrow {}^{241}_{95}\text{Am} \rightarrow {}^{237}_{93}\text{Np} \rightarrow {}^{233}_{91}\text{Pa} \rightarrow {}^{233}_{92}\text{U}$$

11.23 The isotope can decay by either positron emission or electron capture since the atomic number decreases by 1 but the mass number remains the same.

$$^{148}_{69}\text{Tm} \rightarrow {}^{0}_{1}\text{e} + {}^{148}_{68}\text{Er} \quad \textit{or} \quad {}^{148}_{69}\text{Tm} + {}^{0}_{-1}\text{e} \rightarrow {}^{148}_{68}\text{Er}$$

11.24 The half-life is approximately 3.5 years.

11.25 The curve doesn't represent nuclear decay. According to the curve, half of the sample has decayed after 5 days. Half of the remaining sample should have decayed after 10 days, but on this curve the second half-life is shown at 13 days. A decay curve should approach zero after six half-lives, but this curve shows 10% activity remaining at that time.

Radioactivity

11.26 A substance is said to be radioactive if it emits radiation by decay of an unstable nucleus.

11.28

Nuclear Reaction	*Chemical Reaction*
involves change in an atom's nucleus	involves change in an atom's outer shell electrons
usually produces a different element	never produces a different element
different isotopes have different behavior in a nuclear reaction	different isotopes have the same behavior in a chemical reaction
rate is unaffected by a change in temperature or by a catalyst	rate changes with a change in temperature or by using a catalyst
rate is the same, whether the atom is in a compound or uncombined	
energy change is millions of times larger for a nuclear reaction	

11.30 The symbol for an α particle is $^{4}_{2}\text{He}$.

11.32 Outside of the body, gamma radiation has the highest penetrating power, and α radiation has the lowest penetrating power.

11.34 Ionizing radiation causes cell damage by breaking bonds in DNA. The resulting damage may lead to mutation, cancer, or cell death.

11.36 A neutron in the nucleus decomposes to a proton and an electron, which is emitted as a β particle.

Nuclear Decay and Transmutation

11.38 A nuclear equation is balanced if the number of nucleons is the same on both sides and if the sums of the charges on the nuclei and on any other elementary particles are the same on both sides.

11.40 For an atom emitting an α particle, the atomic number decreases by two, and the mass number decreases by four.
For an atom emitting a β particle, the atomic number increases by one, and the mass number is unchanged.

11.42 In nuclear fission, bombardment of a nucleus causes fragmentation in many different ways to yield a large number of smaller fragments. Normal radioactive decay of a nucleus produces an atom with a similar mass and yields a predictable product.

11.44

(a) ${}^{35}_{16}S \rightarrow {}^{0}_{-1}e + {}^{35}_{17}Cl$ (b) ${}^{24}_{10}Ne \rightarrow {}^{0}_{-1}e + {}^{24}_{11}Na$

(c) ${}^{90}_{38}Sr \rightarrow {}^{0}_{-1}e + {}^{90}_{39}Y$

11.46

(a) ${}^{140}_{55}Cs \rightarrow {}^{0}_{-1}e + {}^{140}_{56}Ba$ (b) ${}^{246}_{96}Cm \rightarrow {}^{4}_{2}He + {}^{242}_{94}Pu$

11.48

(a) ${}^{235}_{92}U + {}^{1}_{0}n \rightarrow {}^{160}_{62}Sm + {}^{72}_{30}Zn + 4\,{}^{1}_{0}n$

(b) ${}^{235}_{92}U + {}^{1}_{0}n \rightarrow {}^{87}_{35}Br + {}^{146}_{57}La + 3\,{}^{1}_{0}n$

11.50

${}^{198}_{80}Hg + {}^{1}_{0}n \rightarrow {}^{198}_{79}Au + {}^{1}_{1}H$

A proton is produced in addition to gold-198.

11.52 The four α decays result in a loss of 16 nucleons from the mass number and a reduction of 8 in atomic number. The β decay results in a gain of 1 in atomic number and no change in mass number. The parent isotope, which has seven more protons and a mass 16 units greater than bismuth-212, is thorium-228.

Half-Life

11.54 If strontium-90 has a half-life of 28.8 years, half of a given quantity of strontium-90 will have decayed after 28.8 years.

11.56 365 ÷ 120 = 3.04, or approximately 3 half-lives.

$$0.050 \text{ g} \times \frac{1}{2} \times \frac{1}{2} \times \frac{1}{2} = 0.0062 \text{ g}$$

Approximately 0.006 grams of ${}^{75}_{34}Se$ will remain after a year.

11.58 If the half-life of mercury–97 is 64.1 hours.,
6 days = 144 hr ; 144/64.1 = 2.3, or approximately 2 half-lives
27 days = 648 hr ; 648/64.1 = approximately 10 half-lives
5.0 ng x 1/2 x 1/2 = approx. 1 ng of mercury-197 remains after 6 days.
5.0 ng x $(1/2)^{10}$ = approx. 5 x 10^{-3} ng of mercury-197 remains after 27 days.

Measuring Radioactivity

11.60 The inside walls of a Geiger counter tube are negatively charged, and a wire in the center is positively charged. Radiation ionizes argon gas inside the tube, which creates a conducting path for current between the wall and the wire. The current is detected, and the Geiger counter makes a clicking sound.

11.62 In a scintillation counter, a phosphor emits a flash of light when struck by radiation. The number of flashes are counted and converted to an electrical signal.

11.64 According to Table 11.6, any amount of radiation above 25 rems produces detectable effects in humans.

11.66

$$28 \text{ mCi} \times \frac{1 \text{ mL}}{12 \text{ mCi}} = 2.3 \text{ mL}$$

11.68

$$\frac{I_1}{I_2} = \frac{d_2^2}{d_1^2}; \quad I_1 = 300.0 \text{ rem}; \; I_2 = 25 \text{ rem}; \; d_1^2 = (2.0 \text{ m})^2 = 4.0 \text{ m}^2; \; d_2^2 = ?$$

$$d_2^2 = \frac{d_1^2 \times I_1}{I_2} = \frac{4.0 \text{ m}^2 \times 300.0 \text{ rem}}{25 \text{ rem}} = 48 \text{ m}^2$$

$d_2 = 6.9$ m

Applications

11.70 (1) *In vivo procedures* take place inside the body and assess the functioning of organs or body systems.
(2) *Therapeutic procedures* are used to kill diseased tissue.
(3) *Body imaging* techniques, which include radiopharmaceutical imaging, CAT scans and PET, show body structure and function.

11.72 The purpose of food irradiation is to kill harmful microorganisms by exposing food to ionizing radiation, which destroys the genetic material of the microorganisms.

11.74 The body-imaging techniques CT and PET are noninvasive and yield a large array of images that can be processed by computer to produce a three-dimensional image of an organ.

11.76 The leather is too new. The age of the leather sample is so much smaller than the half-life of $^{14}CO_2$ that the ratio of ^{14}C to ^{12}C is almost the same as the atmospheric ratio.

General Questions and Problems

11.78 Nuclear reactions occur spontaneously, and no substance can "react with" radioactive emissions to neutralize them.

11.80

(a) $^{99}_{42}Mo \rightarrow {}^{0}_{-1}e + {}^{99}_{43}Tc$ ^{99}Mo decays to Tc-99*m* by β emission.

(b) $^{98}_{42}Mo + {}^{1}_{0}n \rightarrow {}^{99}_{42}Mo$

11.82

(a) $^{238}_{94}Pu \rightarrow {}^{4}_{2}He + {}^{234}_{92}U$

(b) The metal case serves as a shield to protect the wearer from α radiation.

11.84 Embryos and fetuses are particularly susceptible to the effects of radiation because their cells divide frequently.

11.86 Nuclear fusion produces few radioactive by-products, and the deuterium fuel used is abundant and inexpensive. Drawbacks include providing high enough temperatures and holding materials long enough for nuclei to react.

11.88

(a) $^{253}_{99}Es + {}^{4}_{2}He \rightarrow {}^{256}_{101}Md + {}^{1}_{0}n$ (b) $^{250}_{98}Cf + {}^{11}_{5}B \rightarrow {}^{257}_{103}Lr + 4\,{}^{1}_{0}n$

11.90

$^{10}_{5}B + {}^{1}_{0}n \rightarrow {}^{7}_{3}Li + {}^{4}_{2}He$

11.92 Alpha particles are used for the bombardment.
$^{238}_{92}U + 3\,{}^{4}_{2}He \rightarrow {}^{246}_{98}Cf + 4\,{}^{1}_{0}n$

Self-Test for Chapter 11

Multiple Choice

1. Bombardment of a uranium-235 atom with a neutron produces three neutrons, which can go on to bombard three more U-235 atoms. How many neutrons are produced after the fourth cycle?
(a) 12 (b) 36 (c) 81 (d) 108

2. The product of the α emission of $^{146}_{62}Sm$ is
(a) $^{146}_{63}Eu$ (b) $^{144}_{61}Pm$ (c) $^{144}_{60}Nd$ (d) $^{142}_{60}Nd$

3. A half-inch-thick piece of plastic blocks 50% of radiation. How much radiation passes through a one-inch-thick piece of plastic?
(a) 50% (b) 25% (c) 12% (d) 0%

4. The *curie* measures
(a) amount of radioactivity (b) ionizing intensity of radiation (c) amount of radiation absorbed (d) tissue damage

5. A sample of a radionuclide has a half-life of 40 days. How much radioactivity remains after 160 days?
(a) 25% (b) 12.5% (c) 6.25% (d) 0%

6. How many disintegrations per second does one microcurie of a sample emit?
(a) 3.7×10^{10} (b) 3.7×10^{7} (c) 3.7×10^{6} (d) 3.7×10^{4}

7. If a person standing 100 cm from a radiation source approaches to within 10 cm of the source, how much does the intensity of the radiation change?
(a) increases by a hundredfold (b) increases tenfold (c) stays the same (d) decreases tenfold

8. Artificial transmutation was probably used to produce which one of the following radionuclides?
(a) $^{238}_{92}U$ (b) $^{210}_{82}Pb$ (c) $^{60}_{27}Co$ (d) $^{239}_{94}Pu$

9. Which of the following radioisotopes is not medically useful?
(a) $^{131}_{53}I$ (b) $^{14}_{6}C$ (c) $^{24}_{11}Na$ (d) $^{60}_{27}Co$

10. In an experiment by the Curies, aluminum-27 was bombarded with α particles. If each aluminum-27 atom captured one α particle and emitted one neutron, what other atom was produced?
(a) $^{29}_{13}Al$ (b) $^{28}_{14}Si$ (c) $^{30}_{15}P$ (d) $^{31}_{15}P$

Sentence Completion

1. The change of one element to another is called _____.
2. _____ ______ causes the most tissue damage.
3. A chemical compound tagged with a radioactive atom can be used as a ______.
4. All people are exposed to _____ radiation.
5. A nuclear equation is balanced when the number of ______ is the same on both sides of the equation.
6. The age of a sample can be determined by measuring the amount of _____ it contains.
7. The _____ is a unit for measuring the number of radioactive disintegrations per second.
8. In _____ ______, an atom is split apart by neutron bombardment to give small fragments.
9. People who work around radiation sources wear _____ _____ for detection of radiation.
10. PET and CT are techniques for _______ _______.
11. Very light elements release large amounts of energy when they undergo _____ ______.
12. The _____ _____ is the size of a radioactive sample that is needed for a nuclear reaction to be self-sustaining.

True or False

1. If a sample has a half-life of 12 days, it will have decayed completely in 24 days.
2. X-rays are considered to be ionizing radiation.
3. The ratio of carbon-14 to carbon-12 in the atmosphere is constant.
4. Pierre and Marie Curie discovered radioactivity.
5. A β particle travels at nearly the speed of light.
6. An α particle travels at nearly the speed of light.
7. The product of β emission has an atomic number 1 amu smaller than the starting material.
8. A nuclear power plant can undergo a nuclear explosion in an accident.

9. The rad is the unit most commonly used in medicine to measure radiation dosage.

10. Radiation causes injury by ionizing molecules.

11. Most of the known radioisotopes are naturally occurring.

12. Many isotopes undergo nuclear fission.

Match each entry on the left with its partner on the right.

1. Rutherford	(a) Alpha particle
2. $^{245}_{96}Cm$	(b) Used in cancer therapy
3. $t_{1/2}$	(c) Discovered radioactivity
4. $^{0}_{-1}e$	(d) Neutron
5. Becquerel	(e) Used for archeological dating
6. $^{90}_{38}Sr$	(f) Discovered α and β particles
7. $^{1}_{0}n$	(g) Natural radioactive element that undergoes fission
8. P. and M. Curie	(h) Discovered radium
9. $^{60}_{27}Co$	(i) Transuranium element
10. $^{4}_{2}He$	(j) Component of radioactive waste
11. $^{14}_{6}C$	(k) Beta particle
12. $^{235}_{92}U$	(l) Half-life

Chapter 12 – Introduction to Organic Chemistry: Alkanes

Chapter Outline

I. Introduction to Organic Chemistry (Sections 12.1–12.5).
  A. The nature of organic molecules (Section 12.1).
    1. Carbon always forms four bonds.
    2. Almost all of the bonds in organic molecules are covalent.
      a. These bonds are polar covalent bonds when carbon forms a bond to an element on the far left of the periodic table.
      b. Carbon can form multiple bonds by sharing more than two electrons.
    3. Organic molecules have specific three-dimensional shapes.
    4. In addition to hydrogen, oxygen and nitrogen are often present in organic molecules.
    5. Organic molecules are low-melting and -boiling, relative to inorganic compounds.
    6. Organic molecules are usually insoluble in water and don't conduct electricity.
  B. Functional groups (Section 12.2).
    1. A functional group is an atom or group of atoms that has a characteristic reactivity.
    2. The chemistry of organic molecules is determined by functional groups.
    3. Functional groups fall into three categories.
      a. Hydrocarbons.
      b. Compounds with C–X single bonds, where X is electronegative.
      c. Compounds with C=O double bonds.
  C. Structures of organic molecules: alkane isomers (Sections 12.3–12.4).
    1. When hydrocarbons contain more than three carbons, there is more than one way to arrange the carbon atoms.
      a. Some alkanes are straight-chain alkanes.
      b. Other alkanes are branched.
    2. Compounds with the same formula but different orders of connecting the carbon atoms are called constitutional isomers.
      Constitutional isomers have different structures and different properties.
    3. Drawing structures (Section 12.4).
      a. Condensed structures are simpler to draw than structural formulas.
      b. In condensed structures, C—H and C—C single bonds are implied, rather than drawn.
      c. Vertical bonds are often shown for clarity.
      d. Occasionally, parentheses are used to show a row of $—CH_2—$ groups.
  D. The shapes of organic molecules (Section 12.5).
    1. The groups around a C—C bond are free to assume an infinite number of conformations.
    2. Molecules adopt the least crowded conformation.
    3. Two structures with identical connections between atoms are identical, no matter how they are drawn.

II. Alkanes (Sections 12.6–12.8).
  A. Naming alkanes (Section 12.6).
    1. Straight-chain alkanes.
      a. Count the carbons.
      b. Find the root name.
      c. Add *-ane* to the root name.

2. Alkyl groups.
   a. Remove a hydrogen from an alkane and replace -ane with -yl.
   b. More than one alkyl group can be formed from some alkanes.
      i. Isopropyl and propyl are the two groups that can be formed from propane.
      ii. Four groups can be formed from butane.
      iii. Alkyl groups can be substituents on a straight chain.
3. Substitution patterns.
   a. Primary carbon: $R–CH_3$.
   b. Secondary carbon: $R–CH_2–R'$.
   c. Tertiary carbon:

```
   R'
   |
R–CH–R
```

   d. Quaternary carbon:

```
  R'
  |
R–C–R'
  |
  R"
```

4. Naming branched-chain alkanes.
   a. Name the main chain by finding the longest continuous chain of carbons and naming it.
   b. Number the carbons in the main chain, starting from the end nearer the first branch point.
   c. Identify and number each branching substituent according to its point of attachment to the main chain.
   d. Write the name as a single word.

B. Properties of alkanes (Section 12.7).
   1. The boiling points and melting points of alkanes increase with the number of carbons.
   2. Alkanes are insoluble in water but are soluble in nonpolar organic solvents.
   3. Alkanes are colorless and odorless.
   4. Alkanes are flammable.
   5. Alkanes with four or fewer carbons are gases, those from C_5 to C_{15} are liquids, and those with more than 15 carbons are solids.

C. Reactivity of alkanes (Section 12.8).
   1. Alkanes are very unreactive.
   2. Reactions that alkanes undergo:
      a. Combustion: alkane + O_2 —> CO_2 + H_2O.
      b. Halogenation: alkane + X_2 —> halogenated alkane + HCl.

III. Cycloalkanes (Sections 12.9–12.10).

A. Properties of cycloalkanes (Section 12.9).
   1. Cycloalkanes contain rings of carbon atoms.
   2. Cyclopropane and cyclobutane are more reactive than other cycloalkanes.
   3. Cyclohexane exists in a chair-like conformation.
   4. Cycloalkanes have properties similar to those of acyclic alkanes.
   5. Free rotation is not possible around the carbon–carbon bonds of a cycloalkane ring.

B. Drawing and naming cycloalkanes (Section 12.10).
   1. Drawing cycloalkanes.
      The cycloalkane ring is represented as a polygon.
   2. Naming cycloalkanes.
      a. Use the cycloalkane as the parent.
      b. Number the substituents.
         i. Start numbering at the group that has alphabetical priority.
         ii. Proceed around the ring to give to the second group the lowest possible number.

Solutions to Chapter 12 Problems

12.1

(a)

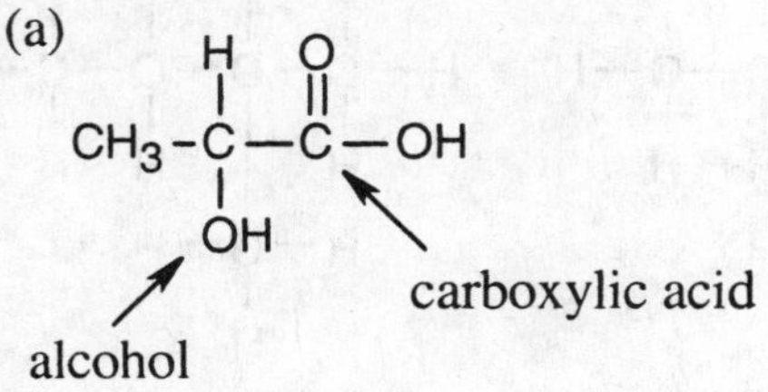
alcohol
carboxylic acid

Lactic acid

(b)

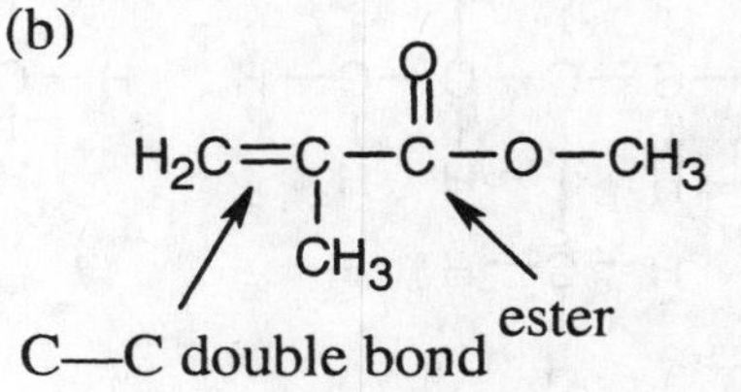
C—C double bond
ester

Methyl methacrylate

(c)

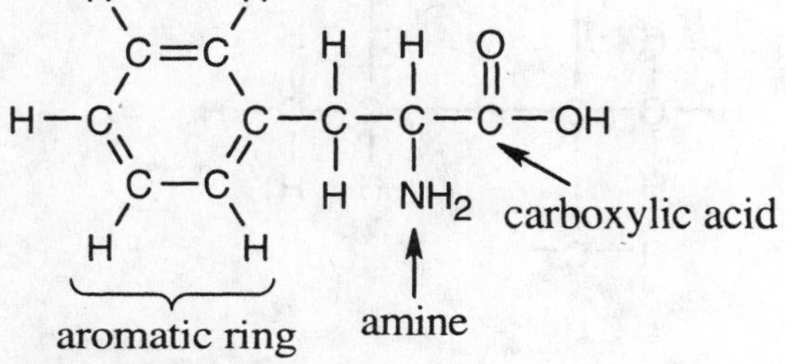
carboxylic acid
amine
aromatic ring

Phenylalanine

12.2

(a)

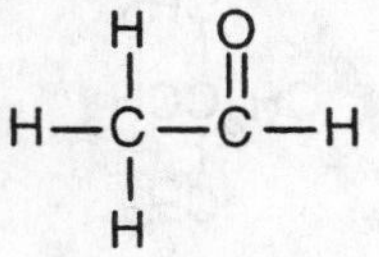

an aldehyde

(b)

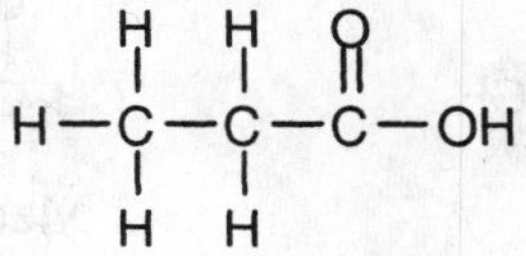

a carboxylic acid

12.3

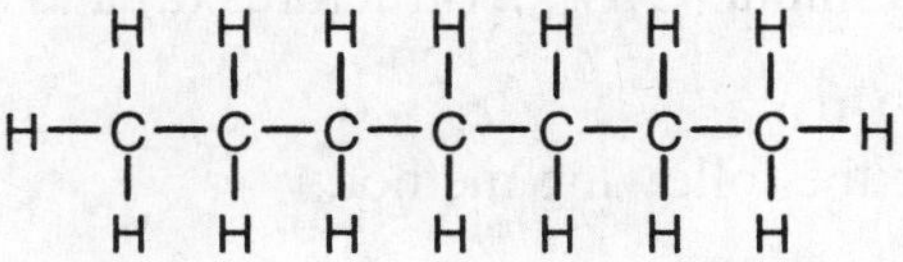

C_7H_{16} Heptane

12.4 There are eight branched-chain heptanes:

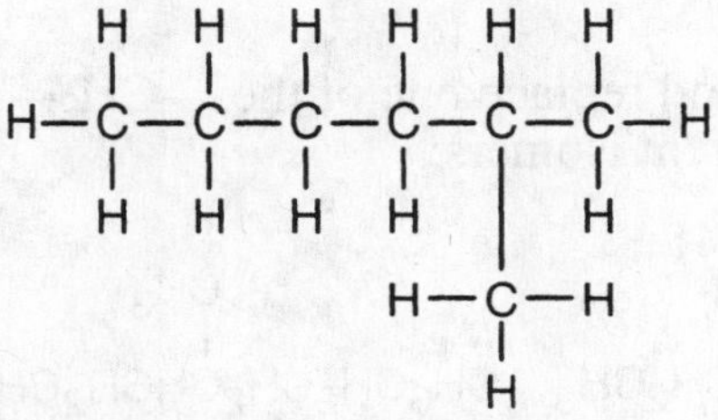

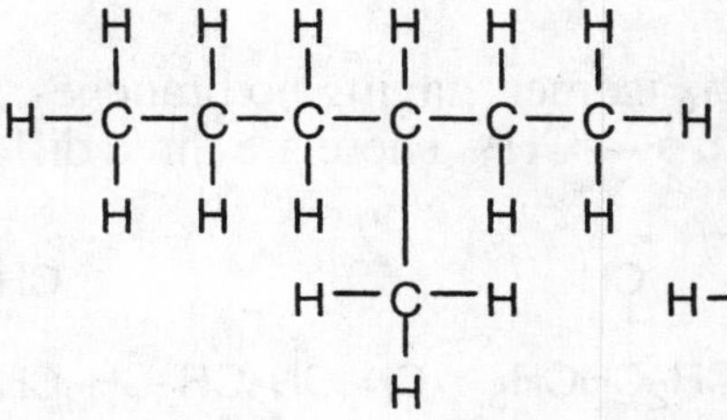

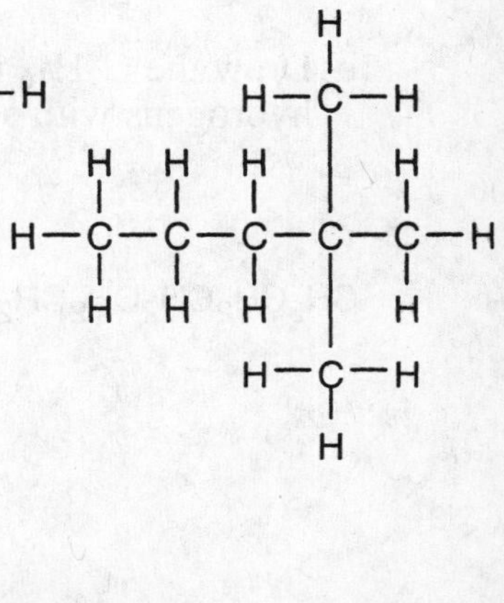

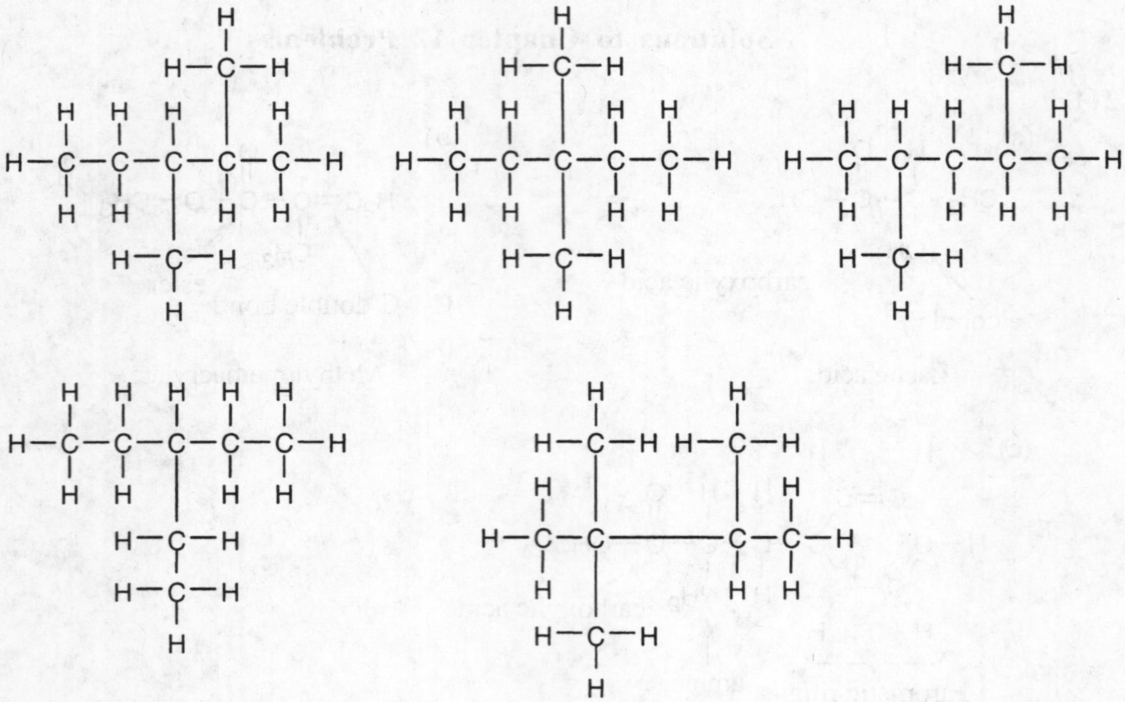

12.5

(a)

$CH_3CH_2CH_2CH_2CH_3$

Pentane

(b)

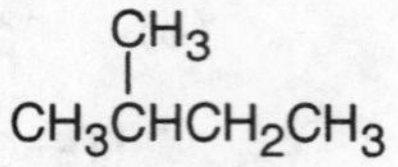

2-Methylbutane

(c)

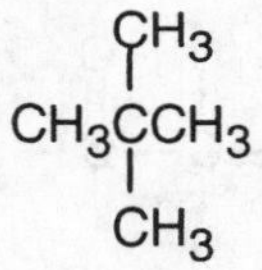

2,2-Dimethylpropane

12.6 All three structures have the same molecular formula (C_7H_{16}). Structures (a) and (c) are identical.

12.7 To solve this problem in a systematic way, use the following method:

(a) Draw the isomer of C_8H_{18} having no branches:

$CH_3CH_2CH_2CH_2CH_2CH_2CH_2CH_3$

(b) Draw the C_7H_{16} isomer having no branches, and replace one of the —CH_2— hydrogens with a —CH_3. There are three different isomers:

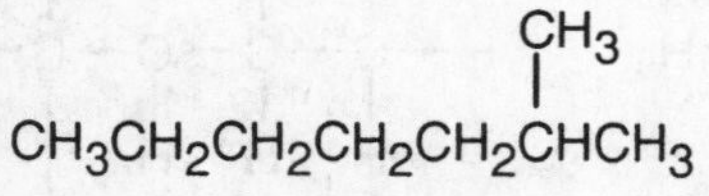

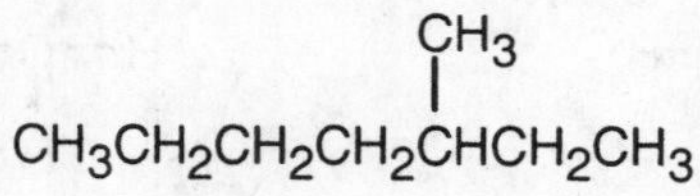

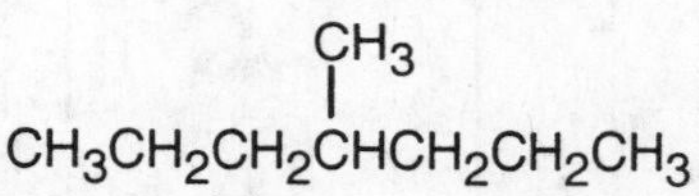

(c) Continue with the C_6, C_5, and C_4 isomers having no branches, and replace the different kinds of hydrogens with —CH_3 or —CH_2CH_3 groups, making sure that you don't draw the same isomer.

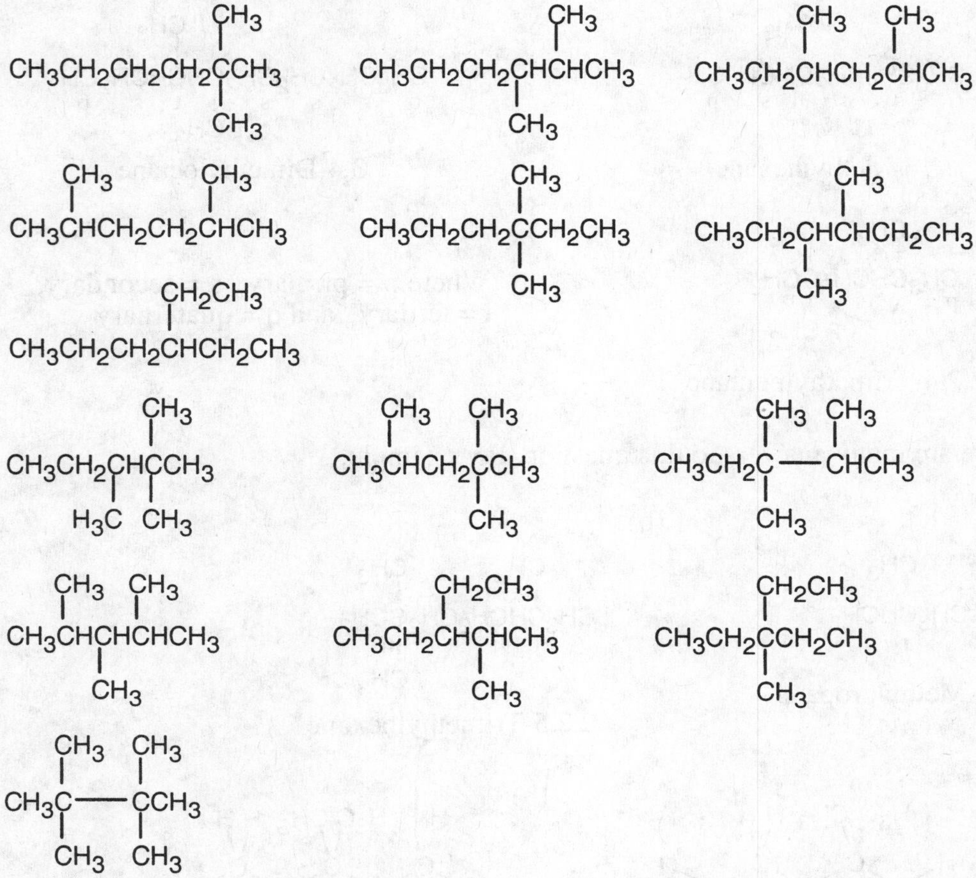

12.8

(a)

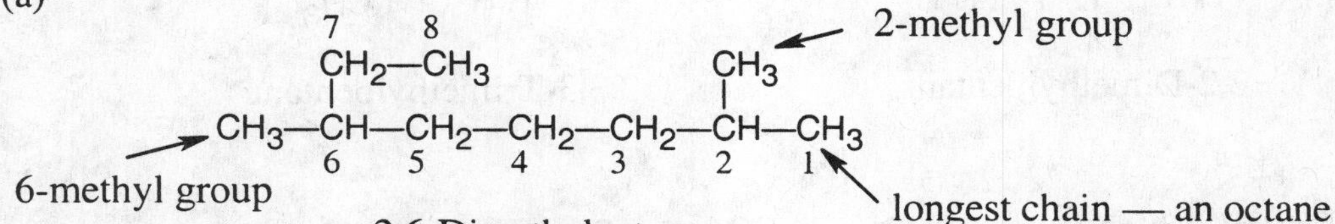
2-methyl group
6-methyl group
longest chain — an octane

2,6-Dimethyloctane

(b)

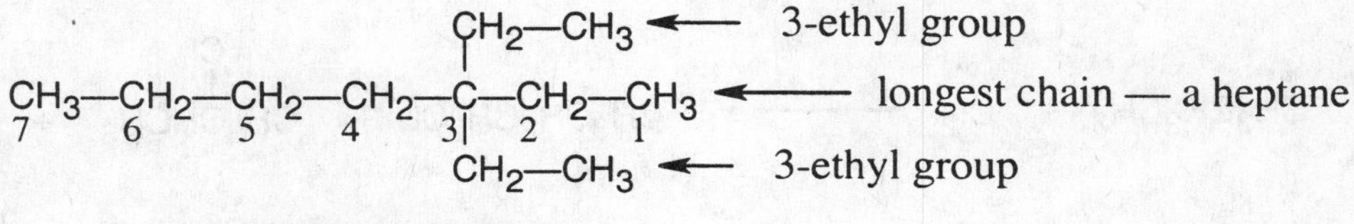
3-ethyl group
longest chain — a heptane
3-ethyl group

3,3-Diethylheptane

12.9 To answer this problem, draw the straight-chain hydrocarbon corresponding to the parent name, and replace —H's with the groups indicated.

(a)

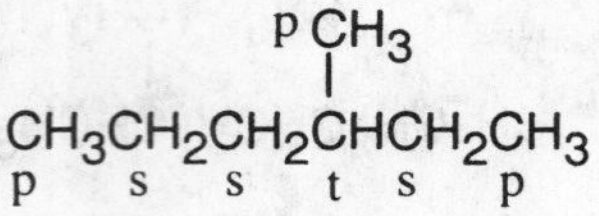

3-Methylhexane

(b)

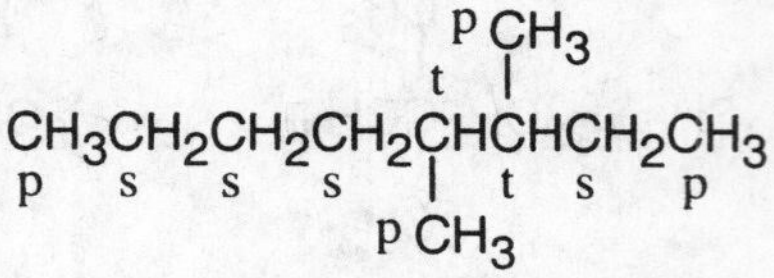

3,4-Dimethyloctane

(c)

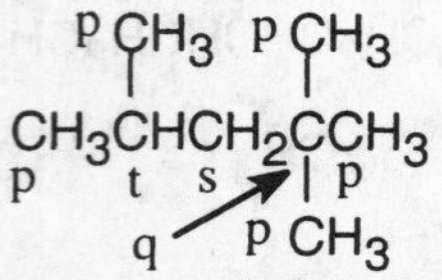

2,2,4-Trimethylpentane

Where p = primary, s = secondary, t = tertiary, and q = quaternary

12.10 There are many answers to this question. For example,

(a)

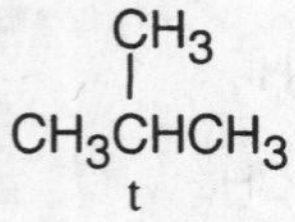

2-Methylpropane

(b)

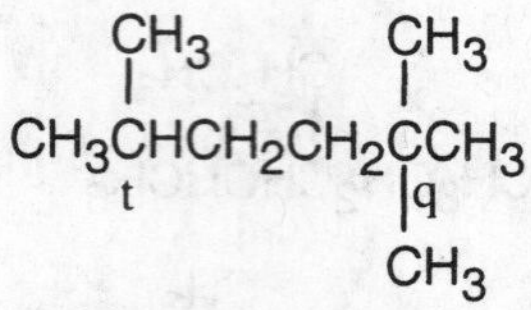

2,2,5-Trimethylhexane

12.11

(a)

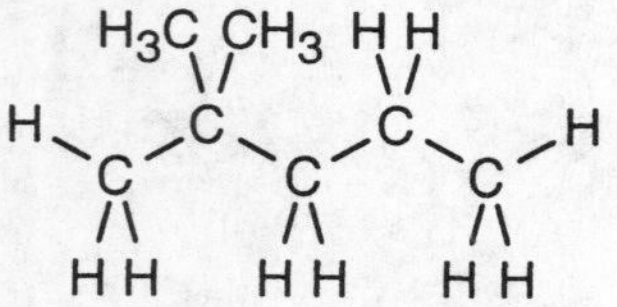

2,2-Dimethylpentane

(b)

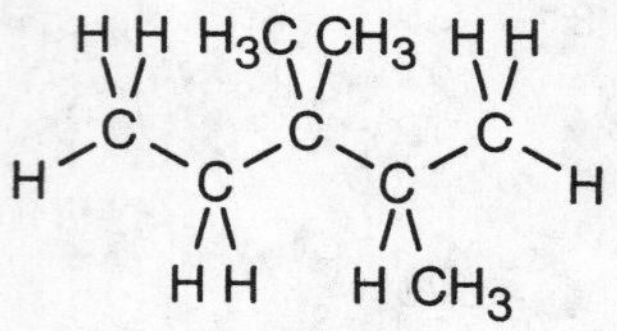

2,3,3-Trimethylpentane

12.12

$$2\ CH_3CH_3 + 7\ O_2 \longrightarrow 4\ CO_2 + 6\ H_2O$$

12.13

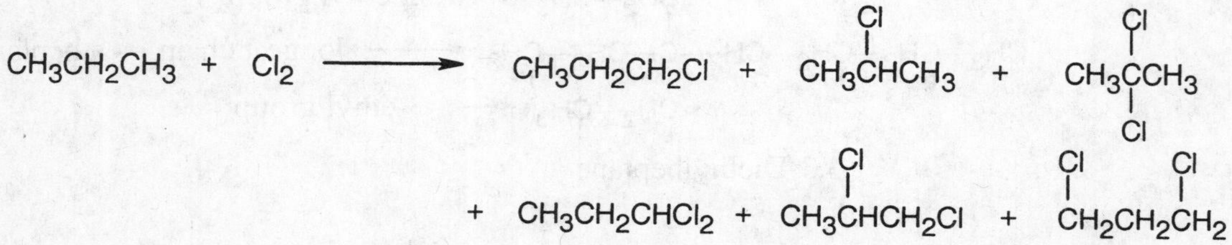

Six different mono- and disubstitution products can be formed from the reaction of propane with chlorine.

12.14

(a)

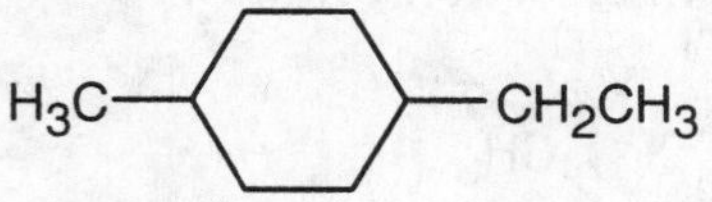
H3C
CH2CH3

1-Ethyl-4-methylcyclohexane

The parent ring is a cyclohexane. The two substituents are an ethyl group and a methyl group. The ethyl group receives the smaller number because it has alphabetical priority.

(b)

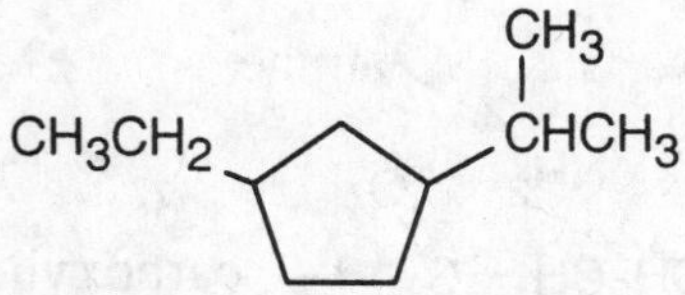
CH3
CH3CH2
CHCH3

1-Ethyl-3-isopropylcyclopentane

The parent ring is a cyclopentane. The two substituents are an ethyl group and an isopropyl group The ethyl group receives the smaller number because it has alphabetical priority.

12.15

(a)

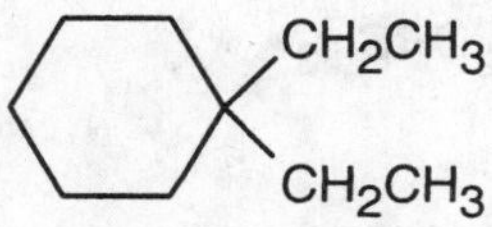
CH2CH3
CH2CH3

1,1-Diethylcyclohexane

(b)

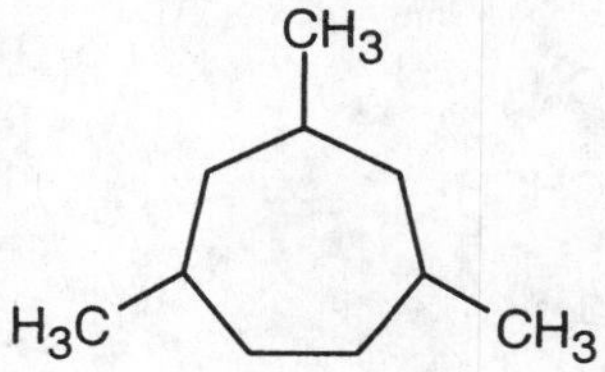
CH3
H3C
CH3

1,3,5-Trimethylcycloheptane

12.16

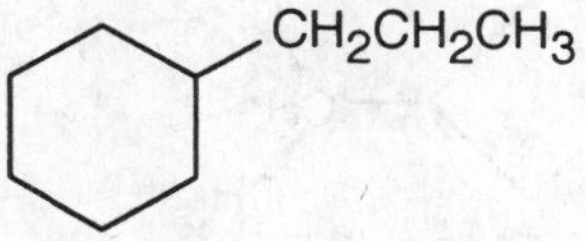
CH2CH2CH3

Propylcyclohexane

Understanding Key Concepts

12.17

(a)

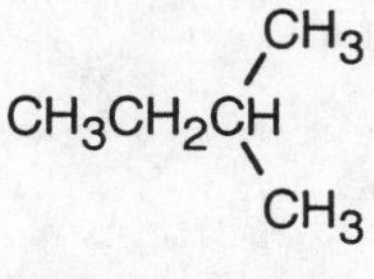
CH3
CH3CH2CH
CH3

12 hydrogens

(b)

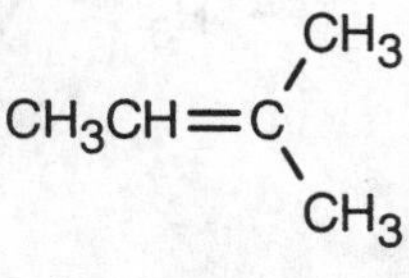
CH3
CH3CH=C
CH3

10 hydrogens

(c)

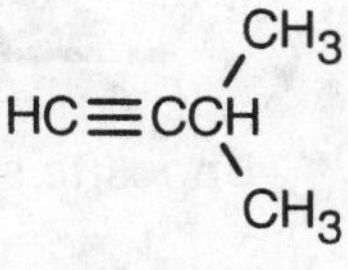
CH3
HC≡CCH
CH3

8 hydrogens

12.18

(a)

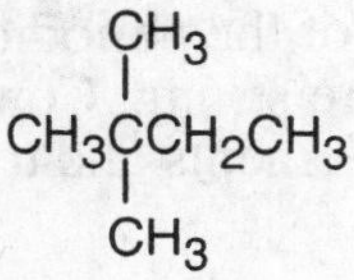
CH3
CH3CCH2CH3
CH3

(b)

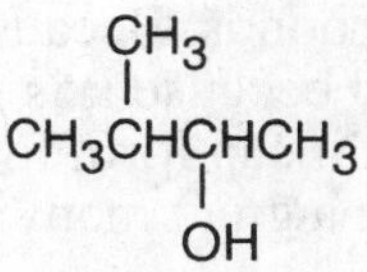
CH3
CH3CHCHCH3
OH

12.19 In a line drawing, a carbon is assumed to be at the intersection of lines.

(a)

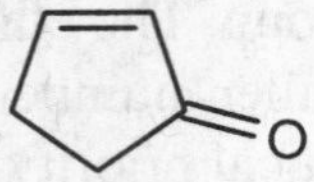
O

(b)

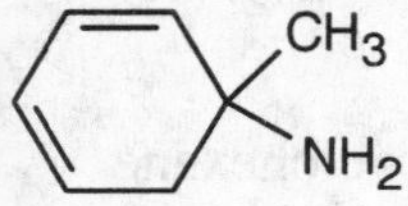
CH3
NH2

12.20

(a)

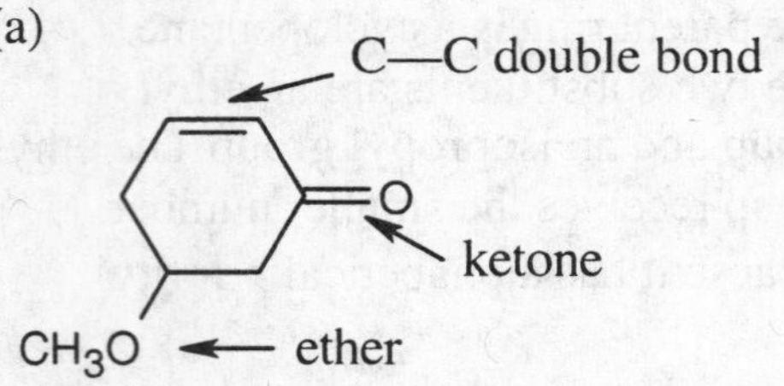
C—C double bond
O
ketone
CH3O
ether

(b)

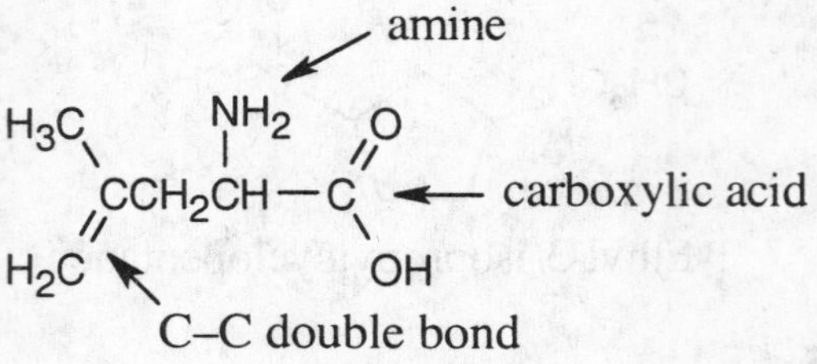
amine
H3C
NH2
O
CCH2CH—C
carboxylic acid
H2C
OH
C–C double bond

12.21

(a)

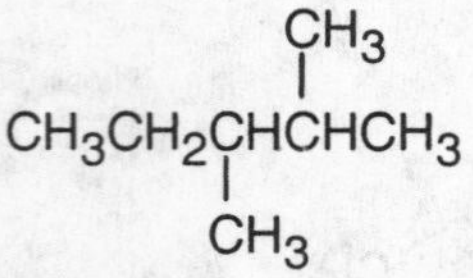
CH3
CH3CH2CHCHCH3
CH3

2,3-Dimethylpentane

(b)

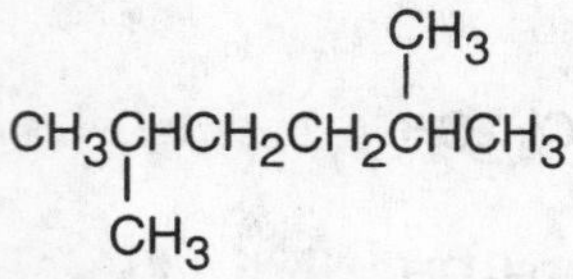
CH3
CH3CHCH2CH2CHCH3
CH3

2,5-Dimethylhexane

12.22

(a)

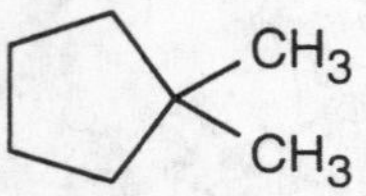
CH3
CH3

1,1-Dimethylcyclopentane

(b)

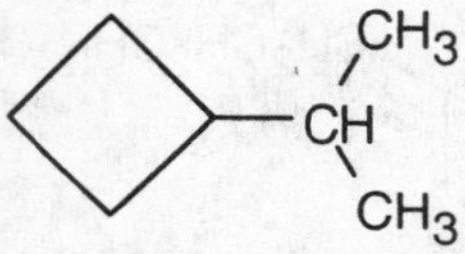
CH3
CH
CH3

Isopropylcyclobutane

12.23 In one of the isomers (b), the methyl groups are on the same side of the ring, and in the other isomer (a), they are on opposite sides.

(a)

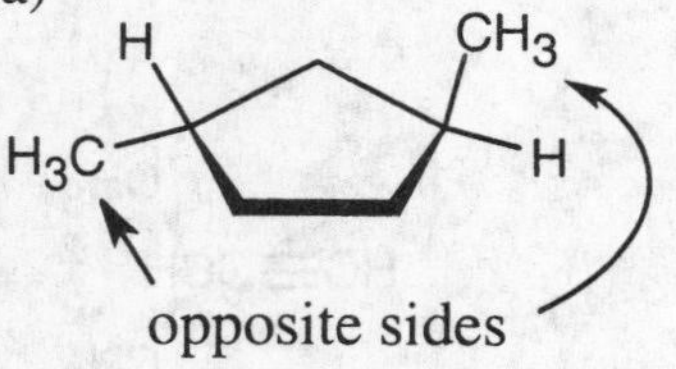
H
CH3
H3C
H
opposite sides

(b)

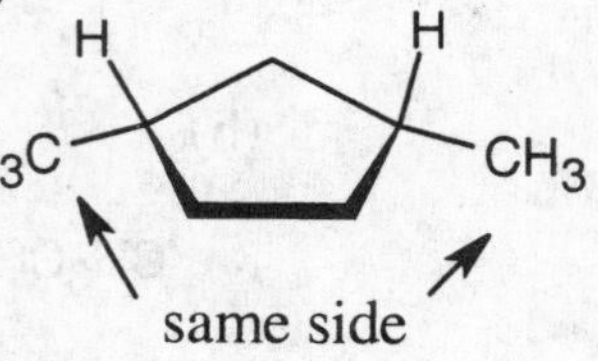
H
H
H3C
CH3
same side

Organic Molecules and Functional Groups

12.24 If you look at the periodic table you will see that carbon belongs to group 4A, whose elements can form four bonds. Because carbon is in the middle of the periodic table, these bonds are covalent, and because it is in period 2, these bonds are strong. Consequently, carbon is unique in that it can form four strong bonds to other elements and to other carbon atoms, making possible a great many different compounds.

12.26 Most organic compounds don't dissolve in water because they are nonpolar. They don't conduct electricity because they are covalent, not ionic.

12.28 A polar covalent bond is a covalent bond in which electrons are shared unequally, being more attracted to one atom than the other. For example, the electrons in the C–Br bond of bromomethane are attracted more strongly to the electronegative bromine than to carbon.

12.30

(a)

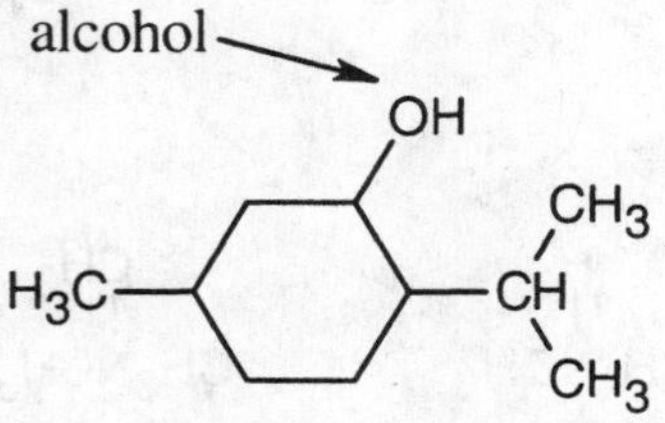
alcohol
OH
CH3
H3C
CH
CH3

Menthol

(b)

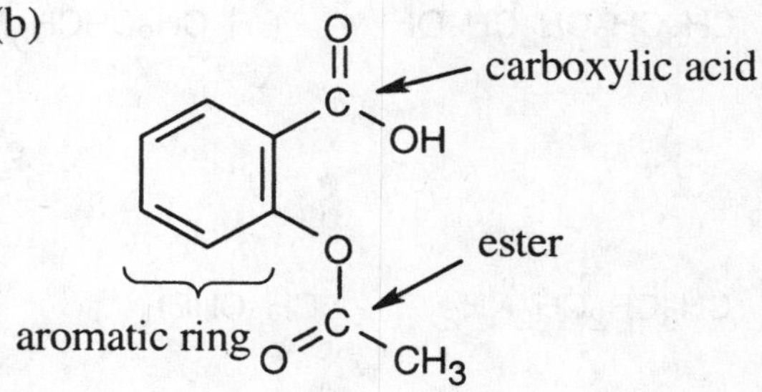
carboxylic acid
O
C
OH
O
ester
C
O
CH3
aromatic ring

Aspirin

12.32 There are many possible answers to each of these questions. For example,

(a) $CH_3CH_2CH_2C(=O)CH_3$ — ketone

(b) $CH_3CH_2CH_2C(=O){-}OCH_2CH_3$ — ester

(c) $H_2N{-}CH_2C(=O){-}OH$ — amine, carboxylic acid

Alkanes and Isomers

12.34 For two compounds to be isomers, they must have the same molecular formula but different structures.

12.36 A primary carbon is bonded to one other carbon; a secondary carbon is bonded to two other carbons; a tertiary carbon is bonded to three other carbons; and a quaternary carbon is bonded to four other carbons.

12.38 There are many possible answers to this question and the following question. For example,

(a)

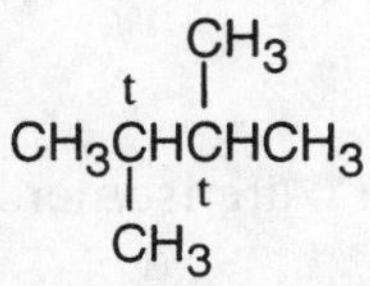
CH3
t
CH3CHCHCH3
t
CH3

2,3-Dimethylbutane

(b)

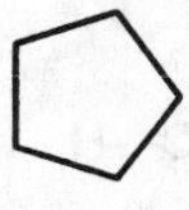

Cyclopentane

12.40

$$CH_3CH_2CH_2OH \qquad \underset{\displaystyle \overset{OH}{|}}{CH_3CHCH_3} \qquad CH_3CH_2-O-CH_3$$

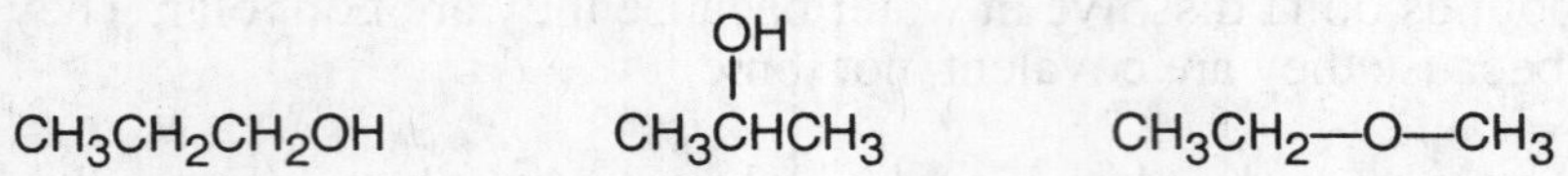

12.42

(a)

$$CH_3CH_2CH_2CH_2OH \qquad \underset{\displaystyle \overset{OH}{|}}{CH_3CH_2CHCH_3} \qquad \underset{\displaystyle \overset{CH_3}{|}}{CH_3CHCH_2OH} \qquad \underset{\displaystyle \underset{CH_3}{|}}{\overset{OH}{\overset{|}{CH_3CCH_3}}}$$

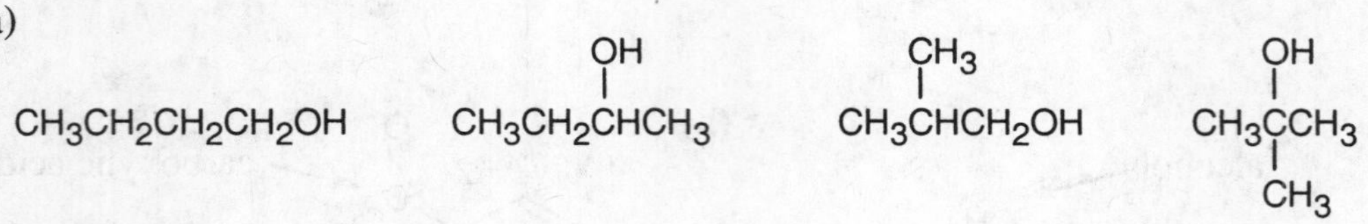

(b)

$$CH_3CH_2CH_2NH_2 \qquad \underset{\displaystyle \overset{NH_2}{|}}{CH_3CHCH_3} \qquad \underset{\displaystyle \overset{H}{|}}{CH_3CH_2NCH_3} \qquad \underset{\displaystyle \overset{CH_3}{|}}{CH_3NCH_3}$$

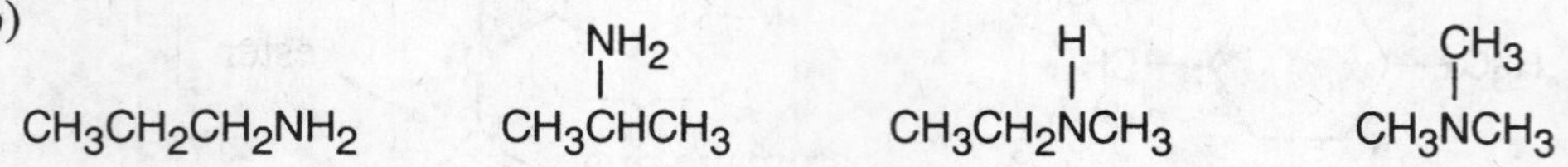

(c)

$$\underset{\displaystyle \overset{O}{\|}}{CH_3CH_2CH_2CCH_3} \qquad \underset{\displaystyle \overset{O}{\|}}{CH_3CH_2CCH_2CH_3} \qquad \underset{\displaystyle \underset{CH_3}{|}}{\overset{O}{\overset{\|}{CH_3CHCCH_3}}}$$

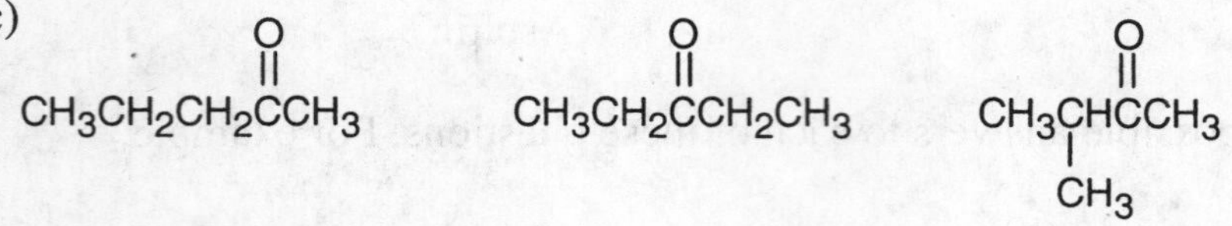

12.44

(a)

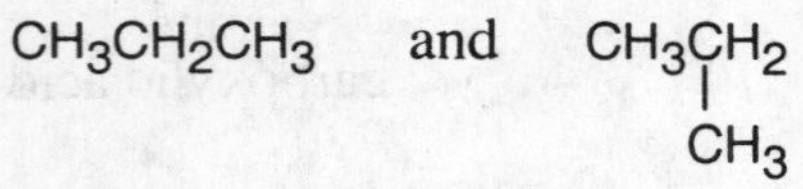

$$CH_3CH_2CH_3 \quad \text{and} \quad \underset{\displaystyle \overset{}{\underset{CH_3}{|}}}{CH_3CH_2} \quad \text{are identical.}$$

(b)

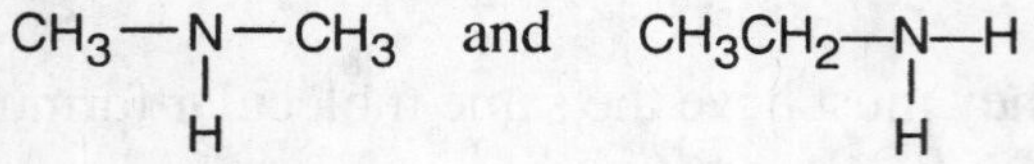

$$\underset{\displaystyle \underset{H}{|}}{CH_3-N-CH_3} \quad \text{and} \quad \underset{\displaystyle \underset{H}{|}}{CH_3CH_2-N-H} \quad \text{are isomers.}$$

(c)

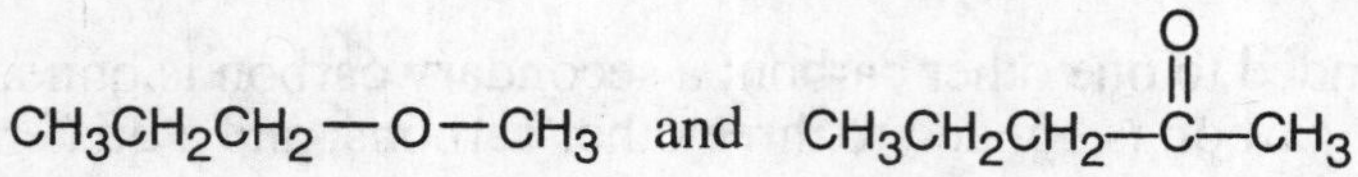

$$CH_3CH_2CH_2-O-CH_3 \quad \text{and} \quad \underset{\displaystyle \overset{O}{\|}}{CH_3CH_2CH_2-C-CH_3} \quad \text{are unrelated.}$$

(d)

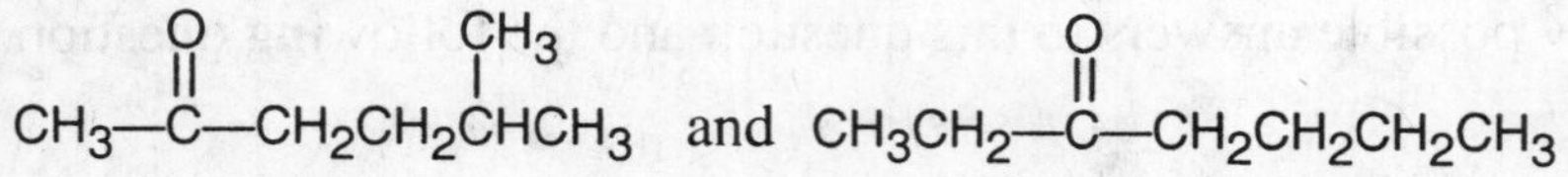

$$\underset{\displaystyle \overset{O}{\|}}{CH_3-C}-\underset{\displaystyle \overset{CH_3}{|}}{CH_2CH_2CHCH_3} \quad \text{and} \quad \underset{\displaystyle \overset{O}{\|}}{CH_3CH_2-C}-CH_2CH_2CH_2CH_3 \quad \text{are isomers.}$$

(e)

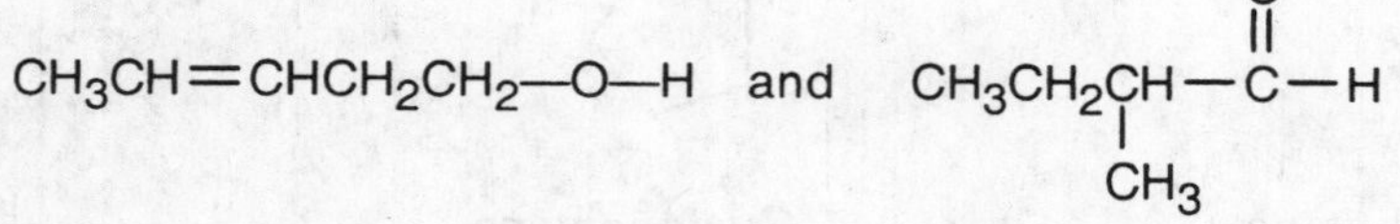

$$CH_3CH=CHCH_2CH_2-O-H \quad \text{and} \quad \underset{\displaystyle \underset{CH_3}{|}}{CH_3CH_2CH}-\underset{\displaystyle \overset{O}{\|}}{C}-H \quad \text{are isomers.}$$

12.46 All three structures have a carbon atom with five bonds.

(a) (b) (c)

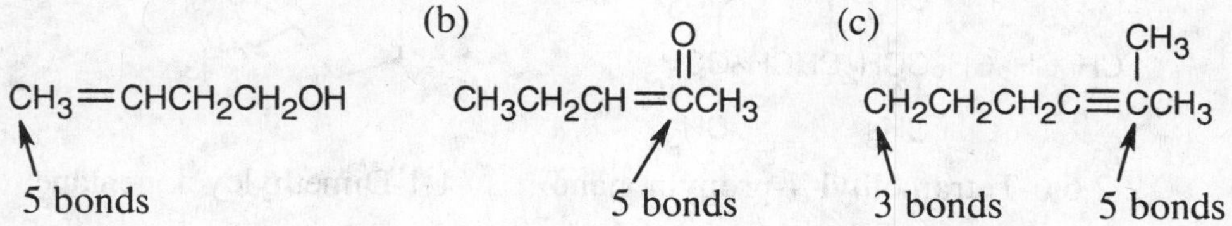
CH3=CHCH2CH2OH
5 bonds
O
CH3CH2CH=CCH3
5 bonds
CH3
CH2CH2CH2C≡CCH3
3 bonds
5 bonds

Naming Alkanes

12.48

(a)

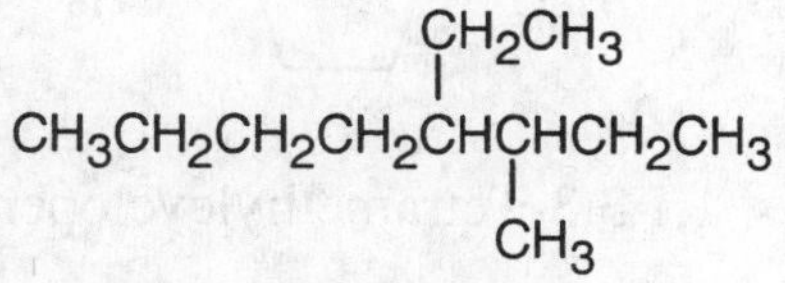
CH2CH3
CH3CH2CH2CH2CHCHCH2CH3
CH3

4-Ethyl-3-methyloctane

(b)

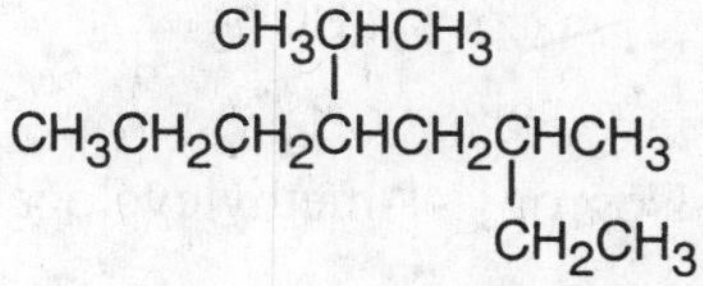
CH3CHCH3
CH3CH2CH2CHCH2CHCH3
CH2CH3

5-Isopropyl-3-methyloctane

(c)

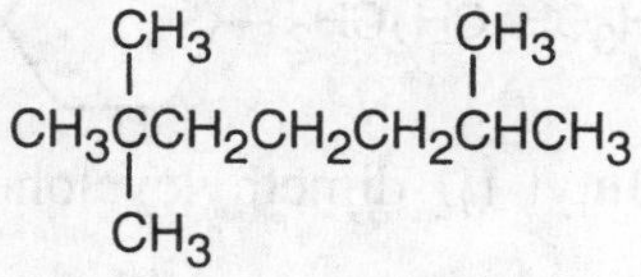
CH3 CH3
CH3CCH2CH2CH2CHCH3
CH3

2,2,6-Trimethylheptane

(d)

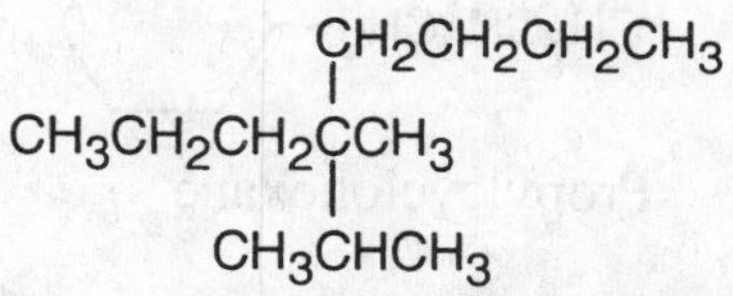
CH2CH2CH2CH3
CH3CH2CH2CCH3
CH3CHCH3

4-Isopropyl-4-methyloctane

(e)

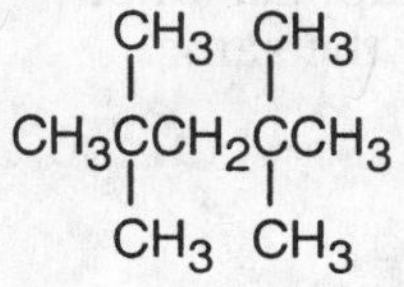
CH3 CH3
CH3CCH2CCH3
CH3 CH3

2,2,4,4-Tetramethylpentane

(f)

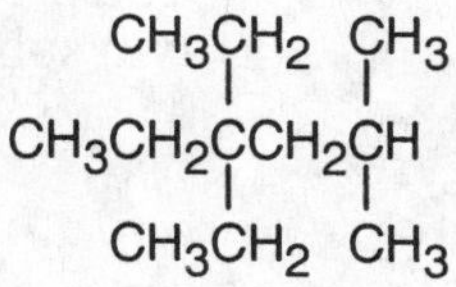
CH3CH2 CH3
CH3CH2CCH2CH
CH3CH2 CH3

4,4-Diethyl-2-methylhexane

(g)

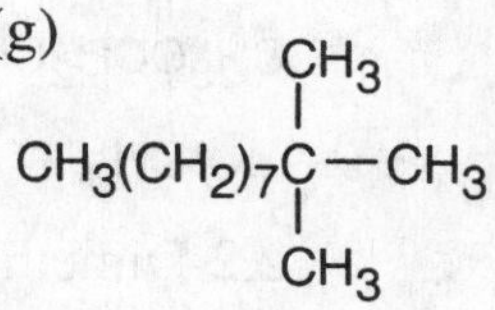
CH3
CH3(CH2)7C—CH3
CH3

2,2-Dimethyldecane

12.50

(a)

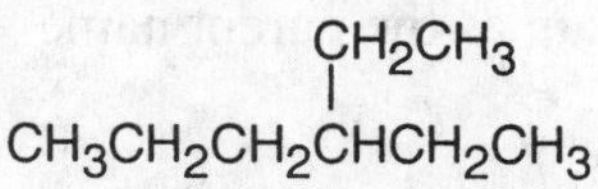
CH2CH3
CH3CH2CH2CHCH2CH3

3-Ethylhexane

(b)

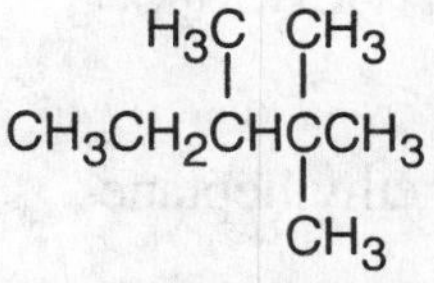
H3C CH3
CH3CH2CHCCH3
CH3

2,2,3-Trimethylpentane

(c)

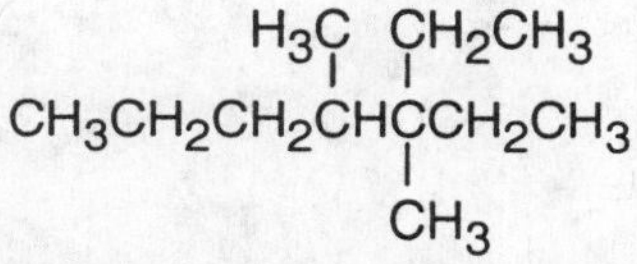
H3C CH2CH3
CH3CH2CH2CHCCH2CH3
CH3

3-Ethyl-3,4-dimethylheptane

(d)

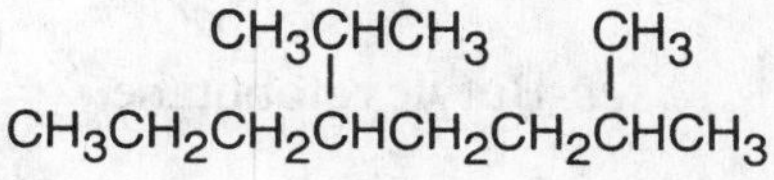
CH3CHCH3 CH3
CH3CH2CH2CHCH2CH2CHCH3

5-Isopropyl-2-methyloctane

(e)

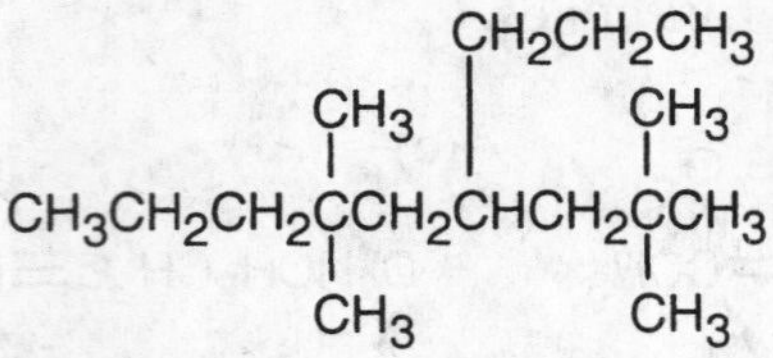

2,2,6,6-Tetramethyl-4-propylnonane

(f)

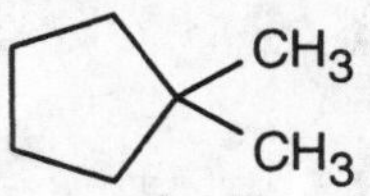

1,1-Dimethylcyclopentane

12.52

(a)

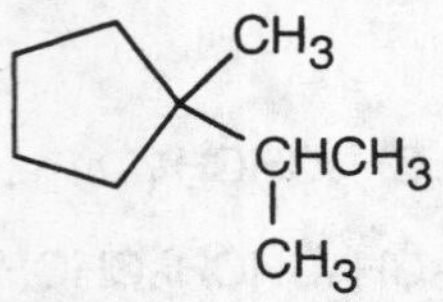

1-Isopropyl-1-methylcyclopentane

(b)

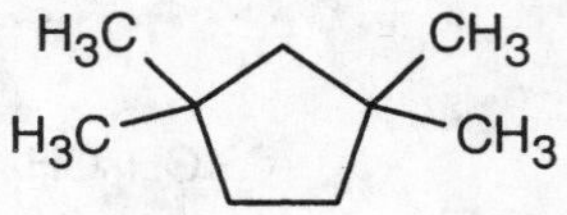

1,1,3,3-Tetramethylcyclopentane

(c)

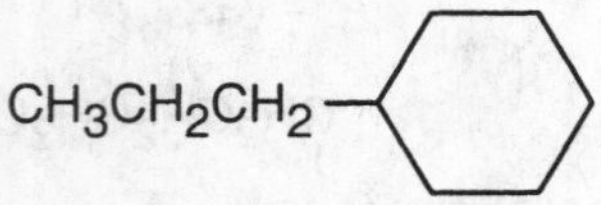

Propylcyclohexane

(d)

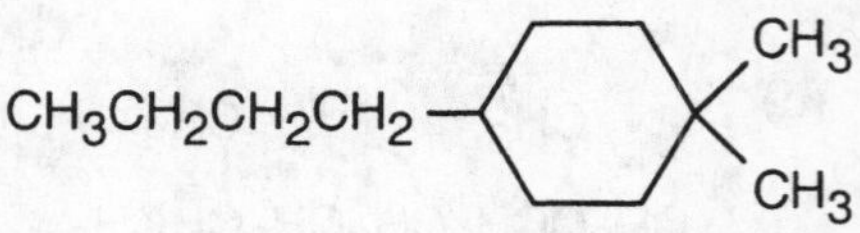

4-Butyl-1,1-dimethylcyclohexane

12.54

	Structure	*Error*
(a)	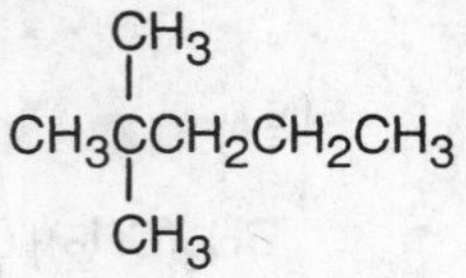 2,2-Dimethylpentane	The prefix *di-* must appear when two substituents are the same.
(b)	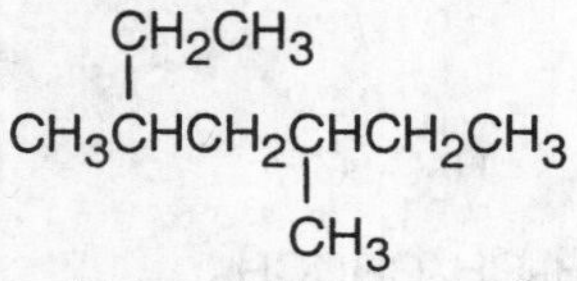 3,5-Dimethylheptane	You must choose the longest carbon chain as the parent name.
(c)	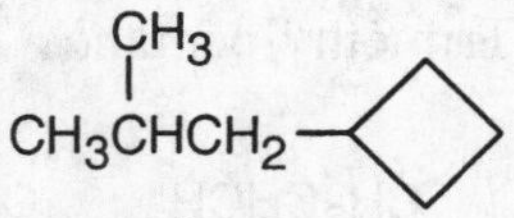 *sec*-Butylcyclobutane	This compound is an alkyl-substituted cycloalkane.

12.56

$CH_3CH_2CH_2CH_2CH_2CH_2CH_3$

Heptane

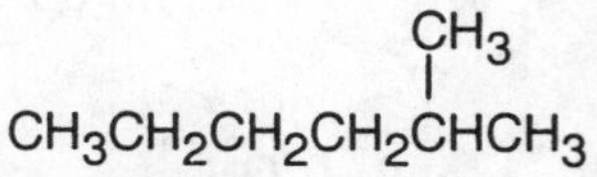

2-Methylhexane

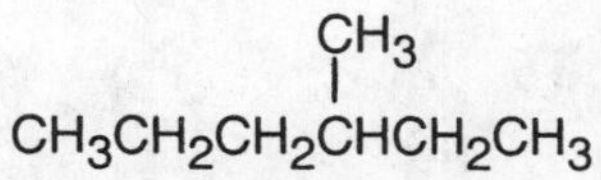

3-Methylhexane

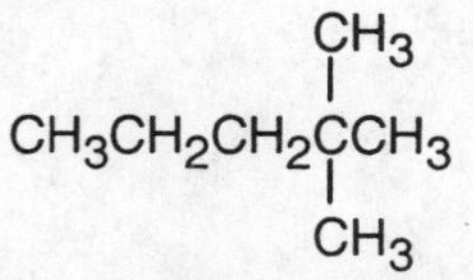

2,2-Dimethylpentane

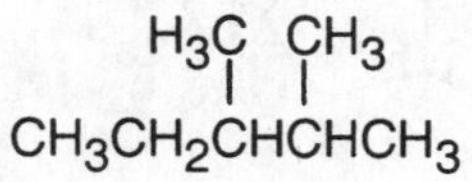

2,3-Dimethylpentane

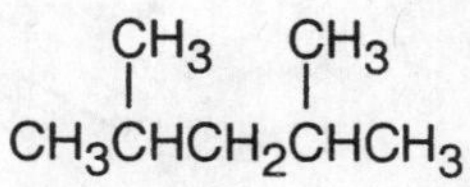

2,4-Dimethylpentane

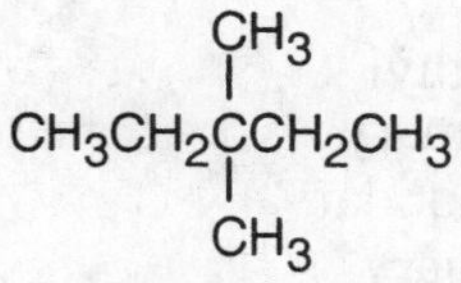

3,3-Dimethylpentane

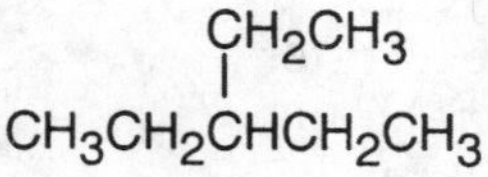

3-Ethylpentane

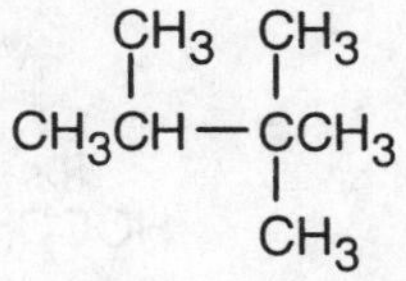

2,2,3-Trimethylbutane

Reactions of Alkanes

12.58

$$CH_3CH_2CH_3 + 5\ O_2 \longrightarrow 3\ CO_2 + 4\ H_2O$$

12.60

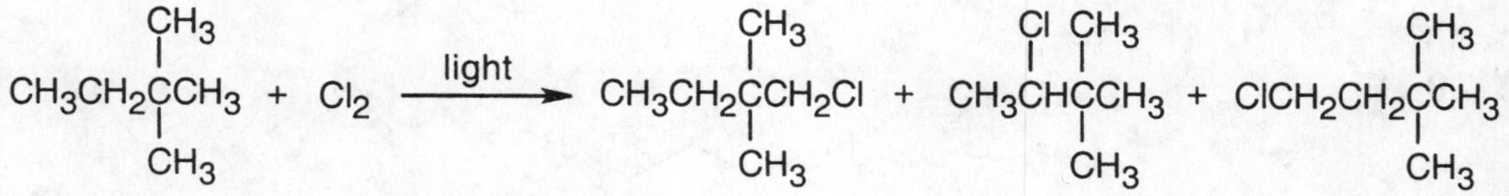

Applications

12.62 A synthetically produced version of a compound and a "natural" compound have the same properties because their chemical structures are identical.

12.64 Natural gas consists of $C_1 - C_4$ hydrocarbons and is a gas at room temperature. Petroleum consists of other alkanes, some of which are very high boiling.

General Questions and Problems

12.66

(a)

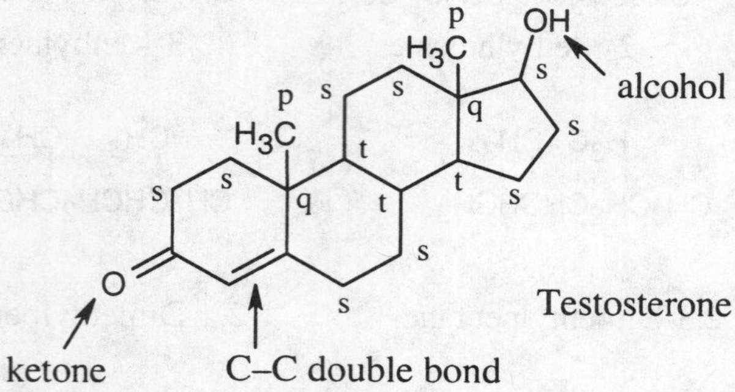
p
OH
H_3C
alcohol
H_3C
ketone
C–C double bond
Testosterone

p = primary
s = secondary
t = tertiary
q = quaternary

(b)

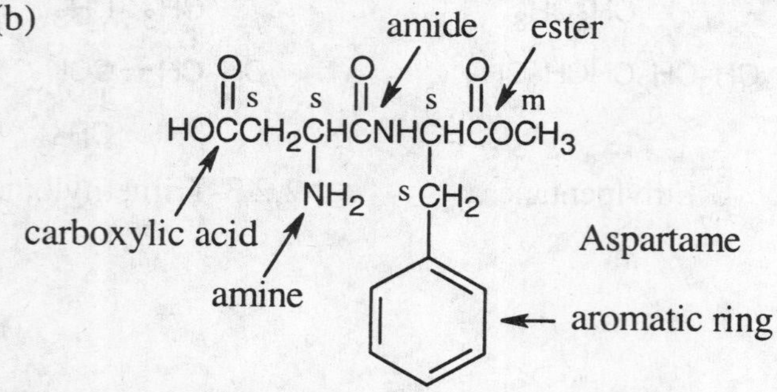
amide
ester
HOCCH2CHCNHCHCOCH3
NH2
CH2
carboxylic acid
amine
Aspartame
aromatic ring

m = methyl
p = primary
s = secondary
t = tertiary
q = quaternary

12.68 Because carbon forms only four bonds, the largest number of hydrogens that can be bonded to three carbons is eight.

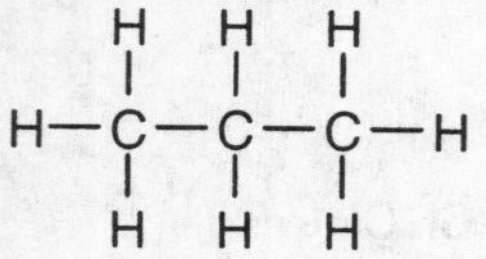

C_3H_8

12.70

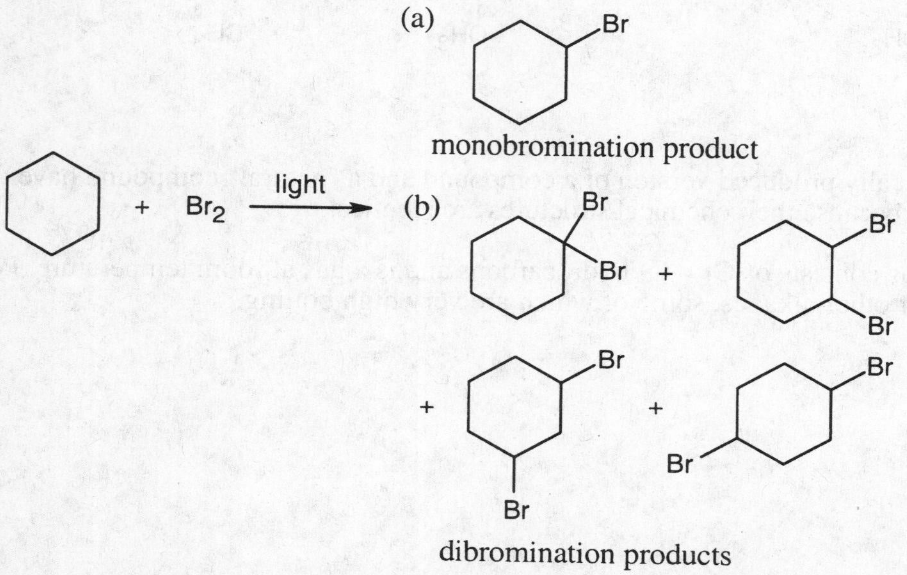
(a)
Br
monobromination product
+ Br2
light
(b)
Br
Br
+
Br
Br
+
Br
Br
+
Br
Br
dibromination products

12.72 Other structures are also possible.

(a)

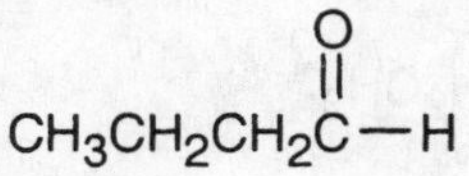

(b)

$CH_3CH_2CH_2CH{=}CHCH_2Br$

(c)

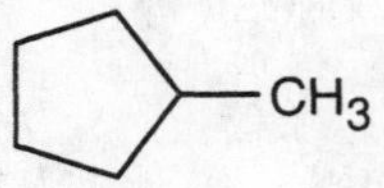

(d)

$CH_3CH{=}CHCH{=}CH_2$

Self-Test for Chapter 12

Multiple Choice

1. Which of the following functional groups doesn't contain a carbon–oxygen double bond?
(a) ether (b) aldehyde (c) ketone (d) ester

2. In which of the following alkanes are carbons not tetrahedral?
(a) ethane (b) propane (c) cyclopropane (d) cyclohexane

3. How many products can result from chlorination of ethane? (Include products with more than one chlorine.)
(a) 2 (b) 4 (c) 6 (d) 9

4. How many branched-chain isomers of C_6H_{14} are there?
(a) 2 (b) 3 (c) 4 (d) 5

5. Which of the following condensed structures doesn't represent a cycloalkane?
(a) C_3H_6 (b) C_4H_{10} (c) C_5H_{10} (d) C_6H_{12}

6.

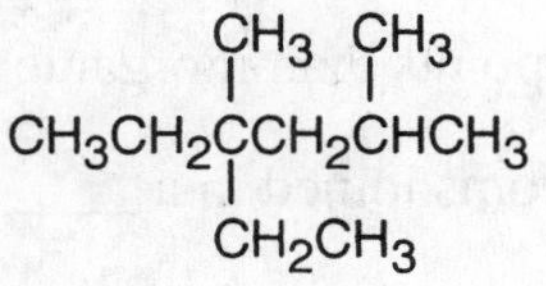

The correct name for the above structure is
(a) 3-ethyl-3,5-dimethylhexane (b) 3-methyl-3-*sec*-butylpentane
(c) 2,4-dimethyl-4-ethylhexane (d) 4-ethyl-2,4-dimethylhexane

7. How many secondary carbons are in the structure shown in Problem 6?
(a) 1 (b) 2 (c) 3 (d) 4

8. Which of the following structures is incorrectly drawn?

(a) 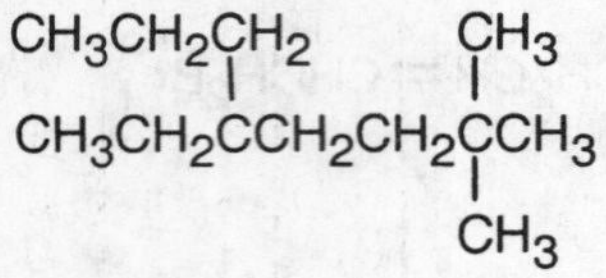

(b) 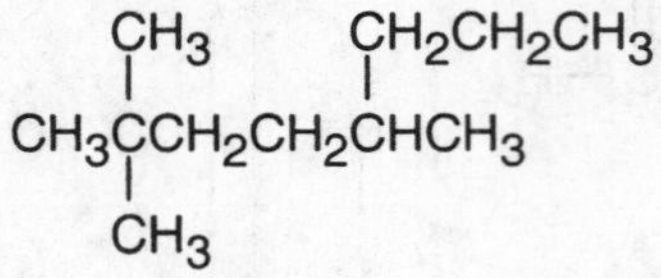

(c) 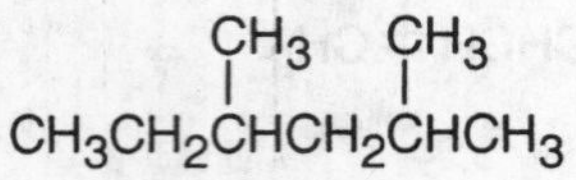

(d) 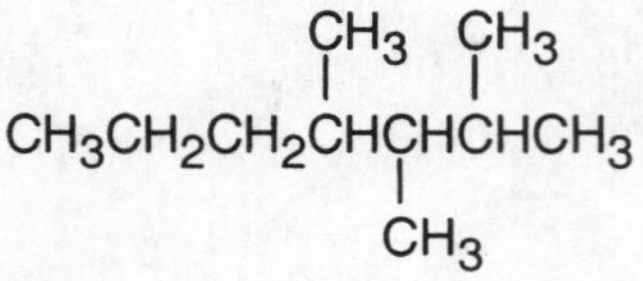

9. How many moles of O_2 are necessary for the complete combustion of one mole of C_6H_{12}?
(a) 4 (b) 6 (c) 9 (d) 10

10. Which alkyl group has a quaternary carbon?
(a) *tert*-butyl (b) isobutyl (c) *sec*-butyl (d) butyl

Sentence Completion

1. C_{20} to C_{36} alkanes are known as _____.
2. Alkynes are compounds that contain _____ bonds.
3. Alcohols and ethers are functional groups that contain _____.
4. Mixtures of hydrocarbons can be separated by _____.
5. A __________ is a shorthand way of drawing a chemical structure.
6. A _____ carbon is bonded to four other carbons.
7. Organic compounds generally have _____ melting points than inorganic compounds.
8. Cycloalkanes are compounds that contain carbon atoms joined in a _____.
9. Organic molecules are named by the _____ system.
10. Compounds with the same formula but different structures are called _____.
11. _______ is the reaction of an alkane with oxygen.
12. A straight-chain alkane is ______ boiling than a branched-chain alkane.

True or False

1. Cyclohexane and hexane are isomers.
2. A molecule with the formula C_5H_{12} can have the root name pentane, butane, or propane.
3. A cyclohexane ring is flat.

4. The correct name of the following alkane is 1,3-dimethylpentane.

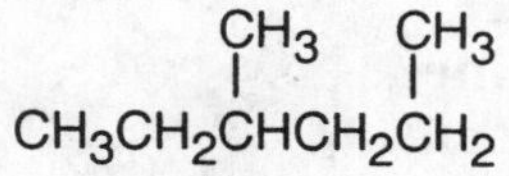
CH3 CH3
CH3CH2CHCH2CH2

5. The compound 2,3-dimethylbutane has only primary and tertiary carbons.

6. Acyclic alkanes and cycloalkanes have similar chemical reactivity.

7. The C—Cl bond in CH_3Cl is ionic.

8. The compound 1,4-dimethylcyclohexane is correctly named.

9. Alkanes with one to four carbons exist as gases at room temperature.

10. Compounds with many functional groups are more reactive than compounds with few functional groups.

11. 2-Methylpentane and 3-methylpentane have nearly identical boiling points.

12. At room temperature, an alkane exists in a single conformation.

Match each entry on the left with its partner on the right.

1. RCH=O	(a) Contains polar covalent bonds
2. C_5H_{12}	(b) Butyl group
3. $CH_3CH(CH_3)_2$	(c) Ketone
4. $CH_3CH_2CH_2CH_3$	(d) Natural gas
5. $CH_3CH_2CH_2$—	(e) Formula of methylcyclobutane
6. $R_2C=O$	(f) Branched-chain alkane
7. CH_2Cl_2	(g) An alkene
8. $C_{30}H_{62}$	(h) Propyl group
9. C_5H_{10}	(i) Aldehyde
10. $CH_3CH_2CH_2CH_2$—	(j) Formula of 2-methylbutane
11. $CH_3CH=CH_2$	(k) A solid
12. CH_4	(l) Straight-chain alkane

Chapter 13 – Alkenes, Alkynes, and Aromatic Compounds

Chapter Outline

I. Alkenes and alkynes (Sections 13.1–13.7).
  A. Introduction (Section 13.1).
    1. Alkenes are compounds that have double bonds (—C=C—).
    2. Alkynes are compounds that have triple bonds (—C≡C—).
  B. Naming alkenes and alkynes (Section 13.2).
    1. Find the longest chain containing the double or triple bond and name the parent compound by adding *-ene* or *-yne* to the root.
    2. Number the carbons in the main chain, beginning at the end nearer the multiple bond.
      a. If the bond is an equal distance from each end, begin numbering at the end nearer the first branch point.
      b. Cyclic alkenes are named cycloalkenes, and the double-bond carbons are carbons 1 and 2.
    3. Write out the full name.
      a. Number the substituents, and list them alphabetically.
      b. Indicate the position of the multiple bond by giving it the number of the first carbon in the bond.
      c. If more than one bond is present, use the endings *-diene*, *-triene*, *-tetraene*.
  C. Cis–trans isomerism in alkenes (Section 13.3).
    1. Atoms attached to a double bond lie in a plane.
    2. If each end of the bond is bonded to two different groups, isomerism can result.
      a. When the larger groups are on the same side of the bond, the isomer is cis.
      b. When the larger groups are on opposite sides of the bond, the isomer is trans.
  D. Properties of alkenes and alkynes (Section 13.4).
    1. Nonpolar, insoluble in water, flammable.
    2. Alkane-like in physical properties.
    3. Alkenes show cis–trans isomerism.
    4. Both alkenes and alkynes react at the multiple bond to form addition products.
  E. Organic reactions (Sections 13.5 – 13.7).
    1. Types of organic reactions (Section 13.5).
      a. Addition reactions occur when two reactants add to form a single product.
      b. Elimination reactions occur when a reactant splits into two products.
      c. Substitution reactions occur when two reactants exchange parts.
      d. Rearrangement reactions occur when a single reactant undergoes a rearrangement of bonds to yield an isomeric product.
    2. Reaction of alkenes and alkynes (Sections 13.6 – 13.7).
      a. Addition reactions (Section 13.6).
        i. Alkene + H_2 —> alkane (hydrogenation).
           Alkyne + 2 H_2 —> alkane.
        ii. Alkene + X_2 —> dihaloalkane (X = halogen) (halogenation).
        iii. Alkene + HX —> alkyl halide.
           Direction of addition: X is bonded to the more substituted carbon (Markovnikov's rule).
        iv. Alkene + H_2O —> alcohol (hydration).
           Addition also follows Markovnikov's rule.
      b. Mechanism of addition reactions, using HBr addition as an example (Section 13.7).
        i. H^+ adds to the alkene to form a carbocation.
        ii. Br^- adds to the carbocation to form the product.

F. Alkene polymers (Section 13.8).
   1. Simple alkenes of the type $H_2C=CHZ$ (monomer) can add to each other in long chains.
   2. The reaction is started by an initiator, which adds to an alkene to form a reactive intermediate.
   3. The reactive intermediate starts the growth of the chain.
   4. The product is a chain-growth polymer.
   5. Varying –Z varies the properties of the polymer.
   6. Properties of polymers also depend on chain length and degree of branching.

II. Aromatic compounds (Sections 13.9–13.11).
   A. Structure of benzene (Section 13.9).
      1. Benzene is a flat, six-membered ring containing three double bonds.
         a. All carbons in benzene are equivalent.
         b. The structure of benzene is an average of the two conventional structures.
         c. This phenomenon is known as resonance.
      2. Despite having double bonds, benzene is less reactive than alkenes.
      3. Aromatic compounds are nonpolar, water-insoluble, volatile, and flammable.
      4. Some aromatic compounds are toxic and carcinogenic.
   B. Naming aromatic compounds (Section 13.10).
      1. Use "benzene" as the parent name.
      2. For monosubstituted benzenes, the name of the substituent is followed by *-benzene* (no number needed).
      3. For disubstituted benzenes:
         a. Ortho-disubstituted benzenes have substituents in the 1,2 positions of the ring.
         b. Meta-disubstituted benzenes have substituents in the 1,3 positions of the ring.
         c. Para-disubstituted benzenes have substituents in the 1,4 positions of the ring.
      4. Many aromatic compounds have trivial names.
   C. Reactions of aromatic compounds (Section 13.11).
      Aromatic compounds undergo substitution reactions.
         a. Aromatic ring + HNO_3 $\xrightarrow{H_2SO_4}$ Nitroaromatic ring
         b. Aromatic ring + X_2 $\xrightarrow{FeX_3}$ Haloaromatic ring
         c. Aromatic ring + SO_3 $\xrightarrow{H_2SO_4}$ Aromatic sulfonic acid

Solutions to Chapter 13 Problems

13.1

(a)

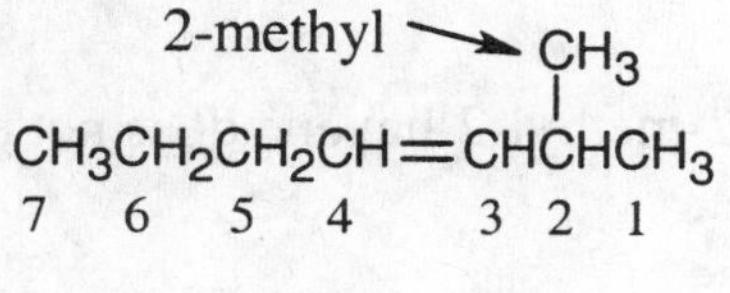

2-methyl
CH3
CH3CH2CH2CH=CHCHCH3
7 6 5 4 3 2 1

2-Methyl-3-heptene

(b)

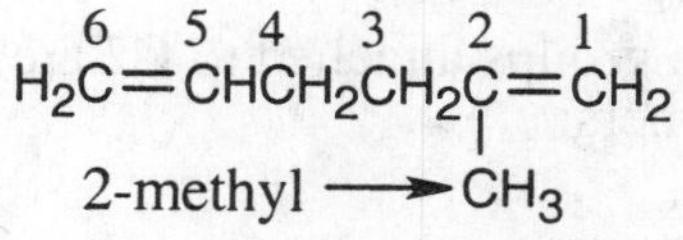

6 5 4 3 2 1
H2C=CHCH2CH2C=CH2
2-methyl
CH3

2-Methyl-1,5-hexadiene

13.2

(a)

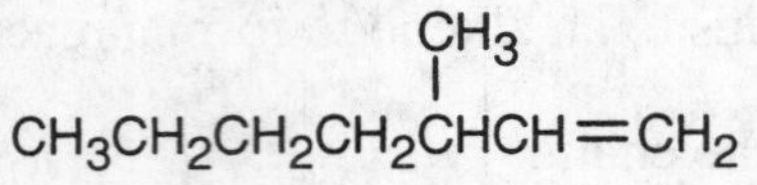

3-Methyl-1-heptene

(b)

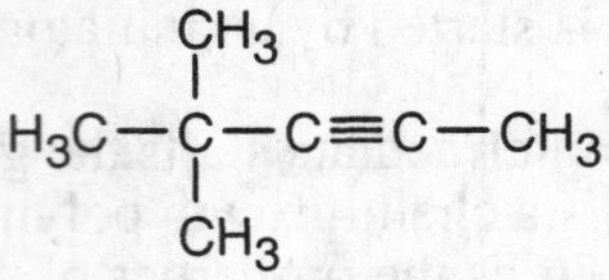

4,4-Dimethyl-2-pentyne

(c)

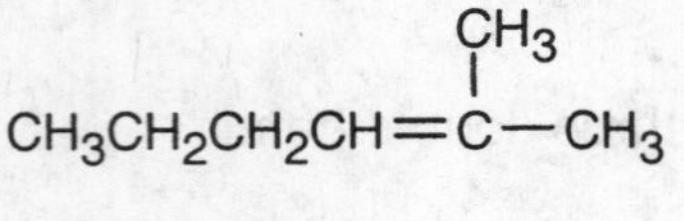

2-Methyl-2-hexene

(d)

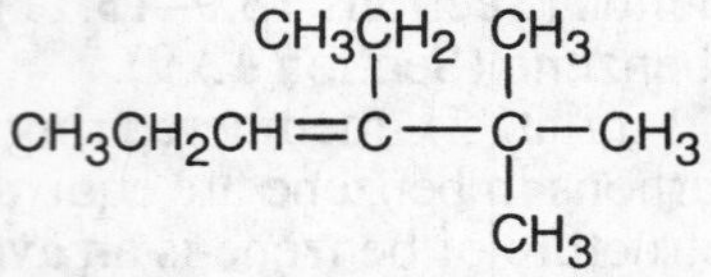

3-Ethyl-2,2-dimethyl-3-hexene

13.3

(a)

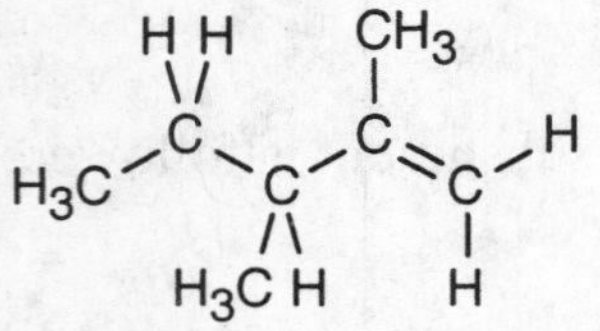

2,3-Dimethyl-1-pentene

(b)

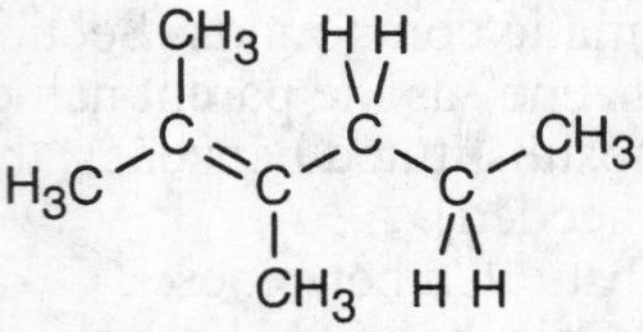

2,3-Dimethyl-2-hexene

13.4 (a) Attached to C3: —H, $—CH_2CH_3$
Attached to C4: —H, $—CH_2CH_2CH_3$

Since each of the double-bond carbons has two different groups attached to it, 3-heptene exists as cis–trans isomers:

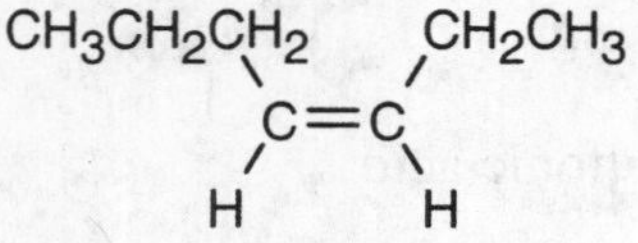

cis-3-Heptene

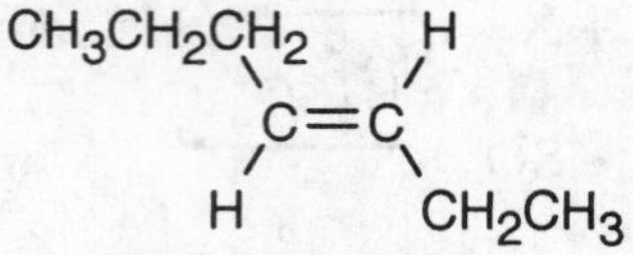

trans-3-Heptene

(b) Attached to C2: $—CH_3$, $—CH_3$
Attached to C3: —H, $—CH_2CH_2CH_3$

Since the two groups attached to C2 are identical, 2-methyl-2-hexene does not exist as cis–trans isomers:

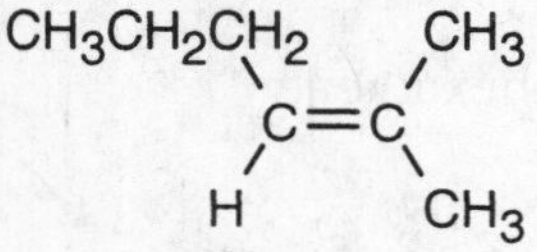

2-Methyl-2-hexene

(c) Attached to C2: —H, —CH_3
Attached to C3: —H, —$CH_2CH(CH_3)_2$

Since each carbon has two different groups attached to it, 5-methyl-2-hexene exists as cis–trans isomers:

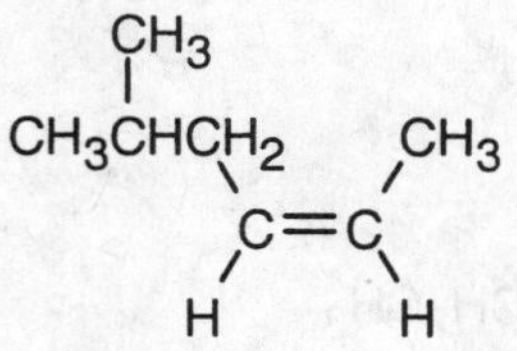

cis-5-Methyl-2-hexene

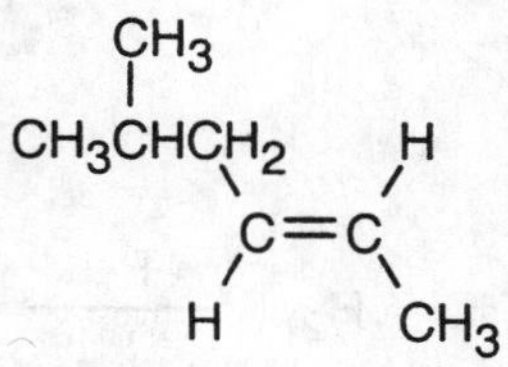

trans-5-Methyl-2-hexene

13.5

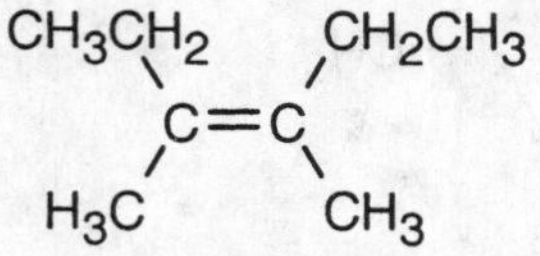

cis-3,4-Dimethyl-3-hexene

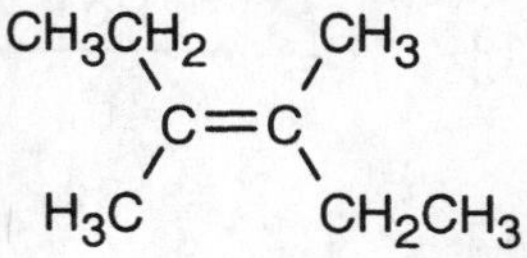

trans-3,4-Dimethyl-3-hexane

13.6

(a)

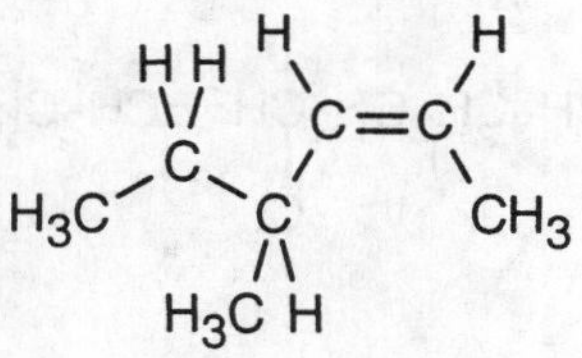

cis-4-Methyl-2-hexene

(b)

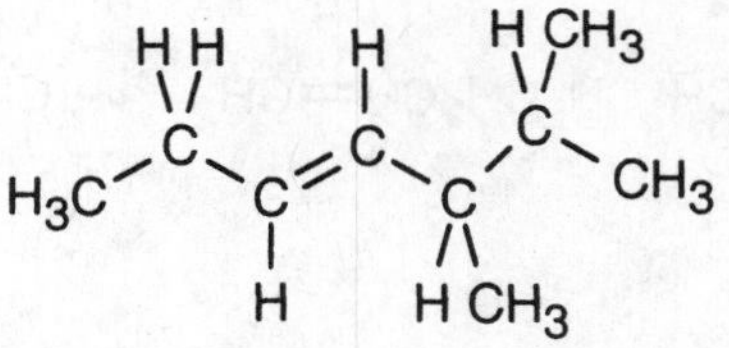

trans-5,6-Dimethyl-3-heptene

13.7

(a) $CH_3Br + NaOH \longrightarrow CH_3OH + NaBr$

This reaction is a substitution because two reagents exchange parts to give two different products.

(b) $H_2C{=}CH_2 + HCl \longrightarrow CH_3CH_2Cl$

This reaction is an addition because two reactants combine to give one product.

(c) $CH_3CH_2Br \longrightarrow H_2C{=}CH_2 + HBr$

In this elimination reaction, two products are formed from one reactant.

13.8

(a) $CH_3CH_2CH=CH_2$ + H_2 $\xrightarrow{\text{Pd}}$ $CH_3CH_2CH_2CH_3$

(b)
$$\begin{array}{c} H_3C \qquad CH_3 \\ \diagdown \quad / \\ C=C \\ / \quad \diagdown \\ H \qquad H \end{array} \quad + \quad H_2 \quad \xrightarrow{\text{Pd}} \quad CH_3CH_2CH_2CH_3$$

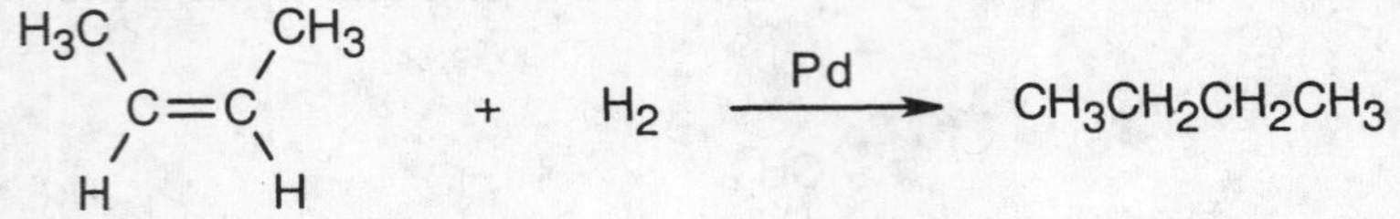

(c)
$$\begin{array}{c} H_3C \qquad H \\ \diagdown \quad / \\ C=C \\ / \quad \diagdown \\ H \qquad CH_3 \end{array} \quad + \quad H_2 \quad \xrightarrow{\text{Pd}} \quad CH_3CH_2CH_2CH_3$$

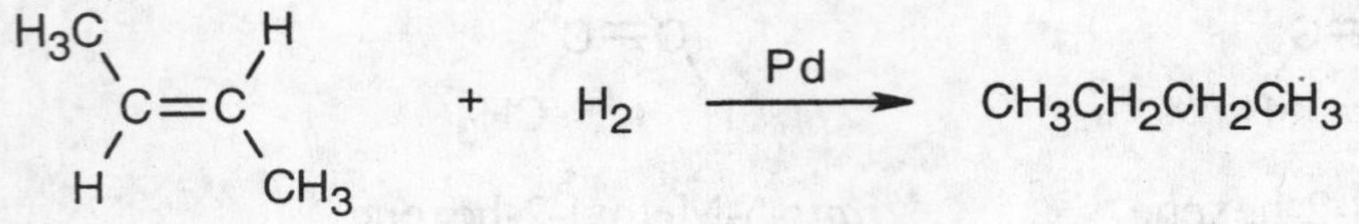

(d)

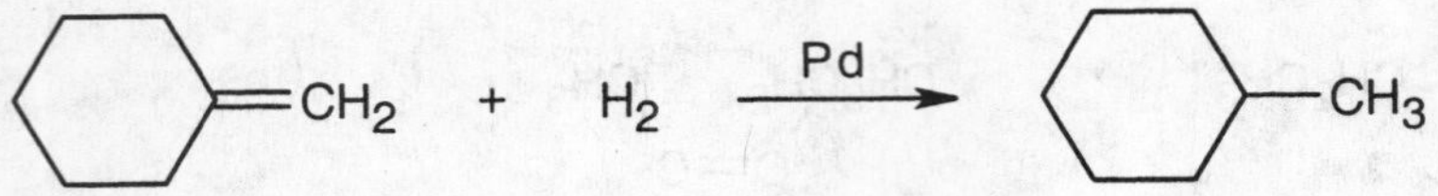

13.9

(a)
$$\begin{array}{c} CH_3 \\ | \\ CH_3C=CH_2 \end{array} \quad + \quad Br_2 \quad \longrightarrow \quad \begin{array}{c} CH_3 \\ | \\ CH_3C-CH_2Br \\ | \\ Br \end{array}$$

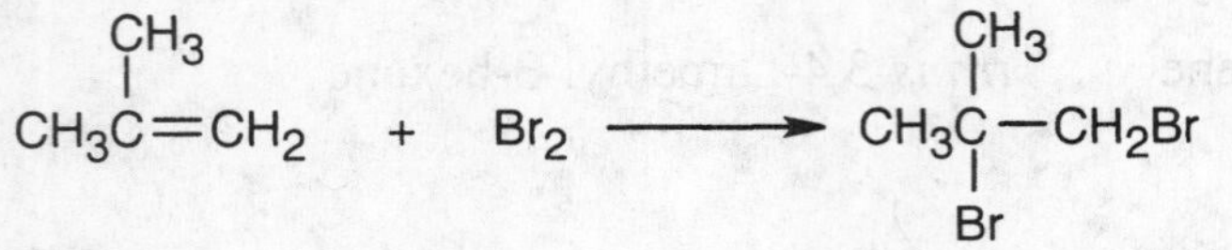

(b) $CH_3CH_2CH_2CH=CH_2$ + Cl_2 $\longrightarrow$ $\begin{array}{c} CH_3CH_2CH_2CH-CH_2Cl \\ | \\ Cl \end{array}$

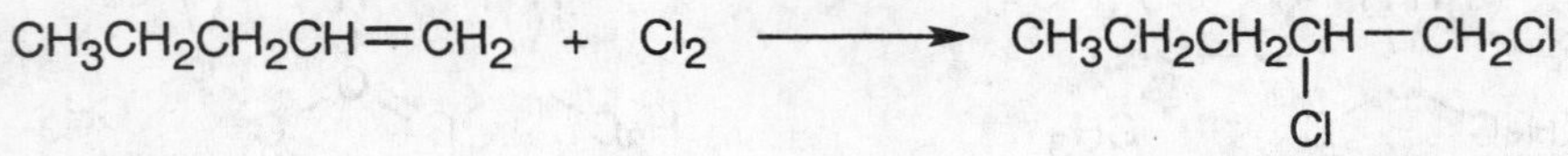

(c)
$$\begin{array}{c} CH_3 \\ | \\ CH_3CH_2CH=CCH_2CHCH_3 \\ | \\ CH_3 \end{array} \quad + \quad Cl_2 \quad \longrightarrow \quad \begin{array}{c} CH_3 \\ | \\ CH_3CH_2CH-CCH_2CHCH_3 \\ | \quad | \quad | \\ Cl \quad Cl \quad CH_3 \end{array}$$

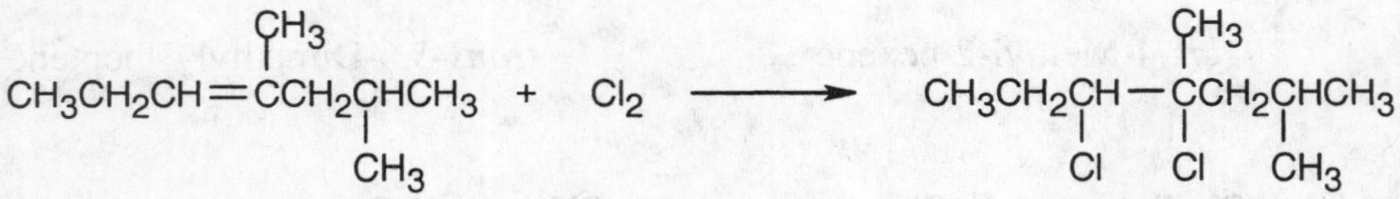

13.10

(a)

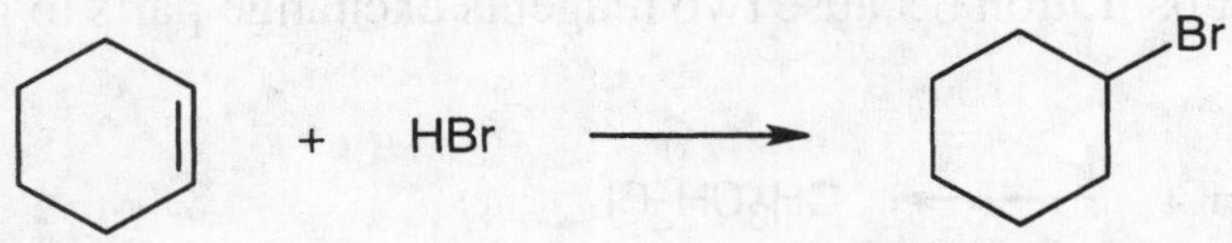

(b) $CH_3CH_2CH_2CH_2CH=CH_2$ + HCl $\longrightarrow$ $\begin{array}{c} CH_3CH_2CH_2CH_2CHCH_3 \\ | \\ Cl \end{array}$

Chlorine bonds to the carbon that has fewer hydrogens.

(c)
$$\begin{array}{c} CH_3 \\ | \\ CH_3CHCH=CH_2 \end{array} \quad + \quad HCl \quad \longrightarrow \quad \begin{array}{c} CH_3 \\ | \\ CH_3CHCHCH_3 \\ | \\ Cl \end{array}$$

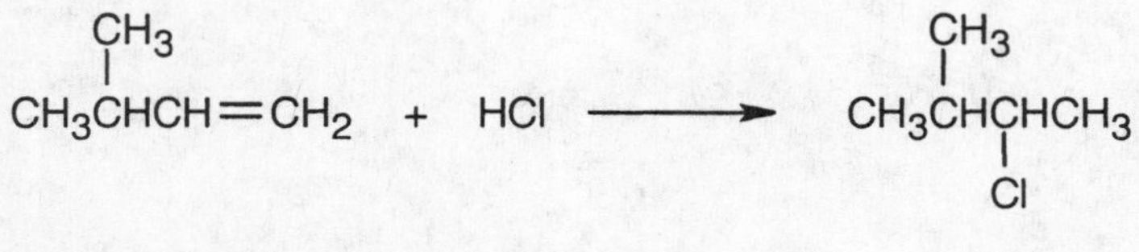

13.11

(a)

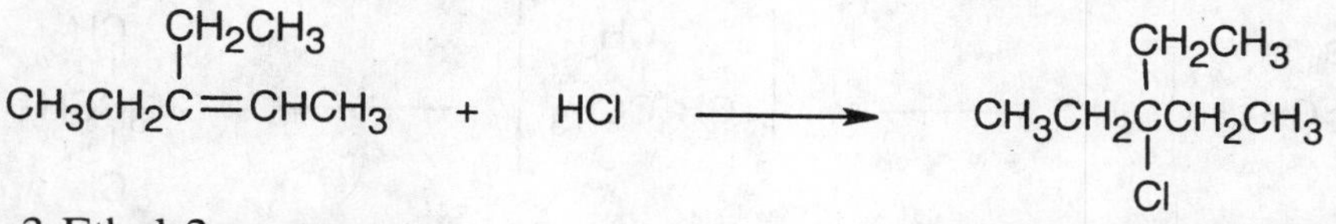

3-Ethyl-2-pentene → 3-Chloro-3-ethylpentane

(b)

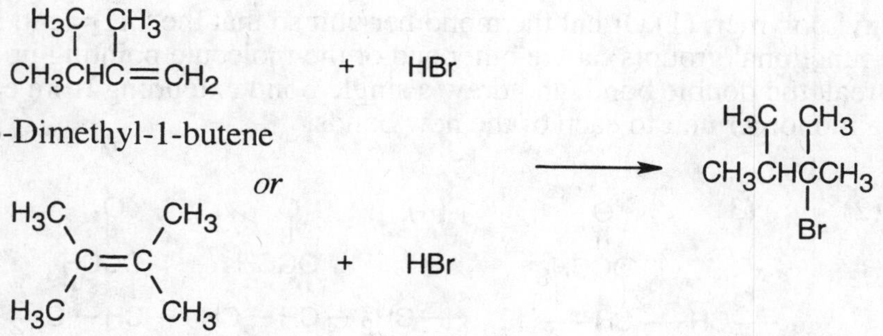

2,3-Dimethyl-1-butene *or* 2,3-Dimethyl-2-butene

13.12

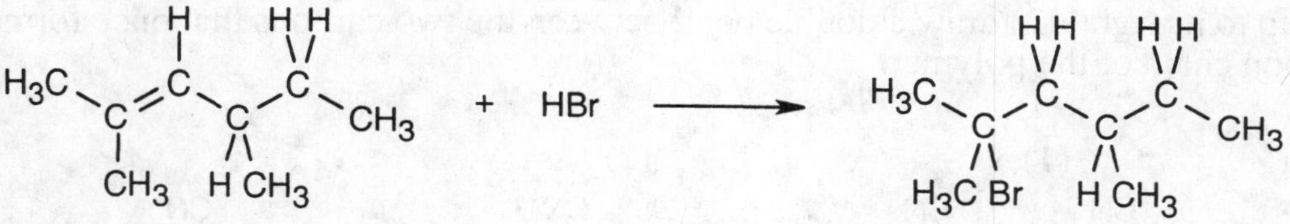

13.13

(a)

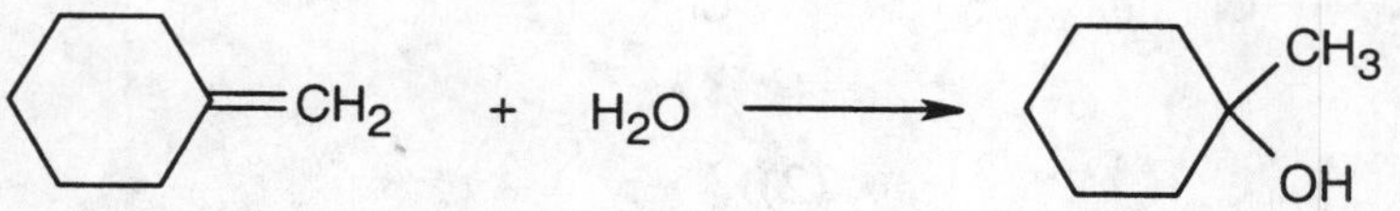

(b)

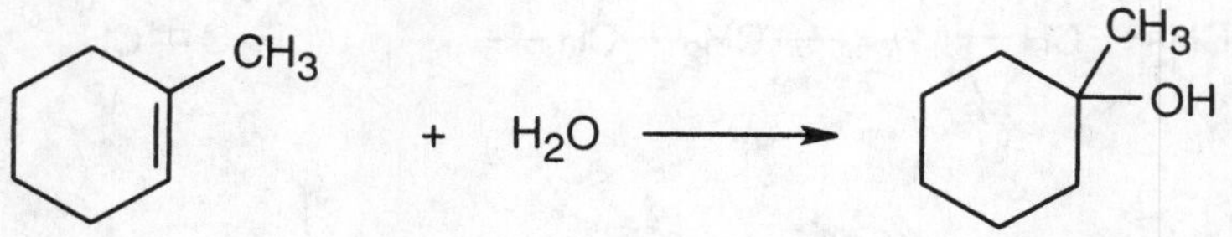

13.14

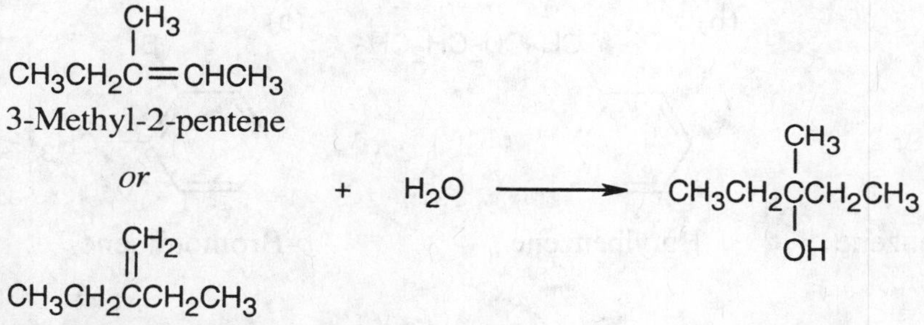

3-Methyl-2-pentene *or* 2-Ethyl-1-butene

13.15

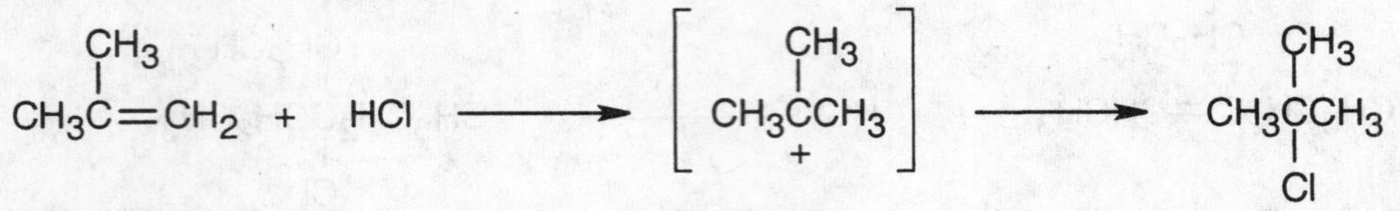

2-Methylpropene | carbocation intermediate | 2-Chloro-2-methylpropane

13.16 To draw a vinyl polymer: (1) Orient the monomer unit so that the CH_2= end is on the left. (2) Draw the functional group(s) at the other end of the molecule pointing up (or up and down). (3) Break the double bond, and draw a single bond extending from each carbon. (4) Connect a monomer unit to each of the new bonds.

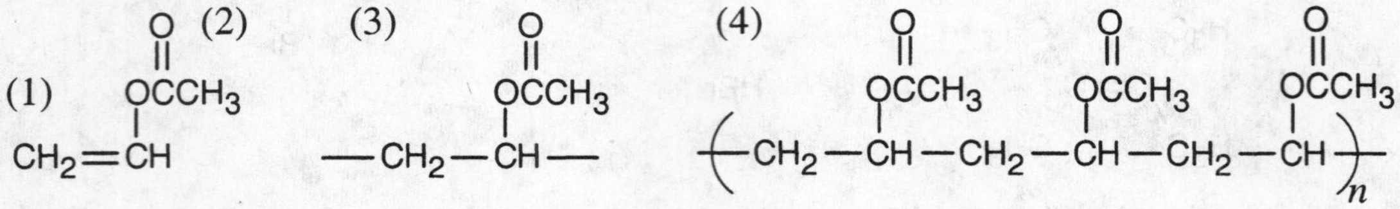

13.17 Reverse the steps in the previous problem to identify the monomer unit of a polymer. (1) Break the bond between the carbon containing the functional group(s) and the —CH_2—. group to its right. (2) draw a double bond between the two carbons that once formed the carbon chain of the polymer.

(a)

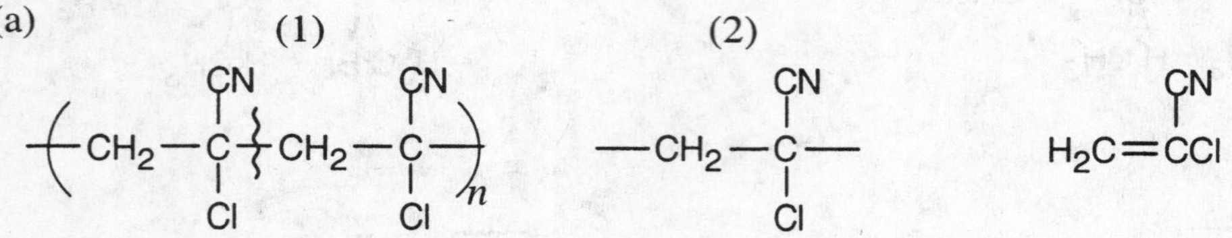

(b)

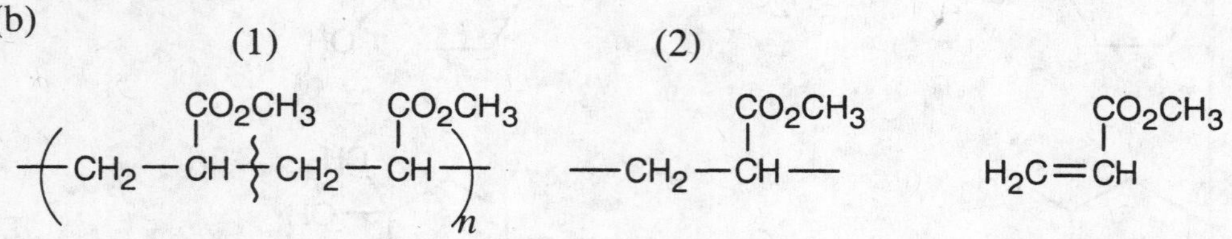

13.18

(a)

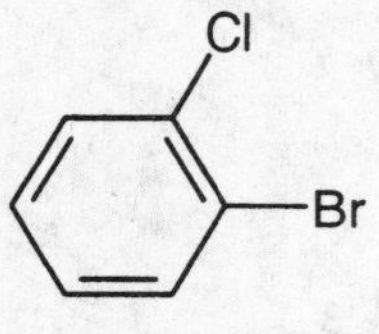

o-Bromochlorobenzene

(b)

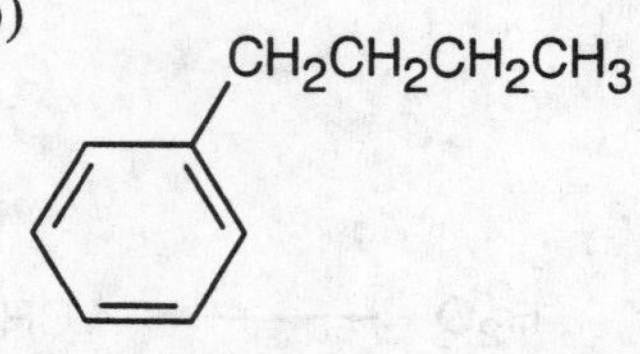

Butylbenzene

(c)

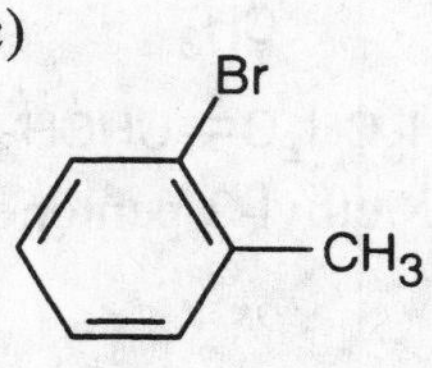

o-Bromotoluene

13.19

(a)

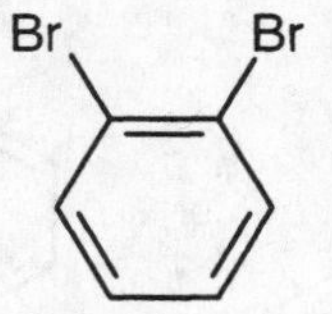

o-Dibromobenzene

(b)

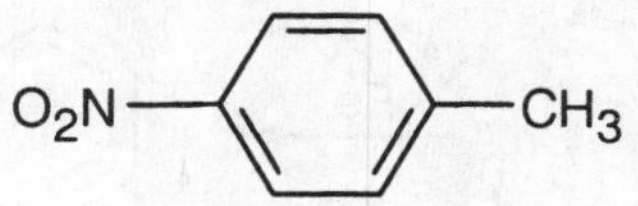

p-Nitrotoluene

(c)

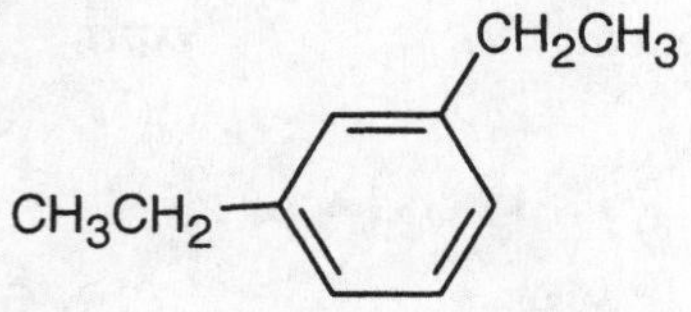

m-Diethylbenzene

(d)

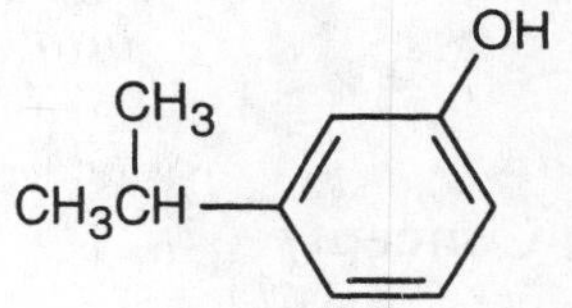

m-Isopropylphenol

13.20

(a)

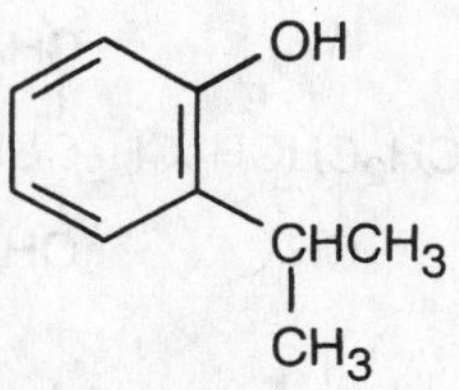

o-Isopropylphenol

(b)

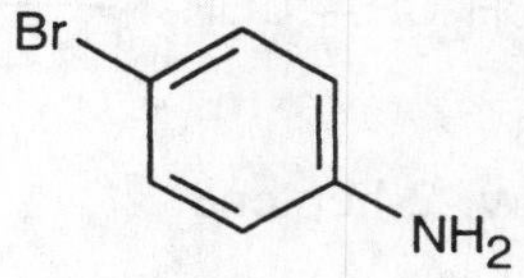

p-Bromoaniline

13.21

(a)

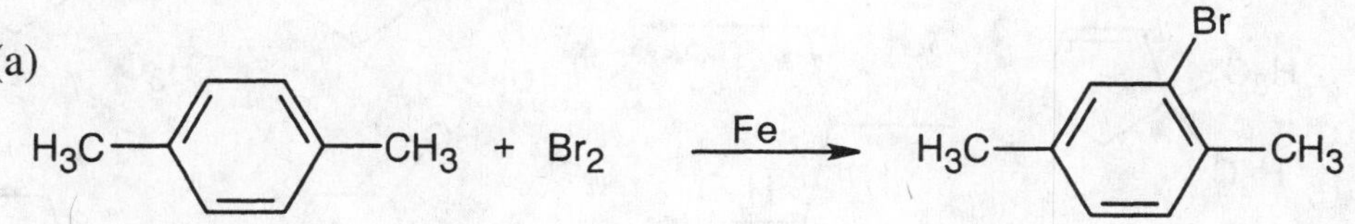

(b)

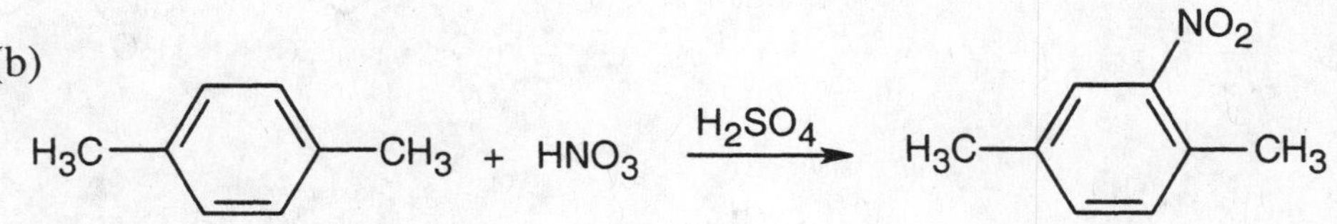

(c)

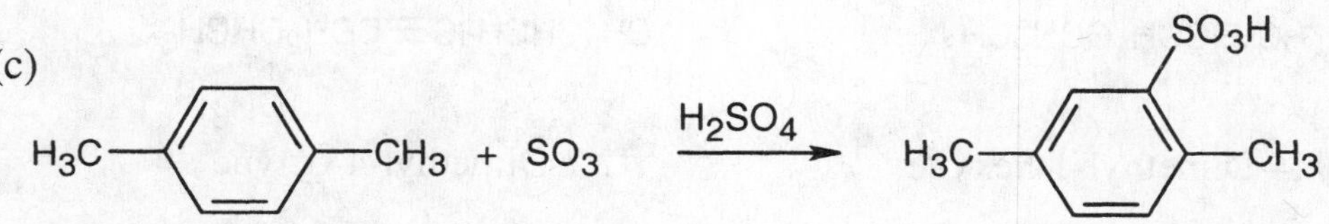

13.22

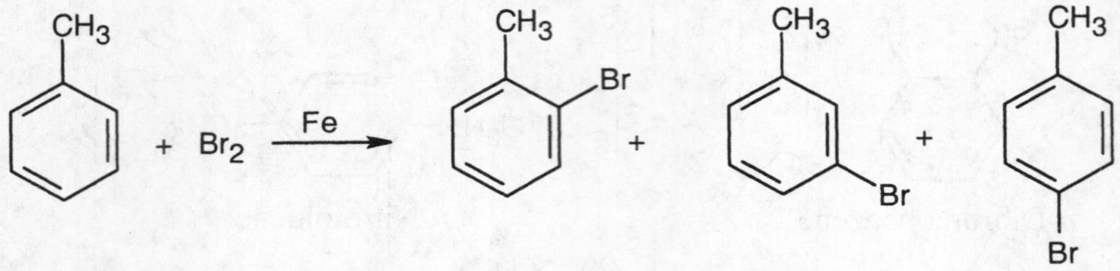

ortho *meta* *para*

Understanding Key Concepts

13.23

(a)

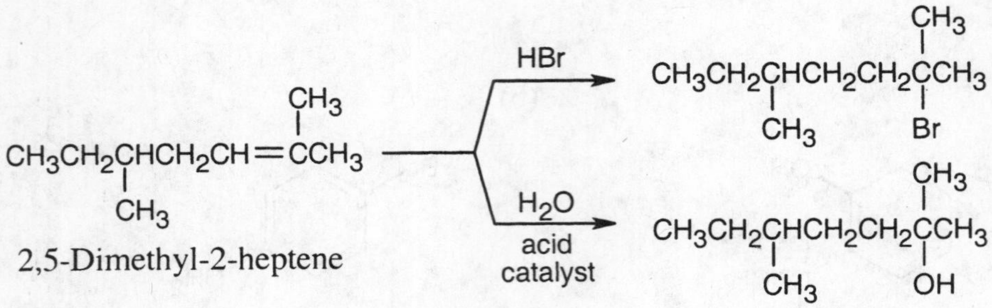

2,5-Dimethyl-2-heptene

(b)

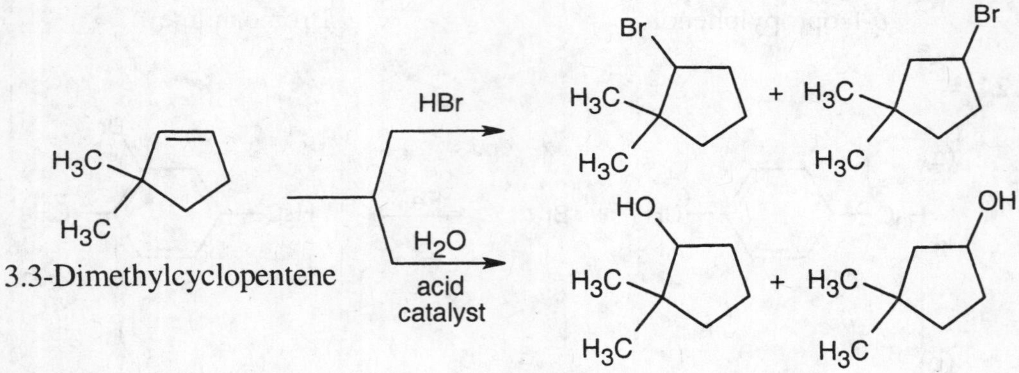

3.3-Dimethylcyclopentene

13.24

(a)

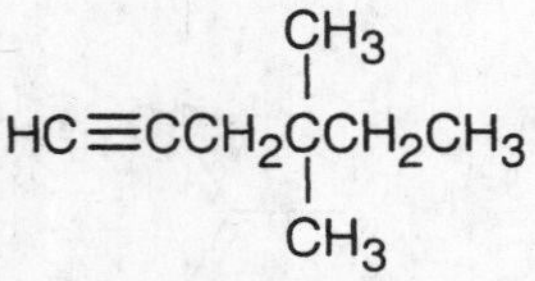

4,4-Dimethyl-1-hexyne

(b)

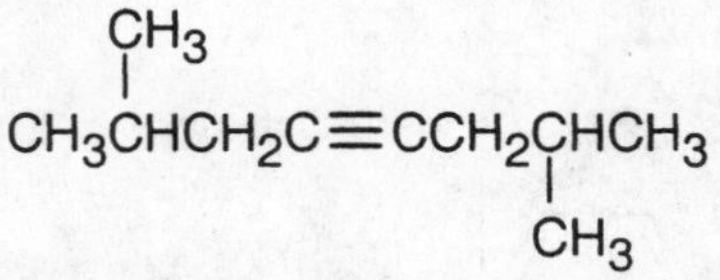

2,7-Dimethyl-4-octyne

13.25

(a)

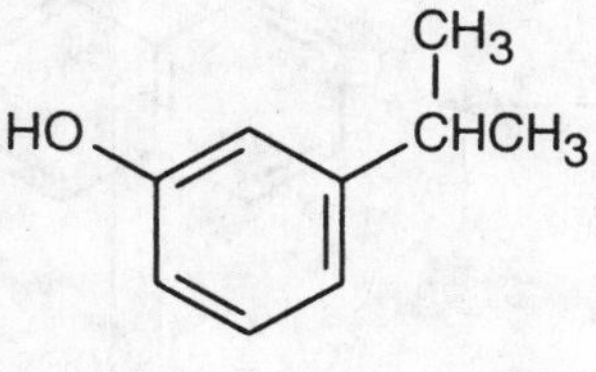

m-Isopropylphenol

(b)

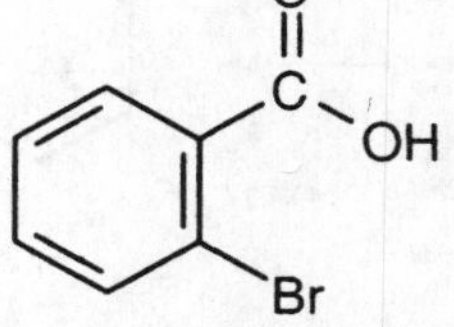

o-Bromobenzoic acid

13.26

(a)

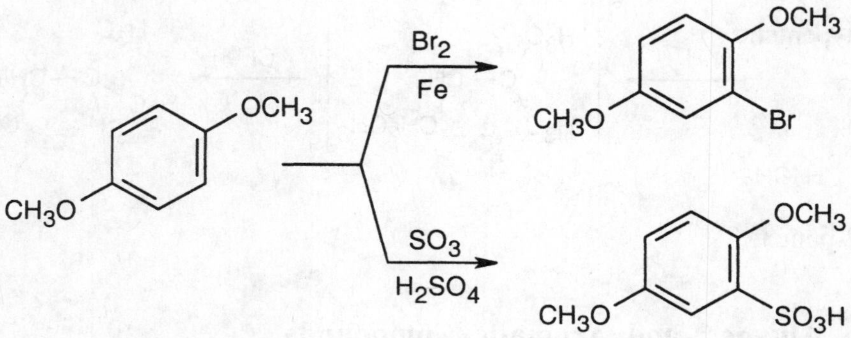

(b)

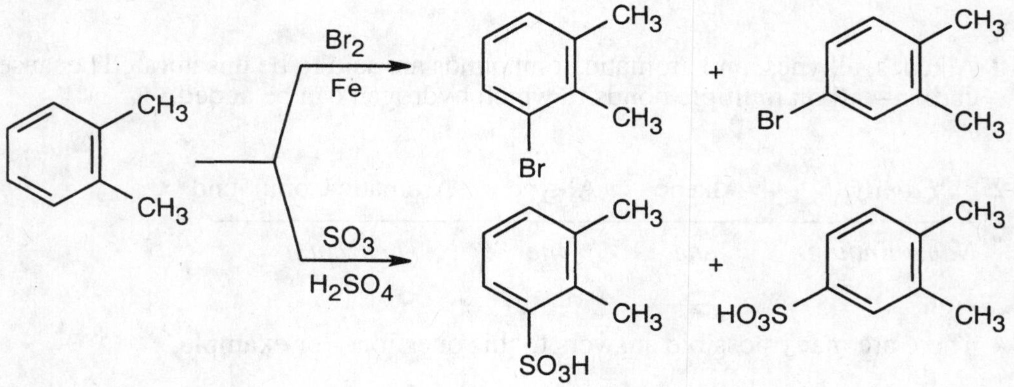

13.27

(a)

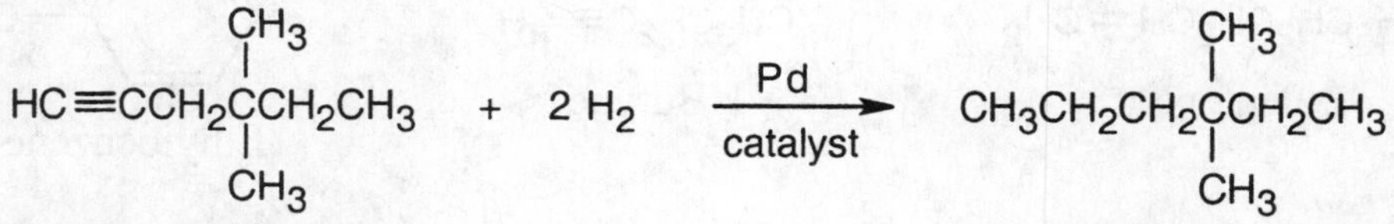

4,4-Dimethyl-1-hexyne

3,3-Dimethylhexane

(b)

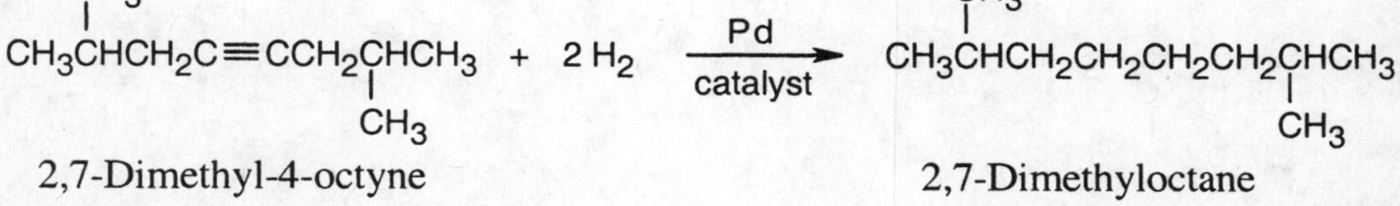

2,7-Dimethyl-4-octyne

2,7-Dimethyloctane

13.28

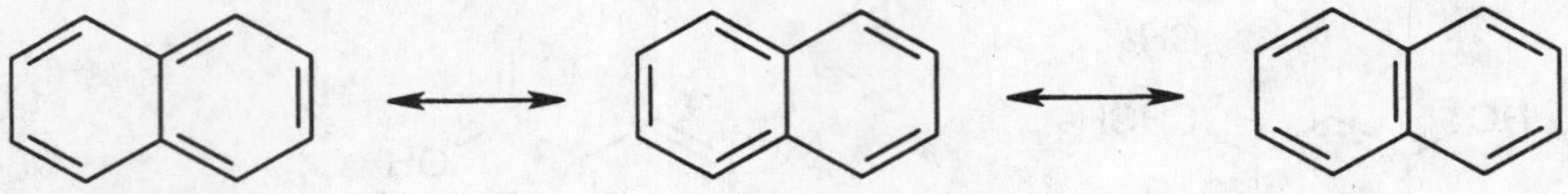

13.29

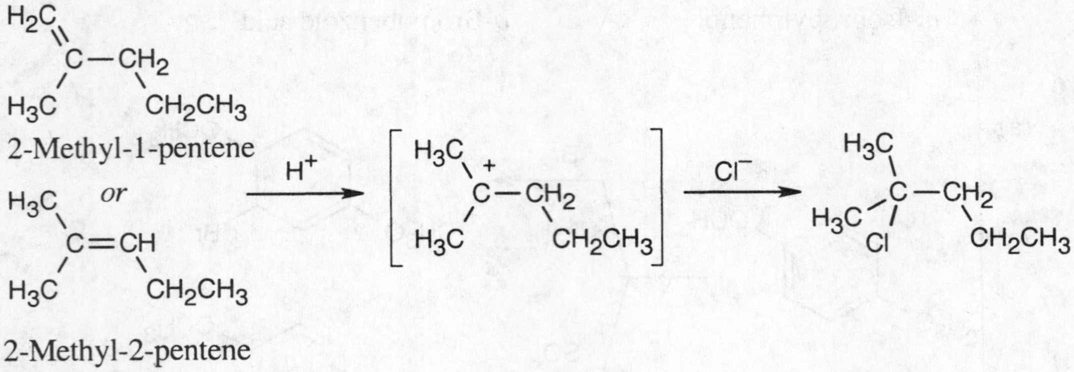
H₂C
C−CH₂
H₃C
CH₂CH₃
2-Methyl-1-pentene
or
H₃C
C=CH
H₃C
CH₂CH₃
2-Methyl-2-pentene
H⁺
H₃C
+
C−CH₂
H₃C
CH₂CH₃
Cl⁻
H₃C
C−CH₂
H₃C
Cl
CH₂CH₃

Naming Alkenes, Alkynes, and Aromatic Compounds

13.30 Alkenes, alkynes, and aromatic compounds are said to be unsaturated because they have carbon–carbon multiple bonds to which hydrogen can be added.

13.32

Family:	Alkene	Alkyne	Aromatic Compound
Name Ending:	*-ene*	*-yne*	*-benzene*

13.34 There are many possible answers to this question. For example,

(a) $CH_3CH_2CH_2CH{=}CH_2$

1-Pentene

(b) $CH_3CH_2C{\equiv}CH$

1-Butyne

(c)

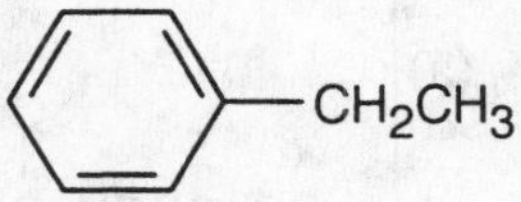
CH₂CH₃

Ethylbenzene

13.36

(a)

$CH_3CH_2CH_2CH{=}CH_2$

1-Pentene

(b)

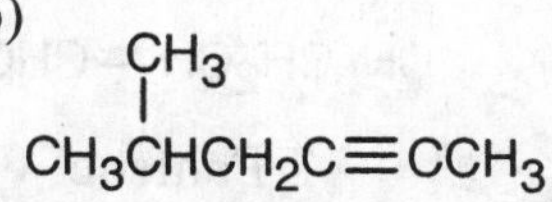

5-Methyl-2-hexyne

(c)

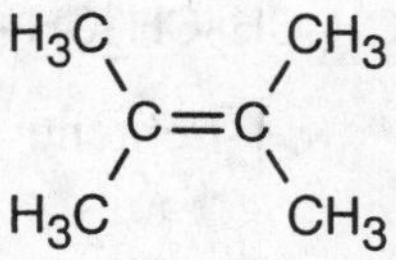

2,3-Dimethyl-2-butene

(d)

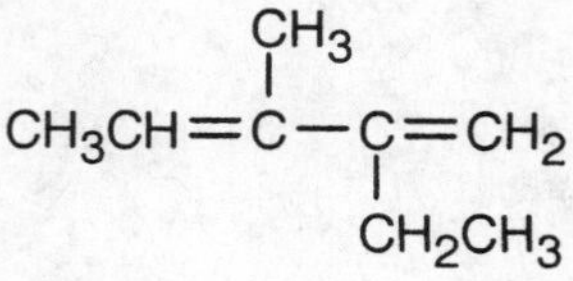

2-Ethyl-3-methyl-1,3-pentadiene

(e)

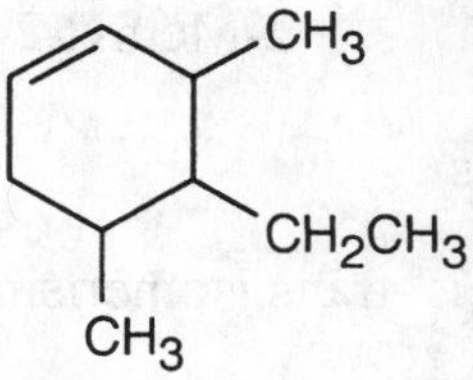

4-Ethyl-3,5-dimethylcyclohexene

(f)

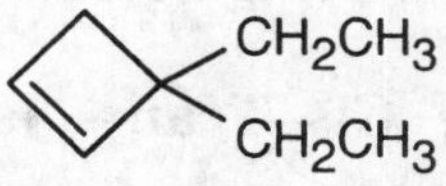

3,3-Diethylcyclobutene

13.38

(a)

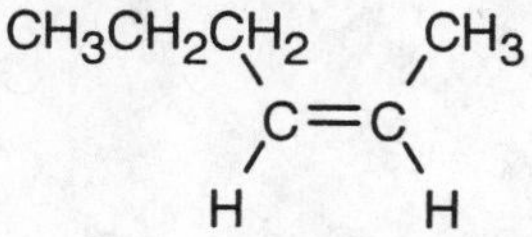

cis-2-Hexene

(b)

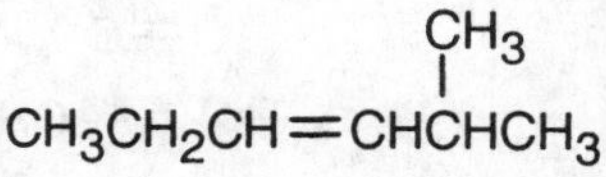

2-Methyl-3-hexene

(c)

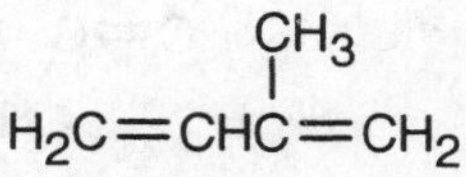

2-Methyl-1,3-butadiene

(d)

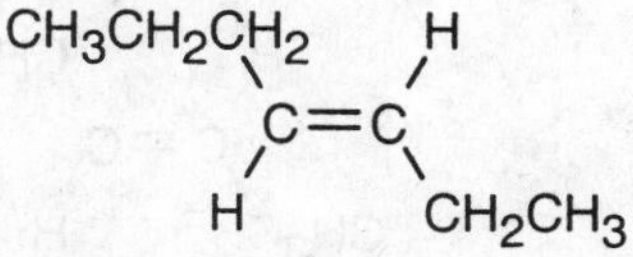

trans-3-Heptene

(e)

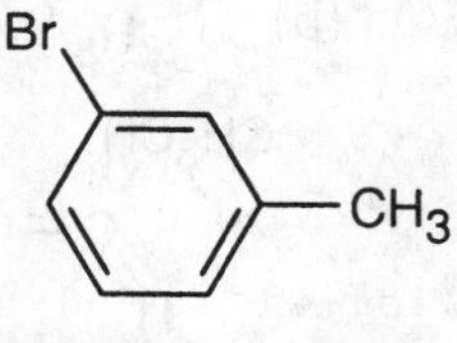

m-Bromotoluene

(f)

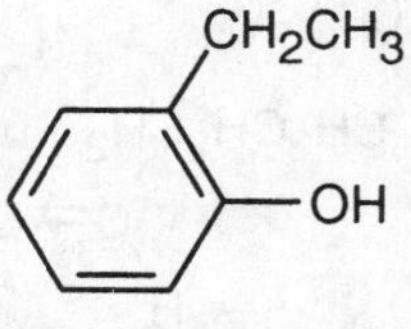

o-Ethylphenol

(g)

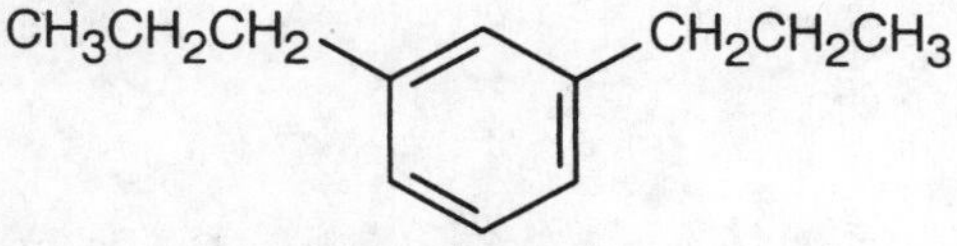

m-Dipropylbenzene

13.40

$CH_3CH_2CH_2C{\equiv}CH$

1-Pentyne

$CH_3CH_2C{\equiv}CCH_3$

2-Pentyne

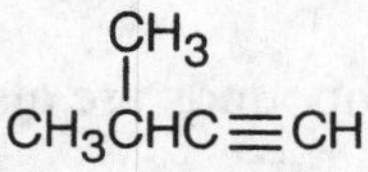

3-Methyl-1-butyne

13.42

$CH_3CH_2CH_2CH{=}CH_2$
1-Pentene

$CH_3CH_2CH{=}CHCH_3$
2-Pentene

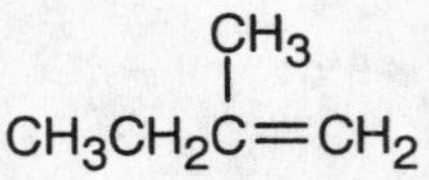
2-Methyl-1-butene

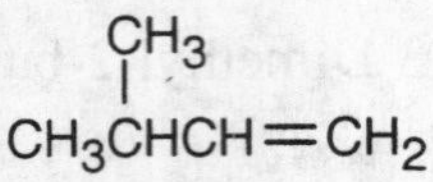
3-Methyl-1-butene

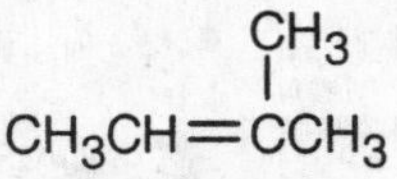
2-Methyl-2-butene

Alkene Cis–Trans Isomers

13.44 For an alkene to show cis–trans isomerism, each carbon of the double bond must be bonded to two different groups.

13.46 Only 2-pentene exists as cis–trans isomers:

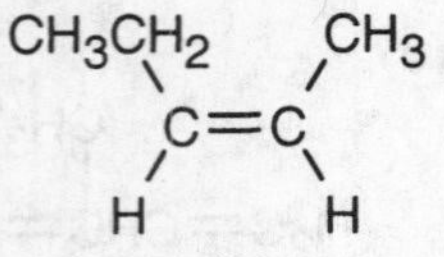
cis-2-Pentene

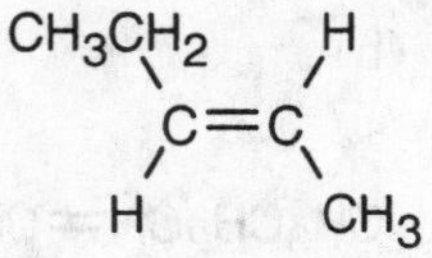
trans-2-Pentene

13.48

(a)
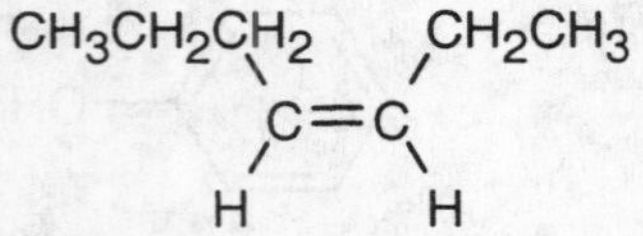
cis-3-Heptene

(b)
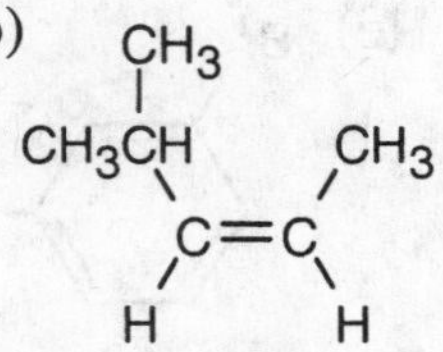
cis-4-Methyl-2-pentene

(c)
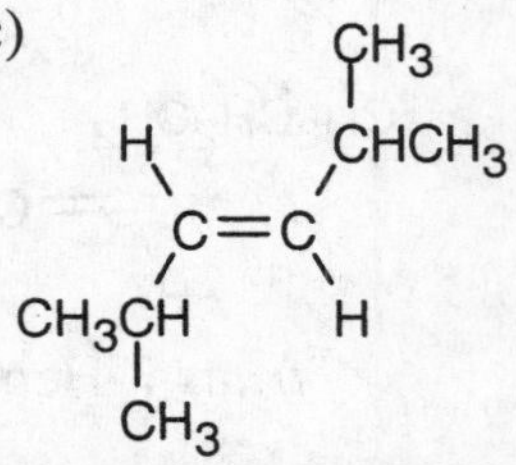
trans-2,5-Dimethyl-3-hexene

13.50 (a) These compounds are identical:

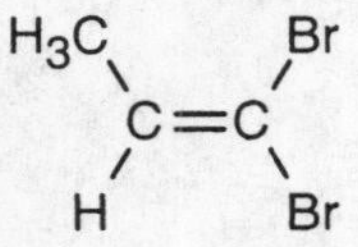
and
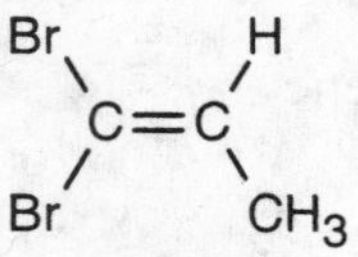

(b) These compounds are also identical:

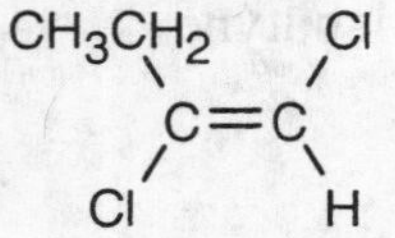
and
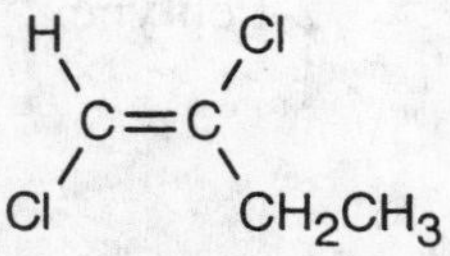

Kinds of Reactions

13.52 In a substitution reaction, two reactants exchange parts to give two new products. In an addition reaction, two reactants add together to form a single product, with no atoms left over.

13.54 The conversion of 2-methyl-2-pentene to 1-hexene would be a rearrangement because it is the conversion of a single reactant into a single product by the reorganization of bonds.

13.56

(a)

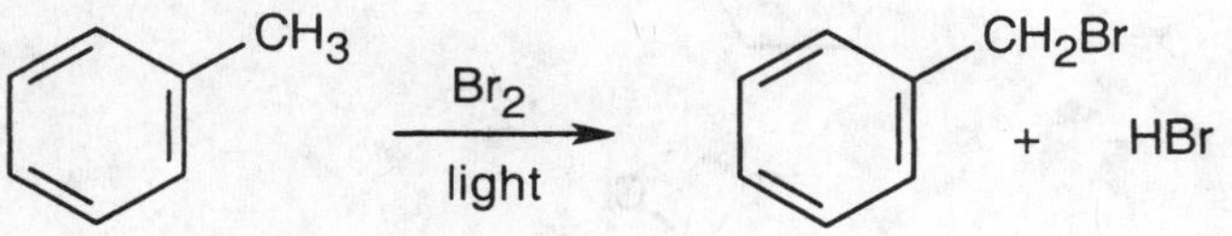
CH3
Br2
light
CH2Br
+ HBr

This reaction is a substitution because two reactants exchange parts to give two new products.

(b)

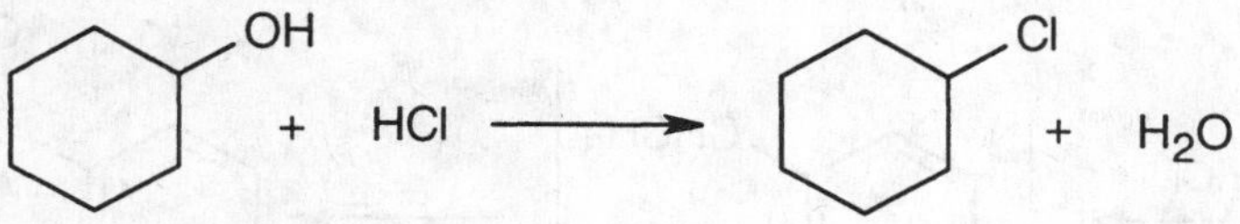
OH
+ HCl
Cl
+ H2O

This is also a substitution reaction.

Reactions of Alkenes and Alkynes

13.58

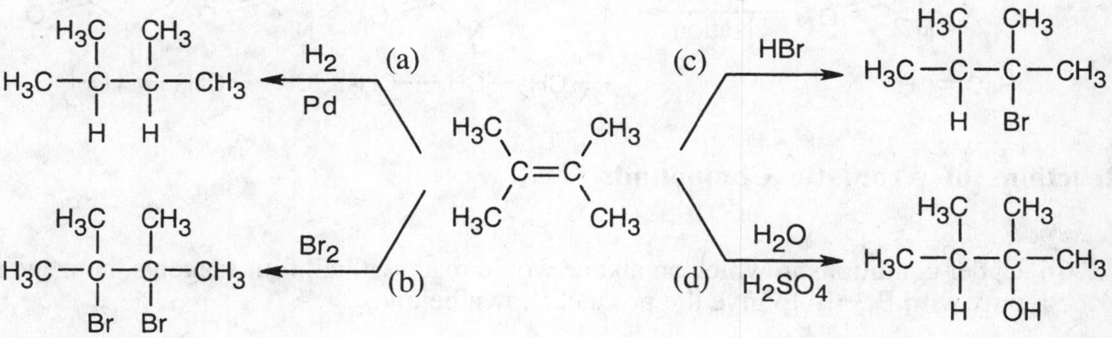
H2
Pd
(a)
Br2
(b)
HBr
(c)
H2O
H2SO4
(d)

13.60

(a)

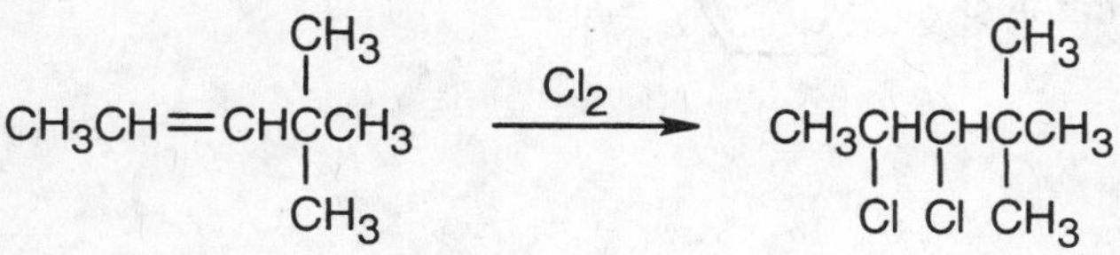
CH3CH=CHCCH3
Cl2
CH3CHCHCCH3

(b)

$$CH_3CH{=}CH_2 \xrightarrow[\text{Pd catalyst}]{H_2} CH_3CH_2CH_3$$

(c)

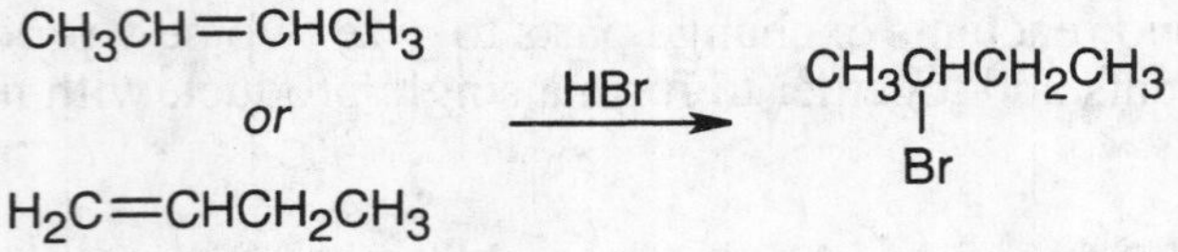
CH3CH=CHCH3
or
H2C=CHCH2CH3
HBr
CH3CHCH2CH3
Br

(d)

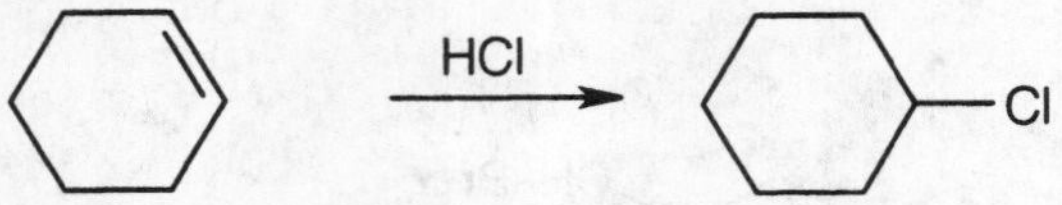
HCl
Cl

(e)

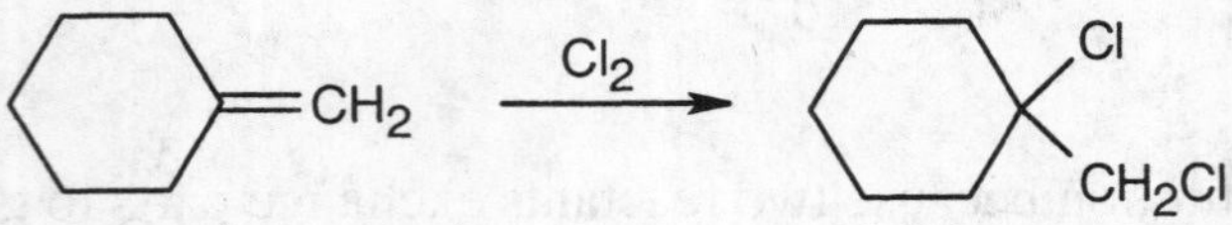
CH2
Cl2
Cl
CH2Cl

13.62

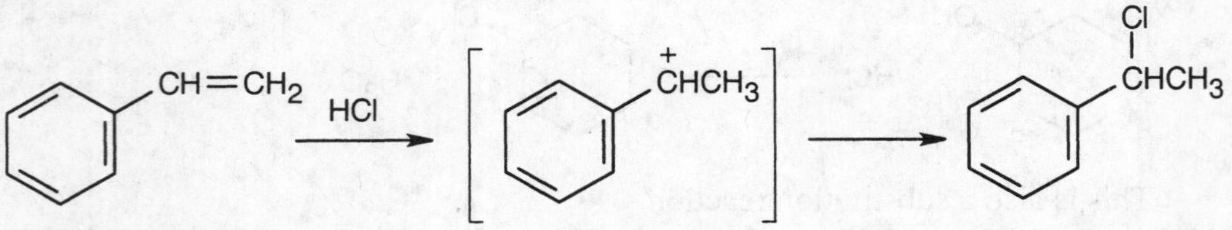
CH=CH2
HCl
+
CHCH3
Cl
CHCH3

13.64

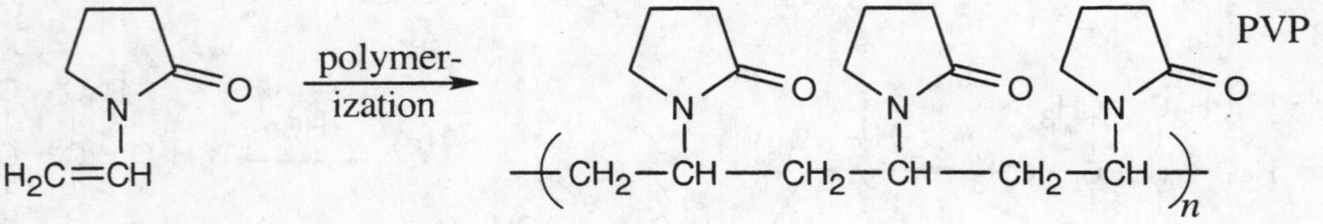
N
O
H2C=CH
polymer-
ization
PVP
CH2—CH — CH2—CH — CH2—CH
n

Reactions of Aromatic Compounds

13.66 Under conditions in which an alkene would react with all four reagents, benzene reacts only with Br_2 (b) to give the product shown below.

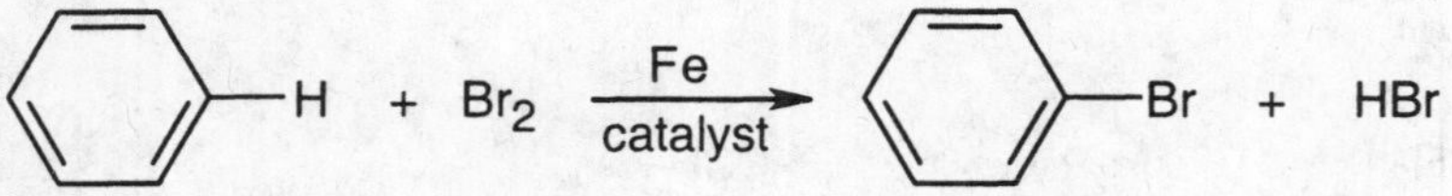
H
+
Br2
Fe
catalyst
Br
+
HBr

13.68

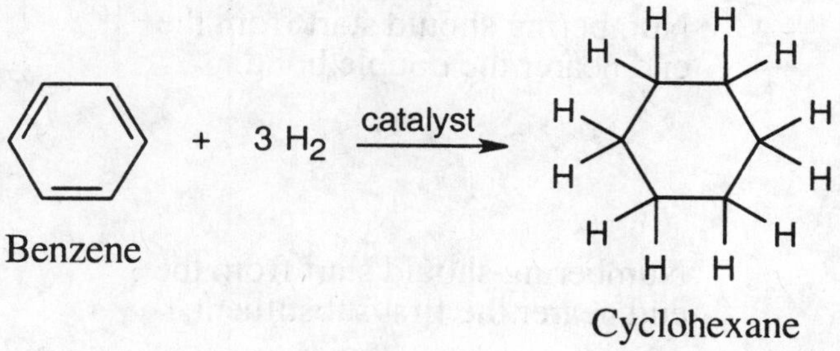
+ 3 H_2
catalyst
Benzene
Cyclohexane

Applications

13.70 The rod cells are responsible for vision in dim light, and the cone cells are responsible for vision in bright light and for color vision.

13.72

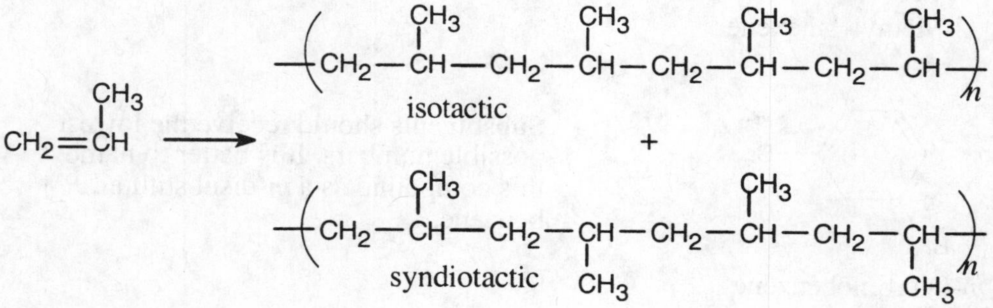
isotactic
+
syndiotactic

13.74 The body attempts to excrete benz[*a*]pyrene by converting it into a water-soluble diol epoxide, which can react with cellular DNA and lead to mutations or cancer.

13.76 Tetrabromofluorescein is colored because it contains many alternating single and double bonds. Since tetrabromofluorescein is purple, it must absorb yellow light. (Yellow is the complement of purple.)

General Questions and Problems

13.78

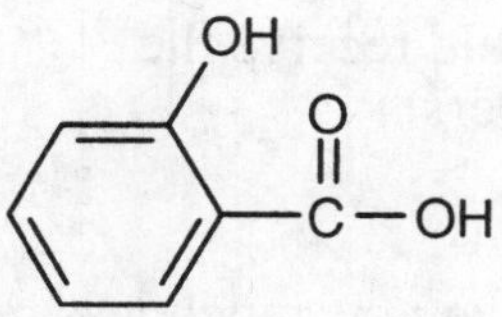

Salicylic acid

13.80 *Structure* — *Error*

(a) $CH_3CH{=}CHCH_2CH(CH_3)CH_3$ (drawn with CH_3 on C-5)

5-Methyl-2-hexene

Numbering should start from the end nearer the double bond.

(b) $CH_3C(CH_3)_2C{\equiv}CCH_2CH_3$ (drawn with two CH_3 groups on C-2)

2,2-Dimethyl-3-hexyne

Numbering should start from the end nearer the first substituent.

(c) $CH_3CH_2CH_2CH_2C(CH_3){=}CH_2$

2-Methyl-1-hexene

The longest chain containing the double bond should be used as the base name.

(d)

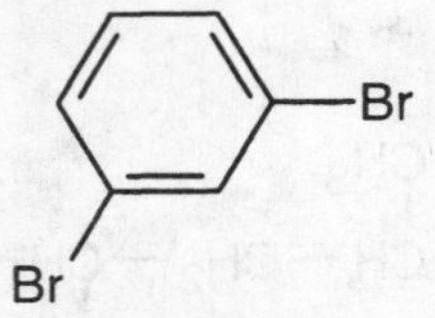

m-Dibromobenzene
(1,3-Dibromobenzene)

Substituents should receive the lowest possible numbers. It is better to name this compound as a *m*-disubstituted benzene.

(e)

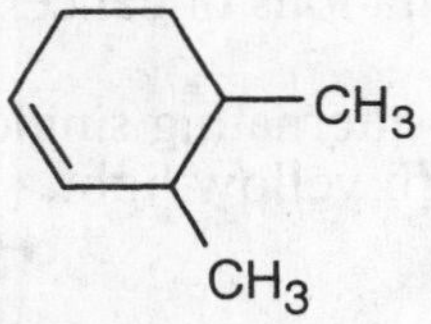

3,4-Dimethylcyclohexene

The double bond receives the lowest number. (For cyclic alkenes, the double bond receives no number but is understood to be between carbons 1 and 2.)

(f) $H_2C{=}CHC(CH_3){=}CHCH_3$

3-Methyl-1,3-pentadiene

The double bonds should receive the lowest possible numbers.

13.82 The same reasoning used in Problem 13.81 applies here. Benzene is much less reactive than alkenes. Thus, treatment of a sample from each bottle with an alkene addition reagent such as Br_2 gives a rapid reaction with cyclohexene but no reaction with benzene.

13.84

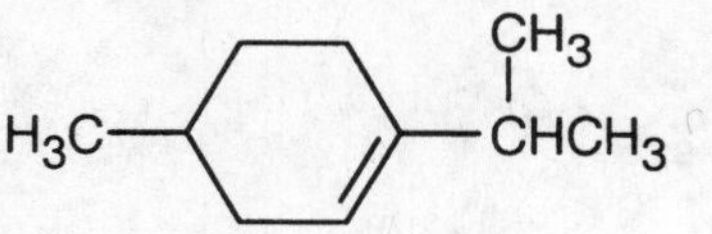
H3C
CH3
CHCH3

Menthene

13.86

(a)

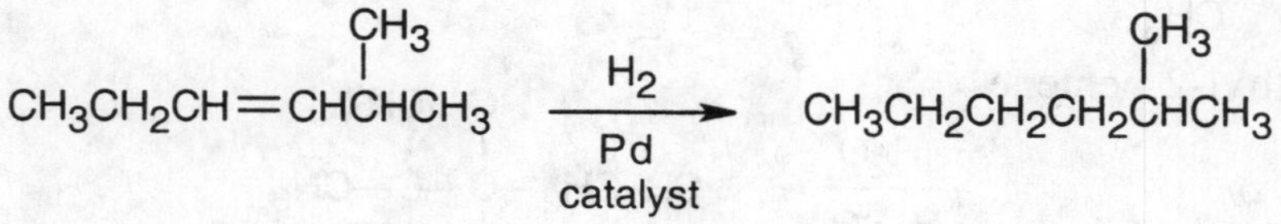
CH3CH2CH=CHCHCH3
CH3
H2
Pd
catalyst
CH3CH2CH2CH2CHCH3
CH3

(b)

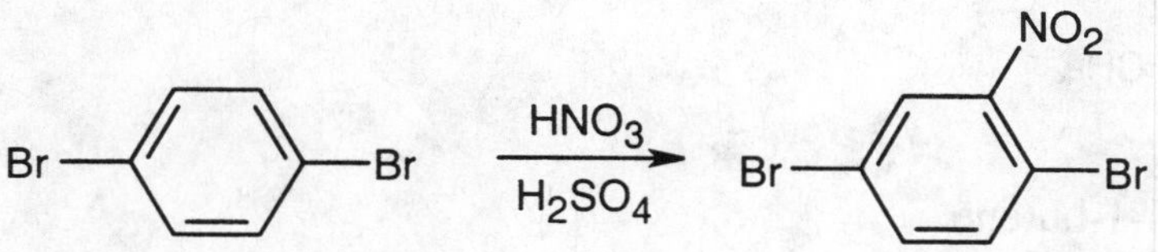
Br
Br
HNO3
H2SO4
NO2
Br
Br

(c)

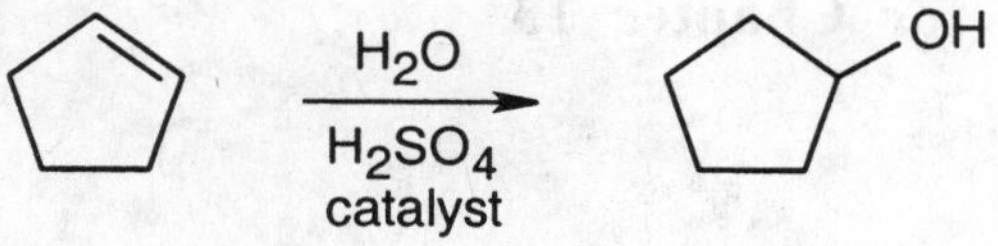
H2O
H2SO4
catalyst
OH

(d)

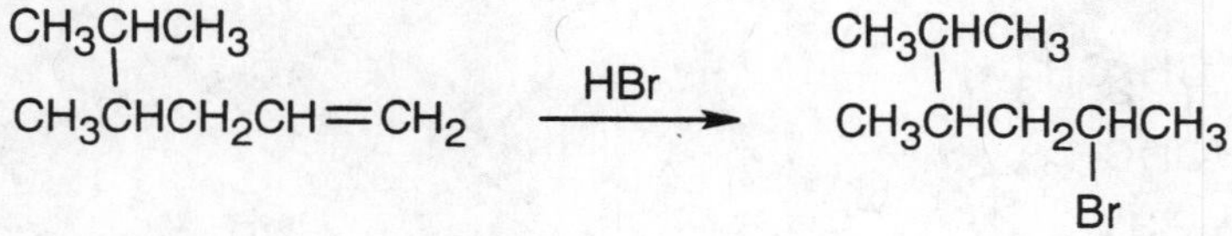
CH3CHCH3
CH3CHCH2CH=CH2
HBr
CH3CHCH3
CH3CHCH2CHCH3
Br

(e)

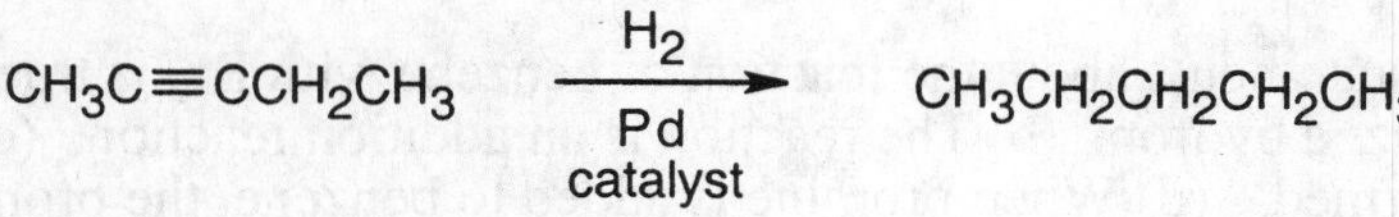
CH3C≡CCH2CH3
H2
Pd
catalyst
CH3CH2CH2CH2CH3

(f)

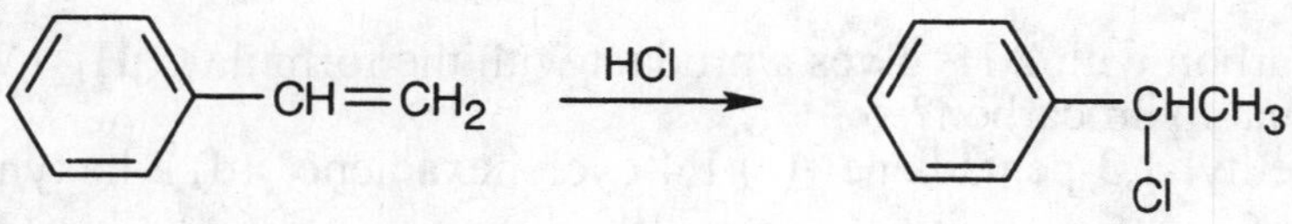
CH=CH2
HCl
CHCH3
Cl

13.88 In contrast to benzene, naphthalene is a solid at room temperature because it has a greater molecular weight and its London forces are greater.

13.90

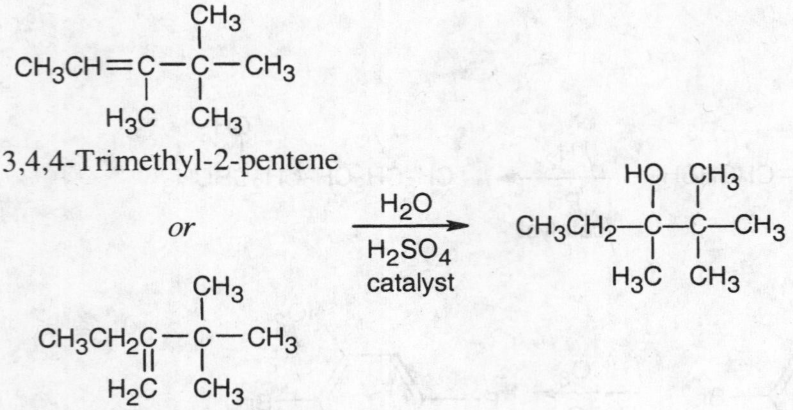
CH3
CH3CH=C—C—CH3
H3C CH3
or
H2O
H2SO4
catalyst
HO CH3
CH3CH2—C—C—CH3
H3C CH3
CH3
CH3CH2C—C—CH3
H2C CH3

3,4,4-Trimethyl-2-pentene

2-Ethyl-3,3-dimethyl-1-butene

Self-Test for Chapter 13

Multiple Choice

1. Which of the following polymers is a hydrocarbon?
(a) Teflon (b) poly(vinyl chloride) (c) Lucite (d) polystyrene

2. 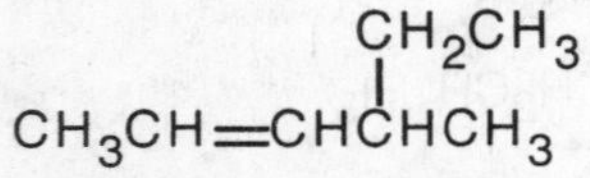
CH2CH3
CH3CH=CHCHCH3

The name of this compound is
(a) 3-methyl-4-hexene (b) 4-methyl-2-hexene (c) 2-ethyl-3-pentene (d) 3-ethyl-2-pentene

3. Which of the following statements about the reaction of benzene with Br_2 is true?
(a) The reaction is catalyzed by iron. (b) The reaction is an addition reaction. (c) Two different products are formed. (d) When bromine is added to benzene, the bromine color disappears.

4. Reaction of a hydrocarbon with 2 H_2 gives a product with the formula C_6H_{12}. Which of the following is the original hydrocarbon?
(a) benzene (b) 3-methyl-1,3-pentadiene (c) 1,4-cyclohexadiene (d) 2-hexyne

5. Which of the following molecules shows cis–trans isomerism?
(a) 2-hexene (b) 2-hexyne (c) 2-methyl-2-pentene (d) 2-ethyl-1-hexene

6. Which of the following statements about carbocations is true?
(a) A carbocation has seven electrons in its outer shell. (b) Two different carbocations can be formed in the reaction of HBr with 3-hexene. (c) A carbocation is an intermediate in the reaction of HBr with an alkene. (d) Carbocations are stable ions.

7. How many isomers with the formula C_5H_8 can be drawn? (Don't include isomers with rings or cis–trans isomers.)
(a) 5 (b) 7 (c) 9 (d) 11

8. Which of the following is probably not a monomer in a polymerization reaction?
(a) $H_2C{=}CHCN$ (b) $H_2C{=}CHCH_3$ (c) $CH_3CH{=}C(CH_3)_2$ (d) $H_2C{=}CCl_2$

9. If toluene reacted with one mole of Cl_2, and each of the products of the reaction reacted with one mole of Cl_2, how many different products could be formed? (Not all of these can be formed in the laboratory.)
(a) 3 (b) 4 (c) 5 (d) 6

10. Which of the following alkenes is not a starting material for 3-bromo-3-methylhexane?
(a) 2-ethyl-1-pentene (b) 3-methyl-2-hexene (c) 3-methyl-3-hexene (d) 4-methyl-2-hexene

Sentence Completion

1. The name of $CH_3CH_2CH_2CH_2C{\equiv}CCH_3$ is _____.

2. Addition of hydrogen to an alkene or alkyne is known as _____.

3. A benzene ring with substituents at the 1 and 4 positions is said to be _____ disubstituted.

4. In the addition of HX to an alkene, the H becomes attached to the carbon that already has _____ H's, and the X becomes attached to the carbon that has _____ H's.

5. Ethanol can be produced by the _____ of ethylene.

6. In the nitration of benzene, H_2SO_4 is used as a _____.

7. The intermediate formed during the addition of HBr to an alkene is called a _____.

8. Compounds with double or triple bonds are said to be _____.

9. _____ is another name for methylbenzene.

10. The reaction of Br_2 with benzene is an example of a _____ reaction.

11. _____ _____ _____ are aromatic compounds consisting of two or more rings joined together by a common bond.

12. Simple alkenes are made by _____ _____ of natural gas and petroleum.

True or False

1. Cis–trans isomers have identical physical properties.
2. Addition of one equivalent of H_2 to an alkyne yields an alkene.
3. Aromatic compounds are less reactive than alkenes.
4. The product of addition of HBr to 1-butene is 1-bromobutane.
5. The reaction of HBr with an alkene is known as halogenation.
6. A compound with the formula C_4H_6 can be either an alkyne or an alkene.
7. 1-Methylcyclohexene can exhibit cis–trans isomerism.
8. Mixing an alkene with water causes the hydration of the double bond.
9. Addition of HBr to an alkene is a two-step reaction.
10. Benzene and 1-butene react with Br_2 under the same reaction conditions.
11. Only aromatic compounds with more than one ring are carcinogenic.
12. Two different compounds result from the reaction of HBr with 2-pentene.

Match each entry on the left with its partner on the right.

1. HNO_3, H_2SO_4	(a) Alkene without cis–trans isomers
2. H_2O, H_2SO_4	(b) Used to hydrogenate an alkene
3. $CH_3C{\equiv}CH$	(c) Polycyclic aromatic hydrocarbon
4. Hydroxybenzene	(d) Addition reaction
5. H_2, Pd	(e) Used to nitrate aromatic compounds
6. $(CH_3)_2CH^+$	(f) Substitution reaction
7. Propene + Br_2	(g) Exhibits cis–trans isomerism
8. Naphthalene	(h) Teflon monomer
9. 2-Methylpropene	(i) Alkyne
10. Benzene + Br_2	(j) Phenol
11. 2-Butene	(k) Used to hydrate an alkene
12. $CF_2{=}CF_2$	(l) Carbocation

Chapter 14 – Some Compounds with Oxygen, Sulfur, or a Halogen

Chapter Outline

I. Compounds containing oxygen (Sections 14.1–14.9).
  A. Introduction (Section 14.1).
    1. In all of these compounds, oxygen forms a single bond to either carbon or hydrogen.
    2. Alcohols (R—OH), phenols (Ar—OH) and ethers (R—O—R) are examples of these compounds.
      a. Many alcohols resemble water in their physical properties.
      b. Alcohols (and phenols) can form hydrogen bonds, which raise their boiling points.
  B. Alcohols (Sections 14.2–14.5).
    1. Common alcohols are methanol, ethanol, isopropanol, ethylene glycol and glycerol (Section 14.2).
    2. Naming alcohols (Section 14.3).
      a. Find the longest chain containing the hydroxyl group, and name the chain by replacing the -e ending of the corresponding alkane with *-ol*.
      b. Number the carbon atoms in the main chain, beginning at the end nearer the –OH group.
      c. Write the name.
        i. Place the number of the —OH group immediately before the parent compound name.
        ii. Number all other substituents according to their positions and list them alphabetically.
      d. Diols are often known as glycols.
      e. Alcohols can be classified according to the number of substituents bonded to the –OH carbon.
        i. If there is one substituent (RCH_2OH), the alcohol is primary.
        ii. If there are two substituents (R_2CHOH), the alcohol is secondary.
        iii. If there are three substituents (R_3COH), the alcohol is tertiary.
    3. Properties of alcohols (Section 14.4).
      a. Hydrogen bonding makes alcohols higher boiling than other compounds of similar mass.
      b. Hydrogen bonding also makes smaller alcohols miscible with water, as well as with organic solvents.
        i. Alcohols of higher mass aren't soluble.
        ii. Diols (glycols) are even more soluble than alcohols of similar mass.
      c. Alcohols are weak acids.
    4. Reactions of alcohols (Section 14.5).
      a. Dehydration: alcohol $\xrightarrow{H_2SO_4}$ alkene + H_2O
      If more than one product is possible, the product with the more substituted double bond will be favored.
      b. Oxidation:
        i. Primary alcohol $\xrightarrow{[O]}$ aldehyde $\xrightarrow{[O]}$ carboxylic acid
        ii. Secondary alcohol $\xrightarrow{[O]}$ ketone
        iii. Tertiary alcohol $\xrightarrow{[O]}$ no reaction

C. Phenols (Sections 14.6–14.7).
  1. Properties of phenols (Section 14.6).
    a. Phenols are named by replacing *-benzene* with *-phenol.*
    b. The properties of phenols are influenced by hydrogen bonding.
      i. Many phenols are water-soluble.
      ii. Phenols are higher boiling than alkylbenzenes.
    c. Phenols are commonly used as disinfectants.
  2. Acidity of alcohols and phenols (Section 14.7).
    a. Alcohols and phenols are weak acids.
      i. Methanol and ethanol are as acidic as water.
      ii. Dissociation of alcohols in water, or reaction of alcohols with sodium metal, produces an alkoxide anion (^-OR).
    b. Phenols are more acidic than water.
      i. K_a of phenol is 1.0×10^{-10}.
      ii. Phenols are soluble in dilute aqueous NaOH.

D. Ethers (Section 14.8).
  1. Names and properties of ethers.
    a. Ethers have two organic groups bonded to the same oxygen.
    b. Ethers are named by identifying the two groups and adding the word "ether."
      i. Some cyclic ethers have common names (ethylene oxide, 1,4-dioxane).
      ii. An —OR group is an alkoxy group.
    c. Properties of ethers.
      i. Ethers are low-boiling and don't form hydrogen bonds.
      ii. Ethers are unreactive.
      iii. Ethers are good solvents for organic compounds.
      iv. Ethers are volatile and flammable.
      v. Ethers are only slightly soluble in water.
      vi. Ethers form explosive peroxides on standing.
  2. Some common ethers.
    a. Diethyl ether is commonly used as a solvent but was formerly an anesthetic.
    b. Ether groups occur in many essential oils.

II. Thiols and disulfides (Section 14.9).
  A. Thiols.
    1. Thiols are the sulfur analogs of alcohols (R–SH).
    2. Naming thiols is similar to naming alcohols, except that the suffix *–thiol* is added to the parent name.
    3. Thiols are important biologically because they occur in proteins.
    4. Thiols stink!
  B. Disulfides.
    1. Reaction of a thiol with a mild oxidizing agent produces a disulfide (RS—SR).
    2. The reverse reaction occurs when a disulfide is treated with a reducing agent.

III. Halogen-containing compounds (Section 14.10).
  A. Haloalkanes are named by considering the halogen as a substituent on a parent alkane.
  B. A few haloalkanes are named by naming the alkyl group and then naming the halide.
  C. Haloalkanes don't occur frequently in nature but are widely used in industry and agriculture.

Solutions to Chapter 14 Problems

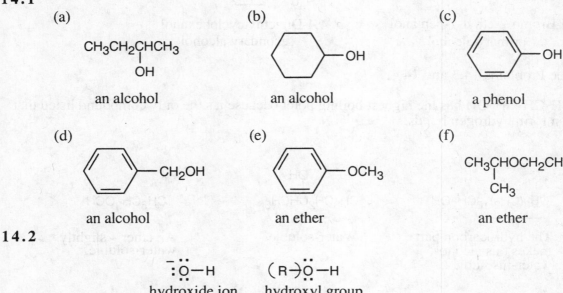

14.1

(a)

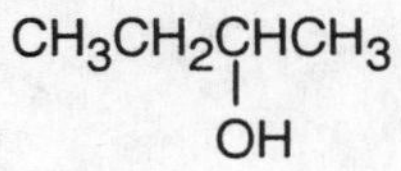

an alcohol

(b)

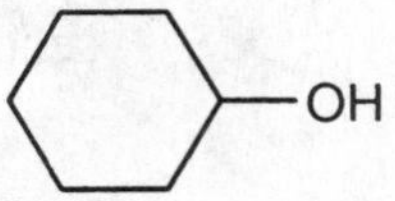

an alcohol

(c)

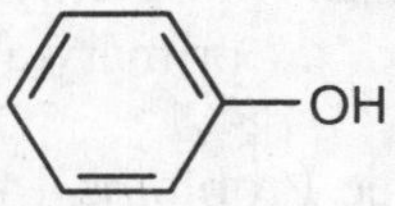

a phenol

(d)

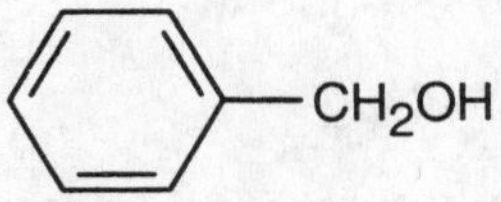

an alcohol

(e)

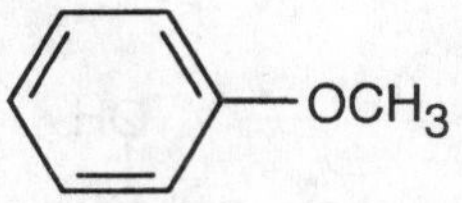

an ether

(f)

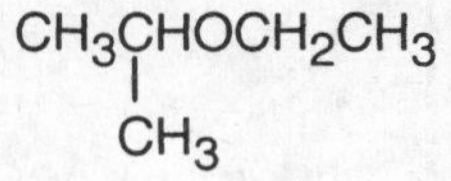

an ether

14.2

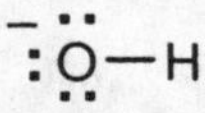

hydroxide ion

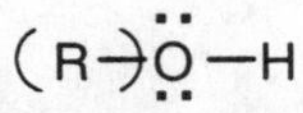

hydroxyl group

A hydroxide ion has three lone electron pairs and a negative charge. A hydroxyl group is an —OH group that is part of an organic molecule.

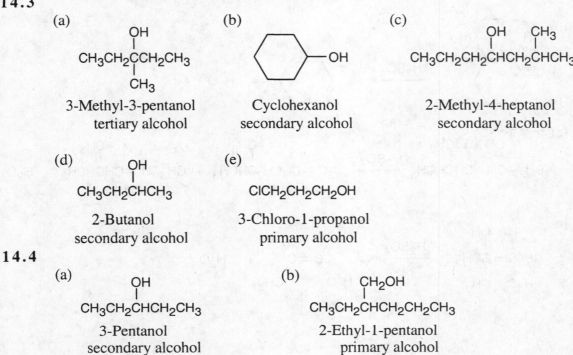

14.3

(a)

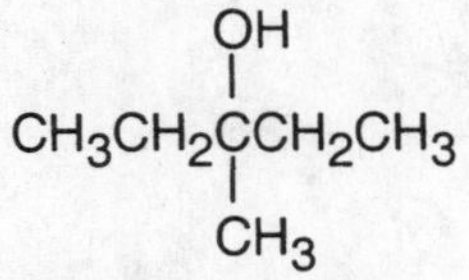

3-Methyl-3-pentanol
tertiary alcohol

(b)

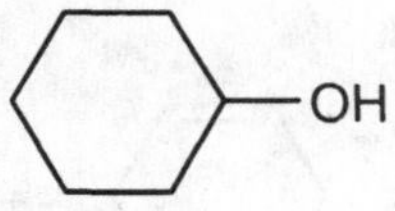

Cyclohexanol
secondary alcohol

(c)

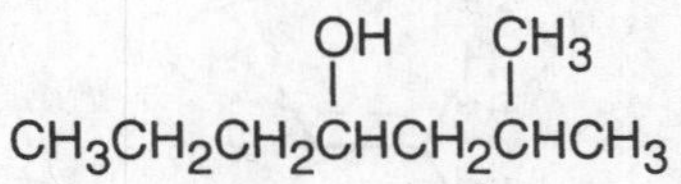

2-Methyl-4-heptanol
secondary alcohol

(d)

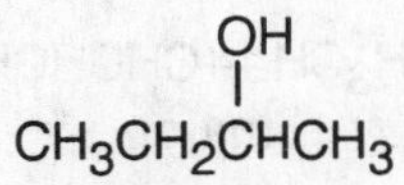

2-Butanol
secondary alcohol

(e)

$ClCH_2CH_2CH_2OH$

3-Chloro-1-propanol
primary alcohol

14.4

(a)

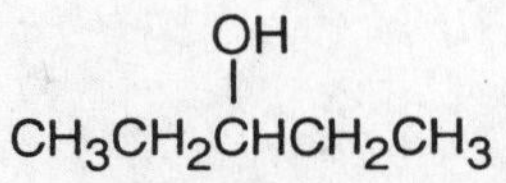

3-Pentanol
secondary alcohol

(b)

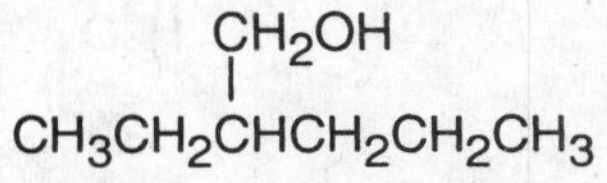

2-Ethyl-1-pentanol
primary alcohol

(c)

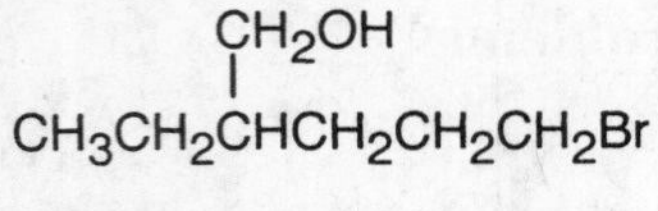

5-Bromo-2-ethyl-1-pentanol
primary alcohol

(d)

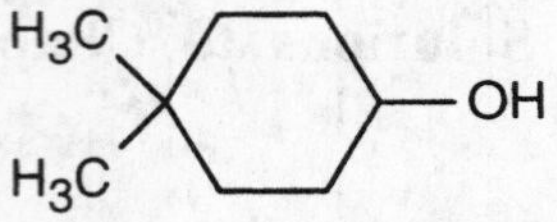

4,4-Dimethylcyclohexanol
secondary alcohol

14.5 See Problems 14.3 and 14.4.

14.6 $CH_3CH_2CH_2OH$ has the highest boiling point because it's the only compound listed that can form hydrogen bonds.

14.7

(a) $CH_3(CH_2)_{10}CH_2OH$

The hydrocarbon part makes this alcohol water-insoluble.

(b)

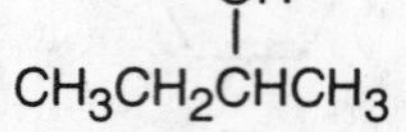

Water-soluble.

(c) $CH_3CH_2OCH_3$

An ether – slightly water-soluble.

14.8

(a)

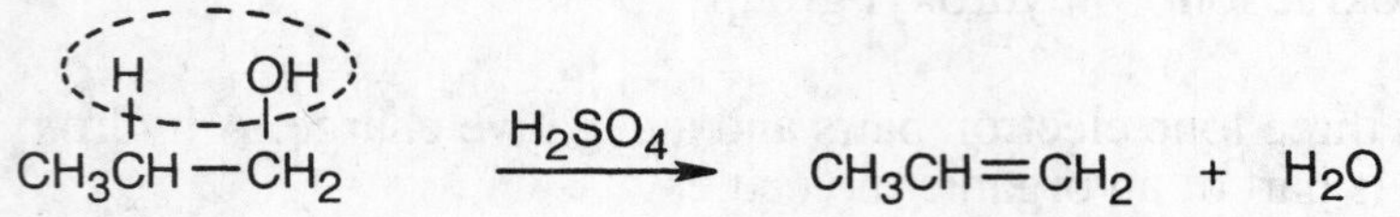

(b)

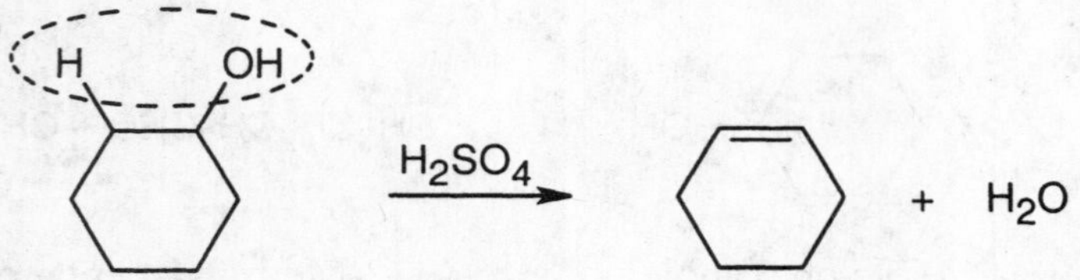

(c)

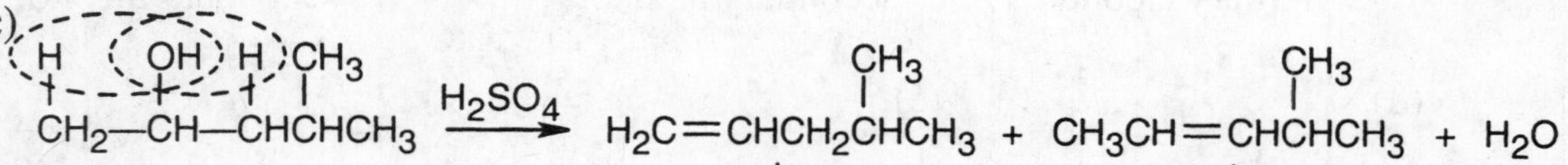
minor
major

14.9

(a)

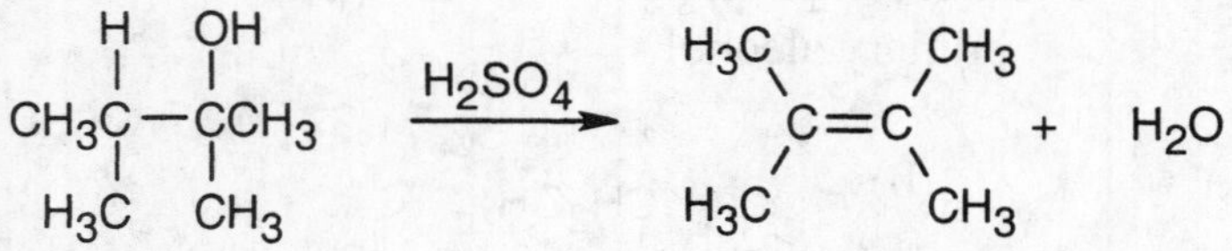

(b)

$$CH_3CH_2\overset{H}{\underset{}{CH}}-\overset{OH}{\underset{}{CH_2}} \xrightarrow{H_2SO_4} CH_3CH_2CH{=}CH_2 \ + \ H_2O$$

or

$$CH_3\overset{H}{\underset{}{CH}}-\overset{OH}{\underset{}{CH}}-\overset{H}{\underset{}{CH_2}} \xrightarrow{H_2SO_4} \underset{minor}{CH_3CH_2CH{=}CH_2} \ + \ \underset{major}{CH_3CH{=}CHCH_3} \ + \ H_2O$$

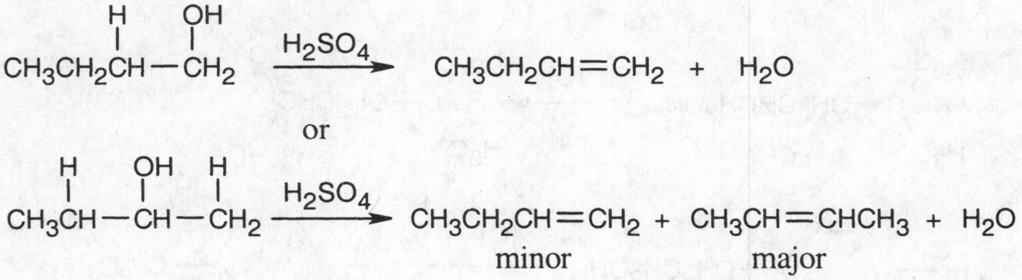

14.10

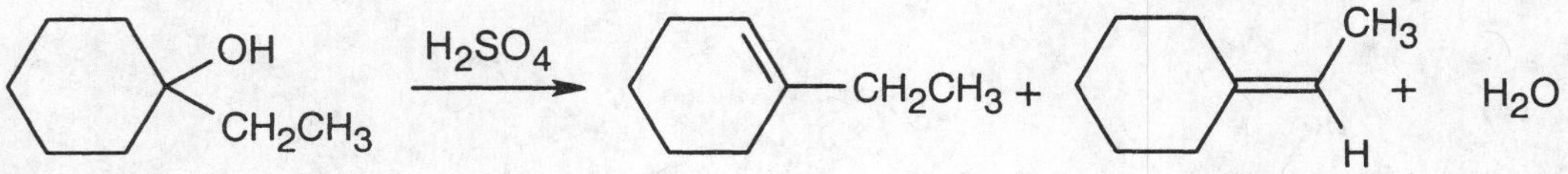

14.11

(a)

$$CH_3CH_2CH_2\overset{OH}{\underset{}{}} \ = \ CH_3CH_2\overset{O-H}{\underset{H}{\overset{|}{C}}{-}H} \xrightarrow{[O]} CH_3CH_2\overset{O}{\overset{\parallel}{C}}{-}H \xrightarrow{[O]} CH_3CH_2\overset{O}{\overset{\parallel}{C}}{-}OH$$

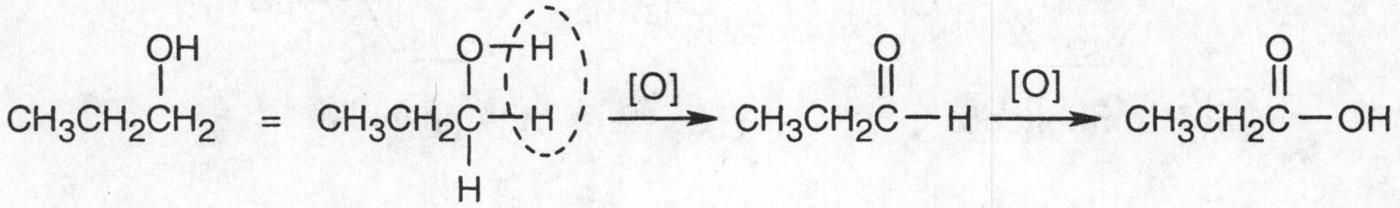

(b)

$$CH_3\overset{OH}{\underset{}{CH}}CH_2CH_2CH_3 \ = \ CH_3\underset{CH_2CH_2CH_3}{\overset{O-H}{\overset{|}{C}}{-}H} \xrightarrow{[O]} CH_3\overset{O}{\overset{\parallel}{C}}CH_2CH_2CH_3$$

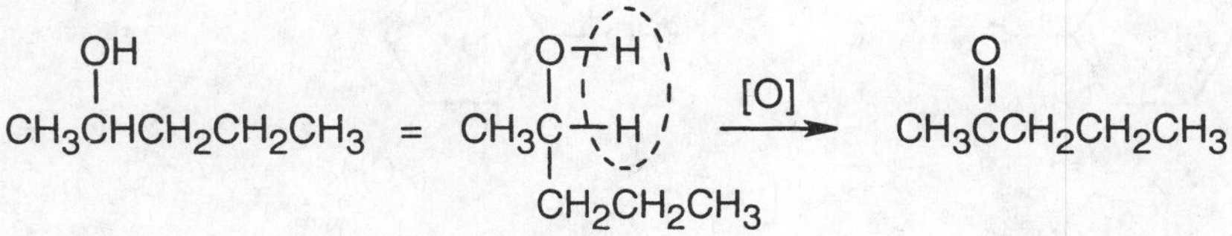

(c)

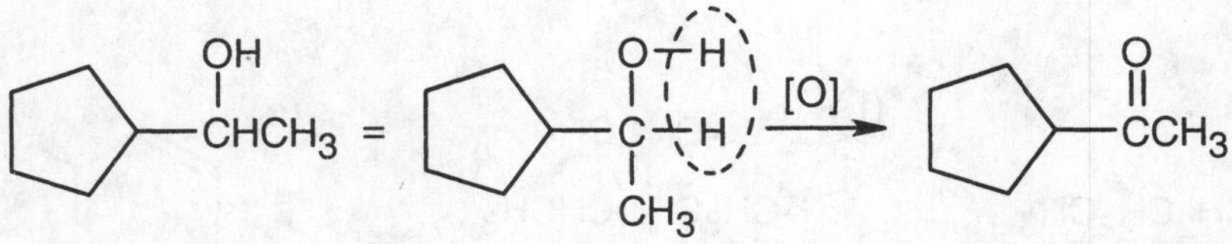

14.12

(a)

$$CH_3\overset{OH}{\underset{}{CH}}CH_3 \xrightarrow{[O]} CH_3\overset{O}{\overset{\parallel}{C}}CH_3$$

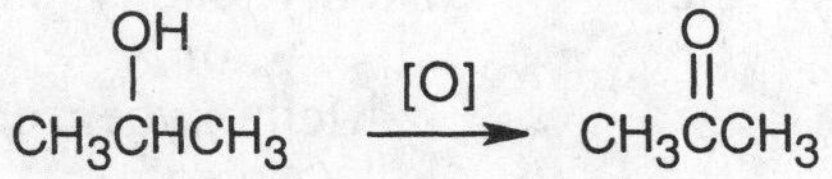

(b)

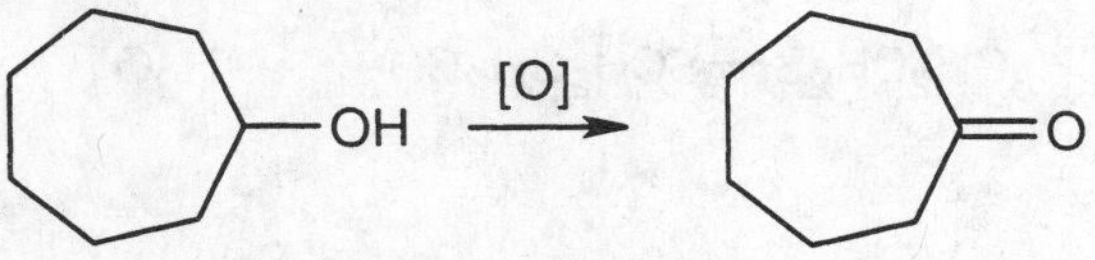

(c)

$$\underset{CH_3CH CH_2CH_2OH}{\overset{CH_3}{|}} \xrightarrow{[O]} \underset{CH_3CHCH_2\overset{O}{\overset{\parallel}{C}}{-}H}{\overset{CH_3}{|}} \xrightarrow{[O]} \underset{CH_3CHCH_2\overset{O}{\overset{\parallel}{C}}{-}OH}{\overset{CH_3}{|}}$$

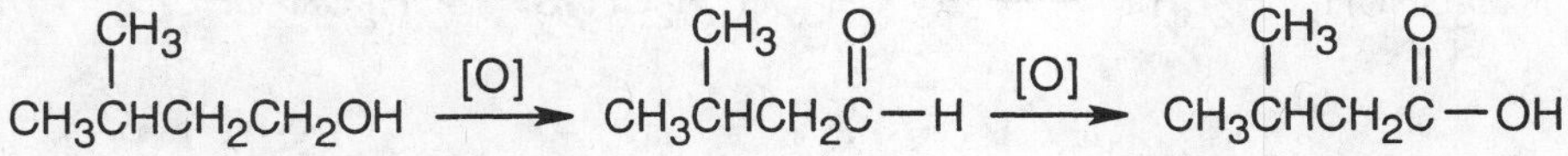

14.13

(a)

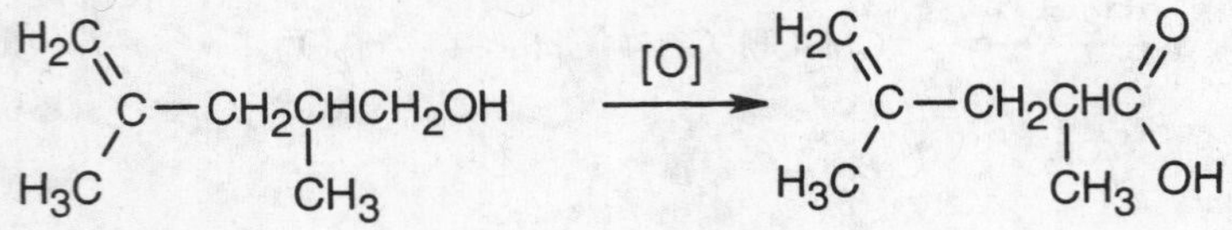

(b)

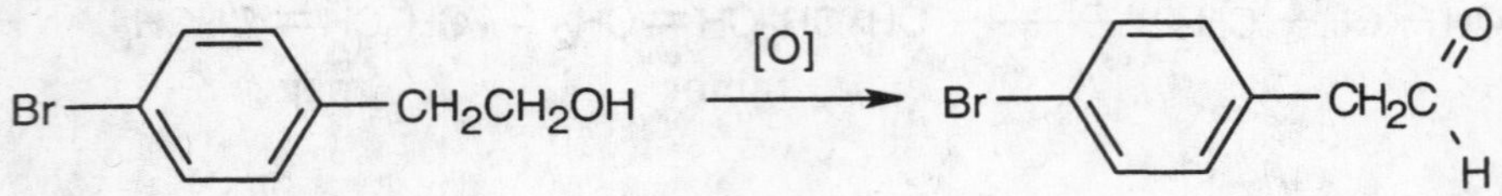

14.14

(a)

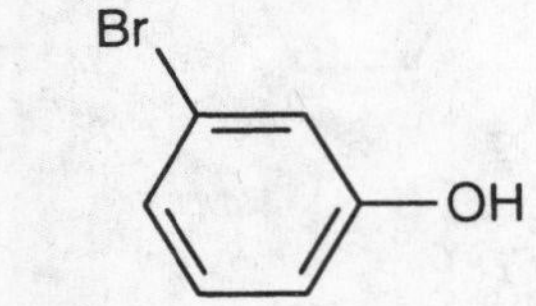

m-Bromophenol

(b)

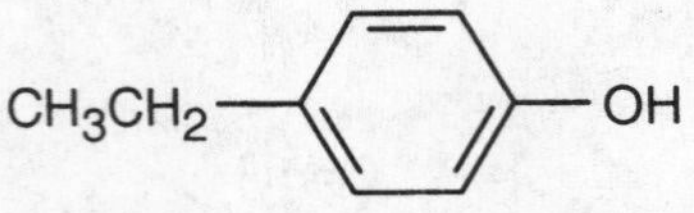

p-Ethylphenol

14.15

(a)

p-Chlorophenol

(b)

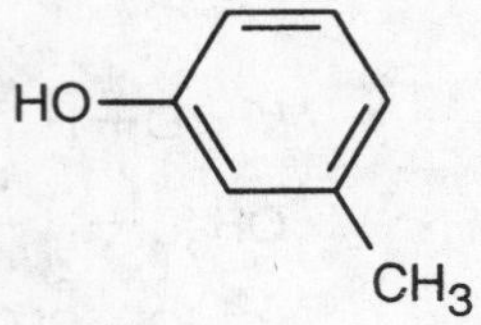

m-Methylphenol (*m*-Cresol)

14.16

(a)

$CH_3OCH_2CH_2CH_3$

Methyl propyl ether

(b)

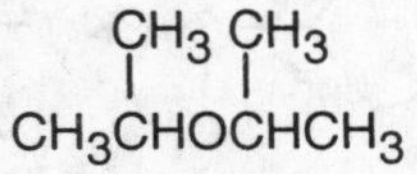

Diisopropyl ether

(c)

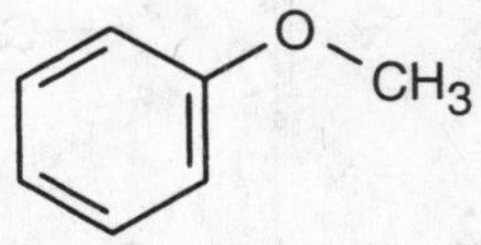

Methyl phenyl ether
or
Methoxybenzene
(Anisole)

14.17

(a)

$$2\ CH_3CH_2CH_2SH \xrightarrow{[O]} CH_3CH_2CH_2S{-}SCH_2CH_2CH_3 + H_2O$$

(b)

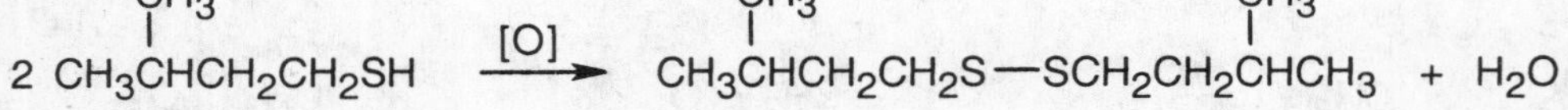

14.18

(a)

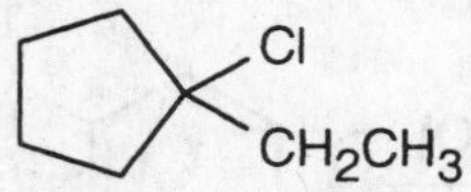

1-Chloro-1-ethylcyclopentane

(b)

$$CH_3CH_2\overset{\overset{\displaystyle CH_3}{|}}{C}HCH_2\overset{\overset{\displaystyle Br}{|}}{C}HCH_2CH_3$$

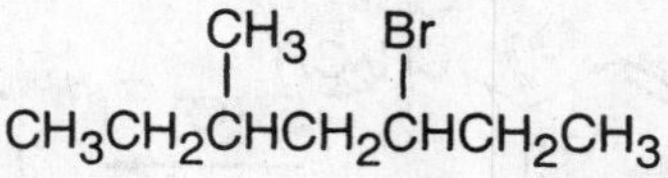

3-Bromo-5-methylheptane

Understanding Key Concepts

14.19

(a)

$$CH_3\overset{\overset{\displaystyle CH_3}{|}}{C}HCH_2\overset{\overset{\displaystyle OH}{|}}{C}HCH_2CH_3$$

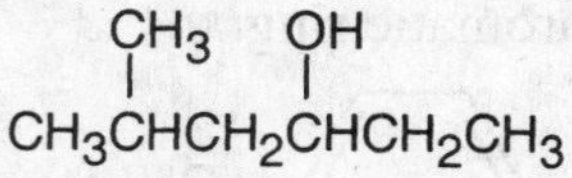

5-Methyl-3-hexanol

(b)

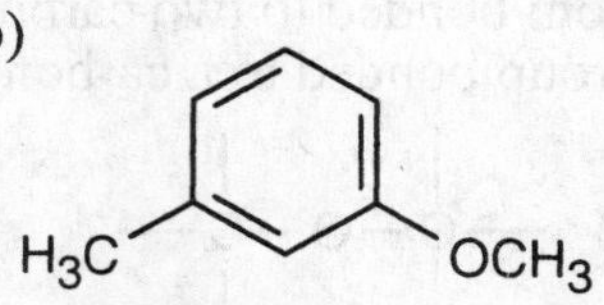

m-Methoxytoluene

(c)

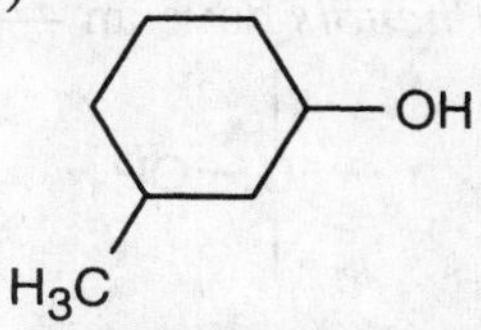

3-Methylcyclohexanol

14.20

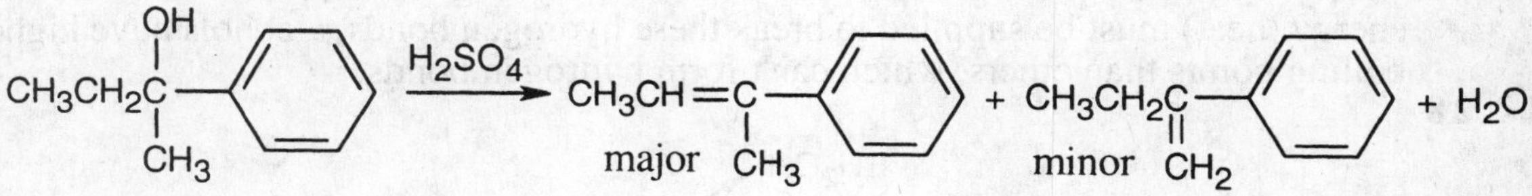

14.21

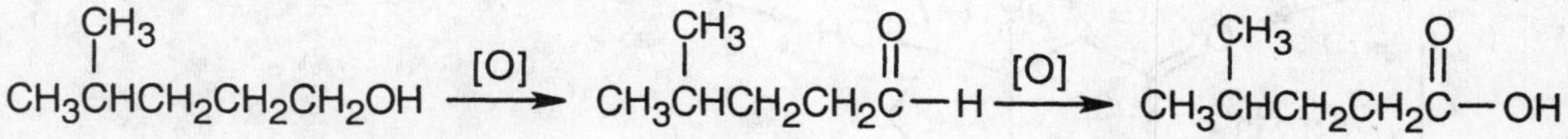

14.22

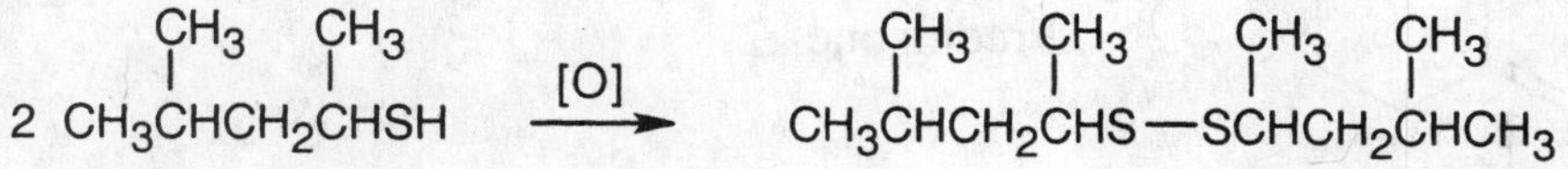

14.23

(a)

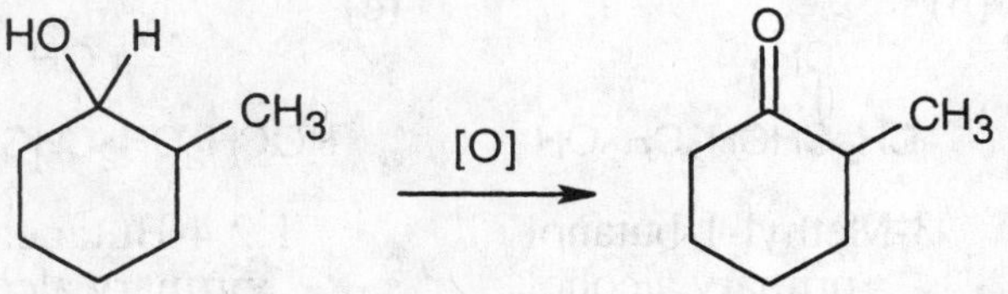

(b)

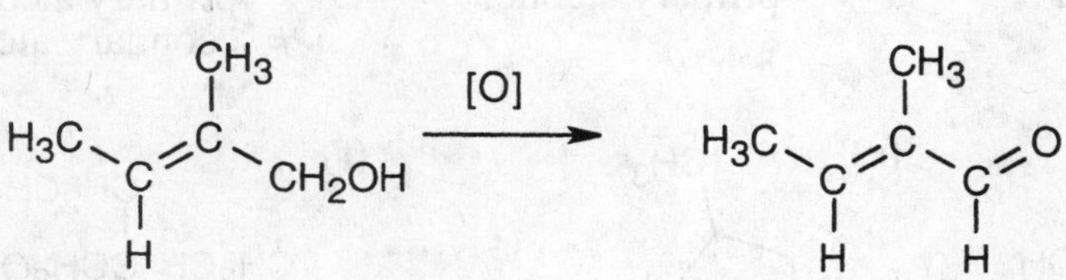

(c)

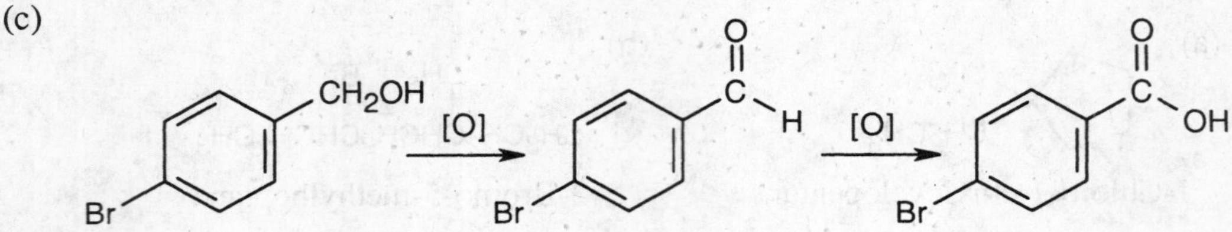
CH2OH
[O]
[O]
Br
Br
Br
O
C
H
O
C
OH

Alcohols, Ethers, and Phenols

14.24 *Alcohols* have an —OH group bonded to an alkane-like carbon atom.
Ethers have an oxygen atom bonded to two carbon atoms.
Phenols have an —OH group bonded to a carbon of an aromatic ring.

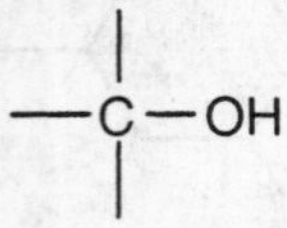

an alcohol

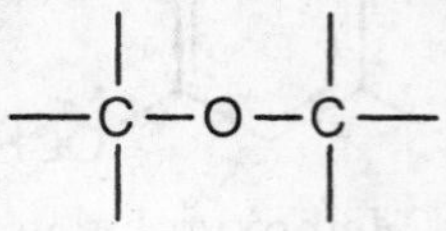

an ether

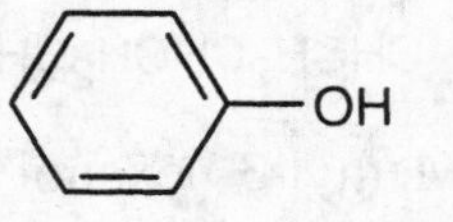

a phenol

14.26 Alcohols contain —OH groups, which can form hydrogen bonds to each other. Since extra energy (heat) must be supplied to break these hydrogen bonds, alcohols have higher boiling points than ethers, which can't form hydrogen bonds.

14.28

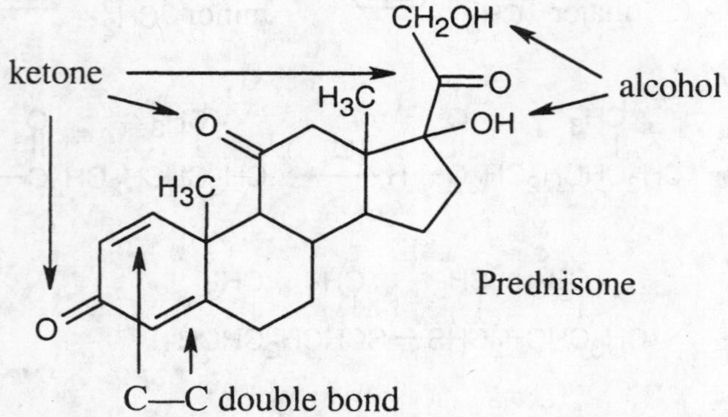
ketone
alcohol
C—C double bond
Prednisone

14.30, 14.34

(a)

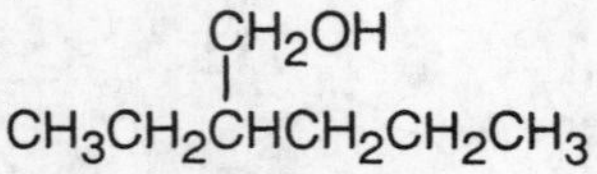

2-Ethyl-1-pentanol
primary alcohol

(b)

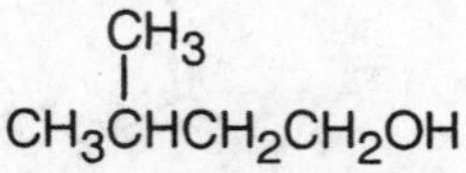

3-Methyl-1-butanol
primary alcohol

(c)

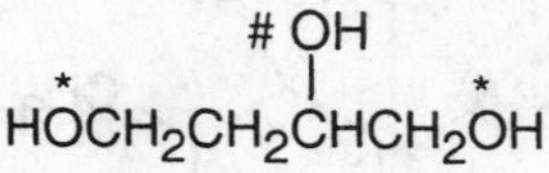

1,2,4-Butanetriol
*primary alcohol
secondary alcohol

(d)

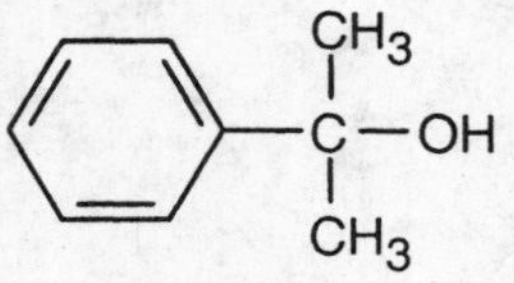

2-Phenyl-2-propanol
tertiary alcohol

(e)

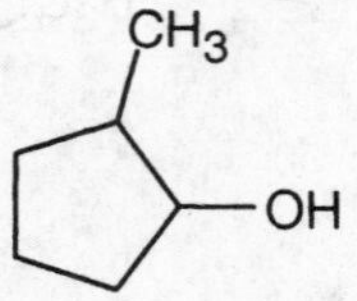

2-Methylcyclopentanol
secondary alcohol

(f)

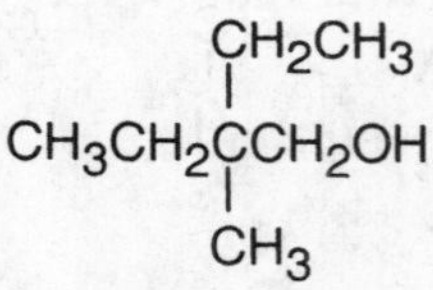

2-Ethyl-2-methyl-1-butanol
primary alcohol

14.32

(a)

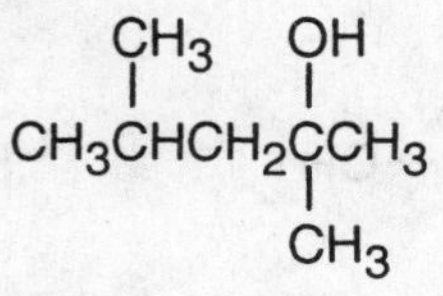

2,4-Dimethyl-2-pentanol

(b)

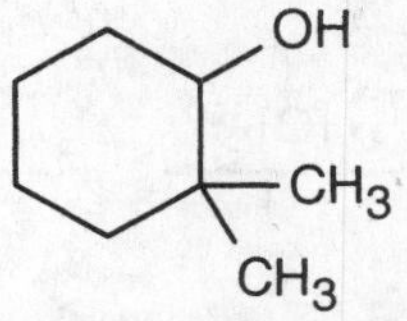

2,2-Dimethylcyclohexanol

(c)

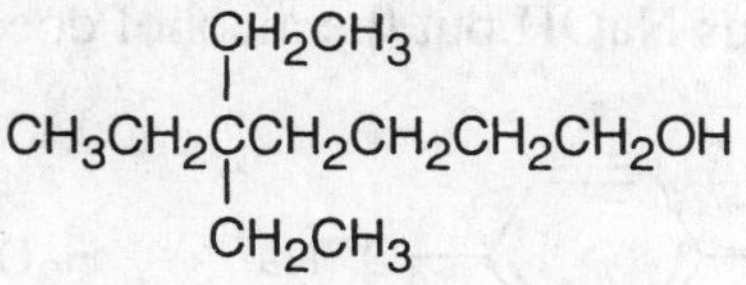

5,5-Diethyl-1-heptanol

(d)

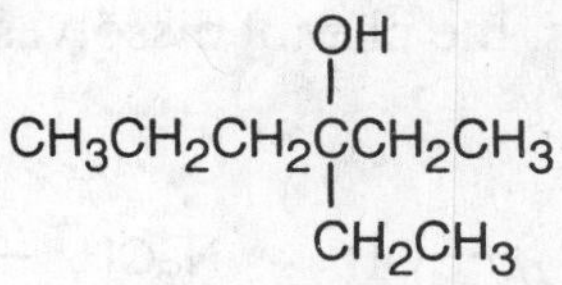

3-Ethyl-3-hexanol

(e)

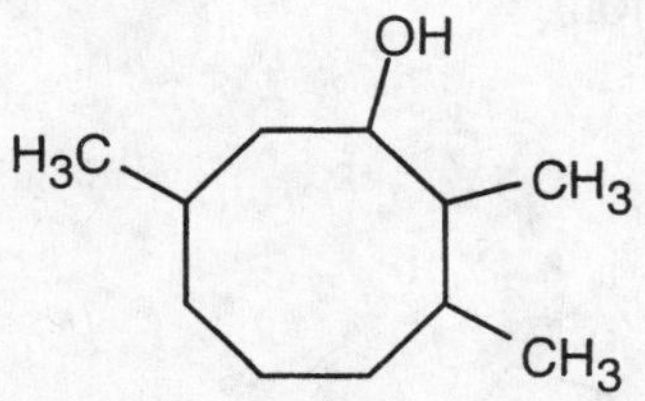

2,3,7-Trimethylcyclooctanol

(f)

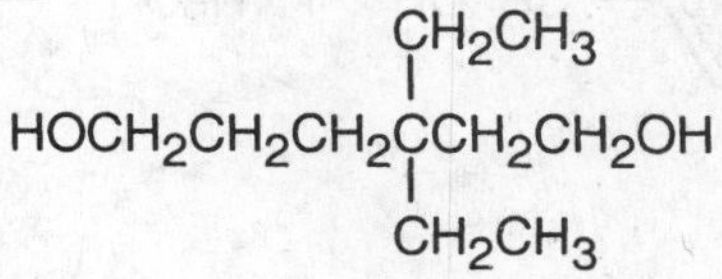

3,3-Diethyl-1,6-hexanediol

14.34 See Problem 14.30

14.36

Compound	*Boiling Point*	*Reason*
Hexanol	Highest	Forms hydrogen bonds
Dipropyl ether	Middle	Polar, but doesn't form hydrogen bonds
Hexane	Lowest	Nonpolar

Reactions of Alcohols

14.38 A ketone is formed on oxidation of a secondary alcohol:

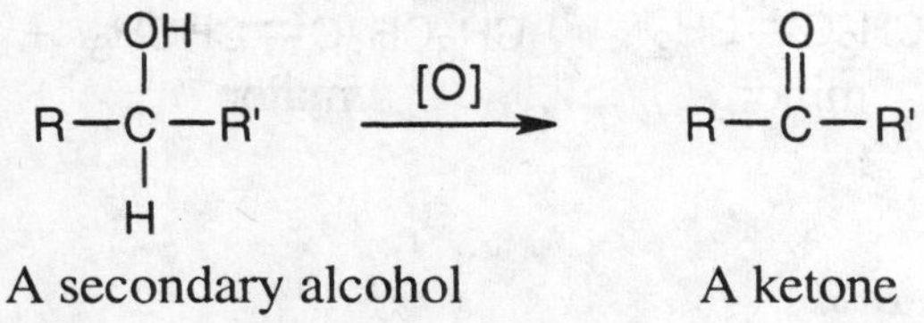

A secondary alcohol   A ketone

14.40 Either an aldehyde or a carboxylic acid can be formed by oxidation of a primary alcohol:

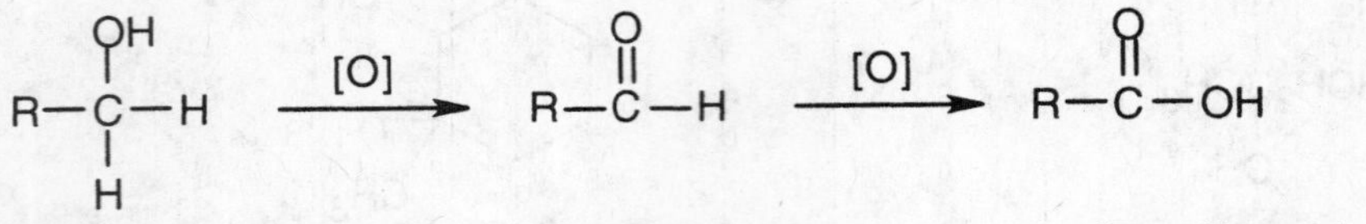

a primary alcohol — an aldehyde — a carboxylic acid

14.42 Phenols are more acidic than alcohols and are converted into their sodium salts on reaction with NaOH. Thus, the phenol dissolves in aqueous NaOH but the alcohol doesn't.

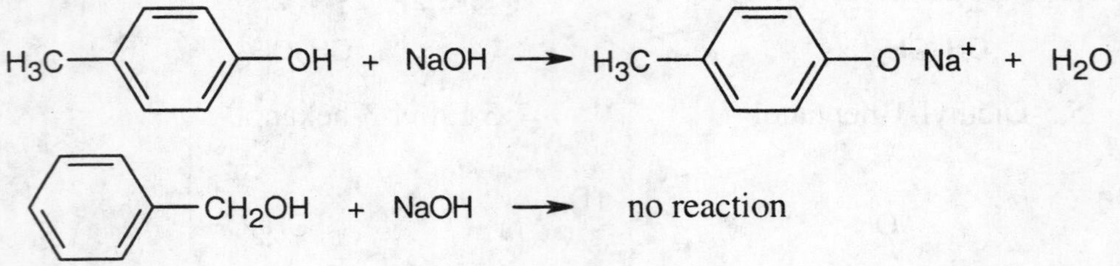
no reaction

14.44

(a)

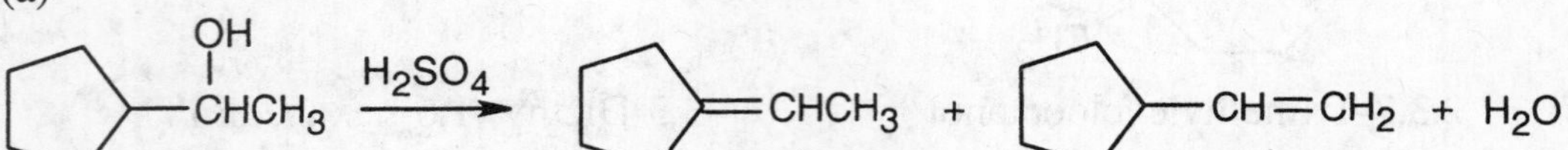

major — minor

or

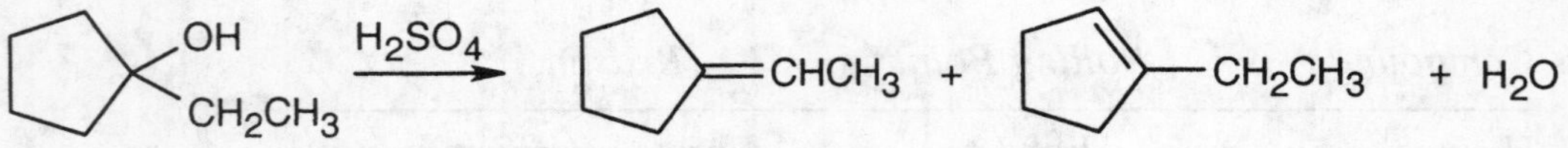

(b)

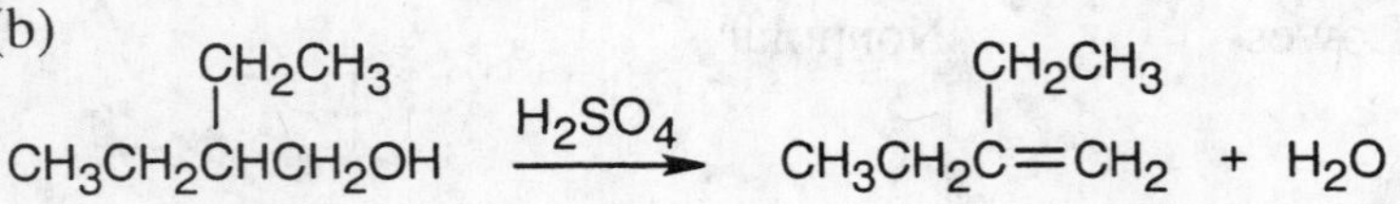

or

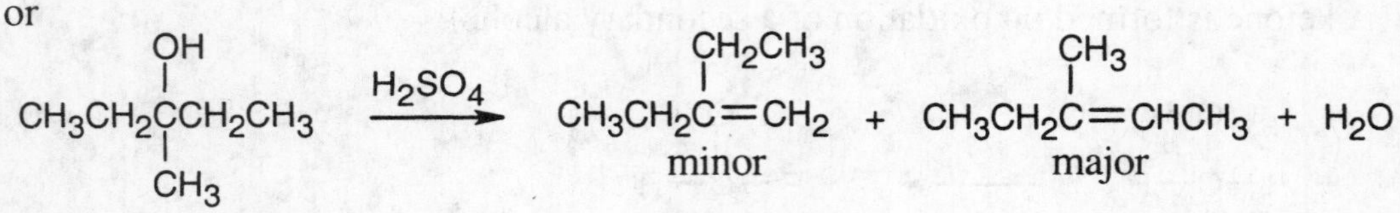

minor — major

(c)

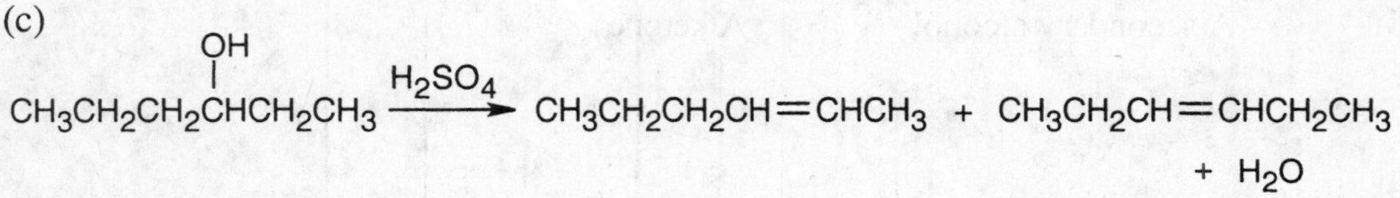

(d)

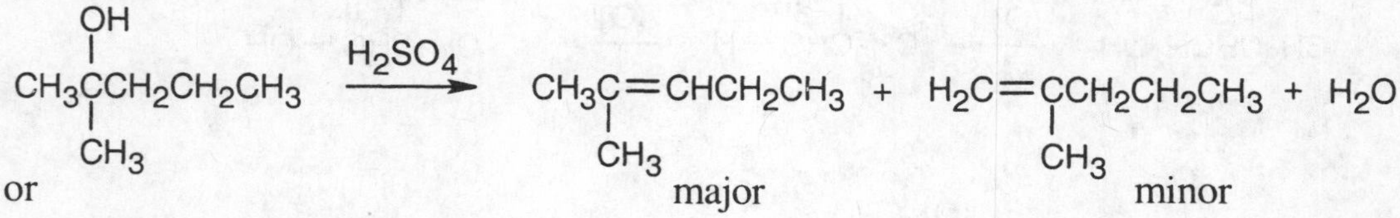

or

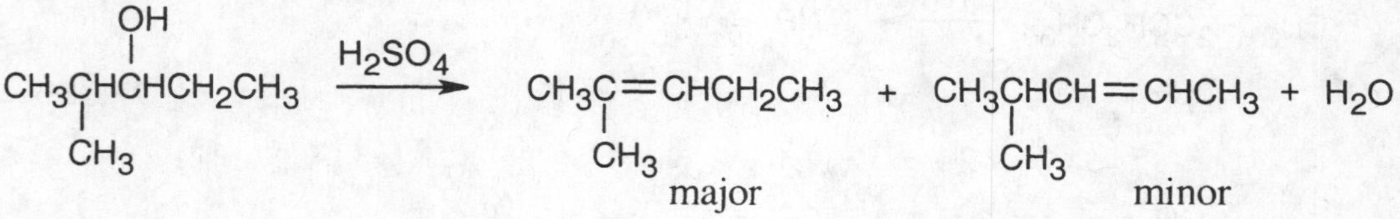

(e)

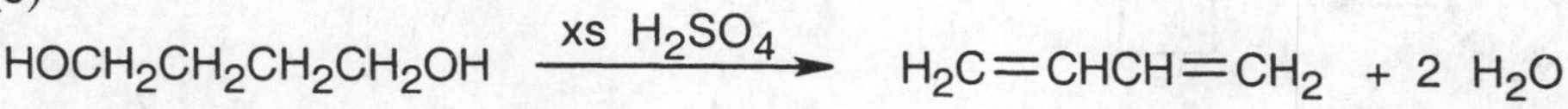

or

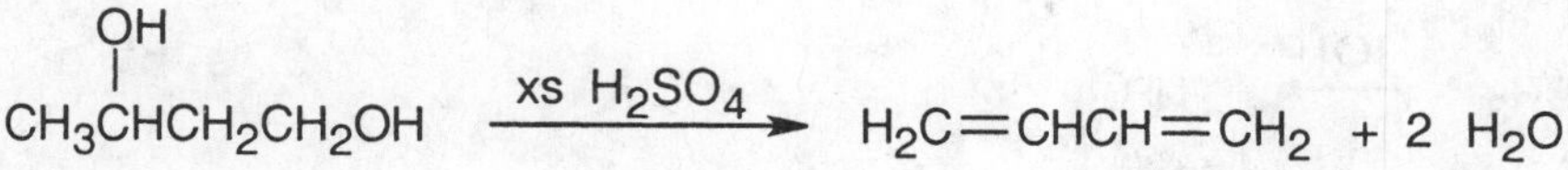

or

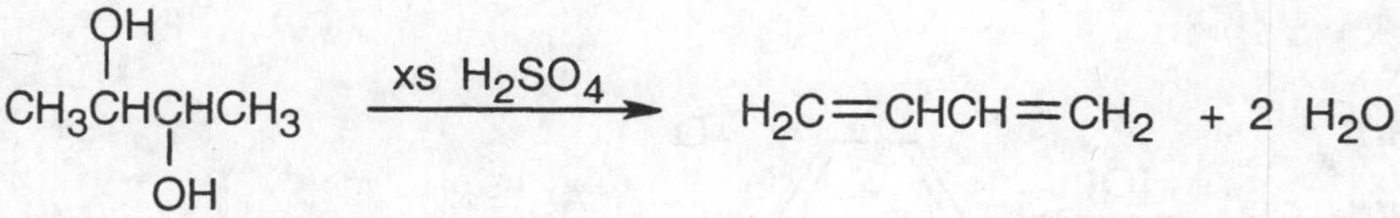

(f)

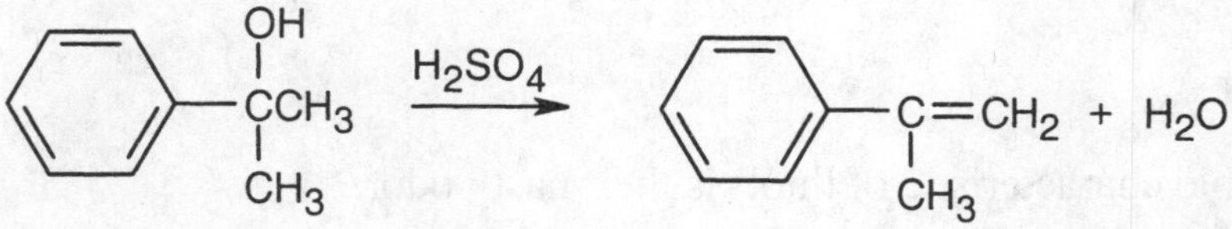

or

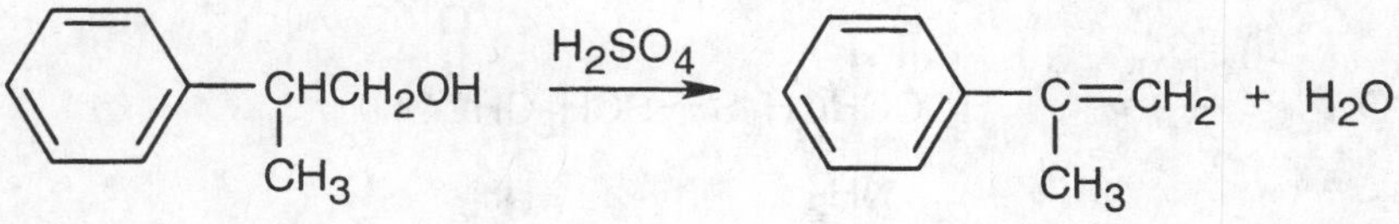

14.46

(a)

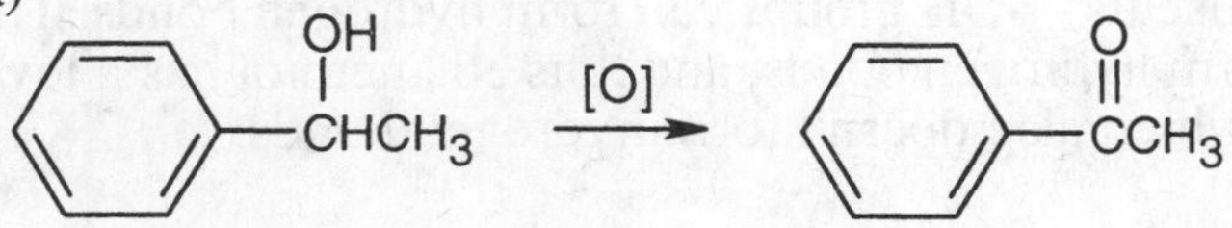

(b)

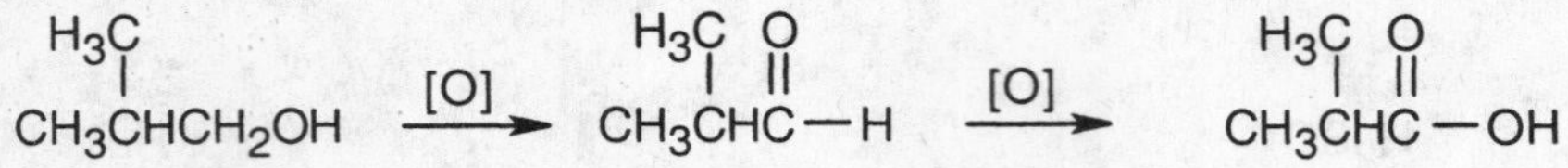
H3C
CH3CHCH2OH
[O]
H3C O
CH3CHC—H
[O]
H3C O
CH3CHC—OH

(c)

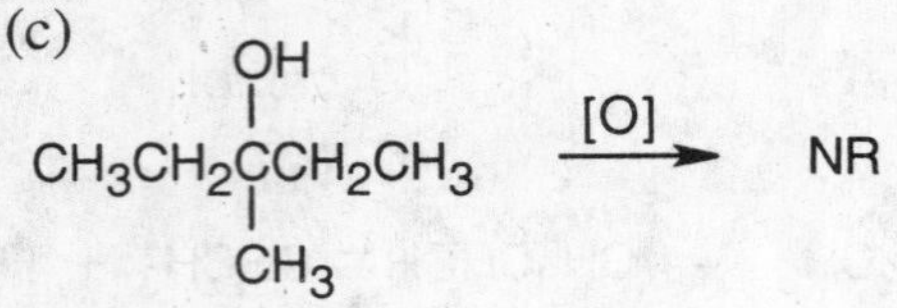
OH
CH3CH2CCH2CH3
CH3
[O]
NR

(d)

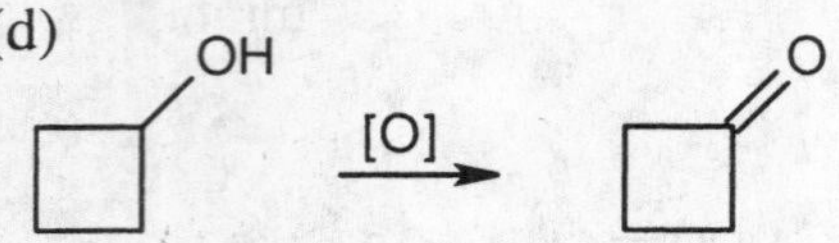
OH
[O]
O

(e)

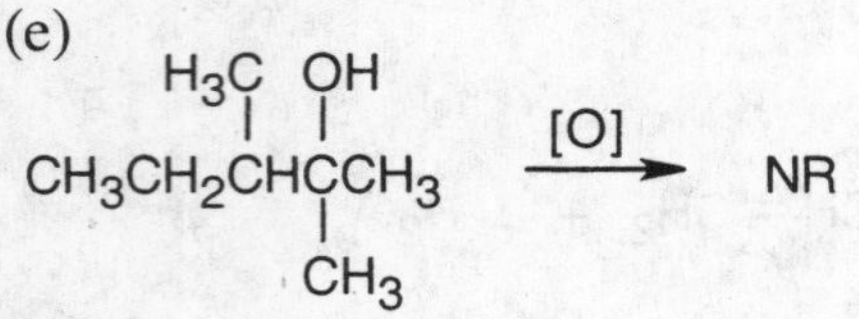
H3C OH
CH3CH2CHCCH3
CH3
[O]
NR

(f)

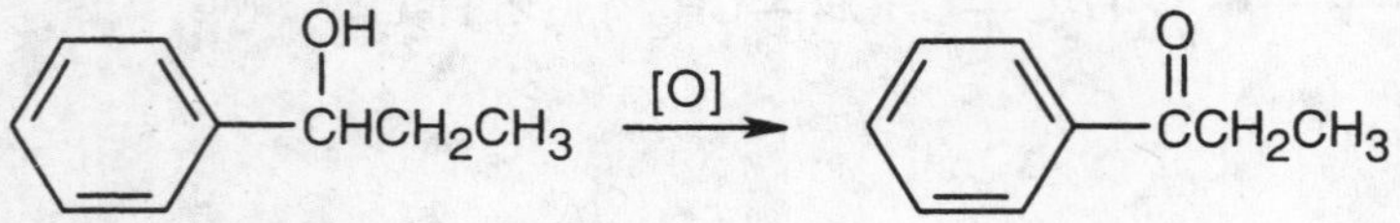
OH
CHCH2CH3
[O]
O
CCH2CH3

Thiols and Disulfides

14.48 The most noticeable characteristic of thiols is their nasty odor.

14.50

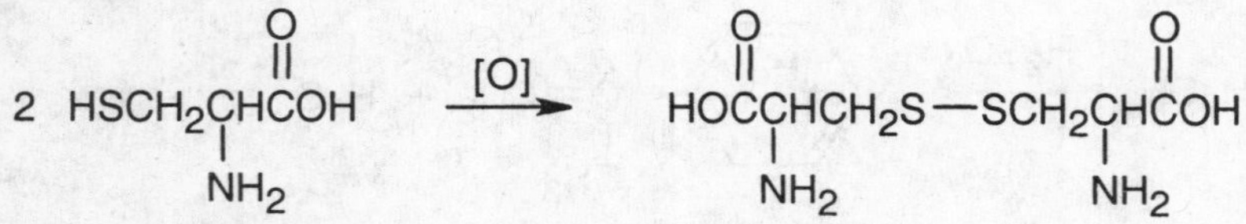
O
2 HSCH2CHCOH
NH2
[O]
O
HOCCHCH2S—SCH2CHCOH
NH2
O
NH2

Cysteine — Cysteine disulfide

14.52 Propanol is high boiling because its —OH groups can form hydrogen bonds. The —SH groups of ethanethiol don't form hydrogen bonds, and thus ethanethiol has a lower boiling point, as does chloroethane, which also doesn't form hydrogen bonds.

Applications

14.54 Ethanol is a depressant. Its effects on the central nervous system are like those of anesthetics and other central nervous system depressants.

14.56 The liver is vulnerable to damage from alcohol because it is the principal site of alcohol metabolism, and toxic products of alcohol metabolism accumulate there.

14.58 A free radical is a reactive species that contains an unpaired electron.

14.60 Diethyl ether was used as the first general anesthetic.

14.62 The ozone layer acts as a shield to protect the earth from intense solar radiation.

General Questions and Problems

14.64 Alcohol isomers of $C_4H_{10}O$:

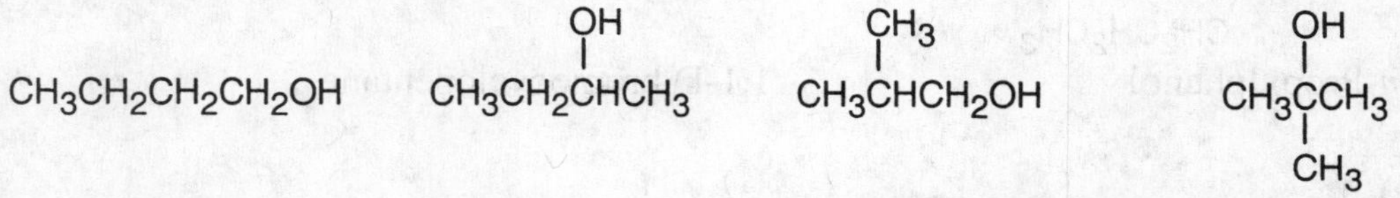

1-Butanol 2-Butanol 2-Methyl-1-propanol 2-Methyl-2-propanol

Ether isomers of $C_4H_{10}O$:

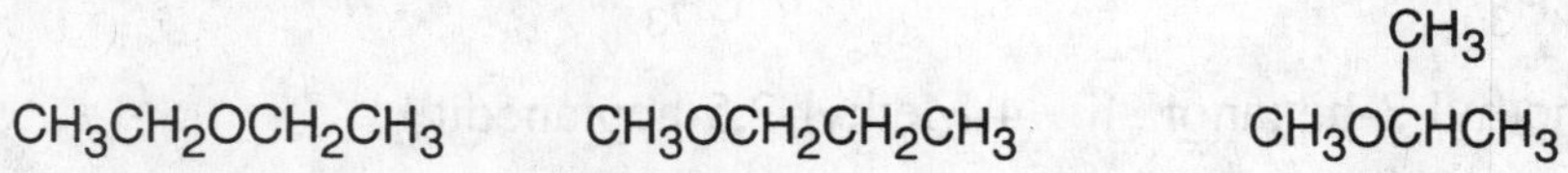

Diethyl ether Methyl propyl ether Isopropyl methyl ether

14.66 $CH_3(CH_2)_8CH_3$	$CH_3(CH_2)_7CH_2OH$
Decane — a hydrocarbon	1-Nonanol — an alcohol
Insoluble in water because it is nonpolar	Insoluble because its hydrocarbon, water-insoluble part, is much larger than its polar hydroxyl group.

14.68 An antiseptic kills microorganisms on living tissue; a disinfectant is toxic and is used only to kill microorganisms on surfaces.

14.70

(a)

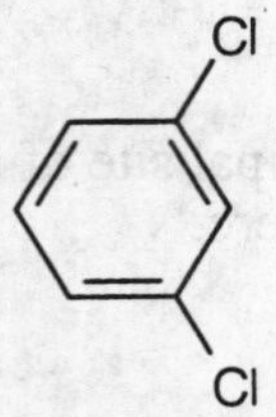

m-Dichlorobenzene

(b)

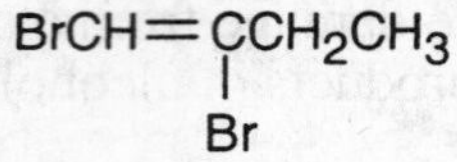

1,2-Dibromo-1-butene

(c)

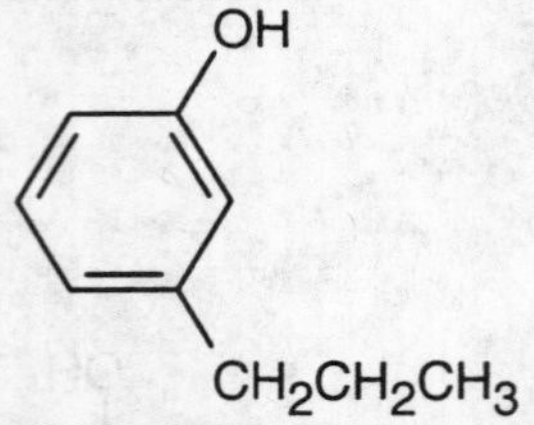

m-Propylphenol

(d)

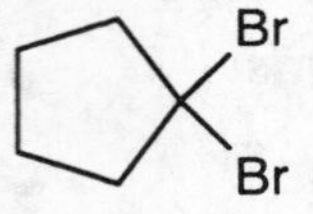

1,1-Dibromocyclopentane

(e)

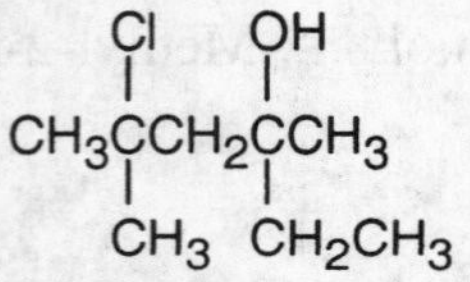

5-Chloro-3,5-dimethyl-3-hexanol

(f)

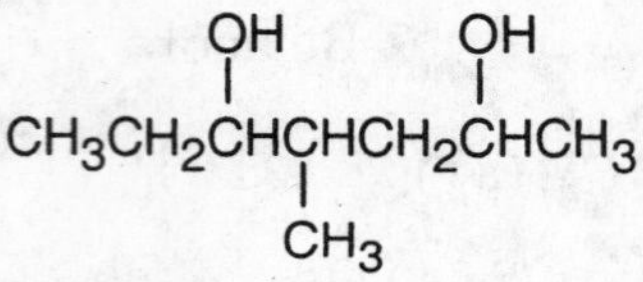

4-Methyl-2,5-heptanediol

(g)

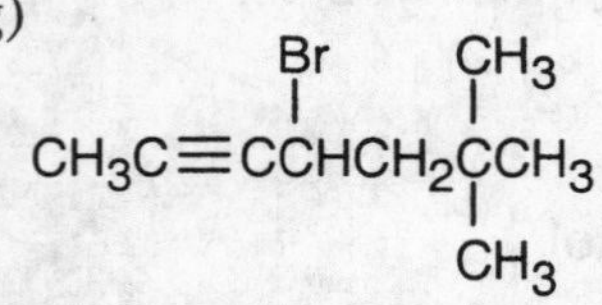

4-Bromo-6,6-dimethyl-2-heptyne

(h)

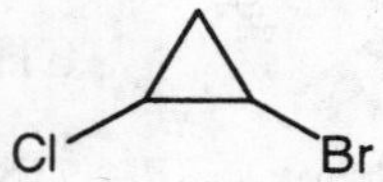

1-Bromo-2-chlorocyclopropane

14.72

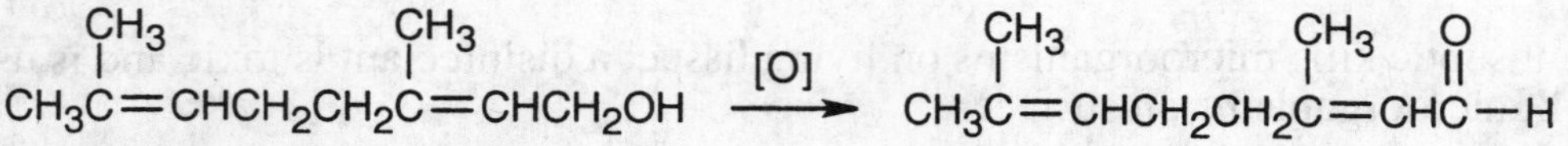

3,7-Dimethyl-2,6-octadiene-1-ol   Citral

14.74

$$CH_3CH_2OH + 3\ O_2 \longrightarrow 2\ CO_2 + 3\ H_2O$$

Self-Test for Chapter 14

Multiple choice:

1. Which of the following alcohols yields an aldehyde on oxidation?
(a) 2-hexanol (b) 2-methyl-2-hexanol (c) 2-methyl-1-hexanol (d) *p*-chlorophenol

2. Which of the following compounds is least acidic?
(a) *p*-chlorophenol (b) 2-butanol (c) HCl (d) acetic acid

3. How many alcohols of the formula $C_4H_{10}O$ are primary alcohols?
(a) 1 (b) 2 (c) 3 (d) 4

4. Which of the following is known as wood alcohol?
(a) CH_3OH (b) CH_3CH_2OH (c) $CH_3CH_2CH_2OH$ (d) $HOCH_2CH_2OH$

5. 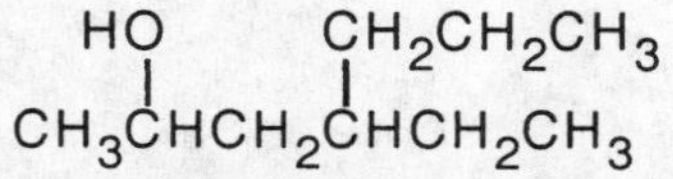
HO
CH2CH2CH3
CH3CHCH2CHCH2CH3
What is the name of the compound shown?
(a) 4-propyl-2-hexanol (b) 4-ethyl-6-heptanol (c) 4-ethylheptanol (d) 4-ethyl-2-heptanol

6. Which of the following is not a property of alcohols?
(a) weakly acidic (b) flammable (c) react with acids (d) low-boiling

7. Which of the following is not a product of dehydration of 2,3-dimethyl-3-pentanol?
(a) 2,3-dimethyl-1-pentene (b) 2,3-dimethyl-2-pentene (c) 3,4-dimethyl-2-pentene
(d) 2-ethyl-3-methyl-1-butene

8. Which of the following is a cyclic ether?
(a) enflurane (b) ethylene oxide (c) methoxybenzene (anisole) (d) methyl cyclohexyl ether

9. An alcohol of the formula $C_5H_{12}O$ forms a carboxylic acid on oxidation yet can't be dehydrated by acid. What is its name?
(a) 1-pentanol (b) 2-methyl-2-butanol (c) 2,2-dimethyl-1-propanol (d) 2-methyl-1-butanol

10. Which reagent doesn't react with alcohols?
(a) Na (b) H_2SO_4 (c) $KMnO_4$ (d) NaOH

Sentence Completion

1. The common name for methanol is _____.

2. Dialcohols are often called _____.

3. Aromatic compounds called _____ react with NaOH to give salts.

4. The dehydration of an alcohol yields an ______.

5. Compounds called _____ are noted for their foul odors.

6. ______ can be used to oxidize an alcohol.

7. Ethers are _____ boiling than alcohols of similar molecular weight.

8. _____ is a phenol used as a food additive.

9. The major product of alcohol dehydration has the ______ number of alkyl groups attached to the double-bond carbons.

10. A ______ ______ is a reactive intermediate containing an unpaired electron.

11. On prolonged contact with air, an ether forms a _______.

12. ______ is another name for a chlorofluorocarbon.

True or False

1. Phenols can form hydrogen bonds.

2. An aldehyde can be formed by oxidation of a secondary alcohol.

3. Two different alkenes result from dehydration of 2-pentanol.

4. Another name for phenol is carbonic acid.

5. Phenols are more acidic than alcohols.

6. Another name for a thiol is a mercaptan.

7. Phenol, isopropyl alcohol, and chloroethane are all antiseptics.

8. Oxidation is the removal of two hydrogen ions.

9. Several halogenated alkanes are used as anesthetics.

10. Under careful reaction conditions, a primary alcohol is oxidized to an aldehyde.

11. Isopropyl alcohol is more toxic than methyl alcohol.

12. Hydrogen bonding accounts for both boiling-point elevation and water solubility.

Match each entry on the left with its partner on the right (use each answer once).

1. CCl_3F	(a) Peroxide
2. $(CH_3)_2CHS—SCH(CH_3)_2$	(b) Thiol
3. $CH_3CH(OH)CH_2CH_2CH_3$	(c) Phenol
4. $CH_3CH_2OCH_3$	(d) Alcohol that is not water soluble
5. CH_3OH	(e) Tertiary alcohol
6. CH_3SH	(f) Forms two alkenes on dehydration
7. $(CH_3)_3C—OH$	(g) Disulfide
8. $CH_3CH_2OOCH_3$	(h) Ether
9. $(CH_3)_3CCOCH_3$	(i) Glycol
10. $CH_3(CH_2)_{10}CH_2OH$	(j) Chlorofluorocarbon
11. $CH_3CH(OH)CH_2OH$	(k) Oxidation product of 3,3-dimethyl-2-butanol
12. C_6H_5OH	(l) Formed from CO and H_2

Chapter 15 – Amines

Chapter Outline

I. General characteristics of amines (Sections 15.1–15.3).
   A. Classification of amines (Section 15.1).
      1. Amines are classified by the degree of substitution at nitrogen.
         a. Primary amines have the structure RNH_2.
         b. Secondary amines have the structure R_2NH.
         c. Tertiary amines have the structure R_3N.
         d. Quaternary ammonium salts have the structure $R_4N^+ X^-$.
      2. The groups bonded to nitrogen may be alkyl or aryl groups and may also contain functional groups.
   B. Naming amines.
      1. Primary amines are named by identifying the alkyl group attached to nitrogen and adding the suffix *-amine*.
      2. Secondary and tertiary amines.
         a. If the groups are identical, the prefix *di-* or *tri-* is added to the name that would be given if the amine were primary.
         b. If the groups are different, the compound is named as an *N*-substituted derivative of a primary amine.
      3. The simplest aromatic amine is aniline.
      4. When the amino group is a substituent, the prefix *amino-* is used.
   C. Properties of amines (Section 15.2).
      1. Amines are basic.
      2. Primary and secondary amines form hydrogen bonds to each other.
      3. Amines can form hydrogen bonds with water.
      4. Simple amines are water-soluble.
      5. Amines have unpleasant odors.
      6. Amines are an important class of biomolecules.
   D. Heterocyclic amines (Section 15.3).
      1. In some nitrogen-containing compounds, nitrogen is part of a ring.
      2. Heterocyclic compounds may be aromatic or nonaromatic.

II. Reactions of amines (Sections 15.4–15.5).
   A. Acid–base reactions of amines (Section 15.4).
      1. Aqueous amines are weak bases that can accept a proton to form ammonium ions. Nonaromatic amines are stronger bases than aromatic amines.
      2. Amines can react with acids to form ammonium salts.
         a. Ammonium cations of alkylamines are named by replacing the ending *-amine* by the ending *-ammonium*.
         b. For cations of heterocyclic amines, *-e* is replaced by *-ium*.
      3. Ammonium salts react with hydroxide ion to yield an amine plus water.
      4. In the body, many amines are present as ammonium ions.
   B. Amine salts (Section 15.5).
      1. Amine salts are composed of an ammonium ion (the cation) and an anion.
      2. Most amine salts are much more soluble in water than the amines from which they were derived.
      3. Sometimes amine salts are written as amine·HX.
      4. An amine can be regenerated from an amine salt by reaction with base.
      5. Amine salts can be formed by reaction of an amine with an alkyl halide.

6. If four alkyl groups are bonded to nitrogen, the compound is a quaternary ammonium salt. Quaternary ammonium salts are usually neither acidic or basic.

III. Alkaloids: amines in plants (Section 15.6).
  1. Many alkaloids are toxic and physiologically active.
  2. Familiar alkaloids are coniine, atropine, solanine, and morphine.

Solutions to Chapter 15 Problems

15.1

(a) $CH_3CH_2CH_2NH_2$
primary amine

(b) $CH_3CH_2NHCH(CH_3)_2$
secondary amine

(c)
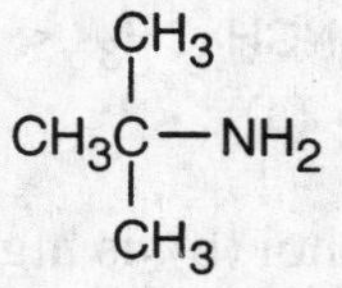
primary amine

(d)
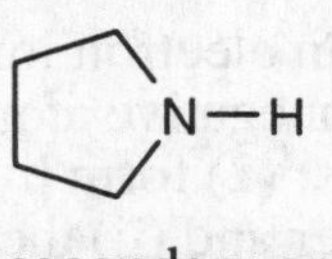
secondary amine

(e)
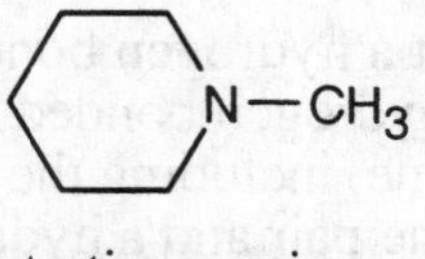
tertiary amine

15.2

(a) (R_4N^+)
tetraalkylammonium ion

(b)
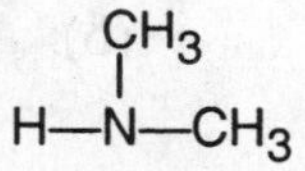
Dimethylamine

(c)
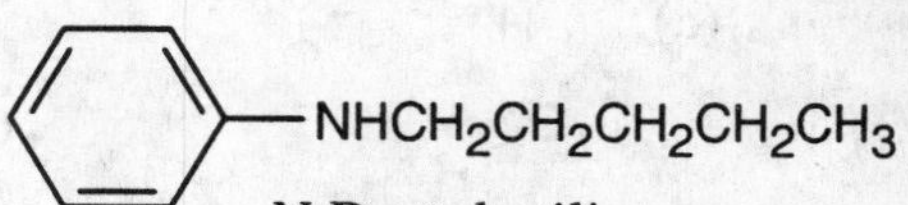
N-Pentylaniline

15.3

(a) $CH_3CH_2CH_2CH_2CH_2NH_2$
Pentylamine

(b)
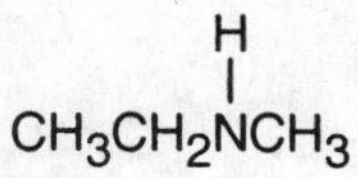
N-Methylethylamine

(c)
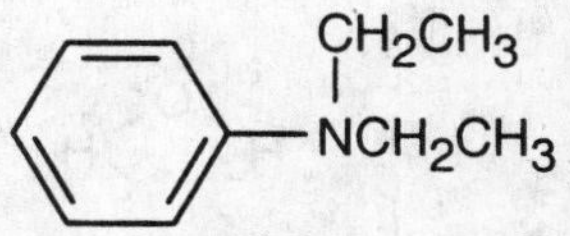
N,*N*-Diethylaniline

(d)
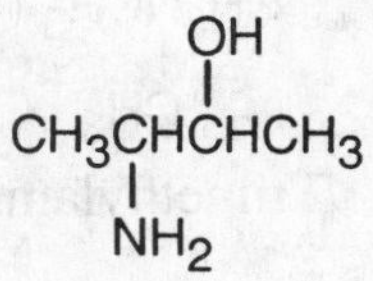
3-Amino-2-butanol

15.4

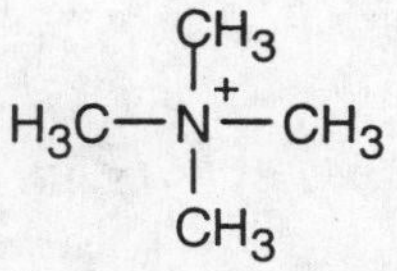
Tetramethylammonium ion

The atoms of tetramethylammonium ion form sixteen bonds (12 C—H bonds and 4 C—N bonds) that contain 32 valence electrons. Four neutral carbon atoms, twelve hydrogen atoms, and one nitrogen atom have a total of 33 valence electrons. Since the ion has one electron fewer than the neutral atoms, the ion has a +1 charge.

15.5

$CH_3CH_2CH_2CH_2NHCH_2CH_3$

N-Ethylbutylamine

15.6

Lowest Boiling ⟶ *Highest Boiling*

$CH_3N(CH_3)CH_2CH_3$ (a) < $CH_3CH_2CH_2CH_2NH_2$ (c) < $CH_3CH_2CH_2CH_2OH$ (b)

Alcohol (b), is highest boiling because —OH bonds of alcohols are more polar and form stronger hydrogen bonds than —NH bonds of amines. Amine (a) is lowest boiling because molecules of (a), a tertiary amine, don't form hydrogen bonds to each other.

15.7 In Section 8.11, we learned that a hydrogen bond forms between an electron lone pair of an electronegative atom and a hydrogen bonded to a second electronegative atom. To draw the structures; (1) draw the amine, including the lone pair electrons; (2) form hydrogen bonds between (i) the amine lone pair and a hydrogen atom of water and (ii) the amine hydrogens bonded to —N and an electron lone pair of water. In (b), only hydrogen bonds of type (i) can form.

(a)

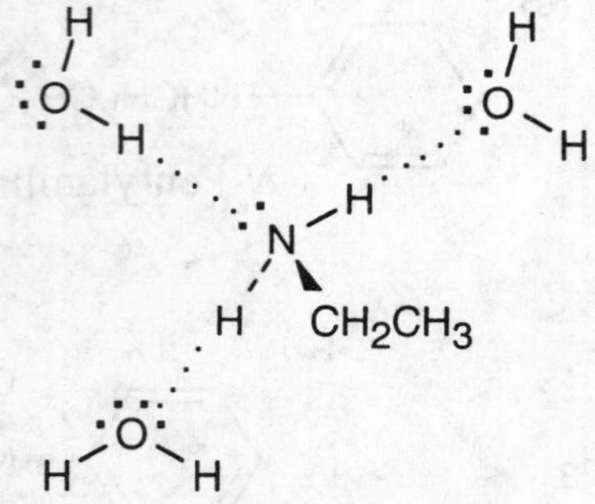
H
O
H
H
O
H
H
N
H
CH2CH3
O
H
H

(b)

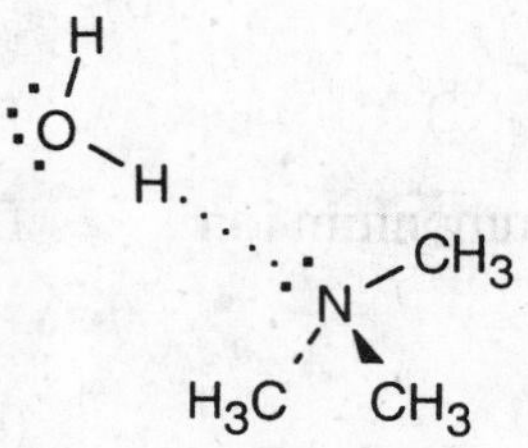
H
O
H
CH3
N
H3C
CH3

15.8

(a)

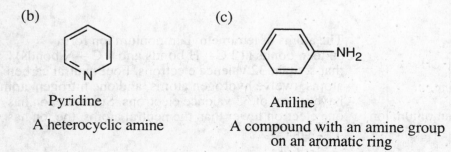

CH_3NH_2	$CH_3CH_2NH_2$	CH_3NHCH_3	$CH_3N(CH_3)CH_3$
Methylamine	Ethylamine	Dimethylamine	Trimethylamine

Amines that are gases at room temperature.

(b)

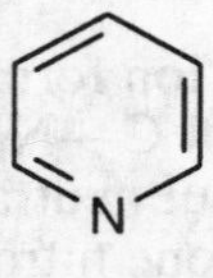
N

Pyridine

A heterocyclic amine

(c)

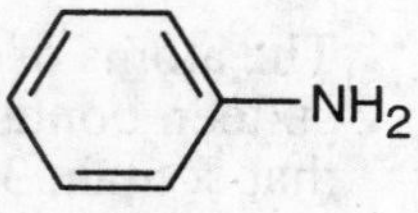
NH2

Aniline

A compound with an amine group on an aromatic ring

15.9

(a)

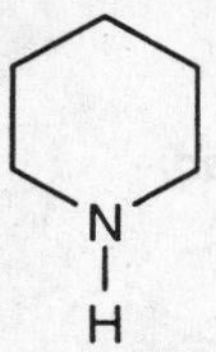

Piperidine
$C_5H_{11}N$

(b)

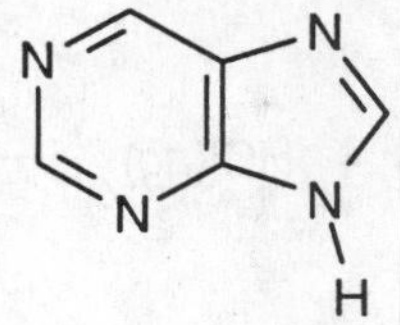

Purine
$C_5H_4N_4$

15.10 In a heterocyclic compound containing nitrogen, nitrogen must form part of the ring. Thus, compounds (a) and (d) are heterocyclic nitrogen compounds.

(a)

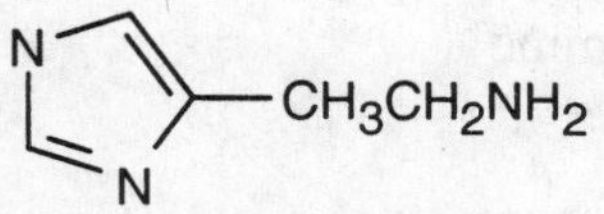
N
CH3CH2NH2
N

heterocyclic nitrogen compound

(b)

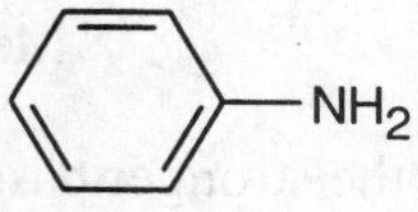
NH2

(c)

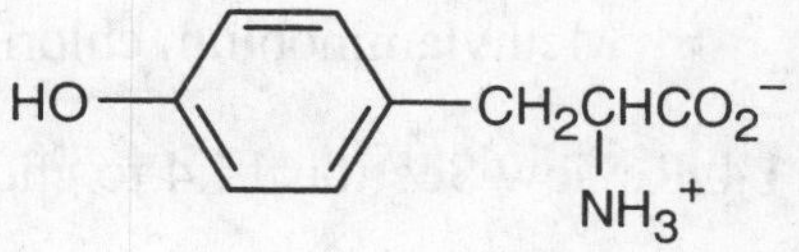
HO
CH2CHCO2−
NH3+

(d)

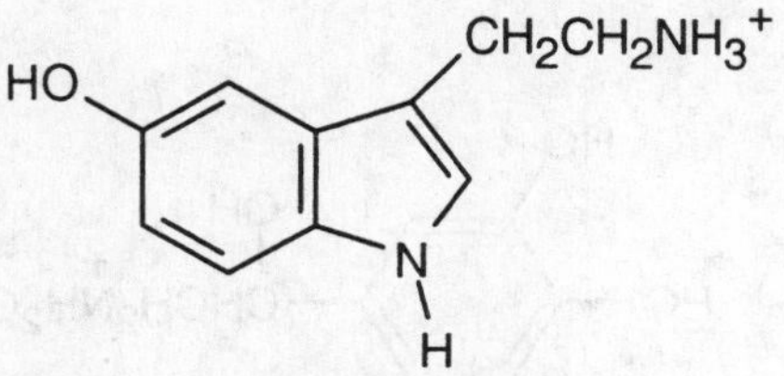
HO
CH2CH2NH3+
N
H

heterocyclic nitrogen compound

15.11

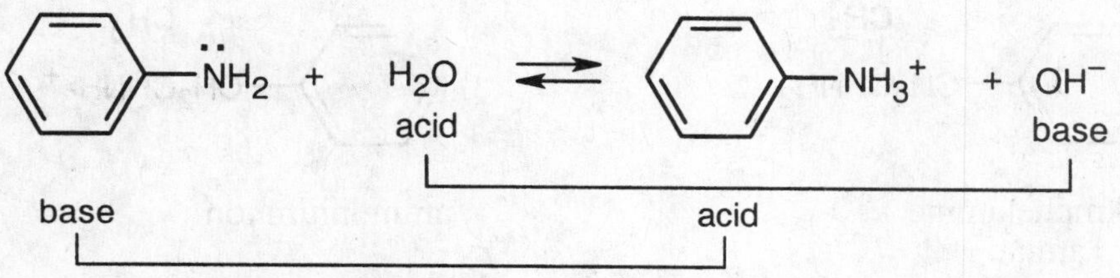
NH2
+
H2O
acid
NH3+
+ OH−
base
base
acid

15.12–15.13

(a)

$$CH_3CH_2\underset{\underset{CH_3}{|}}{C}HNH_2 + HBr(aq) \longrightarrow CH_3CH_2\underset{\underset{CH_3}{|}}{C}HNH_3^+\,Br^-(aq)$$

sec-Butylamine   *sec*-Butylammonium bromide

(b)

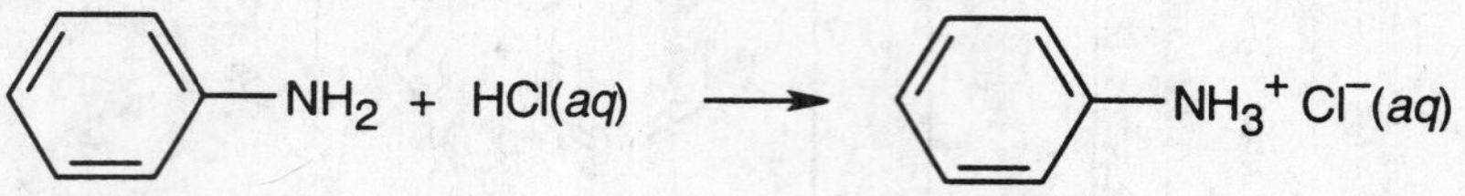

Aniline — Anilinium chloride

(c)

$$CH_3CH_2NH_2 + CH_3COOH(aq) \longrightarrow CH_3CH_2NH_3^+\ CH_3COO^-(aq)$$

Ethylamine — Ethylammonium acetate

(d)

$$CH_3NH_3^+\ Cl^-(aq) + NaOH(aq) \longrightarrow CH_3NH_2 + H_2O\ (l) + NaCl(aq)$$

Methylammonium chloride — Methylamine

15.14 Review Section 15.4 to choose the stronger base.

(a) Ethylamine is a stronger base than ammonia.
(b) Triethylamine (non-aromatic amine) is a stronger base than pyridine (aromatic amine).

15.15

(a)

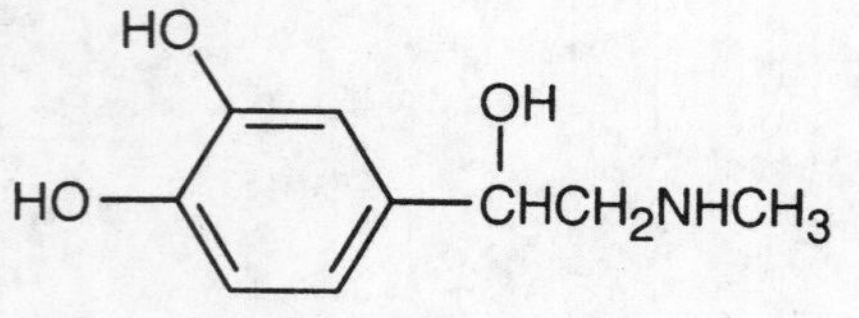

Epinephrine
amine

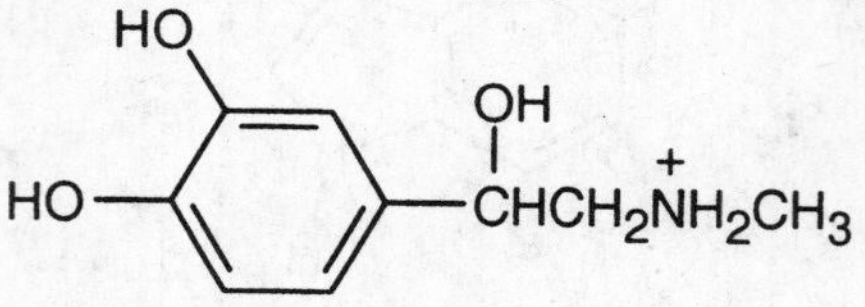

ammonium ion

(b)

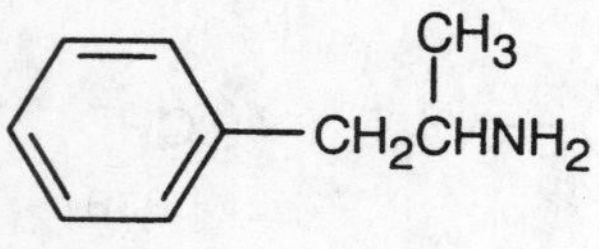

Amphetamine
amine

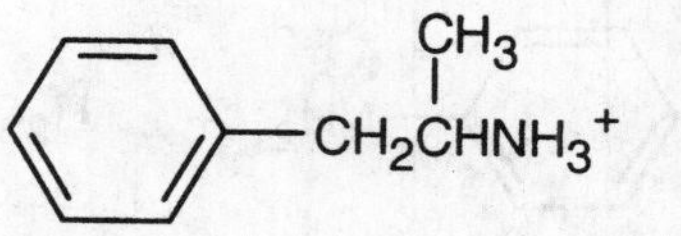

ammonium ion

15.16 – 15.17

(a)

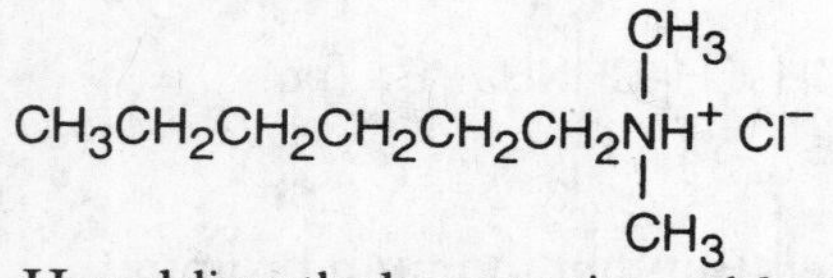

Hexyldimethylammonium chloride
or *N,N*-Dimethylhexylammonium chloride
salt of a tertiary amine

(b)

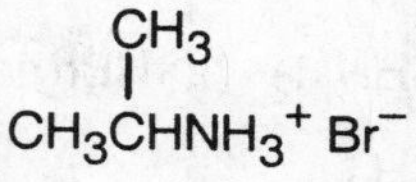

Isopropylammonium bromide

salt of a primary amine

15.18

$$CH_3CH_2CH_2CH_2NH_3^+\ Cl^-(aq) + NaOH\ (aq) \longrightarrow CH_3CH_2CH_2CH_2NH_2 + H_2O\ (l) + NaCl\ (aq)$$

15.19 Benadryl has the general antihistamine structure illustrated below. Attached to the central skeleton ($–Z–CH_2CH_2N–$) of Benadryl are two methyl groups bonded to nitrogen ($R = –CH_3$) and two phenyl groups ($R' = R'' = C_6H_5–$) bonded to Z ($Z = –CHO–$).

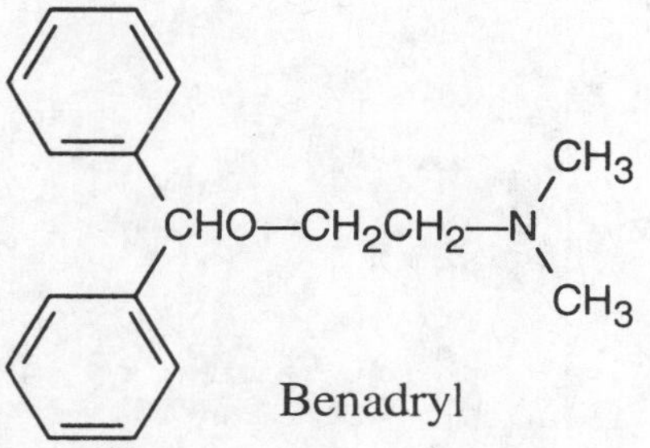
CH3
CHO—CH2CH2—N
CH3

Benadryl

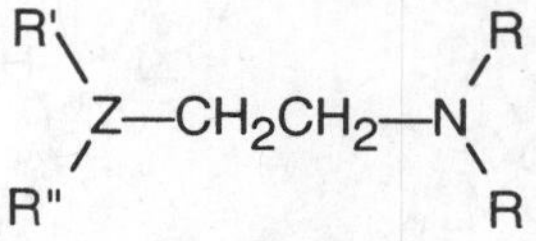
R'
R
Z—CH2CH2—N
R"
R

general antihistamine structure

15.20

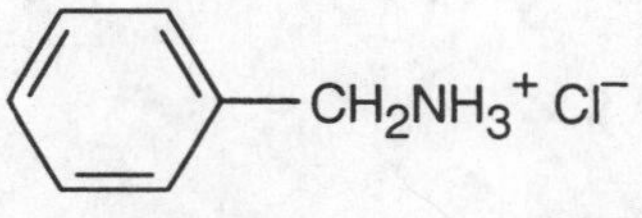
CH2NH3+ Cl−

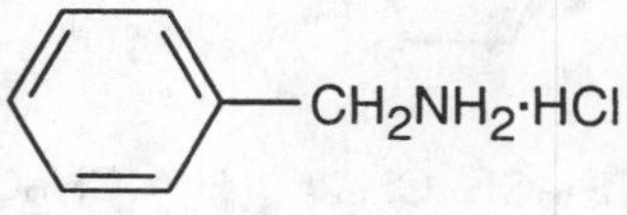
CH2NH2·HCl

Benzylammonium chloride

Understanding Key Concepts

15.21 (a)

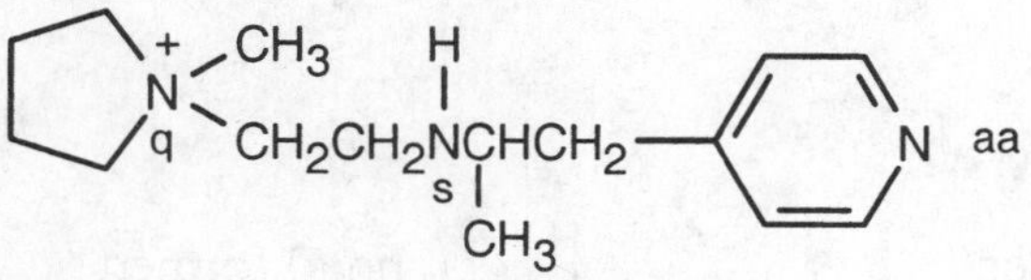
CH3
H
N
q
CH2CH2NCHCH2
s
CH3
N aa

s = secondary
q = quaternary
aa = aromatic amine

(b) The secondary amine group can provide a hydrogen bond. The aromatic amine can accept hydrogen bonds from primary and secondary amine groups but not from other tertiary amine groups. The quaternary group doesn't participate in hydrogen bonding.

15.22

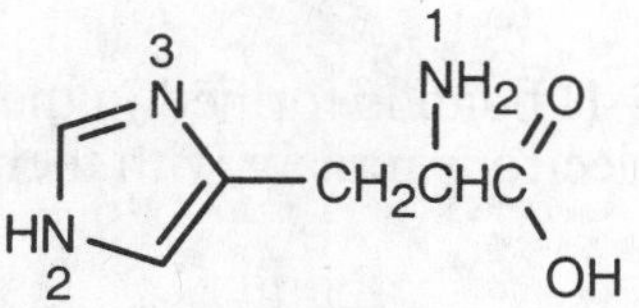
3
N
1
NH2
O
CH2CHC
HN
2
OH

Histidine

(a) All amine groups (as well as the carboxylic acid group) can participate in hydrogen bonding. Nitrogen "3" can accept a hydrogen bond but can't provide one.
(b) Histidine is likely to be water-soluble because it can form hydrogen bonds with water.

15.23

(a)

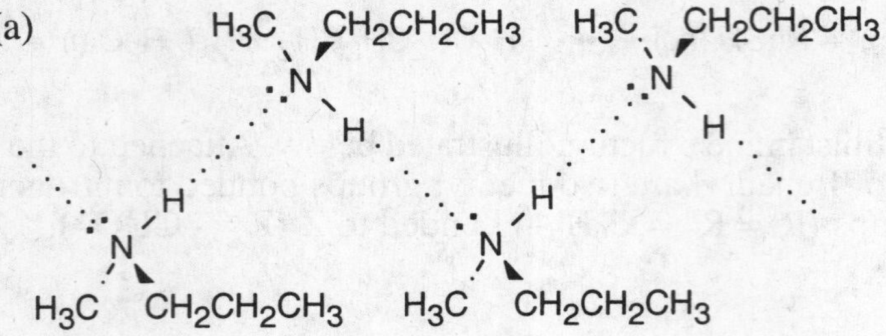

(b)

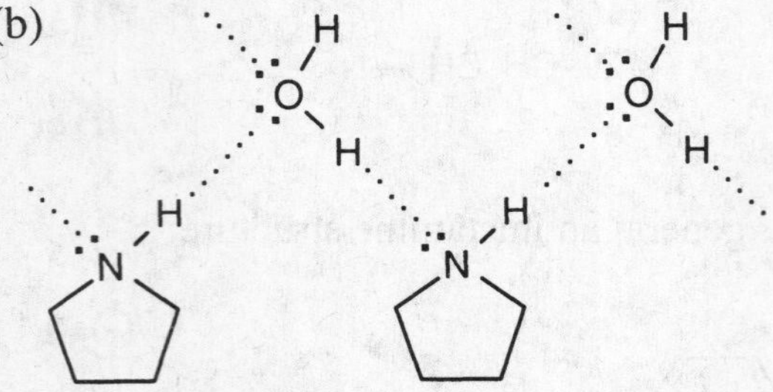

(c)

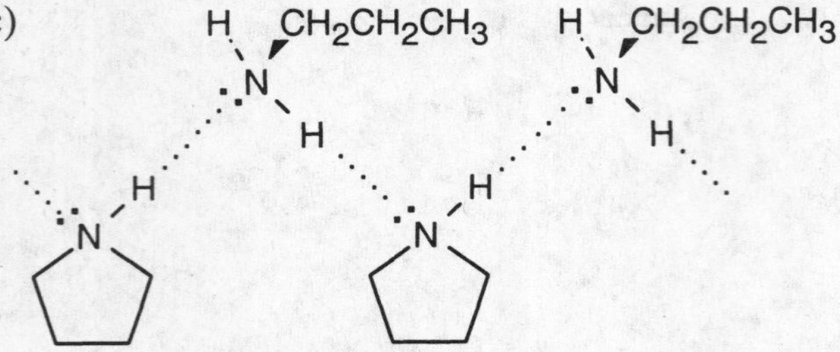

15.24

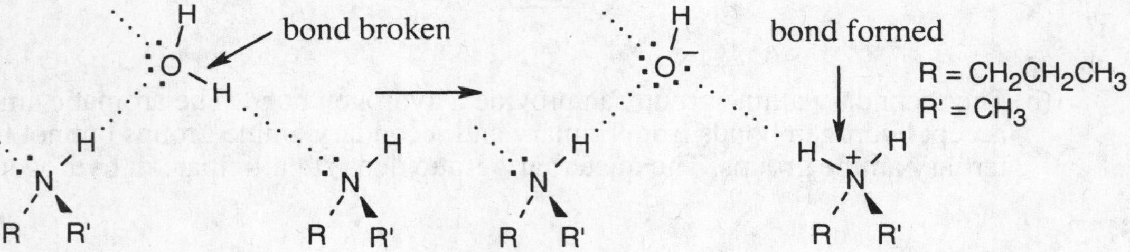
bond broken
bond formed
R = CH2CH2CH3
R' = CH3

An O—H bond of water is broken, and a N—H bond is formed in the reaction to form OH^-, an ammonium ion and an amine. The electrons remain with their original atoms.

15.25

Most basic ⟶ *Least basic*

$(CH_3)_2NH$ > NH_3 > 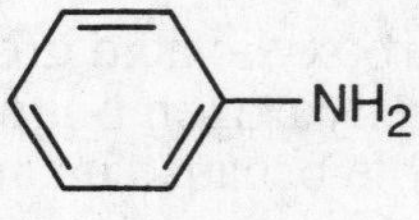

15.26

(a)

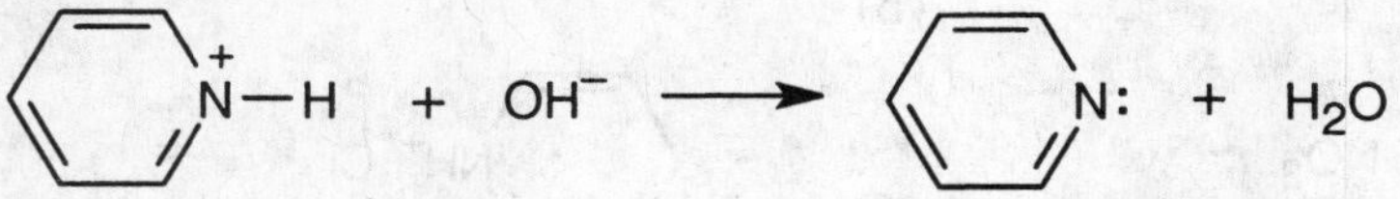

(b)

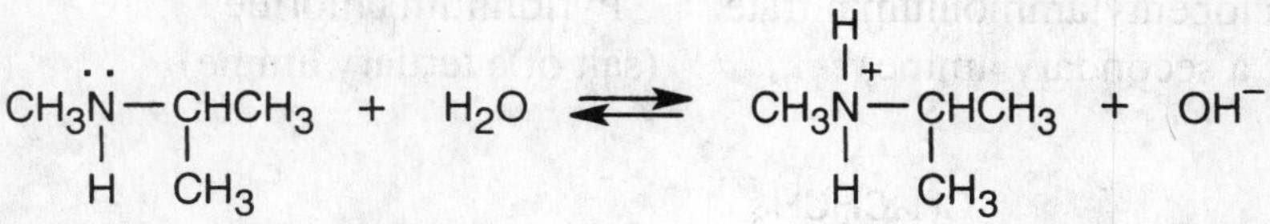

(c)

$$(CH_3)_4N^+ \quad + \quad OH^- \longrightarrow \text{no reaction}$$

(d)

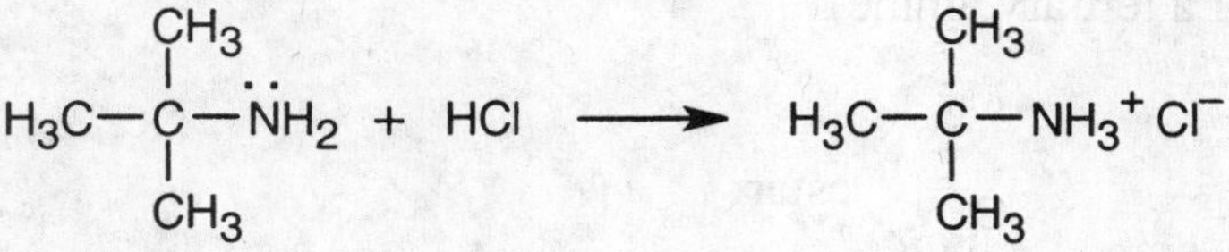

Amines and Ammonium Salts

15.28

(a)

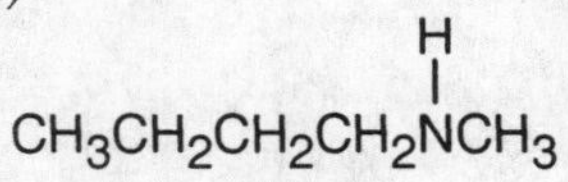

N-Methylbutylamine

(b)

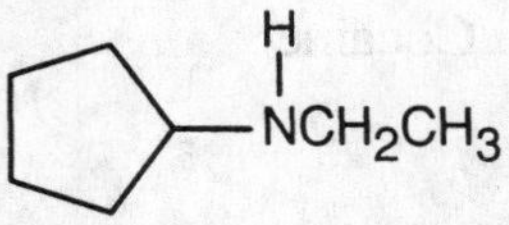

N-Ethylcyclopentylamine

(c)

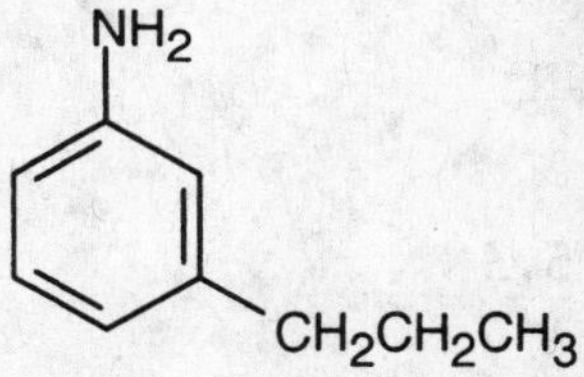

m-Propylaniline

15.30

(a)

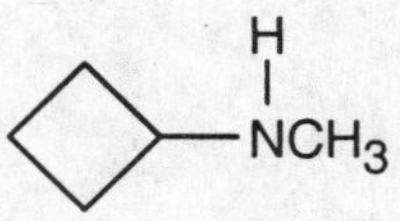

N-Methylcyclobutylamine
secondary amine

(b)

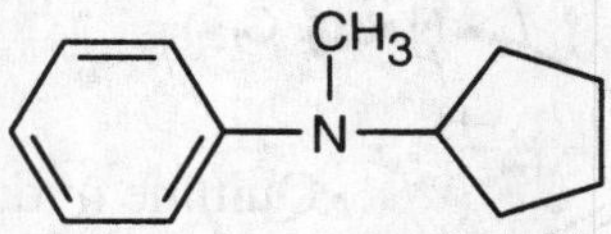

N-Cyclopentyl-*N*-methylaniline
tertiary amine

15.32 Diethylamine is a stronger base than diethyl ether because amines are more basic than ethers.

15.34

(a)

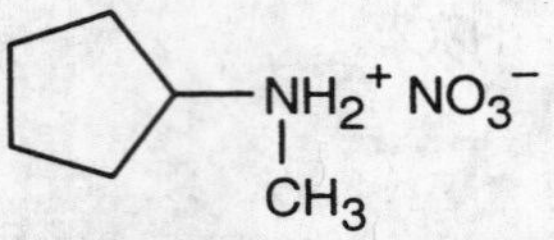
NH2+ NO3−
CH3

N-Methylcyclopentylammonium nitrate
(salt of a secondary amine)

(b)

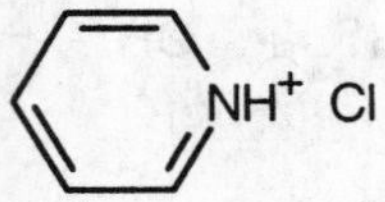
NH+ Cl

Pyridinium chloride
(salt of a tertiary amine)

(c)

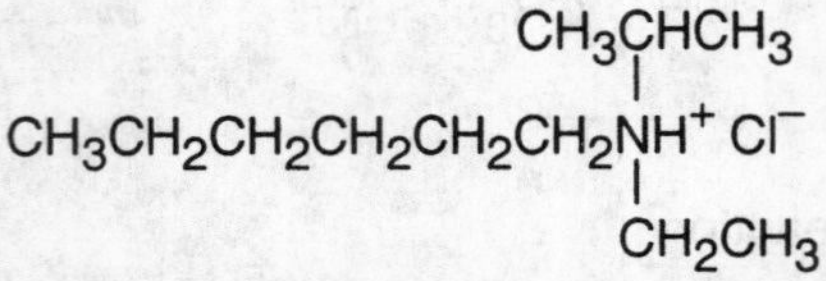
CH3CHCH3
CH3CH2CH2CH2CH2CH2NH+ Cl−
CH2CH3

N-Ethyl-*N*-isopropylhexylammonium chloride
(salt of a tertiary amine)

15.36

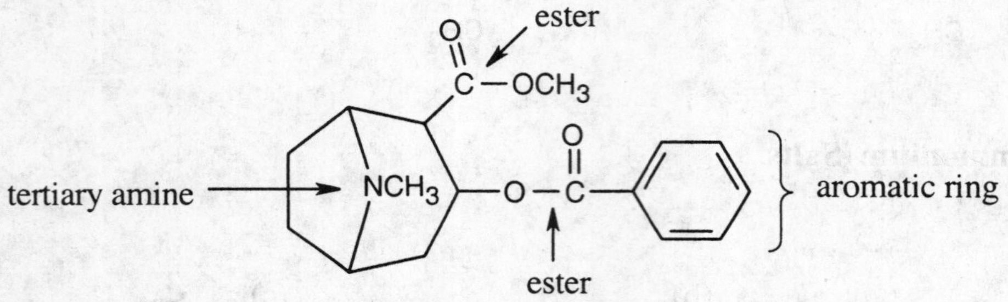
ester
O
C−OCH3
O
tertiary amine
NCH3
O−C
aromatic ring
ester

Cocaine

15.38

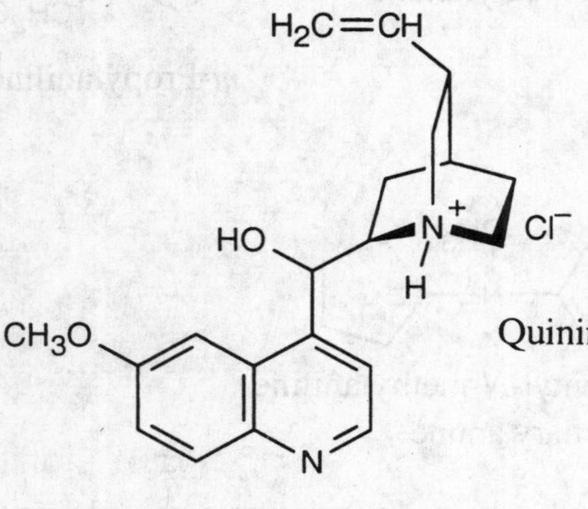
H2C=CH
HO
N+
H
Cl−
CH3O
N

Quinine hydrochloride

The nonaromatic nitrogen is protonated first because it is more basic.

Reactions of Amines

15.40

(a)

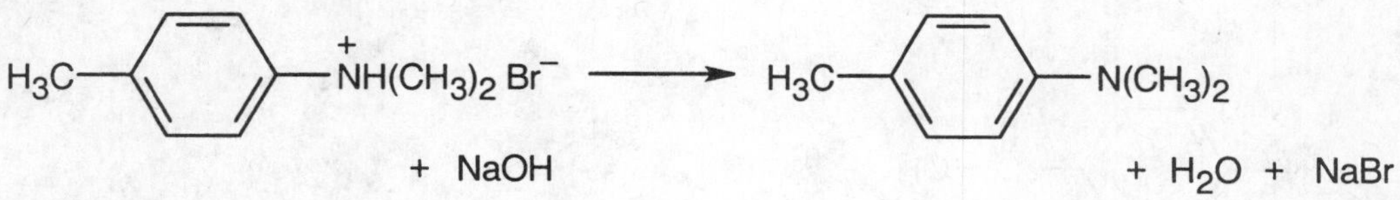
H3C
NH(CH3)2 Br⁻
+ NaOH
H3C
N(CH3)2
+ H2O + NaBr

(b)

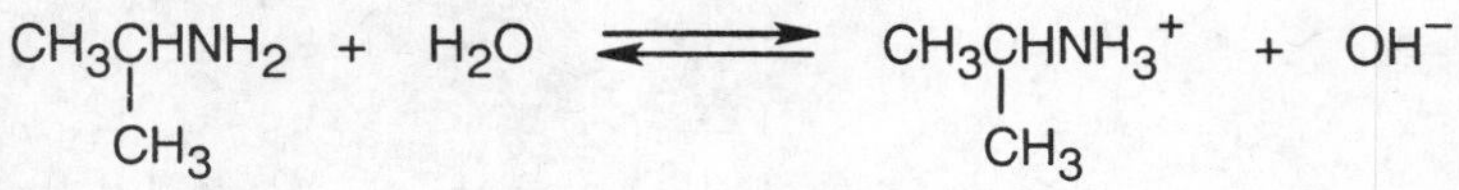
CH3CHNH2 + H2O
CH3
CH3CHNH3+ + OH⁻
CH3

(c)

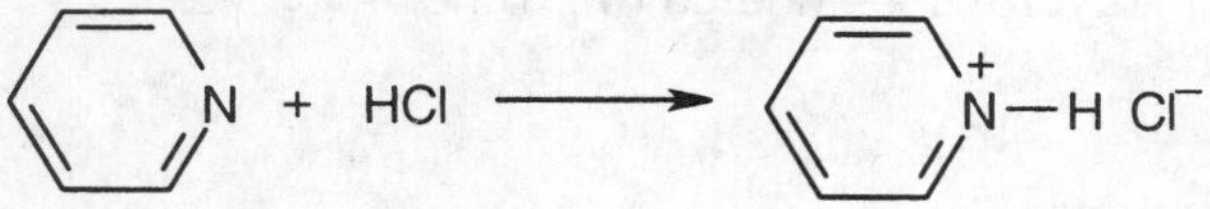
N + HCl
N—H Cl⁻

15.42 Choline doesn't react with HCl because its nitrogen atom isn't basic.

Applications

15.44 Functions that have been attributed to NO include (1) lowering of blood pressure, (2) memory enhancement, (3) relief of angina pain, (4) destruction of parasites, and (5) promotion of wound healing.

15.46

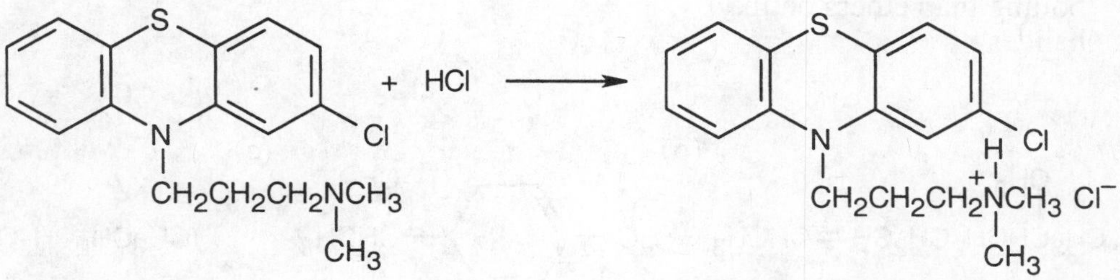
S
N
Cl
CH2CH2CH2NCH3
CH3
+ HCl
S
N
H Cl
CH2CH2CH2NCH3 Cl⁻
CH3

Promazine Promazine hydrochloride

The nitrogen that is not part of a ring is protonated because it is more basic.

15.48 (a) Toxicologists work in three major areas. Clinical toxicologists are involved with the treatment of people harmed by toxic agents. Forensic toxicologists deal with the effects of toxic agents as they apply to criminal cases. Environmental toxicologists study the environmental impact of toxic substances.
(b) When working with a new toxin, a researcher needs to know the structure of the toxin, its mode of action at the molecular level, and a mechanism to reverse its effects.

General Questions and Problems

15.50 Decylamine is much less soluble in water than ethylamine because it resembles a hydrocarbon more than it resembles an amine.

15.52

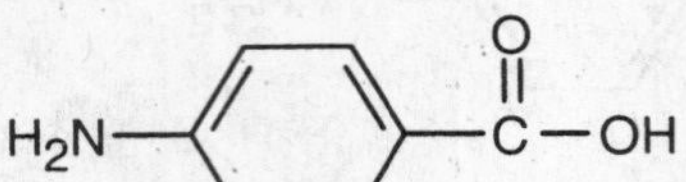
H2N
O
C—OH

PABA

15.54

Acyclovir — related to purine

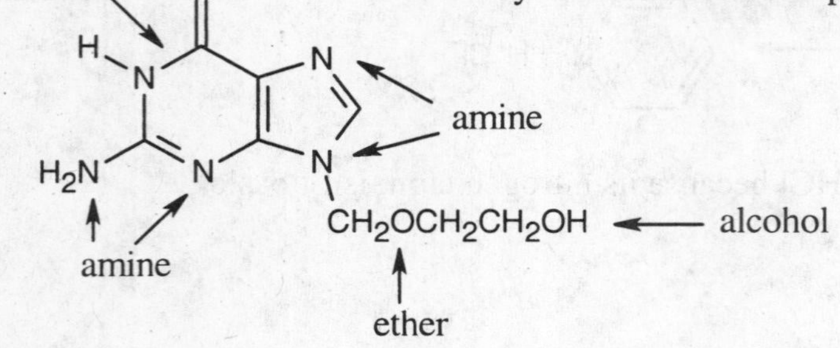
amide
amine
amine
alcohol
ether
CH2OCH2CH2OH

15.56

	Amines	*Alcohols*
(a)	foul smelling	pleasant smelling
(b)	basic	not basic
(c)	lower boiling, due to weaker hydrogen bonds, but higher boiling than ethers or alkyl halides	higher boiling, due to strong hydrogen bonds

15.58

(a)

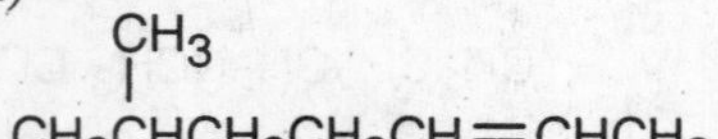
CH3
CH3CHCH2CH2CH=CHCH3

6-Methyl-2-heptene

(b)

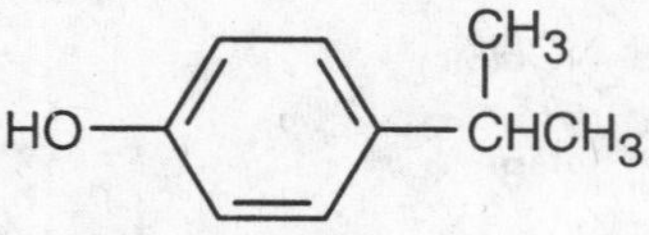
HO
CH3
CHCH3

p-Isopropylphenol

(c)

$(CH_3CH_2CH_2CH_2)_2NH$

Dibutylamine

15.60 Molecules of hexylamine can form hydrogen bonds to each other. Heat must be supplied to break these hydrogen bonds, and thus the boiling point of hexylamine is higher than that of triethylamine, a tertiary amine whose molecules don't hydrogen-bond to each other.

15.62 Psilocin is related to indole.

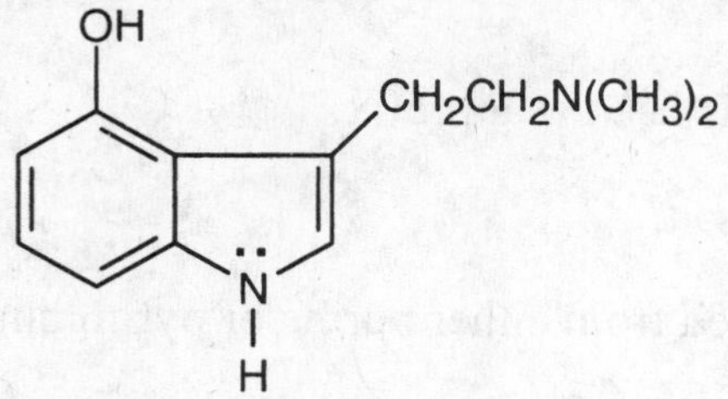
OH
CH2CH2N(CH3)2
N
H

Psilocin

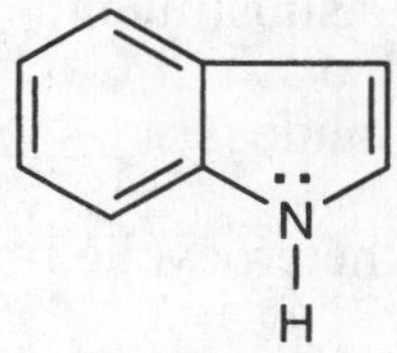
N
H

Indole

15.64 Pyridine is soluble in water because the ring nitrogen can form hydrogen bonds with water. No hydrogen bonding is possible for benzene.

Self-Test for Chapter 15

Multiple choice:

1. Which of the following amines is heterocyclic?
(a) aniline (b) cyclohexylamine (c) pyridine (d) amphetamine

2. Which of the following amines is a secondary amine?
(a) *N*-methylaniline (b) histamine (c) triethylamine (d) codeine

3. The name of the compound shown below is:
(a) ethylcyclopentylamine (b) cyclopentylethylamine (c) *N*-cyclopentylethylamine
(d) *N*-ethylcyclopentylamine

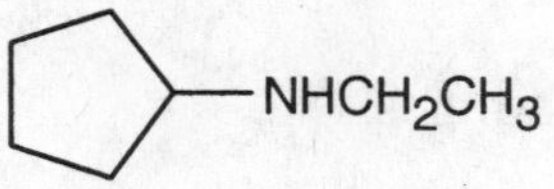
NHCH2CH3

4. An amine and its ammonium salt differ in all respects except
(a) charge (b) solubility (c) carbon skeleton (d) basicity

5. Which of the following amines has the highest boiling point?
(a) triethylamine (b) hexylamine (c) tetramethylammonium chloride (d) dipropylamine

6. Which of the following is an alkaloid?
(a) atropine (b) amphetamine (c) pyrimidine (d) aniline

7. How many isomers of the formula $C_4H_{11}N$ are secondary amines?
(a) 2 (b) 3 (c) 4 (d) 5

8. All of the following amines have a heterocyclic ring except:
(a) nicotine (b) caffeine (c) morphine (d) aniline

9. Propylamine and trimethylamine differ in all respects except:
(a) formula weight (b) boiling point (c) solubility in water (d) melting point

10. Which of the following is a quaternary ammonium salt?
(a) anilinium chloride (b) triethylpropylammonium chloride (c) pyridinium chloride
(d) trimethylammonium chloride

Sentence Completion

1. When the —NH_2 group is a substituent, _______ is used as a prefix.
2. Tetramethylammonium bromide is a _____ amine salt.
3. _______ contains nitrogen heterocyclic rings derived from either purine or pyrimidine.
4. ______ is the science devoted to poisons.
5. A _______ has a nitrogen atom contained in a ring.
6. _______ are a class of amines derived from plants.
7. Simple amines are water-soluble because of _______ ______.
8. Most amines can be made water-soluble by conversion to _______ salts.
9. Nitric oxide is a molecule that is a ____ _______ because it has an unpaired electron.
10. Ammonia is less basic than _______ _____.

True or False

1. Amine groups in biomolecules are usually protonated in body fluids.
2. Ammonium salts are water-soluble.
3. Tertiary amines are higher boiling than primary or secondary amines.
4. Morphine and codeine are alkaloids.
5. Quaternary ammonium salts are acidic.
6. Caffeine is a heterocyclic amine.
7. Heroin is a naturally occurring alkaloid.
8. The physical properties of low-molecular-weight amines and ammonia are similar.
9. NO is responsible for elevating blood pressure.
10. The correct name for $CH_3CH_2CH_2CH_2NHCH_3$ is methylbutylamine.

Match each item in the left column with its partner on the right (use each answer once).

1.	Trimethylamine	(a) Amino acid
2.	Atropine	(b) Vitamin
3.	Piperidine	(c) Primary aromatic amine
4.	Tetramethylammonium chloride	(d) Tertiary amine
5.	Alanine	(e) Aromatic heterocycle
6.	Dimethylamine	(f) Neurotransmitter
7.	Pyridoxine	(g) Primary amine
8.	Putrescine	(h) Nonaromatic heterocycle
9.	Serotonin	(i) Quaternary ammonium salt
10.	Methylamine	(j) Secondary amine
11.	Pyridine	(k) Diamine
12.	Aniline	(l) Alkaloid

Chapter 16 – Aldehydes and Ketones

Chapter Outline

I. Characteristics of aldehydes and ketones (Sections 16.1–16.4).
  A. The carbonyl group (Section 16.1).
    1. Carbonyl groups are polarized, with carbon having a partial positive charge and oxygen having a partial negative charge.
    2. Carbonyl groups are planar, with a 120° bond angle.
    3. Carbonyl compounds can be divided into two groups:
      a. In aldehydes and ketones, the carbonyl carbon is bonded to atoms that don't attract electrons strongly.
      b. In carboxylic acids, esters, anhydrides and amides, the carbonyl carbon is bonded to nitrogen or oxygen.
  B. Naming aldehydes and ketones (Section 16.2).
    1. Aldehydes are named by replacing the suffix of the parent compound with *-al*.
      a. For substituted aldehydes, the carbon chain is numbered with the aldehyde carbon as carbon 1.
      b. Aldehydes with common names are formaldehyde, acetaldehyde and benzaldehyde.
    2. Ketones are named by replacing the suffix of the parent compound with *-one*.
      a. Numbering starts at the end nearer the carbonyl carbon.
      b. Ketones with common names include acetone and acetophenone.
      c. Sometimes, ketones are named by naming the two alkyl groups, followed by the word "ketone".
  C. Properties of aldehydes and ketones (Section 16.3).
    1. Aldehydes and ketones are polar.
    2. Aldehydes and ketones don't hydrogen-bond with each other.
    3. Aldehydes and ketones are soluble in organic solvents.
    4. Simple aldehydes and ketones are water-soluble because they can hydrogen-bond with water.
    5. Aldehydes and ketones have distinctive odors.
    6. Aldehydes and ketones are flammable.
  D. Common aldehydes and ketones (Section 16.4).
    1. Formaldehyde.
      a. Formaldehyde is an irritating component of smog.
      b. Formaldehyde is used as a disinfectant and as a preservative.
      c. Formaldehyde-containing polymers are used in building materials.
    2. Acetaldehyde.
    3. Acetone.
      a. Acetone is a commonly used organic solvent.
      b. Acetone is a product of fat metabolism.

II. Reactions of aldehydes and ketones (Sections 16.5–16.7).
  A. Oxidation (Section 16.5).
    1. Aldehydes can be oxidized to carboxylic acids.
      a. Tollens' reagent converts aldehydes to carboxylic acids and leaves a shiny silver residue on the flask.
      b. Benedict's reagent leaves a brick-red precipitate.
    2. Ketones don't react with most oxidizing agents.

B. Reduction (Section 16.6).
  1. Reducing agents reduce aldehydes to primary alcohols and ketones to secondary alcohols in a two-step reaction.
    a. Hydride ion adds to the carbonyl carbon.
    b. Hydrogen ion adds to the carbonyl oxygen.
  2. In the body, the coenzyme NADH is the reducing agent.

C. Formation of hemiacetals and acetals (Section 16.7).
  1. Hemiacetals.
    a. An alcohol can add to an aldehyde or ketone to form a hemiacetal.
      i. The negatively polarized alcohol oxygen adds to the positively polarized carbonyl carbon.
      ii. The reaction is reversible: Hemiacetals easily revert to an aldehyde or ketone.
    b. Although hemiacetals are often too unstable to isolate, the hemiacetals of sugars are stable.
  2. Acetals.
    a. Hemiacetals can react with a second molecule of an alcohol to form an acetal.
    b. Acetals are stable and can be isolated.
  3. Acetal hydrolysis.
     Aqueous acid reacts with acetals to regenerate the original aldehyde or ketone, plus alcohol.

Solutions to Chapter 16 Problems

16.1

(a)

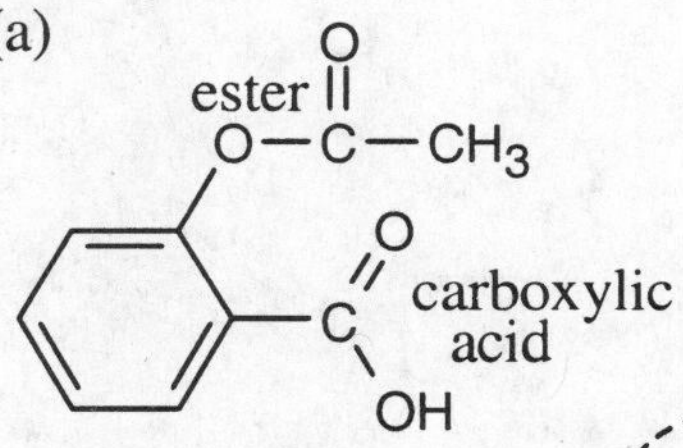
ester
carboxylic acid

Aspirin

(b)

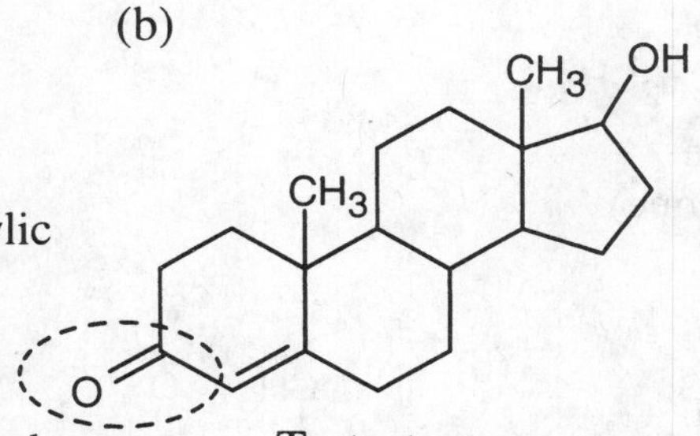
ketone

Testosterone

(c)

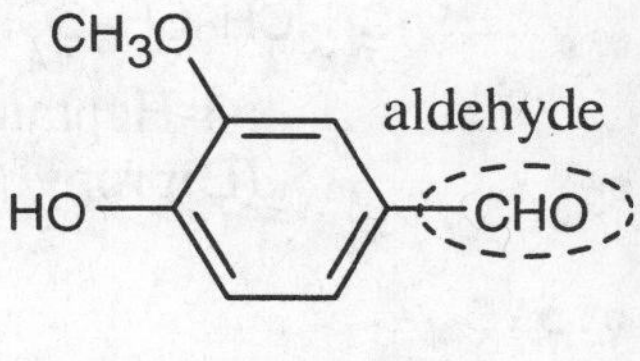
aldehyde

Vanillin

(d) $C_4H_9COCH_3$ — ketone

(e) C_4H_9CHO — aldehyde

(f) $C_4H_9COOCH_3$ — ester

16.2

(d)

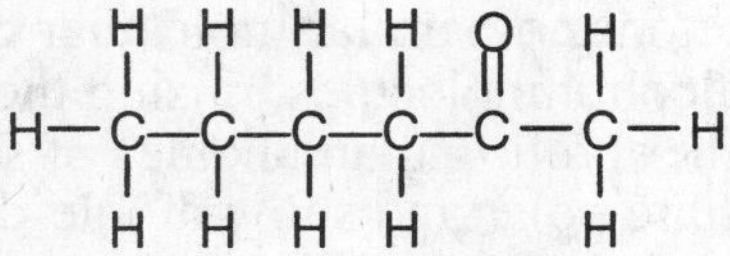

(e)

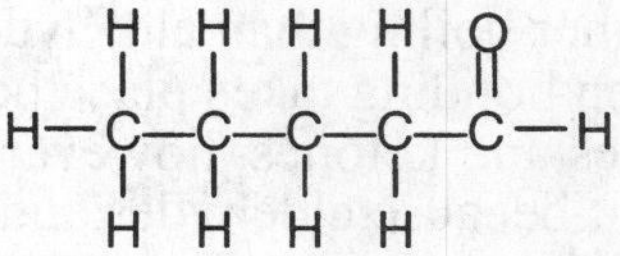

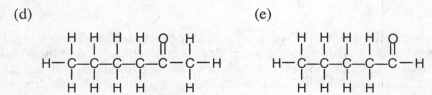

16.3

(a)

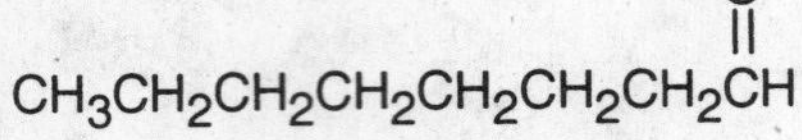

Octanal

(b)

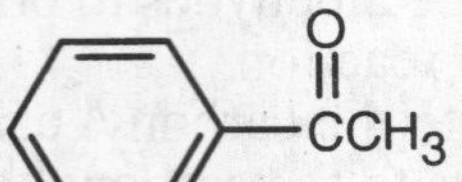

Methyl phenyl ketone

(c)

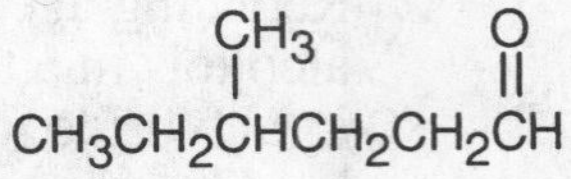

4-Methylhexanal

(d)

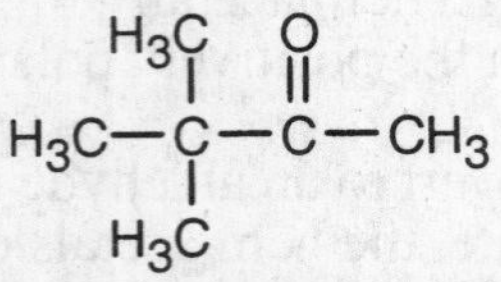

tert-Butyl methyl ketone

16.4

(a)

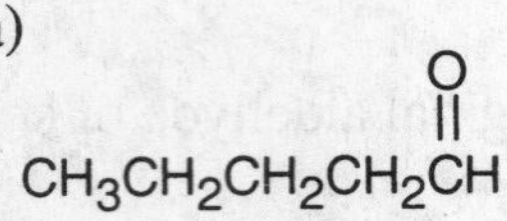

Pentanal

(b)

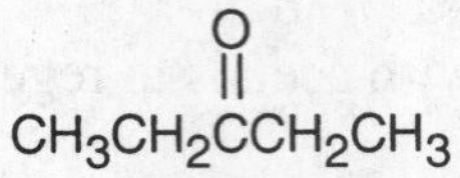

3-Pentanone
(Diethyl ketone)

(c)

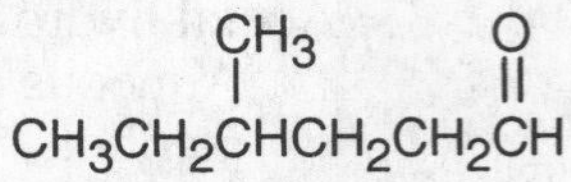

4-Methylhexanal

(d)

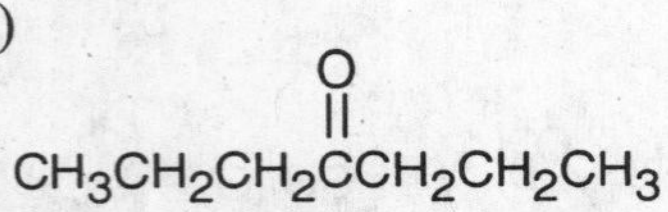

4-Heptanone
(Dipropyl ketone)

16.5

(a)

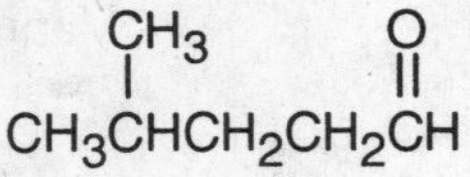

$C_6H_{12}O$

4-Methylpentanal
an aldehyde

(b)

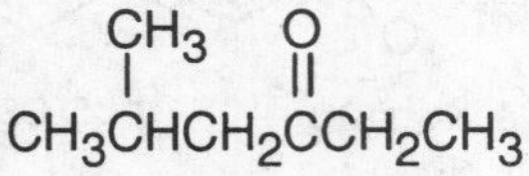

$C_7H_{14}O$

5-Methyl-3-hexanone
a ketone

16.6 The illustrated ketone, 3-pentanone, is a polar, flammable liquid with a boiling point close to 100°C.

16.7 Alcohols are higher boiling than aldehydes and ketones of similar molecular weight because hydrogen bonding takes place between alcohol molecules, raising their boiling points. Aldehydes and ketones, however, are higher boiling than alkanes of similar molecular weight because aldehydes and ketones are polar and show dipole-dipole interactions, which elevate their boiling points relative to the boiling points of alkanes.

16.8

(a)

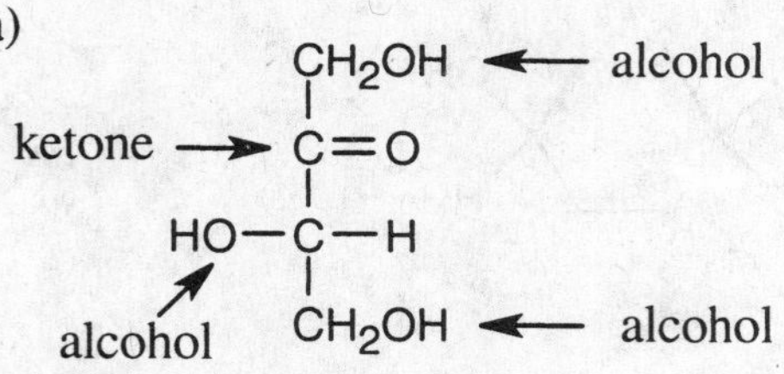
CH2OH
alcohol
ketone
C=O
HO—C—H
alcohol
CH2OH
alcohol

(b)

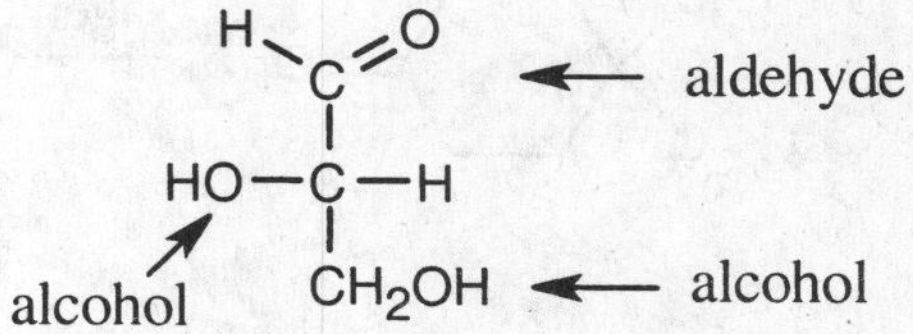
aldehyde
HO—C—H
alcohol
CH2OH
alcohol

(c)

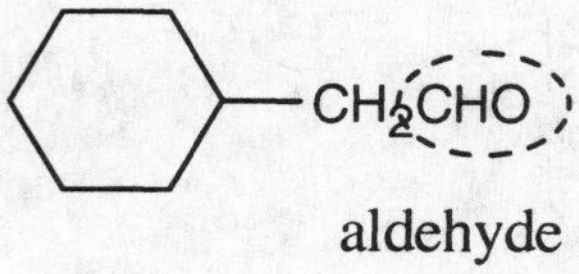
CH2CHO
aldehyde

(d)

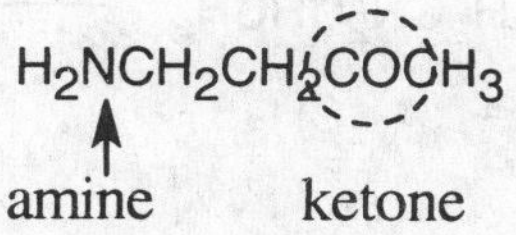
H2NCH2CH2COCH3
amine
ketone

16.9

(a)

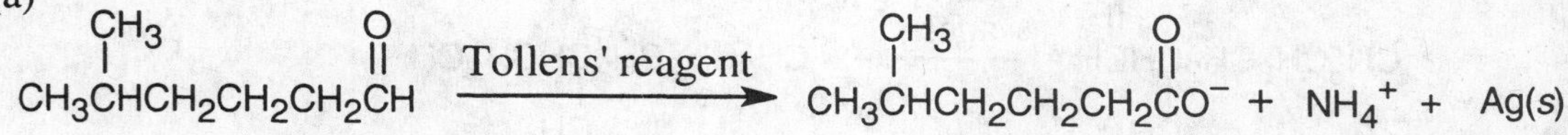
Tollens' reagent
NH4+
Ag(s)

(b)

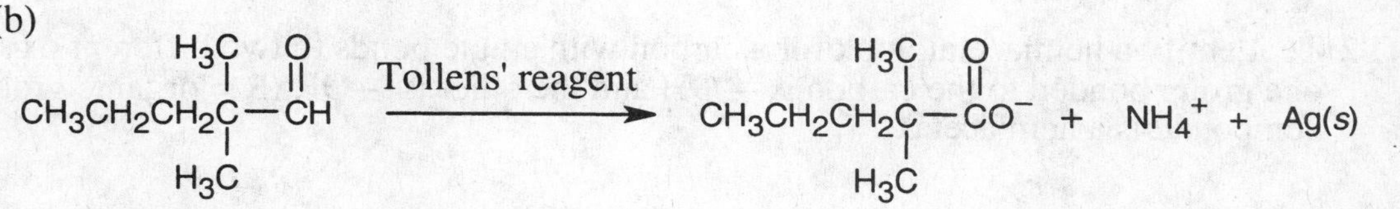
Tollens' reagent
NH4+
Ag(s)

(c)

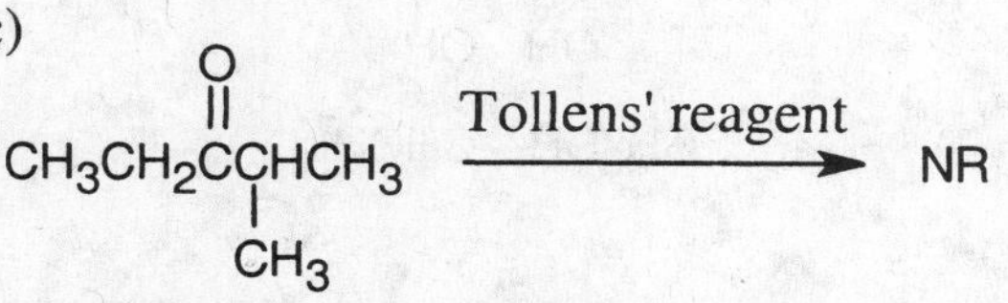
Tollens' reagent
NR

16.10 First, draw the aldehyde or ketone so that the C=O group is vertical. Next, break the double bond, and add one hydrogen to the carbon and one to the oxygen. Finally, redraw the product as a condensed structure.

(a)

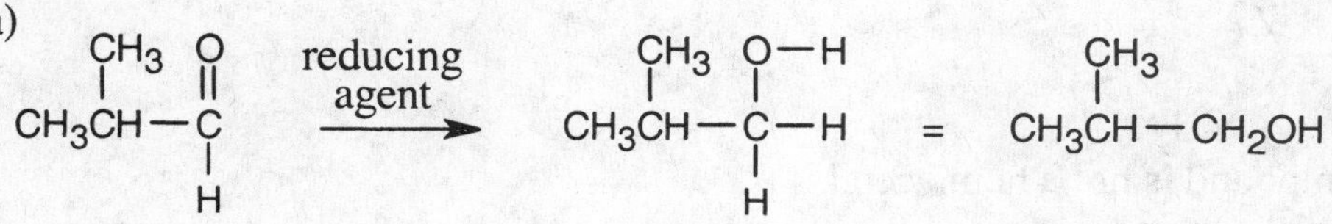
reducing agent
CH3CH—CH2OH

(b)

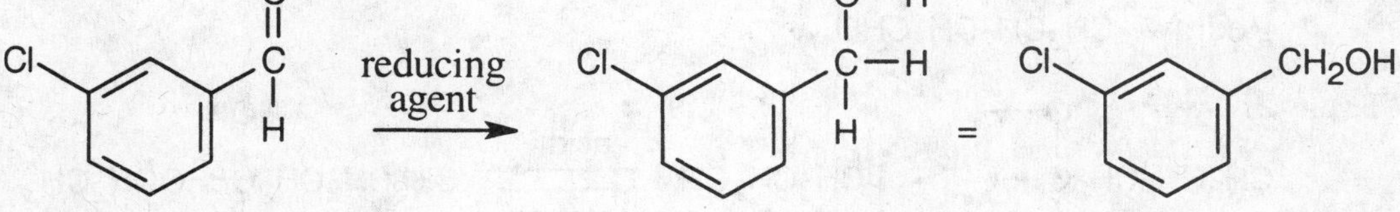
reducing agent
CH2OH

(c)

reducing agent
OH
H

16.11

(a)

H_3C
H_3C
O
reducing
agent
H_3C
H_3C
OH
H

(b)

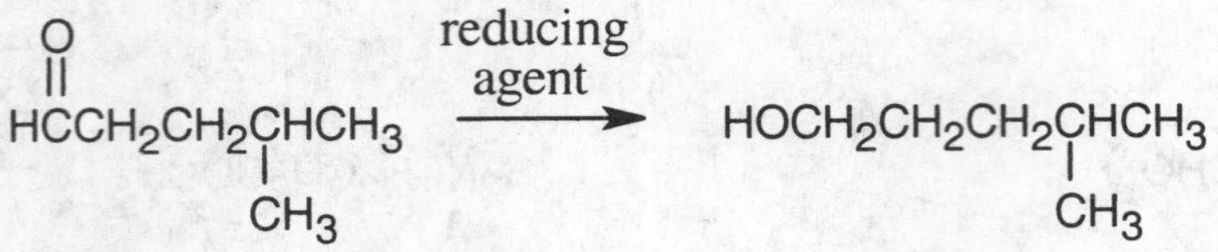

$HCCH_2CH_2CHCH_3$
CH_3
reducing
agent
$HOCH_2CH_2CH_2CHCH_3$
CH_3

(c)

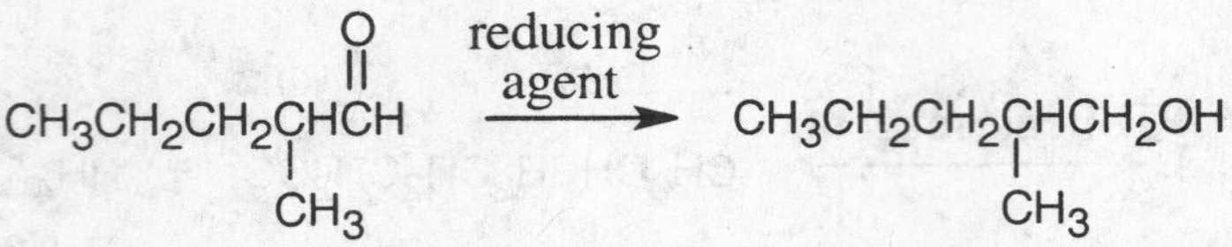

$CH_3CH_2CH_2CHCH$
CH_3
reducing
agent
$CH_3CH_2CH_2CHCH_2OH$
CH_3

16.12 To identify a hemiacetal, look for a carbon with single bonds to two different oxygens. If one group bonded to the carbon is —OH and the other is —OR (R = organic group), the compound is a hemiacetal.

(a)

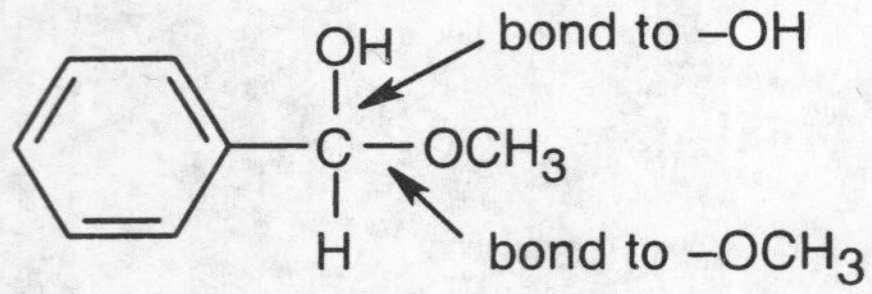

OH
bond to –OH
$C-OCH_3$
H
bond to $-OCH_3$

This compound is a hemiacetal.

(b)

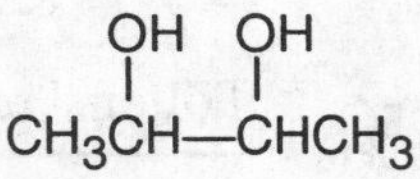

OH OH
$CH_3CH—CHCH_3$

This compound is not a hemiacetal.

(c)

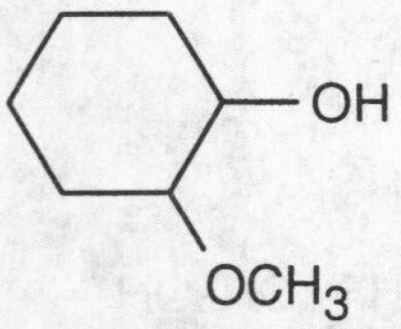

OH
OCH_3

This compound is not a hemiacetal.

16.13

(a)

Redraw $CH_3CH_2CH_2CHO$ as

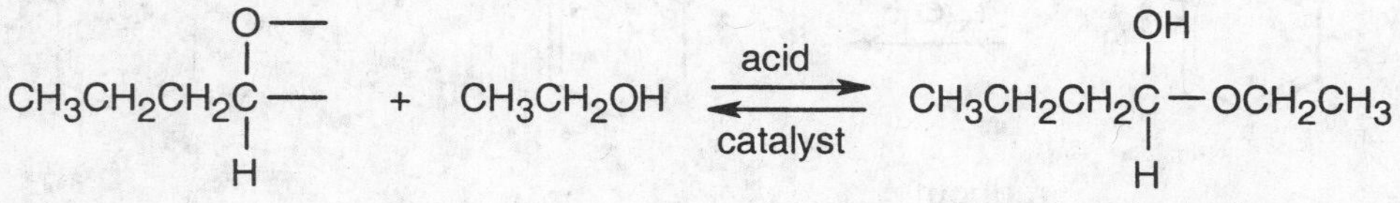

O—
$CH_3CH_2CH_2C—$
H
+ CH_3CH_2OH
acid
catalyst
OH
$CH_3CH_2CH_2C-OCH_2CH_3$
H

hemiacetal

The hemiacetal is formed by adding –H to oxygen and $-OCH_2CH_3$ to carbon.

(b)

Redraw $CH_3CH_2\overset{\overset{O}{\|}}{C}CH_2CH(CH_3)_2$ as

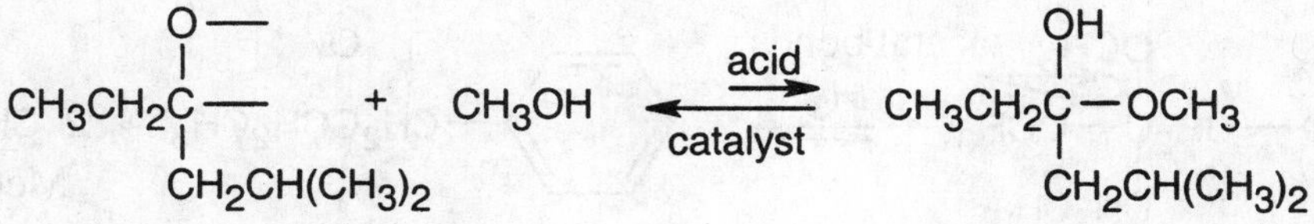

hemiacetal

The equilibrium favors starting material.

16.14 Replace the —H bonded to oxygen with the alkyl part of the alcohol reagent to arrive at the structure of the acetal.

(a)

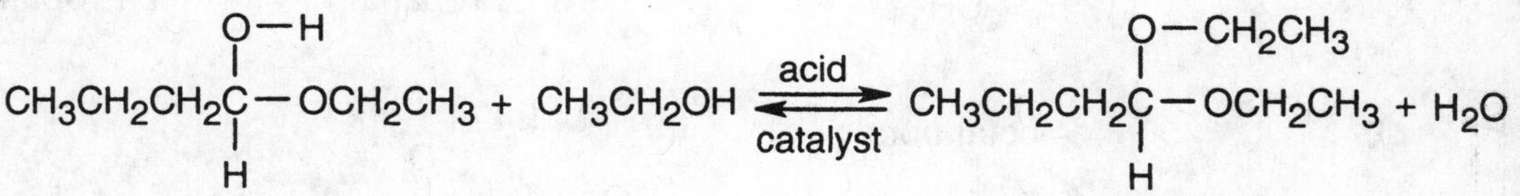

acetal

(b)

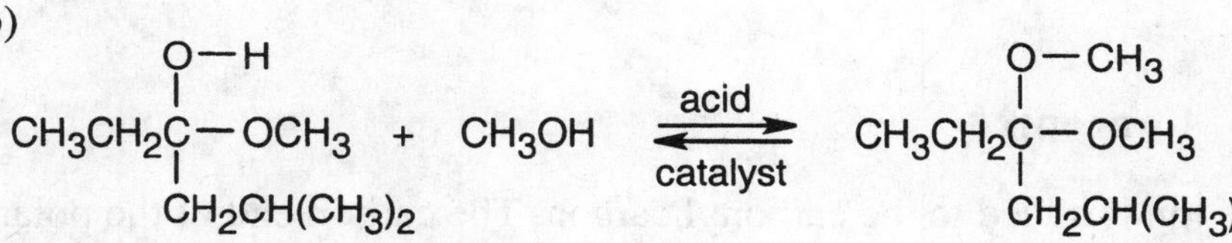

acetal

16.15 Follow the instructions for Worked Example 16.5. If one carbon is bonded to two —OR groups, the compound is an acetal.

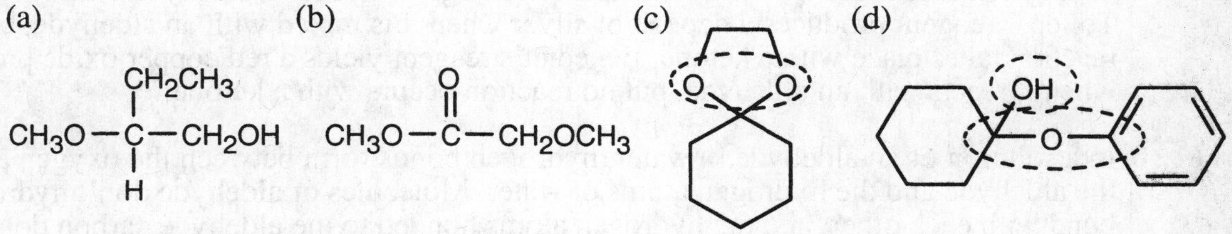

(a) neither acetal nor hemiacetal

(b) neither acetal nor hemiacetal

(c) acetal

(d) hemiacetal

16.16 If the carbon that bears the —OH or —OR groups also has a —H *and* an —R group bonded to it, the original compound was an aldehyde. If the carbon has two —R groups bonded to it, the original compound was a ketone. Thus, both acetal (c) and hemiacetal (d) were formed from ketones.

16.17 Find the two –OR groups that form the acetal. Remove them and replace them with =O to form the original aldehyde or ketone. Add –H to the –OR groups to form the original alcohol.

(a)

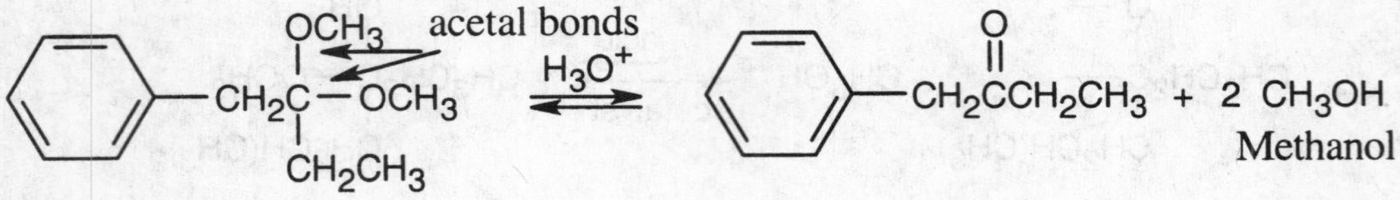
acetal bonds
Methanol

(b)

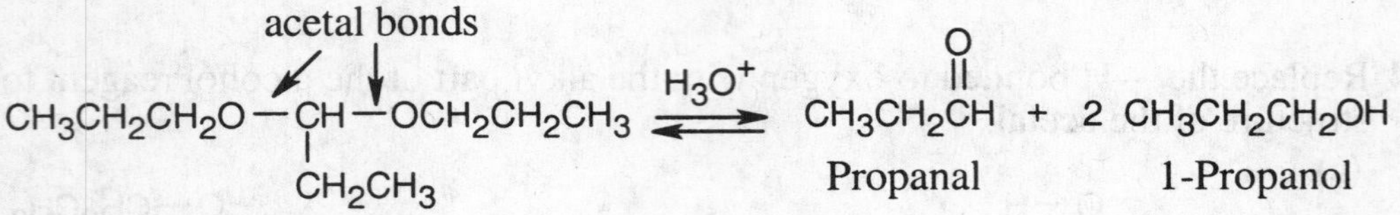
acetal bonds
Propanal
1-Propanol

(c)

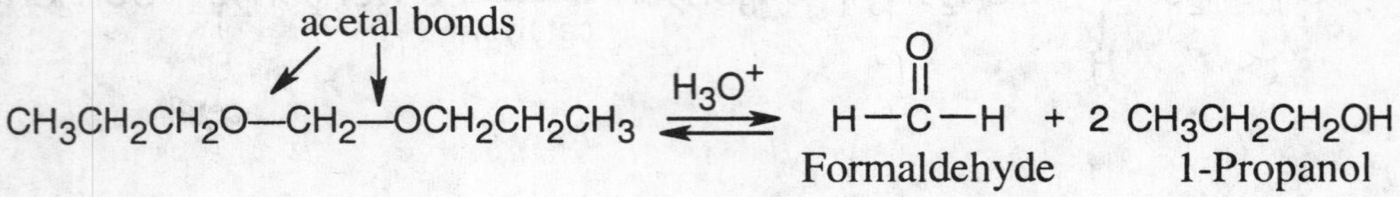
acetal bonds
Formaldehyde
1-Propanol

Understanding Key Concepts

16.18 (a) The hydride ion is added to the carbonyl carbon. The carbon end of the polar C=O bond has a partial positive charge, and thus reaction with negatively charged reagents occurs at carbon.
(b) The top arrow (reaction to the right) represents reduction, and the bottom arrow (reaction to the left) represents oxidation.

16.19 Aldehydes can be oxidized to carboxylic acids, but ketones cannot. Two tests that can distinguish aldehydes from ketones take advantage of selective aldehyde oxidation. Tollens' reagent produces a deposit of silver when it is mixed with an aldehyde, but no reaction takes place with a ketone. Benedict's reagent yields a red copper oxide precipitate when it reacts with an aldehyde, but no reaction occurs with a ketone.

16.20 In a solution of an aldehyde in water, hydrogen bonds form between the oxygen atoms of the aldehyde and the hydrogen atoms of water. Molecules of aldehyde don't hydrogen-bond with each other, and the hydrogen atoms bonded to the aldehyde carbon don't take part in hydrogen bonding.

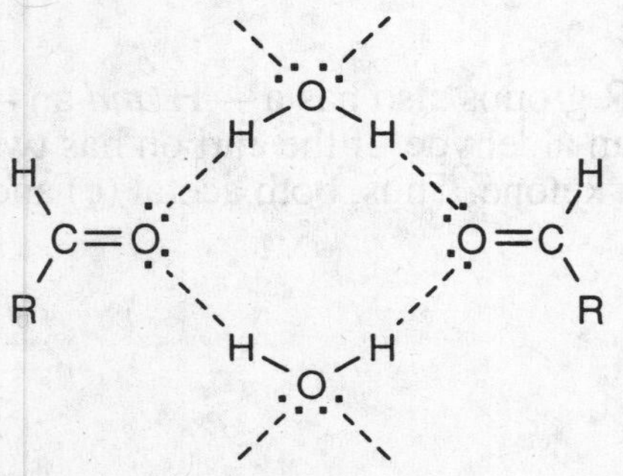

16.21 (a) Under acidic conditions, an alcohol adds to the carbonyl group of an aldehyde to form a hemiacetal. Although some hemiacetals are stable, most hemiacetals are either reconverted to aldehydes or further react with a second molecule of the alcohol to form acetals. The yield of acetal can be improved if the water by-product is removed from the reaction mixture, driving the equilibrium to the right.

(b)

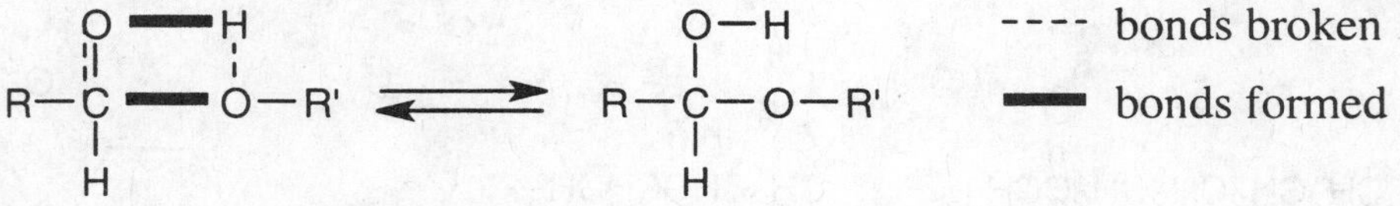
---- bonds broken
bonds formed

16.22 In solution, glucose exists primarily in the cyclic hemiacetal form shown below because it is more stable in this form.

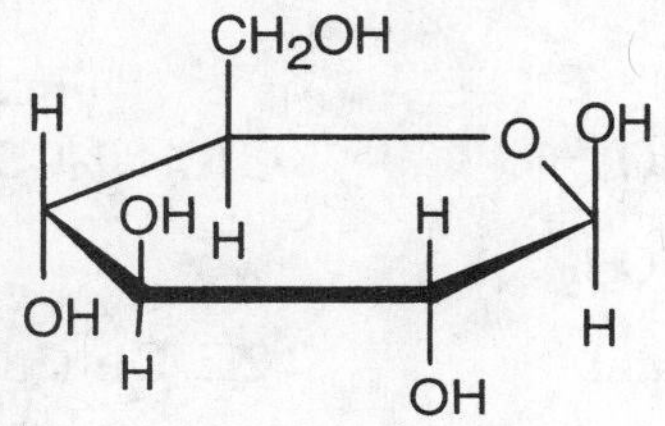

16.23 One equivalent of an alcohol adds to the carbonyl group of an aldehyde or ketone to form a hemiacetal. Two equivalents of alcohol add to the carbonyl group to yield an acetal.

Aldehydes and Ketones

16.24

(a) 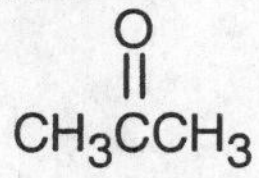

(b) 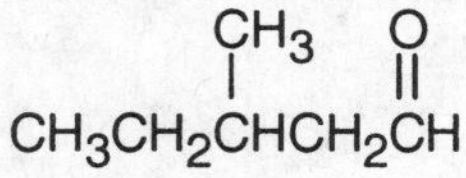

(c) 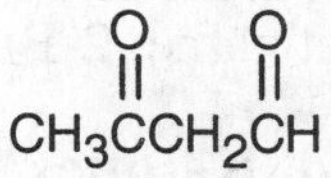

(d) 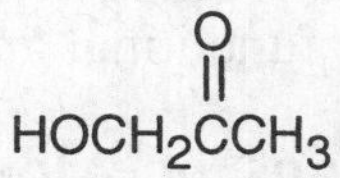

16.26

(a) 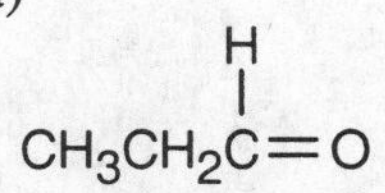

aldehyde

(b) 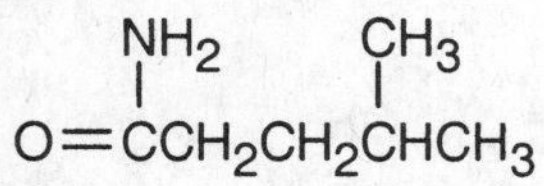

amide

(c) $CH_3CH_2-O-CH=CH_2$

no carbonyl group

(d) 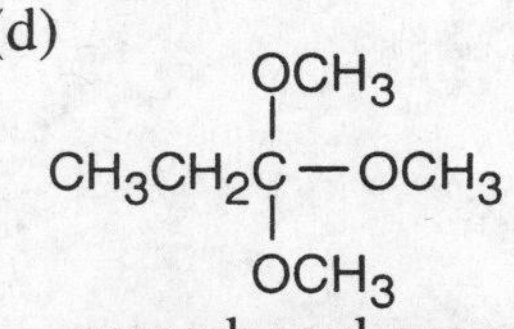

no carbonyl group

(e) 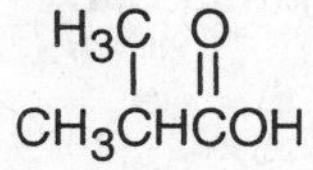

carboxylic acid

(f) 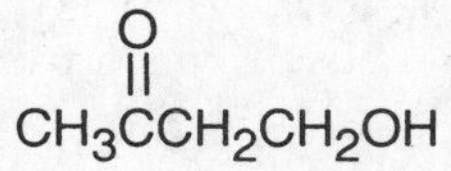

ketone

Structure (a) is an aldehyde, and structure (f) is a ketone.

16.28

(a)

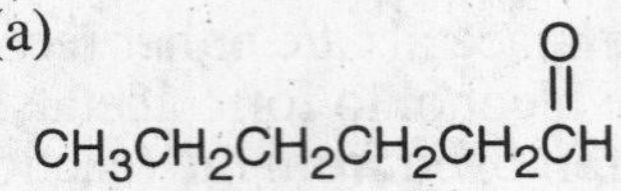

Hexanal

(b)

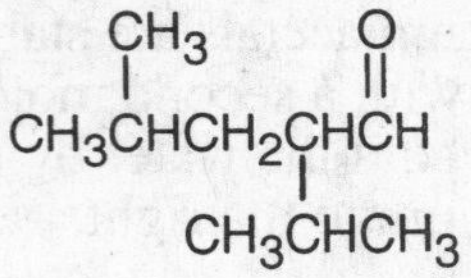

2-Isopropyl-4-methylpentanal

(c)

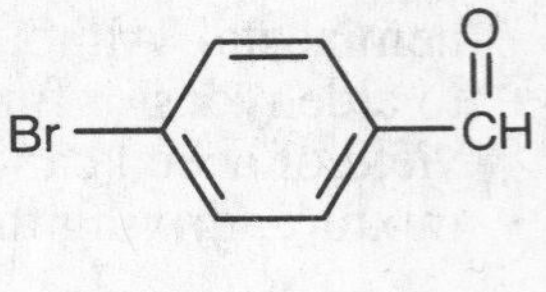

p-Bromoobenzaldehyde

(d)

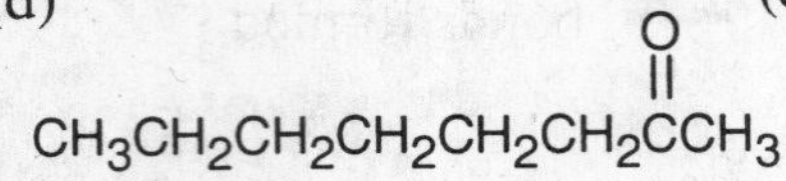

2-Octanone

(e)

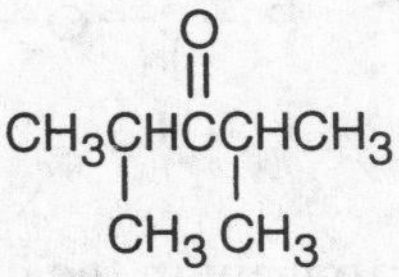

2,4-Dimethyl-3-pentanone

(f)

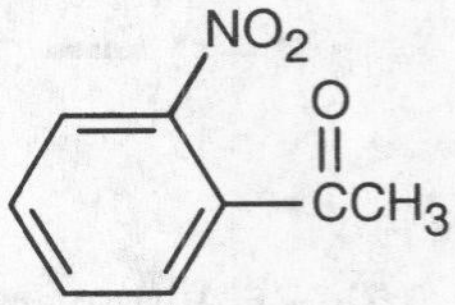

o-Nitroacetophenone

16.30

(a)

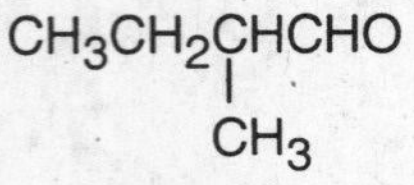

2-Methylbutanal

(b)

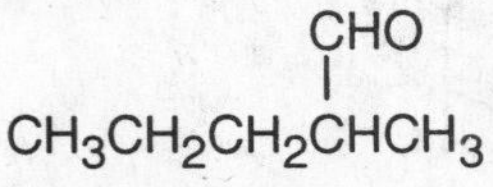

2-Methylpentanal

(c)

$(CH_3)_3CCHO$

2,2-Dimethylpropanal

(d)

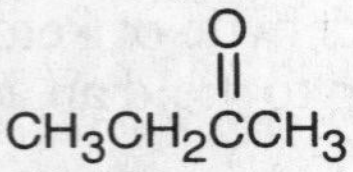

2-Butanone

(e)

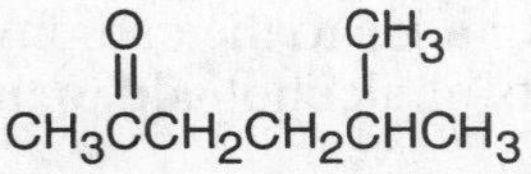

5-Methyl-2-hexanone

16.32 (a) (b)The names 1-butanone and 4-butanone are incorrect because a ketone group can't occur at the end of a carbon chain.
(c) Numbering must start at the end of the carbon chain that is closer to the ketone functional group. Correct name: 2-Butanone.

Reactions of Aldehydes and Ketones

16.34 A *hemiacetal* is produced when an aldehyde reacts with an alcohol in a 1:1 ratio. No second product is formed.

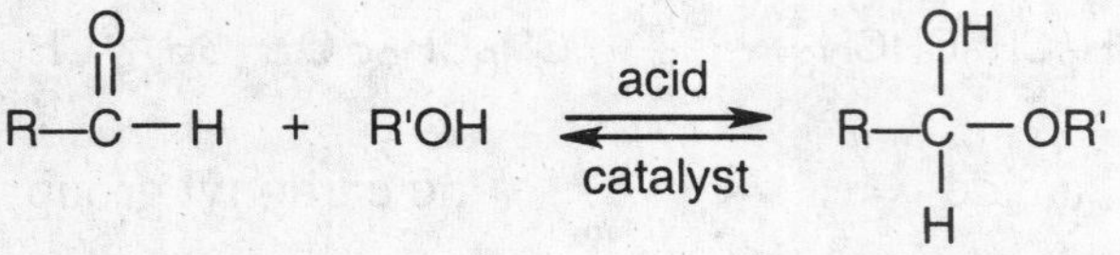

hemiacetal

16.36 Remember that only aldehydes react with Tollens' reagent. Ketones are not oxidized.

	Compound	*Tollens' Product*	*Reduction Product*
(a)	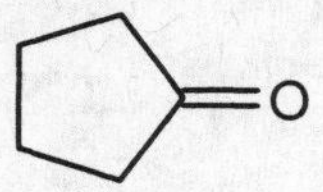	no reaction	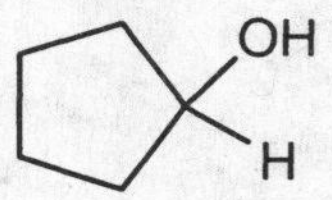
(b)	$CH_3CH_2CH_2CH_2CH_2\overset{O}{\overset{\|}{C}}H$	$CH_3CH_2CH_2CH_2CH_2\overset{O}{\overset{\|}{C}}OH$	$CH_3CH_2CH_2CH_2CH_2CH_2OH$
(c)	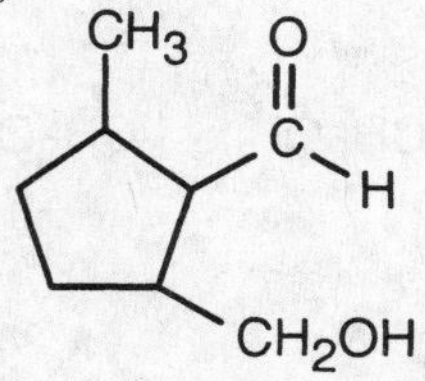	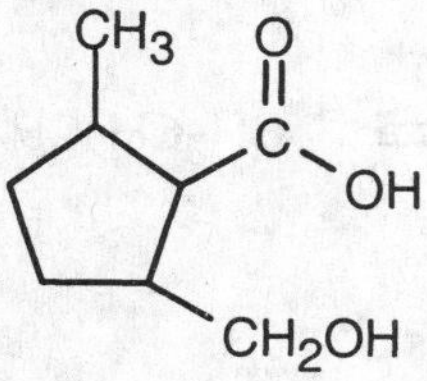	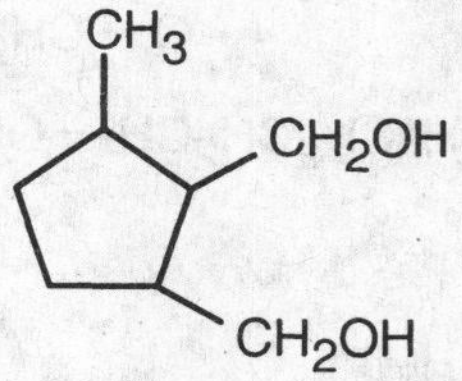

16.38

	Carboxylic acid	*Aldehyde*	*Primary Alcohol*
(a)	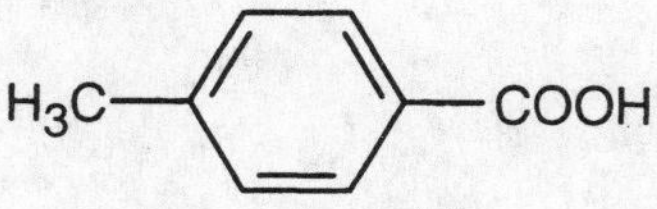	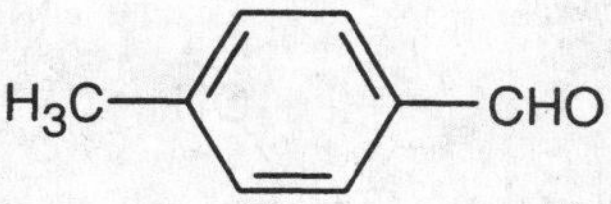	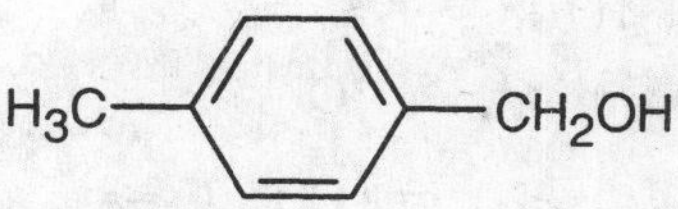
(b)	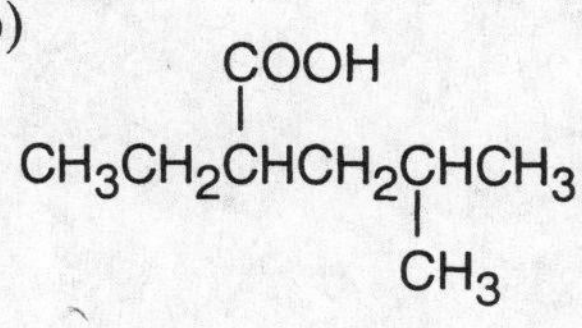	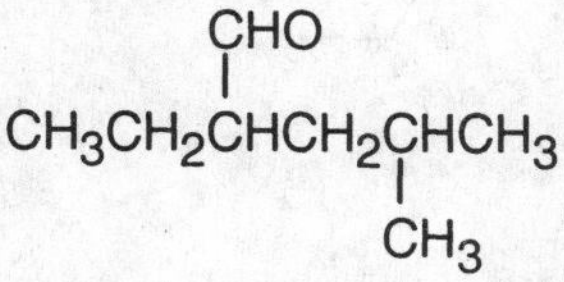	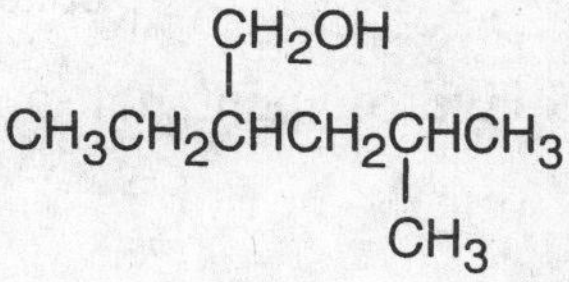
(c)	$CH_3CH{=}CHCOOH$	$CH_3CH{=}CHCHO$	$CH_3CH{=}CHCH_2OH$

16.40

(a)

$$CH_3CH_2\overset{\overset{\displaystyle O}{\|}}{C}CH_3 \;+\; CH_3CH_2CH_2OH \;\underset{\text{catalyst}}{\overset{\text{acid}}{\rightleftharpoons}}\; CH_3CH_2\overset{\overset{\displaystyle OH}{|}}{\underset{\underset{\displaystyle CH_3}{|}}{C}}{-}OCH_2CH_2CH_3$$

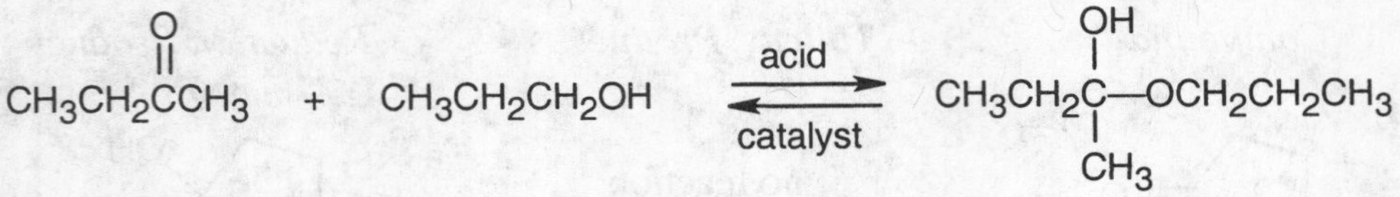

(b)

$$CH_3CH_2CH_2\overset{\overset{\displaystyle O}{\|}}{C}H \;+\; (CH_3)_2CHOH \;\underset{\text{catalyst}}{\overset{\text{acid}}{\rightleftharpoons}}\; CH_3CH_2CH_2\overset{\overset{\displaystyle OH}{|}}{\underset{\underset{\displaystyle H}{|}}{C}}{-}OCH(CH_3)_2$$

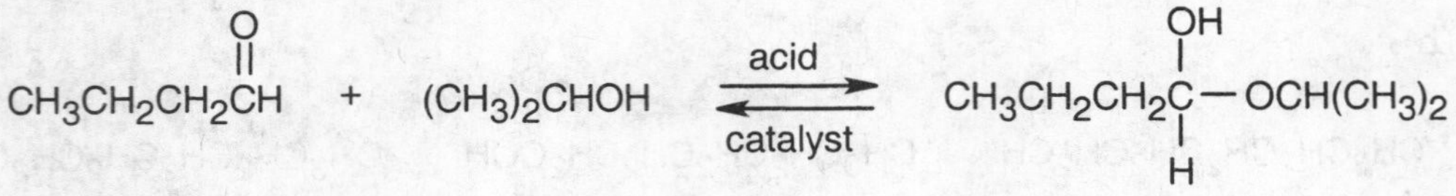

(c)

$$CH_3CH_2CH_2\overset{\overset{\displaystyle O-CH_2CH_3}{|}}{C}H{-}OCH_3 \;\overset{H_3O^+}{\rightleftharpoons}\; CH_3CH_2CH_2\overset{\overset{\displaystyle O}{\|}}{C}H \;+\; CH_3CH_2OH \;+\; CH_3OH$$

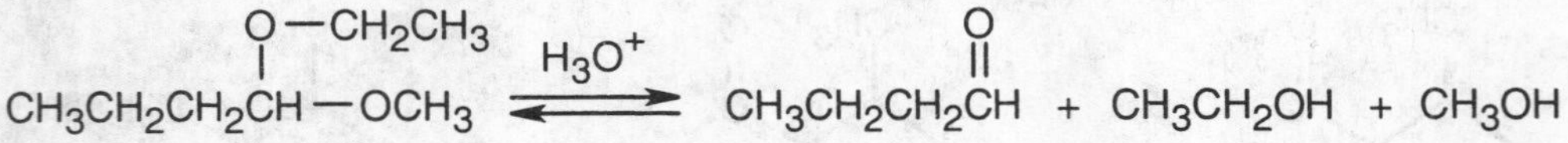

(d)

$$\rightleftharpoons \quad \overset{H_3C}{\underset{H_3C}{>}}C{=}O \;+\; HOCH_2CH_2OH$$

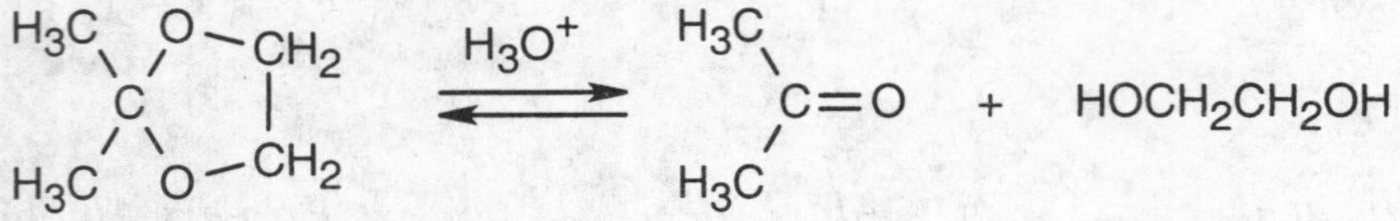

16.42

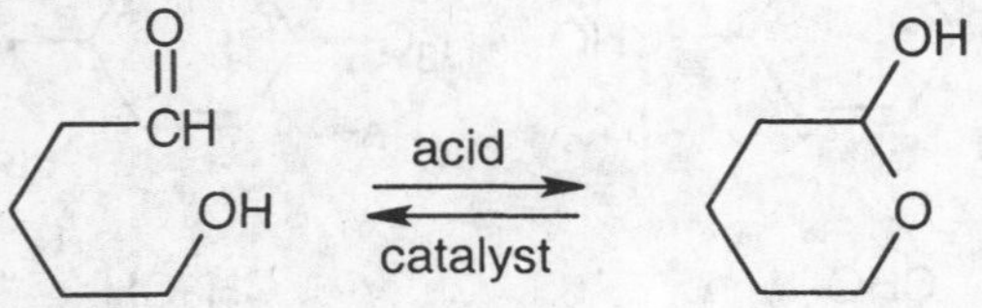

5-Hydroxypentanal

16.44

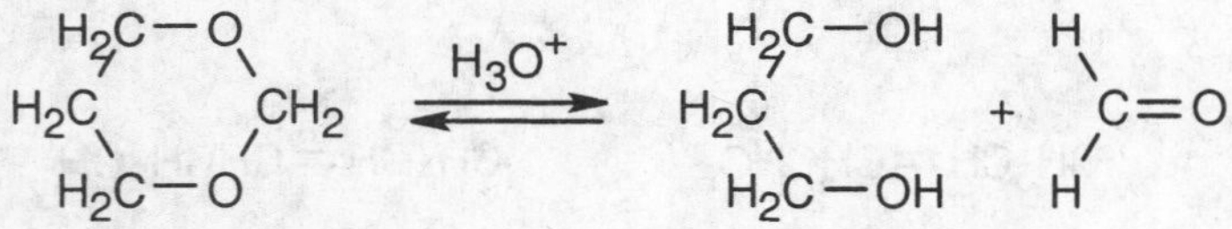

16.46

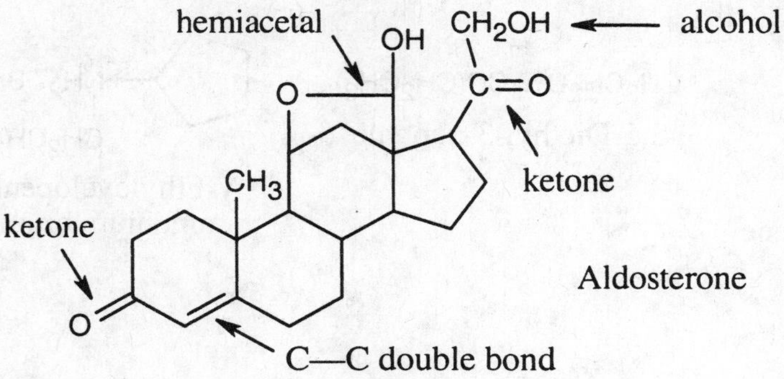
hemiacetal
OH
CH2OH
alcohol
O
C=O
ketone
CH3
ketone
O
C—C double bond

Aldosterone

The hemiacetal group is derived from an aldehyde because the hemiacetal carbon has a hydrogen atom bonded to it.

Applications

16.48

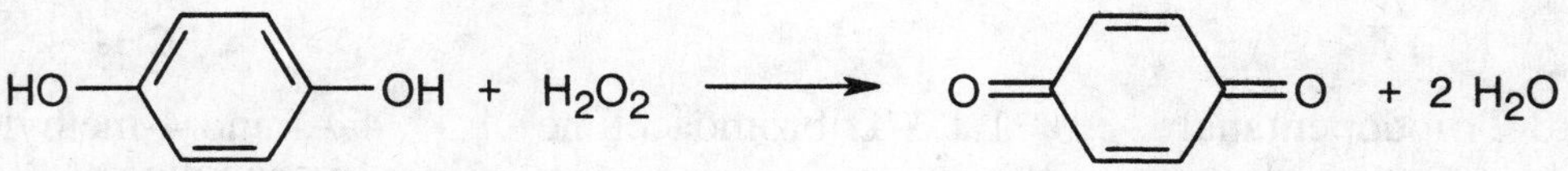
HO
OH + H2O2
O
O + 2 H2O

When *p*-dihydroxybenzene is oxidized, hydrogen peroxide is reduced.

16.50 Vanillin is an aromatic molecule with a polar hydroxyl group. The solvent of choice for extraction of vanillin from vanilla beans should also be polar, organic and nontoxic. Ethanol is a good choice.

16.52 (a) There are several advantages to using *in vitro* testing for acute toxicity. *In vitro* testing is relatively inexpensive, and many more tests can be performed for the same cost. In addition, animals don't have to be sacrificed for *in vitro* testing.
(b) Since *in vitro* testing is performed on cultured cells that are identical, the results of testing may not be reliable for organisms that have many different kinds of cells.

General Questions and Problems

16.54

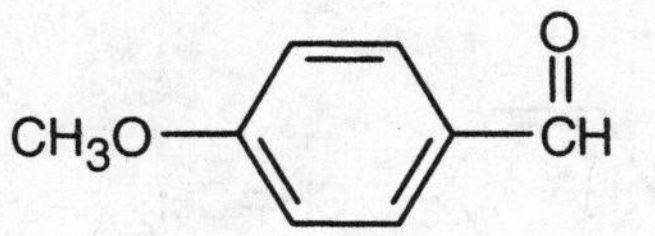
O
CH3O
CH

p-Methoxybenzaldehyde

16.56 The portion of the odor due to aldehyde is less stable because aldehydes are easily oxidized to carboxylic acids.

16.58

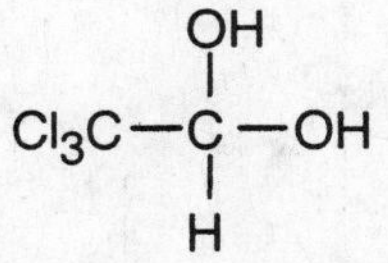
OH
Cl3C—C—OH
H

Chloral hydrate

16.60

(a)

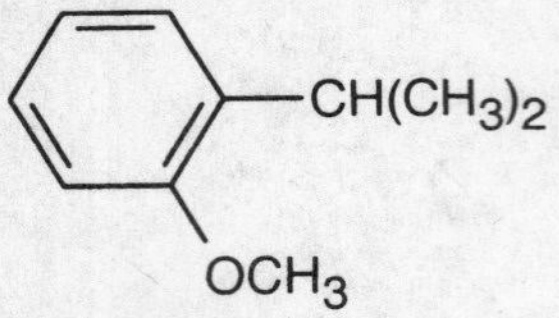

o-Isopropylmethoxybenzene
or
o-Isopropylanisole

(b)

$CH_3CH_2C\equiv CC(CH_2CH_3)_3$

5,5-Diethyl-3-heptyne

(c)

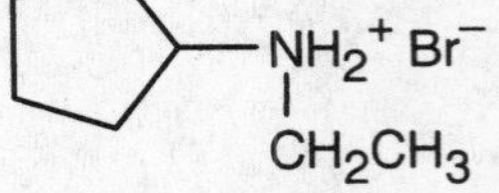

N-Ethylcyclopentylammonium bromide

(d)

$(CH_3CH_2)_2N(CH_2)_5CH_3$

N,N-Diethylhexylamine

16.62

(a)

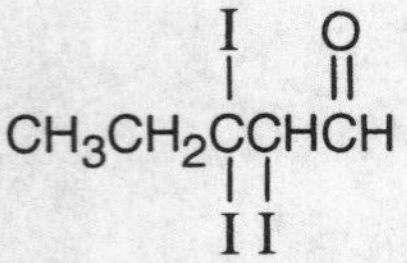

2,3,3-Triiodopentanal

(b)

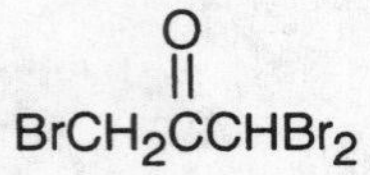

1,1,3-Tribromoacetone

(c)

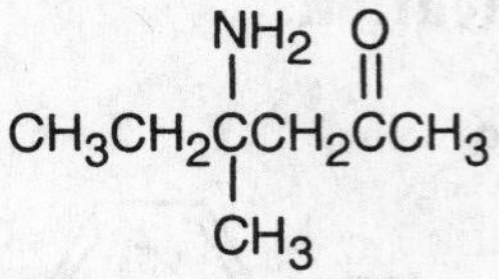

4-Amino-4-methyl-2-hexanone

16.64

(a)

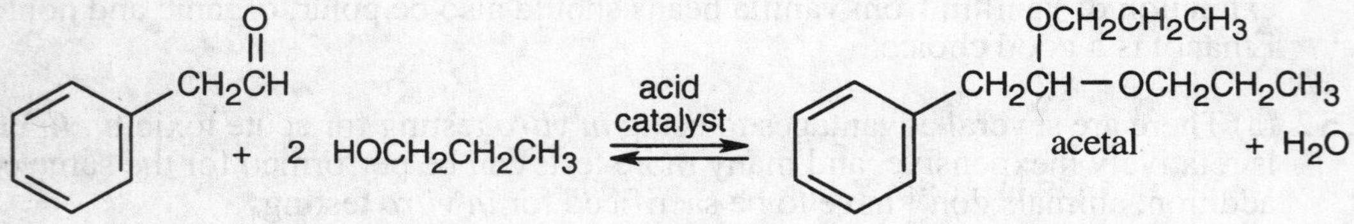

(b)

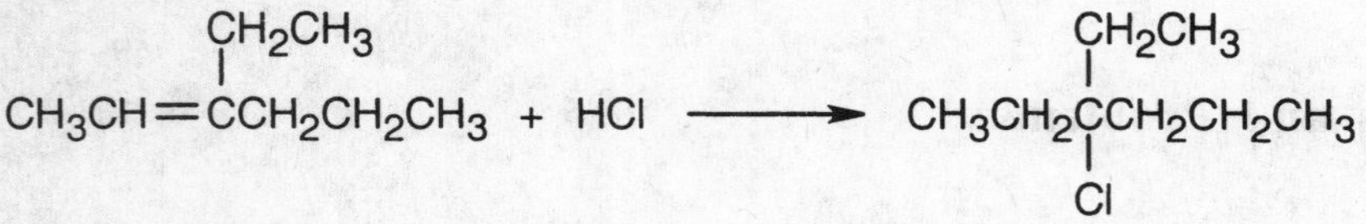

(c)

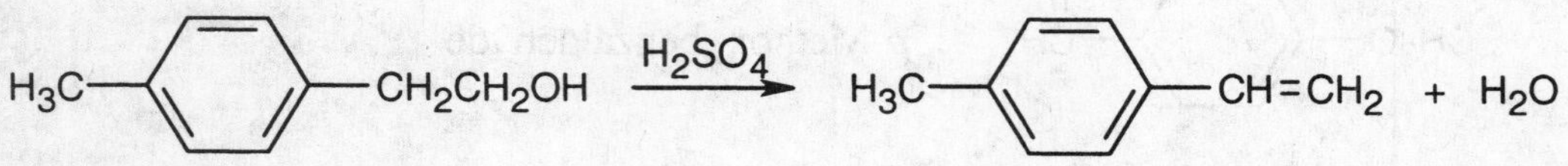

16.66 1-Butanol (boiling point [bp] 117°C) is the highest boiling of the three compounds because it forms stronger hydrogen bonds than does butylamine (bp 78°C). Butanal (bp 75°C) is polar but doesn't form hydrogen bonds.

Self-Test for Chapter 16

Multiple choice:

1. Which of the following alcohols can't be produced by reduction of an aldehyde or ketone? (a) 2-pentanol (b) cyclohexanol (c) 2-methyl-2-pentanol (d) 2-methyl-1-butanol

2. The term "LD_{50}" refers to (a) 50% of the amount of a substance that will kill a population (b) the amount of a substance that will kill 50% of a population (c) the name of a substance, 50% of which will kill a population (d) none of the above

3. 3-Pentanone is unlikely to undergo which of the following reactions? (a) oxidation (b) reduction (c) acetal formation (d) hemiacetal formation

4. Vanillin contains all of the following functional groups except (a) aldehyde (b) ether (c) aromatic ring (d) ketone

5. How many ketone isomers of the formula $C_6H_{12}O$ are there? (a) 4 (b) 5 (c) 6 (d) 7

6. Which of the following aldehydes is least soluble in water? (a) propanal (b) benzaldehyde (c) formaldehyde (d) acetaldehyde

7. Which of the following compounds undergoes reaction with Tollens' reagent? (a) 3-methyl-3-pentanol (b) glucose (c) acetone (d) cyclohexanone dimethyl acetal

8. The main difference between aldehydes and ketones is (a) reactivity (b) solubility (c) flammability (d) polarity

9. Formaldehyde is used for all of the following except (a) polymers (b) disinfectant (c) preservative (d) food additive

10. Which of the following statements about 3-heptanone is true? (a) It undergoes reaction with Benedict's reagent. (b) It forms a cyclic acetal with 1,3-propanediol. (c) It is soluble in water. (d) It is a solid at room temperature.

Sentence Completion

1. Aldehydes, esters, and ketones are all _____ compounds.

2. The shiny product of oxidation of an aldehyde by Tollens' reagent is _____.

3. _____ is a reaction that converts an acetal to an aldehyde or a ketone.

4. A carbonyl group is polarized, with a partial _____ charge on carbon and a partial _____ charge on oxygen.

5. _____ is a ketone that is widely used as a solvent.

6. Chronic exposure to the aldehyde _____ can cause symptoms resembling those of alcoholism.

7. Bonds to the carbonyl carbon of esters and amides are _____ polar than the bonds to the carbonyl carbon of ketones and aldehydes.

8. The conversion of an aldehyde or ketone into an alcohol is said to be a _____ reaction.

9. Formaldehyde is widely used as a _____.

10. The initial product of reaction between a ketone or aldehyde and an alcohol is called a _____.

11. _______ reagent is used to detect sugar in urine.

12. _______ can be detected on the breath during starvation.

Match each entry on the left with its partner on the right (use each answer once).

1. $AgNO_3$, NH_3, H_2O	(a) Reagent used to form an acetal
2. $CH_3CH_2COCH_3$	(b) Reduces carbonyl groups to alcohols
3. CH_3CH_2COOH	(c) An amide
4. CH_3OH, H^+ catalyst	(d) Product of an aldehyde plus Tollens' reagent
5. CH_3CH_2OH	(e) Tollens' reagent
6. $CH_3CH_2COOCH_3$	(f) Colored product of Benedict's test
7. $CH_3CH(OH)CH_3$	(g) Formaldehyde
8. NADH	(h) Product of aldehyde reduction
9. CH_3CHO	(i) Yields secondary alcohol when reduced
10. Cu_2O	(j) Ester
11. HCHO	(k) Can be oxidized to a ketone
12. CH_3CONH_2	(l) Product of primary alcohol oxidation

True or False

1. Glucose contains an acetal link.
2. A bombardier beetle protects itself by secreting benzoquinone.
3. Ketones are oxidized by Tollens' reagent to carboxylic acids.
4. The reduction of aldehydes and ketones is carried out by using NaOH.
5. An acetal is an alternative name for an ester.
6. Only aldehydes form acetals.
7. An aldehyde group always occurs at the end of a carbon chain.
8. In the chemical industry, formaldehyde is used to synthesize polymers.
9. NAD^+ reduces ketones and aldehydes to alcohols.
10. Acetaldehyde results from the oxidation of ethanol.
11. Both aldehydes and ketones can be reduced to alcohols.
12. Aldehydes and ketones are not capable of forming hydrogen bonds.

Chapter 17 – Carboxylic Acids and Their Derivatives

Chapter Outline

I. Properties and names of carboxylic acids and derivatives (Section 17.1).
  A. General characteristics.
    1. Groups bonded to the carbonyl carbon are electron-attracting.
      a. In carboxylic acids, —OH is bonded to the carbonyl carbon.
      b. In amides, —NH_2 is bonded to the carbonyl carbon.
      c. In esters, —OR is bonded to the carbonyl carbon.
    2. All of these functional groups undergo carbonyl group substitution reactions.
  B. Carboxylic acids.
    1. Properties.
      a. All have high boiling points.
      b. Carboxylic acids can form hydrogen bonds with each other.
      c. Smaller carboxylic acids are water-soluble.
      d. Volatile carboxylic acids have sharp odors.
    2. Naming carboxylic acids
      a. For simple carboxylic acids, the *-e* of the corresponding alkane is replaced by *-oic acid.*
      b. Many simple carboxylic acids have common names.
      c. For dicarboxylic acids, *-dioic acid* replaces the *-e* of the corresponding alkane.
      d. The group remaining when a carboxylic acid loses —OH is an acyl group.
      e. Unsaturated carboxylic acids are named by using *-enoic acid.*
      f. In some cases, the carbon next to the —COOH group is referred to as the α carbon.
  C. Esters.
    1. Properties.
      a. Esters are lower boiling than carboxylic acids.
      b. Esters have pleasant odors.
      c. Simple esters are liquids.
    2. Naming esters
    Ester names have two parts.
      a. The —OR fragment has the name of the alkyl group R.
      b. The remaining portion is the name of the parent carboxylic acid, with *-ate* replacing *-oic acid.*
  D. Amides.
    1. Properties.
      a. Amides are higher boiling than carboxylic acids; most are solids.
      b. Amides are not basic.
    2. Naming amides.
      a. An amide has the name of the parent acid, with *-amide* replacing *-oic acid.*
      b. If nitrogen is substituted, the alkyl substituents are specified, preceded by *N-* (to indicate that the substituents are bonded to nitrogen).

II. Carboxylic acids (Sections 17.2–17.4).
  A. Common carboxylic acids (Section 17.2).
    1. Acetic acid.
      a. Acetic acid is a common laboratory solvent.
      b. Acetic acid is formed from fermentation of fruit in the presence of ample O_2.
    2. Citric acid.

B. Acidity of carboxylic acids (Section 17.3).
   1. Carboxylic acids are weak acids, with $pK_a \sim 10^{-5}$.
   2. Carboxylate anions are given the name of the parent carboxylic acid, with *-ate* replacing *-oic acid.*
   3. Carboxylic acids react with base to give carboxylic acid salts.
      a. The amount of salt or acid present depends on pH.
      b. Carboxylic acid salts are much more soluble in water than the parent acids.

C. Reactions of carboxylic acids (Section 17.4).
   1. Ester formation.
      a. $\text{carboxylic acid} + \text{alcohol} \underset{\text{catalyst}}{\overset{H^+}{\rightleftharpoons}} \text{ester} + H_2O$
      b. Esterification reactions are reversible.
   2. Amide formation.
      a. Carboxylic acid + ammonia (or an amine) ——> amide + H_2O
      b. Acid anhydride + ammonia (or an amine) ——> amide + carboxylic acid

III. Esters, amides, and carboxylic acid anhydrides (Sections 17.5–17.7).

A. Aspirin and other over-the-counter carboxylic acid derivatives (Section 17.5).
   1. Aspirin.
      a. Aspirin is a salicylic acid ester.
      b. Aspirin causes pain relief, reduces fever and reduces inflammation.
      c. Aspirin's side effects include gastric bleeding and gastric upset.
   2. Acetaminophen is an amide that can be used in place of aspirin.
   3. Benzocaine and lidocaine are amides that are used as topical anesthetics.

B. Hydrolysis of esters and amides (Section 17.6).
   1. Esters.
      a. $\text{Ester} + H_2O \xrightarrow{\text{acid catalyst}} \text{carboxylic acid} + \text{alcohol}$
      b. $\text{Ester} + H_2O \xrightarrow{\text{base}} \text{carboxylate anion} + \text{alcohol}$
   2. Amides.

$$\text{Amide} + H_2O \xrightarrow{\text{acid or base}} \text{carboxylic acid} + \text{amine (or ammonia)}$$

C. Polyesters and polyamides (Section 17.7).
   1. Nylons are polyamides formed in the reaction of a diacid with a diamine.
   2. Polyesters result from the reaction of a diacid with a dialcohol.

IV. Phosphoric acid derivatives (Section 17.8).

A. Structure of phosphate esters.
   1. Phosphoric acid has three ionizable hydrogens and can form three different anions.
   2. Phosphates can react with alcohols at one, two or three oxygens.
   3. Mono- and diphosphate esters are present as anions.

B. Phosphate esters in the body.
   1. In the body, phosphate esters exist as anions.
   2. In the body, phosphate esters can form anhydrides.
      a. Diphosphates and triphosphates are the anhydrides that occur in living things.
      b. Triphosphate esters are used for energy storage in the body.

Solutions to Chapter 17 Problems

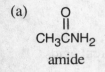

17.1

(a)

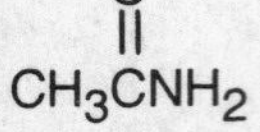

amide

(b) CH_3OCH_3

none (ether)

(c) CH_3COOH

carboxylic acid

(d) $CH_3COOCH_2CH_3$

ester

(e) CH_3COCH_3

none (ketone)

(f) $CH_3CH_2CONHCH_3$

amide

(g) $CH_3CH_2NH_2$

none (amine)

(h)

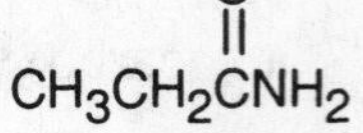

amide

17.2

(a)

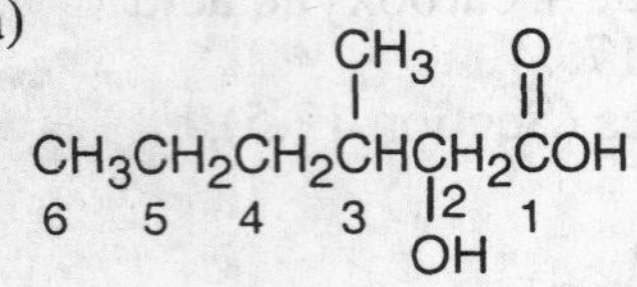

2-Hydroxy-3-methylhexanoic acid

(b)

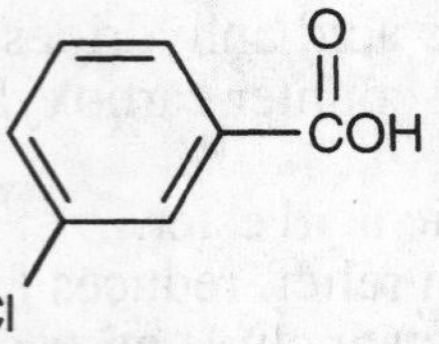

m-Chlorobenzoic acid

17.3

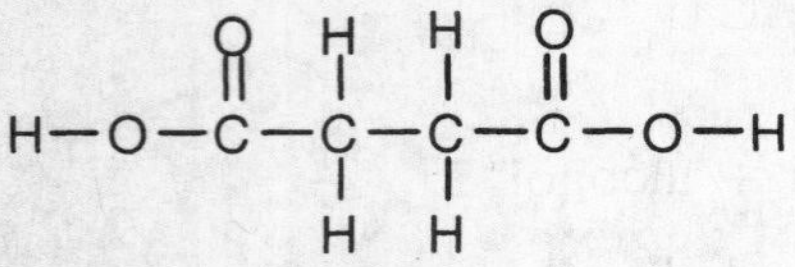

Succinic acid

17.4

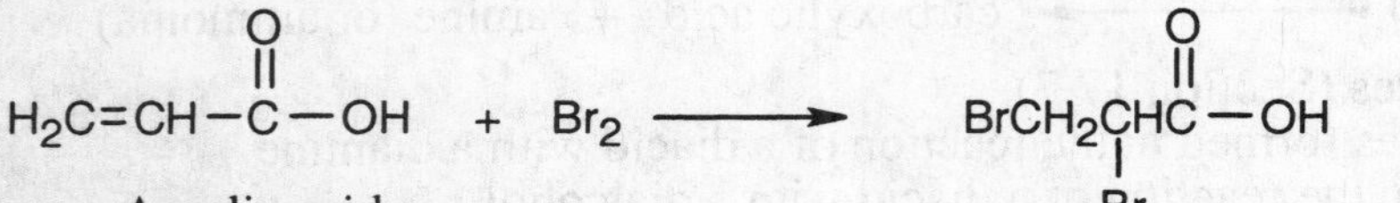

Acrylic acid (Propenoic acid)

2,3-Dibromopropanoic acid

17.5

(a) from benzoic acid

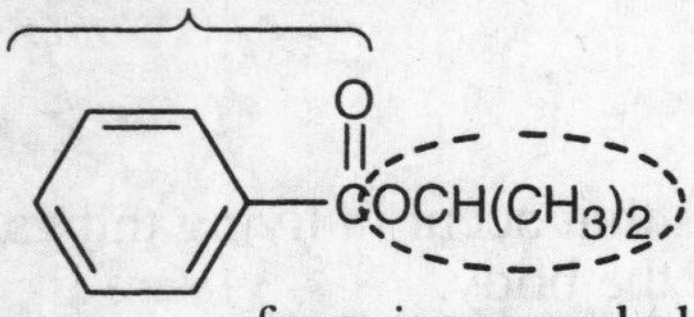

from isopropyl alcohol

Isoropyl benzoate

(b) from propanoic acid

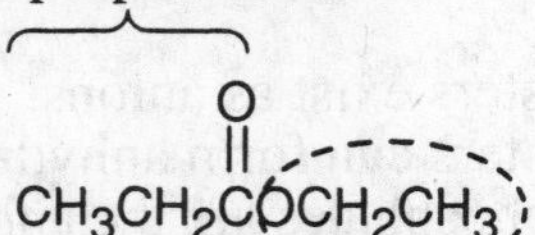

from ethanol

Ethyl propanoate

(c) from crotonic acid

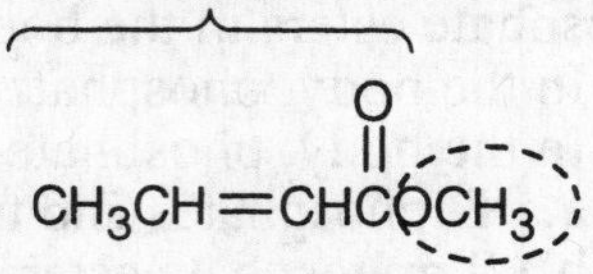

from methanol

Methyl crotonate

17.6 (a) CH_3OCH_3

Low boiling.
Polar, but doesn't form hydrogen bonds.

(b) CH_3COOH

Highest boiling.
Forms strongest hydrogen bonds.

(c) $CH_3CH_2CH_3$

Lowest boiling.
Doesn't form hydrogen bonds.

17.7

More soluble	*Less soluble*	*Reason*
(a) $CH_3CH_2CH_2COOH$	$C_8H_{17}COOH$	The large hydrocarbon part of $C_8H_{17}COOH$ makes it insoluble in water.
(b) $(CH_3)_2CHCOOH$	$CH_3CH_2COOCH(CH_3)_2$	Carboxylic acids form stronger hydrogen bonds with water.

17.8

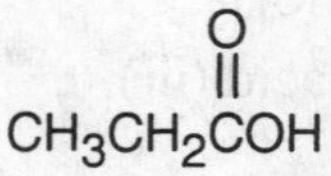

Propanoic acid
(Propionic acid)

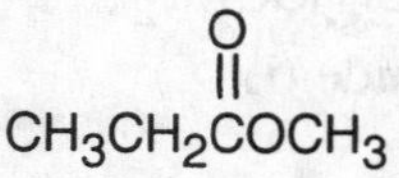

Methyl propanoate
(Methyl propionate)

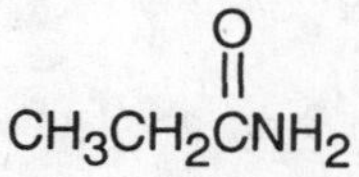

Propanamide
(Propionamide)

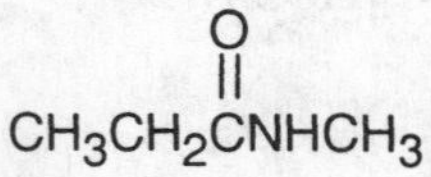

N-Methylpropanamide
(*N*-Methylpropionamide)

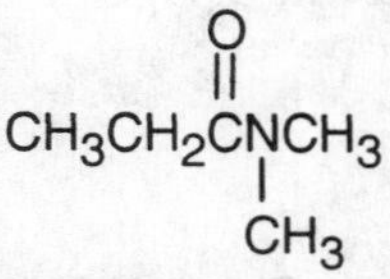

N,N-Dimethylpropanamide
(*N,N*-Dimethylpropionamide)

17.9

(a)

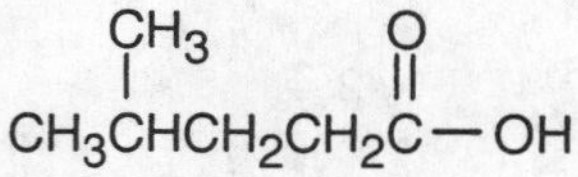

4-Methylpentanoic acid

(b)

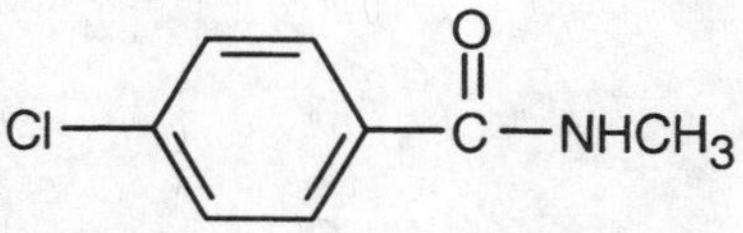

N-Methyl-*p*-chlorobenzamide

17.10

(a)

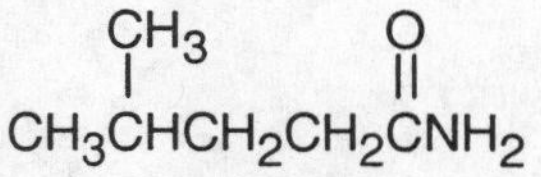

4-Methylpentanamide

(b)

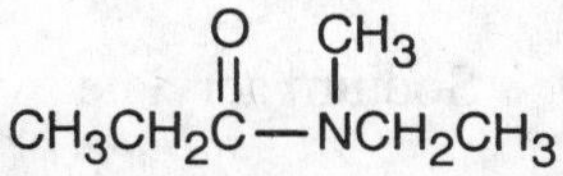

N-Ethyl-*N*-methylpropanamide

17.11

(a)

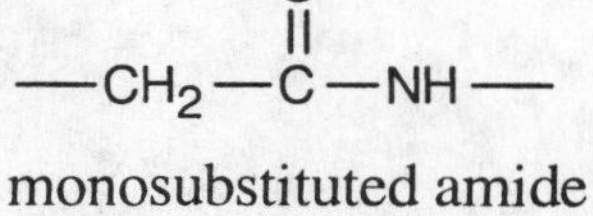

monosubstituted amide (ii)

(b)

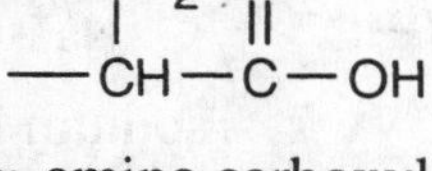

α-amino carboxylic acid (i)

(c)

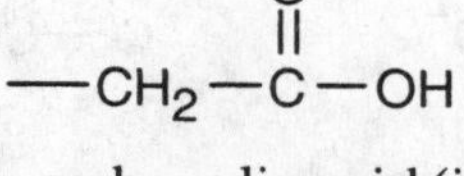

carboxylic acid (iv)

(d)

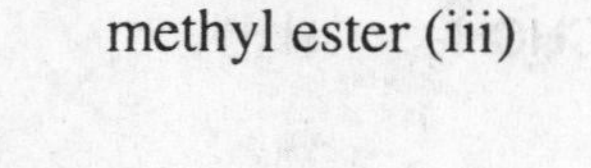

methyl ester (iii)

17.12

(a) CH_3COOCH_3 ester (ii)

(b) RCONHR amide (i)

(c) C_6H_5COOH carboxylic acid (iii)

(d) $CH_3CH_2C(=O)N(CH_3)_2$ amide (i)

(e) $CH_3CH_2CH_2CONH_2$ amide (i)

(f) $HOOCCH_2CH(CH_3)CH_3$ carboxylic acid (iii)

17.13

(a) $C_6H_5C(=O)NH_2$ amide (C_7H_7NO)

(b) $CH_3CH_2C(=O)OH$ carboxylic acid ($C_3H_6O_2$)

(c) $CH_3C(=O)OCH_2CH_3$ ester ($C_4H_8O_2$)

17.14

(a)

$$CH_3CH_2CH_2C(=O){-}OH + KOH \longrightarrow CH_3CH_2CH_2C(=O){-}O^-K^+ + H_2O$$

(b)

$$2\ CH_3CH_2CH_2CH(CH_3)C(=O){-}OH + Ba(OH)_2 \longrightarrow \left[CH_3CH_2CH_2CH(CH_3)C(=O){-}O^-\right]_2 Ba^{2+} + 2\ H_2O$$

17.15

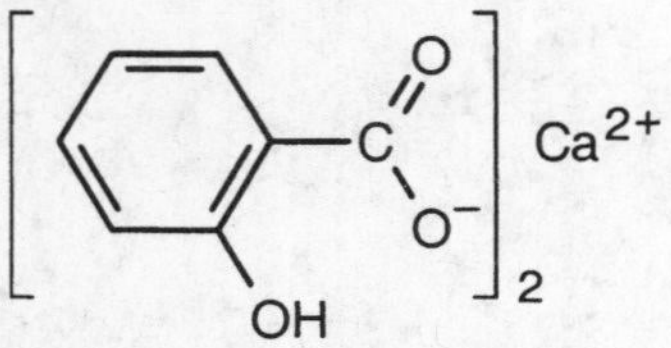

Calcium salicylate

$H_2C{=}CHC(=O){-}O^-\ Na^+$

Sodium acrylate

17.16 When sodium acetate and disodium glutarate are dissolved in water, acetate ion, glutarate ion and sodium ion are present.

$CH_3C(=O){-}O^-$ acetate ion

$^-O{-}C(=O)CH_2CH_2CH_2C(=O){-}O^-$ glutarate ion

Na^+ sodium ion

17.17 Redraw the structures so that the alcohol hydroxyl group and the —OH group of the carboxylic acid are facing each other. Remove water, and draw the ester bond.

$$H{-}C(=O){-}OH + H{-}O{-}CH_2CH(CH_3)CH_3 \xrightleftharpoons[\text{catalyst}]{H^+} H{-}C(=O){-}O{-}CH_2CH(CH_3)CH_3 + H_2O$$

17.18

(a)

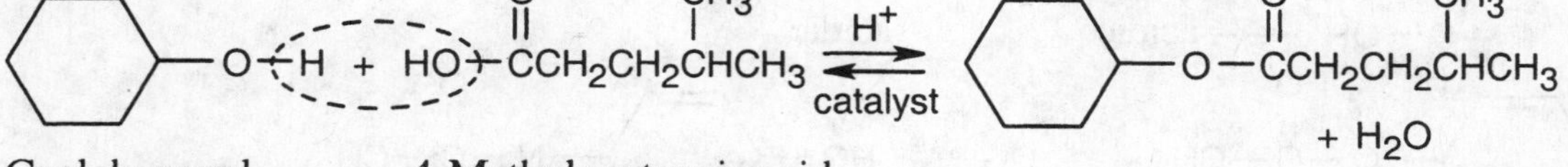

Cyclohexanol 4-Methylpentanoic acid

(b)

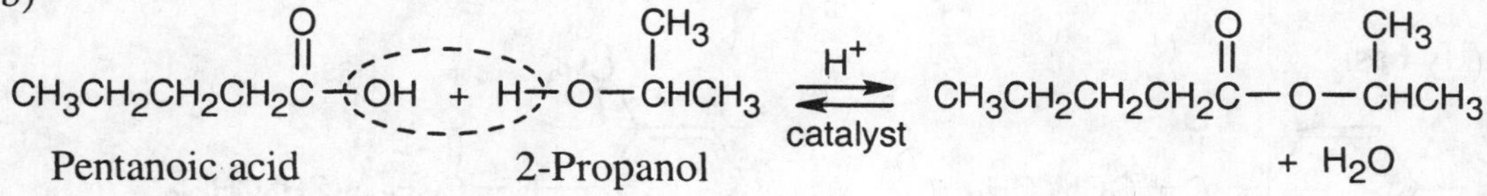

Pentanoic acid 2-Propanol

17.19 Use the technique shown in Problem 17.17 to draw the amide product.

(a)

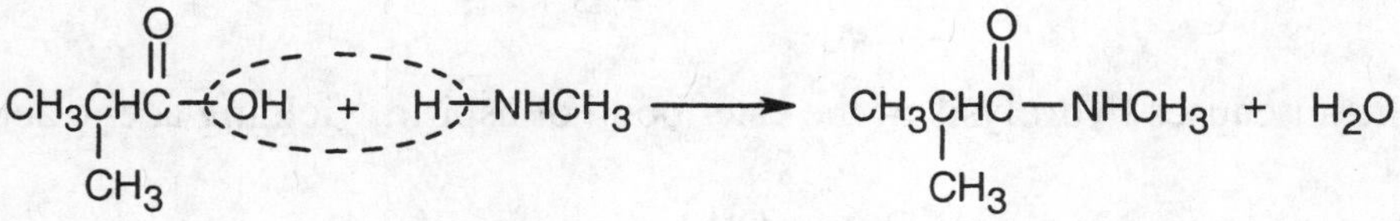

(b)

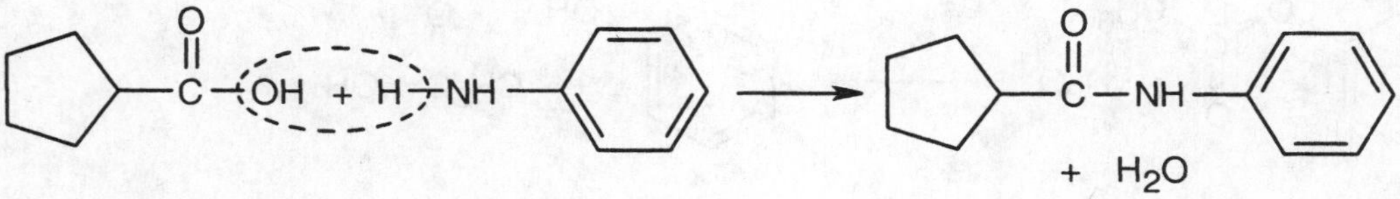

17.20

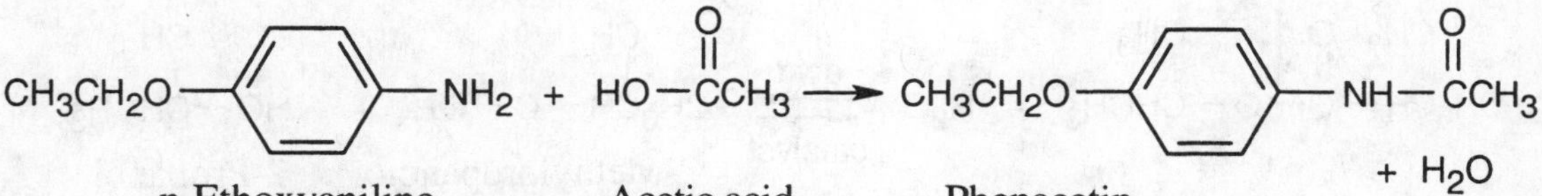

p-Ethoxyaniline Acetic acid Phenacetin

17.21

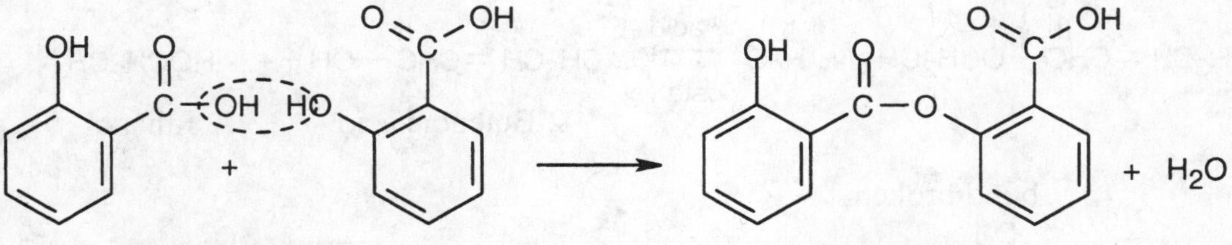

Salicylic acid Salsalate

17.22

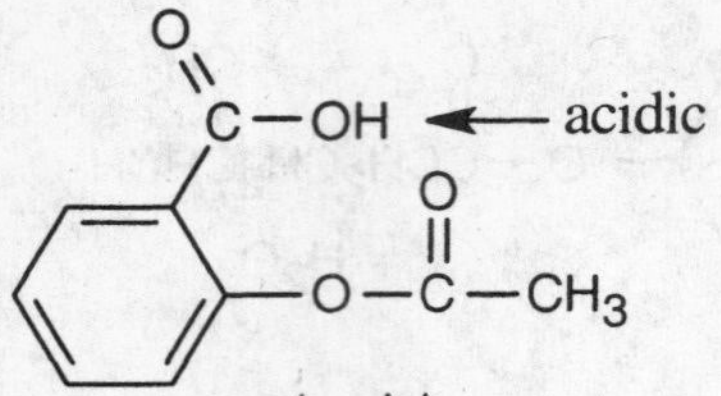
C—OH
acidic
O—C—CH3

Aspirin

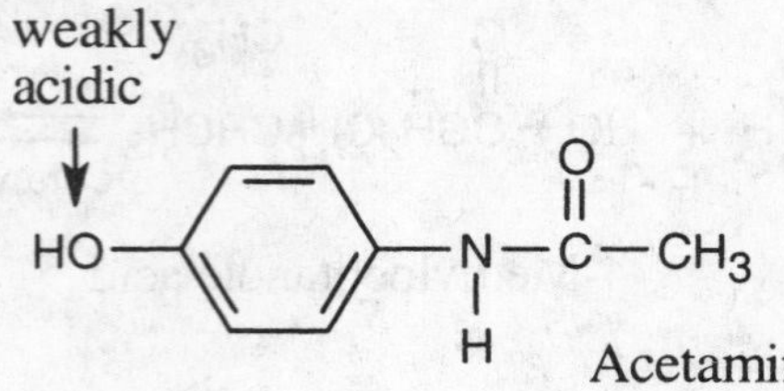
weakly
acidic
HO
N—C—CH3
H

Acetaminophen

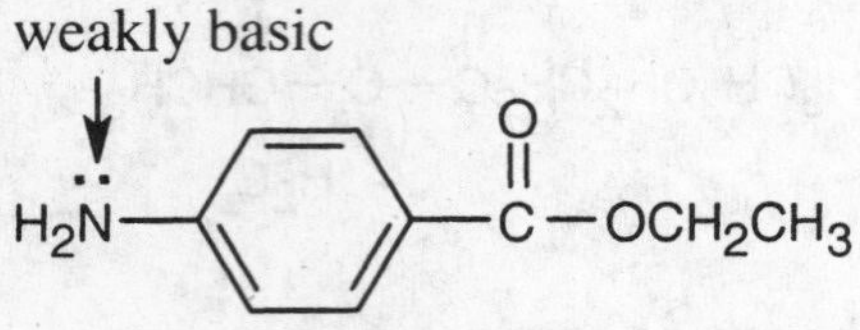
weakly basic
H2N
C—OCH2CH3

Benzocaine

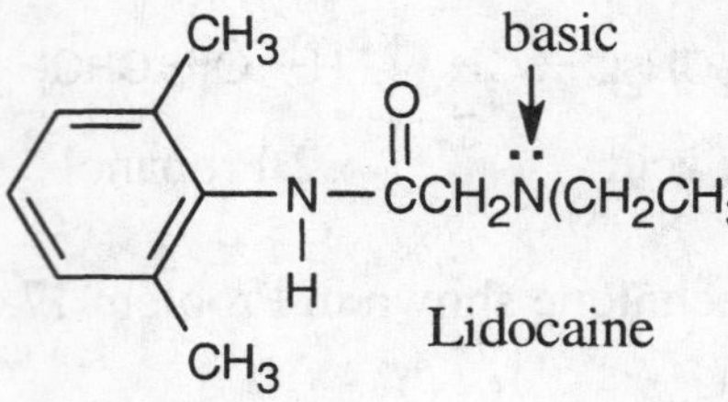
CH3
basic
N—CCH2N(CH2CH3)2
H
CH3

Lidocaine

17.23 Moisture in the air causes hydrolysis of the ester bond of aspirin, yielding acetic acid.

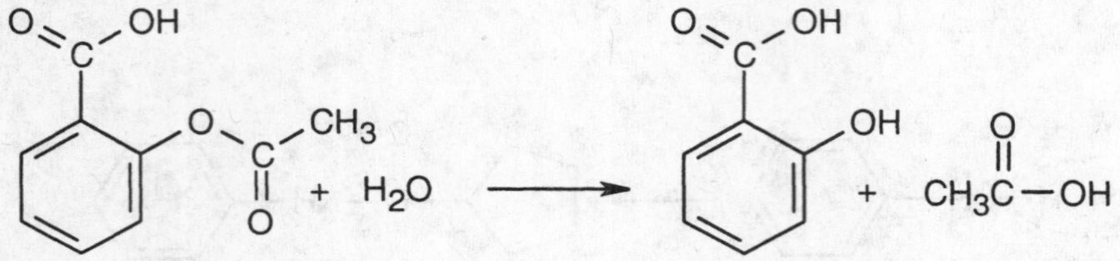

17.24

(a)

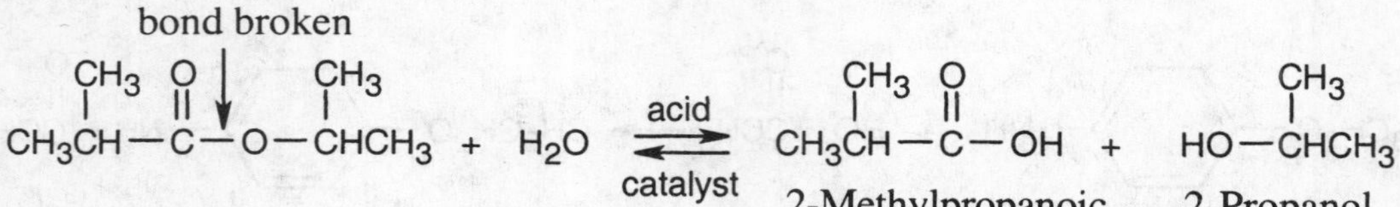
bond broken
acid
catalyst

2-Methylpropanoic acid   2-Propanol

(b)

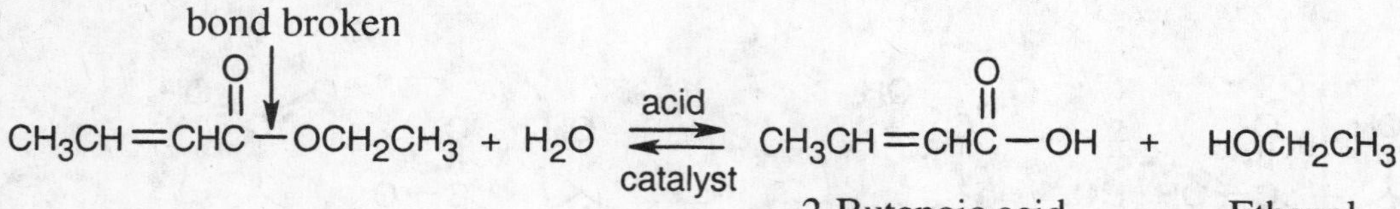
bond broken
acid
catalyst

2-Butenoic acid   Ethanol

(c)

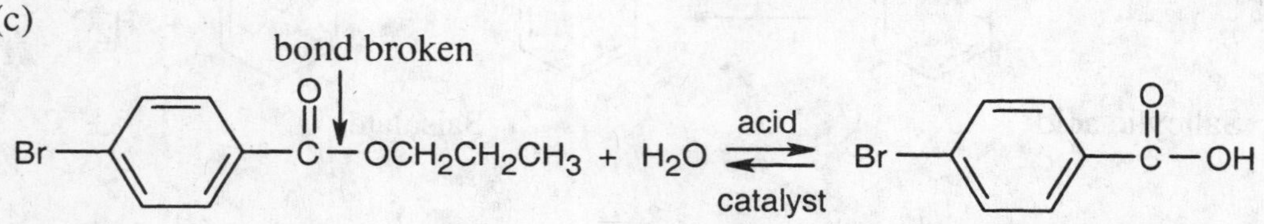
bond broken
acid
catalyst

p-Bromobenzoic acid

+ $HOCH_2CH_2CH_3$

1-Propanol

17.25

(a)

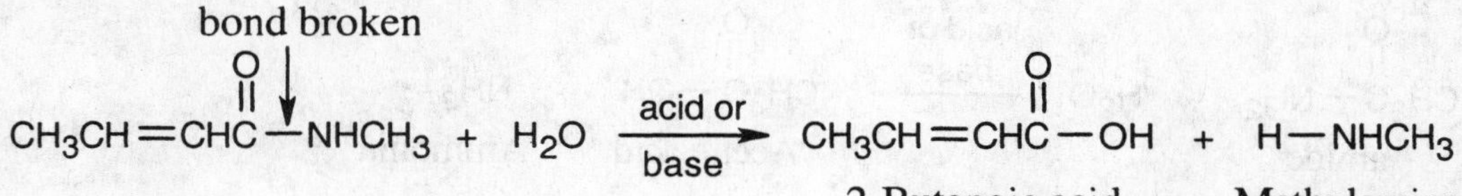
bond broken
acid or
base

2-Butenoic acid Methylamine

(b)

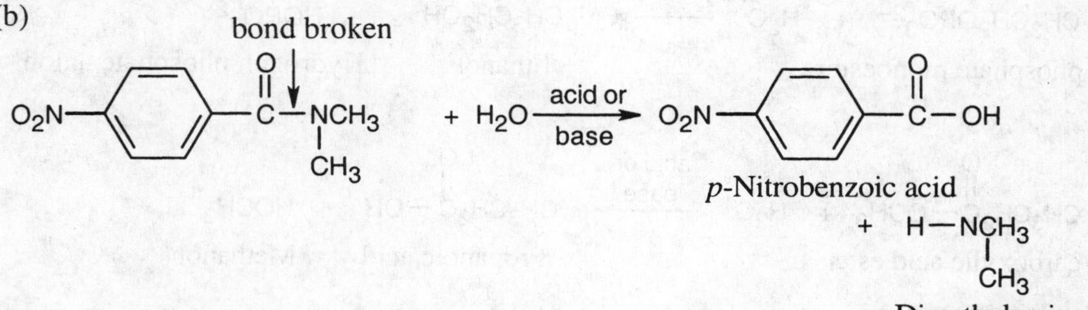
bond broken
acid or
base

p-Nitrobenzoic acid

Dimethylamine

17.26 As in problems 17.17–17.19, draw the reacting partners so that the atoms involved in the reaction face each other. Remove one molecule of water for each bond formed.

(a)

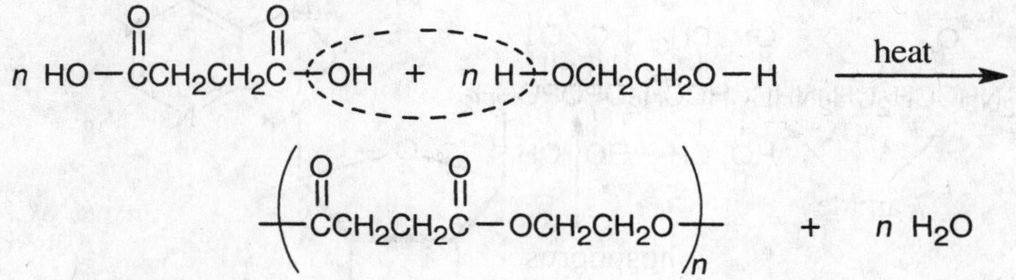
heat

(b)

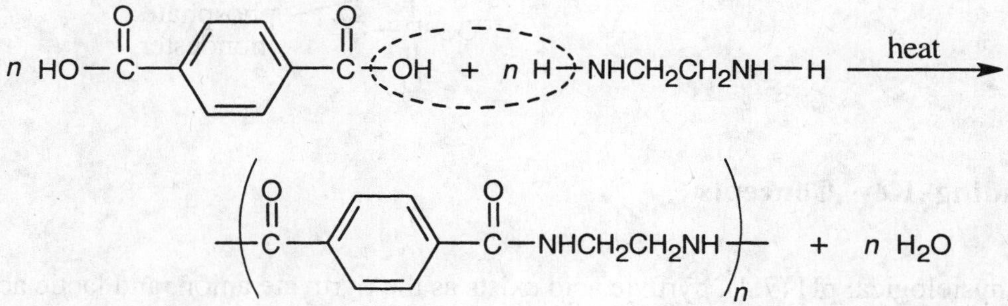
heat

17.27

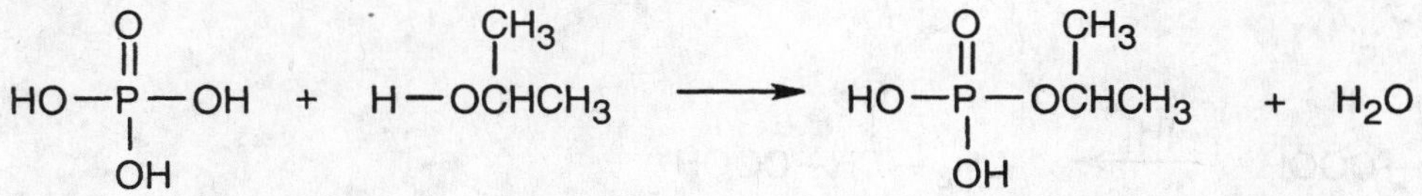

Isopropyl phosphate (unionized)

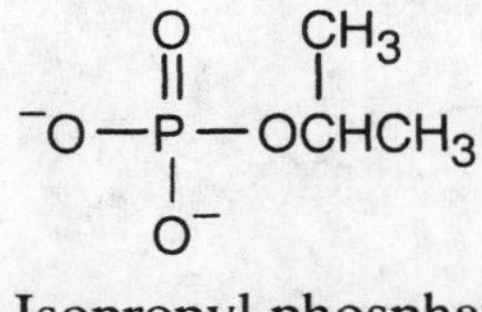

Isopropyl phosphate (ionized)

17.28

(a)

$$CH_3C(=O)-NH_2 + H_2O \xrightarrow{\text{acid or base}} CH_3C(=O)-OH + NH_3$$

amide → Acetic acid + Ammonia

(b)

$$CH_3CH_2OPO_3^{2-} + H_2O \longrightarrow CH_3CH_2OH + HOPO_3^{2-}$$

phosphate monoester → Ethanol + Hydrogen phosphate anion

(c)

$$CH_3CH_2C(=O)-OCH_3 + H_2O \xrightarrow{\text{acid or base}} CH_3CH_2C(=O)-OH + HOCH_3$$

carboxylic acid ester → Propanoic acid + Methanol

17.29

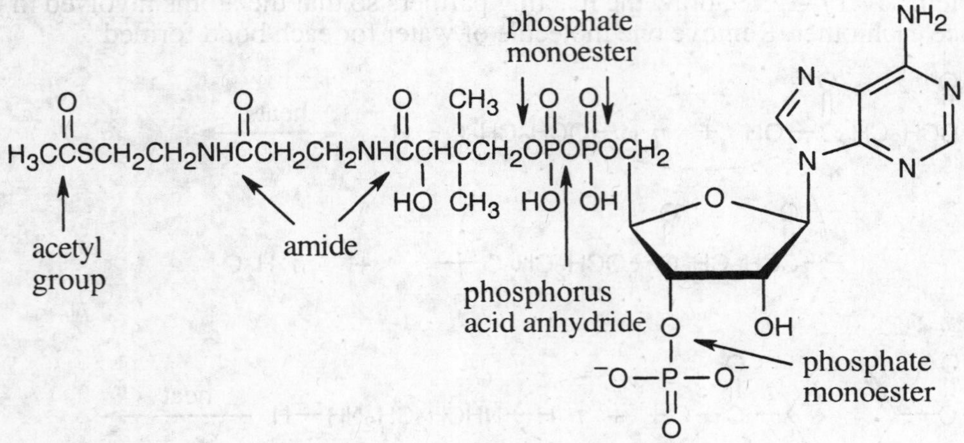
phosphate monoester
acetyl group
amide
phosphorus acid anhydride
phosphate monoester

Understanding Key Concepts

17.30

(a) At physiological pH (7.4), pyruvic acid exists as the pyruvate anion, and lactic acid exists as the lactate anion.

(b)

$$CH_3-C(=O)-COOH \xrightarrow{[H]} CH_3-CH(OH)-COOH$$

Pyruvic acid → Lactic acid

(c) Hydrogen bonds between the carboxylate oxygen and water are shown. In addition, the carbonyl oxygens can also hydrogen-bond with water. For lactate, hydrogen bonding takes place between the hydroxyl hydrogen and water (shown below), as well as between molecules of lactate. You would expect pyruvate and lactate to have comparable solubility in water.

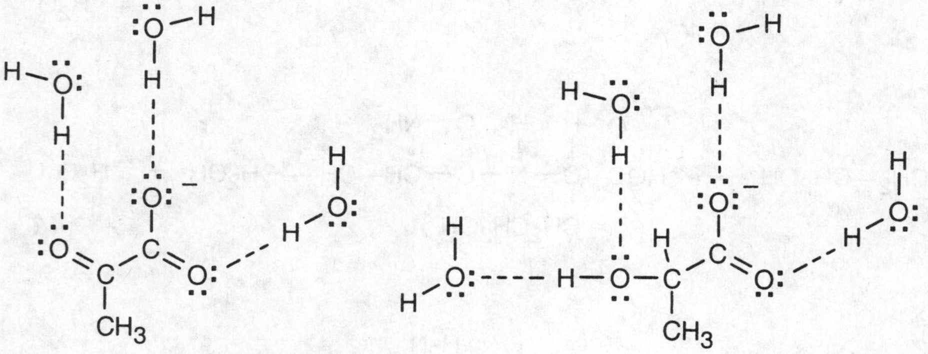

17.31

(a) Under conditions that favor amide hydrolysis (H_2O, plus either acid or base), the acetyl group can be removed from *N*-acetylglucosamine.

(b)

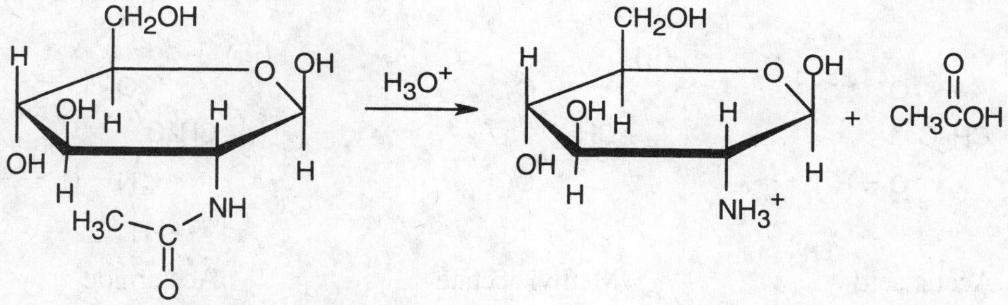

17.32

(a) Glycerate and phosphate are connected by a phosphate ester linkage.
(b)

1,3-Bisphosphoglycerate 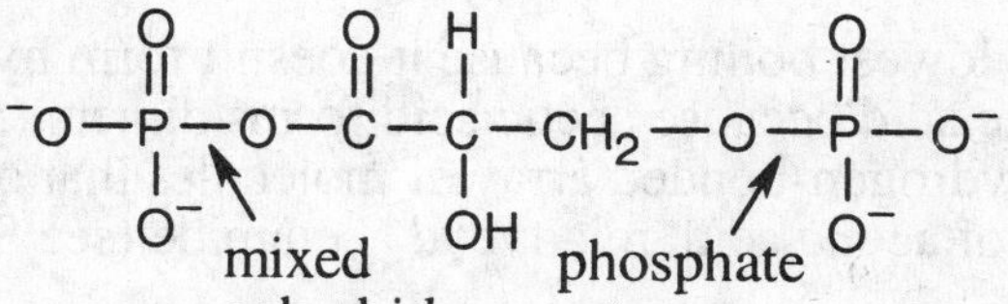
mixed anhydride linkage
phosphate ester linkage

17.33

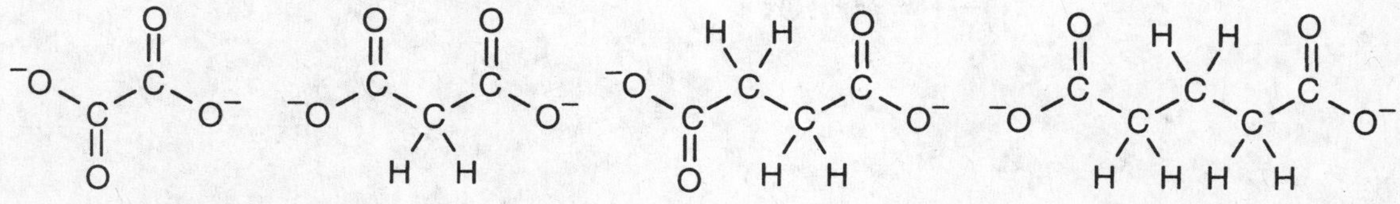

Oxalate Malonate Succinate Glutarate

17.34

(a)

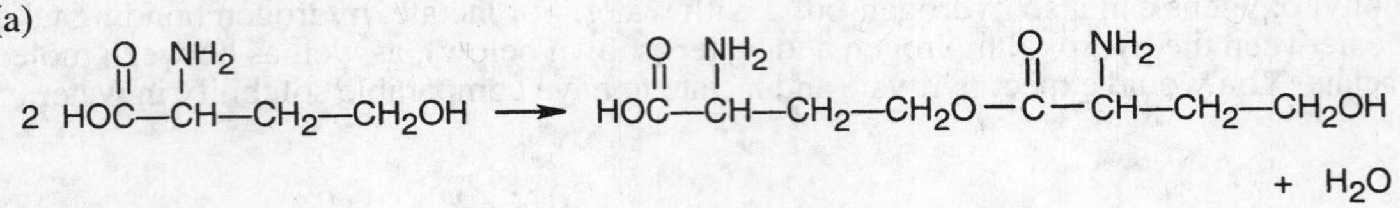

(b)

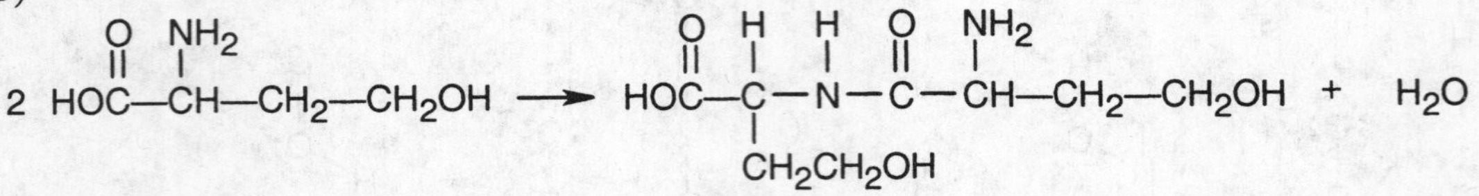

(c)

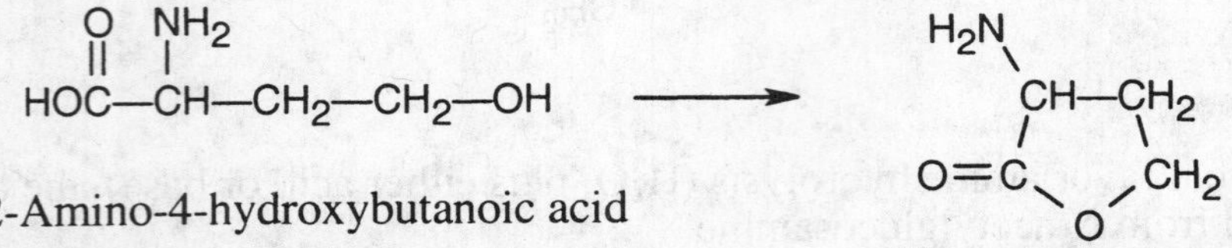

2-Amino-4-hydroxybutanoic acid
(2-Amino-4-hydroxybutyric acid)

Homoserine lactone

17.35

(a) (i)

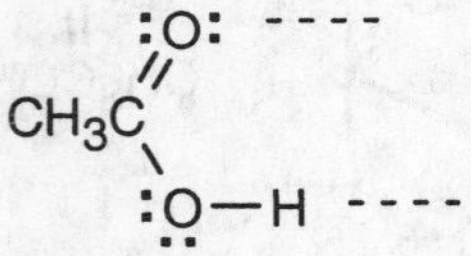

Acetic acid

(ii)

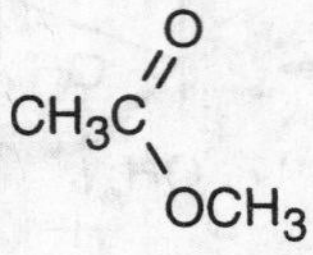

Methyl acetate

(iii)

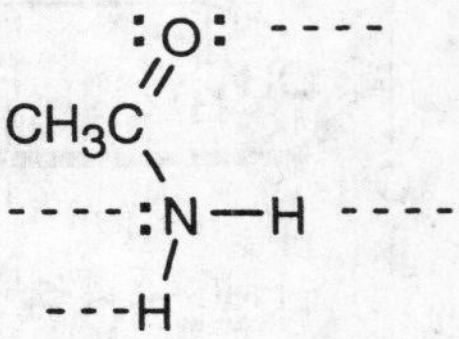

Acetamide

(b) *Lowest boiling* ——————> *Highest boiling*
Methyl acetate   Acetic acid   Acetamide

Methyl acetate is lowest boiling because it doesn't form hydrogen bonds.Acetamide is higher boiling than acetic acid because acetic acid forms dimers (pictured). These dimers do not form the extensively hydrogen-bonded array of molecules that occurs in acetamide, and they lower the boiling point of acetic acid, relative to acetamide (see Section 17.1).

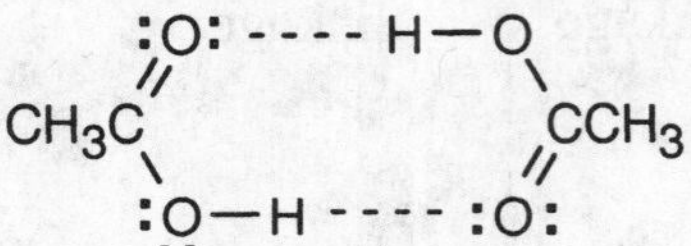

17.36 The hydrolyzed bonds are indicated on the structure.

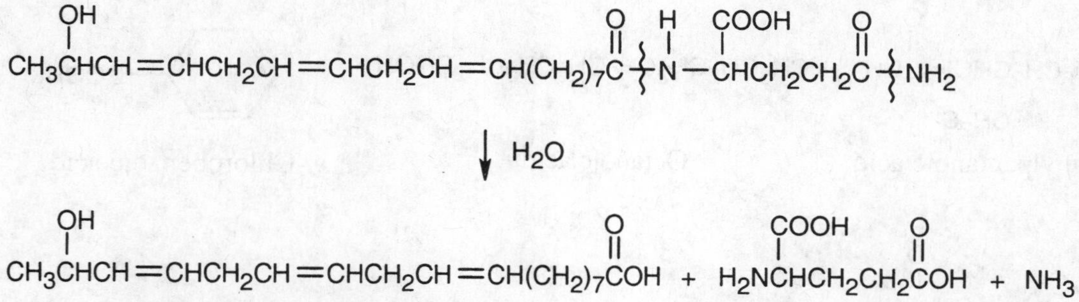

17-Hydroxylinolenic acid Glutamic acid Ammonia

17.37

(a)

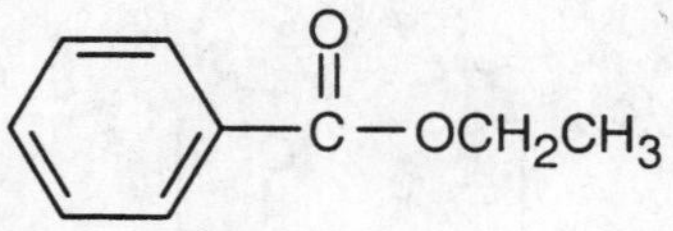

Ethyl benzoate

(b)

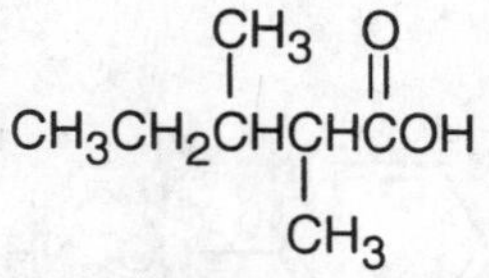

2,3-Dimethylpentanoic acid

(c)

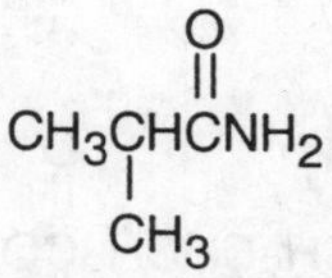

2-Methylpropanamide

(d)

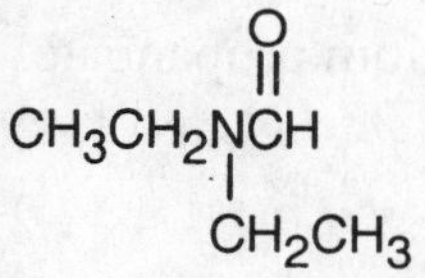

N,N-Diethylformamide

Compound (b) is acidic. The other compounds are neither acidic nor basic.

Carboxylic Acids

17.38

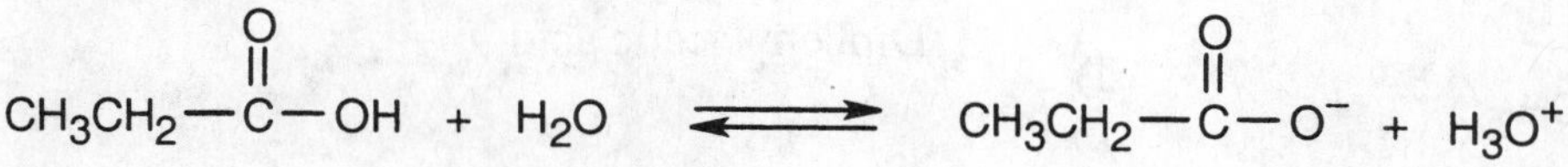

17.40

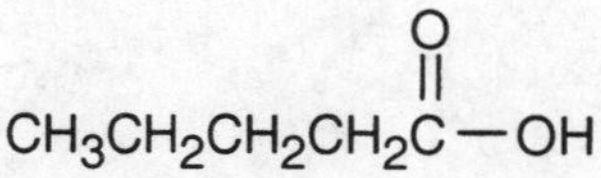

Pentanoic acid

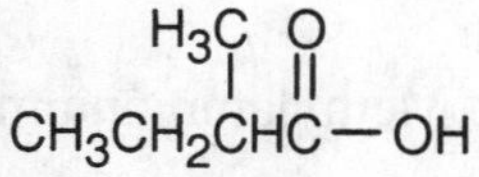

2-Methylbutanoic acid

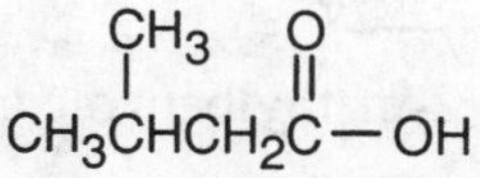

3-Methylbutanoic acid

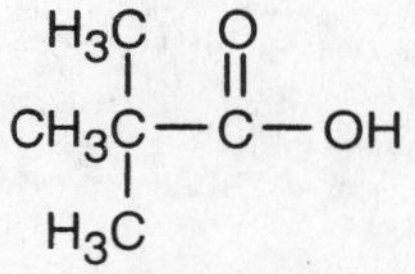

2,2-Dimethylpropanoic acid

17.42

(a)

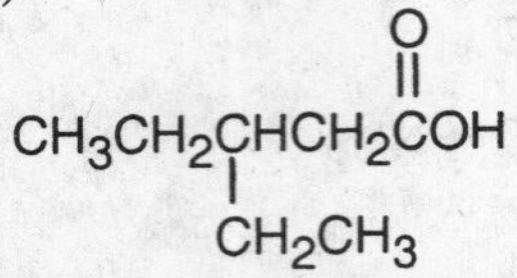

3-Ethylpentanoic acid

(b)

$CH_3CH_2CH_2CH_2CH_2CH_2CH_2COOH$

Octanoic acid

(c)

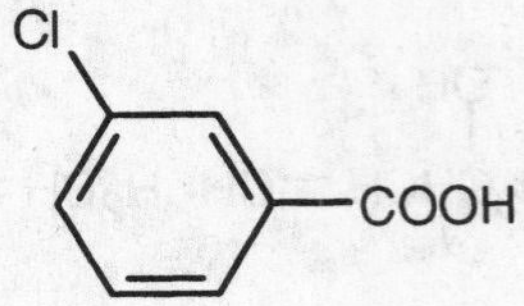

m-Chlorobenzoic acid

(d)

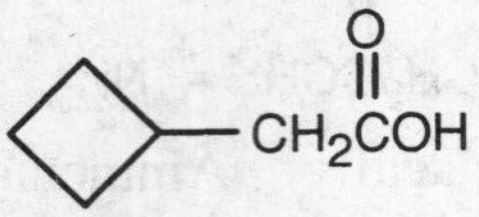

Cyclobutylacetic acid

17.44

(a)

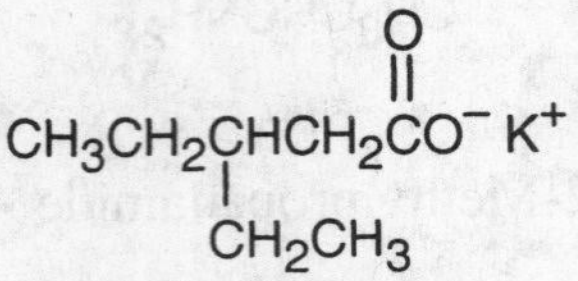

Potassium 3-ethylpentanoate

(b)

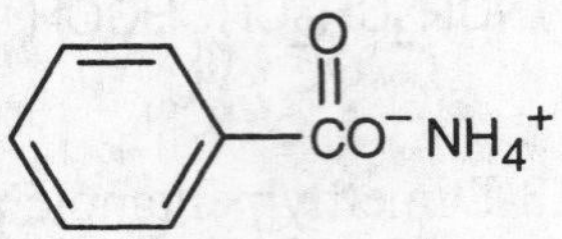

Ammonium benzoate

(c)

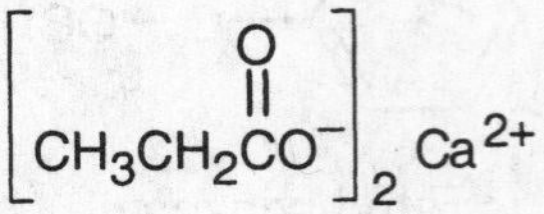

Calcium propanoate

17.46

(a)

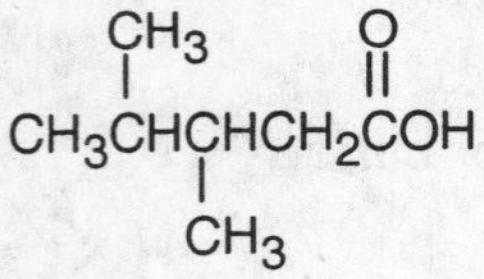

3,4-Dimethylpentanoic acid

(b)

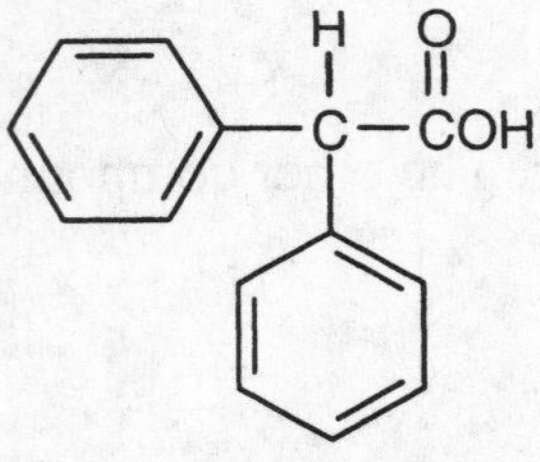

Diphenylacetic acid

(c)

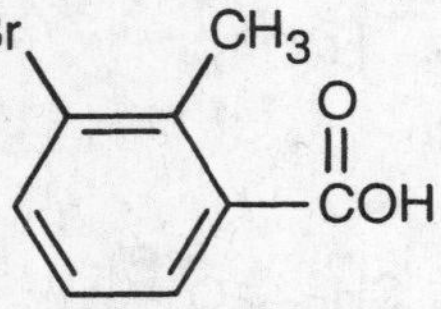

3-Bromo-2-methylbenzoic acid

(d)

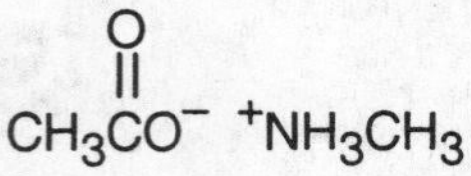

Methylammonium acetate

17.48

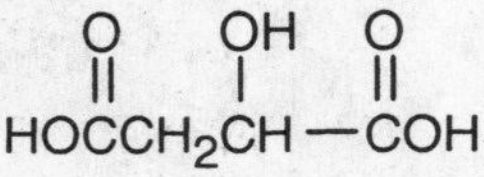

Malic acid

17.50

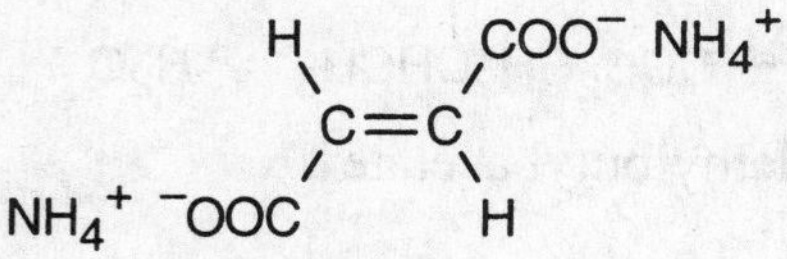
H
COO⁻ NH4+
C=C
NH4+ ⁻OOC
H

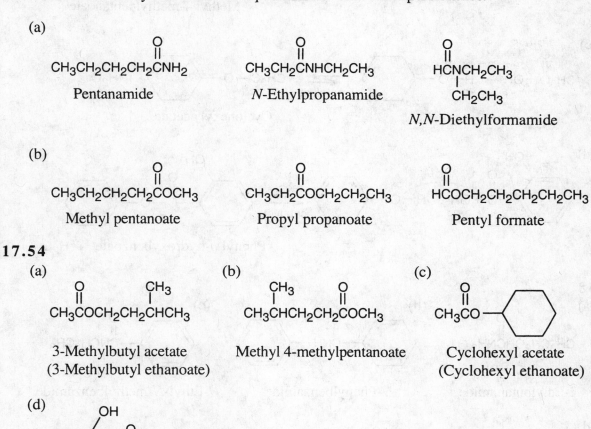

Diammonium fumarate

Esters and Amides

17.52 There are many answers to this question. Here are some possibilities:

(a)

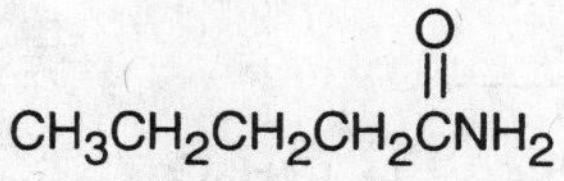
O
CH3CH2CH2CH2CNH2

Pentanamide

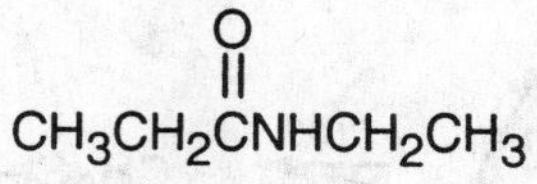
O
CH3CH2CNHCH2CH3

N-Ethylpropanamide

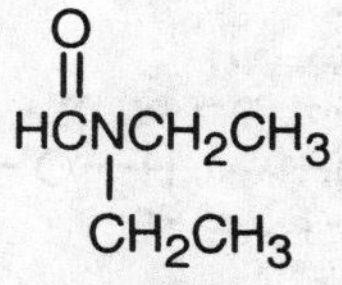
O
HCNCH2CH3
CH2CH3

N,N-Diethylformamide

(b)

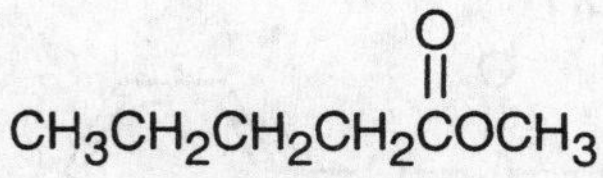
O
CH3CH2CH2CH2COCH3

Methyl pentanoate

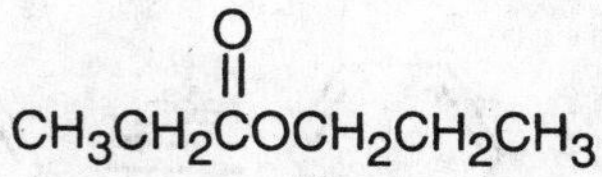
O
CH3CH2COCH2CH2CH3

Propyl propanoate

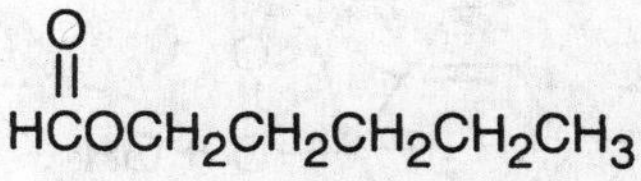
O
HCOCH2CH2CH2CH2CH3

Pentyl formate

17.54

(a)

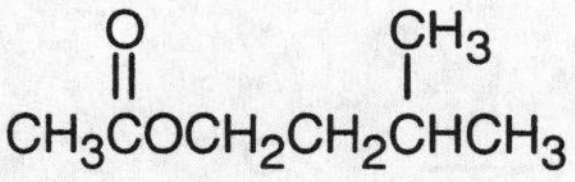
O
CH3
CH3COCH2CH2CHCH3

3-Methylbutyl acetate
(3-Methylbutyl ethanoate)

(b)

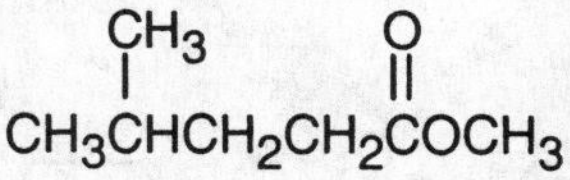
CH3
O
CH3CHCH2CH2COCH3

Methyl 4-methylpentanoate

(c)

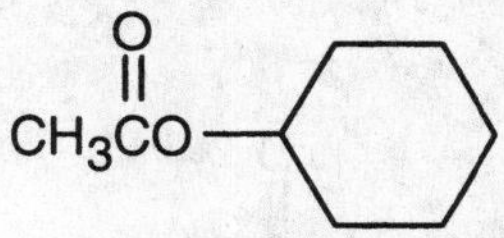
O
CH3CO

Cyclohexyl acetate
(Cyclohexyl ethanoate)

(d)

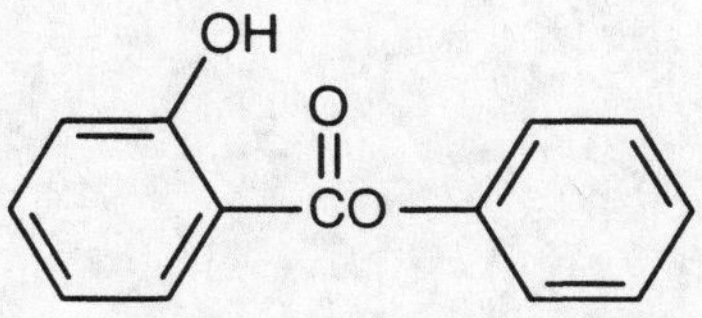
OH
O
CO

Phenyl *o*-hydroxybenzoate

17.56

(a)

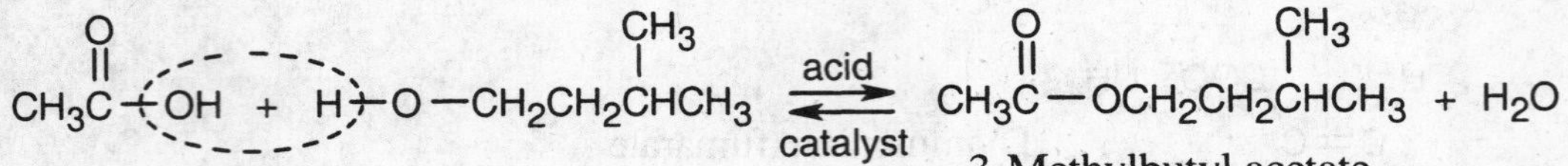

3-Methylbutyl acetate

(b)

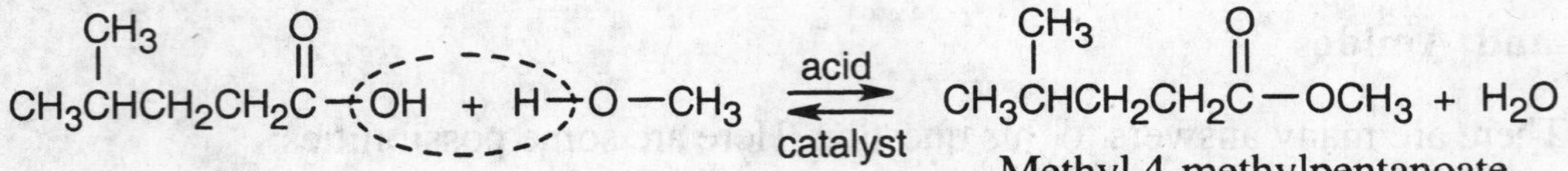

Methyl 4-methylpentanoate

(c)

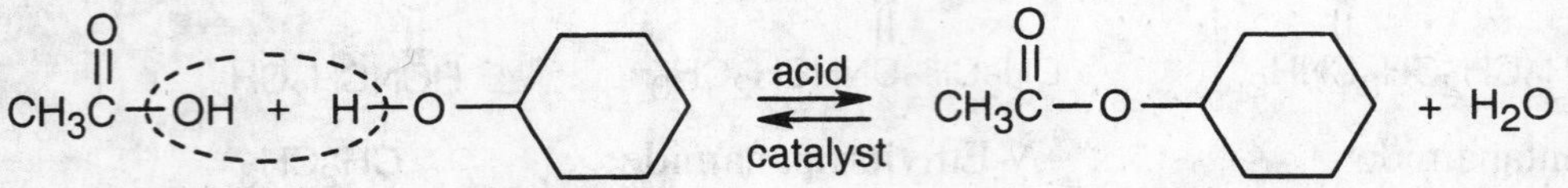

Cyclohexyl acetate

(d)

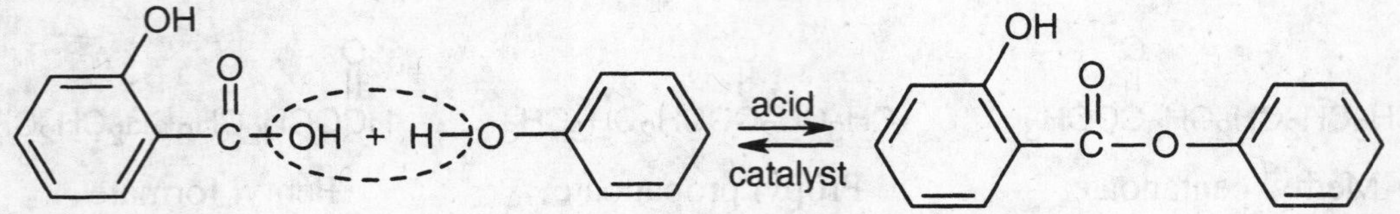

Phenyl *o*-hydroxybenzoate + H_2O

17.58

(a)

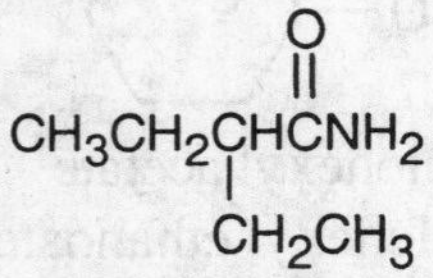

2-Ethylbutanamide

(b)

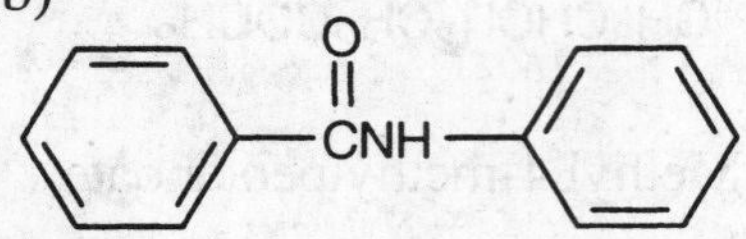

N-Phenylbenzamide

(c)

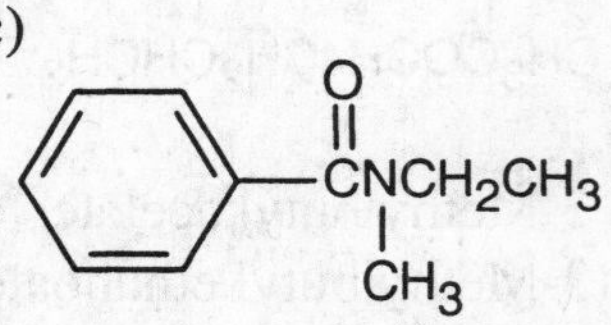

N-Ethyl-*N*-methylbenzamide

(d)

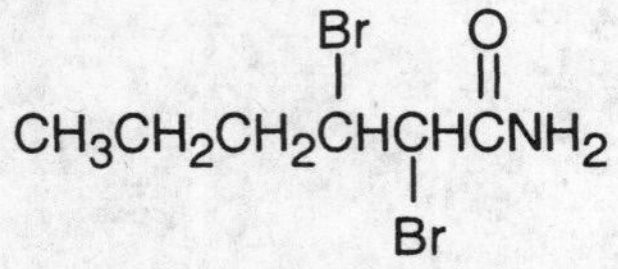

2,3-Dibromohexanamide

17.60

(a)

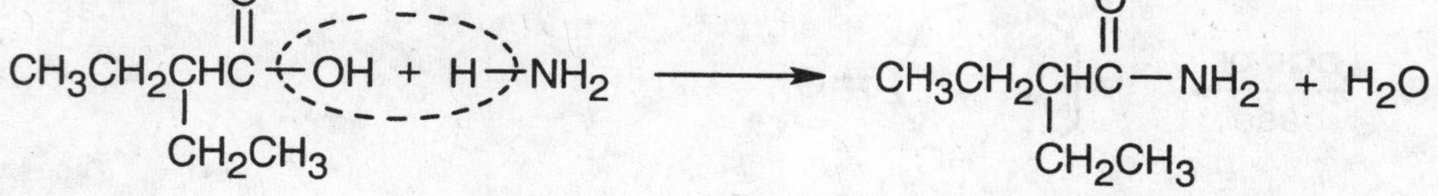

2-Ethylbutanamide

(b)

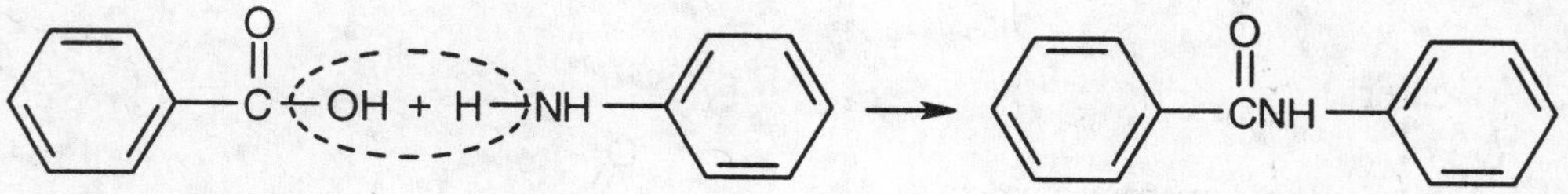

N-Phenylbenzamide + H_2O

(c)

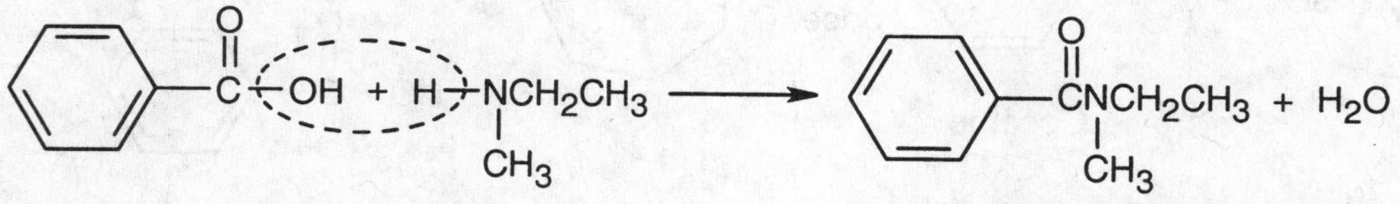

N-Ethyl-*N*-methylbenzamide

(d)

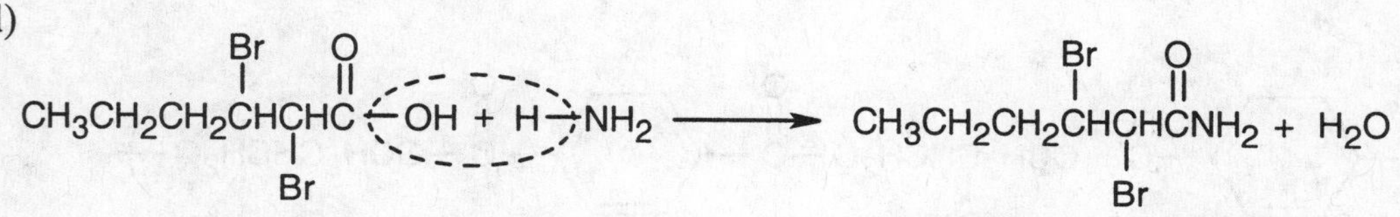

2,3-Dibromohexanamide

Reactions of Carboxylic Acids and Their Derivatives

17.62

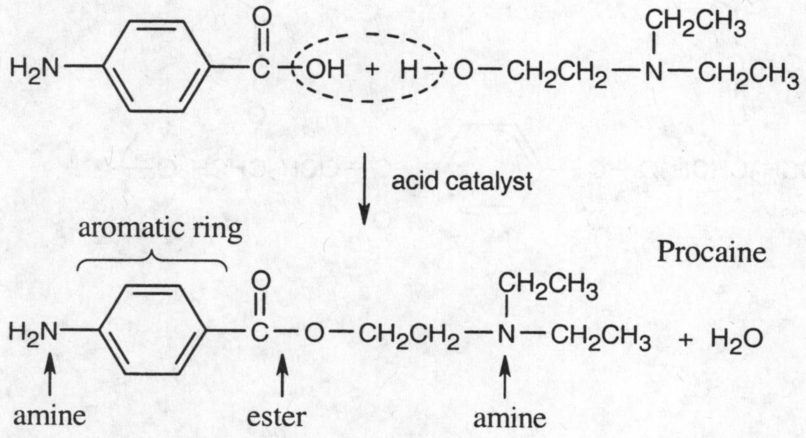
acid catalyst
aromatic ring
Procaine
amine
ester
amine

17.64

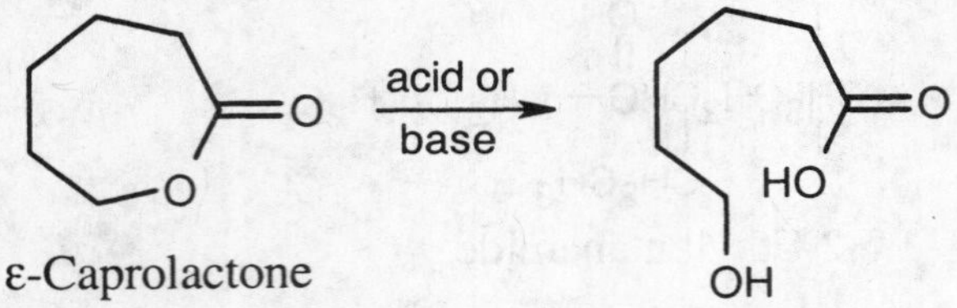
acid or
base
HO
OH
ε-Caprolactone

17.66

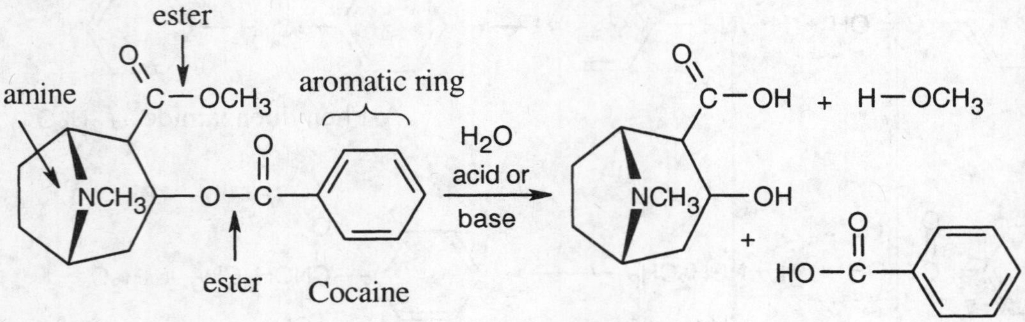
ester
amine
aromatic ring
NCH3
ester
Cocaine
H2O
acid or
base
C−OH
H−OCH3
NCH3
OH
HO−C

Polyesters and Polyamides

17.68

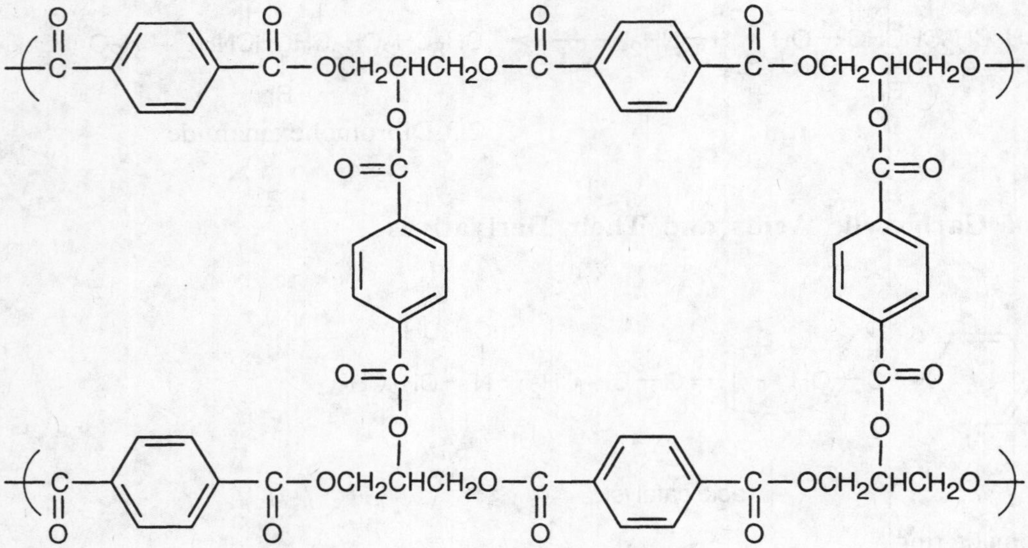
C−OCH2CHCH2O−C
C−OCH2CHCH2O

Phosphate Esters and Anhydrides

17.70

$$\begin{array}{c} CH_2OH \\ | \\ C=O \quad\quad O \\ | \quad\quad\quad || \\ CH_2-O-P-O^- \\ | \\ O^- \end{array} \;+\; H_2O \;\longrightarrow\; \begin{array}{c} CH_2OH \\ | \\ C=O \\ | \\ CH_2OH \end{array} \;+\; \begin{array}{c} O \\ || \\ HO-P-O^- \\ | \\ O^- \end{array}$$

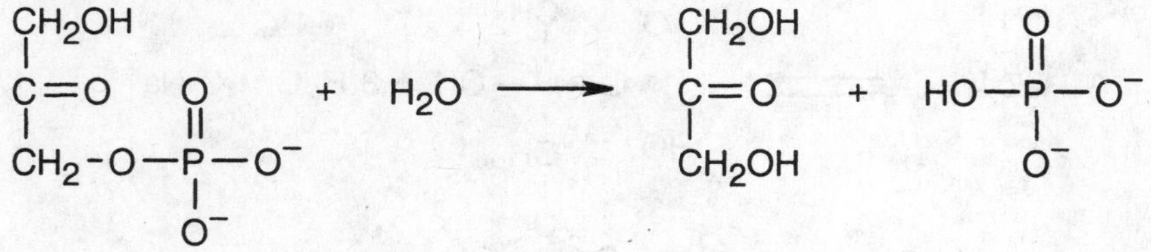

The products of hydrolysis are dihydroxyacetone and hydrogen phosphate anion.

17.72

$$\begin{array}{c} O \quad\quad\quad O \\ || \quad\quad\quad || \\ HO-P-O-C-CH_3 \\ | \\ OH \end{array}$$

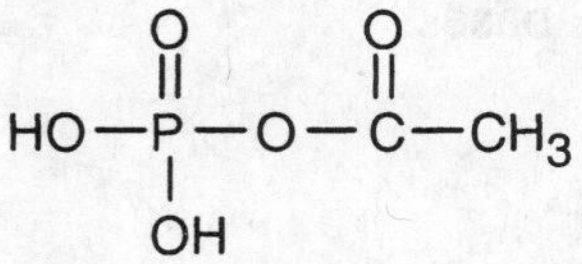

Acetyl phosphate

17.74

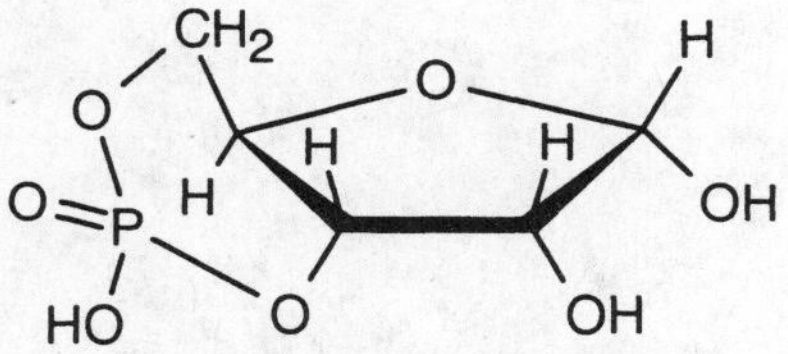

A cyclic phosphate diester

A cyclic phosphate diester is formed when one phosphate forms ester bonds with two hydroxyl groups in the same molecule.

Applications

17.76

$$\begin{array}{c} O \\ || \\ CCl_3COH \end{array} \;\text{Trichloroacetic acid} \quad\quad\quad \begin{array}{c} O \\ || \\ CH_3CHCOH \\ | \\ OH \end{array} \;\text{Lactic acid}$$

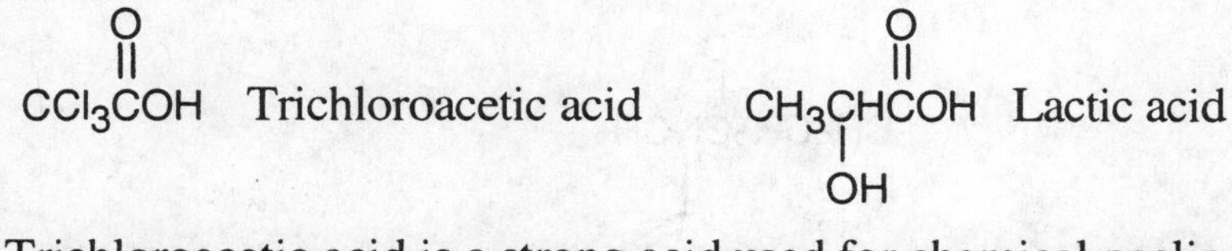

Trichloroacetic acid is a strong acid used for chemical peeling of the skin, and for removing scars and wrinkles. Lactic acid is a weaker acid used for wrinkle removal and skin moisturizing.

17.78

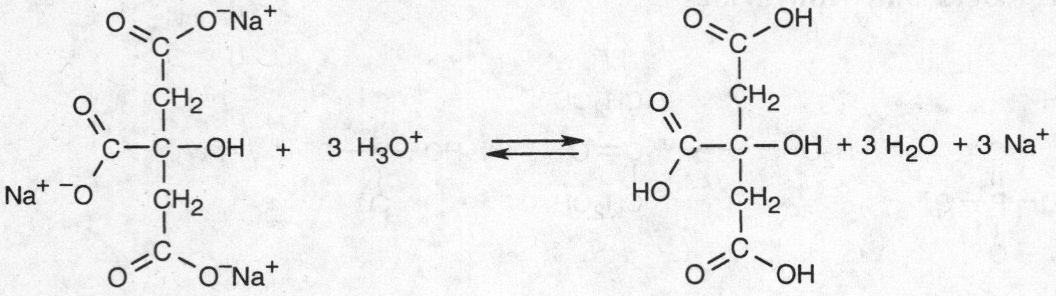

Trisodium citrate

Citric acid

17.80 Kevlar is a polyamide formed from *p*-benzenedicarboxylic acid and *p*-diaminobenzene. Because it is an amide, it can be hydrolyzed by strong acids and bases.

General Questions and Problems

17.82

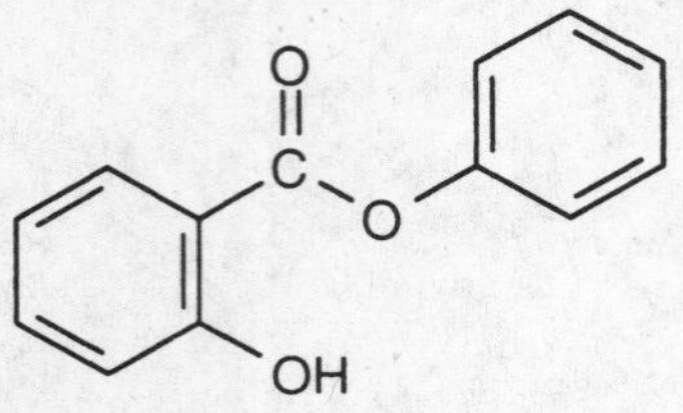

Salol (Phenyl salicylate)

17.84 (1) Measure the pH of solutions of the two compounds. Benzoic acid is acidic; benzaldehyde is nonacidic.

(2) Benzaldehyde reacts with Tollens' reagent to form a silver mirror; benzoic acid doesn't react with Tollens' reagent.

17.86

(a)

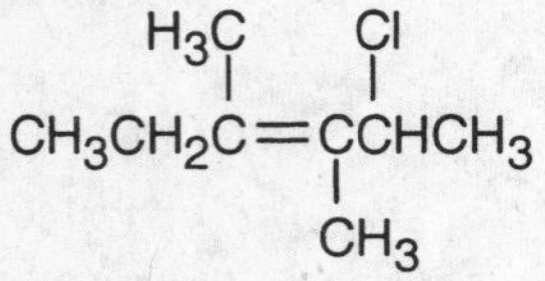

2-Chloro-3,4-dimethyl-3-hexene

(b)

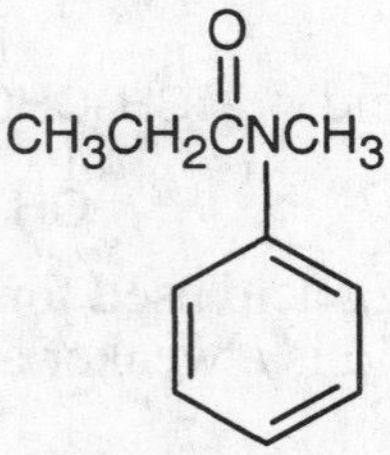

N-Methyl-*N*-phenylpropanamide

(c)

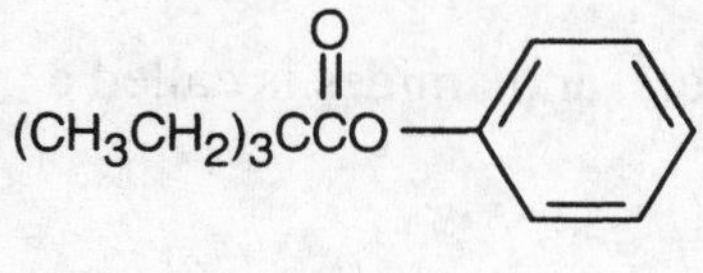

Phenyl 2,2-diethylbutanoate

(d)

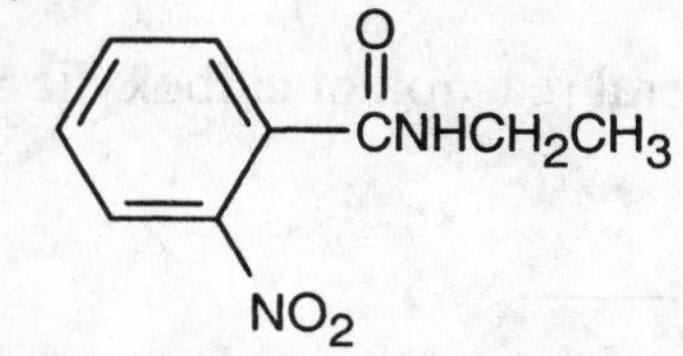

N-Ethyl-*o*-nitrobenzamide

Self-Test for Chapter 17

Multiple Choice

1. Which of the following amides does not form hydrogen bonds?
(a) benzamide (b) formamide (c) *N*-methylformamide (d) *N,N*-dimethylformamide

2. Which of the following statements about phosphoric acid anhydrides is untrue?
(a) Energy is released when triphosphate anhydrides react with water.
(b) Both mono- and dianhydrides occur in the body.
(c) Hydrolysis of phosphate ester anhydrides yields caustic products.
(d) Two molecules of water are necessary to completely hydrolyze a triphosphate anhydride.

3. Which class of compounds is lowest boiling?
(a) carboxylic acid esters (b) amides (c) carboxylic acids (d) carboxylic acid salts

4. The common name of an *-enoic* acid is
(a) succinic acid (b) benzoic acid (c) oxalic acid (d) acrylic acid

5. Amide bonds occur in all of the following except
(a) nylon (b) Dacron (c) urea (d) proteins

6. In the reaction $CH_3COOH + CH_3OH \rightleftharpoons CH_3COOCH_3 + H_2O$, the yield of CH_3COOCH_3 can be improved by
(a) distilling off the CH_3COOCH_3 (b) removing the water (c) using more CH_3COOH and CH_3OH (d) all of the above

7. Reaction of methanol with oxalic acid in the presence of an acid catalyst forms
(a) methyl oxalate (b) dimethyl oxalate (c) methyl acetate (d) reaction doesn't occur

8. Polypropylene and nylon resemble each other in which respect?
(a) They are both polymers. (b) They are both hydrocarbons. (c) Concentrated acid will dissolve them. (d) An initiator is needed for polymerization to occur.

9. Which of the following compounds is an α-amino acid?
(a) $H_2NCH_2CH_2C(=O)OH$ (b) $H_2NC(=O)CH_2CH_3$ (c) $H_2NCH_2C(=O)OCH_3$ (d) $H_2NCH_2C(=O)OH$

10. How many amides of the formula C_3H_7NO can be drawn?
(a) 3 (b) 4 (c) 5 (d) 6

Complete the following sentences:

1. The most common general reaction of carboxylic acids, esters, and amides is called a _____ _____ reaction.

2. Kevlar is a type of ________.

3. A carboxylic acid can be dissolved in water by converting it into its _____ _____.

4. The reaction of a carboxylic acid with an alcohol in the presence of an acid catalyst is called an _____ reaction.

5. In carboxylic acids, esters, and amides, the carbonyl-group carbon is bonded to an atom that strongly _____ electrons.

6. Carboxylic acids are named by using the name ending ___ ____.

7. $CH_3CH_2COOCH_2CH_2CH_3$ is named _____ _____.

8. Many flavors and fragrances are due to _____.

9. ________ is the transfer of a —PO_3^{2-} group from one molecule to another.

10. Long-chain carboxylic acids can be found in nature as components of _____.

11. The reaction of an ester with aqueous NaOH to yield a salt and an alcohol is called a _____ reaction.

12. Malonic acid is also known as ________ acid.

True or False

1. A carboxylic acid salt is more soluble in water than a carboxylic acid.

2. A *saponification* reaction is the acid-catalyzed hydrolysis of an ester.

3. Amides and amines are both basic.

4. A carboxylic acid is higher boiling than an ester of the same molecular weight.

5. Basic hydrolysis of ethyl acetate yields acetic acid and ethanol.

6. The compound $HCON(CH_3)_2$ is named dimethylformamide.

7. Nitrate esters are important in living systems.

8. Acetic acid is about 1% dissociated in a 1 M aqueous solution.

9. Carboxylic acids are either solids or liquids at room temperature.

10. Esterification can be brought about by treating a carboxylic acid with an alcohol in the presence of NaOH.

11. Pyrophosphoric acid is a phosphate ester.

12. Propanamide is higher boiling than methyl acetate.

Match each entry on the left with its partner on the right.

1. $CH_3COOH + CH_3OH + HCl$	(a) Amide hydrolysis
2. $HOOCCH_2COOH$	(b) Ester hydrolysis
3. $(CH_3COO^-)_2Mg^{2+}$	(c) Thioester
4. $CH_3COOCH_3 + NaOH, H_2O$	(d) *-enoic* acid
5. HCOOH	(e) Phosphate ester
6. $CH_3CH{=}CHCOOH$	(f) Dioic acid
7. $CH_3CONH_2 + NaOH, H_2O$	(g) Amide
8. CH_3OPO_3H	(h) Polyester
9. Nylon	(i) Formic acid
10. Dacron	(j) Ester formation
11. Acetyl-SCoA	(k) Acid salt
12. Benzocaine	(l) Polyamide

Chapter 18 – Amino Acids and Proteins

Chapter Outline

I. Introduction to biochemistry and proteins (Sections 18.1–18.2).
  A. Biochemistry (Section 18.1).
    1. Biochemistry is the study of the structure and function of biomolecules.
    2. The principal classes of biomolecules are proteins, carbohydrates, lipids, and nucleic acids.
    3. Biomolecules range in size from small organic molecules to polymers with millions of subunits.
    4. The three-dimensional shape of biomolecules is critical to their ability to function.
  B. Proteins (Section 18.2).
    1. Proteins are polymers of amino acids.
    2. The bonds that form between amino acids are amide bonds (peptide bonds).
      a. Two amino acids bond together to form a dipeptide.
      b. Three amino acids bond together to form a tripeptide.
      c. A chain with 10–100 amino acids is a polypeptide.
      d. The atoms that form a peptide bond have a planar relationship.
    3. There are four levels of protein structure.
      a. "Primary structure" refers to the sequence of amino acids that form peptide bonds.
      b. "Secondary structure" refers to the organization of polypeptide chains into a regular pattern.
      c. "Tertiary structure" refers to the overall shape of the protein molecule.
      d. "Quaternary structure" refers to the organization of proteins composed of several polypeptide chains.
    4. Proteins have numerous functions in living things.
      Among these functions are structure, support, storage, transport, and control of biochemical reactions.

II. Amino acids (Sections 18.3–18.6).
  A. Structure of amino acids (Section 18.3).
    1. Twenty amino acids commonly occur in nature.
      a. All twenty are α-amino acids.
      b. Nineteen of the twenty amino acids are primary amines.
    2. In this book, each amino acid is represented by a three-letter code.
    3. Amino acids are classified as neutral, acidic, or basic.
      Of the common amino acids, fifteen are neutral, three are basic, and two are acidic.
    4. Amino acid side chains are classified as hydrophilic (polar) or hydrophobic (nonpolar).
      a. Hydrophobic side chains cluster in the middle of a protein.
      b. Hydrophilic side chains are positioned on the surface of the protein.
  B. Acid-base properties of amino acids (Section 18.4).
    1. Amino acids exist as dipolar zwitterions.
      a. Amino acids have properties similar to salts: They are high-melting and soluble in water.
      b. Amino acids can react as acids or bases.
    2. The pH at which the number of positive charges on an amino acid equals the number of negative charges is called the isoelectric point (pI).
      a. Neutral amino acids have pIs in the range 5.0–6.5.
      b. Acidic amino acids are negatively charged at physiological pH.

C. Chirality and amino acids (Sections 18.5–18.6).
   1. Chirality (Section 18.5).
      a. Chirality is the property of handedness.
      b. An object that lacks a plane of symmetry is chiral.
   2. Molecular handedness (Section 18.6).
      a. A carbon that is bonded to four different atoms or groups of atoms is a chiral carbon atom.
      b. The two mirror-image forms of a chiral molecule are enantiomers, or optical isomers.
         i. Optical isomers are one kind of stereoisomer.
         ii. Optical isomers are identical in all properties except for their effect on polarized light.
      c. All amino acids except for glycine are chiral.
      d. Only one of a pair of enantiomeric amino acids occurs naturally.

III. Proteins (Sections 18.7–18.12).
A. Primary protein structure (Sections 18.7–18.8).
   1. The repeating chain of peptide bonds and α carbons is known as the protein backbone (Section 18.7).
      a. The atoms that form the peptide bond lie in a plane.
      b. The amino-terminal end of the peptide is written on the left, and the carboxy-terminal end is on the right.
      c. A peptide is named by listing the residues in order, from left to right.
   2. Protein function is dependent on the exact sequence of amino acids in protein primary structure.
   3. Primary structure is responsible for the shape of a protein molecule.
      In sickle-cell anemia, a change in only one amino acid is responsible for the disease.
   4. Several types of interactions determine protein shape (Section 18.8).
      a. Noncovalent interactions.
         i. Hydrogen bonds can occur between atoms on the protein backbone.
         ii. Hydrogen bonds can occur between side-chains of amino acids or between side-chain amino acids and the polypeptide backbone.
         iii. Ionic interactions can occur between ionized acidic and basic amino acids; these are called salt bridges.
         iv. Hydrophobic interactions occur between nonpolar side chains.
      b. Covalent interactions. The thiol groups of cysteine residues form disulfide bonds.

B. Secondary protein structure (Section 18.9).
   1. Secondary structure refers to the ordered relationships of backbone atoms resulting from hydrogen bonding.
   2. There are two types of secondary structures.
      a. The α-helix is a right-handed coil formed by hydrogen bonds between an N—H group and a carbonyl group four amino acids away.
      b. The β-sheet occurs when polypeptide chains line up next to each other, and hydrogen bonds form between adjacent chains.
   3. Fibrous and globular proteins show examples of secondary structure.
      a. Some fibrous proteins are composed almost entirely of α-helices.
      b. Globular proteins have smaller regions of α-helix and β-sheet secondary structure.
   4. The parts of the polypeptide chain not involved in a secondary structural element are called random coil segments.

C. Tertiary protein structure (Section 18.10).
   1. Tertiary structure.
      a. Tertiary structure describes the overall shape of proteins.

b. The interactions responsible for tertiary structure may be between amino acids many units apart.
c. Interactions described in Section 18.7 give each protein its unique three-dimensional shape.
2. Examples.
a. Ribonuclease – a globular protein.
Hydrophobic side-chains congregate in the middle, and hydrophilic side chains are distributed on the outside.
b. Myoglobin – a globular protein.
i. Myoglobin has eight α-helix segments.
ii. A heme group is embedded within the polypeptide chain.

D. Quaternary structure (Section 18.11).
1. Quaternary structure describes the noncovalent interactions between the polypeptide chains of proteins that consist of more than one chain.
2. Examples.
a. Collagen is formed by several tropocollagen strands overlapping lengthwise.
b. Hemoglobin consists of four polypeptide chains held together by hydrophobic interactions.
3. Classification of proteins.
a. Proteins can be classified as simple or conjugated.
b. Proteins can be classified as fibrous or globular.

F. Chemical properties of proteins (Section 18.12).
1. Hydrolysis.
Polypeptide amide bonds can be cleaved by acid or enzymes to yield amino acids.
2. Denaturation.
a. Denaturation disturbs a protein's shape without disrupting primary structure.
b. Denaturation changes the properties of proteins.
c. Denaturation can be caused by various agents.
i. Heat disturbs side-chain interactions.
ii. Mechanical agitation.
iii Detergents disrupt the interactions of hydrophobic side chains.
iv. Organic compounds disrupt hydrogen bonds.
v. pH changes disrupt salt bridges.
vi. Inorganic salts disrupt salt bridges.
3. Occasionally, denatured proteins can undergo renaturation.

Solutions to Chapter 18 Problems

18.1 Amino acids containing an aromatic ring: phenylalanine, tyrosine, tryptophan

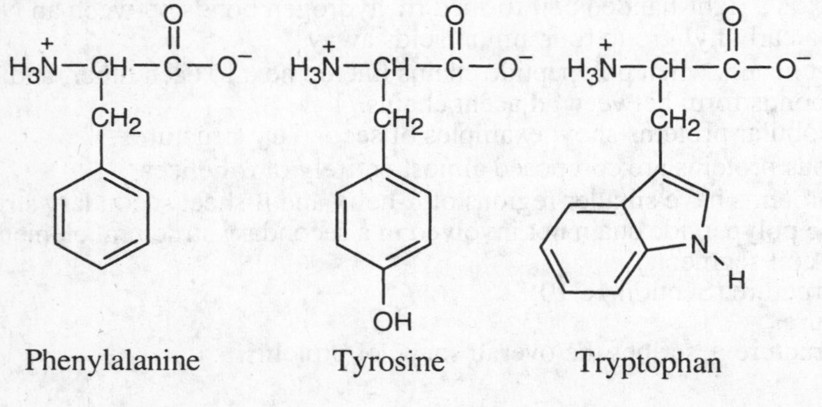

Phenylalanine Tyrosine Tryptophan

Amino acids containing sulfur: cysteine, methionine

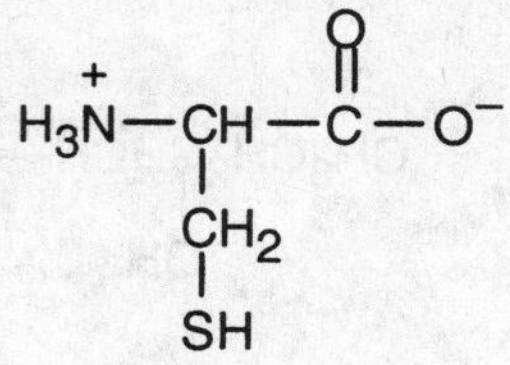

$H_3\overset{+}{N}-CH-C(=O)-O^-$
CH_2
SH

Cysteine

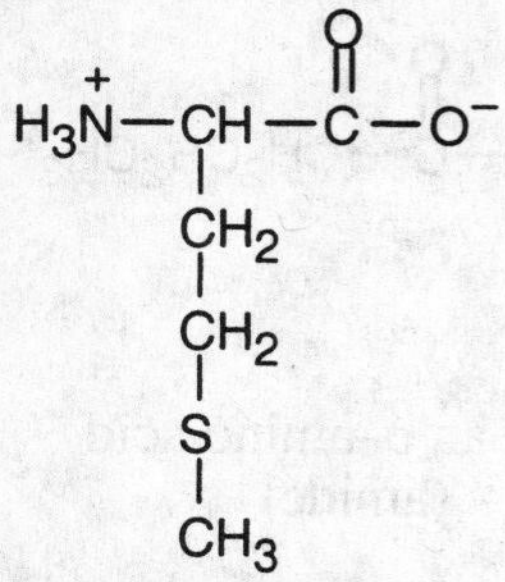

$H_3\overset{+}{N}-CH-C(=O)-O^-$
CH_2
CH_2
S
CH_3

Methionine

Amino acids that are alcohols: serine, threonine, tyrosine (a phenol)

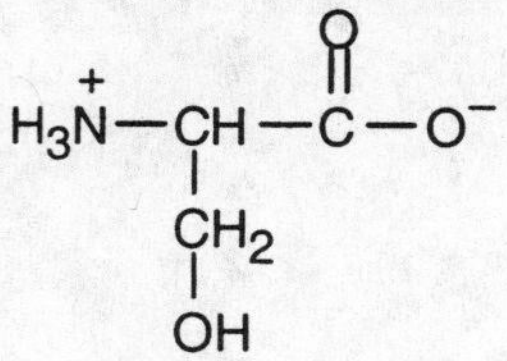

$H_3\overset{+}{N}-CH-C(=O)-O^-$
CH_2
OH

Serine

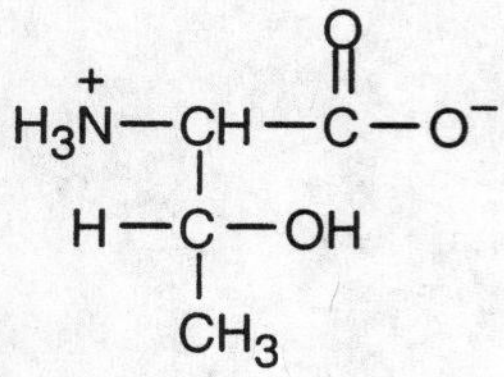

$H_3\overset{+}{N}-CH-C(=O)-O^-$
H—C—OH
CH_3

Threonine

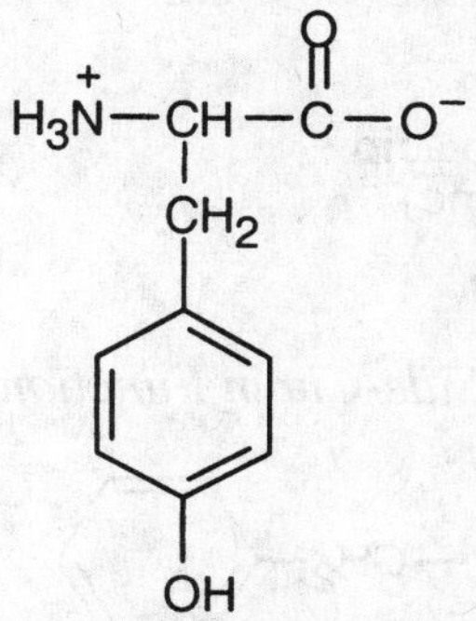

$H_3\overset{+}{N}-CH-C(=O)-O^-$
CH_2
OH

Tyrosine

Amino acids with alkyl group side chains: alanine, valine, leucine, isoleucine

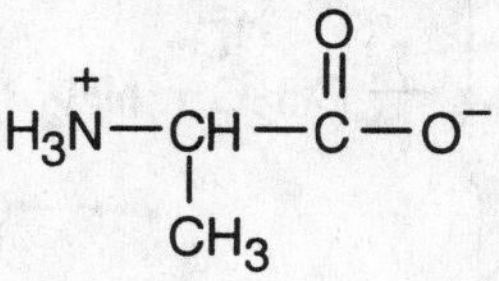

$H_3\overset{+}{N}-CH-C(=O)-O^-$
CH_3

Alanine

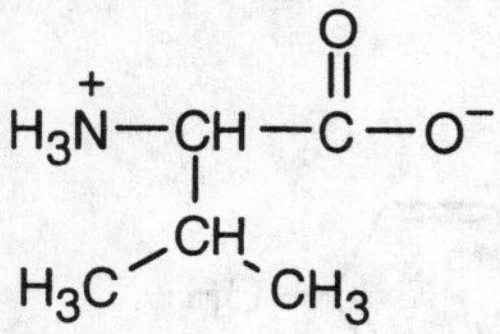

$H_3\overset{+}{N}-CH-C(=O)-O^-$
CH
H_3C
CH_3

Valine

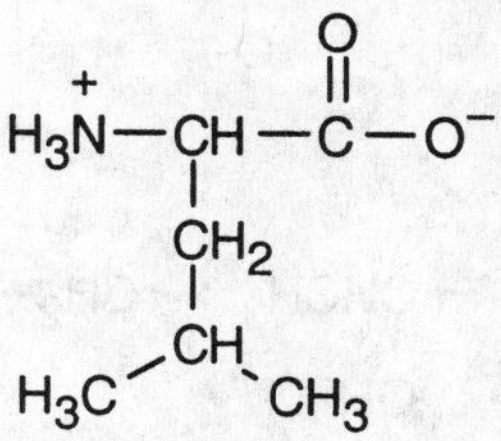

$H_3\overset{+}{N}-CH-C(=O)-O^-$
CH_2
CH
H_3C
CH_3

Leucine

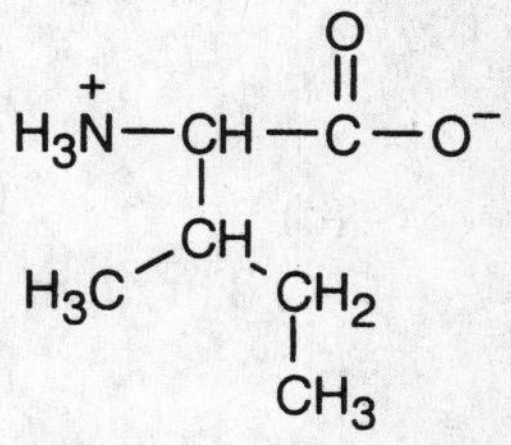

$H_3\overset{+}{N}-CH-C(=O)-O^-$
CH
H_3C
CH_2
CH_3

Isoleucine

18.2

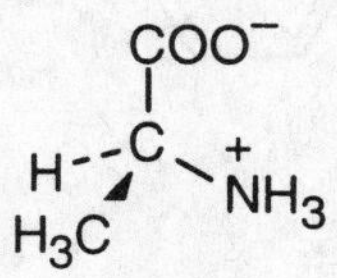

COO^-
H
C
$\overset{+}{N}H_3$
H_3C

Alanine

18.3 Two dipeptides of alanine (nonpolar) and serine (polar) can be drawn.

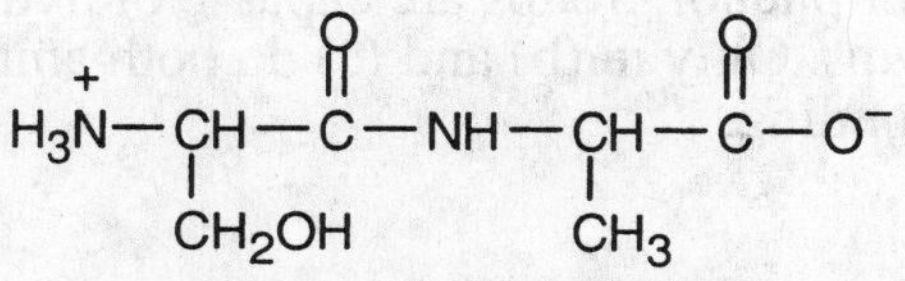

$H_3\overset{+}{N}-CH-C(=O)-NH-CH-C(=O)-O^-$
CH_2OH
CH_3

Serine Alanine

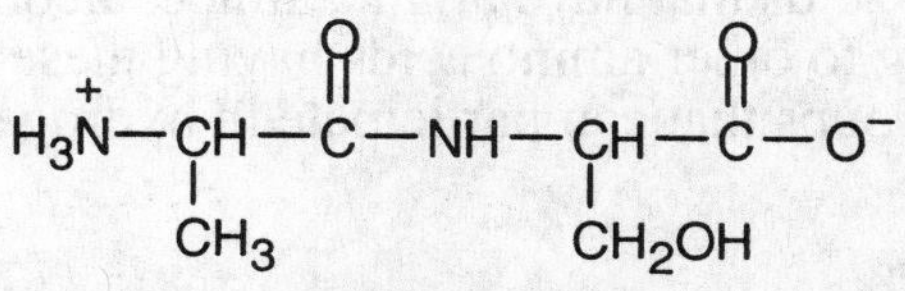

$H_3\overset{+}{N}-CH-C(=O)-NH-CH-C(=O)-O^-$
CH_3
CH_2OH

Alanine Serine

18.4

(a)

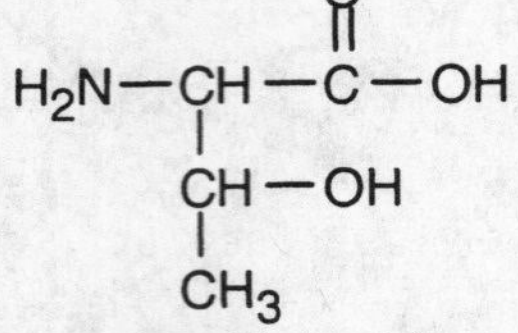

α-amino acid
(Threonine)

(b)

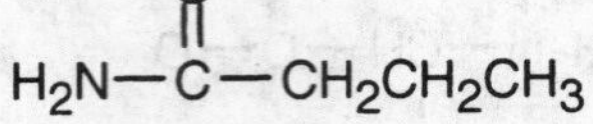

not an α-amino acid
(amide)

(c)

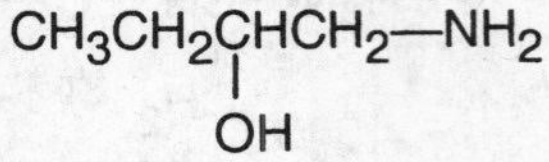

not an α-amino acid
(amino alcohol)

(d)

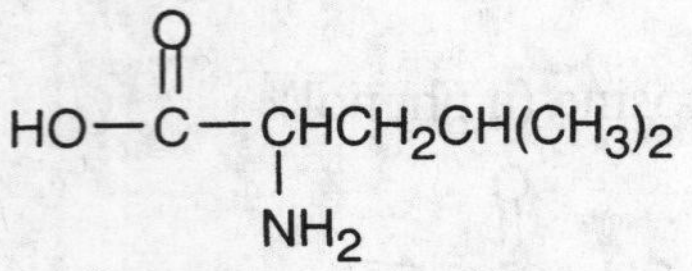

α-amino acid
(Leucine)

18.5

Side-Chain Functional Groups: *Hydrogen Bonding?*

(a) Phe, Thr

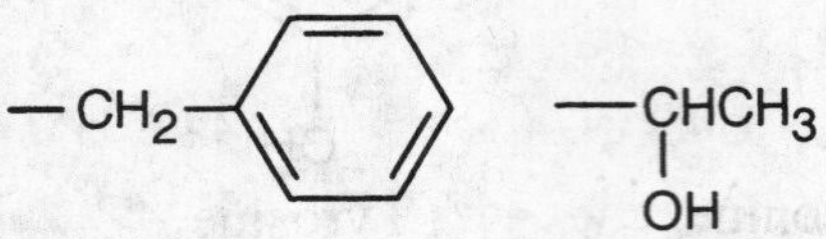

no

(b) Asn, Ser

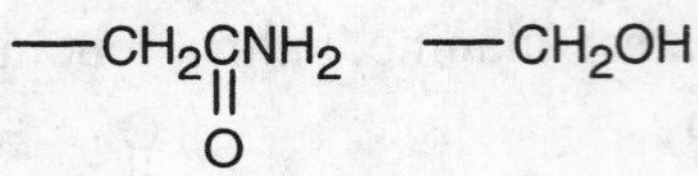

yes

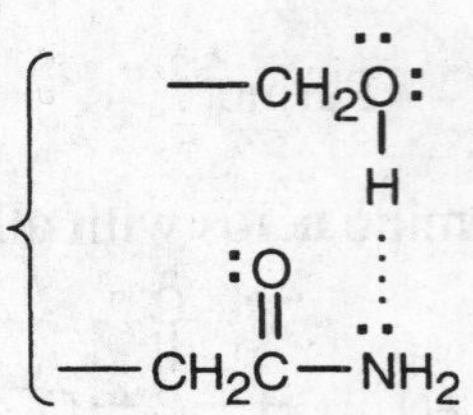

(c) Thr, Tyr

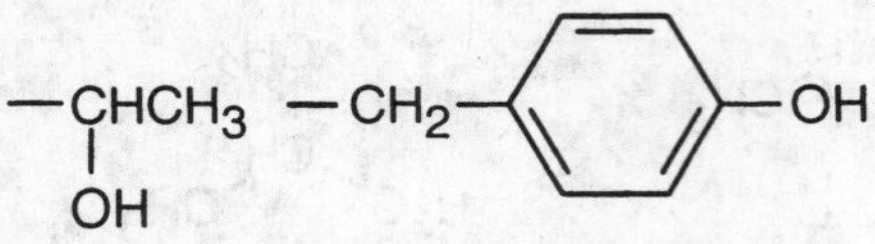

yes

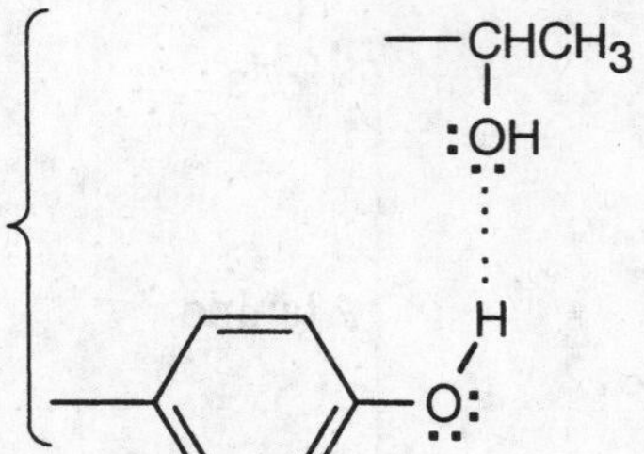

(d) Gly, Trp

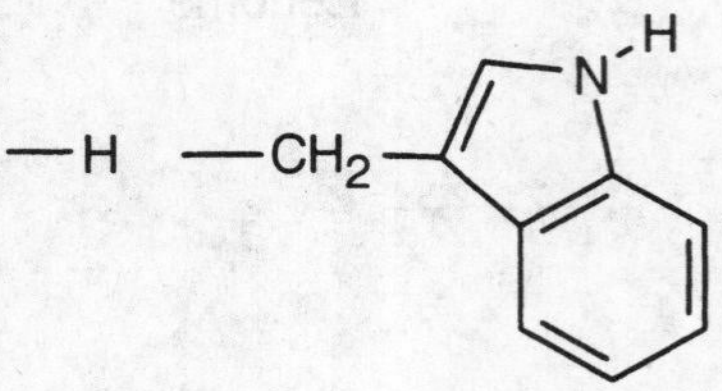

no

Amino acids that have amine, amide, alcohol, or phenol groups are capable of hydrogen bonding to other amino acids having these groups. Only in (b) and (c) do both amino acids have groups that can participate in hydrogen bonding.

18.6

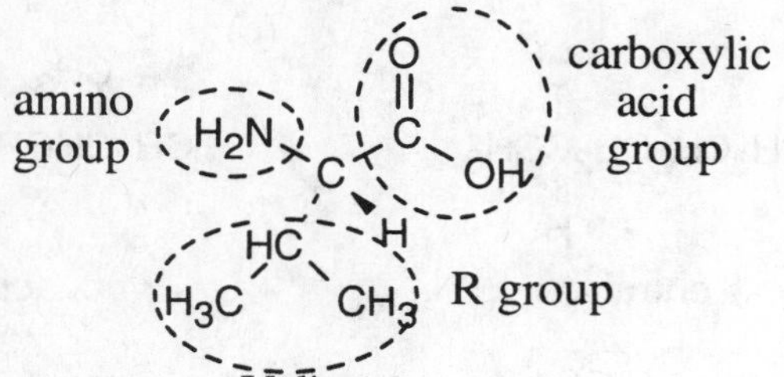
amino group
carboxylic acid group
R group

Valine

18.7

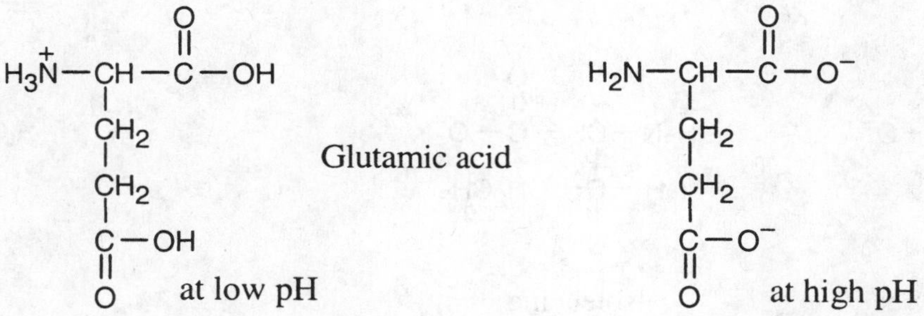
Glutamic acid
at low pH
at high pH

At low pH, both of the carboxylic acid groups and the amino group are protonated. At high pH, the carboxylic acid groups exist as carboxylate anions and the amino group is not protonated.

18.8 In the zwitterionic form of an amino acid, the —NH_3^+ group is an acid (because it can donate H^+), and the —COO^- group is a base (because it can accept H^+).

18.9 Chiral: (a) chair (b) jar (d) scissors

18.10 Handed: wrench, shoe, bottle cap
Not handed: thumb tack, pencil, eraser

Many other answers are possible.

18.11

2-Aminopropane 2-Aminobutane

2-Aminopropane is achiral because no carbon has four different groups bonded to it. 2-Butanol is chiral because four different groups are bonded to carbon 2 (—H, —CH_3, —NH_2 and —CH_2CH_3).

18.12

(a)

$$CH_3CH_2\underset{\underset{H}{|}}{\overset{\overset{Cl}{|}}{C}}CH_2CH_3$$

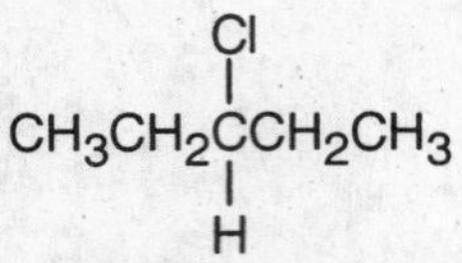

achiral

(b)

$$CH_3CH_2CH_2\overset{*}{\underset{\underset{H}{|}}{\overset{\overset{Cl}{|}}{C}}}CH_3$$

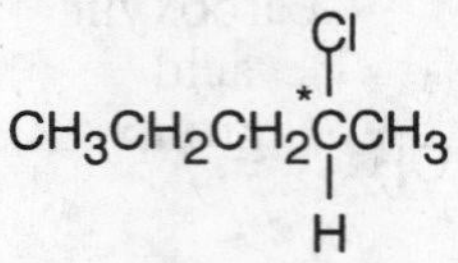

chiral

(c)

$$CH_3\underset{|}{\overset{\overset{CH_3}{|}}{CH}}CH_2\overset{*}{\underset{\underset{H}{|}}{\overset{\overset{CH_3}{|}}{C}}}CH_2CH_3$$

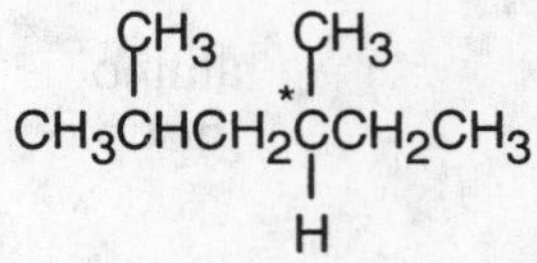

chiral

The starred carbon atoms in (b) and (c) each have four different groups bonded to them.

18.13 Threonine and isoleucine each have two chiral carbon atoms (starred in the following structures).

$$\overset{+}{H_3N}-\overset{*}{\underset{|}{CH}}-\overset{\overset{O}{||}}{C}-O^-$$
$$H-\overset{*}{\underset{|}{C}}-OH$$
$$CH_3$$

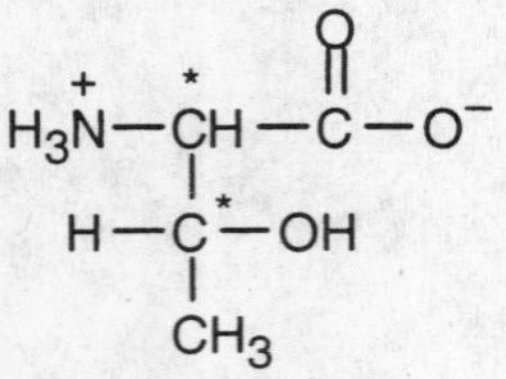

Threonine

$$\overset{+}{H_3N}-\overset{*}{\underset{|}{CH}}-\overset{\overset{O}{||}}{C}-O^-$$
$$H-\overset{*}{\underset{|}{C}}-CH_2CH_3$$
$$CH_3$$

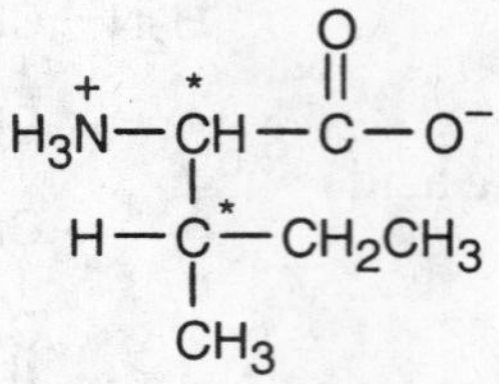

Isoleucine

18.14

$$H-\underset{\underset{Br}{|}}{\overset{\overset{H}{|}}{C}}-\underset{\underset{Cl}{|}}{\overset{\overset{H}{|}}{C}}-H$$

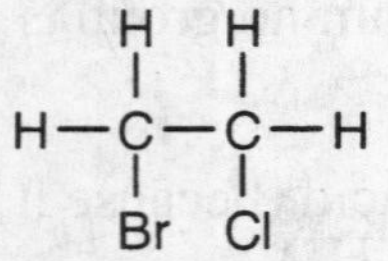

$$H-\underset{\underset{H}{|}}{\overset{\overset{H}{|}}{C}}-\overset{*}{\underset{\underset{Cl}{|}}{\overset{\overset{H}{|}}{C}}}-Br$$

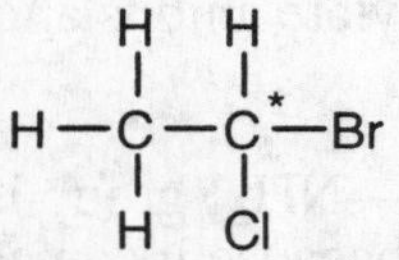

The starred carbon in the second isomer is chiral because four different groups (–H, –Cl, –Br, –CH$_3$) are bonded to it.

18.15 (a) Gly–Ser–Tyr   Tyr–Ser–Gly   Ser–Tyr–Gly
        Gly–Tyr–Ser   Tyr–Gly–Ser   Ser–Gly–Tyr

(b)

$$\overset{+}{H_3N}-CH_2-\overset{\overset{O}{||}}{C}-NH-\underset{\underset{CH_2OH}{|}}{CH}-\overset{\overset{O}{||}}{C}-NH-\underset{\underset{CH_2}{|}}{CH}-\overset{\overset{O}{||}}{C}-O^-$$

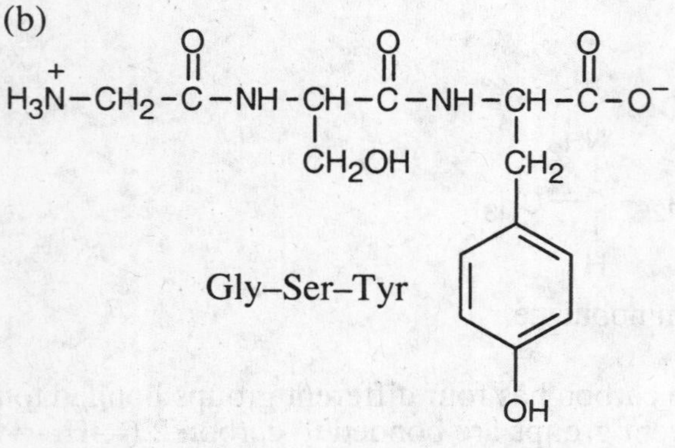

Gly–Ser–Tyr

$$\overset{+}{H_3N}-CH_2-\overset{\overset{O}{||}}{C}-NH-\underset{\underset{CH_2}{|}}{CH}-\overset{\overset{O}{||}}{C}-NH-\underset{\underset{CH_2OH}{|}}{CH}-\overset{\overset{O}{||}}{C}-O^-$$

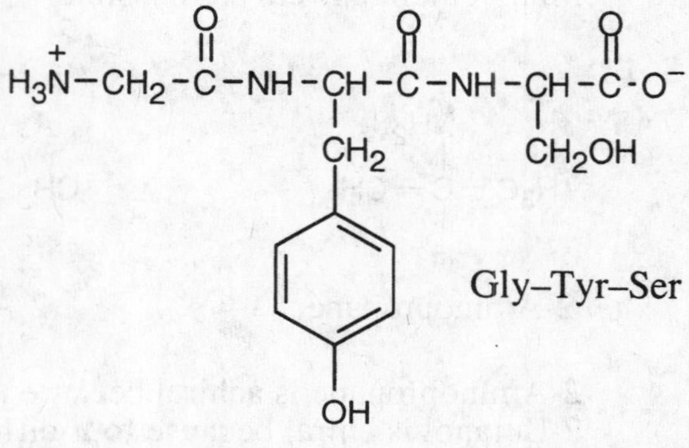

Gly–Tyr–Ser

18.16 Val–His–Ala His–Ala–Val Ala–His–Val
Val–Ala–His His–Val–Ala Ala–Val–His

18.17

(a)

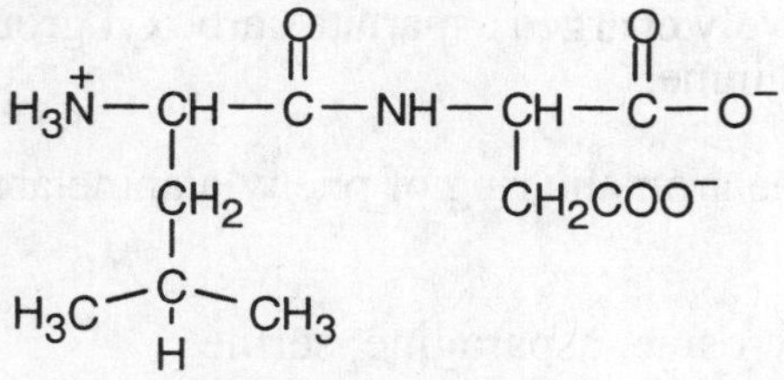

Leu–Asp

Leucine (Leu) Aspartate (Asp)

(b)

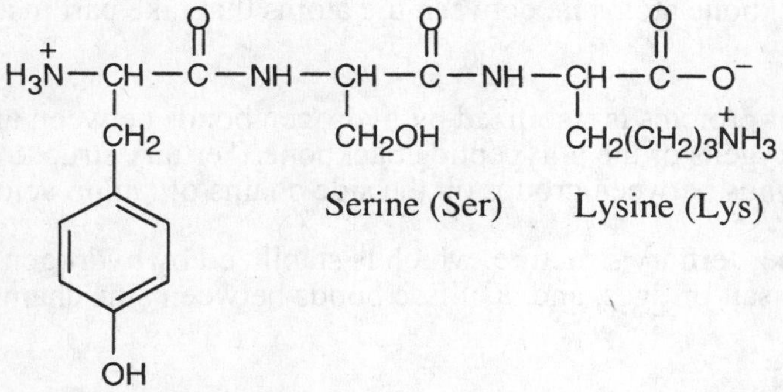

Tyr–Ser–Lys

Tyrosine (Tyr) Serine (Ser) Lysine (Lys)

18.18

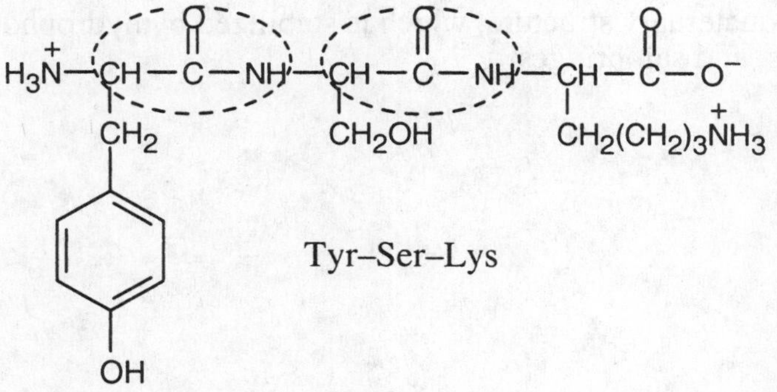

Tyr–Ser–Lys

18.19 Chymotrypsin breaks peptide bonds on the carboxylate side of aromatic amino acids. Table 18.3 shows that Phe, Tyr and Trp are the three aromatic acids that are found in proteins. Vasopressin contains Phe and Tyr, and three fragments result from treatment of vasopressin with chymotrypsin.

Asp–Tyr⌇Phe⌇Glu–Asn–Cys–Pro–Lys–Gly

↓ Chymotrypsin

Asp–Tyr + Phe + Glu–Asn–Cys–Pro–Lys–Gly

18.20 (a) Glutamine and tyrosine interact through *hydrogen bonds* between the terminal —NH_2 group of glutamine and the —OH of tyrosine.

(b) Leucine and proline are pulled together through *hydrophobic interactions* between the alkyl side chain of leucine and the ring portion of proline.

(c) A *salt bridge* occurs between the negatively charged aspartate carboxyl group and the positively charged terminal group of arginine.

(d) The alkyl side chain of isoleucine and the aromatic ring of phenylalanine are held together by *hydrophobic interactions.*

18.21 (a) Hydrogen bonds from side chains: tyrosine, asparagine, serine.
(b) Hydrophobic group interactions: alanine, isoleucine, valine, leucine.

18.22 In an α-helix, a carbonyl oxygen forms a hydrogen bond with an amide hydrogen twelve atoms away. Thus, 11 backbone atoms lie between the atoms that take part in an α-helix hydrogen bond.

18.23 The secondary structure of proteins is stabilized by hydrogen bonds between amide nitrogens and carbonyl oxygens of the polypeptide backbone. Tertiary structure is stabilized by hydrogen bonds between groups on the side chains of amino acids.

18.24 (a) This statement describes tertiary structure, which is stabilized by hydrogen bonds, hydrophobic interactions, salt bridges, and disulfide bonds between side chains on the same polypeptide chain.

(b) This statement describes secondary structure (α-helix), which is stabilized by hydrogen bonds between amide hydrogen atoms and carbonyl oxygen atoms on the polypeptide backbone.

(c) This statement describes quaternary structure, which is stabilized by hydrophobic interactions, hydrogen bonds, and salt bridges.

Understanding Key Concepts

18.25 Peptides that contain neither acidic nor basic amino acids have a net charge of +1 at pH = 1 because both the *N*-terminal amino group and the *C*-terminal carboxylic acid group are protonated. At pH = 11, these peptides have a net charge of –1, because the *N*-terminal group is uncharged and the *C*-terminal group is a carboxylate anion. At pH = 7, these peptides have a net charge of zero.

(a) Val–Gly–Leu

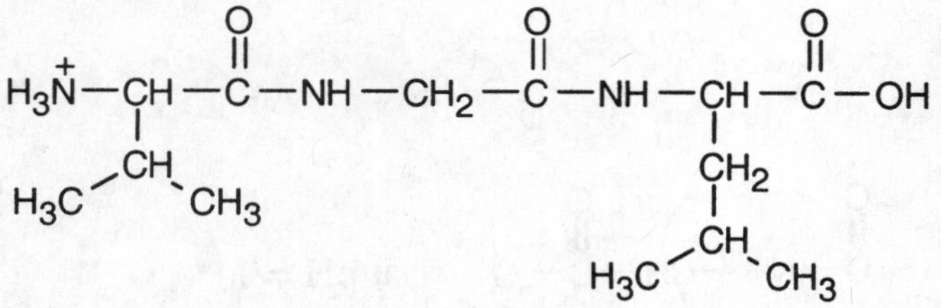

at pH = 1

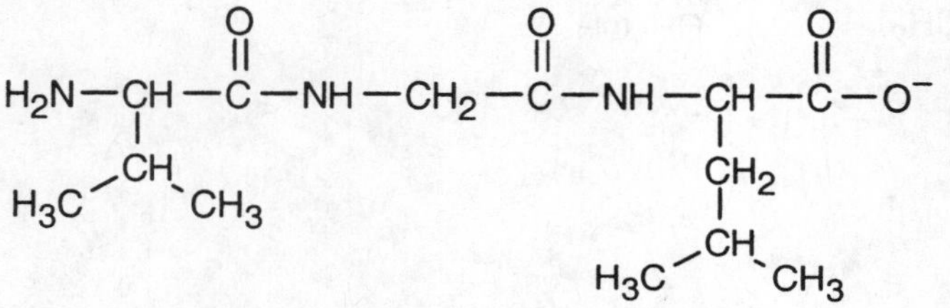

at pH = 11

(b) Arg–Lys–His

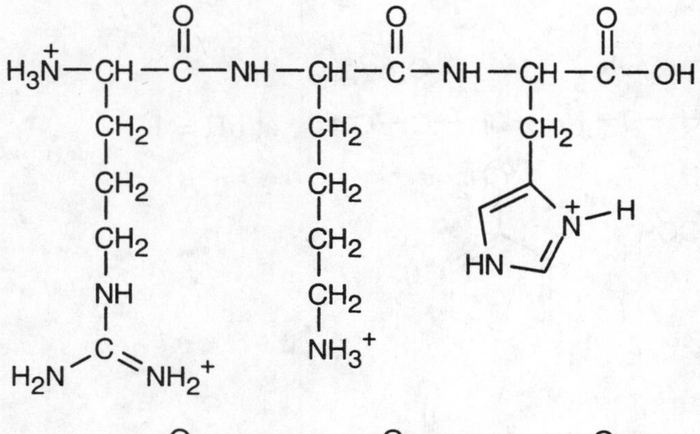

at pH = 1

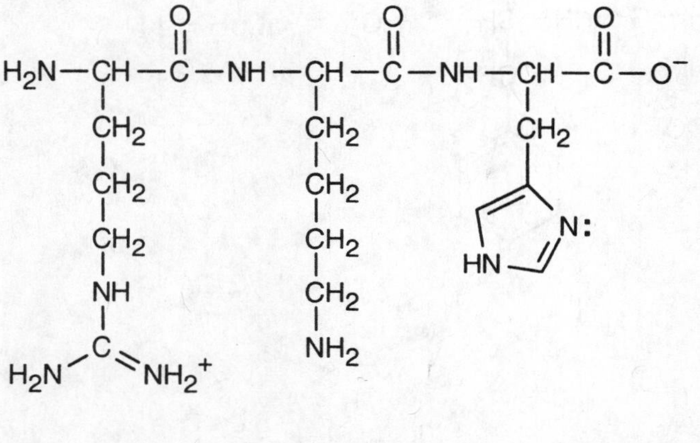

at pH = 11

(c) Tyr–Pro–Ser

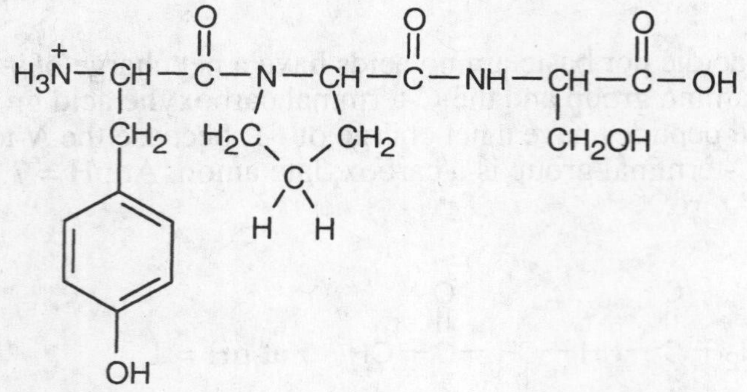

at pH = 1

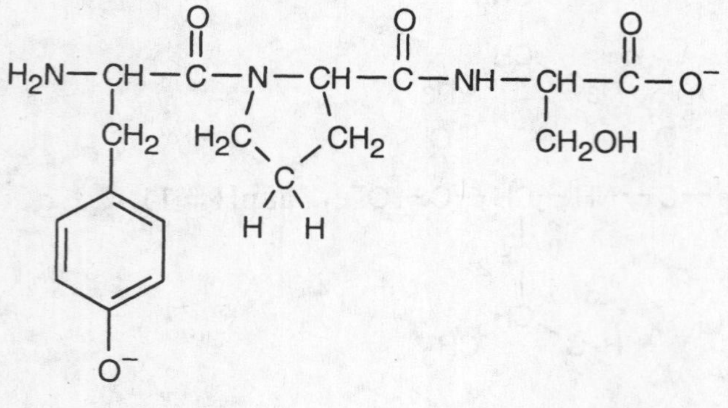

at pH = 11

(d) Glu–Asp–Phe

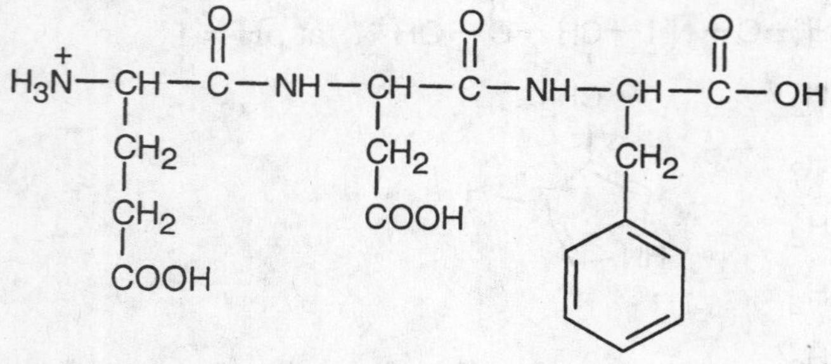

at pH = 1

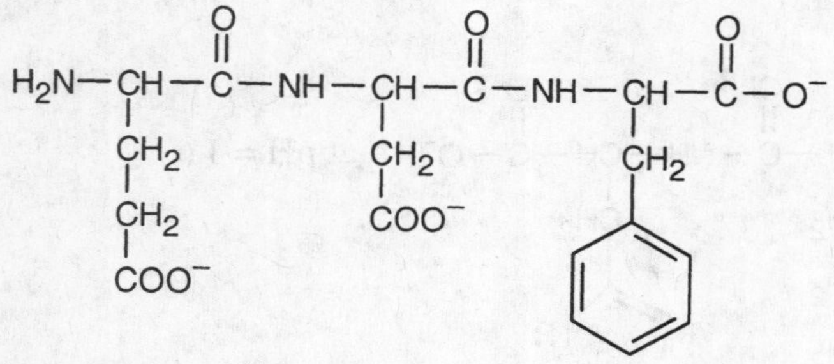

at pH = 11

(e) Gln–Ala–Asn

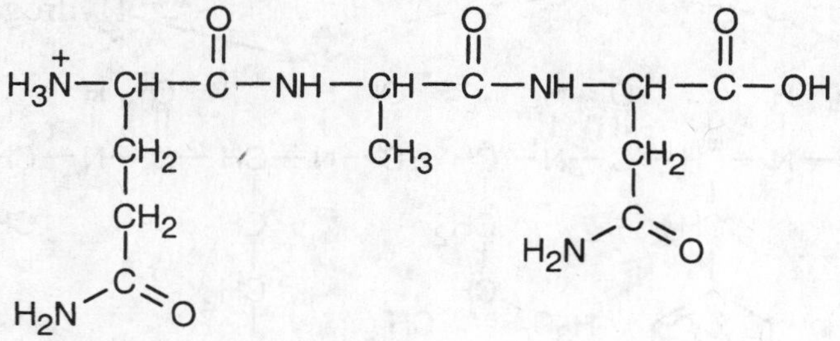

at pH = 1

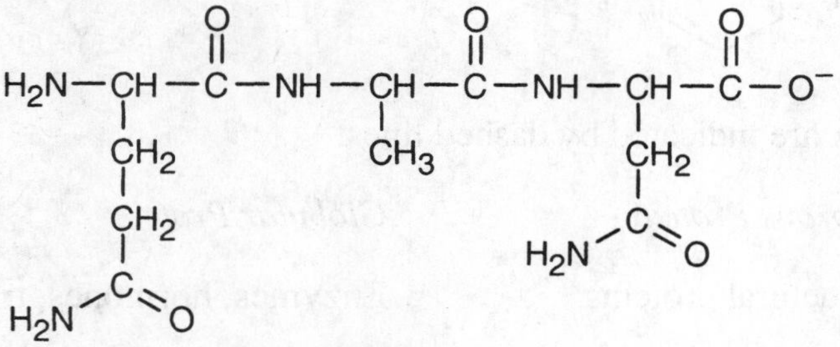

at pH = 11

(f) Met–Trp–Cys

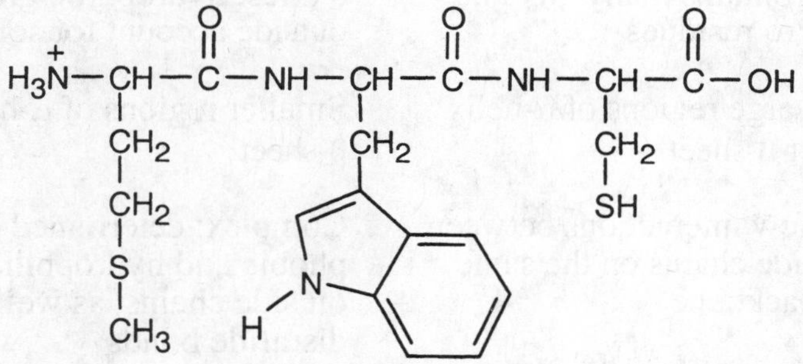

at pH = 1

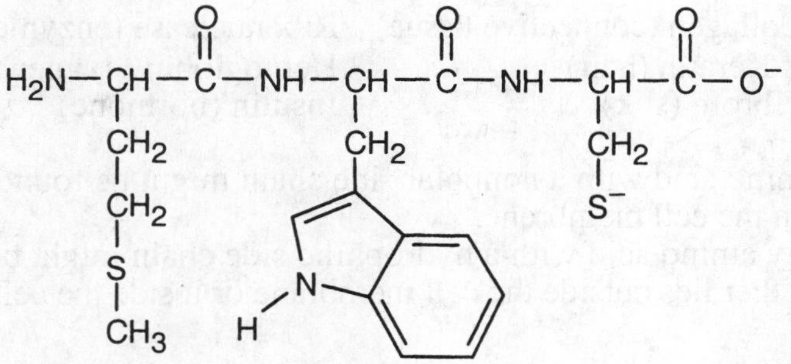

at pH = 11

18.26 In order for two amino acids to interact, they must both be of the same type (both polar or both nonpolar, for example).

(a) The pairs Pro...Leu and Ile...Val show hydrophobic interactions because they are both nonpolar. The pair Tyr ...Phe also shows hydrophobic interactions.
(b) Arg...Asp and His...Glu show ionic interactions because they are both charged.
(c) Thr...Glu form hydrogen bonds.

18.27

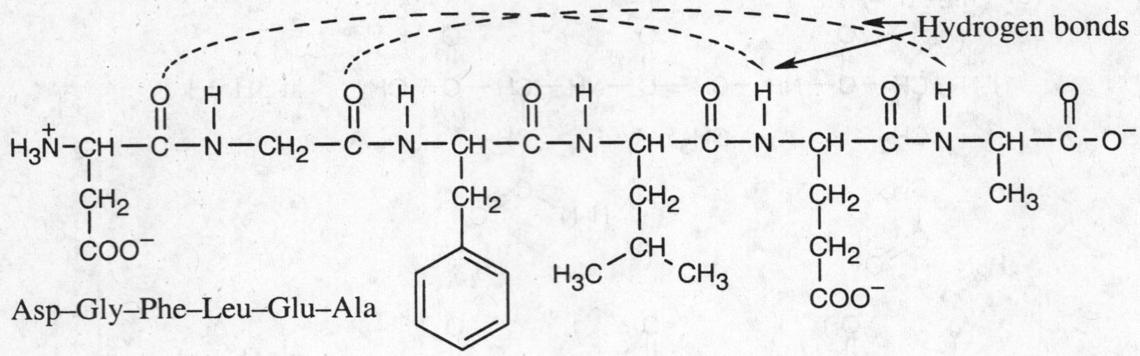
Hydrogen bonds
Asp–Gly–Phe–Leu–Glu–Ala

Hydrogen bonds in an α-helix are indicated by dashed lines.

18.28

	Fibrous Protein	*Globular Protein*
Biological function:	Structural proteins	Enzymes, hormones, transport
Water solubility:	Water-insoluble	Usually water-soluble
Amino acid composition:	Contains many Gly and Pro residues	Varies; hydrophilic groups on the outside account for solubility
Secondary structure:	Large regions of α-helix or β-sheet	Smaller regions of α-helix or β-sheet
Tertiary Structure:	Few interactions between side chains on the same backbone	Complex: determined by hydrophobic and hydrophilic groups on side chains, as well as by disulfide bonds
Examples:	Collagen (connective tissue) α-Keratin (hair) Fibroin (silk)	Ribonuclease (enzyme) Hemoglobin (oxygen transport) Insulin (hormone)

18.29 (a) Leu, Phe, Ala, or any amino acid with a nonpolar side chain might be found in the part of the protein that lies within the cell membrane.
(b),(c) Asp, Lys, Thr, or any amino acid with a hydrophilic side chain might be found in the part of the protein that either lies outside the cell membrane or inside the cell membrane.

Amino Acids

18.30 When referring to an amino acid, the prefix "α" means that the amino group is bonded to the carbon next to the —COOH carbon. In other words, the —NH_2 and —COOH groups are bonded to the same carbon.

18.32

(a)

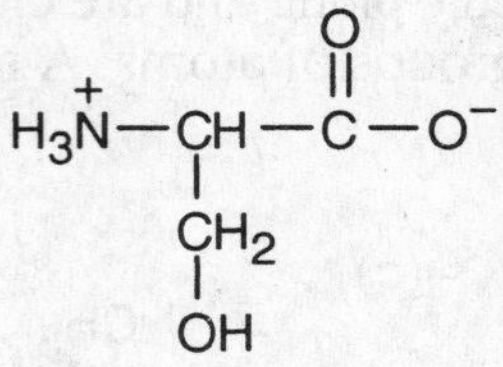

Serine (Ser)

(b)

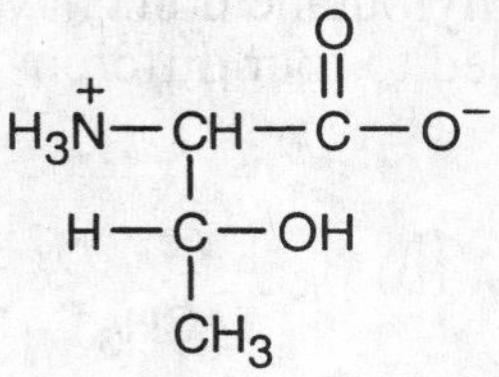

Threonine (Thr)

(c)

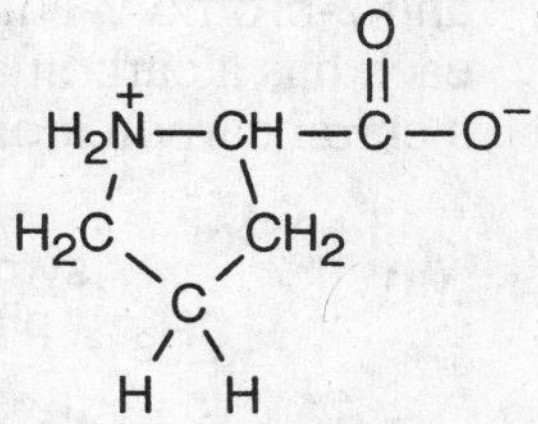

Proline (Pro)

18.34

(a)

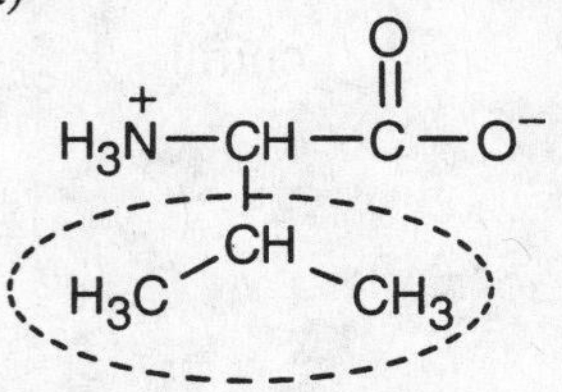

Valine (Val)

(b)

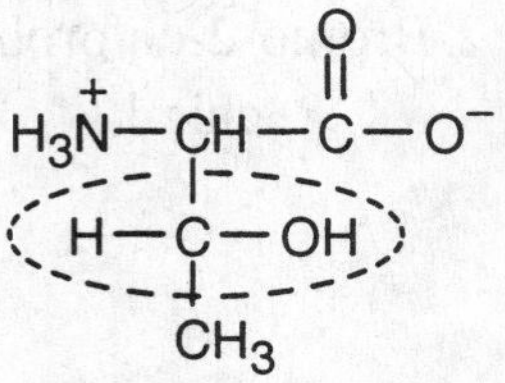

Threonine (Thr)

18.36 At a neutral pH (pH = 5 – 8), an amino acid with a pI less than 5 is negatively charged, and an amino acid with a pI greater than 8 is positively charged. Otherwise, an amino acid has no net charge at neutral pH and is neutral. Phenylalanine (pI = 5.5), proline (pI = 6.3), and asparagine (pI = 5.4) are all neutral.

18.38

(a)

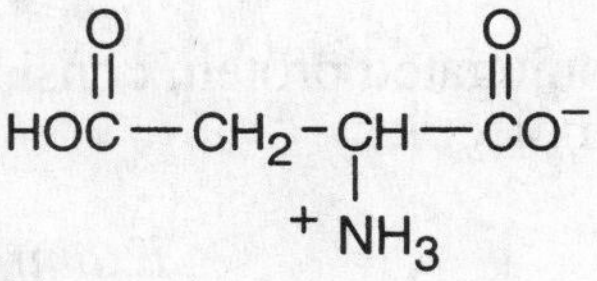

This structure represents aspartic acid at pH = 3, its isoelectric point. (low pH)

(b)

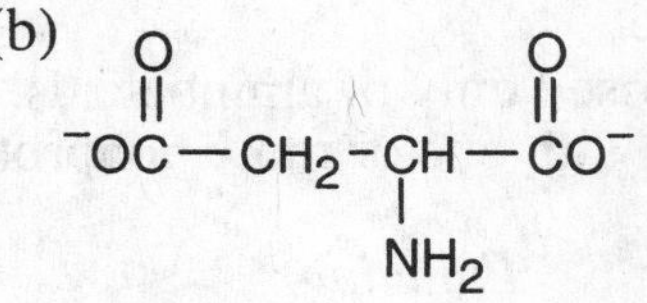

This structure represents aspartic acid at pH = 13. (high pH)

(c)

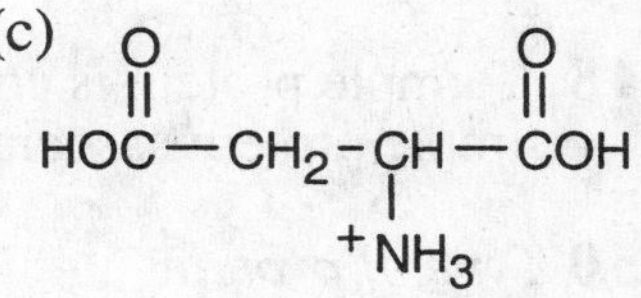

This structure represents aspartic acid at pH = 1 (low pH)

Handedness in Molecules

18.40 A chiral object is one that has handedness. Examples include a glove and a car.

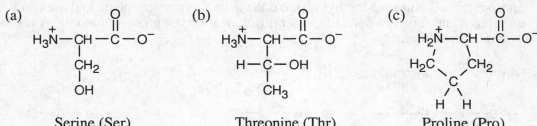

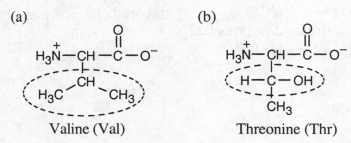

18.42 Chiral: (a) shoe (c) light bulb (because of screw threads)
Achiral: (b) bed

18.44 2-Bromo-2-chloropropane has a symmetry plane and is achiral. 2-Bromo-2-chlorobutane and 2-bromo-2-chloro-3-methylbutane don't have a symmetry plane and are chiral because each has a carbon atom bonded to four different atoms or groups of atoms. A star indicates a chiral carbon atom.

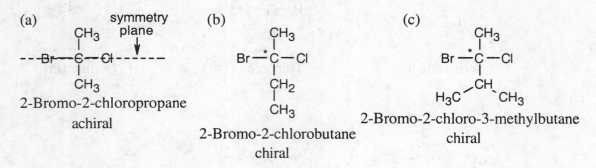

(a)

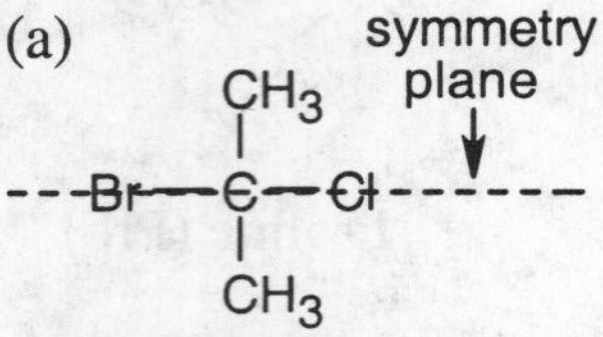
symmetry
plane
CH3
Br
C
Cl
CH3

2-Bromo-2-chloropropane

achiral

(b)

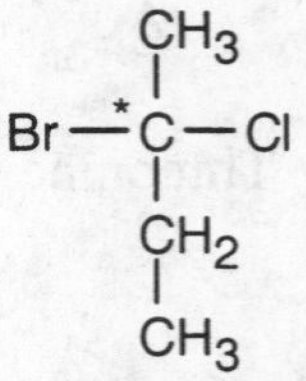
CH3
Br
C
Cl
CH2
CH3

2-Bromo-2-chlorobutane

chiral

(c)

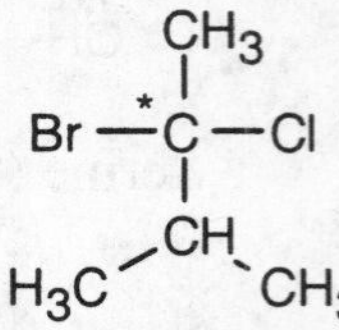
CH3
Br
C
Cl
CH
H3C
CH3

2-Bromo-2-chloro-3-methylbutane

chiral

18.46

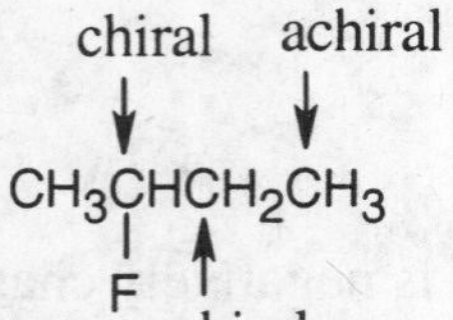
chiral
achiral
CH3CHCH2CH3
F
achiral

Peptides and Proteins

18.48 A simple protein is composed only of amino acids. A conjugated protein consists of a simple protein associated with one or more nonprotein molecules.

18.50

Type of protein	*Function*	*Example*
Enzymes:	Catalyze biochemical reactions	Ribonuclease
Hormones:	Regulate body functions	Insulin
Storage proteins:	Store essential substances	Myoglobin
Transport proteins:	Transport substances through body fluids	Serum albumin
Structural proteins:	Provide shape and support	Collagen
Protective proteins:	Defend the body against foreign matter	Immunoglobulins
Contractile proteins	Do mechanical work	Myosin and actin

18.52 The disulfide bonds between two cysteine residues help to stabilize a protein's tertiary structure.

18.54 (a) *Hydrophobic interactions* occur between hydrocarbon side chains of amino acids. In a protein, these side chains cluster in the center of the molecule to exclude water, and are responsible for the nearly spherical tertiary shape of globular proteins. Alanine and isoleucine take part in hydrophobic interactions.

(b) *Salt bridges* occur between negatively charged and positively charged amino acid side chain groups. They can stabilize the tertiary structure of a protein by connecting two distant parts of a polypeptide chain or by pulling the protein backbone together in the middle of the chain. They can also stabilize quaternary structure by bringing together two polypeptide chains. Lysine and aspartate can form salt bridges.

18.56 When a protein is denatured, its three-dimensional structure is disrupted, and its ability to catalyze reactions is impaired. Primary structure is not affected by denaturation.

18.58 Ala–Ser–Tyr Ser–Ala–Tyr Tyr–Ser–Ala
Ala–Tyr–Ser Ser–Tyr–Ala Tyr–Ala–Ser

18.60 Amino acids with polar side chains (glutamate and lysine, for example) are likely to be found on the outside of a globular protein, where they can form hydrogen bonds with water and with each other. Amino acids with nonpolar side chains (alanine and isoleucine, for example) are likely to be found on the inside of globular proteins, where they can escape from water.

18.62 If a diabetic took insulin orally, digestive enzymes would catalyze its hydrolysis, and the individual amino acids would be absorbed as food.

18.64

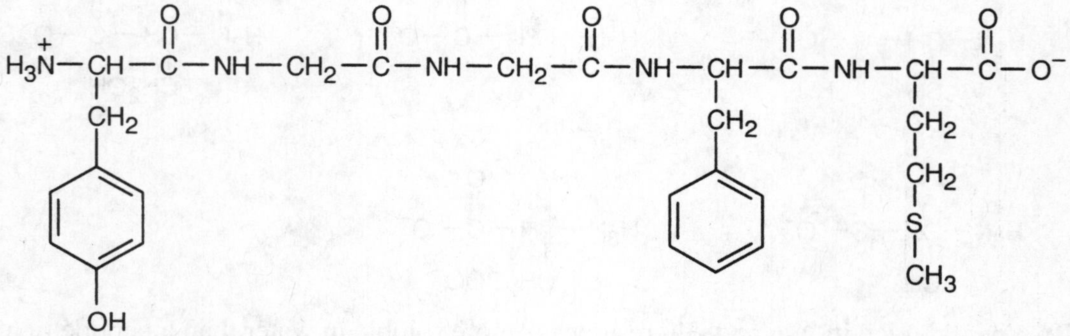

N-terminal amino acid Tyr – Gly – Gly – Phe – Met C-Terminal amino acid

Properties and Reactions of Amino Acids and Proteins

18.66

(a)

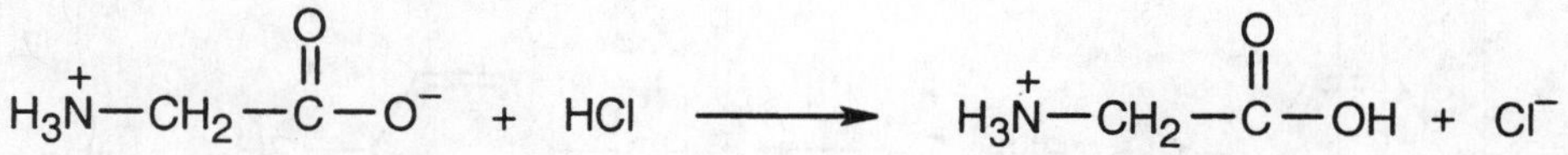

(b)

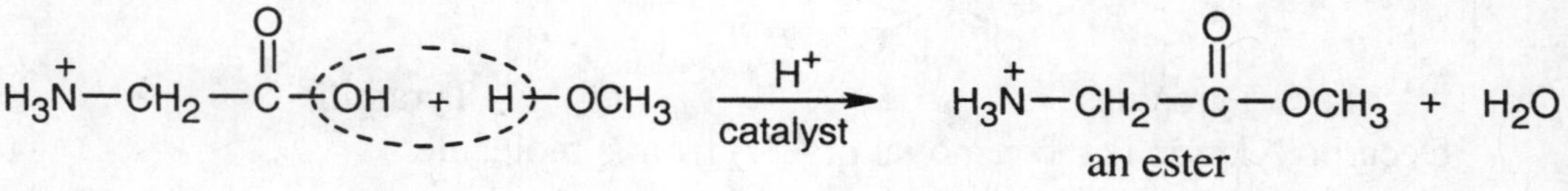

18.68

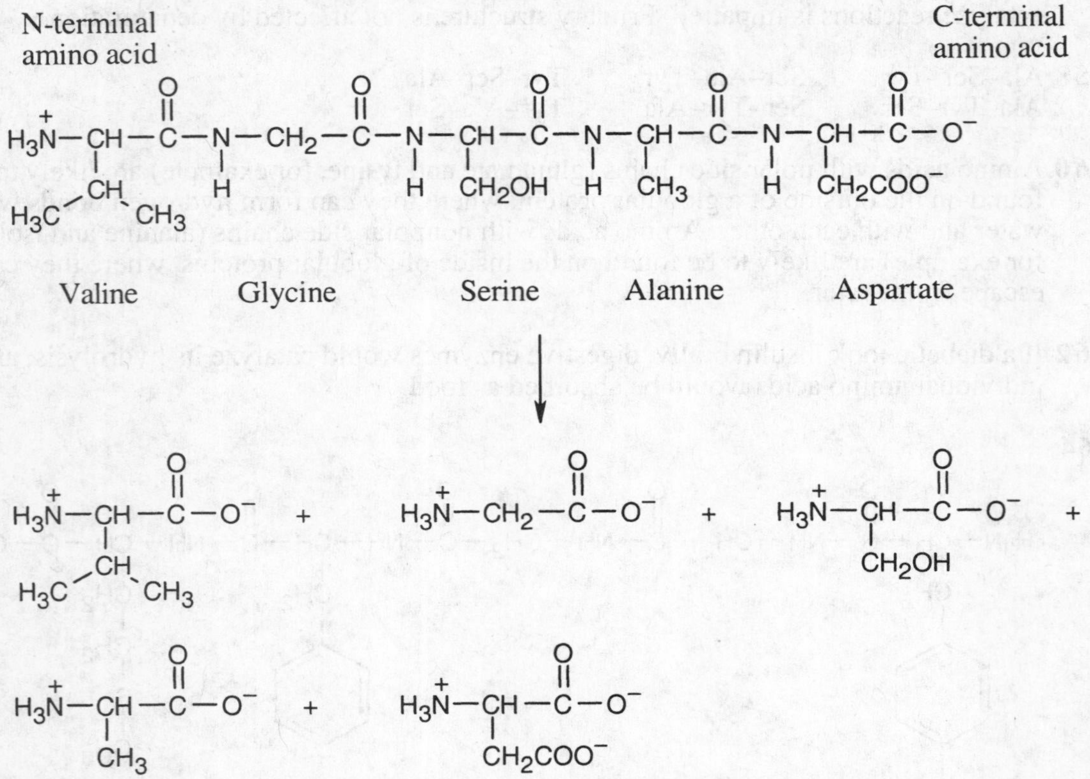

N-terminal amino acid
C-terminal amino acid
Valine
Glycine
Serine
Alanine
Aspartate

18.70 A peptide rich in Arg and Glu residues is more soluble in water than a peptide rich in Val and Gly residues. The side chains of Arg and Glu are polar and are better solvated by water than the nonpolar, hydrophobic side chains of Val and Gly.

Applications

18.72

(a)

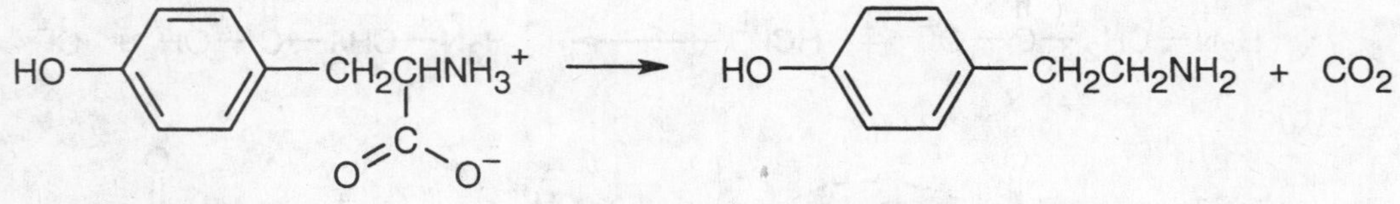

Tyrosine Tyramine

Decarboxylation is the removal of CO_2 from a molecule.

(b)

Phenelzine Tyramine

Like tyramine, phenelzine has an amino group on a two-carbon chain that is bonded to an aromatic ring. Phenelzine resembles tyramine, and it inhibits the enzyme that removes the amino group from tyramine.

18.74 An incomplete protein lacks one or more of the nine essential amino acids.

18.76 Casein and egg white protein are well-balanced proteins because they must provide complete nutrition to newborn and embryonic organisms. It is thus not surprising that they are also well-balanced proteins for human growth and development.

18.78 You need to remember these facts to answer this question.
(1) In a peptide, the acidic and basic amino acids determine the charge of the peptide.
(2) An amino acid that is acidic is negatively charged at a neutral pH, and a basic amino acid is positively charged at a neutral pH.
(3) A positively charged molecule migrates to the cathode (–), and a negatively charged molecule migrates to the anode (+).

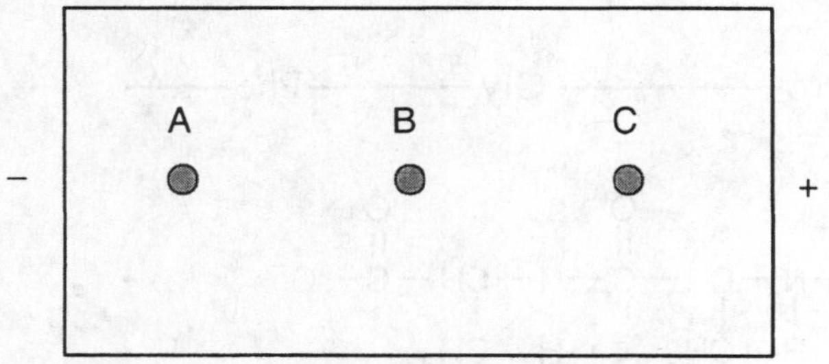
A
B
C
–
+

A = Lys–Trp

B = Ala–Cys

C = Glu–Tyr

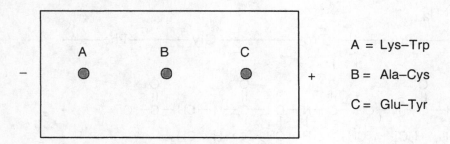

18.80 Osteogenesis imperfecta is a dominant genetic defect in which improperly synthesized collagen leads to frequent bone fractures.

18.82 It was hard to believe that a protein could duplicate itself and cause disease. It was also hard to accept that a form of protein might be responsible for inherited disease, might be transmitted between individuals, and might arise spontaneously.

18.84 A combination of grains, legumes, and nuts in each meal provides all of the essential amino acids.

General Questions and Problems

18.86 Pineapple that is canned has been heated to inactivate enzymes. Thus, no enzymatic hydrolysis occurs when canned pineapple is added to gelatin.

18.88 (a) Bradykinin:

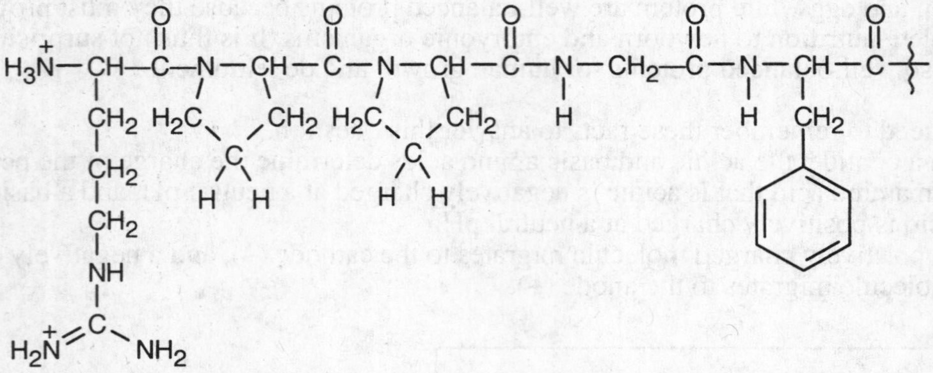

Arg——Pro——Pro——Gly——Phe—⌇

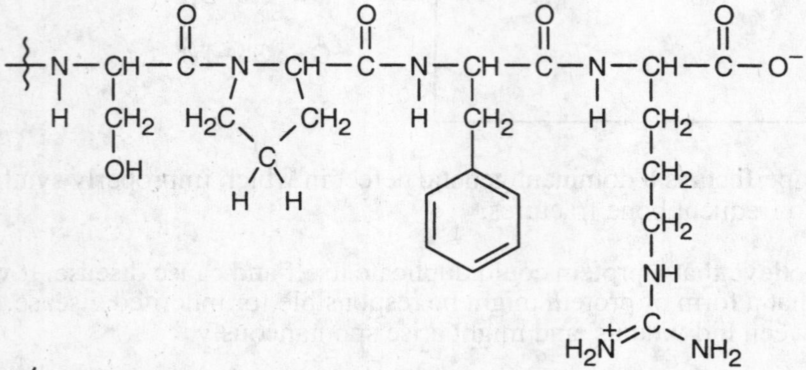

⌇—Ser——Pro——Phe——Arg

(b) The rigid proline rings introduce kinks and bends in bradykinin and prevent hydrogen bonds from forming (because proline has no hydrogens to form hydrogen bonds).

18.90 After oxidation, the formerly chiral carbon is no longer bonded to four different groups and thus isn't chiral.

18.92

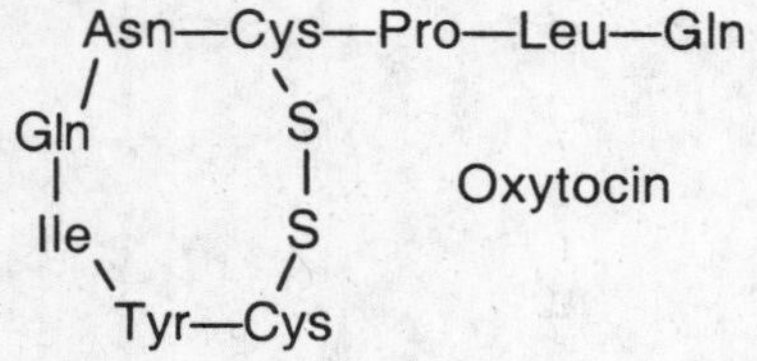
Asn—Cys—Pro—Leu—Gln
Gln
Ile
Tyr—Cys
S
S
Oxytocin

18.94 Amino acids that can form hydrogen bonds contain the following functional groups: amine, alcohol, amide, carboxylic acid (carboxylate). These amino acids are arginine, aspartic acid, asparagine, glutamic acid, glutamine, histidine, lysine, serine, threonine, and tyrosine. Shown below is hydrogen bonding between asparagine and serine.

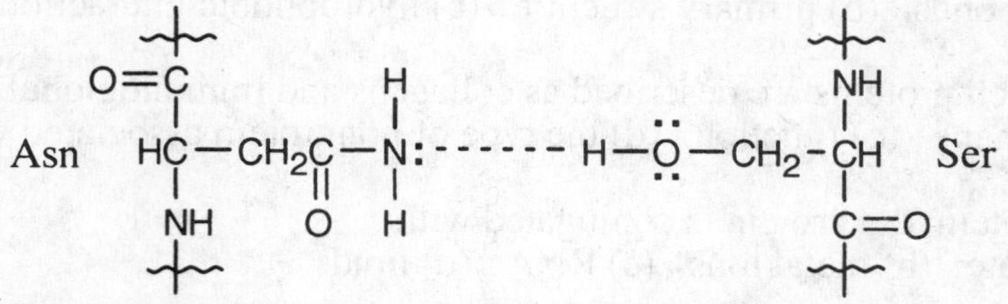

Hydrogen bonds between the amino acids and water:

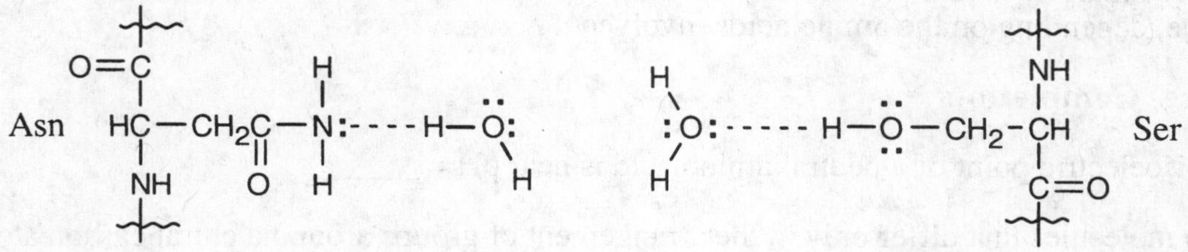

18.96 Polar, hydrophilic amino acids that can form hydrogen bonds with water are found on the outside of globular proteins. Examples: (b) Glu (e) Ser.
Nonpolar amino acids that have small side chains are found in fibrous proteins. Examples: (a) Ala (f) Val. Phe and Leu are nonpolar but are too bulky to be often found in fibrous proteins.

18.98 If an aspartate residue were substituted for a glutamate residue, a health problem might not occur because both amino acids have similar physical properties and chemical behavior.

Self-Test for Chapter 18

Multiple Choice

1. Which level of protein structure doesn't involve hydrogen bonds?
(a) primary (b) secondary (c) tertiary (d) quaternary

2. Which of the following amino acids has a hydrophobic side chain?
(a) asparagine (b) threonine (c) histidine (d) phenylalanine

3. The isoelectric point of an amino acid is 7.6. Which of the following statements about it is untrue?
(a) At pH = 7.6, the number of positive charges equals the number of negative charges.
(b) It is a basic amino acid.
(c) At pH = 5.5, both the carboxylic acid group and the amine group are protonated.
(d) It forms salt bridges when it is part of a polypeptide chain.

4. Which of the following organic molecules is chiral?
(a) 1-pentanol (b) 2-pentanol (c) 3-pentanol (d) 2-methyl-2-butanol

5. How many tetrapeptides can be formed from alanine, lysine, and two valines?
(a) 6 (b) 12 (c) 18 (d) 24

6. Which of the following is an amino acid with a nitrogen heterocyclic ring?
(a) histidine (b) threonine (c) tyrosine (d) cysteine

7. Addition of heavy metal ions to a protein disrupts which structural element?
(a) hydrogen bonds (b) primary structure (c) hydrophobic interactions (d) disulfide bonds

8. A table in which proteins are described as collagens and immunoglobulins classifies them by
(a) size (b) shape (c) function (d) the type of nonprotein associated with them

9. In a nucleoprotein, the protein is conjugated with
(a) carbohydrate (b) metal ions (c) RNA (d) lipids

10. Substitution of one amino acid for another in a polypeptide chain disrupts
(a) secondary structure (b) tertiary structure (c) isoelectric point (d) all or none of the above, depending on the amino acids involved

Sentence Completion

1. The isoelectric point of a neutral amino acid is near pH = ______.

2. Two molecules that differ only in the arrangement of groups around a chiral carbon atom are called _______.

3. Amino acids exist as dipolar ions called ______.

4. The repeating chain of amide bonds in a peptide is called the _____.

5. A disulfide bond between two cysteines in the same chain produces a _____ in the peptide.

6. A protein bonded to a carbohydrate is called a _____.

7. _____ structure refers to how the entire protein is folded and coiled into a specific three-dimensional shape.

8. In the secondary structure called a _____ _____, polypeptide chains line up in a parallel arrangement held together by hydrogen bonds.

9. The tripeptide Ser-Gln-Lys contains side chains that are ______.

10. The amino acids methionine and cysteine are the only two that contain the element _____.

11. A chain with fewer than 50 amino acids is called a ______.

12. _______ interactions pull nonpolar side chains together to exclude water.

True or False

1. All amino acids have at least one chiral carbon atom.
2. Tyrosine and valine can react to form a dipeptide.
3. Protein denaturation disrupts the primary structure of a protein.
4. Lysylalanine is identical to alanyllysine.
5. Some amino acids have an isoelectric point near 10.
6. Simple proteins are more common than conjugated proteins.
7. β-Sheets and α-helices occur mostly in fibrous proteins.
8. Amino acids are quite water-soluble.
9. Proteins, as well as amino acids, have isoelectric points.
10. Both fibrous and globular proteins are water-soluble.
11. Proteins may be classified by biological function.
12. 2-Butanol has a chiral carbon atom.

Match each entry on the left with its partner on the right.

1. Isoleucine	(a) Achiral amino acid
2. Insulin	(b) Secondary structure
3. Glycylglycine	(c) Fibrous protein
4. Glycine	(d) Amino acid that is a secondary amine
5. β-Sheet	(e) Amino acid with hydrocarbon side chain
6. Aspartic acid	(f) Globular protein
7. Collagen	(g) Peptide hormone
8. Cysteine	(h) Basic amino acid
9. Albumin	(i) Aromatic amino acid
10. Arginine	(j) Dipeptide
11. Proline	(k) Acidic amino acid
12. Tryptophan	(l) Can form disulfide bridges

Chapter 19 – Enzymes and Vitamins

Chapter Outline

I. Introduction to enzymes (Sections 19.1–19.3).
   A. Catalysis by enzymes (Section 19.1).
      1. Enzymes are globular proteins that catalyze biochemical reactions.
         a. The active site is the region of the enzyme where catalysis takes place.
         b. The reactant in an enzyme-catalyzed reaction is called the substrate.
         c. Some enzymes are specific for one particular substrate, whereas others catalyze reactions involving a number of substrates.
         d. Most enzymes are specific with respect to stereochemistry.
      2. Enzymes affect only the rate of reaction and not the position of equilibrium.
      3. The catalytic efficiency of an enzyme is measured by its turnover number.
   B. Enzyme cofactors (Section 19.2).
      1. Many enzymes include protein portions and nonprotein portions that are called cofactors.
      2. The cofactors, called coenzymes, are either metal ions or small organic molecules.
      3. Enzymes can obtain from cofactors chemically reactive groups not available as side chains.
      4. Some cofactors are covalently bonded; others serve as cosubstrates.
   C. Enzyme classification (Section 19.3).
      1. Classes of enzymes.
         a. Oxidoreductases catalyze oxidation–reduction reactions.
         b. Transferases catalyze the transfer of a specific group from one substrate to another.
         c. Hydrolases catalyze the hydrolysis of substrates.
         d. Isomerases catalyze the isomerization of substrates.
         e. Lyases catalyze the addition or elimination of small molecules.
         f. Ligases catalyze the bonding of two substrate molecules.
      2. Naming enzymes.
         a. The first part of the name identifies the substrate.
         b. The second part of the name identifies the enzyme subclass.

II. Enzyme function (Sections 19.4–19.6).
   A. How enzymes work (Section 19.4).
      1. Models for representing enzyme action.
         a. The shape of the active site is complementary to the shape of the substrate. This description of enzyme–substrate is called the lock-and-key model.
         b. A more modern interpretation of enzyme–substrate interaction is the induced-fit model.
            i. In this model, an enzyme is flexible enough to change shape to fit the spatial requirement of the substrate.
            ii. The enzyme and substrate induce each other to change shape.
      2. Mechanism of enzyme catalysis.
         a. An enzyme–substrate complex is formed when the substrate migrates to the active site, and atoms that will take part in the reaction are held in place (proximity effect).
         b. Reactants are positioned at the exact distance necessary for reaction to occur (orientation effect).
         c. The active site provides the kinds of functional groups necessary for catalysis (catalytic effect).
         d. The activation energy for reaction is lowered by introducing strain into the bonds of the substrate (energy effect).

C. Effect of concentration on enzyme activity (Section 19.5).
  1. When substrate concentration varies, and enzyme concentration remains constant:
    a. Additional substrate increases the rate until all active sites are occupied.
    b. At this point, reaction rate becomes constant.
    c. The enzyme is said to be saturated.
  2. Under most conditions, reaction rate is controlled by enzyme efficiency.
     The upper limit to reaction rate is about 10^8 collisions per mole per second.
  3. When substrate concentration is high, and enzyme concentration varies:
    a. Additional enzyme increases the reaction rate.
    b. The increase in reaction rate is directly proportional to enzyme concentration.

D. Influence of temperature and pH on enzymes (Section 19.6).
  1. Temperature.
    a. All enzymes have an optimum temperature for greatest catalytic efficiency. In the human body, this temperature is 37°C.
    b. At temperatures above 50–60°C, enzymes denature.
  2. pH.
    a. Enzymes also have an optimum pH.
    b. If pH is too high or too low, enzymes lose their ability to catalyze reactions.

III. Enzyme regulation (Sections 19.7–19.9).

A. General strategies of control (Section 19.7).
  1. Activation is any process that increases the action of an enzyme.
  2. Inhibition is any process that slows or stops the action of an enzyme.

B. Feedback and allosteric control.
  1. Feedback control.
    a. The product of a series of reactions is an inhibitor for the first reaction.
    b. This strategy keeps excessive amounts of products from accumulating.
  2. Allosteric control.
    a. Most enzymes are regulated by allosteric control.
    b. Allosteric enzymes have more than one polypeptide chain.
    c. Allosteric enzymes have catalytic sites and regulatory sites.
    d. Binding of a positive regulator increases reaction rate.
    e. Binding of a negative regulator decreases reaction rate.

C. Enzyme inhibition (Section 19.8).
  1. Reversible noncompetitive inhibition.
    a. An inhibitor binds to the enzyme at a site other than the active site and changes the shape of the enzyme.
    b. The enzyme is a less effective catalyst, and reaction rate is slowed.
    c. The inhibitor doesn't compete with the substrate.
  2. Reversible competitive inhibition.
    a. In competitive inhibition, a substrate that resembles the normal substrate occupies the enzyme's active site.
    b. Competitive inhibition is reversible.
      i. The degree of inhibition can be regulated by controlling the amounts of substrate and inhibitor.
      ii. Increasing the concentration of substrate displaces inhibitor from the active site.
  3. Irreversible inhibition.
     The inhibitor bonds covalently to the active site, and the enzyme is irreversibly inhibited.

D. Covalent modification and genetic control (Section 19.9).
  1. Zymogens.
    a. Some enzymes(zymogens) are synthesized in a form that differs from their catalytic form.
    b. Zymogens are activated by enzymatic addition or removal of a part of the zymogen.

c. Enzymes that might injure the body if constantly present in their active form are synthesized as zymogens.
2. Phosphorylation/dephosphorylation.
Phosphate groups can be added to serine and threonine side chains to activate certain enzymes.
3. Genetic control.
a. Synthesis of some enzymes is regulated by genes.
b. Genetic control is used for enzymes needed only at certain stages of development.

IV. Vitamins (Section 19.10).
A. Vitamins are small organic molecules that must be supplied in the diet.
B. Vitamins are classified by solubility.
1. Water-soluble vitamins are either coenzymes or precursors to coenzymes.
Water-soluble vitamins include vitamin C and the B vitamins.
2. Fat-soluble vitamins are stored in the body's fatty tissues.
a. Vitamin A is important for vision.
b. Vitamin D regulates calcium absorption.
c. Vitamin E is an antioxidant.
d. Vitamin K is involved in blood clotting.

Solutions for Chapter 19 Problems

19.1 Acetylcholinesterase catalyzes a maximum of 10,000 (10^4) reactions per second.

19.2 There are two reasons: (1) The enzyme might catalyze reactions within the eye if it were not removed. (2) Saline is sterile and is isotonic with body fluids.

19.3 Most vitamin/mineral supplements contain the listed metal ion cofactors (iron, zinc, copper, manganese, molybdenum, vanadium, cobalt, and nickel), as well as containing selenium and boron.

19.4 Vitamin-derived coenzymes are not synthesized in the body and must be provided in the diet. Other coenzymes are normally synthesized in the body.

19.5 (a) Pyruvate kinase catalyzes the transfer of a phosphate group to or from pyruvate.
(b) Succinyl CoA synthetase catalyzes the formation of a bond between succinyl CoA and another substrate.
(c) Glucose-6-phosphate isomerase catalyzes the isomerization of glucose 6-phosphate.
(d) Malate dehydrogenase catalyzes the removal of two —H from malate.

19.6 (a) The enzyme is named urease. (b) The enzyme is sucrase.

19.7 Alanine aminotransferase is a transferase. It catalyzes the transfer of an amino group from alanine to a second substrate.

19.8 In this lyase reaction, water adds to fumarate (substrate) to give L-malate (product).

19.9 Reaction (a) might be catalyzed by a decarboxylase because it involves a loss of CO_2. Reaction (b) isn't catalyzed by a decarboxylase.

19.10 Acidic, basic, and polar side chains can take part in catalytic activity and in holding the substrate in the active site. Nonpolar side chains can take part in holding the enzyme in the active site but are not likely to be involved in catalytic activity.

19.11 If an enzyme is saturated with substrate, substrate molecules are bound to all of the active sites. (a) Increasing the substrate concentration has no effect on the rate because there are no empty sites where the added substrate can bind. (b) Adding more enzyme increases the rate because more enzyme–substrate complexes can form.

19.12 The rate of the reaction shown in Figure 19.7a is greater at 30°C than at 20°C. The rate is somewhat greater at 40°C than at 25°C.

19.13 The rate of the reaction catalyzed by trypsin is much greater at pH = 8 than at pH = 10.

19.14

(a) (b)

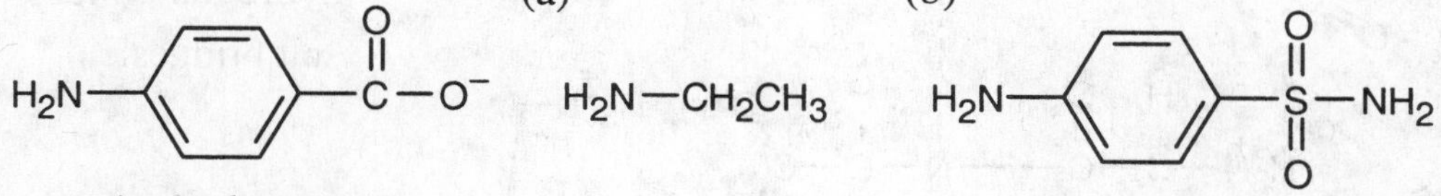

p-Aminobenzoate

Structure (b) is a possible competitive inhibitor for the enzyme that has *p*-aminobenzoate (PABA) as a substrate because it resembles PABA both in shape and in the type of functional groups present.

19.15 A product of an enzyme-catalyzed reaction that resembles the substrate might be a competitive inhibitor for the enzyme.

19.16 (a) *Covalent modification*, either by activation of a zymogen or by phosphorylation-dephosphorylation, is a type of enzyme regulation that occurs when an enzyme must be quickly activated.
(b) *Competitive inhibition* by use of a drug can regulate an overactive enzyme.
(c) *Genetic control* regulates enzymes that are needed only during certain stages of development.
(d) *Covalent modification* by phosphorylation–dephosphorylation can regulate enzymes that are needed for quick energy. Alternatively, *feedback control* can regulate glucose production. When glucose levels are adequate, glucose inhibits the enzyme that catalyzes its formation. When glucose levels drop, the enzyme is no longer inhibited, and glucose is formed.

19.17 Vitamin A is fat-soluble because it has a long hydrocarbon chain. Vitamin C is water-soluble because it has polar hydroxyl groups.

19.18 The difference among these compounds occurs at the functional group at the end of the hydrocarbon chain. In retinal, a —CHO group (aldehyde) replaces the —CH_2OH group; in retinoic acid, the —CH_2OH group becomes a —COOH group.

19.19 Vitamins can be enzyme cofactors; some are antioxidants; they aid absorption of calcium and phosphate ions; they are used in synthesis of visual pigments; they are involved in the synthesis of blood-clotting factors.

Understanding Key Concepts

19.20

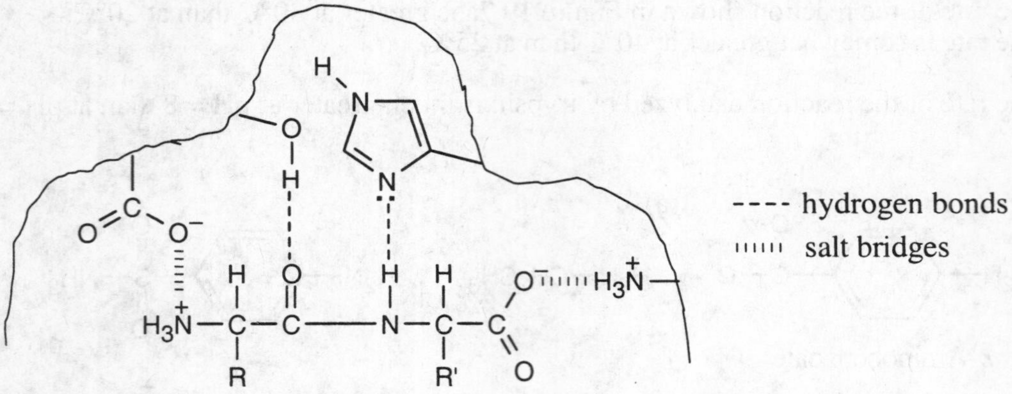

H
N
O
H
N
C
O^-
H
O
H
H
O^-
$H_3\overset{+}{N}$
$H_3\overset{+}{N}$
C
C
N
C
C
R
R'
O
---- hydrogen bonds
''''' salt bridges

19.21

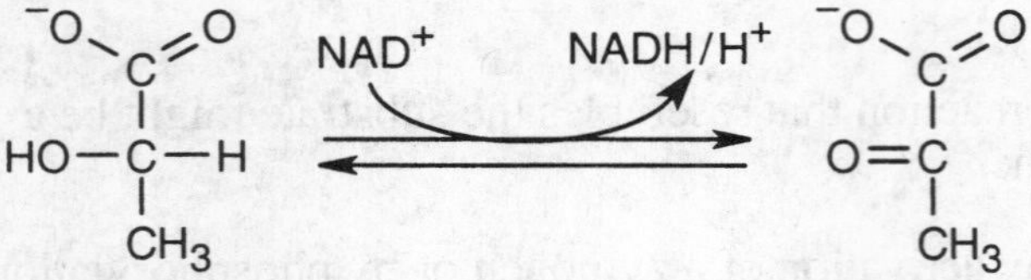

NAD^+
$NADH/H^+$
HO—C—H
CH_3
O=C
CH_3

L–Lactate Pyruvate

(a) The enzyme that catalyzes the above reaction is an oxidoreductase.
(b) The enzyme belongs to the dehydrogenase subclass.
(c) L-Lactate is the substrate for the above enzyme.
(d) Pyruvate is the product.
(e) The enzyme is named L-lactate dehydrogenase.

19.22 The enzyme in Problem 19.21 will most likely not use D-lactate as a substrate because most enzymes are "handed" and catalyze the reaction of only one enantiomer of a pair of enantiomers. It is possible that D-lactate might act as a competitive inhibitor of the enzyme.

19.23 The coenzyme needed for the above reaction is NAD^+ (nicotinamide adenine dinucleotide), which is an oxidizing agent and includes the vitamin niacin.

19.24 (a) Increasing the substrate concentration at constant inhibitor concentration increases the rate when substrate concentration is low. Very soon, however, a maximum rate is reached, and adding more substrate does not change the rate of reaction. This maximum rate is always lower than the rate of the uninhibited reaction.
(b) Decreasing the inhibitor concentration at constant substrate concentration increases the rate of reaction. As inhibitor concentration is decreased, more inhibitor dissociates from the enzyme, leaving active enzyme that is free to react with substrate.

19.25 (a) *Allosteric regulation* (either positive or negative) occurs when a regulator binds to the enzyme at a site other than the active site. This binding changes the shape of the enzyme and alters the catalytic ability of the enzyme.
(b) In *covalent modification*, the activity of an enzyme is influenced by the addition or removal of a group that is covalently bonded to the enzyme.
(c) *Inhibition* is any process that stops or slows down an enzyme's ability to catalyze a reaction. Noncompetitive inhibition can be a type of allosteric regulation (see part (a)). Competitive inhibition occurs when an inhibitor reversibly occupies an enzyme's active site. Irreversible inhibition results when an inhibitor covalently binds to an enzyme and destroys its ability to catalyze a reaction.
(d) In *genetic control*, hormones control the synthesis of enzymes.

19.26 (a) Feedback inhibition (b) Irreversible inhibition (c) Genetic control
(d) Noncompetitive inhibition

19.27 The amino acids (from left to right): aspartate, serine, glutamine, arginine, histidine. Arginine and histidine are basic, and aspartate is acidic.

Structure and Classification of Enzymes

19.28 (a) A *hydrolase* catalyzes the hydrolysis (bond breaking by addition of water) of a substrate.
(b) An *isomerase* catalyzes the isomerization of a substrate.
(c) A *lyase* catalyzes the addition of a small molecule to a double bond of a substrate, or the elimination of a small molecule from a substrate to form a double bond.

19.30 (a) Maltase (b) Fumarase (c) DNAse

19.32 An enzyme is a large three-dimensional molecule with a catalytic site into which a substrate can fit. Enzymes are specific in their action because only one or a few molecules have the appropriate shape and functional groups to fit into the catalytic site.

19.34 (a) A *hydrolase* catalyzes this reaction, which is the hydrolysis of a peptide bond.
(b) A *lyase* catalyzes this reaction.
(c) An *oxidoreductase* catalyzes the introduction of a double bond into a molecule by removal of H_2.

19.36 (a) A *kinase* catalyzes the transfer of a phosphate group between substrates.
(b) A *decarboxylase* catalyzes the replacement of CO_2 by —H.
(c) A *ligase* catalyzes the formation of a new bond between two substrates.

19.38 A urease is a hydrolase because it catalyzes the hydrolysis of urea to ammonia and carbonic acid.

19.40 (a) Niacin (B_3) (b) Pantothenic acid (B_5) (c) Folic acid

Enzyme Function and Regulation

19.42 In the lock-and-key model of enzyme action, the active site of an enzyme has a specific shape (lock) into which only a specific substrate (key) can fit. In the induced-fit model, the shape of the active site changes to accommodate the substrate.

19.44 The amino acid residues involved in the active site can be brought close to each other by protein folding without being near each other in the polypeptide chain.

19.46 To function in the very acidic environment of the stomach, an enzyme must be active at a low pH. To function in the intestine, an enzyme must have high catalytic activity at a pH near neutral. Each enzyme has an optimum pH for catalysis, and an enzyme that is most active at neutral pH will not be active in a strongly acidic environment.

19.48

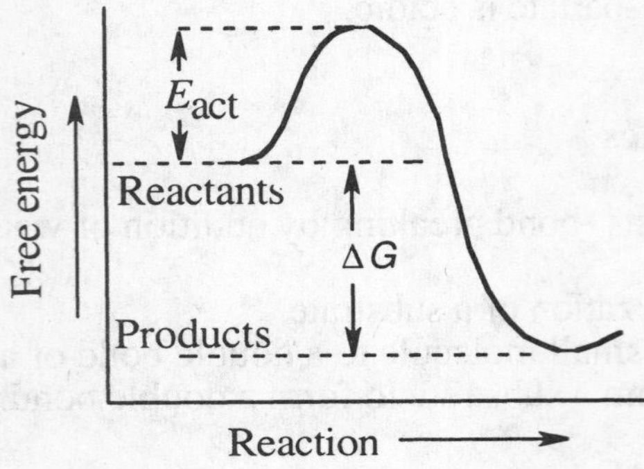
Eact
Reactants
ΔG
Products
Free energy
Reaction

19.50 The rate of reaction increases as the substrate concentration increases, up to a point where all enzyme catalytic sites are occupied. The reaction rate then levels off, and adding more substrate doesn't increase the reaction rate.

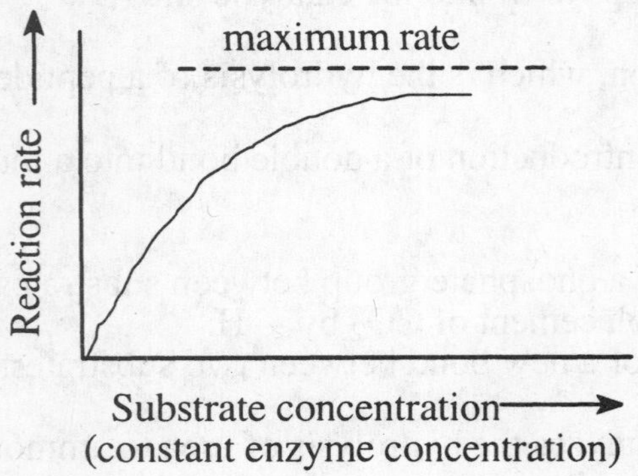
maximum rate
Reaction rate
Substrate concentration
(constant enzyme concentration)

19.52 (a) Raising the temperature of the enzyme-catalyzed reaction from 37°C to 60°C drastically decreases the rate of reaction.
(b) Raising the pH of the enzyme-catalyzed reaction from 6 to 11 will probably decrease the rate of reaction, since most enzymes have their optimum rates at close to neutral pH. However, if the enzyme has a rate optimum near 11, then the increase in pH will increase the rate of reaction.
(c) Adding a heavy-metal salt either stops the reaction or decreases the rate of the enzyme-catalyzed reaction because heavy metals bind to enzymes, causing irreversible inhibition.

19.54 *Competitive inhibition* occurs when the structure of a second substrate closely resembles that of the normal substrate for an enzyme. The second substrate can occupy the active site and thereby inhibit binding at the active site of the usual substrate. Competitive inhibition is usually reversible.

Noncompetitive inhibition occurs when an inhibitor binds to the enzyme at a location other than the active site. The conformation of the enzyme changes, and the enzyme is inactivated or its catalytic ability is reduced. Noncompetitive inhibition is reversible.

Irreversible inhibition occurs when a molecule covalently bonds to the active site of an enzyme. The active site is thus irreversibly inactivated, and enzyme activity stops.

In competitive inhibition, the inhibitor bonds noncovalently to the active site. In noncompetitive inhibition, the inhibitor binds noncovalently with a group away from the active site. In irreversible inhibition, the inhibitor forms a covalent bond at the active site.

19.56 Graph C represents the activity of Eco R1 after EDTA has been added. When EDTA is first added, the rate levels off as EDTA chelates the Mg^{2+} ions. When all Mg^{2+} has been removed, the enzyme is no longer active and the rate approaches zero.

19.58 Papain works by catalyzing hydrolysis of the bee toxin responsible for swelling.

19.60 Positive regulators change the shape of the active site so that the rate of the enzyme-catalyzed reaction increases. Negative regulators change the shape of the active site so that the enzyme is a less effective catalyst.

19.62 "Feed-forward activation" occurs when the first product of a series of reactions activates enzymes needed for later steps in the sequence. "Feed–forward activation" is a mechanism of enzyme regulation that might be useful when it is important to quickly activate an enzyme or to remove a rapidly accumulating product.

19.64 Phosphorylation of a serine or threonine residue of an enzyme replaces a polar –OH group with a charged phosphate group. If this replacement occurs near the active site of an enzyme, the activity of the enzyme might be either increased or inhibited, depending on the enzyme mechanism.

Vitamins

19.66 Water-soluble vitamins act as cofactors for enzymes and make it possible for enzymes to catalyze biochemical reactions. The relationship between fat-soluble vitamins and enzymes is less clear.

19.68 The four fat-soluble vitamins are vitamins A, D, E, and K. All except vitamin E are stored in the body and are toxic when ingested in large amounts.

Applications

19.70 (1) Enzymes produce only one enantiomer of a desired product. (2) Enzymes can be used to synthesize products that are difficult to produce by nonbiological pathways. (3) Enzyme-catalyzed reactions often take place without producing dangerous or wasteful by-products.

19.72 Two strategies keep the enzyme active: (1) The organism synthesizes chaperonins, enzymes that return a protein to its active form; (2) the protein itself is rigid and resists heat denaturation.

19.74 Enzyme activity must be monitored under standard conditions because activity is affected by pH, temperature, and substrate concentration. The standard is the unit (u), which is the amount of enzyme that converts one micromole of substrate to product at defined standard conditions of pH, temperature and substrate concentration.

19.76 The body excretes excess water-soluble vitamins, but fat-soluble vitamins accumulate in tissues.

19.78 Listings for vitamin A, vitamin C, iron, and calcium are mandatory on food labels because they are considered to be of greatest importance in maintaining good health.

General Questions and Problems

19.80

$$1.6 \text{ mg riboflavin} \times \frac{100 \text{ mL apple juice}}{0.014 \text{ mg riboflavin}} = 11{,}000 \text{ mL} = 11 \text{ L apple juice}$$

19.82 Because competitive inhibition is reversible, addition of a large amount of the normal substrate will reverse the binding of the inhibitor, and the rate of reaction of the normal substrate will return to its usual value. The effects of noncompetitive inhibition can't be reversed by addition of excess substrate.

19.84 If valine replaced serine, the enzyme would be inactivated because the —OH functional group of serine is essential for enzyme activity. If aspartate replaced glutamate, the effect would probably be minor because both amino acids have the same functional groups.

Self-Test for Chapter 19

Multiple choice:

1. A subclass of enzyme that catalyzes cleavage of peptide bonds is a
(a) lipase (b) dehydrase (c) protease (d) reductase

2. Which of the following is an enzyme cofactor?
(a) thiamine (b) tocopherol (c) hexokinase (d) trypsin

3. The ability of enzymes to bring reactants together is known as the
(a) orientation effect (b) catalytic effect (c) proximity effect (d) energy effect

4. Fat-soluble vitamins serve all of the following functions except
(a) promotion of bone growth (b) acting as an antioxidant (c) aiding night vision
(d) preventing anemia

5. Which of the following enzymes probably requires a coenzyme that is reduced during reaction?
(a) transferase (b) oxidase (c) isomerase (d) dehydrase

6. The most likely control mechanism for reactions that occur during embryonic development is
(a) feedback control (b) genetic control (c) zymogens (d) allosteric control

7. Snake venom probably causes its effects by
(a) noncompetitive inhibition (b) competitive inhibition (c) allosteric control
(d) irreversible inhibition

8. Why does the rate of enzymatic reactions decrease as temperature is lowered?
(a) Salt bridges are disrupted. (b) The shape of the active site is changed. (c) Reactions are slower at lower temperatures. (d) The enzyme begins to denature.

9. If an enzyme is saturated, adding more substrate will
(a) increase reaction rate (b) have no effect on reaction rate (c) decrease reaction rate
(d) have varying effects, depending on the enzyme

10. In which of the following types of enzyme regulation can adding large amounts of substrate restore an enzyme's reaction rate to its maximum value?
(a) feedback inhibition (b) irreversible inhibition (c) noncompetitive inhibition
(d) competitive inhibition

Sentence Completion

1. An enzyme called a _____ catalyzes the isomerization of a chiral center.

2. _____ are enzymes that have slightly different structures but that catalyze the same reaction.

3. Vitamin __ is necessary for the synthesis of blood-clotting factors.

4. In the _____ - _____ model of enzyme action, an enzyme can change its shape slightly to fit different substrates.

5. In _____ inhibition, an inhibitor changes the shape of an enzyme by binding at a location other than the active site.

6. If the temperature becomes too high, enzymes begin to _____.

7. The catalytic activity of an enzyme is measured by its _____ _____.

8. A type of covalent modification of an enzyme involves addition or removal of a ______ group.

9. The _______ effect is responsible for bringing substrate and catalytic sites together.

10. The upper limit of any enzyme's rate of reaction is ___collisions per mole per second.

11. An ______ enzyme has more than one chain and has binding sites for both substrate and regulator.

12. An enzyme that is synthesized in a form different from its active form is called a ______.

Tell whether each of the following statements is true or false:

1. 98.6°F is the optimum temperature for most enzymes.
2. In an enzyme-substrate complex, the substrate is in its lowest energy shape.
3. Noncompetitive inhibition is irreversible.
4. A dehydrogenase catalyzes the loss of H_2O from a substrate.
5. At the active site, the enzyme and substrate are held together by covalent bonds.
6. Vitamins may be small organic molecules or inorganic ions.
7. Chymotrypsinogen is a zymogen.
8. β-Carotene is the active form of vitamin A.
9. Copper, cobalt, and selenium are essential enzyme cofactors.
10. Heavy metals cause irreversible inhibition of enzymes.
11. As enzyme concentration is increased, the reaction rate eventually levels off.
12. The side chains of serine and threonine are sites of covalent modification.

Match each entry on the left with its partner on the right.

1. Papain	(a) Deficiency causes anemia
2. Vitamin D	(b) Occurs away from an enzyme's active site
3. Competitive inhibition	(c) Nonspecific enzyme
4. Kinase	(d) Catalyzes hydrolysis of ester groups in lipids
5. Alanine transaminase	(e) Protein part of enzyme, plus cofactor
6. Cofactor	(f) Deficiency causes scurvy
7. Noncompetitive inhibition	(g) Transfers a phosphate group between substrates
8. Vitamin B_6	(h) Fat-soluble vitamin
9. Lipase	(i) Occurs at an enzyme's active site
10. Vitamin C	(j) Metal ion or small organic molecule
11. Active enzyme	(k) Specific enzyme
12. Lyase	(l) Catalyzes loss of small molecule from substrate

Chapter 20 – Chemical Messengers

Chapter Outline

I. Introduction to chemical messengers (Section 20.1).
   A. Control of vital functions is accomplished by chemical messengers.
      1. The messengers interact with the cells of a target tissue.
      2. The message is delivered by interaction between the chemical messengers and receptors.
      3. Noncovalent interactions draw messengers and receptors together.
      4. The results of the interaction are chemical changes within the target cell.
   B. Two kinds of chemical messengers are important in the body.
      1. Hormones are the chemical messengers of the endocrine system.
         a. Hormones travel through the bloodstream.
         b. The responses produced by hormones are slow but long-lasting.
      2. The chemical messengers of the nervous system are neurotransmitters.
         a. Signals travel very quickly along nerve fibers.
         b. Neurotransmitters carry the message of the signal across the gap that separates one nerve fiber from the next fiber.
         c. The effects of neurotransmitters are very short-lived.

II. Hormones (Sections 20.2–20.5).
   A. Hormones and the endocrine system (Section 20.2).
      1. The endocrine system consists of all the glands that secrete hormones.
      2. The endocrine glands are managed by the hypothalamus in three different ways.
         a. Direct neural control by a nervous system pathway from the hypothalamus.
         b. Direct release of hormones from the hypothalamus.
         c. Indirect control by release of regulatory hormones.
      3. There are three types of hormones.
         a. Polypeptide hormones.
         b. Steroid hormones.
         c. Amino acid derivatives.
      4. The signal of a hormone enters cells in either of two ways.
         a. Steroid hormones pass through the hydrophobic cell membrane.
         b. Other hormones bind with receptors in the cell wall.
   B. How hormones work: epinephrine (Section 20.3).
      1. Epinephrine carried in the bloodstream binds to a receptor on the surface of a cell.
      2. The hormone–receptor complex interacts with a nearby G protein, causing it to bind GTP.
      3. This complex activates the enzyme adenylate cyclase, which resides in the cell membrane.
      4. Adenylate cyclase catalyzes production within the cell of the second messenger, cyclic AMP.
      5. Cyclic AMP initiates reactions that activate glycogen phosphorylase, which catalyzes release of glucose from storage.
      6. After the emergency, a phosphodiesterase catalyzes hydrolysis of cyclic AMP to AMP.
   C. Types of hormones (Sections 20.4–20.5).
      1. Amino acid derivatives (Section 20.4).
         a. Many amino acid derivatives are also neurotransmitters.
            Examples include epinephrine, dopamine, and norepinephrine.
         b. Thyroxine is an iodine-containing hormone that regulates the synthesis of various enzymes.

2. Polypeptide hormones.
   a. TRH and TSH control the thyroid gland.
   b. Vasopressin and oxytocin are small cyclic polypeptides.
   c. Insulin regulates glucose metabolism.
3. Steroid hormones (Section 20.5).
   a. Mineralocorticoids (such as aldosterone) regulate ionic balance in cellular fluid.
   b. Glucocorticoids (such as cortisone) regulate inflammation.
   c. Sex hormones.
      i. Androgens (male hormones) include testosterone and androsterone.
      ii. Female hormones include estrogens and progestins.
      iii. There are also hundreds of synthetic hormones of all types.

III. Neurotransmitters (Sections 20.6–20.10).

A. General features of neurotransmitters (Section 20.6).
1. A nerve impulse is transmitted along a neuron by variations in electric potential.
2. Neurotransmitters convey the impulse across the synaptic cleft from a presynaptic neuron to a postsynaptic neuron.
3. The impulse is transmitted down the next neuron, and the preceding process is repeated.
4. Neurotransmitters are synthesized and stored in vesicles in the presynaptic neuron.
5. After transmission, the neurotransmitter is inactivated in one of two ways.
   a. A chemical change inactivates the neurotransmitter.
   b. The neurotransmitter is returned to the presynaptic neuron.
6. Most neurotransmitters are amines.
7. Some neurotransmitters act directly, and others rely on second messengers.

B. How neurotransmitters work: acetylcholine (ACh) (Section 20.7).
1. Events of neurotransmission.
   a. An impulse arrives at the presynaptic neuron.
   b. The vesicles move to the cell membrane, fuse with it, and release ACh.
   c. ACh crosses the synaptic cleft and binds to receptors on the postsynaptic neuron.
   d. A change in the permeability of the postsynaptic neuron initiates the nerve impulse in that neuron.
   e. Acetylcholinesterase in the synaptic cleft catalyzes the decomposition of ACh.
   f. Choline is reabsorbed into the presynaptic neuron, and new ACh is synthesized.
2. Interactions of drugs at ACh synapses.
   a. To have an effect a drug must connect with a receptor.
   b. Drugs that are agonists prolong the biochemical response of a receptor.
      Nicotine at a low dose is an example of an agonist.
   c. Drugs that are antagonists block the normal response of a receptor.
      Antagonists can be either competitive (tubocurarine) or irreversible (nerve gas).

C. Histamine and antihistamines (Section 20.8).
1. Histamine is the neurotransmitter responsible for the symptoms of allergic reactions.
2. Antihistamines are drugs that are histamine receptor antagonists.

D. Monoamines (Sections 20.9–20.10).
1. Serotonin, norepinephrine, and dopamine are neurotransmitters active in the brain (Section 20.9).
2. Since these neurotransmitters affect mood, drugs have been created to affect the concentration of these neurotransmitters at synapses.
   a. Tricyclic antidepressants (Elavil) prevent the reuptake of serotonin and norepinephrine from the synaptic cleft.
   b. MAO inhibitors (Nardil) inhibit the enzyme that breaks down monoamine neurotransmitters.
   c. SSRI antidepressants (Prozac) inhibit only the reuptake of serotonin.

3. Dopamine.
   a. Dopamine plays a role in emotion, thought and behavior through interactions with five different kinds of receptors in the brain.
   b. Dopamine levels are responsible for many types of behaviors.
      i. An oversupply of dopamine is associated with schizophrenia.
      ii. An undersupply of dopamine is responsible for Parkinson's disease.
      iii. An ample supply of dopamine is responsible for a feeling of well-being.
   c. Drugs such as heroin, cocaine, marijuana, and alcohol increase dopamine levels.

E. Neuropeptides (Section 20.10).
The brain has receptors for small polypeptides (enkephalins) that also act as receptors for opiates.

IV. Drug discovery and drug design (Section 20.11).
   A. Plants were the first source of drugs.
   Today, ethnobotanists seek new plant sources of drugs in remote regions.
   B. In the nineteenth century, simple drugs (benzocaine, phenacetin) were synthesized in chemical laboratories.
   C. Combinatorial chemistry generates large masses of related compounds and screens them for possible effectiveness as drugs.
   D. Supercomputers and molecular graphics are increasingly used in drug design.

Solutions to Chapter 20 Problems

20.1

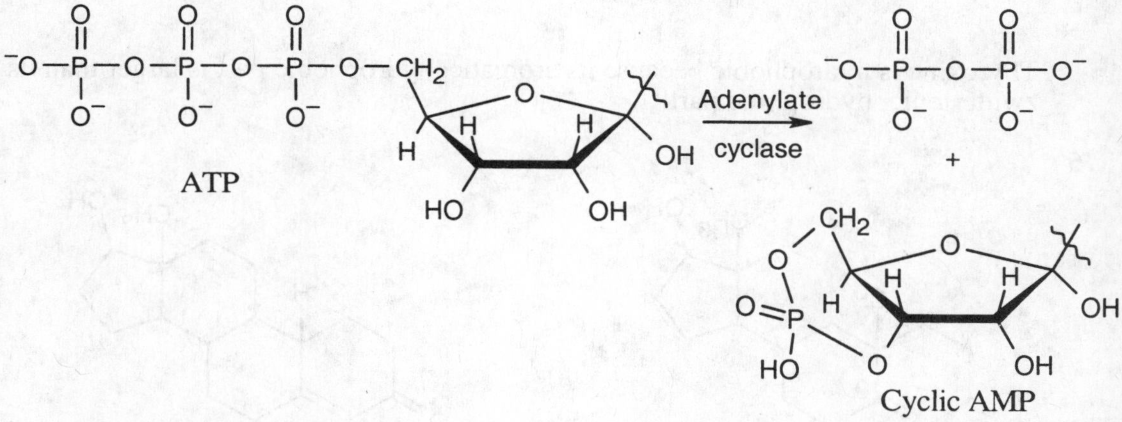
ATP
Adenylate
cyclase
Cyclic AMP

If you redraw the reaction shown in Figure 20.3, you can see the anion that is a by-product of the conversion of ATP to cyclic AMP. The anion (PP_i) is $P_2O_7^{4-}$.

20.2 The heterocyclic rings of caffeine and theobromine resemble the heterocyclic rings of cyclic AMP. It is possible that these two molecules could act as inhibitors to one of the enzymes that inactivates cAMP.

20.3

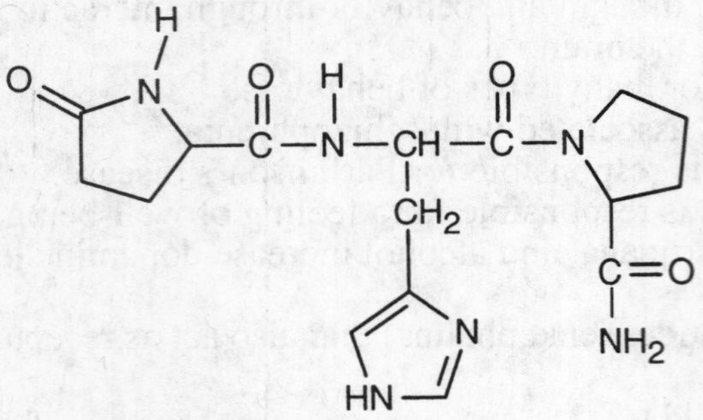
H
O
N
O
H
O
C
N
CH
C
N
CH2
C=O
N
NH2
HN

Glu His Pro

The tripeptide is Glu–His–Pro. Glutamic acid has formed a cyclic amide (lactam).

20.4

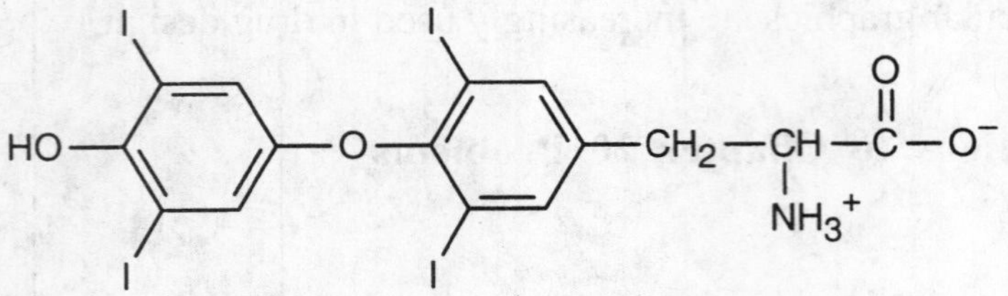
I
I
HO
O
CH2
CH
C
O
O⁻
NH3+
I
I
Thyroxine

Thyroxine is hydrophobic because its aromatic, hydrophobic part is larger than its zwitterionic, hydrophilic part.

20.5

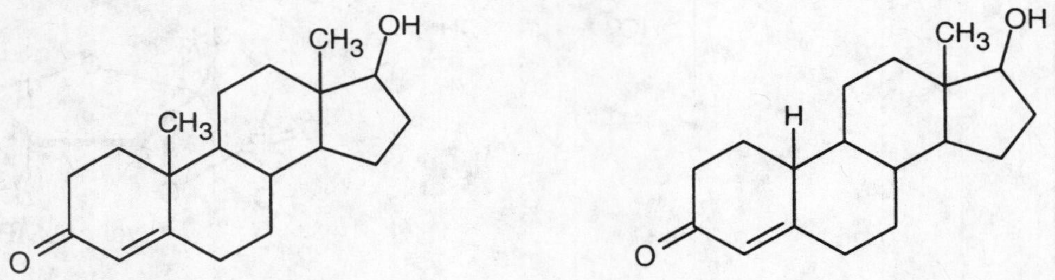
CH3
OH
CH3
O
CH3
OH
H
O

Testosterone Nandrolone

Nandrolone and testosterone are identical except for the presence in testosterone of a methyl group between the first two rings that is absent in nandrolone.

20.6

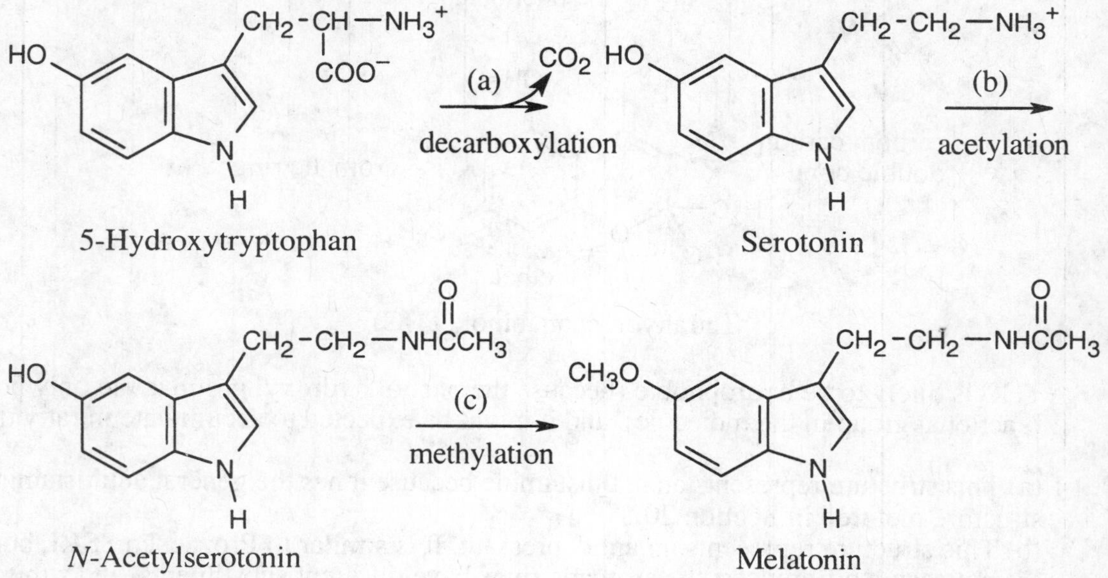
HO
CH_2-CH—NH_3^+
COO^-
N
H
(a)
CO_2
decarboxylation
HO
CH_2-CH_2—NH_3^+
N
H
(b)
acetylation
5-Hydroxytryptophan
Serotonin
HO
O
CH_2-CH_2—NHCCH$_3$
N
H
(c)
methylation
CH_3O
O
CH_2-CH_2—NHCCH$_3$
N
H
N-Acetylserotonin
Melatonin

(a) decarboxylation (2)
(b) acetylation (3)
(c) methylation (1)

20.7

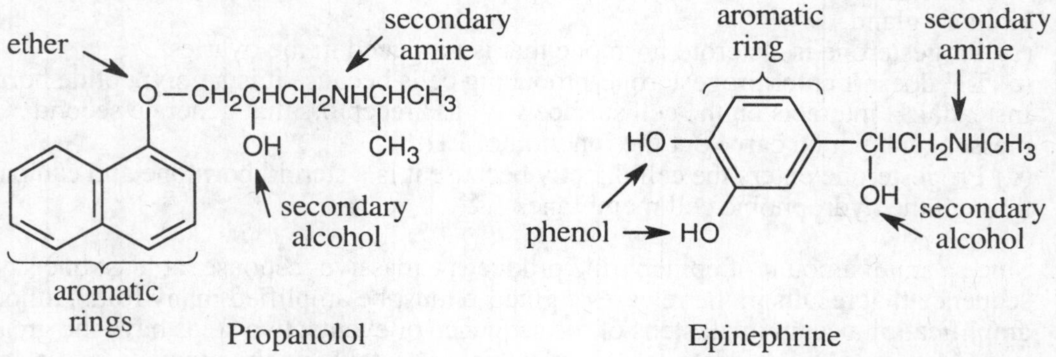
ether
secondary amine
O—$CH_2CHCH_2NHCHCH_3$
OH
CH_3
secondary alcohol
aromatic rings
Propanolol
aromatic ring
secondary amine
HO
$CHCH_2NHCH_3$
OH
phenol
HO
secondary alcohol
Epinephrine

Both structures have aromatic rings and have secondary alcohol and secondary amine functional groups. Propranolol has a naphthalene aromatic ring system and has an ether group. Epinephrine has an aromatic ring with two phenol groups. The compounds have different carbon skeletons in their side chains.

20.8 Malathion, with an LD_{50} of 1000–1375 mg/kg, is the best choice because its lethal dose is highest, and it is thus the least harmful pesticide of the three.

20.9 An agonist (black widow spider venom) prolongs the biochemical response of a receptor. An antagonist (botulinus toxin) blocks or inhibits the normal response of a receptor.

20.10

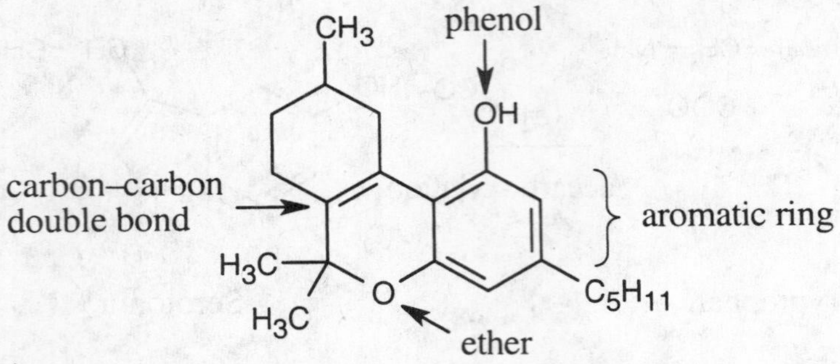
CH3
phenol
OH
carbon–carbon
double bond
aromatic ring
H3C
H3C
O
C5H11
ether

Tetrahydrocannabinol (THC)

THC is likely to be hydrophobic (because the phenol hydroxyl group is the only polar functional group in the molecule), and it might be expected to accumulate in fatty tissue.

20.11 (a) This structure represents an antihistamine because it has the general antihistamine structure pictured in Section 20.8.
(b) This structure represents an antidepressant. It is similar to Prozac, an SSRI, but there are noticeable differences; the aromatic rings have different substituents, and a third ring is present in the compound pictured.

Understanding Key Concepts

20.12 (a) Luteinizing hormone (LH) is a polypeptide hormone that is produced in the anterior pituitary gland.
(b) Progesterone is a steroid hormone that is produced in the ovaries.
(c) LH doesn't enter progesterone-producing cells because it is a polypeptide hormone. Instead, LH interacts on the cell surface with LH receptors that generate second messengers, which carry out the function of LH.
(d) Progesterone enters the cell directly because it is a steroid hormone and can pass through the hydrophobic cell membrane.

20.13 Since a small amount of epinephrine produces a massive response, at least one step in the sequence that results in the release of glucose must be amplified many fold. Although amplification occurs in all steps of the sequence of events, two steps have the greatest amplification. (1) Adenylate cyclase is capable of catalyzing the production of a great number of cAMP molecules. (2) The kinase enzymes phosphorylated as a result of cAMP activation (Section 19.9) quickly catalyze the breakdown of glycogen to release large amounts of glucose.

20.14 (a) Insulin, a polypeptide hormone, is involved in type I diabetes.
(b) In unaffected individuals, insulin is released by the pancreas. The pancreas fails to produce insulin in individuals with type I diabetes.
(c) Insulin is transported through the bloodstream to cells that need it.
(d) Insulin doesn't enter cells because it is a polypeptide hormone and can't pass through the hydrophobic cell membrane. Instead, it binds with a cell surface receptor, which generates a second messenger within the cell.

20.15 Neurotransmitters can act either by binding to receptors or by activating second messengers.

20.16 The transmission of a nerve impulse may be terminated by an enzyme that converts the neurotransmitter to an inactive form. It is also possible for the neurotransmitter to be returned to the presynaptic neuron.

20.17 Elevated concentrations of dopamine in the brain result in a "high" feeling. All of these drugs increase the concentration of dopamine in the brain. The brain attempts to return to its normal state by decreasing the number of dopamine receptors and by decreasing their sensitivity. Consequently, more of the drug is required to achieve the same effect, leading to addiction.

Chemical Messengers

20.18 A vitamin is usually an enzyme cofactor, whereas a hormone regulates enzyme activity.

20.20 A hormone transmits a chemical message from an endocrine gland to a target tissue. A neurotransmitter carries an impulse between neighboring nerve cells. Neurotransmitters act rapidly and with short duration, whereas hormones act more slowly and produce effects of longer duration.

20.22 Hormones are molecules of different sizes and types that travel through the bloodstream and regulate the rates of biochemical reactions without directly taking part in the reactions. A hormone is detected by a receptor, either at a cell surface or within the cell.

Hormones and the Endocrine System

20.24 The body's endocrine system manufactures and secretes hormones, which regulate the functioning of biochemical reaction pathways.

20.26 The three major classes of hormones are polypeptide hormones, steroid hormones, and hormones that are derivatives of amino acids.

20.28 Enzymes are proteins, whereas hormones vary greatly in structure. Some hormones are polypeptides, some are proteins, some are steroids, and some are derivatives of amino acids.

20.30 Steroid hormones travel through the bloodstream to target tissues. Because they are lipids, they are able to pass through the cell membrane. Receptors for steroid hormones occur either in intracellular fluid or in the nucleus.

How Hormones Work: Epinephrine

20.32 Epinephrine is produced in the adrenal medulla and released as a result of a nervous system signal from the hypothalamus. It is produced when the body needs an instant response to stress. At target tissues, epinephrine stimulates the production of glucose as a source of energy to deal with whatever stress is at hand.

20.34 The second messenger initiates reactions that activate glycogen phosphorylase, the enzyme responsible for releasing glucose from storage. When the message is ready to be terminated, the enzyme phosphodiesterase converts cyclic AMP to AMP.

Hormones

20.36 Insulin is an example of a polypeptide hormone that contains 51 amino acids in two chains that are linked by disulfide bridges. It is stored in the pancreas and is released in response to high glucose levels in the blood. The hormone stimulates cells to take up glucose for use or storage.

20.38 *Mineralocorticoids* include aldosterone.
Glucocorticoids include hydrocortisone and cortisone.
Sex hormones include testosterone, androsterone, estrone, estradiol, and progesterone.

20.40 Both thyroxine and steroid hormones have large nonpolar regions and can cross a cell membrane to activate the synthesis of enzymes.

20.42 *Hormone* — *Class*

(a) — amino acid derivative

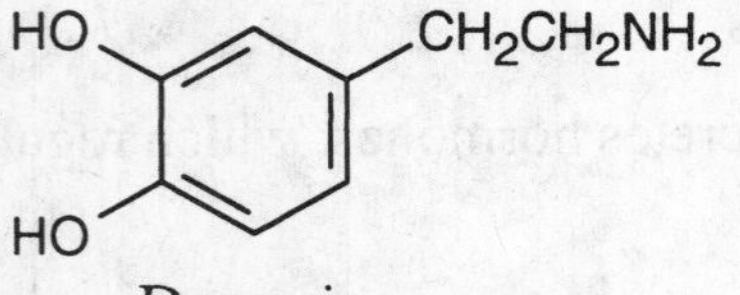
HO
$CH_2CH_2NH_2$
HO

Dopamine

(b) Insulin — polypeptide hormone

(c) — steroid hormone

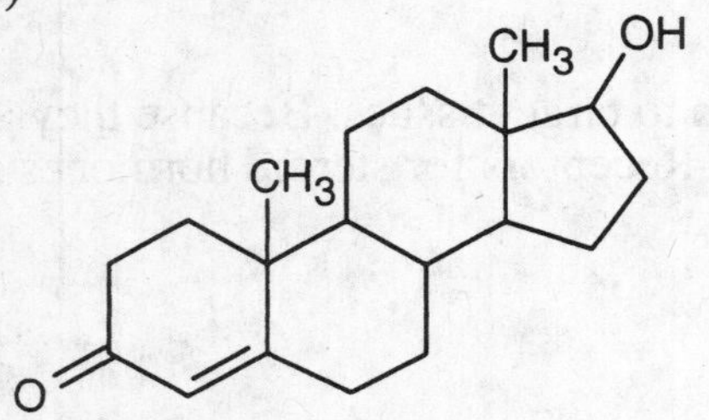
CH_3
OH
CH_3
O

Testosterone

Neurotransmitters

20.44 A synapse is the gap between two nerve cells (neurons). Neurotransmitters released by one neuron cross the synapse to receptors on a second neuron and transmit the nerve impulse.

20.46 A nerve impulse arrives at the presynaptic end of a neuron. The nerve impulse stimulates the movement of a vesicle, containing neurotransmitter molecules, to the cell membrane. The vesicle fuses with the cell membrane and releases the neurotransmitter, which crosses the synaptic cleft to a receptor site on the postsynaptic end of a second neuron. After reception, the cell transmits an electrical signal down its axon and passes on the impulse. Enzymes then deactivate the neurotransmitter so that the neuron can receive the next impulse. Alternatively, the neurotransmitter may be returned to the presynaptic neuron.

20.48 (1) Neurotransmitter molecules are released from a presynaptic neuron in response to an impulse. (2) The neurotransmitter molecules cross the synaptic cleft. (3) The neurotransmitter molecules bind to receptors on the target cell.

20.50 Enkephalins are called "neurohormones" because they are secreted in the central nervous system and have receptors in brain tissue.

Chemical Messengers and Drugs

20.52 Drugs that are agonists interact with receptors to produce or prolong the normal response of the receptor. Antagonists block or inhibit the normal response of a receptor.

20.54 Three families of drugs used to treat depression are tricyclic antidepressants (Elavil), monoamine oxidase inhibitors (Nardil), and selective serotonin reuptake inhibitors (Prozac).

20.56 Both cocaine and amphetamines increase dopamine levels in the brain. Cocaine blocks reuptake of dopamine, and amphetamines accelerate release of dopamine.

20.58 When it was discovered that the brain had receptors for neurotransmitters that came from plants, scientists reasoned that there must also be animal neurotransmitters that acted on the same receptors. It seems to be a coincidence that the brain receptors that respond to animal neurotransmitters also respond to plant neurotransmitters.

20.60 An ethnobotanist works in remote regions of the world to learn what indigenous people have discovered about the healing power of plants.

20.62 Studies of the exact size and shape of biomolecules give scientists information about receptor sites of molecules of interest. This information allows scientists to design drugs with properties suitable for the desired drug–receptor interaction with the target biomolecule.

Applications

20.64 Homeostasis is the maintenance of a constant internal environment in the body.

20.66 Plants must synthesize hormones in the cells where they are needed because plants don't have endocrine systems, nor do they have a continuously circulating fluid like blood.

20.68 Epibatidine acts as a painkiller by binding to an acetylcholine receptor in the central nervous system (like nicotine) rather than to an opioid receptor (like morphine).

General Questions and Problems

20.70 The *hormone receptor* recognizes the hormone and sets into motion the series of reactions that result in the response of the cell to hormonal stimulation.
The hormone–receptor complex interacts with the *G protein* and causes it to bind GTP. The G protein mediates the reaction between the receptor and adenylate cyclase.
The G protein–GTP complex activates *adenylate cyclase*, which catalyzes the formation of the second messenger, cyclic AMP. Cyclic AMP initiates the reactions that the hormone is designed to stimulate.

20.72 Signal amplification is the process in which a small signal induces a response much larger in magnitude than the original signal. For hormones, this amplification begins with the activation of the G protein; one hormone–receptor complex can activate many G protein–GTP complexes. Each G protein–GTP complex, in turn, can activate many molecules of adenylate cyclase, which can stimulate production of many molecules of cyclic AMP. The importance of signal amplification is that a small amount of hormone can cause a very large response.

20.74 With the exception of the circled groups, testosterone and progesterone are identical.

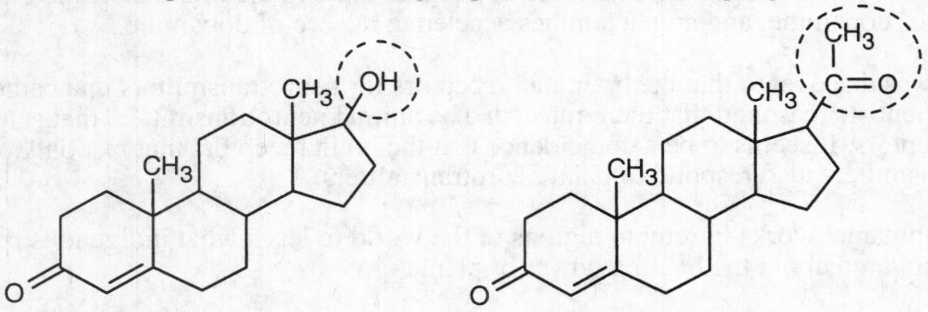
CH3
OH
CH3
O
CH3
C=O
CH3
CH3
O

Testosterone Progesterone

20.76 The craving for chocolate might be explained by the stimulation of dopamine receptors by anandamides, producing feelings of satisfaction similar to those produced by THC. The effect of chocolate consumption may be a milder version of marijuana's effects.

20.78 Testosterone can be converted to androsterone by reduction of the ketone group and the double bond in the first ring, and by oxidation of the hydroxyl group in the five-membered ring. Estradiol can be converted to estrone by oxidation of the —OH group in the five-membered ring. Most of these changes occur as a result of oxidations and reductions.

Self–Test for Chapter 20

Multiple Choice

1. Which of the following compounds is an acetylcholine agonist?
(a) nicotine (b) succinylcholine (c) tubocurarine (d) atropine

2. Which of the following hormones regulates the balance of Na^+ and K^+ ions in cellular fluid?
(a) androsterone (b) progesterone (c) aldosterone (d) cortisone

3. Cocaine affects the brain because it
(a) accelerates the release of dopamine (b) blocks reuptake of dopamine (c) raises the level of endorphins (d) all of the above

4. An effective antihistamine has all of the structural elements listed except
(a) an ethylamine skeleton (b) a tertiary amine (c) an ether oxygen (d) two bulky –R groups.

5. Which of the following compounds is a neurotransmitter but not a hormone?
(a) dopamine (b) norepinephrine (c) epinephrine (d) acetylcholine

6. Which of the following compounds does not reside in the cell membrane?
(a) cyclic AMP (b) epinephrine receptor (c) adenylate cyclase (d) G protein

7. Hormones and neurotransmitters have all of the following in common except
(a) They both regulate reaction rates. (b) They both can be amino acid derivatives. (c) They both interact with receptors at target tissues. (d) They both travel through the bloodstream.

8. Which of the following events doesn't occur in "fight or flight"?
(a) Epinephrine crosses the cell membrane. (b) Epinephrine stimulates production of cyclic AMP. (c) Glucose is released from storage. (d) Cyclic AMP is converted to AMP.

9. Control of the endocrine system occurs in the
(a) pancreas (b) pituitary gland (c) adrenal glands (d) hypothalamus

10. Which of the following isn't a site for hormone receptors?
(a) outer cell surface (b) cytoplasm within the cell (c) cell nucleus (d) bloodstream

Sentence Completion

1. ________ is a life-threatening allergic response.

2. In direct neural control, the hypothalamus controls the release of hormones by the ____ gland.

3. Neurotransmitter molecules are stored in ______.

4. _______ is the neurotransmitter responsible for the symptoms of allergic reactions.

5. Nerves that rely on acetylcholine as their neurotransmitter are referred to as ______ nerves.

6. The hormone ______ prepares the uterus to receive a fertilized egg.

7. An ______ is a neuropeptide that acts at opiate receptors.

8. A person who studies the healing powers of plants from remote regions is a _________.

9. One neuron is separated from another by a gap called a _____ _____.

10. Heroin, alcohol, and cocaine all produce an elevated level of the neurotransmitter ______.

11. The hormone _______ contains iodine atoms.

12. After an emergency, the enzyme ________ catalyzes hydrolysis of cyclic AMP to AMP.

True or False

1. Only steroid hormones can cross the cell membrane to activate enzymes.

2. Cocaine accelerates the release of dopamine.

3 In direct release of hormones, hormones move through the bloodstream to the posterior pituitary gland, where they are stored until needed.

4. Some neurotransmitters can act directly; others use second messengers.

5. Acetylcholine is synthesized at postsynaptic neurons.

6. Choline is a quaternary ammonium ion.

7. Epinephrine reduces blood pressure and slows the heart rate.

8. An enlarged thyroid gland is a symptom of excess iodine in the diet.

9. Polypeptide hormones vary greatly in size.

10. Succinylcholine is a competitive antagonist for acetylcholine.

Match each entry on the left with its partner on the right.

1. Androgen	(a) Polypeptide hormone
2. Tricyclic antidepressant	(b) Progesterone
3. Acetylcholine agonist	(c) Cortisone
4. Natural estrogen	(d) ACTH
5. Second messenger	(e) Testosterone
6. Oxytocin	(f) Norethindrone
7. Regulatory hormone	(g) Cyclic AMP
8. MAO inhibitor antidepressant	(h) Amitriptyline (Elavil)
9. Synthetic estrogen	(i) Fluoxetine (Prozac)
10 Acetylcholine antagonist	(j) Phenelzine (Nardil)
11. Glucocorticoid	(k) Nicotine
12 SSRI inhibitor antidepressant	(l) Atropine

Chapter 21 – The Generation of Biochemical Energy

Chapter Outline

I. Energy and cells (Sections 21.1–21.3).
  A. Energy requirements for living things (Section 21.1).
    1. Energy must be released from food gradually.
    2. Energy must be stored in a readily accessible form.
    3. The rate of release of energy from storage must be finely controlled.
    4. Just enough energy must be released as heat to maintain body temperature.
    5. Energy in a form other than heat must be available to drive reactions that aren't spontaneous at body temperature.
  B. Free energy and biochemical reactions (Section 21.2).
    1. In favorable chemical reactions, free energy is released.
      a. Favorable reactions occur when heat is released and/or disorder increases.
      b. These reactions are described as exergonic.
      c. In favorable reactions, the products are more stable than the reactants.
      d. Favorable reactions have a negative value for ΔG.
    2. Free energy must be provided for unfavorable chemical reactions to take place.
      a. Unfavorable reactions are described as endergonic.
      b. Energy must be supplied in order for endergonic reactions to proceed.
      c. In unfavorable reactions, the products are less stable than the reactants.
      d. Unfavorable reactions have a positive value for ΔG.
  C. The cell and energy (Section 21.3).
    1. Simple organisms have prokaryotic cells.
    2. More complicated organisms have eukaryotic cells.
      These cells have membrane-enclosed nuclei and organelles.
    3. Structure of eukaryotic cells.
      a. Everything between the cell membrane and the nuclear membrane is the cytoplasm.
      b. The fluid of the cytoplasm is the cytosol.
      c. The most important organelles are the mitochondria.
        i. Mitochondria consist of a smooth outer membrane and a folded inner membrane.
        ii. The space between the two membranes is the intermembrane space.
        iii. The space enclosed by the inner membrane is the mitochondrial matrix.
        iv. Most of the energy-producing reactions of the cell begin in the mitochondrial matrix.

II. Metabolism (Sections 21.4–21.7).
  A. Overview of metabolism (Section 21.4).
    1. A sequence of reactions in metabolism is known as a metabolic pathway.
      a. Pathways may be linear, cyclic or spiral.
      b. Pathways that break molecules apart are known as catabolic pathways.
      c. Pathways that build molecules are known as anabolic pathways.
    2. Catabolism consists of four phases.
      a. Digestion occurs in the mouth and small intestine.
      b. Small molecules are degraded in the cell to yield acetyl-SCoA.
      c. Acetyl groups are oxidized to yield CO_2, H_2O, and energy.
      d. Some of the energy is transferred to ATP and reduced coenzymes.

B. Strategies of metabolism (Sections 21.5–21.7).
1. ATP and energy transfer (Section 21.5).
a. ATP contains two phosphoric anhydride bonds and a phosphate ester bond.
b. Hydrolysis of one phosphate anhydride bond provides –7.3 kcal/mol of energy.
c. Synthesis of ATP from ADP and phosphate requires +7.3 kcal/mol of energy.
d. Synthesis of ATP occurs when there is energy to store, and hydrolysis of ATP occurs when energy is needed.
2. Metabolic pathways and coupled reactions (Section 21.6).
a. In any reaction, the amount of energy consumed or released is the same, no matter what the path.
b. The overall energy change for a series of reactions can be found by adding up the free energy changes for the individual steps.
c. A reaction that is energetically unfavored can take place if it is coupled with a reaction that is energetically favored.
i. The phosphorylation of glucose can take place by coupling with the conversion of ATP to ADP.
ii. ATP can be synthesized by coupling with the transfer of a phosphoryl group from phosphoenolpyruvate.
3. Oxidized and reduced coenzymes (Section 21.7).
a. Many biochemical reactions are redox reactions.
i. Oxidation may be loss of electrons, loss of hydrogen, or addition of oxygen.
ii. Reduction may be gain of electrons, gain of hydrogen, or removal of oxygen.
iii. Reductions and oxidations always occur together.
b. Common redox coenzymes are NAD^+, $NADP^+$ and FAD (written in the oxidized form).
i. $NAD^+$and $NADP^+$ are used to oxidize alcohols to carbonyl compounds.
ii. FAD catalyzes the formation of a double bond.
c. The energy stored in $FADH_2$, $NADH/H^+$, and $NADPH/H^+$ is passed on to ATP.

III. Metabolic pathways (Sections 21.8–21.10).
A. The citric acid cycle (Section 21.8).
1. Oxidation of two-carbon acyl groups from acetyl-SCoA to CO_2 occurs in the citric acid cycle.
2. The citric acid cycle is a closed loop of eight reactions in which the product of step 8 is a reactant in step 1.
3. The cycle operates only if
a. Acetyl groups are available.
b. NAD^+ and FAD are in their oxidized form.
c. Oxygen is available.
4. A summary of steps:
a. Steps 1, 2: Preparation.
i. Acetyl-SCoA + oxalate —> citrate.
ii. Citrate is isomerized to isocitrate.
b. Steps 3, 4: Oxidative decarboxylation.
i. Isocitrate is oxidized and decarboxylated to form α-ketoglutarate, with reduction of NAD^+.
ii. α-Ketoglutarate is decarboxylated to form succinyl-SCoA and reduced NAD^+.
c. Step 5: Phosphorylation.
Succinyl-SCoA + GDP —> succinate + HSCoA + GTP.
d. Step 6: Oxidation of succinate.
Succinate + FAD —> fumarate + $FADH_2$.
e. Steps 7, 8: Regeneration of oxaloacetate.
i. Fumarate + H_2O —> malate.
ii. Malate + NAD^+ —> oxaloacetate + $NADH/H^+$.

5. Net result of citric acid cycle:
   a. Production of four reduced coenzyme molecules.
   b. Conversion of an acetyl group to two CO_2 molecules.
   c. Production of one GTP.

B. The electron transport chain and production of ATP (Section 21.9).
   1. The end product of the electron transport chain is water in the reaction :
      $O_2 + 4\,e^- + 4\,H^+ \longrightarrow 2\,H_2O$
   2. The reactions of the electron transport chain are coupled to oxidative phosphorylation.
   3. Enzymes for electron transport are embedded in the mitochondrial membrane.
   4. Features of the electron transport chain:
      a. Hydrogen and electrons from NADH and $FADH_2$ enter the respiratory chain from the mitochondrial matrix.
      b. Electrons pass from weaker to stronger electron acceptors.
      c. Some of the energy released is used to transport H^+ into the intermembrane space.
      d. The H^+ concentration gradient creates a potential energy difference that is crucial for ATP synthesis.
      e. H^+ ions can return to the complex only by passing through a channel that is part of the ATP synthase complex.
         The energy that they release drives the phosphorylation of ATP.
   5. Various cofactors, including iron–sulfur clusters and cytochromes, are involved in electron transport.
   6. Ultimately, electrons are passed on to oxygen, which combines with H^+ to form H_2O.
   7. The energy needed for ATP synthesis is provided by the passage of H^+ ions through the ATP synthase enzyme complex.
   8. The passage of electrons from one mol NADH produces from 2.5 to 3 mol ATP.

C. Harmful oxygen by-products and antioxidants (Section 21.10).
   1. Oxygen can be consumed in other redox reactions besides electron transport.
   2. The products of these reactions may be H_2O_2, the $\cdot OH^-$ radical, or superoxide ion $\cdot O_2^-$.
   3. People are protected from the harmful effects of these species by several enzymes, as well as by antioxidants and vitamins A, C, and E.

Solutions to Chapter 21 Problems

21.1 Use two facts to solve this problem:

(1) A reaction with a negative ΔG is exergonic, and a reaction with a positive ΔG is endergonic.
(2) A reaction with a larger negative ΔG releases more energy than a reaction with a smaller negative ΔG.

Thus, reactions (a) and (c) are exergonic, and reaction (b) is endergonic. Reaction (a) releases the most energy, because its ΔG has a larger negative value than the ΔG's of the other reactions.

21.2 The amount of energy produced by both processes is the same.

21.3 (a) Oxidation of glucose is exergonic, and photosynthesis is endergonic.
(b) Sunlight provides the energy for the endergonic pathway.

21.4 (a) Carbohydrates are digested in the mouth, stomach, and small intestine to yield sugars, which are degraded in the cytosol to pyruvate. Pyruvate is converted to acetyl-SCoA, which enters the citric acid cycle and is oxidized to CO_2. The reduced coenzymes that are generated by oxidation of acetyl-SCoA enter the electron-transport chain and are used in the production of ATP by oxidative phosphorylation.

(b) The products of amino acid catabolism can enter the central metabolic pathway as pyruvate, as acetyl-SCoA, and as citric acid cycle intermediates.

21.5

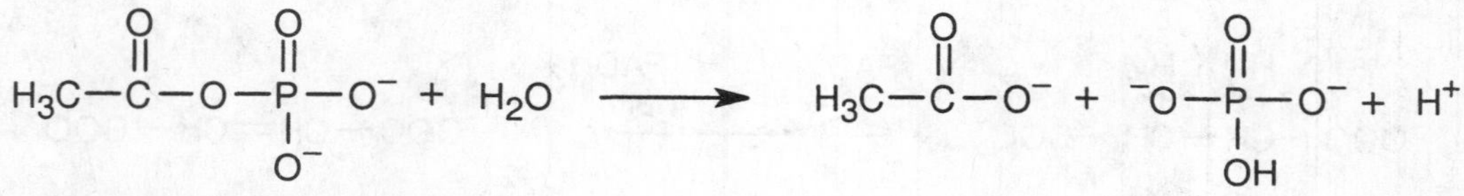

Acetyl phosphate

21.6 This strategy ensures that an exergonic reaction only occurs when the energy it releases is needed.

21.7

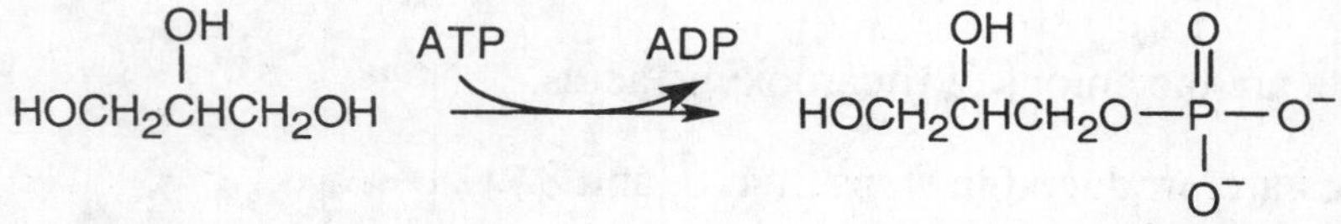

Glycerol Glycerol 1-phosphate

21.8 If a metabolic pathway that breaks down a molecule is exergonic, the reverse of that pathway (synthesis) *must* be endergonic. The only way to synthesize the product is to couple the energetically unfavorable reactions with other reactions that are energetically favorable in a pathway that differs from the reverse of the breakdown pathway.

21.9

$$\text{Acetyl phosphate} + H_2O \longrightarrow \text{Acetate} + HOPO_3^{2-} + H^+ \qquad \Delta G = -10.3 \text{ kcal/mol}$$

$$\text{ADP} + HOPO_3^{2-} + H^+ \longrightarrow \text{ATP} + H_2O \qquad \Delta G = +7.3 \text{ kcal/mol}$$

$$\text{Acetyl phosphate} + \text{ADP} \longrightarrow \text{Acetate} + \text{ATP} \qquad \Delta G = -3.0 \text{ kcal/mol}$$

The reaction is favorable because ΔG is negative.

21.10 Yes. If you look at the structure of FAD shown in Section 21.7, you will see that ADP appears on the right side of the FAD molecule.

21.11 The hydrogen atoms removed are circled.

Step 3:

$$^-OOC-C(OH)(H)-CH(COO^-)-CH_2COO^- \xrightarrow{NAD^+ \rightarrow NADH/H^+} {}^-OOC-C(=O)-CH_2CH_2COO^- + CO_2$$

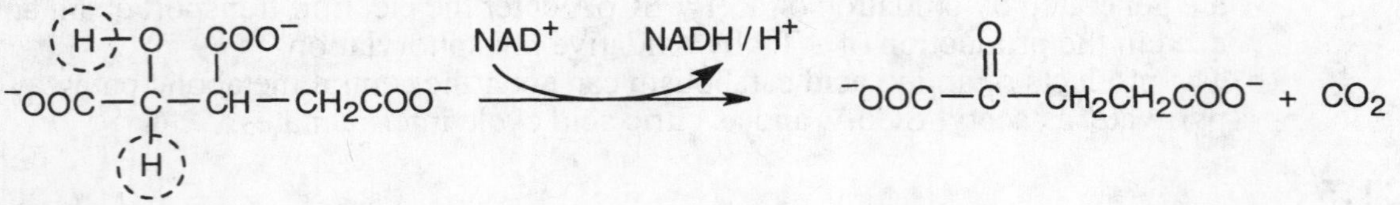

Step 6:

$$^-OOC-CH(H)-CH(H)-COO^- \xrightarrow{FAD \rightarrow FADH_2} {}^-OOC-CH=CH-COO^-$$

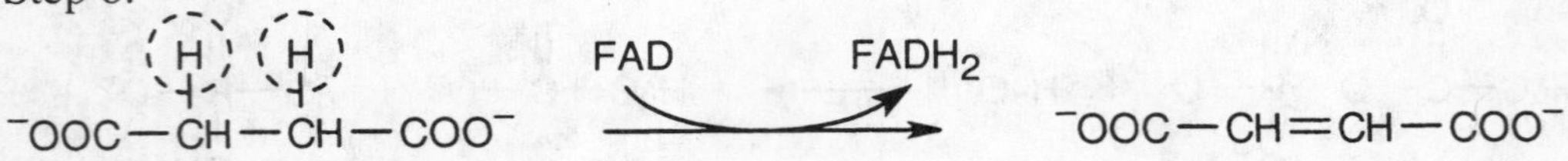

Step 8:

$$^-OOC-CH_2-C(O-H)(H)-COO^- \xrightarrow{NAD^+ \rightarrow NADH/H^+} {}^-OOC-CH_2-C(=O)-COO^-$$

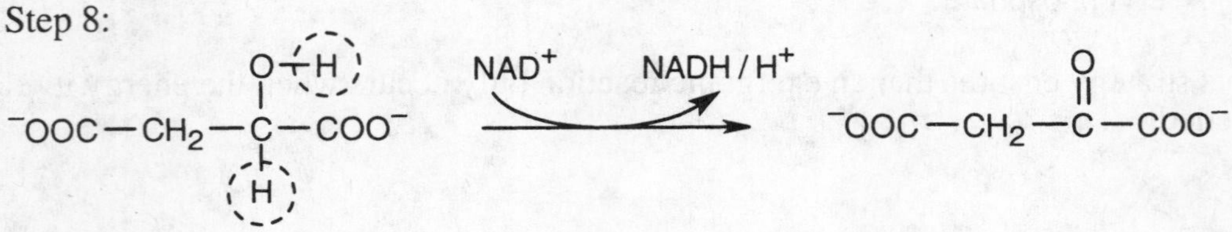

21.12 Citrate and isocitrate are the anions of tricarboxylic acids.

21.13 Reduced coenzymes are produced in steps 3, 4, 6, and 8.

21.14 In Step 6 of the citric acid cycle, succinate dehydrogenase catalyzes the removal of two hydrogens from succinate to yield fumarate. The hydrogens are transferred to the coenzyme FAD to produce the reduced coenzyme $FADH_2$.

21.15 α-Ketoglutarate and oxaloacetate are α-keto acids.

21.16 Isocitrate has two chiral carbon atoms.

21.17 Steps 1–4 correspond to the first stage, and Steps 5–8 correspond to the second stage.

21.18 The pH is higher in the mitochondrial matrix.

21.19 O_2 is the final electron acceptor. When H^+ ions move from a region of high concentration to a region of low concentration, energy is released that is used in ATP synthesis.

Understanding Key Concepts

21.20 (a) Exergonic reaction:
$$\text{Succinyl phosphate} + H_2O \longrightarrow \text{Succinate} + HOPO_3^{2-} + H^+$$
(b) Endergonic reaction:
$$ADP + HOPO_3^{2-} + H^+ \longrightarrow ATP + H_2O \qquad \Delta G = +7.3 \text{ kcal/mol}$$

21.21 (a) Production of acetyl-SCoA from glucose is a result of Stage 2 of food metabolism.
(b) The digestion of starch to glucose occurs in Stage 1 of food metabolism.
(c) The reactions shown represent the citric acid cycle and occur in Stage 3 of food metabolism.
(d) The synthesis of ATP takes place in Stage 4 of digestion (electron-transport chain).

21.22 When ATP "drives" a reaction, energy from ATP hydrolysis is used to allow another reaction to proceed. In this case, the reaction that forms fatty acid-SCoA from a fatty acid and coenzyme A is endergonic and is unfavorable in the absence of ATP. When the energy from hydrolysis of ATP is used to drive the reaction, the formation of fatty acid-SCoA can take place. Coupling is the metabolic strategy in which the energy from an energetically favorable reaction can be used to allow an energetically unfavorable reaction to take place.

21.23 In the steps of the citric acid cycle in which acetyl groups are oxidized to CO_2, NAD^+ is an acceptor of hydride ions, forming NADH. The hydrogen ions that are removed in an oxidation using NAD^+ are released to the mitochondrial matrix. NADH transfers electrons to the enzymes and coenzymes of the electron transport chain in the fourth stage of metabolism. Ultimately, the hydrogen ions combine with reduced oxygen to form H_2O.

21.24

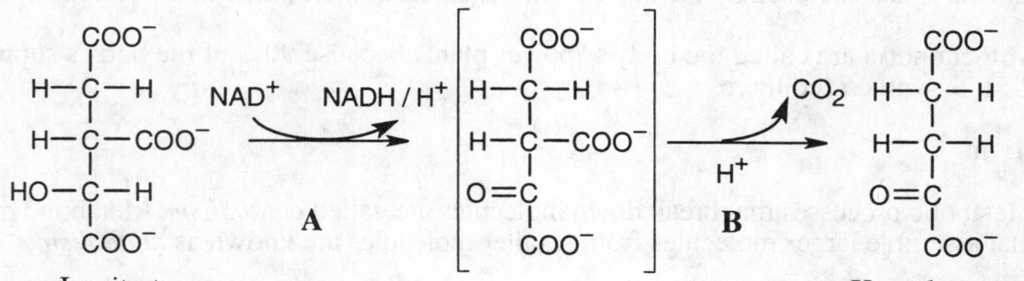
COO⁻
H—C—H
H—C—COO⁻
HO—C—H
COO⁻
NAD⁺
NADH / H⁺
A
COO⁻
H—C—H
H—C—COO⁻
O=C
COO⁻
CO₂
H⁺
B
COO⁻
H—C—H
H—C—H
O=C
COO⁻

Isocitrate α-Ketoglutarate

(a) The coenzyme NAD^+ is involved with reaction **A**.
(b) CO_2 is evolved and an H^+ is added in reaction **B**.
(d) The product of Step **A** is a β-keto acid because its ketone group is two carbons away from the carboxylic acid group bonded to the middle carbon.

21.25

Step	*Reaction*	*Reaction Type*	*Type of Enzyme*
1.	Oxaloacetate —> Citrate	Addition	Lyase
2.	Citrate —> Isocitrate	Isomerization	Isomerase
3.	Isocitrate —> α-Ketoglutarate	Oxidation, loss of CO_2	Oxidoreductase
4.	α-Ketoglutarate—>Succinyl-SCoA	Oxidation, loss of CO_2	Oxidoreductase; lyase
5.	Succinyl-SCoA —> Succinate	Hydrolysis, phosphorylation	Ligase
6.	Succinate —> Fumarate	Oxidation	Oxidoreductase
7.	Fumarate —> Malate	Addition of H_2O	Lyase
8.	Malate —> Oxaloacetate	Oxidation	Oxidoreductase

21.26 Metals are better oxidizing and reducing agents. Also, they can accept and donate electrons in one-electron increments.

Free Energy and Biochemical Reactions

21.28 For a reaction to be favorable, it must release energy and thus have a negative ΔG.

21.30 Enzymes only increase the rate of reaction and have no effect on either the magnitude or the sign of ΔG.

21.32 Reactions (a) and (c) are exergonic; reaction (b) is endergonic. Reaction (a) proceeds farthest toward products at equilibrium because it has the largest negative value for ΔG.

Cells and their Structure

21.34 Prokaryotic cells are found in bacteria and algae. Eukaryotic cells are found in all other organisms.

21.36 See Figure 21.3 in Section 21.3.

21.38 A mitochondrion is egg-shaped and consists of a smooth, outer membrane and a folded inner membrane. The intermembrane space lies between the outer and inner membranes, and the space enclosed by the inner membrane is called the *mitochondrial matrix*.

21.40 Mitochondria are called the body's "power plant" because 90% of the body's supply of ATP is synthesized there.

Metabolism

21.42 Metabolic processes that break down molecules are called *catabolism*. Metabolic processes that assemble larger molecules from smaller molecules are known as *anabolism*.

21.44 *First* ————————————————> *Last*
digestion, citric acid cycle, electron transport, oxidative phosphorylation

Strategies of Metabolism

21.46 ATP is called a high-energy molecule because energy is released when ATP transfers a phosphoryl group to other molecules.

21.48 An ATP molecule transfers a phosphoryl group to another molecule in exergonic reactions.

21.50

$$\text{1,3-Bisphosphoglycerate} + H_2O \longrightarrow \text{3-Phosphoglycerate} + HOPO_3^{2-} + H^+ \qquad \Delta G = -11.8 \text{ kcal/mol}$$

$$ADP + HOPO_3^{2-} + H^+ \longrightarrow ATP + H_2O \qquad \Delta G = +7.3 \text{ kcal/mol}$$

$$\text{1,3-Bisphosphoglycerate} + ADP \longrightarrow \text{3-Phosphoglycerate} + ATP \qquad \Delta G = -4.5 \text{ kcal/mol}$$

The reaction is favorable because ΔG is negative.

21.52 The hydrolysis of fructose 6-phosphate ($\Delta G = -3.3$ kcal/mol) is not favorable for phosphorylating ADP ($\Delta G = +7.3$ kcal/mol) because the overall value of ΔG (+ 4.0 kcal/mol) is positive.

21.54 (a) FAD is reduced when a molecule is dehydrogenated.
(b) FAD is an oxidizing agent.
(c) FAD oxidizes $—CH_2CH_2—$ to $—CH{=}CH—$.
(d) Dehydrogenation converts FAD to $FADH_2$.
(e)

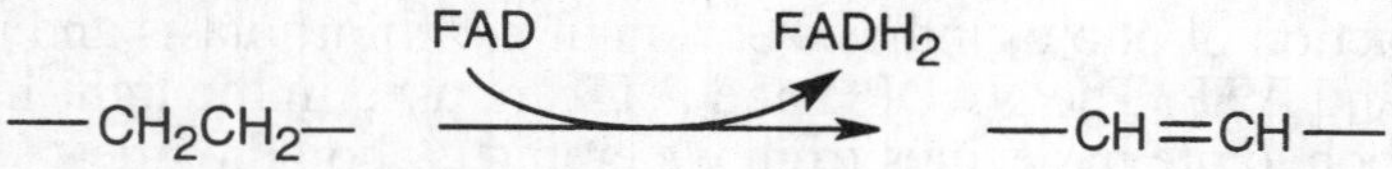
FAD
FADH2
—CH2CH2—
—CH=CH—

The Citric Acid Cycle

21.56 The citric acid cycle is also known as the Krebs cycle or the tricarboxylic acid cycle.

21.58 The two acetyl-SCoA carbons are oxidized to CO_2 in the citric acid cycle.

21.60 Three molecules of $NADH/H^+$ and one molecule of $FADH_2$ are produced in each turn of the citric acid cycle.

21.62 Step 6 (succinate → fumarate) stores energy as $FADH_2$.

The Electron Transport Chain/Oxidative Phosphorylation

21.64 The two primary functions of the electron transport chain are the conversion of ADP to ATP and the oxidation of the coenzymes NADH and $FADH_2$.

21.66 The ultimate products of the electron transport chain are water, energy in the form of ATP, and the oxidized coenzymes FAD and NAD^+.

21.68 $NADH/H^+$ and FAD are found in the mitochondrial matrix, and Cyt *c* and CoQ are found in the inner mitochondrial membrane.

21.70 *First* ——————————————————> *Last*
NADH, coenzyme Q, cytochrome *c*

21.72 If $FADH_2$ and NADH weren't reoxidized, the body's supply of the oxidized forms of these coenzymes would be depleted, and the citric acid cycle would stop.

21.74 Oxidative phosphorylation refers to formation of ATP from the reactions of reduced coenzymes as they are oxidized in the electron-transport chain.

21.76 (a) ATP is the energy-carrying product.
(b) H_2O and oxidized coenzymes are the other two products.

Applications

21.78 Basal metabolic rate is the minimum amount of energy per unit time needed for breathing, maintaining body temperature, circulating blood, and keeping all body organs functioning.

21.80 Daily activities such as walking use energy, and thus the body requires a larger caloric intake than that needed to maintain basal metabolism.

21.82 When ATP production is decoupled, oxygen consumption increases because the proton gradient disappears, more water is formed, and more oxygen is used.

21.84 A seal has more brown fat because it needs to generate more body heat than a cat does.

21.86 The light-dependent reaction of photosynthesis occurs in the chloroplasts and is used to produce O_2, NADPH, and ATP. The NADPH and ATP are used in the light-independent reaction to produce carbohydrate molecules from water and carbon dioxide.

General Questions and Problems

21.88 The breakdown of molecules for energy must occur in several steps to avoid the production of large amounts of heat, to allow for storage of energy, and to control the rate of metabolism. Stepwise breakdown also allows energetically favorable steps to be coupled with other energetically unfavorable reactions.

21.90 Evidently, the isomer with a cis double bond cannot act as a substrate for the enzyme that is responsible for the next step in the citric acid cycle.

21.92 Electrons from the oxidation of reduced coenzymes pass through the electron-transport chain. Ultimately, the electrons are used to reduce O_2, which combines with H^+ ions to form H_2O.

21.94 Enzymes at the site of injury (catalase, in particular) catalyze the decomposition of hydrogen peroxide to oxygen, which bubbles from the wound.

21.96 Energy from combustion is released to the surroundings as heat and is wasted. Energy from metabolic oxidation is released in several steps and is stored in each step so that is available for use in other metabolic processes.

21.98 Oxygen debt occurs because the increased metabolic rate due to running consumes oxygen in the electron-transport chain. Panting is the body's attempt to resupply tissues with oxygen.

Self-Test for Chapter 21

Multiple Choice

1. Which of the following oxygen by-products isn't produced in the human body?
(a) O_2^- (b) O_3 (c) HO· (d) H_2O_2

2. The hydrolysis of which of the following substrates can be coupled with the reaction ADP + phosphate —> ATP to produce an energetically favorable reaction?
(a) glucose 6-phosphate (b) glucose 1-phosphate (c) creatine phosphate
(d) fructose 6-phosphate

3. Which of the following cofactors isn't held in a fixed position in electron transport?
(a) coenzyme Q (b) FMN (c) iron–sulfur clusters (d) cytochrome a

4. Which of the following reactions is an oxidation?
(a) Fe^{3+} —> Fe^{2+} (b) CH_3COOH —> CH_3CHO
(c) $CH_3CH_2CH_2COOH$ —>$CH_3CH{=}CHCOOH$ (d) CH_3COOCH_3—> $CH_3COOH + CH_3OH$

5. All of the following statements about electron transport are true except
(a) A concentration gradient is established between the inner membrane and the mitochondrial matrix. (b) Electrons are passed from weaker electron acceptors to stronger electron acceptors. (c) A greater amount of energy is produced from oxidation of NADH than from oxidation of $FADH_2$. (d) Some of the enzyme cofactors in the electron transport chain are mobile.

6. All of the following reactions are oxidations except:
(a) isocitrate —> α-ketoglutarate (b) α-ketoglutarate —> succinyl-SCoA
(c) succinate —> fumarate (d) fumarate —> malate

7. Which of the following citric acid cycle enzymes is an isomerase?
(a) citrate synthetase (b) aconitase (c) succinyl-SCoA synthetase (d) fumarase

8. Which coenzyme is not an oxidizing agent?
(a) FAD (b) Coenzyme Q (c) Acetyl-SCoA (d) NAD^+

9. All of the following reactions have positive ΔG except
(a) photosynthesis (b) hydrolysis of acetyl-SCoA (c) formation of ATP from ADP
(d) formation of glucose 6-phosphate

10. Which of the following metabolic pathways doesn't occur in mitochondria?
(a) oxidative phosphorylation (b) ATP synthesis (c) citric acid cycle (d) degradation of carbohydrates

Sentence Completion

1. _____ cells are found in higher organisms.

2. A → B → C is known as a _____ _____.

3. ATP is synthesized from _____ and _____.

4. A reaction that requires energy in order to take place is said to be energetically _____.

5. The citric acid cycle is also known as the _____ and as the _____ - _____ cycle.

6. α-Ketoglutaric acid reacts with acetyl-SCoA to yield _____ and _____.

7. Reactions that use the coenzyme _____ remove two hydrogens from an alcohol to yield a ketone.

8. A complete citric acid cycle yields _____ molecules of ATP.

9. _____ is the material that fills the interior of a cell.

10. _____ is a fast-acting enzyme that catalyzes the decomposition of reactive oxygen species.

11. The reaction succinate —> fumarate is catalyzed by _____ _____ .

12. _____ _____ is the minimal amount of energy required to stay alive.

True or False

1. ATP is a higher-energy molecule than ADP.

2. Both prokaryotic and eukaryotic cells are found in higher organisms.

3. Anabolism is the breakdown of high-energy molecules.

4. In a reaction that is energetically unfavorable, the energy of the products is less than the energy of the reactants.

5. The third and fourth stages of digestion take place in the mitochondria.

6. A reaction that is energetically unfavorable can use ATP as an energy source.

7. $FADH_2$ donates two electrons to cytochrome *c* in the respiratory chain.

8. FAD removes two hydrogens from a carbon chain to yield a double bond.

9. Release of heat and increase in order contribute to making a reaction favorable.

10. ATP is synthesized only in the respiratory chain.

11. In the synthesis of ATP from ADP, a phosphate ester bond is formed.

12. The reactions of the citric acid cycle may be exergonic or endergonic.

Match each entry on the left with its partner on the right.

1. Mitochondrion	(a) Uses energy
2. Oxidative phosphorylation	(b) Yields one molecule of H_2O
3. Isocitrate	(c) Releases energy
4. Anabolic reaction	(d) Site of energy production in cell
5. Succinyl-SCoA → succinate	(e) Reduces NAD^+ to $NADH/H^+$
6. Citric acid cycle	(f) Tricarboxylic acid
7. Malate → oxaloacetate	(g) Contains an iron atom
8. Catabolic reaction	(h) Subcellular structure
9. Respiratory chain	(i) Reduces FAD to $FADH_2$
10. Cytochrome	(j) ATP synthesis
11. Succinate → fumarate	(k) Yields 2 molecules of CO_2
12. Organelle	(l) Yields acetyl-SCoA plus ATP

Chapter 22 – Carbohydrates

Chapter Outline

I. General information about carbohydrates (Sections 22.1–22.3).
  A. Classification of carbohydrates (Section 22.1).
    1. By complexity.
      a. Monosaccharides don't yield smaller molecules when hydrolyzed.
      b. Disaccharides are composed of two monosaccharides.
      c. Polysaccharides are composed of a large number of monosaccharides.
    2. By carbonyl group.
      a. Aldoses contain an aldehyde carbonyl group.
      b. Ketoses contain a ketone carbonyl group.
    3. By number of carbons in a monosaccharide unit.
      Prefixes (*tri-*, *tetra-*, *penta-*) indicate the number of carbons in the monosaccharide.
  B. Handedness (Section 22.2–22.3).
    1. General characteristics of handed molecules (Section 22.2).
      a. Compounds having a carbon bonded to four different groups are chiral.
        i. A compound with a chiral carbon can exist in either a right-handed form (D) or a left-handed form (L).
        ii. These two forms are called enantiomers.
        iii. An "optically active" compound rotates the plane of plane-polarized light.
        iv. Enantiomers rotate the plane of plane-polarized light to the same extent but in opposite directions.
      b. Compounds having n chiral centers can have 2^n possible stereoisomers.
        i. Some of these isomers are enantiomers.
        ii. Stereoisomers that are not mirror images are diastereomers.
        iii. Some chiral compounds have fewer than the predicted number of stereoisomers because of symmetry.
    2. D and L sugars (Section 22.3).
      a. Stereoisomers can be drawn as Fischer projections.
        i. In these projections, the chiral carbon is drawn as the intersection of two perpendicular lines.
        ii. Bonds that point out of the page are shown as horizontal lines.
        iii. Bonds that point back into the page are vertical lines.
        iv. In sugars, the carbonyl group is at or near the top of a Fischer projection.
      b. Monosaccharides are divided into two families.
        i. In D sugars, the —OH group bonded to the chiral carbon farthest from the carbonyl group points to the right.
        ii. In L sugars, the —OH group bonded to the chiral carbon farthest from the carbonyl group points to the left.
        iii. Most of the carbohydrates that occur naturally are D stereoisomers.
      c. Fischer projections of molecules with more than one chiral carbon are drawn by stacking the chiral centers on top of each other.
      d. The enantiomer of a Fischer projection can be drawn by reversing the horizontal substituents on each chiral carbon.

II. Monosaccharides (Sections 22.4–22.6).
  A. Structure of monosaccharides (Section 22.4).
    1. Monosaccharides with five or more carbons can form cyclic internal hemiacetals.

a. The hemiacetal carbon (C1) can have two stereoisomeric forms.
b. Stereoisomers that differ in configuration only at the hemiacetal carbon are called anomers and are diastereomers.

2. Fischer projections can be converted to cyclic Haworth projections.
   a. In a Haworth projection of the β anomer, the —CH_2OH group and the anomeric —OH group are on the same side of the ring.
   b. In a Haworth projection of the α anomer, the —CH_2OH group and the anomeric —OH group are on opposite sides of the ring.
   c. Groups that are on the left in a Fischer projection point up in a Haworth projection.
   d. Groups that are on the right in a Fischer projection point down in a Haworth projection.
   e. The —CH_2OH group at C6 points up in D sugars.
3. In solution, glucose exists as a mixture of open chain glucose (0.02%), the α anomer (36%), and the β anomer (64%).
   a. Any mixture of glucose anomers achieves the same percent of anomers in solution.
   b. This phenomenon is called mutarotation.

B. Important monosaccharides (Section 22.5).
1. Glucose is the most important monosaccharide in human metabolism.
2. Galactose.
   a. Galactose differs from glucose only in the configuration at C4.
   b. Galactose is a component of the disaccharide lactose.
   c. Galactosemia is an inherited disorder of galactose metabolism.
3. Fructose.
   a. Fructose is a component of the disaccharide sucrose.
   b. Fructose is a ketohexose.
4. Ribose and 2-deoxyribose.
   a. These monosaccharides are aldopentoses.
   b. In 2-deoxyribose, the —OH group at C2 is replaced by –H.
   c. Both of these sugars occur as components of nucleic acids.

C. Reactions of monosaccharides (Section 22.6).
1. Reaction with oxidizing agents.
   a. Aldoses can be oxidized to carboxylic acids.
   b. In basic solution, ketoses can also be oxidized to carboxylic acids.
      Ketoses and aldoses are in equilibrium with an intermediate enediol.
   c. Carbohydrates that react with oxidizing agents are called reducing sugars.
2. Reaction with alcohols.
   a. Hemiacetals react with alcohols to form acetals that are called glycosides.
   b. The bond between the anomeric carbon atom and the oxygen of the —OR group is a glycosidic bond.
3. Formation of a bond between two monosaccharides.
   a. Glycosidic bonds can form between two monosaccharides or between a monosaccharide and another molecule.
      i. These bonds may have either α or β orientation.
      ii. Glycosides are not reducing sugars.
   b. Bonds between monosaccharides in more complex carbohydrates are also glycosidic bonds.
      The bond is described by specifying the positions of the connected carbon atoms and by using α or β to indicate the orientation.
   c. Hydrolysis is the cleavage of a glycosidic bond.

III. Important disaccharides (Section 22.7).
  A. Maltose.
    1. Maltose consists of two glucose molecules joined by an α-1,4 glycosidic bond.
    2. Maltose occurs in prepared foods and occurs in the body as a product of starch digestion.
    3. Maltose is a reducing sugar.
  B. Lactose.
    1. Lactose consists of a β-D-glucose molecule joined to a β-D-galactose molecule by a β-1,4 glycosidic linkage.
    2. Lactose is a reducing sugar.
    3. Lactose occurs in milk.
    4. Lactose intolerance is a metabolic disorder in which lactose can't be digested.
  C. Sucrose.
    1. Sucrose consists of an α-D-glucose molecule joined to a β-D-fructose molecule by a glycosidic bond connecting the two anomeric carbons.
    2. Sucrose isn't a reducing sugar.
    3. Sucrose is the most common disaccharide.

IV. Important biomolecules derived from carbohydrates (Section 22.8).
  A. Chitin is a polymer of *N*-acetyl-D-glucosamine that occurs in the shells of shellfish and in insects.
  B. Cartilage and tendons consist of protein fibers and polysaccharides composed of β-D-glucuronic acid and *N*-acetyl-D-glucosamine or galactose derivatives.
  C. Hyaluronate and chondroitin 6-sulfate are present in joints, tendons and cartilage.
  D. Heparin is a polysaccharide that contains sulfate groups and that functions as an anticoagulant.
  E. Glycoproteins contain carbohydrates bonded to proteins and have important functions at cell surfaces.

V. Polysaccharides (Section 22.9).
  A. Polysaccharides consist of hundreds to thousands of monosaccharides connected by glycosidic bonds.
  B. Cellulose.
    1. Cellulose consists of thousands of β-D-glucose units connected by glycosidic bonds.
    2. Chains of cellulose fibers can form hydrogen bonds.
    3. Humans can't digest cellulose.
  C. Starch.
    1. Starch consists of glucose units joined by α-1,4 glycosidic bonds.
    2. There are two kinds of starch.
      a. Amylose consists of hundreds of glucose units joined by α-1,4 glycosidic bonds and is soluble in hot water.
      b. Amylopectin is much larger than amylose, also contains α-1,6 branches every 25 units, and is insoluble in water.
      c. Starch is digested in the small intestine by α-amylase.
  D. Glycogen.
    1. Glycogen resembles amylopectin but is larger and has more branches.
    2. In humans and animals, glycogen is used for carbohydrate storage.

Solutions to Chapter 22 Problems

22.1 The name of a monosaccharide consists of three parts:
(1) the prefix *aldo*- (if the carbonyl group is an aldehyde) or *keto*-(if the carbonyl group is a ketone);
(2) a number prefix, such as *tri*-, *tetr*-, *pent*-, *hex*- (to show the number of carbons in the monosaccharide);
(3) the suffix *-ose*, which indicates that the compound is a sugar).

(a)

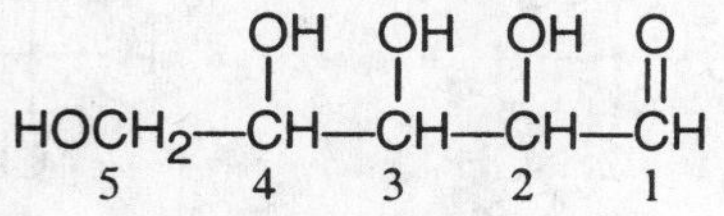

An aldopentose

(b)

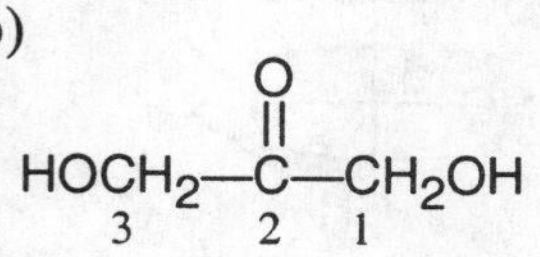

A ketotriose

(c)

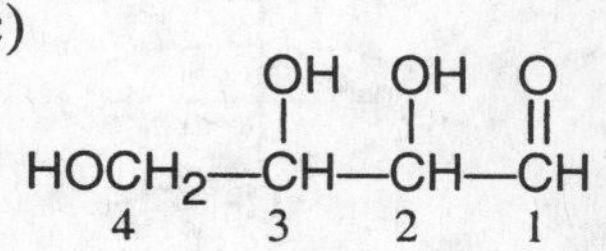

An aldotetrose

22.2

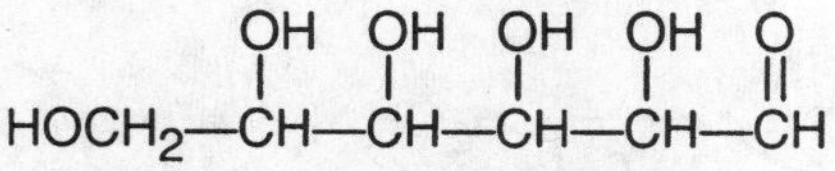

An aldohexose

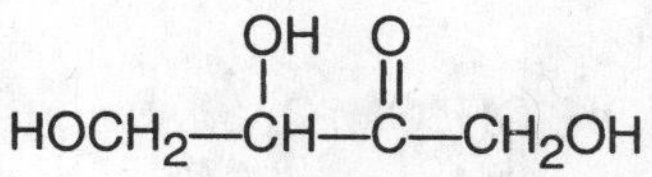

A ketotetrose

22.3 An aldopentose (see illustration in Section 22.1) has three chiral carbon atoms. Using the fact that a molecule with *n* chiral carbons has 2^n stereoisomers, we calculate that an aldopentose has a maximum of $2^3 = 8$ stereoisomers.

22.4

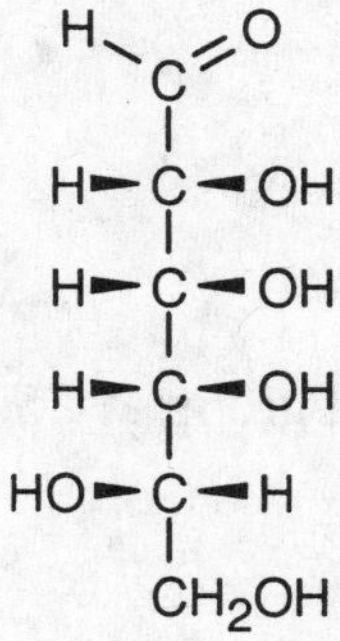

(a)

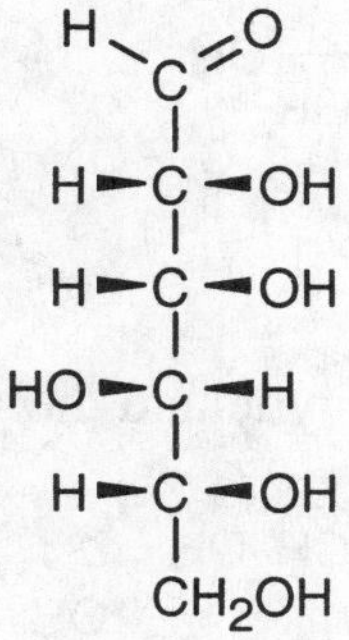

(b)

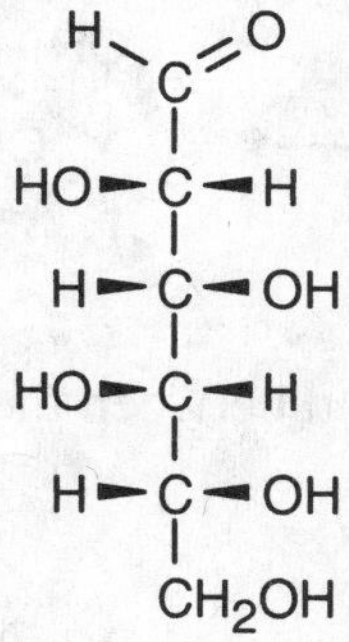

(c)

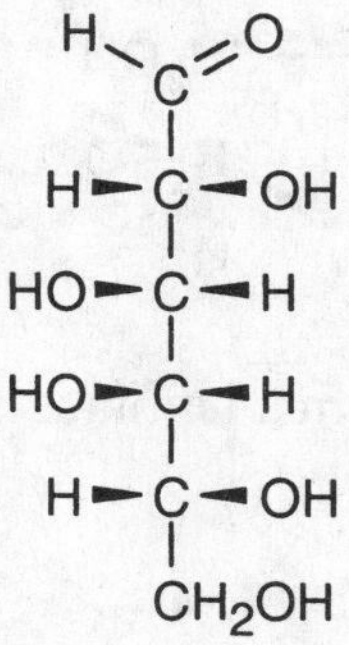

(d)

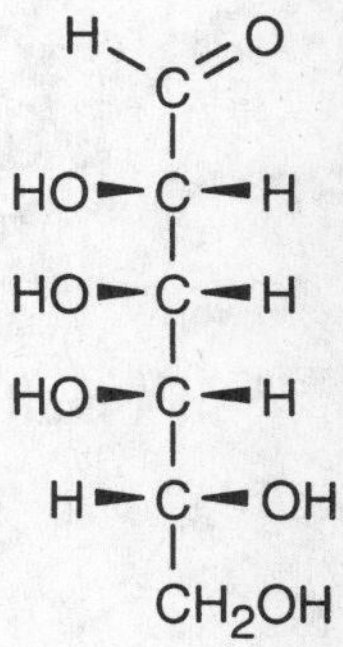

If the monosaccharide shown on the left were to look in the mirror, it would see monosaccharide (d), its enantiomer.

22.5 The bottom carbon is not chiral. The orientations of the hydroxyl groups bonded to the chiral carbons must be shown in order to indicate which stereoisomer is pictured.

22.6 The enantiomers are mirror images. The –OH bonded to the chiral carbon farthest from the carbonyl group points to the right in the D enantiomer and to the left in the L enantiomer.

(a) (b)

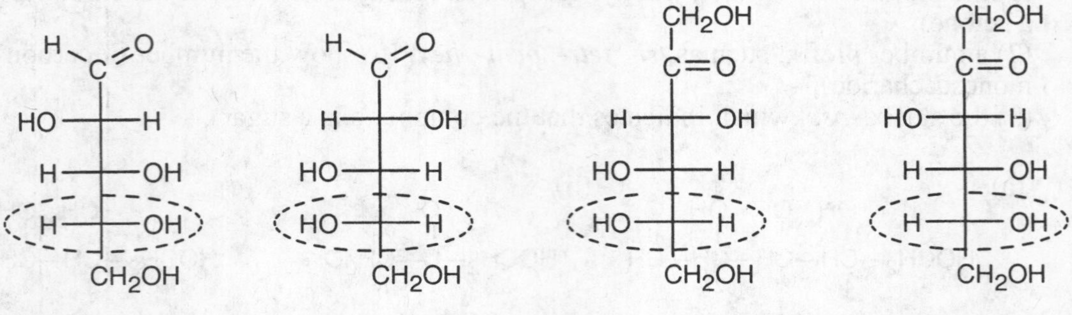

A D-aldopentose — An L-aldopentose — An L-ketohexose — A D-ketohexose

22.7 First, coil D-talose into a circular shape:

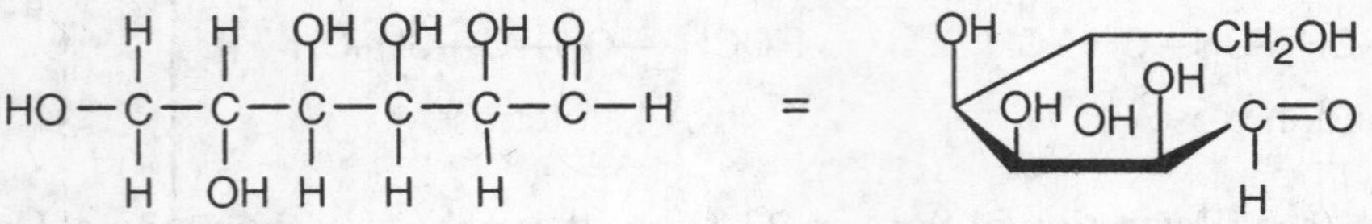

Next, rotate around the indicated single bond between C4 and C5 so that the —CH_2OH group (C6) points up.

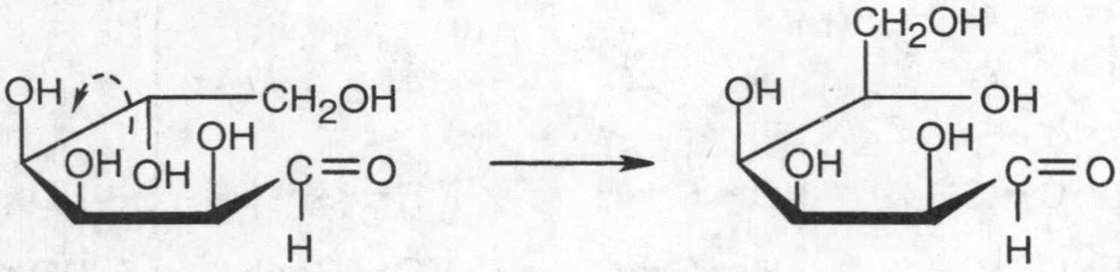

Finally, form a hemiacetal bond between the aldehyde and the —OH group at C5.

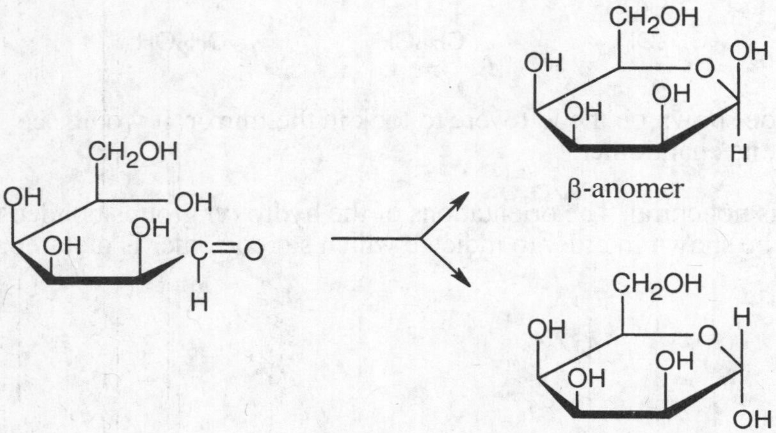

β-anomer

α-anomer

22.8 Reverse the series of steps shown in Problem 22.7. First, break the hemiacetal bond.

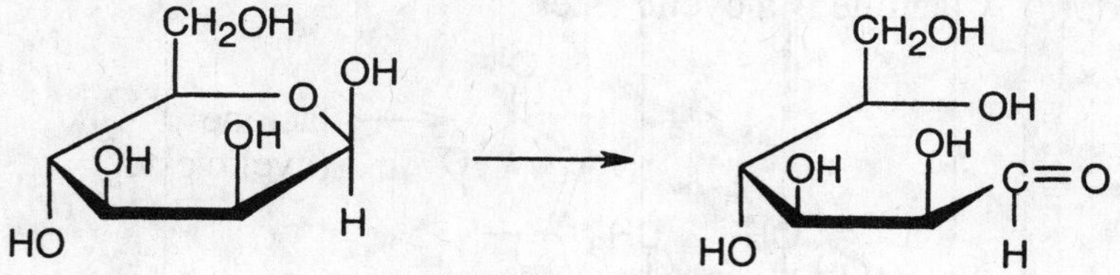

Rotate around the single bond between C4 and C5 so that the hydroxyl group on C5 points down.

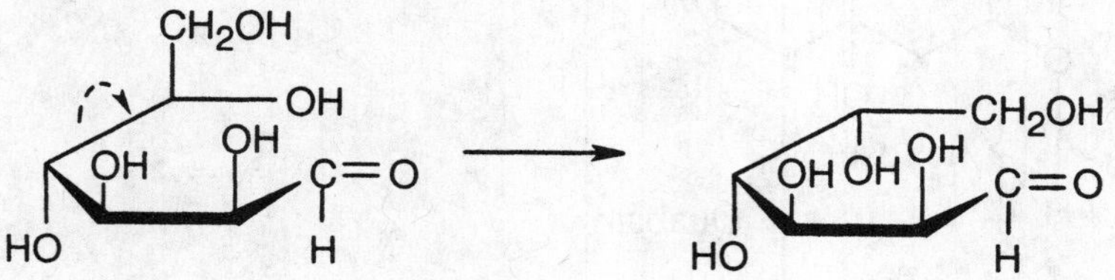

Uncoil D-mannose to arrive at the Fischer projection.

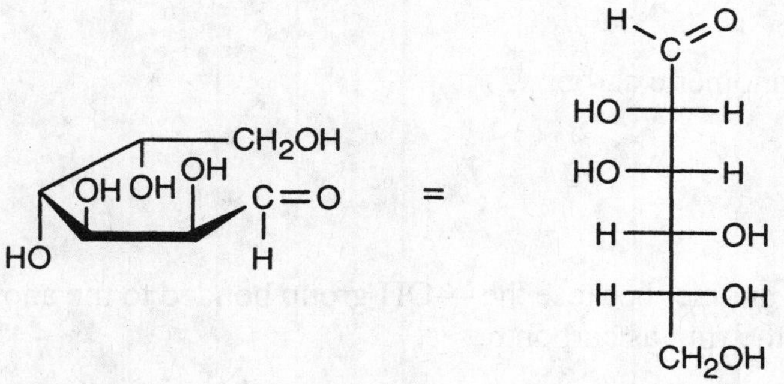

D-Mannose

22.9 (a) The monosaccharide is a hexose. It is an α-anomer because the anomeric oxygen is on the opposite side of the ring from carbon 6. (b) The tetracyclic ring system resembles the ring system of a steroid. (c) A lactone is a cyclic ester.

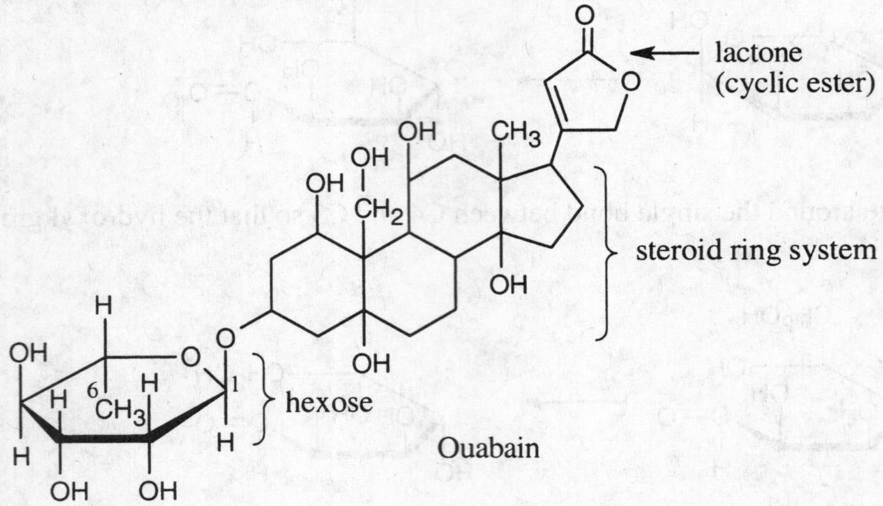
lactone
(cyclic ester)
steroid ring system
hexose

Ouabain

22.10

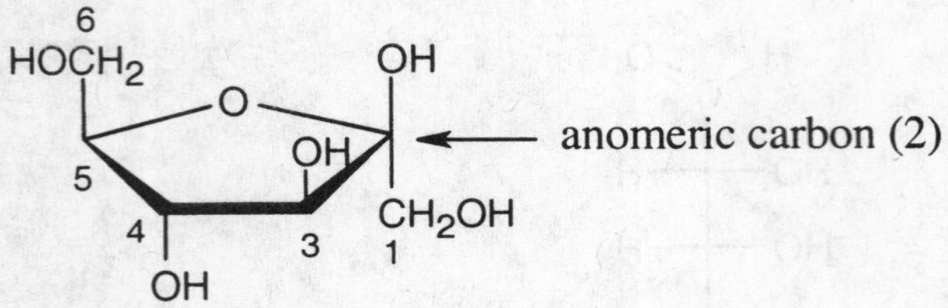
anomeric carbon (2)

The drawing represents the β anomer because the —OH group bonded to the anomeric carbon is on the same side of the ring as carbon 6.

22.11 Chiral carbons are starred. Remember that anomeric carbons and all other carbons bonded to four different groups are chiral.

(a)

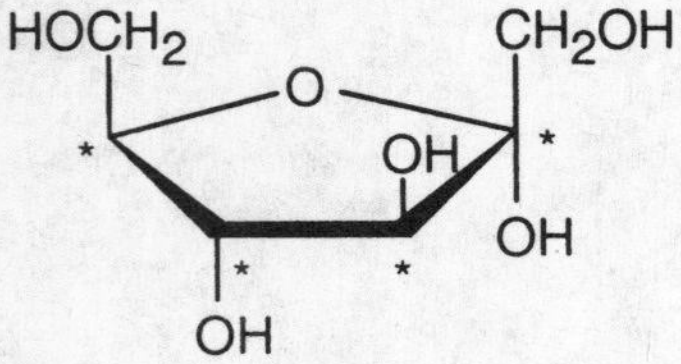

α-D-Fructose

(b)

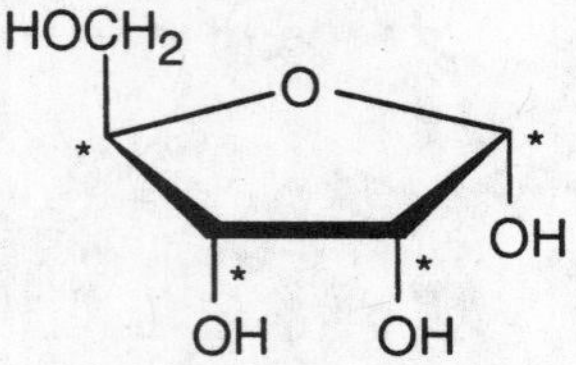

α-D-Ribose

(c)

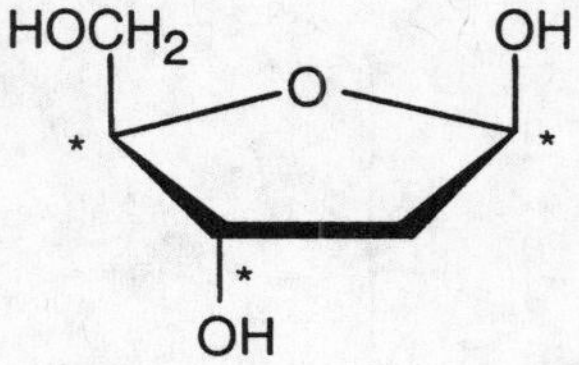

β-D-2-Deoxyribose

22.12

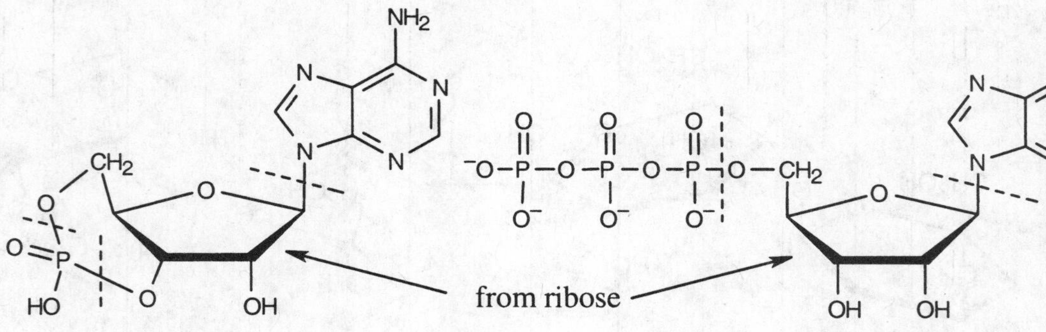
from ribose

cyclic AMP ATP

22.13

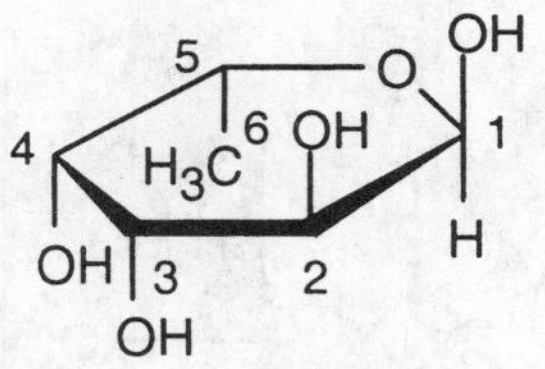

L-Fucose

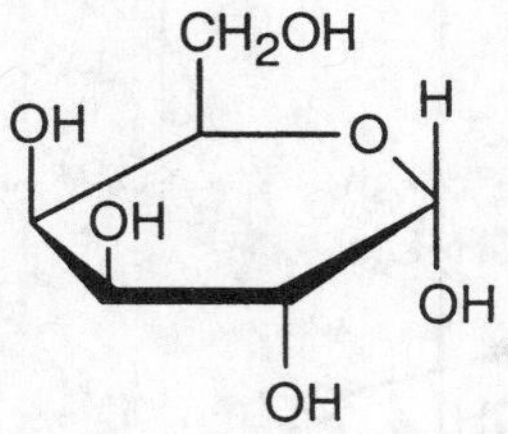

α-D-Galactose

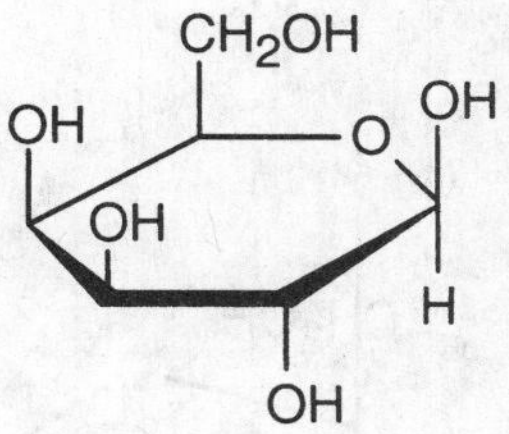

β-D-Galactose

(a) L-Fucose is an α anomer because the anomeric hydroxyl group is on the opposite side of the hemiacetal ring from carbon 6.

(b) L-Fucose is missing a hydroxyl group on carbon 6.

(c) The —OH group at carbon 2 that is below the plane of the ring in D-galactose is above the plane of the ring in L-fucose. The —OH groups that are above the plane of the ring in D-galactose are below the plane of the ring in L-fucose.

(d) 6-Deoxy-L-galactose is a correct name for L-fucose.

22.14

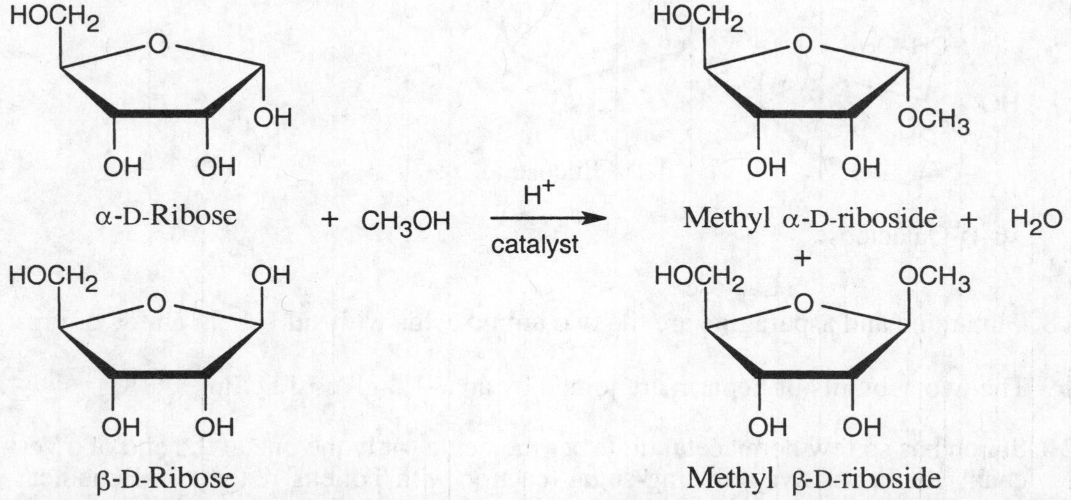
α-D-Ribose
+ CH3OH
H+
catalyst
Methyl α-D-riboside + H2O
+
β-D-Ribose
Methyl β-D-riboside

The two products are acetals because reaction with methanol occurs at the hemiacetal hydroxyl group, producing a compound with two —OR groups.

22.15 Cellobiose has a β-1,4 glycosidic link.

22.16

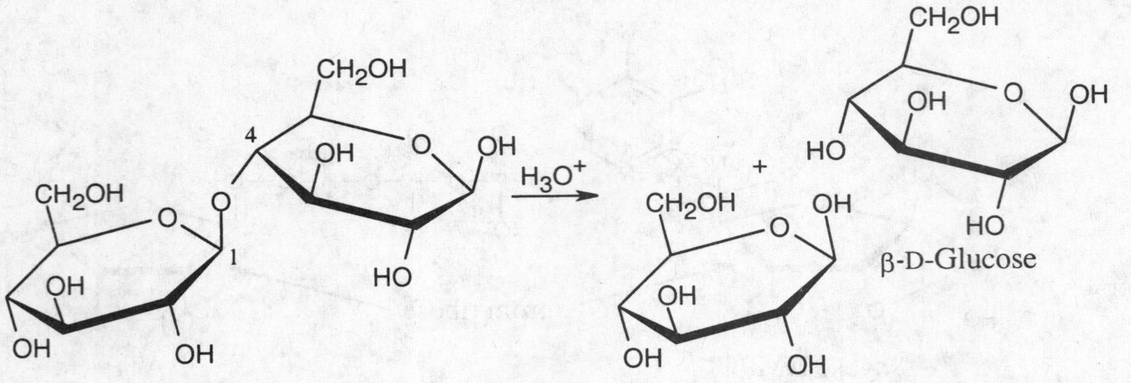

Cellobiose β-D-Glucose β-D-Glucose

22.17

(a)

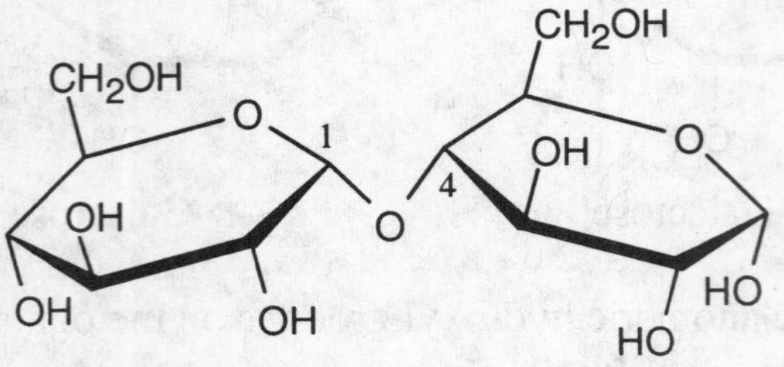

α-D-Glucose α-D-Glucose

Maltose

(b)

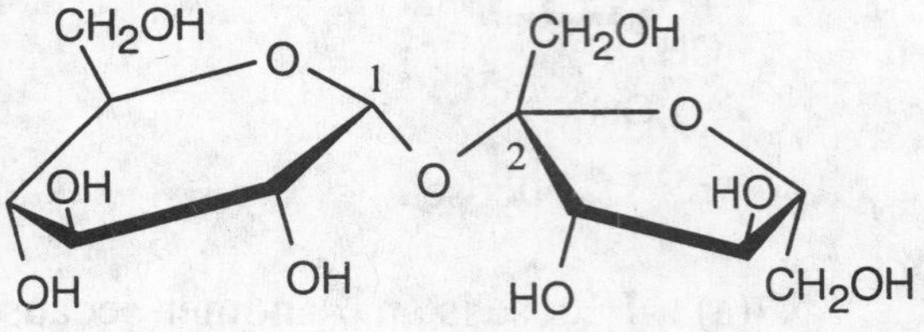

α-D-Glucose β-D-Fructose

Sucrose

(c)

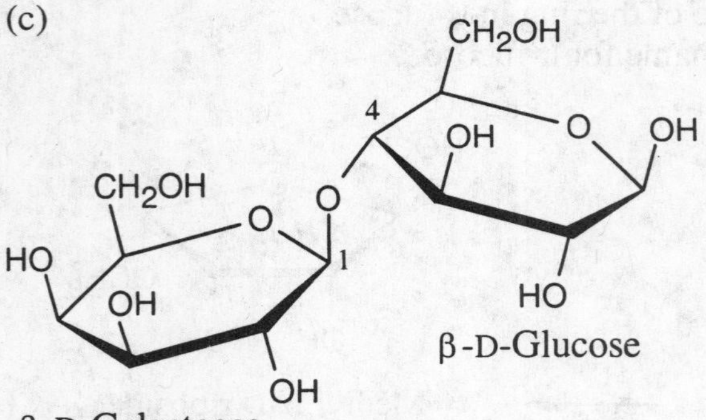

β-D-Galactcose β-D-Glucose

Lactose

22.18 Glutamine and asparagine are the two amino acids with side-chain amide groups.

22.19 The two subunits of heparin are joined by an α-1,4 glycosidic link.

22.20 Starch has so few hemiacetal units per molecule (only the one at the end of a very long chain) that a positive reducing-sugar reaction with Tollens' reagent or Benedict's reagent is undetectable.

Understanding Key Concepts

22.21

Starch $\xrightarrow{\text{Amylase}}$ Maltose $\xrightarrow{\text{Maltase}}$ Glucose

polysaccharide — disaccharide — monosaccharide

Starch is a large polysaccharide consisting of many glucose subunits connected by α-1,4 glycosidic bonds. α-Amylase hydrolyzes these bonds to yield maltose, a disaccharide, and maltase cleaves the α-1,4 glycosidic bond of maltose to give the monosaccharide glucose.

22.22 (a) The two fructose molecules are diastereomers and anomers; they are stereoisomers that aren't mirror images. (b) D-Galactose and L-galactose are enantiomers. (c) L-Allose and D-glucose are diastereomers.

22.23 (a), (b)

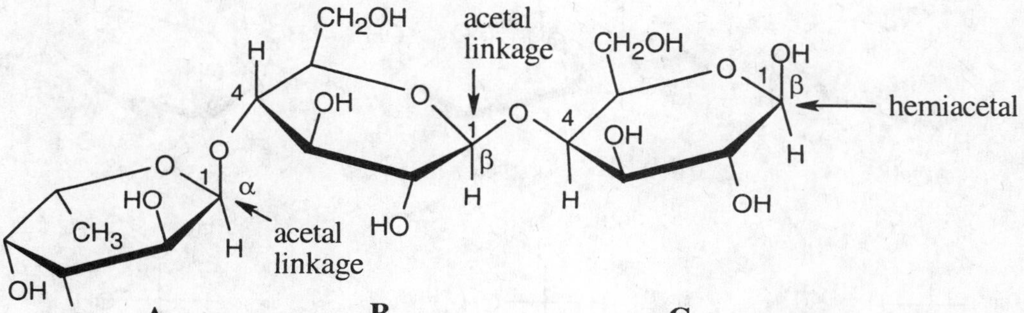
acetal linkage
hemiacetal
acetal linkage
CH_2OH
CH_3

A α anomer — **B** β anomer — **C** β anomer

(c) The linkage between monosaccharide **A** and monosaccharide **B** is an α-1,4 link that connects carbon 1 of **A** to carbon 4 of **B**.

(d) The linkage between monosaccharide **B** and monosaccharide **C** is an β-1,4 link that connects carbon 1 of **B** to carbon 4 of **C**.

22.24 (a) None of the three monosaccharides are identical, and none are enantiomers.

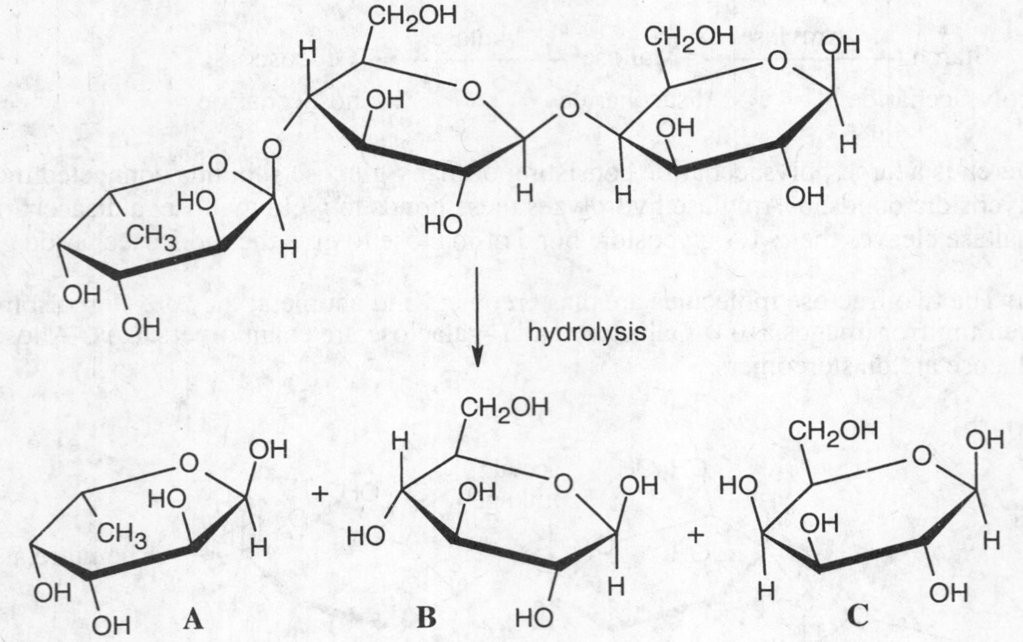
hydrolysis
A
B
C

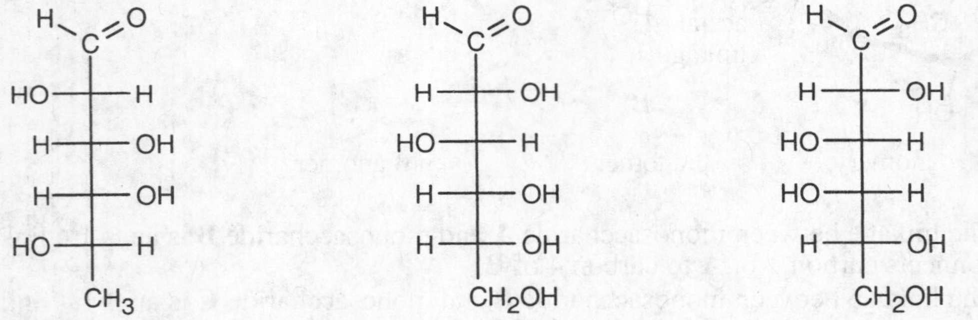

L-Fucose D-Glucose D-Galactose

22.25 Monosaccharide **C** (D-galactose) is oxidized by an oxidizing agent because it is the only one of the three monosaccharides that has a hemiacetal in equilibrium with an open-chain aldehyde. Isolation and identification of the resulting carboxylic acid also identifies the terminal hemiacetal monosaccharide.

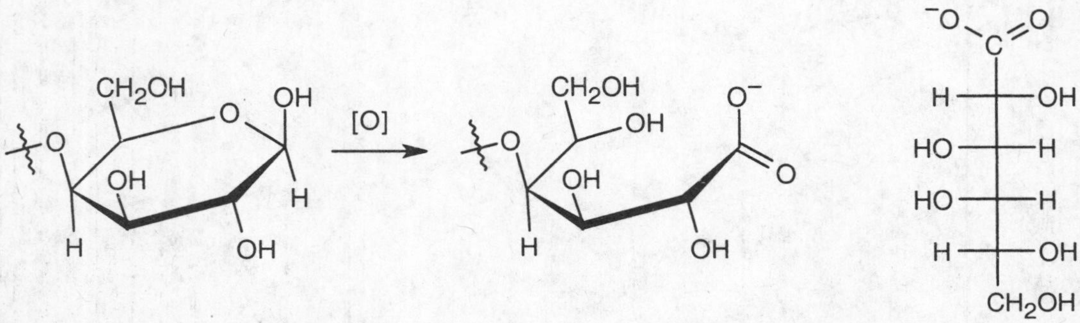
[O]

22.26 Monosaccharides **B** and **C** are the components of lactose, but **B** and **C** would have to be connected **C–B**, instead of **B–C**, in order for lactose to be part of the trisaccharide.

22.27

Polysaccharide	*Linkage*	*Branching?*
Cellulose	β-1,4	no
Amylose	α-1,4	no
Amylopectin	α-1,4	yes: α-1,6 branches occur ~ every 25 units
Glycogen	α-1,4	yes: even more α-1,6 branches than in amylopectin

22.28 In solution, an equilibrium exists between open-chain glucose and its cyclic hemiacetal forms. The open chain form reacts with the oxidizing agent, and, according to Le Châtelier's principle, the equilibrium shifts to produce more of the open-chain form, which is also oxidized. Ultimately, all of the glucose is oxidized to gluconate.

Classification and Structure of Carbohydrates

22.30 The family-name ending for a sugar is *-ose*.

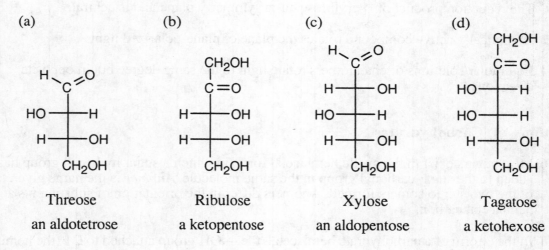

22.32

(a) (b) (c) (d)

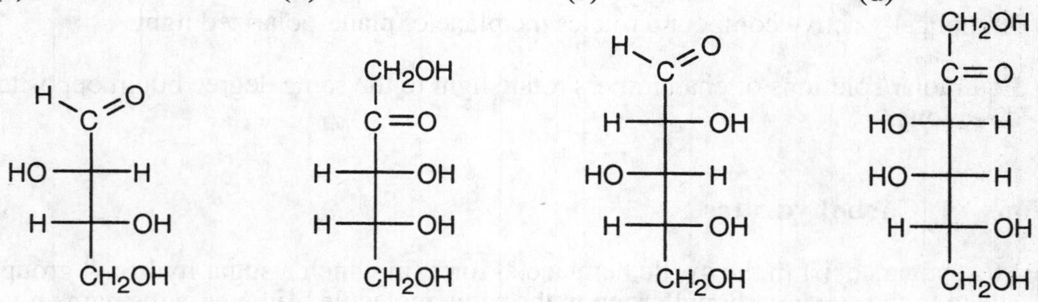

Threose, an aldotetrose | Ribulose, a ketopentose | Xylose, an aldopentose | Tagatose, a ketohexose

22.34

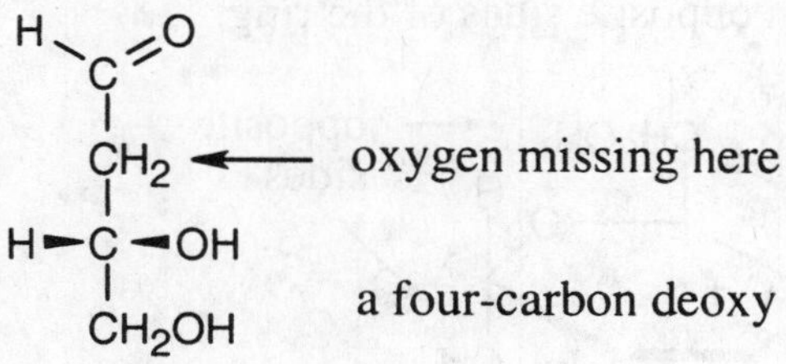
oxygen missing here

a four-carbon deoxy sugar

22.36 *Glucose* occurs in most food, especially fruits and vegetables, and in all living organisms.
Galactose occurs in brain tissue and as a component of lactose (milk sugar).
Fructose occurs in honey and in many fruits.
Ribose occurs in nucleic acids.

Handedness in Carbohydrates

22.38 *Enantiomers* are stereoisomers that are mirror images.

22.40

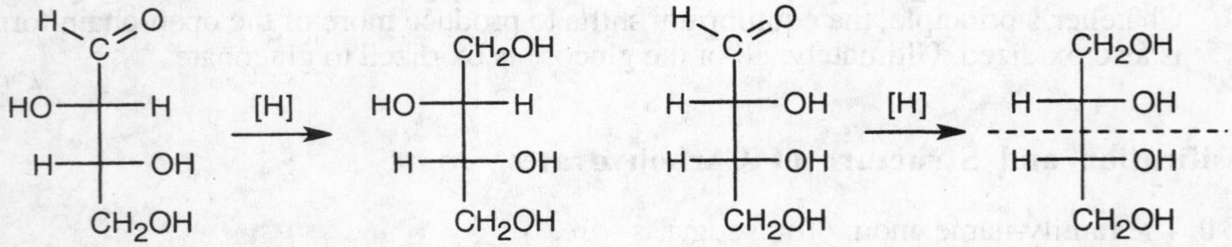
[H]
[H]

D-Threose chiral D-Erythrose achiral

The reduction product of D-erythrose has a symmetry plane and is achiral.

22.42 An optically active compound rotates the plane of plane-polarized light.

22.44 Equimolar solutions of enantiomers rotate light to the same degree but in opposite directions.

Reactions of Carbohydrates

22.46 Most sugars exist in the cyclic hemiacetal form, in which a sugar hydroxyl group has added to the sugar carbonyl group in the same molecule. *Anomer* is the name given to each of the two stereoisomers formed. Anomers differ in the orientation of substituents at the hemiacetal carbon.

22.48 In the β form of a carbohydrate hemiacetal, the —OH group attached to C1 (the hemiacetal carbon) is on the same side of the ring as the —CH_2OH group. In the α form, the —OH group at C1 and the —CH_2OH group are on opposite sides of the ring.

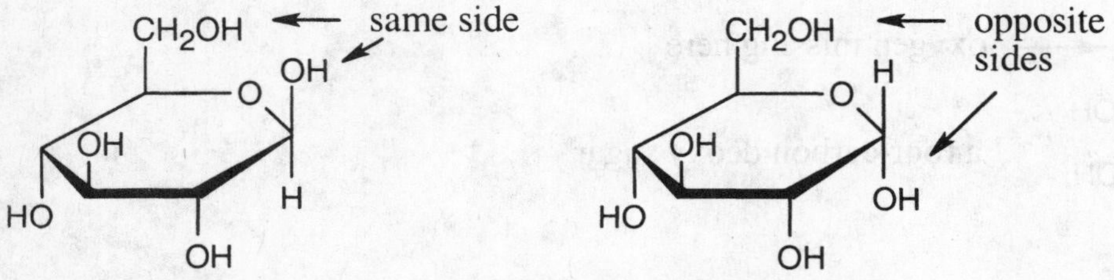
same side
opposite sides

a β anomer an α anomer

22.50

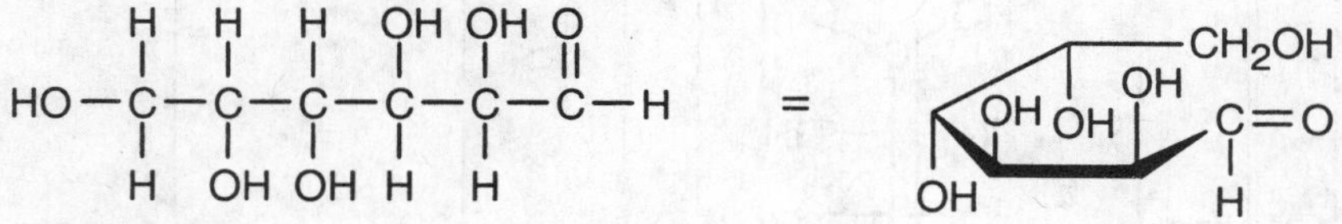

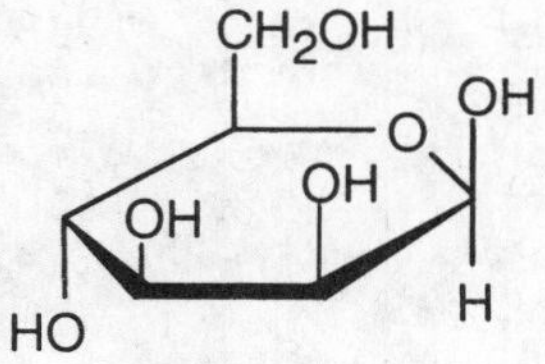

β-D-Mannose

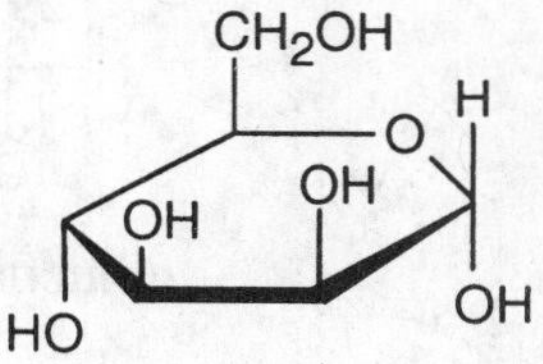

α-D-Mannose

22.52

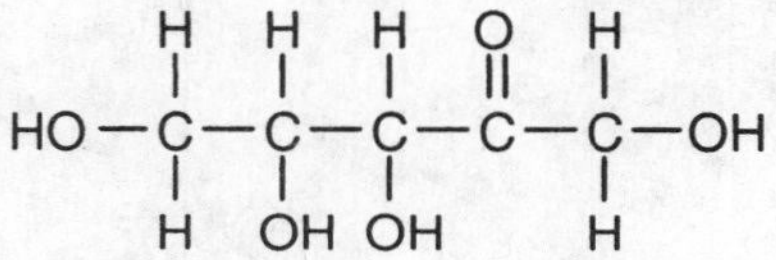

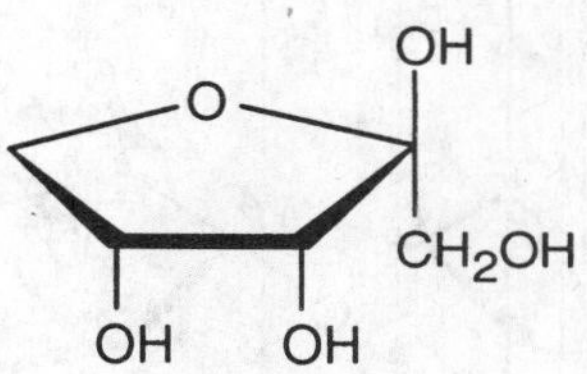

β-D-Ribulose

22.54

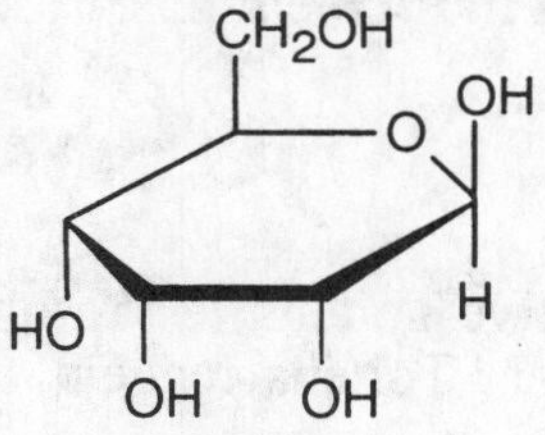

β-D-Allose

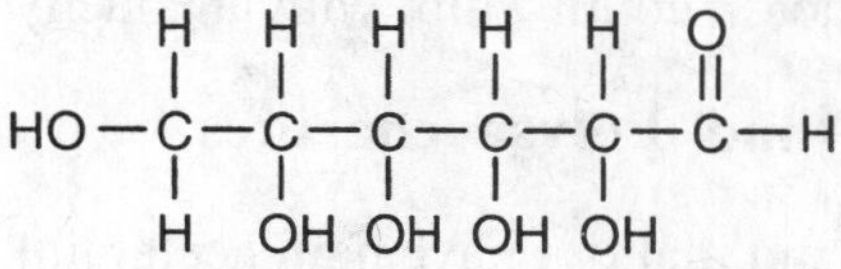

22.56

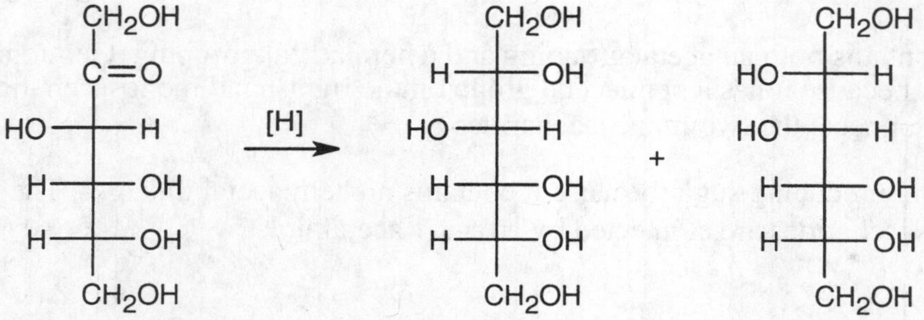

D-Fructose Sorbitol Mannitol

22.58

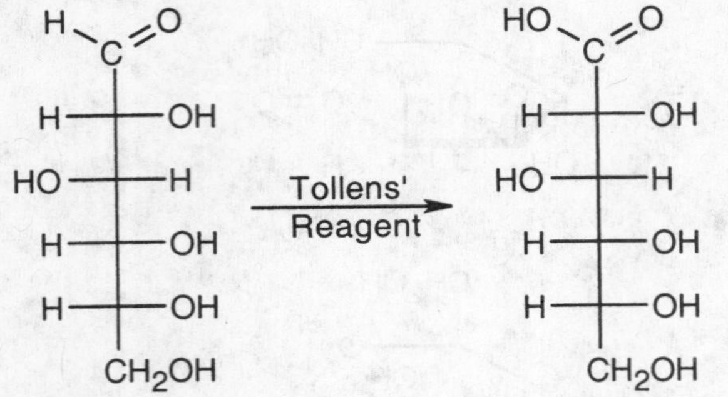
H
C
O
H
OH
HO
H
H
OH
H
OH
CH2OH
Tollens'
Reagent
HO
C
O
H
OH
HO
H
H
OH
H
OH
CH2OH

D-Glucose Gluconic acid

22.60 A *glycoside* is the acetal product that results from reaction of the hemiacetal —OH group of a carbohydrate with an alcohol.

22.62

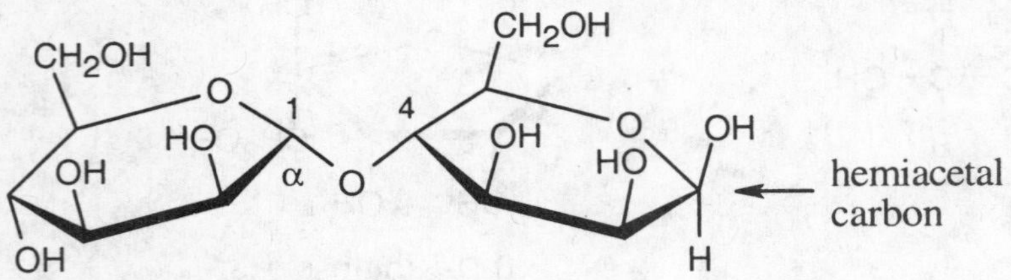
CH2OH
O
1
4
HO
OH
α
O
OH
CH2OH
O
OH
HO
H
OH
hemiacetal
carbon

The product in this problem has a cyclic hemiacetal carbon and is in equilibrium with an open-chain aldehyde that is a reducing sugar. The glycosides in Problem 22.61 are acetals and are not in equilibrium with an aldehyde.

Disaccharides and Polysaccharides

22.64 Lactose and maltose have hemiacetal linkages that give positive Tollens' test results. Sucrose has no hemiacetal group and is thus unreactive toward Tollens' reagent.

22.66 Amylose, a major component of the human diet, consists of α-D-glucose units linked by α-1,4 glycosidic bonds. Cellulose, used by plants as a structural material, consists of β-D-glucose units linked by β-1,4 glycosidic bonds.

22.68 Gentiobiose contains both an acetal grouping and a hemiacetal grouping. Gentiobiose is a reducing sugar because it has a hemiacetal group on the right-hand monosaccharide unit. A β-1,6 linkage connects the two monosaccharides.

22.70 Trehalose is a nonreducing sugar because it contains no hemiacetal linkages. The two D-glucose monosaccharides are connected by an α-1,1 acetal link

22.72

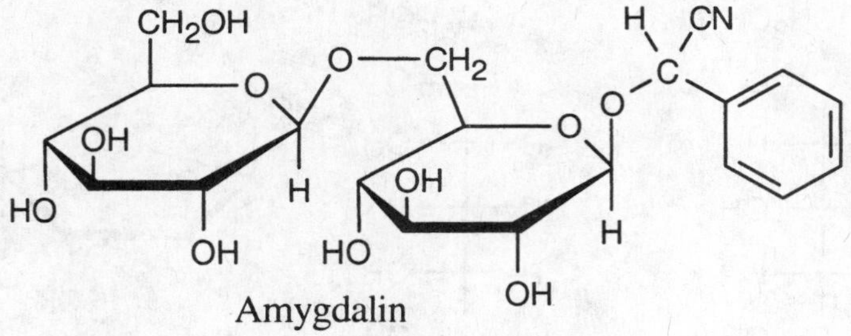

Amygdalin

Applications

22.74 Enzyme-catalyzed reactions are usually stereospecific and produce only one enantiomer of the compound of interest.

22.76 Starch, a polysaccharide, is an example of a complex carbohydrate in the diet. Glucose and fructose are simple carbohydrates found in the diet. Soluble and insoluble fiber are complex carbohydrates that can't be hydrolyzed to simple carbohydrates, and most of them pass undigested through the body.

22.78 Most of a plant cell wall is composed of cellulose (a polymer of β-D-glucose) in a matrix of pectin, lignin, and hemicellulose.

22.80 Penicillin inhibits the enzyme that synthesizes peptidoglycan polypeptide bridges. Since mammals don't contain this enzyme, penicillin doesn't harm mammalian cells.

22.82 People with type O blood can receive blood only from other donors that have type O blood. People with type AB blood can give blood only to other people with type AB blood because antibodies to AB blood are present in the blood of people having any of the other blood types.

22.84 Pectin and vegetable gum are two kinds of soluble fiber, which can be found in fruits, barley, oats, and beans.

General Questions and Problems

22.86

D-Ribose

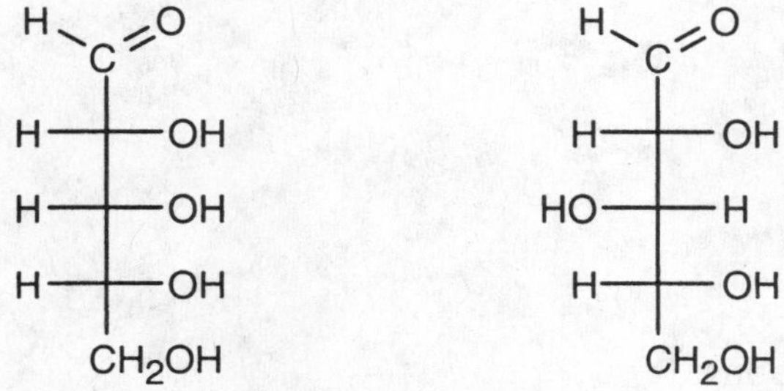

D-Xylose

D-Ribose and D-xylose are diastereomers and differ in all properties listed.

22.88

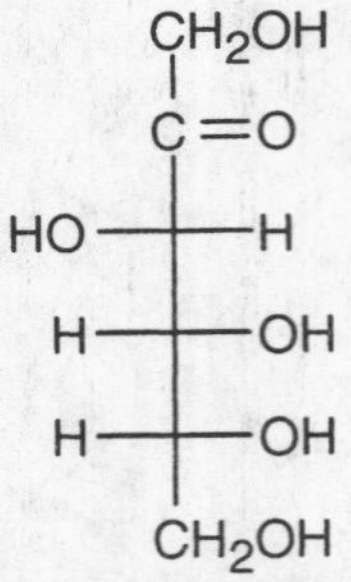

D-Fructose

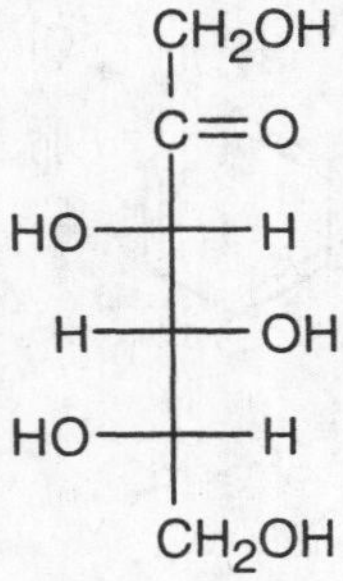

L-Sorbose

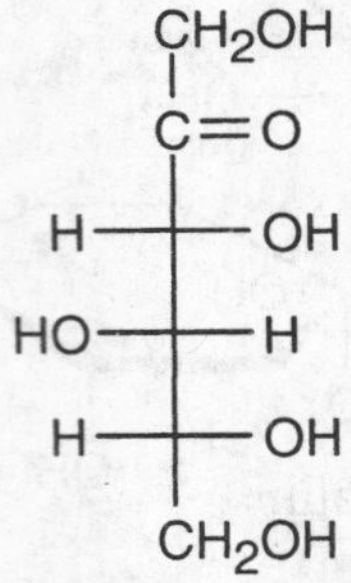

D-Sorbose

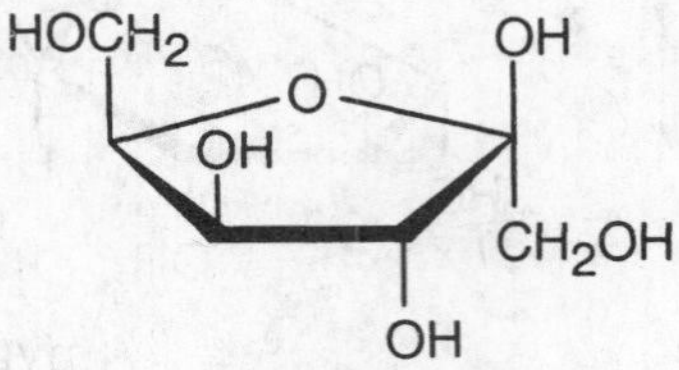

β-D-Sorbose

22.90

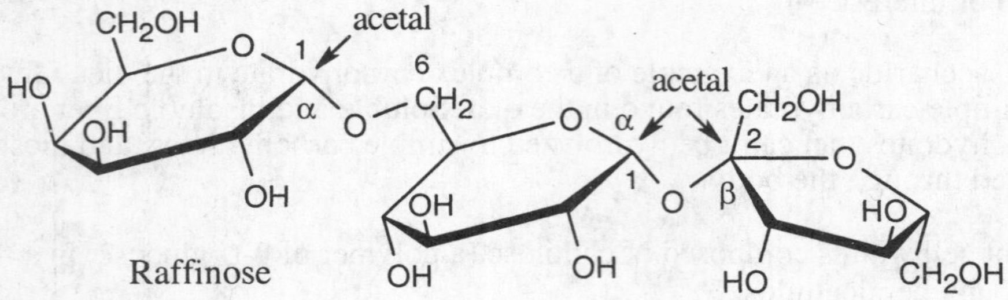

Raffinose

22.92 The sweet taste of a partially chewed cracker is due to the enzymatic breakdown of starch to glucose.

22.94 Lactose intolerance is an inability to digest lactose. Symptoms include bloating, cramps, and diarrhea.

22.96 Symptoms of the disease galactosemia, which results when the body lacks an enzyme needed to digest galactose, include

In infancy: vomiting, enlarged liver, failure to thrive

Eventual: liver failure, mental retardation, cataracts

22.98

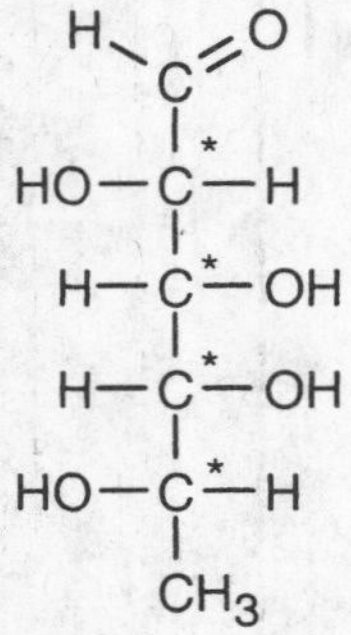

L-Fucose has four chiral carbons.

Self-Test for Chapter 22

Multiple Choice

1. One of these disaccharides is not a reducing sugar. Which one?
(a) sucrose (b) maltose (c) lactose (d) cellobiose

2. Which one of the following bonds doesn't occur in common polysaccharides?
(a) α-1,4 bonds (b) α-1,6 bonds (c) β-1,4 bonds (d) β-1,6 bonds

3. The compound shown is
(a) The α anomer of a ketopentose (b) the α anomer of an aldohexose (c) the β anomer of an aldopentose (d) the β anomer of a ketohexose

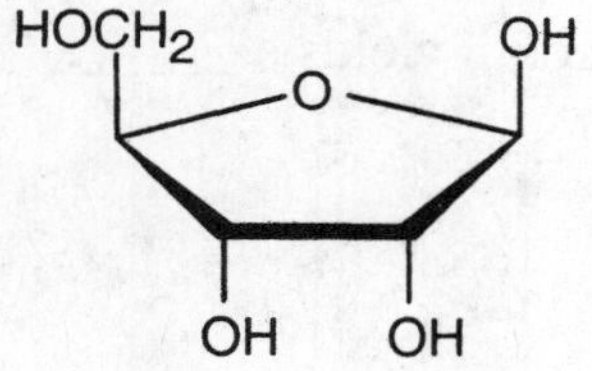

HOCH2
OH
O
OH
OH

4. Oxidation of the aldotetroses pictured in Section 22.2 can be controlled to produce dicarboxylic acids known as tartaric acids. How many stereoisomeric tartaric acids are there?
(a) 1 (b) 2 (c) 3 (d) 4

5. *N*-Acetyl-D-glucosamine is a component of all of the following, except
(a) chitin (b) blood group determinants (c) tendons (d) heparin

6. Humans can't digest cellulose because
(a) Its molecules are too big. (b) Humans don't produce enzymes to digest polysaccharides. (c) Humans can't digest branched polysaccharides. (d) Human enzymes that digest carbohydrates can only hydrolyze α glycosidic bonds.

7. Which blood group is the "universal donor"?
(a) A (b) B (c) AB (d) O

8. Which of the following polysaccharides consists of only α-1,4 glycosidic bonds?
(a) amylopectin (b) cellulose (c) amylose (d) glycogen

9. Which of these errors of carbohydrate metabolism is not life-threatening?
(a) galactosemia (b) lactose intolerance (c) diabetes mellitus (d) blood-group incompatibility

10 How many stereoisomers does an open-chain 2-ketopentose have?
(a) 2 (b) 4 (c) 6 (d) 8

Sentence Completion

1. An object that has handedness is said to be _____.
2. Starch molecules are digested by enzymes called _____.
3. The two mirror image forms of a chiral molecule are called _____.
4. A reaction between an aldehyde carbonyl group and an alcohol hydroxyl group in the same molecule yields a _____ _____.
5. *Levulose* is another name for _____.
6. _____ and _____ are two kinds of starch.
7. The reaction of a monosaccharide with an alcohol yields a _____.
8. _____ is used for food storage in animals.
9. D-Glucose can be classified as a _____.
10. 3-Pentanol is an _____ molecule.
11. A ______ is a stereoisomer that is not an enantiomer.
12. ________have important functions at cell surfaces.

True or False

1. All naturally-occurring carbohydrates are chiral.
2. Glucose is a reducing sugar.
3. In an L sugar, the —OH on the carbon nearest to the carbonyl group points to the left.
4. Humans can digest polysaccharides containing β-1,4 acetal links but not α-1,4 acetal links.
5. Achiral objects possess a plane of symmetry.
6. Crystalline glucose is a mixture of α anomer, β anomer, and open-chain forms.
7. Sucrose contains both acetal and hemiacetal groups.
8. Amylopectin and glycogen contain 1,4 and 1,6 acetal links.
9. An acetal is an ester.
10. Maltose is a disaccharide composed of glucose and galactose.
11. Two diastereomers rotate plane-polarized light in equal amounts but in opposite directions.
12. Not all compounds with n chiral carbons have 2^n stereoisomers.

Match each entry on the left with its partner on the right.

1. Maltose	(a) Aldohexose
2. Cellulose	(b) Glucose
3. Methyl glucoside	(c) Aldotriose
4. Ribose	(d) Glucose + fructose
5. Fructose	(e) Glucose + glucose
6. Glycogen	(f) Polysaccharide of α-D-glucose
7. Dextrose	(g) Galactose + glucose
8. Glucose	(h) Aldopentose
9. Sucrose	(i) Ketohexose
10. Lactose	(j) Acetal
11. Glyceraldehyde	(k) Animal starch
12. Amylose	(l) Polysaccharide of β-D-glucose

Chapter 23 – Carbohydrate Metabolism

Chapter Outline

I. Introduction to carbohydrate metabolism (Sections 23.1–23.2).
   A. Digestion of carbohydrates (Section 23.1).
      1. Digestion is the breakdown of food into small molecules.
      2. The products of digestion are absorbed from the intestinal tract.
      3. Digestion of carbohydrates.
         a. α–Amylase in the mouth breaks starch into smaller polysaccharides and maltose.
         b. α–Amylase in the small intestine further breaks down polysaccharides.
         c. Disaccharides are broken down to monosaccharides in the small intestine.
   B. Overview of glucose metabolism (Section 23.2).
      1. *Glycolysis* is the conversion of glucose to pyruvate; it occurs when energy is needed.
      2. *Glycogenesis* is the synthesis of glycogen from glucose; it occurs when excess glucose is present.
      3. The *pentose phosphate pathway* supplies other monosaccharides; it occurs when these are in short supply.
      4. *Glycogenolysis* is the breakdown of glycogen to glucose units; it occurs when the body needs glucose.
      5. Pyruvate has several fates:
         a. Under normal circumstances, pyruvate is converted to acetyl-SCoA.
         b. When oxygen is lacking, pyruvate is converted to lactate.
         c. When the body is starved for glucose, pyruvate is converted to glucose via *gluconeogenesis*.

II. Glycolysis and pyruvate metabolism (Sections 23.3–23.6).
   A. Glycolysis is the breakdown of glucose to two pyruvates (Section 23.3).
      Glycolysis occurs in the cytosol.
   B. Steps in glycolysis:
      1. Steps 1–3: Phosphorylation.
         a. Step 1: Glucose moves into the cell and is converted to glucose 6-phosphate, with the expenditure of one ATP.
         b. Step 2: Glucose 6-phosphate is isomerized to fructose 6-phosphate.
         c. Step 3: Fructose 6-phosphate is converted to fructose 1,6-bisphosphate, with the expenditure of one ATP.
      2. Steps 4, 5: Cleavage and isomerization.
         a. Step 4: Fructose 1,6-bisphosphate is cleaved to glyceraldehyde 3-phosphate and dihydroxyacetone phosphate.
         b. Step 5: Dihydroxyacetone phosphate is isomerized to glyceraldehyde 3-phosphate.
      3. Steps 6–10: Energy generation.
         a. Step 6: Glyceraldehyde 3-phosphate is phosphorylated and oxidized to 1,3-bisphosphoglycerate: NAD^+ —> $NADH/H^+$.
         b. Step 7: 1,3-Bisphosphoglycerate transfers a phosphate to ADP to yield 3-phosphoglycerate.
         c. Step 8: 3-Phosphoglycerate is isomerized to 2-phosphoglycerate.
         d. Step 9: 2-Phosphoglycerate is dehydrated to phosphoenolpyruvate.
         e. Step 10: Phosphoenolpyruvate transfers a phosphate group to ADP to yield ATP and pyruvate.
   C. End results of glycolysis.
      1. Conversion of glucose to 2 pyruvates.
      2. Production of 2 ATP.
      3. Production of 2 $NADH/H^+$.

D. Entry of other sugars into glycolysis (Section 23.4).
   1. Fructose is converted to fructose 6-phosphate and enters glycolysis.
   2. Mannose is converted to fructose 6-phosphate and enters glycolysis.
   3. Galactose is converted to glucose 6-phosphate and enters glycolysis.
E. Pyruvate metabolism (Section 23.5).
   1. When oxygen is available, pyruvate is converted to acetyl-SCoA, with the conversion of NAD^+ to $NADH/H^+$ and the production of CO_2.
   2. When glucose is in short supply, pyruvate can be converted back to glucose by gluconeogenesis.
   3. Under anaerobic conditions, pyruvate is reduced to lactate, and $NADH/H^+$ is converted to NAD^+.
   4. In yeast, pyruvate is converted to ethanol and CO_2.
F. Energy output in complete catabolism of glucose (Section 23.6).
   1. The total energy output from glucose metabolism is the combined result of
      a. Glycolysis.
      b. Pyruvate —> acetyl-SCoA.
      c. Citric acid cycle of two acetyl-SCoA molecules (and passage of the resulting reduced coenzymes through the respiratory chain).
      d. Passage of two reduced coenzymes from glycolysis through the respiratory chain.
   2. The number of ATP produced depends on
      a. The number of electrons that enter the respiratory chain from reduced coenzymes.
      b. The number of ATP produced per reduced coenzyme.
      c. An estimated 30–38 ATP are produced per mol glucose catabolized.

III. Regulation of glucose metabolism (Sections 23.7–23.9).
A. Regulation of glucose concentration in the blood (Section 23.7).
   1. Hypoglycemia: low blood sugar.
      The hormone glucagon stimulates breakdown of glycogen to glucose to raise blood sugar.
   2. Hyperglycemia: high blood sugar.
      The hormone insulin stimulates passage of glucose into cells to be used in energy production.
B. Fasting and starvation (Section 23.8).
   1. First, glucose is released from glycogen.
   2. Then, glucose is synthesized from proteins via gluconeogenesis.
   3. Then, fats are metabolized to acetyl-SCoA, which enters the citric acid cycle.
   4. As the citric acid cycle is overloaded, acetyl-SCoA is removed by formation of ketone bodies.
   5. Ultimately, the body produces 50% of ATP from ketone bodies.
   6. The body can endure this state for months.
C. *Diabetes mellitus* (Section 23.9).
   1. There are two types of *diabetes mellitus*.
      a. In Type I (juvenile), the pancreas produces insufficient insulin.
         i. Juvenile diabetes is an autoimmune disease, in which insulin-producing cells are destroyed.
         ii. Juvenile diabetes is treated by supplying insulin.
      b. In Type II (adult-onset), insulin doesn't aid the passage of glucose across the cell membrane.
         i. Adult-onset diabetes results when cell receptors fail to recognize insulin.
         ii. Drugs that increase insulin levels are an effective treatment.
   2. Complications of diabetes.
      a. Cataracts may result from buildup of sorbitol in the eye.
      b. Ketoacidosis is caused by buildup of acidic ketones.
      c. Hypoglycemia may be due to an overdose of insulin or to failure to eat.

IV. Other pathways of carbohydrate metabolism (Sections 23.10, 23.11).
   A. Glycogen metabolism (Section 23.10).
      1. Glycogenesis.
         a. Glycogenesis occurs when glucose levels are high.
         b. The pathway to glycogen synthesis:
            Glucose —> Glucose 6-phosphate —> Glucose 1-phosphate —>
            Glucose-UDP —> Glycogen
      2. Glycogenolysis.
         a. Glycogenolysis occurs when there is an immediate need for energy.
         b The pathway of glycogenolysis:
            Glycogen —> Glucose 1-phosphate —> Glucose 6-phosphate —> Glucose
   B. Gluconeogenesis (Section 23.11).
      1. Gluconeogenesis is the synthesis of glucose from any of several small molecules, including lactate, pyruvate, amino acids, and glycerol.
      2. Gluconeogenesis occurs when the body is starved for glucose.
      3. Seven of the steps of gluconeogenesis are reversals of glycolysis steps.
         a. The other three steps are too endergonic, and alternate pathways must be used.
         b. Step 1 of gluconeogenesis:
            Pyruvate —> Oxaloacetate —> Phosphoenolpyruvate
         c. Oxaloacetate is an intermediate that allows amino acids to enter gluconeogenesis.

Solutions to Chapter 23 Problems

23.1 (a) *Glycogenolysis* is the release of glucose units from glycogen.

(b) *Gluconeogenesis* is the synthesis of glucose from lactate or other noncarbohydrates.

(c) *Glycogenesis* is the synthesis of glycogen from glucose.

23.2 The following synthetic pathways have glucose 6-phosphate as their first reactant:
Glycogenesis: synthesis of glycogen from glucose
Pentose phosphate pathway: synthesis of five-carbon sugars from glucose
Glycolysis: conversion of glucose to pyruvate

23.3 (1) In *Step 6*, 1,3-bisphosphoglycerate is synthesized. In *Step 7*, the energy is harvested in ATP as 3-phosphoglycerate is formed.

(2) In *Step 9*, phosphoenolpyruvate is synthesized. In *Step 10*, the energy is harvested in ATP as pyruvate is formed.

23.4 The following steps of glycolysis are isomerizations:
Step 2: Glucose 6-phosphate → Fructose 6-phosphate
Step 5: Dihydroxyacetone phosphate → Glyceraldehyde 3-phosphate
Step 8: 3-Phosphoglycerate → 2-Phosphoglycerate

23.5

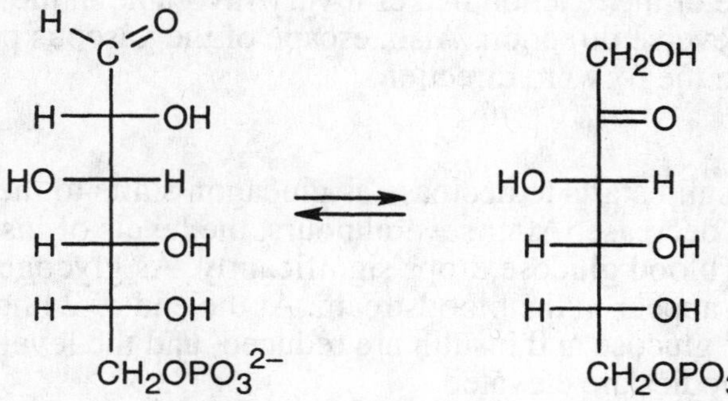

H
C
O
H
OH
HO
H
H
OH
H
OH
$CH_2OPO_3^{2-}$
CH_2OH
O
HO
H
H
OH
H
OH
$CH_2OPO_3^{2-}$

Glucose 6-phosphate Fructose 6-phosphate

23.6 (a) Pyruvate is oxidized to a greater extent than glucose because it has two carbon–oxygen double bonds.
(b) Oxidation occurs *Step 6*, in which glyceraldehyde 3-phosphate is oxidized and phosphorylated to give 1,3 bisphosphoglycerate. NAD^+ is the oxidizing agent.

23.7

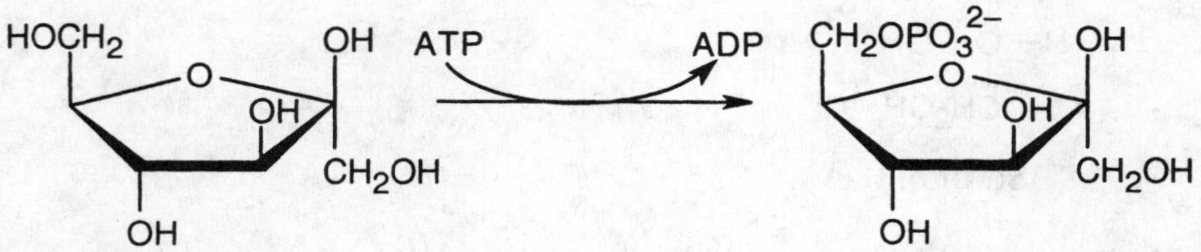

$HOCH_2$
O
OH
OH
CH_2OH
OH
ATP
ADP
$CH_2OPO_3^{2-}$
O
OH
OH
CH_2OH
OH

Fructose Fructose 6-phosphate

Fructose 6-phosphate enters glycolysis at *Step 3*.

23.8

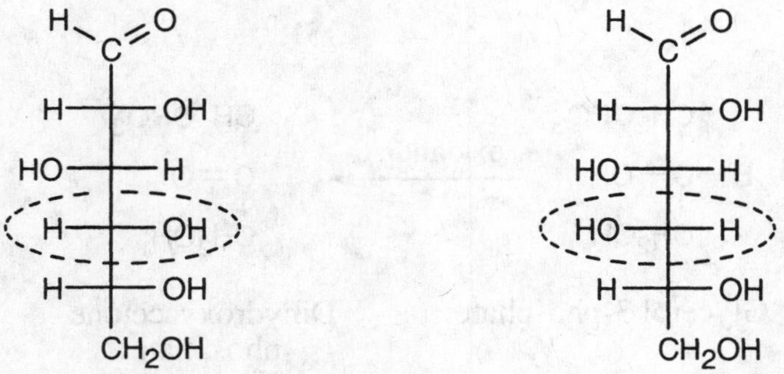

H
C
O
H
OH
HO
H
H
OH
H
OH
CH_2OH
H
C
O
H
OH
HO
H
HO
H
H
OH
CH_2OH

D-Glucose D-Galactose

Glucose and galactose differ in configuration at carbon 4.

23.9 (a) The remaining energy escapes as heat.
(b) The exergonic nature of the reaction makes it very favorable in the forward direction and unfavorable in the reverse direction. Also, escape of the gaseous product drives the reaction to completion in the forward direction.

23.10 As starvation begins, insulin starts to decrease as glucagon starts to increase, while liver glycogen begins a rapid decrease. After several hours, the levels of insulin and glucagon continue to change, and blood glucose drops significantly. As glycogen is used up, fatty acids and ketone bodies appear in the bloodstream. At the end of 24 hours, liver glycogen is depleted, the levels of glucose and insulin are reduced, and the levels of glucagon, free fatty acids, and ketone bodies are elevated.

23.11

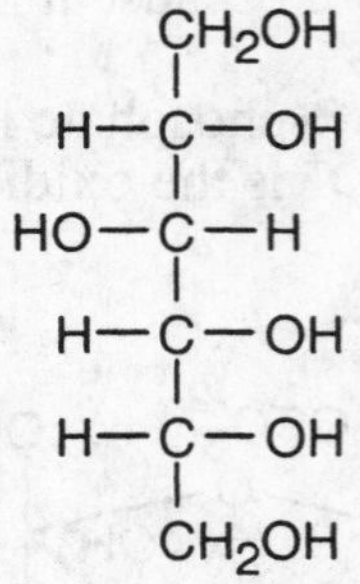

Sorbitol

Sorbitol can't form a cyclic hemiacetal because it doesn't have a carbonyl group.

23.12 (a) The increase in $[H^+]$ drives the equilibrium shown in Section 23.9 to the right, causing the production of CO_2.
(b) This effect is an example of Le Châtelier's principle.

23.13

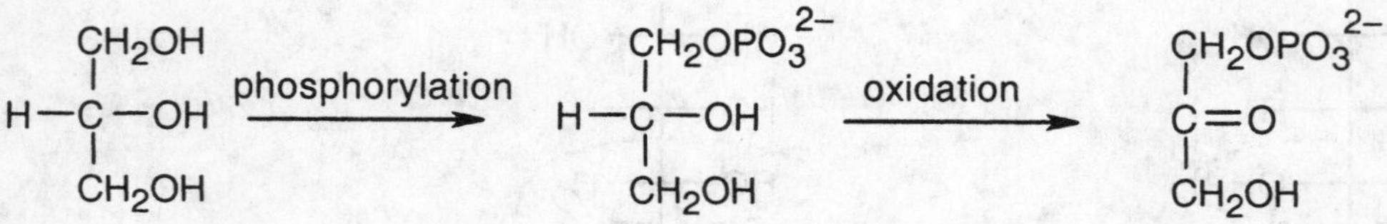
phosphorylation
oxidation

Glycerol   Glycerol 3-phosphate   Dihydroxyacetone phosphate

Understanding Key Concepts

23.14 Most of the enzymes involved with digestion are hydrolases, which catalyze the hydrolysis bonds in large molecules to produce smaller molecules.

23.15 (a) *Glycolysis* occurs when the body needs energy and the supply of glucose is adequate.
(b) *Hydrolysis to free glucose* takes place in the liver when free glucose is needed in cells in other parts of the body. (Only free glucose can be transported in the blood.)
(c) The *pentose phosphate pathway* operates when either ribose 5-phosphate or the reduced coenzyme NADPH is needed.
(d) *Glycogenesis* occurs when the concentration of glucose in the blood is high and the body doesn't need glucose for energy production.

23.16 The energy investments made when glucose is converted to glucose 6-phosphate (Step 1) and when fructose 1-phosphate is converted to fructose 1,6-bisphosphate (Step 3) produce the phosphorylated intermediates needed in later stages of glycolysis. These intermediates take part in the reactions that ultimately repay the initial energy investment. Cleavage of fructose 1,6-bisphosphate at Step 4 generates the two three-carbon molecules whose transformations result in the formation of pyruvate.

23.17 (a) Pyruvate enters into the *citric acid cycle* when the body needs energy. To enter the cycle, pyruvate is first converted to acetyl-SCoA in mitochondria.
(b) In yeast, pyruvate yields *ethanol and* CO_2 in the absence of oxygen.
(c) Pyruvate is *converted to lactate* in muscles and in red blood cells, under anaerobic conditions.
(d) Pyruvate is directed to *gluconeogenesis* when the body needs glucose and both glucose and glycogen are in short supply. Gluconeogenesis takes place in the liver.

23.18

Step	*Enzyme*	*Class*
1	Hexokinase	transferase
2	Glucose 6-phosphate isomerase	isomerase
3	Phosphofructokinase	transferase
4	Aldolase	lyase
5	Triose phosphate isomerase	isomerase
6	Glyceraldehyde 3-phosphate dehydrogenase	oxidoreductase, transferase
7	Phosphoglycerate kinase	transferase
8	Phosphoglycerate mutase	isomerase
9	Enolase	lyase
10	Pyruvate kinase	transferase

Transferases are the most common class of enzymes in glycolysis because several reactions involve phosphate transfers to ADP and from ATP. Ligases are not represented among the enzymes of glycolysis because ligases are involved with the synthesis of larger molecules from smaller molecules, with the expenditure of ATP. Glycolysis is a pathway for the breakdown of larger molecules to smaller molecules, with the eventual generation of ATP.

23.19 (1) Insulin levels rise (g).
(2) Glucose is absorbed by cells (c).
(3) Glycolysis replenishes ATP supplies (b).
(4) Glycogen synthesis occurs (glycogenesis) if there is excess glucose (e).
(5) Blood levels pass through normal to below normal (hypoglycemic) (f).
(6) Glucagon is secreted (a).
(7) The liver releases glucose into the bloodstream (d).

23.20 In the absence of oxygen, the pyruvate product of catabolism of glucose in wine is fermented by yeast enzymes to ethanol and CO_2, which increased the pressure in the bottle and popped the cork.

23.21 Compounds available for gluconeogenesis include pyruvate, lactate, many amino acids, glycerol, and intermediates of the citric acid cycle, especially oxaloacetate. The conversion of fatty acids to glucose occurs in plants, where fatty acids stored in seeds can be used as a source of carbohydrates after germination. Unlike plants, animals don't need carbohydrates as structural materials and are able to obtain all the carbohydrates they need from food.

23.22 (a) No. Molecular oxygen is not involved in any of the steps of glycolysis.
(b) Molecular oxygen is used in electron transport, where it combines with hydrogen ions and with electrons from coenzymes (reduced in the citric acid cycle) to produce water. The reoxidized coenzymes can reenter the citric acid cycle or can be used in glycolysis.

Digestion and Metabolism

23.24 $\text{Sucrose} + H_2O \xrightarrow{\text{Sucrase}} \text{Glucose} + \text{Fructose}$

This process occurs in the mucous lining of the small intestine.

23.26 The major monosaccharide products of digestion are glucose, fructose, and galactose.

23.28 Under aerobic conditions, pyruvate forms acetyl-SCoA.
Under anaerobic conditions, pyruvate forms lactate.
Under fermentation conditions, pyruvate forms ethanol and CO_2.

23.30 *Glycolysis* is the metabolic pathway that catabolizes glucose to pyruvate.
Gluconeogenesis is the process that synthesizes glucose from small molecules when glucose is in short supply.

23.32 In *gluconeogenesis*, glucose is synthesized from small molecules; in *glycogenesis*, glycogen is synthesized from glucose.

23.34

If the Body Needs	*Fate of Intermediates in Pentose Phosphate Pathway*
NADPH	Pentose phosphate intermediates are recycled to glucose 6-phosphate for further production of NADPH.
ATP	Fructose 6-phosphate and glyceraldehyde 3-phosphate (pentose phosphate intermediates) enter glycolysis.
Nucleic acid synthesis	Ribose 5-phosphate is the major product.

Glycolysis

23.36 Pyruvate is the final product of glycolysis. ATP is also formed in the final reaction. NADH is a by-product of an earlier reaction of glycolysis.

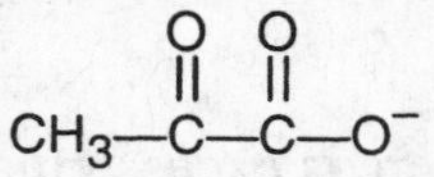

Pyruvate

23.38

Enzyme	*Catalyzes*
(a) Hexokinase	Glucose → Glucose 6-phosphate
(b) Phosphoglycerate mutase	3-Phosphoglycerate → 2-Phosphoglycerate
(c) Glyceraldehyde 3-phosphate dehydrogenase	Glyceraldehyde 3-phosphate → 1,3-Bisphosphoglycerate
(d) Pyruvate kinase	Phosphoenolpyruvate → Pyruvate
(e) Aldolase	Fructose 1,6-bisphosphate → glyceraldehyde 3-phosphate + dihydroxyacetone phosphate

23.40 *Note:* "Direct (or substrate-level) phosphorylation" is formation of ATP as a by-product of a reaction, as opposed to formation of ATP as a byproduct of electron transport.

(a) Glycolysis of 1 mol glucose produces 2 mol ATP as a result of direct phosphorylation. (Actually, 4 mol ATP are produced by phosphorylation, but 2 mol ATP are consumed in steps 1 and 3 of glycolysis.)

(b) Aerobic conversion of pyruvate to acetyl-SCoA doesn't produce ATP by direct phosphorylation.

(c) In the citric acid cycle, 1 mol of acetyl-SCoA produces 1 mol ATP by direct phosphorylation (Step 5). Most of the ATP produced in the citric acid cycle results from passage of the reduced coenzymes NADH and $FADH_2$ through the electron-transport chain.

23.42

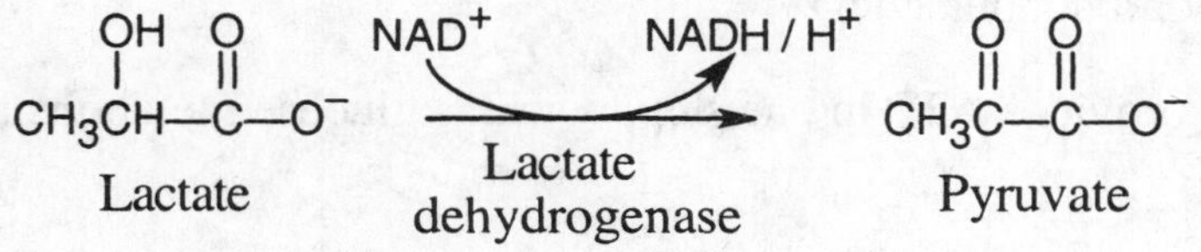
OH O
CH3CH—C—O−
Lactate
NAD+
NADH / H+
Lactate
dehydrogenase
O O
CH3C—C—O−
Pyruvate

23.44 Catabolism of one mole of sucrose produces four moles of acetyl-SCoA.

Regulation of Glucose Metabolism/Metabolism in Diabetes Mellitus

23.46 Insulin is released when blood glucose levels are high and results in passage of glucose into cells, where it is metabolized. Glucagon is released when blood glucose levels are low and results in breakdown of glycogen in the liver to produce glucose.

23.48 As starvation continues, acetyl-SCoA is converted to *ketone bodies* to prevent buildup in the cells.

23.50 In diabetes, excess glucose in the eyes and extremities is converted to sorbitol, which can't be transported out of cells. This elevated sorbitol level changes the osmolarity of tissues and causes cataracts and gangrene.

23.52 *Type I diabetes* is caused by insufficient production of insulin in the pancreas. *Type II diabetes* is caused by the failure of cell membrane receptors to recognize insulin.

23.54 Muscle cells, unlike liver cells, lack an enzyme that converts glucose 6-phosphate to glucose, which can pass into the bloodstream. Consequently, the glucose 6-phosphate product of glycogenolysis in muscle cells enters directly into glycolysis.

23.56 The exact reverse of an energetically favorable reaction must be energetically unfavorable. Since glycogenolysis is energetically favorable, its exact reverse must be energetically unfavorable. Thus, glycogenesis must occur by an alternate pathway.

Glucose Anabolism

23.58 Lactate and pyruvate are two molecules that can serve as starting materials for glucose synthesis.

23.60 Several steps of the exact reverse of the energetically favorable conversion of glucose to pyruvate are energetically unfavorable.

Applications

23.62 Plaque is composed of glycoproteins from saliva, bacteria, dextran, and polysaccharide storage granules released by the bacteria.

22.64 *Similarities:* Both fermentation and lactate production take place in anaerobic environments, both use pyruvate as a starting material, both produce alcohols, and both are reductions that yield NAD^+ as a by-product. *Differences:* Fermentation occurs only in the presence of yeasts, and the products of fermentation are ethanol and CO_2.

23.66 The fasting level of glucose in a diabetic is 140 mg/dL or greater, as compared to an average level of 90 mg/dL for a nondiabetic.

23.68 Creatine phosphate quickly provides ATP in one step, whereas glucose metabolism takes many steps to provide ATP.

23.70 *First used* ————————————————> *Last used*
ATP, creatine phosphate, glucose, glycogen, fatty acids from triacylglycerols

General Questions and Problems

23.72 Pyruvate can cross the mitochondrial membrane because it is the only molecule in glycolysis that is not a phosphate. (Phosphates can't cross the mitochondrial membrane.)

23.74 Fructose and glucose have the same net ATP production because fructose can be phosphorylated to form fructose 6-phosphate, which can enter glycolysis directly as a glycolysis intermediate.

23.76 Glycolysis must be tightly controlled because the body must avoid extreme fluctuations in glucose concentration.

Self-Test for Chapter 23

Multiple Choice

1. The synthesis of glucose from small molecules is called
(a) glycolysis (b) glucogenesis (c) gluconeogenesis (d) glycogenesis

2. Which one of the following substances can cross cell membranes?
(a) glucose 6-phosphate (b) ATP (c) glucose (d) acetyl-SCoA

3. The synthesis of glycogen occurs in the
(a) liver and bloodstream (b) liver and muscles (c) liver and pancreas (d) muscles and pancreas

4. The exact reverse of which of the following steps of glycolysis also occurs in gluconeogenesis?
(a) glucose —> glucose 6-phosphate (b) phosphoenolpyruvate —> pyruvate
(c) fructose 6-phosphate —> fructose 1,6-bisphosphate
(d) 3-phosphoglycerate —> 2-phosphoglycerate

5. When the body needs to synthesize nucleic acids
(a) The oxidative phase of the pentose phosphate path is bypassed. (b) The synthesis of NADPH is increased. (c) Glucose 6-phosphate enters glycolysis. (d) Three-, four-, or seven-carbon sugars are produced.

6. After several weeks of starvation, the body's principal energy source is
(a) protein (b) fat (c) carbohydrate (d) all three

7. Type I *diabetes mellitus* is a disorder of
(a) insufficient insulin production (b) faulty glucose metabolism (c) autoimmune response (d) all three

8. Which of the following is not a route for pyruvate metabolism in the human body?
(a) conversion to acetyl-SCoA (b) reduction to lactate (c) fermentation to alcohol
(d) reformation of glucose

9. Glycogenesis resembles glycogenolysis in that
(a) Both require the coenzyme UTP. (b) Both occur when glucose is in good supply.
(c) Both are stimulated by the hormone epinephrine. (d) Both involve glucose 6-phosphate as an intermediate.

10. Which of the following monosaccharides doesn't enter glycolysis?
(a) ribose (b) mannose (c) galactose (d) fructose

Sentence Completion

1. The ______ – ______ pathway is another name for glycolysis.

2. Step __ of glycolysis involves an oxidation and a phosphorylation.

3. ______ ______ _____catalyzes the formation of acetyl-SCoA from pyruvate.

4. _______ aids in the passage of blood glucose across cell membranes.

5. The first step of glycogenolysis is the formation of ________.

6. Steps ___ and _____ are known as the energy investment part of glycolysis.

7. The metabolic response to ______ resembles starvation.

8. ______ and ______ supply the energy for gluconeogenesis.

9. When pyruvate is converted to acetyl-SCoA, one molecule of ______ is lost.

10. The isomerization of glucose 6-phosphate to fructose 6-phosphate is catalyzed by ______.

11. The hormone ______ stimulates breakdown of glycogen.

12. ______ may be due to an overdose of insulin.

True or False

1. The pentose phosphate pathway is important because it produces NADH.

2. Fructose, galactose, and mannose can all enter the glycolysis pathway.

3. Conversion of glucose 6-phosphate to fructose 6-phosphate requires ATP.

4. Glycogenesis is the exact reverse of glycogenolysis.

5. Hyperglycemia is a high level of blood glucose.

6. The reactions of glycolysis occur in the mitochondria.

7. 36 ATP molecules are produced for each glucose that passes through the glycolysis pathway.

8. Glucagon is the storage form of glucose.

9. All four transformations of pyruvate occur in the human body.

10. Cleavage of fructose 1,6-diphosphate yields two molecules of glyceraldehyde 3-phosphate.

11. Pyruvate is converted to lactate under anaerobic conditions.

12. Each conversion of glyceraldehyde 3-phosphate to pyruvate requires two ADP.

Match each entry on the left with its partner on the right.

1. Glycolysis	(a) Formed by fermentation of pyruvate
2. Hyperglycemia	(b) Formed from pyruvate under anaerobic conditions
3. Enolase	(c) Intermediate in glycogen synthesis
4. Glycogenolysis	(d) Synthesis of glucose from pyruvate
5. UDP-glucose	(e) Catalyzes the cleavage of fructose 1,6-diphosphate
6. Ribose 5-phosphate	(f) Low blood sugar
7. Gluconeogenesis	(g) Synthesis of glycogen from glucose
8. Ethanol	(h) Product of pentose phosphate pathway
9. Hypoglycemia	(i) Catalyzes loss of water from 2-phosphoglyceric acid
10. Glycogenesis	(j) Breakdown of glycogen to glucose
11. Lactate	(k) High blood sugar
12. Aldolase	(l) Breakdown of glucose to pyruvate

Chapter 24 – Lipids

Chapter Outline

I. Structure and classification of lipids (Section 24.1).
  A. Lipids are defined by solubility in nonpolar solvents.
  B. Classification of lipids.
    1. Waxes.
    2. Triacylglycerols.
    3. Glycerophospholipids.
    4. Sphingolipids.
    5. Steroids and eicosanoids.
II. Fatty acids and their esters (Sections 24.2–24.4).
  A. Fatty acids (Section 24.2).
    1. Fatty acids are long-chain carboxylic acids.
    2. Fatty acids are classified by the number of double bonds they have.
      a. Fatty acids with no double bonds are saturated.
      b. Fatty acids with one double bond are monounsaturated.
      c. Fatty acids with more than one double bond are polyunsaturated.
  B. Waxes are esters of long-chain alcohols with fatty acids.
  C. Fats and oils.
    1. Fats and oils are mixtures of esters of glycerol with three fatty acids and are known as triacylglycerols.
    2. Properties of fats and oils (Section 24.3).
      a. Hydrophobic.
      b. Uncharged.
      c. Melting point is determined by the length of the fatty acid side chains and the number of double bonds.
        i. Solid fats have saturated fatty acid side chains.
        ii. Liquid fats have unsaturated fatty acid side chains.
    3. Reactions of triacylglycerols (Section 24.4).
      a. Hydrogenation.
        Control of hydrogenation determines the consistency of a fat.
      b. Hydrolysis.
        i. In the body, enzymes catalyze hydrolysis of triacylglycerols.
        ii. In the laboratory, strong aqueous base is used.
        iii. The resulting fatty acid salts are called soaps.
        iv. Soaps clean because the polar end dissolves in water and the nonpolar end dissolves in grease.
        v. Soap molecules cluster together in water to form micelles; grease is trapped in the middle of a micelle.
III. Cell membrane lipids (Sections 24.5–24.6).
  A. Phospholipids (Section 24.5).
    1. Glycerophospholipids.
      a. Glycerophospholipids are esters of glycerol with two fatty acids and a phosphate group that is bonded to one of a number of different compounds containing an –OH group.
      b. The phospholipid with choline as a phosphate ester is a lecithin.
        i. Lecithins are components of cell membranes.
        ii. Lecithin is often used as an emulsifying agent.

2. Sphingolipids and other membrane lipids.
   a. Sphingolipids are derivatives of the amino alcohol sphingosine.
   b. Sphingolipids consist of
      i. An amide bond between a fatty acid and sphingosine.
      ii. A phosphate ester also bonded to choline.
   c. Sphingomyelins are sphingolipids that are constituents of the coating around nerve fibers.

B. Glycolipids resemble sphingolipids, except that the phosphate group at C1 is replaced by a carbohydrate.
   1. Cerebrosides have a monosaccharide at C1.
      Cerebrosides are found in cell membranes.
   2. Gangliosides have a small polysaccharide at C1.
      Gangliosides are components of neurotransmitters and receptors.

C. Cholesterol (Section 24.6).
   1. Cholesterol has a tetracyclic steroid structure.
   2. Cholesterol serves as a starting material for steroid hormones.
   3. Cholesterol is a component of cell membranes that helps maintain the structure of the membrane.

IV. Cell membranes (Sections 24.7–24.8).

A. Structure of cell membranes (Section 24.7).
   1. Cell membranes are composed of two parallel layers of phospholipids, called a *lipid bilayer.*
   2. The nonpolar tails are clustered in the middle, and the polar heads point inward and outward.
   3. The fluid-mosaic model of a cell membrane explains the more complex structural details.
      a. Glycolipids and cholesterol are in the lipid part and provide membrane structure.
      b. Glycoproteins (20%) mediate the action of cell contents with the outer environment.
         i. Some proteins form channels to allow specific molecules to enter or leave.
         ii. Glycoproteins that extend through the bilayer are called integral proteins.
         iii. Glycoproteins that are partially embedded are peripheral proteins.
         iv. The carbohydrate portions act as receptors for enzymes and neurotransmitters.
      c. The membrane is fluid and doesn't rupture.
         Fluidity of the membrane increases with the amounts of saturated and unsaturated fatty acids in the lipid portion.

B. Transport across cell membranes (Section 24.8).
   1. Passive transport.
      a. Simple diffusion.
         i. Gases and small nonpolar molecules diffuse through the bilayer.
         ii. Small hydrophilic molecules pass through channels formed by integral proteins.
      b. Facilitated diffusion.
         Facilitated diffusion is passive transport, but proteins help solutes to pass across the membrane.
   2. Active transport.
      a. Ions and other substances that maintain concentration gradients inside and outside the cell move by active transport.
      b. Active transport requires an expenditure of energy and involves changing the shape of an integral protein.

V. Eicosanoids (Section 24.9).

A. General information.
   1. Eicosanoids are derivatives of 20-carbon fatty acids.
   2. Eicosanoids are synthesized from arachidonic acid.
   3. Eicosanoids are short-term messengers.

B. There are three classes of eicosanoids.
   1. Thromboxanes promote aggregation of blood platelets during clotting.
   2. Prostaglandins.
      a. Prostaglandins consist of a five-membered ring with two side chains.
      b. Biological effects include blood pressure lowering, stimulation of uterine contractions, and lowering the extent of gastric secretions.
   3. Leukotrienes mediate inflammatory and allergic responses.

Solutions to Chapter 24 Problems

24.1 The circled groups can be used to identify lipid families.

(a)

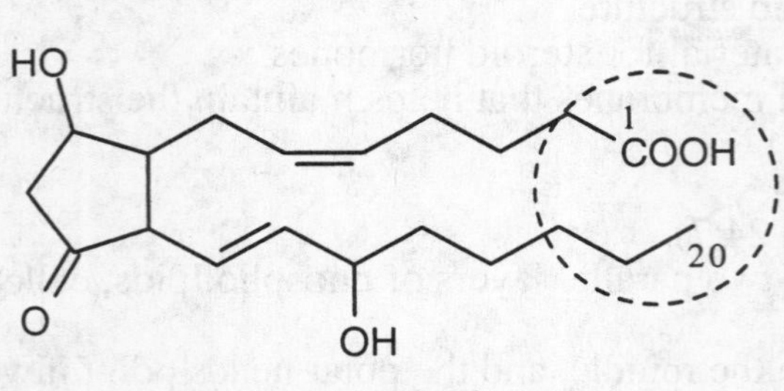
HO
1
COOH
20
O
OH
an eicosanoid

(b)

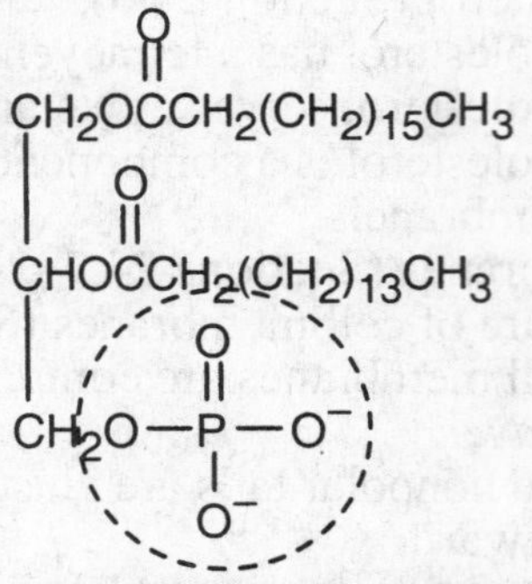
CH2OCCH2(CH2)15CH3
CHOCCH2(CH2)13CH3
CH2O—P—O−
O−
a glycerophospholipid

(c)

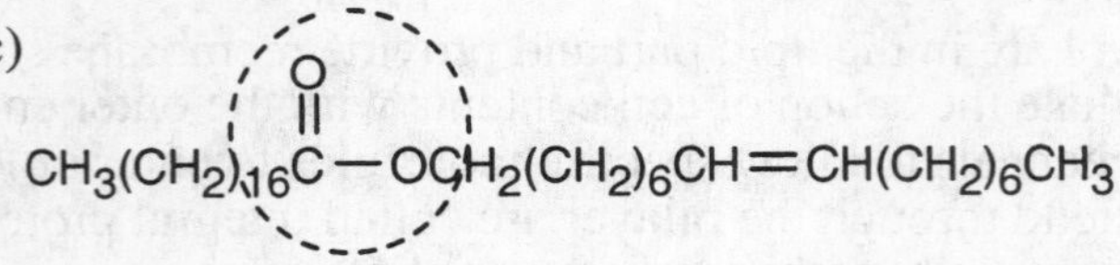
CH3(CH2)16C—OCH2(CH2)6CH=CH(CH2)6CH3
a wax

24.2

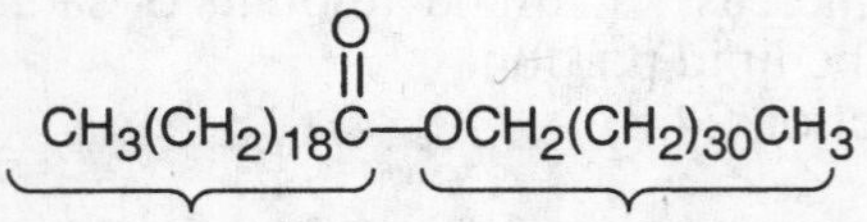
CH3(CH2)18C—OCH2(CH2)30CH3
from C_{20} carboxylic acid   from C_{32} alcohol

24.3

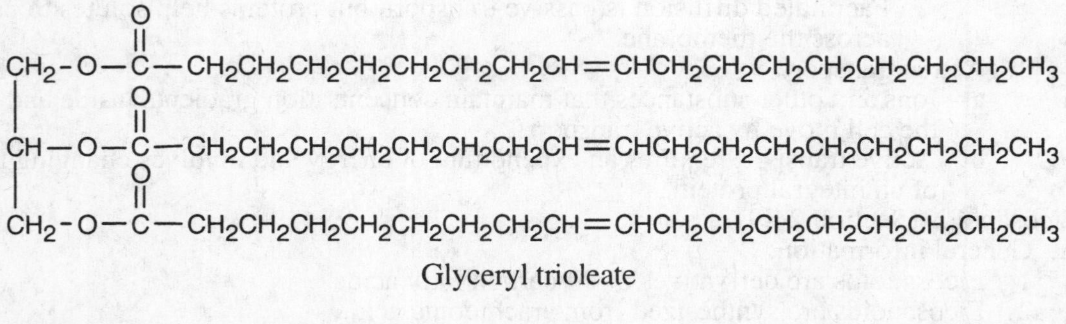
CH2-O—C—CH2CH2CH2CH2CH2CH2CH2CH=CHCH2CH2CH2CH2CH2CH2CH2CH3
CH—O—C—CH2CH2CH2CH2CH2CH2CH2CH=CHCH2CH2CH2CH2CH2CH2CH2CH3
CH2-O—C—CH2CH2CH2CH2CH2CH2CH2CH=CHCH2CH2CH2CH2CH2CH2CH2CH3
Glyceryl trioleate

24.4 (a) Butter has the largest percentage of saturated fatty acids.
(b) Soybean oil has the largest percentage of polyunsaturated fatty acids.

24.5

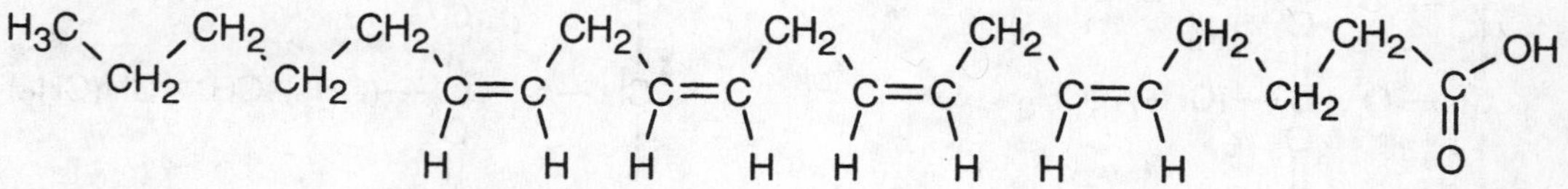

Arachidonic acid

24.6 The starred carbon of the triacylglycerol pictured below is bonded to four different groups and is chiral. (Whenever two different fatty acids are bonded to carbon 1 and carbon 3 of glycerol, carbon 2 is chiral.)

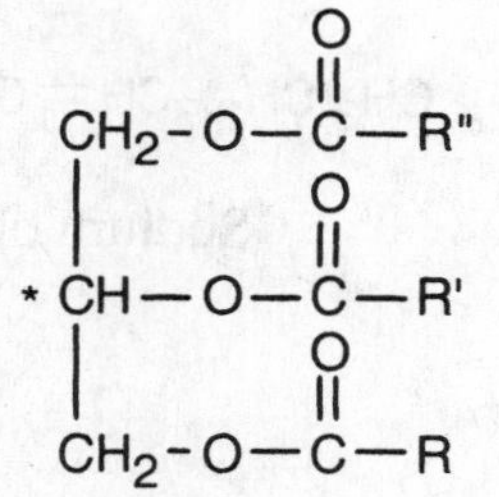

24.7 London forces bind the nonpolar segments of lipids together. These forces are generally weak, but when there are many such interactions, their total contribution is relatively large. Lipids don't mix with water because the hydrogen bonds between water molecules are stronger than the forces between lipid molecules or between water molecules and lipid molecules.

24.8 Glyceryl trioleate (Problem 24.3)

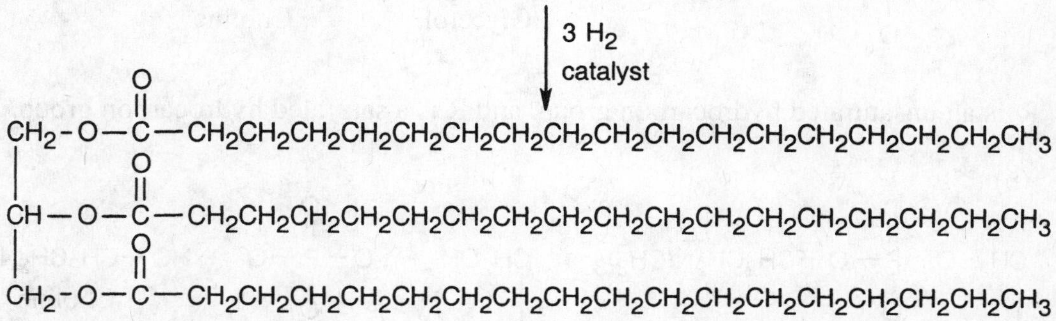

Glyceryl tristearate

The acyl groups of the triacylglycerol are derived from stearic acid.

24.9

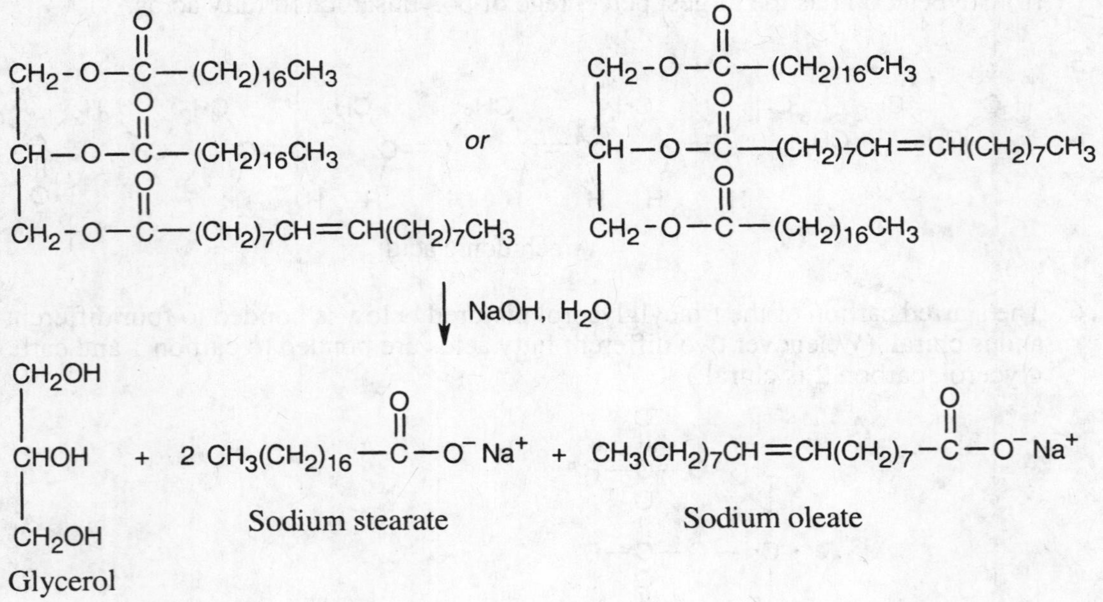
or
NaOH, H2O
Sodium stearate
Sodium oleate
Glycerol

24.10

(a)

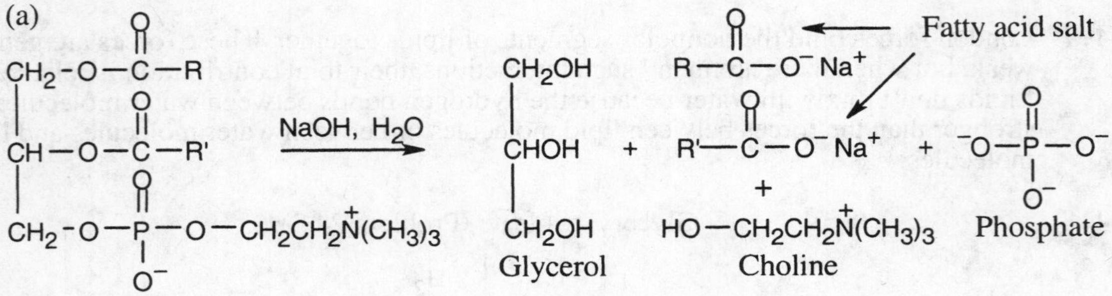
Fatty acid salt
NaOH, H2O
Glycerol
Choline
Phosphate

R' is an unsaturated hydrocarbon group, and R is a saturated hydrocarbon group.

(b)

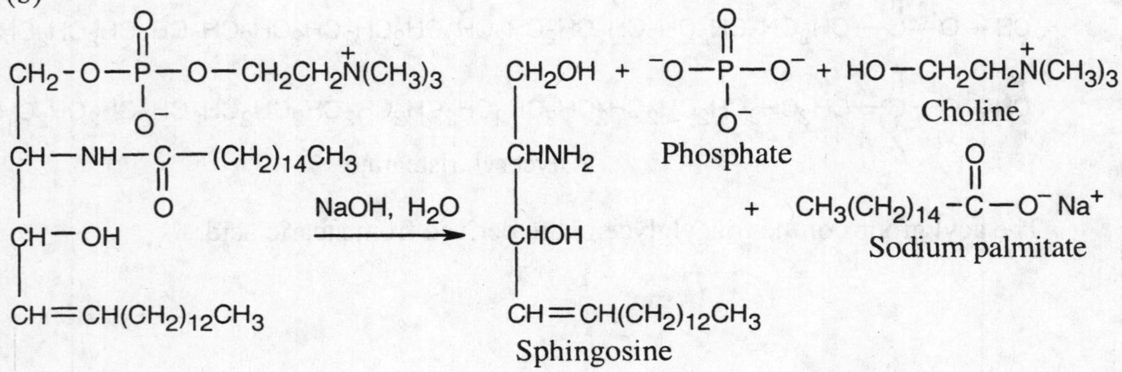
NaOH, H2O
Choline
Phosphate
Sodium palmitate
Sphingosine

24.11

$(CH_3)_3\overset{+}{N}CH_2CH_2O-\overset{\overset{\displaystyle O}{\|}}{\underset{\underset{\displaystyle O^-}{|}}{P}}-O-CH_2$

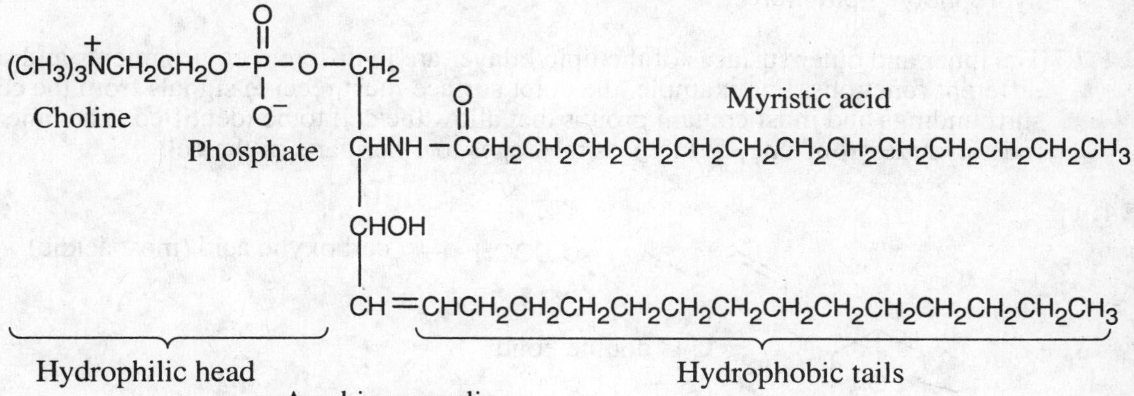

Choline

Phosphate

$CHNH-\overset{\overset{\displaystyle O}{\|}}{C}CH_2CH_2CH_2CH_2CH_2CH_2CH_2CH_2CH_2CH_2CH_2CH_2CH_3$ Myristic acid

$CHOH$

$CH=CHCH_2CH_2CH_2CH_2CH_2CH_2CH_2CH_2CH_2CH_2CH_2CH_2CH_3$

$\underbrace{\qquad\qquad}$ Hydrophilic head $\underbrace{\qquad\qquad}$ Hydrophobic tails

A sphingomyelin

24.12

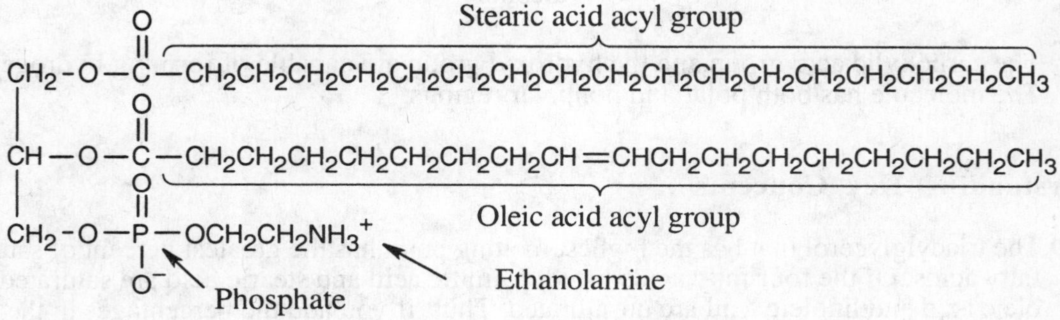

Stearic acid acyl group

$CH_2-O-\overset{\overset{\displaystyle O}{\|}}{C}-CH_2CH_2CH_2CH_2CH_2CH_2CH_2CH_2CH_2CH_2CH_2CH_2CH_2CH_2CH_2CH_2CH_3$

$CH-O-\overset{\overset{\displaystyle O}{\|}}{C}-CH_2CH_2CH_2CH_2CH_2CH_2CH_2CH=CHCH_2CH_2CH_2CH_2CH_2CH_2CH_2CH_3$

Oleic acid acyl group

$CH_2-O-\overset{\overset{\displaystyle O}{\|}}{\underset{\underset{\displaystyle O^-}{|}}{P}}-OCH_2CH_2NH_3^+$ Ethanolamine

Phosphate

A glycerophospholipid

24.13

$CH_3(CH_2)_{12}-CH=CH-CH-OH$

$\overset{\overset{\displaystyle O}{\|}}{R-C}-NH-CH$

$CH_2-O-\overset{\overset{\displaystyle O}{\|}}{\underset{\underset{\displaystyle O^-}{|}}{P}}-OCH_2-\overset{\overset{\displaystyle NH_3^+}{|}}{\underset{\underset{\displaystyle H}{|}}{C}}-COO^-$

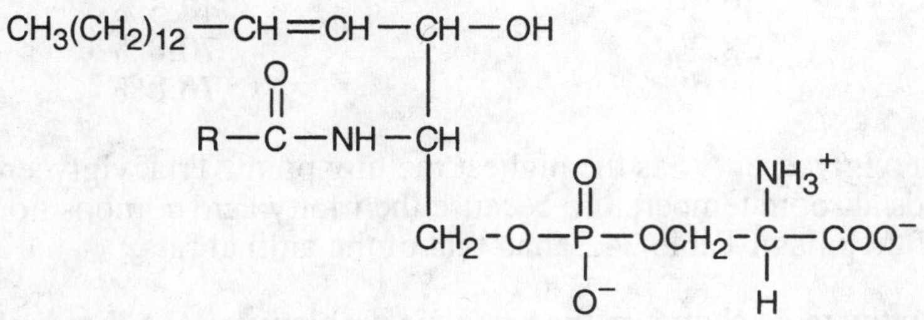

The illustrated structure is a phospholipid (a) because it contains a phosphate group. It is a sphingolipid (c) because it has a sphingosine backbone. It is a lipid (e) because it is soluble in nonpolar solvents. It contains a phosphate ester group (f).

24.14 Integral membrane proteins must be hydrophobic to remain in the hydrophobic environment of a cell membrane. They must contain many amino acids with nonpolar side chains and must be folded so that the hydrophobic regions face outward.

24.15 You would predict that NO would cross a lipid bilayer by simple diffusion because it is small and relatively nonpolar.

24.16 Glucose 6-phosphate has a charged phosphate group and can't pass through the hydrophobic lipid bilayer.

24.17 The inner and outer surfaces of the lipid bilayer are in different environments and serve different functions. For example, the outer surface must receive signals from the cell's surroundings and must contain groups that allow the cell to be identified. The inner surface must include groups needed to pass messages to other parts of the cell.

24.18

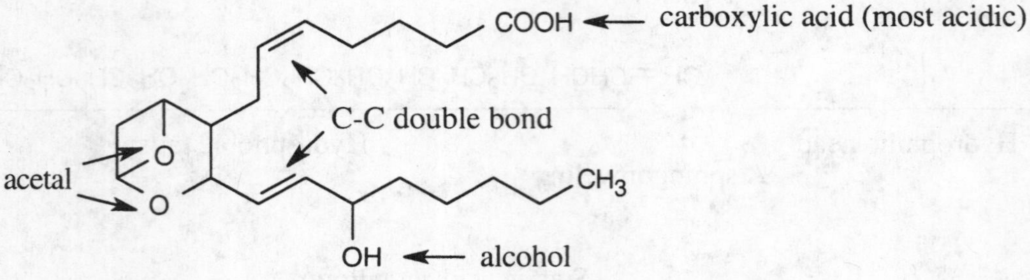
COOH
carboxylic acid (most acidic)
C-C double bond
acetal
O
O
CH3
OH
alcohol

The carboxylic acid group and the hydroxyl group are capable of forming hydrogen bonds. The molecule has both polar and nonpolar regions.

Understanding Key Concepts

24.19 The triacylglycerol that has the highest melting point has the greatest percent of saturated fatty acids. Of the four fatty acids listed, palmitic acid and stearic acid are saturated, and oleic acid and linoleic acid are unsaturated. Thus, if you add the percentages in the table, you arrive at a new table.

Triacylglycerol	*Percent Saturated Fatty Acids*	*Percent Unsaturated Fatty Acids*
Triacylglycerol A	49.2%	47.5%
Triacylglycerol B	28.9%	70.8%
Triacylglycerol C	19.5%	76.8%

This table shows that triacylglycerol A has the highest melting point. Triacylglycerols B and C are probably liquids at room temperature because their fatty acid composition more closely resembles that of the oils in Table 24.2 than that of the animal fats.

24.20 Three of the fatty acids in the table shown in the previous problem are C_{18} fatty acids (stearic acid, oleic acid, and linoleic acid). When the triacylglycerols are hydrogenated, the unsaturated fatty acids are converted to stearic acid. The composition of the triacylglycerols after hydrogenation can be found by adding the percentages of C_{18} fatty acids.

Triacylglycerol	*Percent C_{16} Fatty Acids*	*Percent C_{18} Fatty Acids*
Triacylglycerol A	21.4%	75.3%
Triacylglycerol B	12.2%	87.5%
Triacylglycerol C	11.2%	85.1%

After hydrogenation, triacylglycerol B would be composed of 12.2% palmitic acid and 87.5% stearic acid. The hydrogenation product of triacylglycerol B closely resembles the hydrogenation product of triacylglycerol C because they have similar percentages of C_{16} fatty acids and C_{18} fatty acids.

24.21

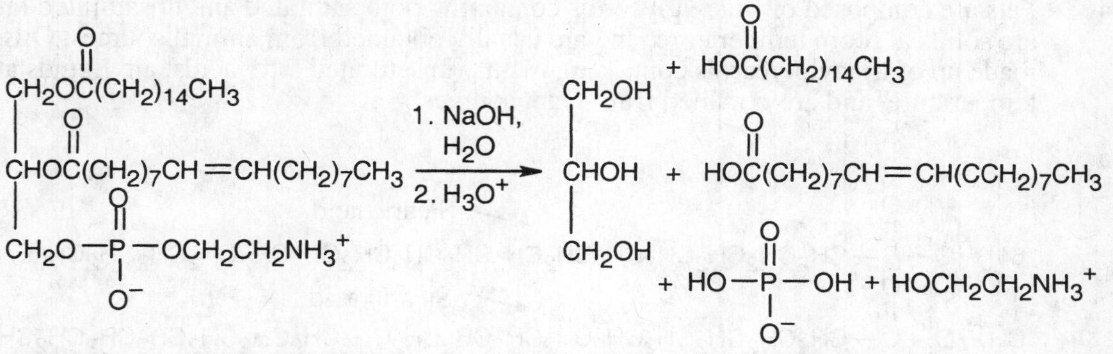

The membrane lipid is a glycerophospholipid that is a phosphatidylethanolamine.

24.22 Because the membrane is fluid, rather than rigid, it is able to flow together after an injury instead of shattering.

24.23

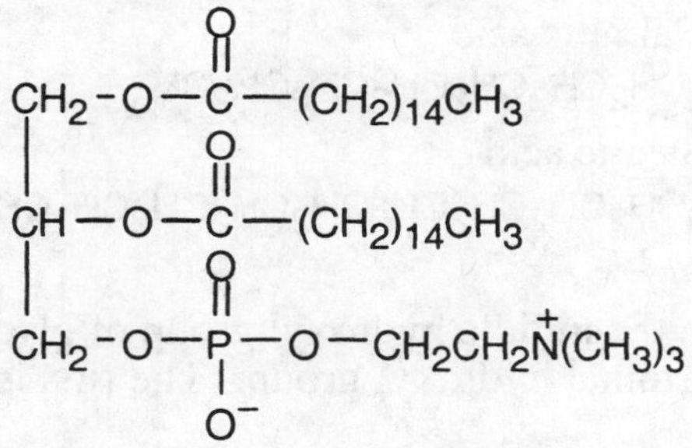

DPPC

The two fatty acids are 16-carbon saturated straight-chain fatty acids.The polar head is situated in lung tissue, and the nonpolar groups protrude into the air space within the alveoli.

Waxes, Fats, and Oils

24.24 A lipid is a naturally occurring organic molecule that dissolves in nonpolar solvents.

24.26 A fatty acid is a long-chain (C_{12}–C_{22}) carboxylic acid having an even number of carbon atoms.

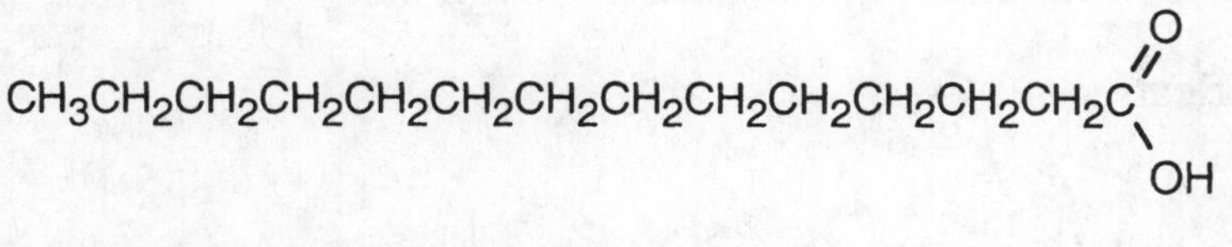

Myristic acid

24.28 The double bonds in naturally occurring fatty acids are cis.

24.30 Linoleic acid and linolenic acid are two essential fatty acids. Vegetable oils and nuts are good sources of these acids.

24.32 A fat or oil is a triester of glycerol with three fatty acids — a triacylglycerol.

24.34 Fats are composed of triacylglycerols containing both saturated and unsaturated fatty acids, are solids at room temperature, and are usually obtained from animal sources. Oils are made up of triacylglycerols containing mainly unsaturated fatty acids, are liquids at room temperature, and are obtained from plant sources.

24.36

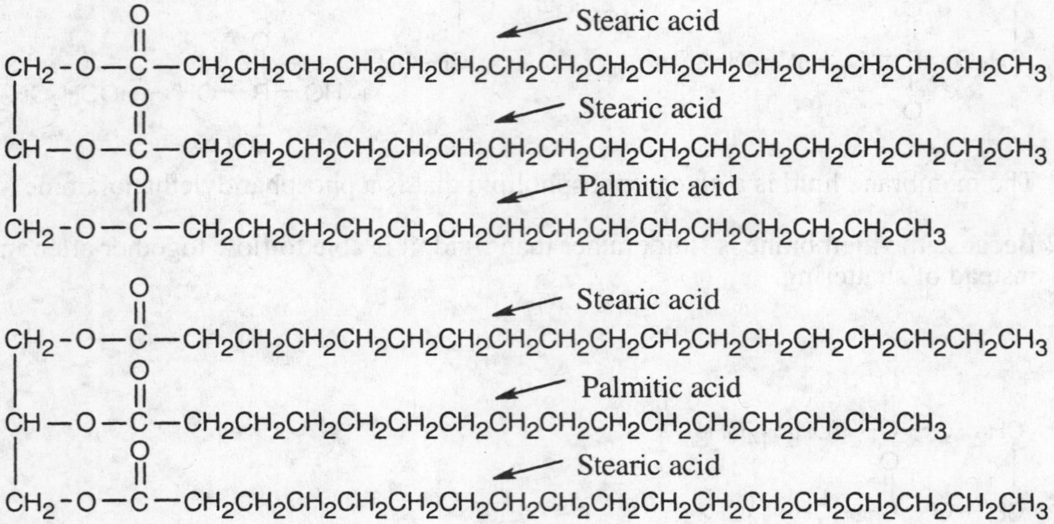
Stearic acid
Stearic acid
Palmitic acid
Stearic acid
Palmitic acid
Stearic acid

In one isomer, palmitic acid forms an ester with the middle hydroxyl group of glycerol; in the other, palmitic acid forms an ester with a terminal hydroxyl group. (The first isomer is chiral.)

24.38 In animals, fats are used for energy storage, as components of cell membranes, and as precursors for steroid hormones.

24.40 Spermaceti is a wax.

Chemical Reactions of Lipids

24.42 If some, but not all, of the double bonds in corn oil were hydrogenated, the resulting product would be a semisolid fat that could be used as margarine.

24.44 The reaction is a saponification.

24.46

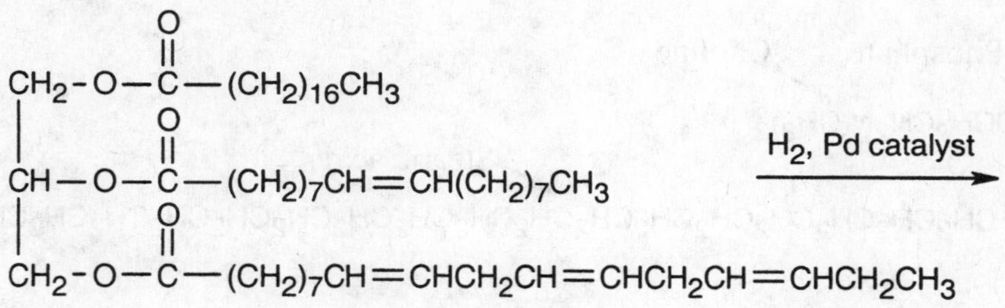
H2, Pd catalyst

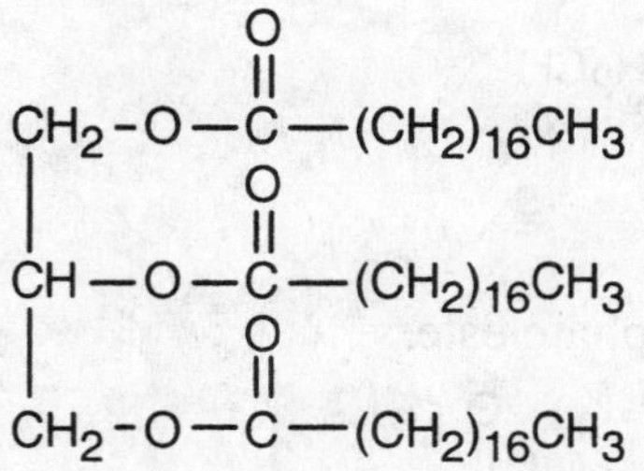

Glyceryl tristearate

Glyceryl tristearate is higher melting than the original lipid because it has no double bonds and can solidify more easily.

Phospholipids, Glycolipids, and Cell Membranes

24.48 Glycerophospholipids have an ionic part (the *head*) and a nonpolar part (the *tail*). The ionic head protrudes outward toward the aqueous environment of the cell or inward toward the cell contents, and the nonpolar tails cluster together to form the membrane. Triacylglycerols don't have an ionic head and thus can't function as membrane components.

24.50 Sphingomyelins and glycolipids are two different kinds of sphingosine-based lipids.

24.52 In a soap micelle, the polar hydrophilic heads are on the exterior, and the hydrophobic tails cluster in the center. In a membrane bilayer, hydrophilic heads are on both the exterior and interior surfaces of the membrane, and the region between the two surfaces is occupied by hydrophobic tails.

24.54 If cell membranes were freely permeable, the concentrations of all substances would be the same on both sides of the cell membrane, and it would be impossible for cells to maintain concentration gradients.

24.56

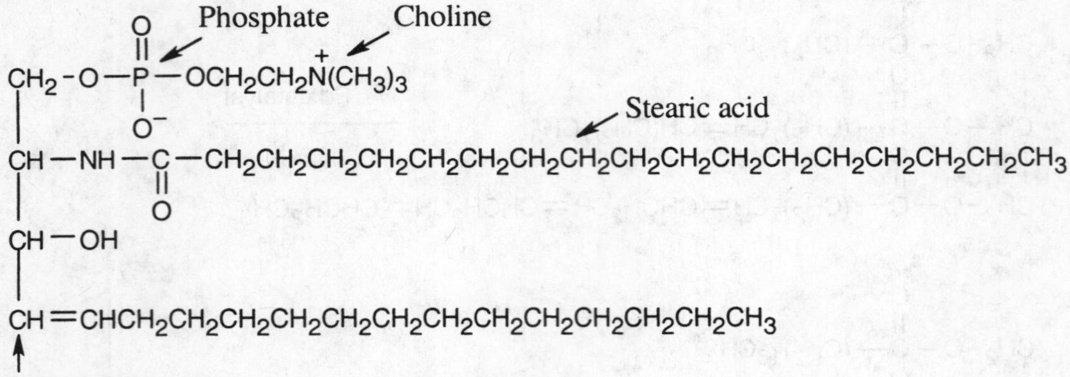
Phosphate
Choline
Stearic acid

Sphingosine a sphingomyelin

24.58 Aqueous NaOH cleaves all ester bonds, including phosphate esters.

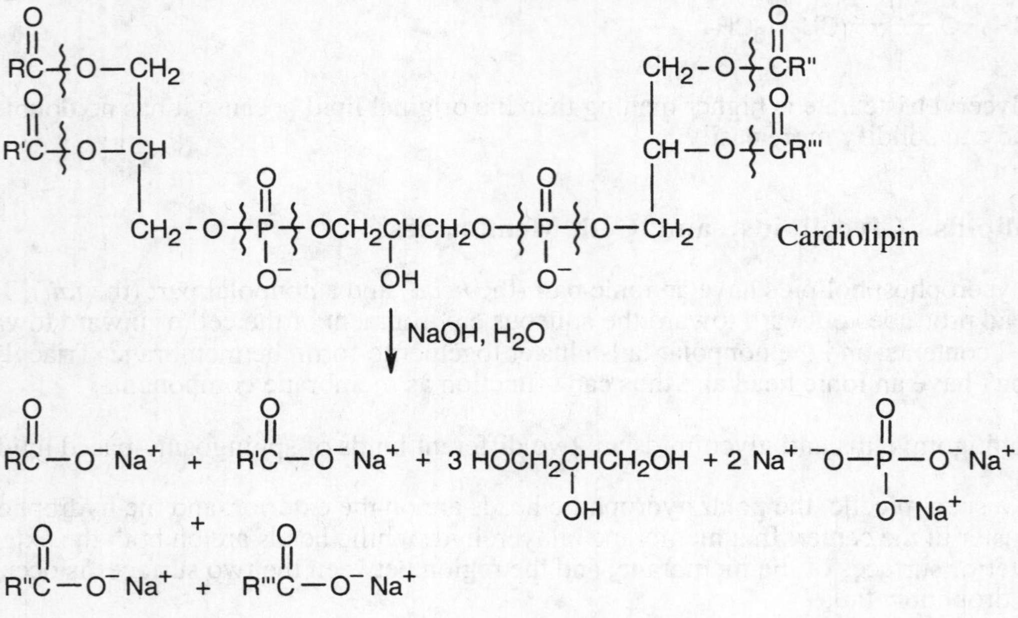
Cardiolipin
NaOH, H_2O

24.60 In both simple diffusion and facilitated diffusion, substances cross cell membranes from areas of high concentration to areas of low concentration. In facilitated diffusion, proteins help substances cross cell membranes.

Eicosanoids

24.62 Eicosanoids are called "local hormones" because they are synthesized near their site of action.

24.64 Arachidonic acid is synthesized from linolenic acid, an essential fatty acid.

24.66 Leukotrienes are responsible for triggering asthmatic attacks, inflammation and allergic reactions, and thus it is desirable to inhibit their synthesis.

24.68 By transferring its acetyl group, aspirin inhibits the enzyme that is responsible for the first step in the conversion of arachidonic acid to prostaglandins.

Applications

24.70 In addition to fats and oils, other foods with high lipid content are meat, fish, poultry, dairy products, nuts, seeds, whole-grain cereals, and prepared foods.

24.72 Detergents and soaps both have hydrocarbon "tails" and polar "heads," and both form micelles, in which the hydrocarbon "tails" surround greasy dirt and aggregate in the center of a cluster. The polar "heads" protrude into the aqueous medium and make the cluster soluble.

24.74 Branched-chain hydrocarbons are no longer used for detergents because they aren't biodegradable. Bacteria in sewage treatment plants can't digest detergents made from branched-chain hydrocarbons, and the undecomposed detergents produce suds in waterways.

24.76 Peanut oil and olive oil are the best sources of monounsaturated fatty acids.

24.78 The liposome fuses with a skin cell and delivers the moisturizer directly to the inside of the skin cell. This is more efficient than applying the moisturizer to the surface of the cell.

General Questions and Problems

24.80

Lipid	*Backbone*	*Groups Attached*
(c) A cerebroside	Sphingosine	A fatty acid, a monosaccharide
(d) Glyceryl trioleate	Glycerol	Three oleic acids
(e) A sphingomyelin	Sphingosine	A fatty acid, a phosphate group, choline or ethanolamine
(f) A lecithin	Glycerol	A saturated fatty acid, an unsaturated fatty acid, a phosphate group, choline

24.82 The fat described in the previous problem is lower melting than a fat composed of linolenic, myristic and stearic acids, because the fat in Problem 24.81 is more unsaturated and thus solidifies at a lower temperature.

24.84 Cholesterol isn't saponifiable because it contains no ester linkages.

24.86 Sphingomyelins, cerebrosides, and gangliosides are abundant in brain tissue.

24.88 Prostaglandins can lower blood pressure, assist in blood clotting, stimulate uterine contractions, lower gastric secretions, and cause some of the pain and swelling associated with inflammation.

24.90

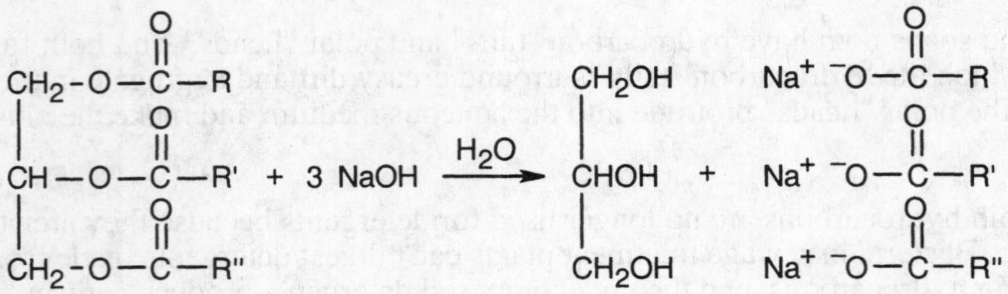

Molar mass of fat = 1500 g

Molar mass of NaOH = 40 g

$$5.0 \text{ g oil} \times \frac{1 \text{ mol}}{1500 \text{ g}} = 3.3 \times 10^{-3} \text{ mol oil}$$

Since 3 mol of NaOH are needed to saponify 1 mol of oil, 9.9×10^{-3} mol of NaOH is needed to saponify 3.3×10^{-3} mol of oil.

$$9.9 \times 10^{-3} \text{ mol NaOH} \times \frac{40 \text{ g}}{1 \text{ mol}} = 0.39 \text{ g NaOH, or approximately } 0.4 \text{ g NaOH}$$

Self-Test for Chapter 24

Multiple Choice

1. Small polar molecules pass through the lipid bilayer by
(a) simple diffusion through the lipid bilayer (b) facilitated transfer (c) active transport (d) simple diffusion through channels

2. Cholesterol is
(a) a male sex hormone (b) a saponifiable lipid (c) a component of cell membranes (d) common to plants and animals

3. Which of the following is not an effect of prostaglandins?
(a) stimulation of allergic response (b) lowering of blood pressure (c) reduction of gastric secretions (d) stimulation of uterine contractions

4. Active transport requires all of the following except
(a) the solutes to be nonpolar organic molecules (b) the expenditure of ATP (c) the need for cells to maintain a concentration gradient between the inside and the outside (d) the assistance of integral proteins

5. Which of the following contain a glycosidic bond?
(a) triacylglycerols (b) sphingomyelins (c) lecithins (d) cerebrosides

6. The basic hydrolysis of which of the following triacylglycerols produces only polyunsaturated fatty acids?
(a) glyceryl trioleate (b) glyceryl tristearate (c) glyceryl linoleate dioleate (d) glyceryl trilinolenate

7. How many different triacylglycerols (including enantiomers!) can be formed from glycerol, two stearic acids, and one oleic acid?
(a) 1 (b) 2 (c) 3 (d) 4

8. Which of the following molecules aren't components of glycolipids?
(a) sphingosine (b) phosphate groups (c) fatty acids (d) sugars

9. A cell membrane is composed of all of the following except
(a) triacylglycerols (b) phosphoglycerides (c) sphingomyelins (d) glycolipids

10. Waxes
(a) are triacylglycerols (b) can be hydrolyzed by base (c) contain no more than thirty carbons (d) are only produced by plants

Sentence Completion

1. A glycolipid contains an _____ link between sphingosine and a sugar.
2. _____ is a mixture of long-chain fatty acid salts.
3. The carboxylate end of a fatty acid is _____ and the organic chain end is _____.
4. _____ and _____ are two components of cell membranes.
5. The common model of a cell membrane is called the _____ _____ model.
6. Steroid structures are based on a _____ ring system.
7. Prostaglandins are synthesized in the body from a fatty acid called _____ acid.
8. Clusters of soap molecules in water are called _____.
9. _____ are phospholipids that are abundant in brain tissue.
10. Phospholipids aggregate in a closed, sheetlike membrane called a _____ _____.
11. _________ are a group of compounds derived from 20-carbon unsaturated fatty acids.
12. ______ proteins are involved with active transport across cell membranes.

True or False

1. Lipids are defined by their physical properties, not by their structure.
2. Saturated fats are lower melting than unsaturated fats.
3. Sphingolipids contain a carboxylic acid ester group.
4. Cholesterol is synthesized by the human body.
5. Sphingosine is a component of both phospholipids and glycolipids.
6. When soap molecules are dissolved in water, they form a lipid bilayer.
7. Cholesterol is a hormone.
8. The main difference between fats and oil is in their melting points.
9. Cerebrosides are a major constituent of the coating around nerve fibers.
10. Waxes and fats are both carboxylic acid esters.
11. Leukotrienes are synthesized in the cells where they act.
12. Facilitated diffusion requires an energy investment.

Match each entry on the left with its partner on the right.

1. Decyl stearate	(a) Extends completely through the cell membrane
2. Prostaglandin	(b) Monounsaturated fatty acid
3. Choline	(c) Partially embedded in the cell membrane
4. Stearic acid	(d) Phosphoglyceride
5. Integral protein	(e) Amino alcohol
6. Glyceryl trilaurate	(f) Saturated fatty acid
7. Cerebroside	(g) Polyunsaturated fatty acid
8. Oleic acid	(h) C_{20} acid with a five-membered ring
9. Lecithin	(i) Sphingolipid
10. Linoleic acid	(j) Fat
11. Sphingomyelin	(k) Glycolipid
12. Peripheral protein	(l) Wax

Chapter 25 – Lipid Metabolism

Chapter Outline

I. Triacylglycerols (Sections 25.1–25.4).
   A. Digestion of triacylglycerols (Section 25.1).
      1. Triacylglycerols (TAGs) pass through the mouth unchanged.
      2. In the stomach, TAGs are broken down into small droplets.
      3. As TAGs pass into the intestines, lipases and bile are produced.
         a. Bile acids solubilize lipid droplets.
         b. Lipases hydrolyze lipids to mono- and diacylglycerols, fatty acids, and glycerol.
      4. Products of TAG digestion are absorbed through the intestinal wall.
         a. Smaller molecules are transported to the liver.
         b. Free fatty acids and acylglycerols are reconverted to triacylglycerols and packaged into lipoproteins (chylomicrons).
   B. Lipoproteins for lipid transport (Section 25.2).
      1. Triacylglycerols and fatty acids enter metabolism from three sources:
         a. Diet.
         b. Storage in adipose tissue.
         c. Synthesis in the liver.
      2. These lipids must be made soluble by association with lipoproteins.
      3. A lipoprotein is a globule of TAGs and fatty acids surrounded by a layer of phospholipids.
      4. Five kinds of lipoproteins are important.
         a. Chylomicrons carry lipids in the diet through the lymphatic system into the blood.
         b. VLDLs carry TAGs from the liver to tissues for storage or energy production.
         c. IDLs carry remnants of VLDLs from peripheral tissues back to the liver for use in synthesis.
         d. LDLs carry cholesterol from the liver to tissues.
         e. HDLs carry cholesterol from cells to the liver, where it is converted to bile acids.
   C. Metabolism of triacylglycerols (Sections 25.3–25.4).
      1. Overview (Section 25.3).
         a. TAGs are hydrolyzed.
            i. TAGs in the diet are hydrolyzed to glycerol and fatty acids by lipoprotein lipase in capillary walls in adipose tissue.
            ii. TAGs in adipocytes are hydrolyzed within the cells, and the fatty acids travel into the bloodstream with albumins.
         b. Glycerol is carried to the liver or kidneys.
            Glycerol is converted to dihydroxyacetone phosphate, which enters glycolysis or gluconeogenesis.
         c. Fatty acids have two fates.
            i. When energy is in good supply, fatty acids are converted to TAGs for storage.
            ii. When energy is needed, fatty acids are metabolized to acetyl-SCoA.
         d. Acetyl-SCoA is used for
            i. Generation of energy via the citric acid cycle and oxidative phosphorylation.
            ii. Biosynthesis of fatty acids.
            iii. Production of ketone bodies.
            iv. Synthesis of steroids.

2. Storage and mobilization of TAGs (Section 25.4).
   a. When blood glucose levels are high, TAGs are synthesized for storage.
      i. The glycerol 3-phosphate needed is made from dihydroxyacetone phosphate, which comes from glycolysis.
      ii. The fatty acyl-SCoAs needed come from digestion or biosynthesis.
      iii. Two fatty acyl-SCoA are added to glycerol 3-phosphate.
      iv. After removal of phosphate from glycerol 3-phosphate, the third fatty acyl-SCoA is added.
   b. When blood glucose levels are low, fatty acids and glycerol are released from adipocytes and enter the bloodstream.

II. Fatty acid oxidation (Sections 25.5–25.7).
   A. Steps in fatty acid oxidation (Section 25.5).
      1. Activation.
         a. Fatty acids react with HSCoA to form fatty acyl-SCoA.
         b. At the same time, ATP is converted to AMP + 2 $HOPO_3^{2-}$.
      2. Transport.
         Fatty acyl-SCoAs are transported across the mitochondrial membrane.
      3. Oxidation (β Oxidation).
         a.

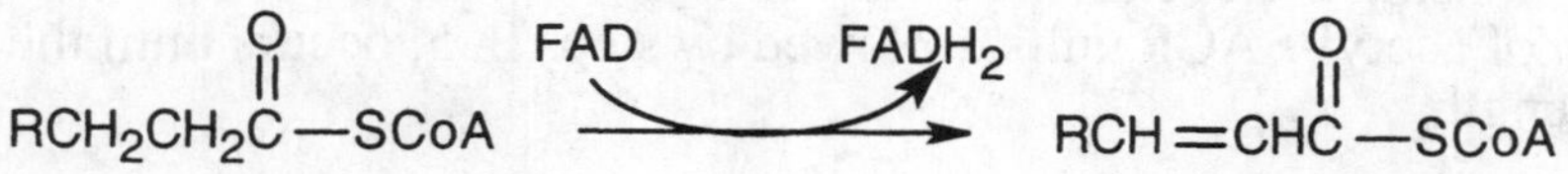
FAD
FADH2
RCH2CH2C—SCoA
RCH=CHC—SCoA

b.

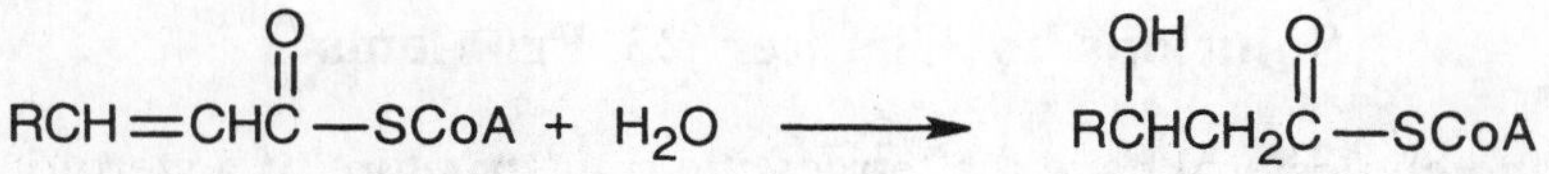
RCH=CHC—SCoA + H2O
RCHCH2C—SCoA

c.

NAD+
NADH/H+
RCHCH2C—SCoA
RCCH2C—SCoA

d.

HSCoA
RCCH2C—SCoA
RC—SCoA + CH3C—SCoA

         e. An n-carbon fatty acid produces $n/2$ acetyl-SCoA.
   B. Energy from fatty acid oxidation (Section 25.6).
      1. The number of molecules of ATP produced from a fatty acid that yields n acetyl-SCoA molecules is $14n - 6$.
      2. Fats produce more than twice the amount of energy per unit weight than carbohydrates do.
   C. Production of ketone bodies (ketogenesis) (Section 25.7).
      1. Ketone bodies are formed when the body produces excess acetyl-SCoA.
      2. Synthesis of ketone bodies.
         a. 2 Acetyl-SCoA —> acetoacetyl-SCoA + HSCoA.
         b. Acetoacetyl-SCoA + acetyl-SCoA —> 3-hydroxy-3-methylglutaryl-SCoA + HSCoA.
         c. 3-Hydroxy-3-methylglutaryl-SCoA —> acetyl-SCoA + acetoacetate.
         d. Acetoacetate + NADH/H^+ —> 3-hydroxybutyrate + NAD^+.
         e. Acetoacetate —> acetone + CO_2.

3. Catabolism of ketone bodies during starvation produces much of the energy that the body needs.
4. When ketone bodies are formed faster than the body can utilize them, ketoacidosis occurs.
   In ketoacidosis, blood pH drops, ketone bodies are excreted in the urine, and coma and death may result.

III. Fatty acid biosynthesis (lipogenesis) (Section 25.8).
  A. Lipogenesis occurs when amino acids and carbohydrates are in good supply.
  B. Lipogenesis resembles fatty acid oxidation but isn't its exact reverse.
     Lipogenesis occurs in the cytosol, and intermediates are carried by ACP.
  C. Mechanism of lipogenesis.
    1. Condensation.
       a. Acetyl-SCoA + HCO_3^- —> H_2O + malonyl-SCoA.
       b. Malonyl-SCoA + HSACP —> malonyl-SACP + HSCoA.
       c. Acetyl-SCoA + HSACP —> acetyl-SACP + HSCoA.
       d. Acetyl-SACP + malonyl-SACP —> acetoacetyl-SACP + SACP + CO_2.
    2. Reduction, using NADPH/H^+.
    3. Dehydration.
    4. Reduction, using the coenzyme NADPH/H^+.
    5. Addition of acetyl-SACP units, followed by steps 2–5, occurs until the chain is the correct length.

Solutions to Chapter 25 Problems

25.1 Both cholate and cholesterol have the tetracyclic ring structure of a steroid. Cholate has more polar functional groups (three —OH groups and one carboxylate group) and is better able to emulsify fats than cholesterol (one —OH group). The hydrophobic side of cholate interacts with TAGs, and the hydrophilic side interacts with the aqueous environment. The less polar cholesterol is more suitable for incorporation into cell membranes. Thus, the two molecules can't change roles.

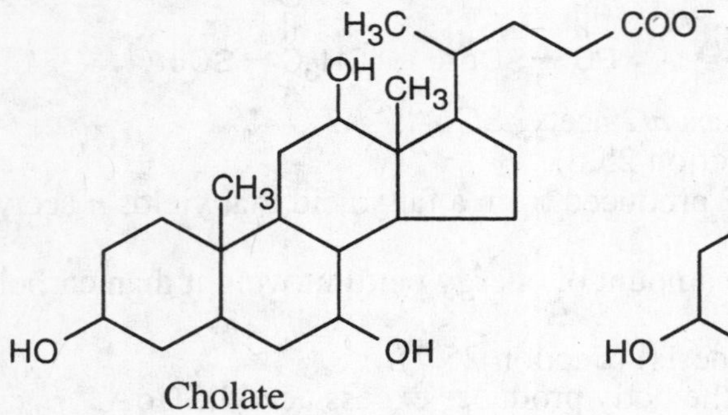
H3C
COO⁻
OH
CH3
CH3
HO
OH
H3C
CH3
CH3
CH3
CH3
HO

Cholate

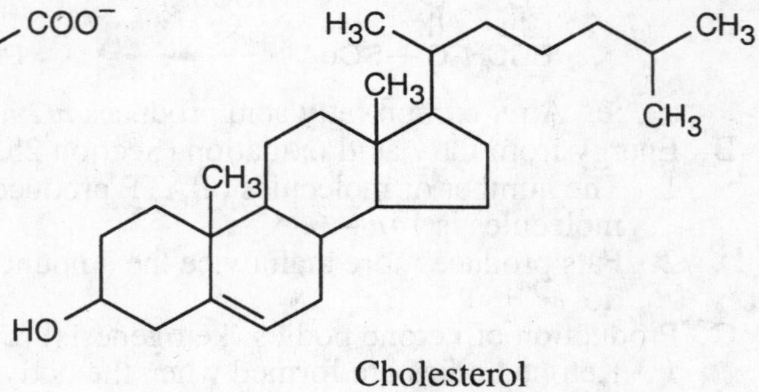

Cholesterol

25.2 The enzyme *triose phosphate isomerase* catalyzes the isomerization of dihydroxyacetone phosphate to glyceraldehyde 3-phosphate, which proceeds through the last five steps of glycolysis to yield pyruvate.

25.3 (a), (b) In *Step 1*, a C=C double bond is introduced, using FAD as the oxidizing agent. In *Step 3*, an alcohol is oxidized to a ketone, using NAD^+ as the oxidizing agent.
(c) In *Step 2*, water is added to a carbon-carbon double bond.
(d) In *Step 4*, HSCoA displaces acetyl-SCoA, producing a chain-shortened acyl-SCoA fatty acid.

25.4

(a)

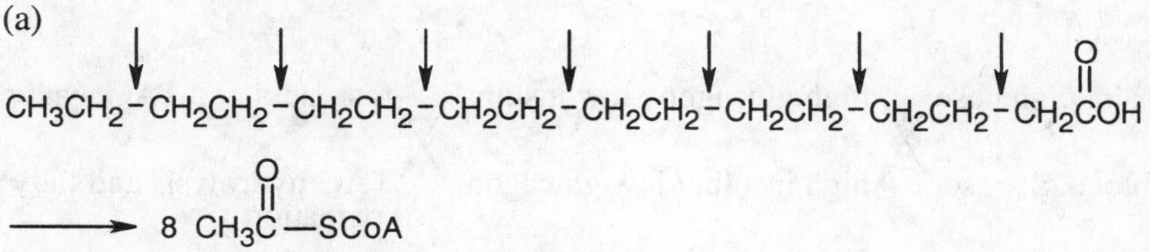
CH3CH2-CH2CH2-CH2CH2-CH2CH2-CH2CH2-CH2CH2-CH2CH2-CH2COH
8 CH3C—SCoA

Seven β oxidations are needed.

(b)

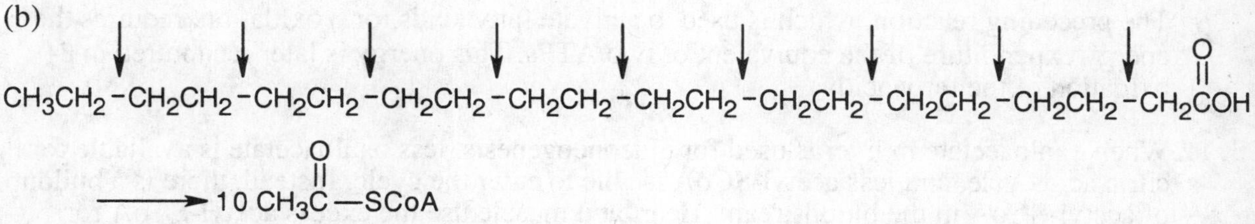
CH3CH2-CH2CH2-CH2CH2-CH2CH2-CH2CH2-CH2CH2-CH2CH2-CH2CH2-CH2CH2-CH2COH
10 CH3C—SCoA

Nine β oxidations are needed.

25.5 In the citric acid cycle, Steps 6 (dehydrogenation of succinate to produce fumarate), 7 (hydration of fumarate to produce malate), and 8 (oxidation of malate to produce oxaloacetate) are similar to the first three reactions of the β oxidation of a fatty acid.

25.6 The formation of 3-hydroxybutyrate from acetoacetate is a reduction (d).

25.7 (a) Acetyl-SCoA provides the acetyl groups used in the synthesis of the ketone bodies. (b) Three acetyl-SCoA molecules are used. (c) During prolonged starvation, the body, including the brain, uses ketone bodies as an energy source.

Understanding Key Concepts

25.8 The NADH and $FADH_2$ produced in β oxidation must be reoxidized in the electron transport system in order for β oxidation to continue. Since oxygen is required to reoxidize these reduced coenzymes in the electron transport system, β oxidation is an aerobic pathway even though oxygen isn't directly involved.

25.9 (a) Chylomicrons have the lowest density because they have the highest percentage of lipids, and lipids are less dense than protein.
(b) Chylomicrons carry TAGs from the diet.
(c) HDL removes cholesterol from circulation and transports it to the liver, where it is converted to bile acids and excreted.
(d) LDL contains "bad" cholesterol, which is deposited in tissues and contributes to atherosclerosis.
(e) HDL has the highest ratio of protein to lipid.
(f) VLDL carries TAGs from the liver to peripheral tissue, where they are used either for storage or for energy generation.
(g) LDL carries cholesterol from the liver to peripheral tissue.

25.10

A	B	C
high blood glucose	high glucagon / low insulin	fatty acid and TAG synthesis
low blood glucose	high insulin / low glucagon	TAG hydrolysis and fatty acid oxidation

25.11 Fatty acid + HSCoA + ATP $\longrightarrow$ Fatty acyl-SCoA + AMP + 2 PO_4^{3-}

The preceding reaction, which is used to activate fatty acids for β oxidation, requires the energy expenditure of the equivalent of two ATPs. This energy is later recaptured in β oxidation of the fatty acid.

25.12 When oxaloacetate in liver is used for gluconeogenesis, less oxaloacetate is available for the citric acid cycle, and less acetyl-SCoA is able to enter the cycle. Instead, there is a buildup of acetyl-SCoA in the bloodstream. Heart and muscle use the excess acetyl-SCoA for synthesis of ketone bodies. Buildup of ketone bodies leads to ketoacidosis, in which blood pH is lowered and the odor of acetone is noticeable in urine and on the breath. Ketoacidosis can lead to dehydration, labored breathing, and death.

25.13 Catabolism of one gram of stored TAG provides more energy than does catabolism of one gram of glycogen. Another reason that stored fats have a higher "energy density" than stored carbohydrates is the association of water with the hydrophilic glycogen molecules, which further reduces the energy yield per gram of glycogen.

25.14 During starvation, glucose is in short supply, and the body responds by producing ketone bodies as a source of energy.

25.15 Table 25.1 summarizes the two pathways, which differ in several ways. (1) Intermediates of oxidation are carried by coenzyme A, whereas intermediates of lipogenesis are carried by acyl carrier protein. (2) The two processes use different enzymes and coenzymes. (3) Oxidation occurs in mitochondria, and synthesis occurs in cytosol.

Digestion and Catabolism of Lipids

25.16 Lipids make you feel full because they slow the rate of movement of food through the stomach.

25.18 Bile emulsifies lipid droplets so that they can be attacked by enzymes.

25.20 The products of pancreatic lipase hydrolysis of triacylglycerols (TAGs) are mono- and diacylglycerols, plus fatty acids and glycerol. The products of lipoprotein lipase (in adipocytes) are fatty acids and glycerol.

25.22 Very-low-density lipoproteins originate in the liver and are used to transport TAGs that have been synthesized in the liver to tissues where they will be used or stored.

25.24 Steps 6–10 of the glycolysis pathway are necessary for converting glyceraldehyde 3-phosphate to pyruvate. These steps include an oxidation (Step 6), a phosphorylation (Step 6), two phosphate transfers to ADP (Steps 7 and 10), an isomerization (Step 8), and a dehydration (Step 9).

25.26 Eight molecules of ATP are formed in the catabolism of glycerol to yield acetyl–SCoA — the 5.5 mentioned in Problem 25.21 and an additional 2.5 in the conversion of pyruvate to acetyl–SCoA (Section 23.5).
A maximum of 18 molecules of ATP are released in the complete catabolism of glycerol to CO_2 and H_2O — the 8 molecules mentioned above and an additional 10 molecules formed when acetyl SCoA is metabolized in the citric-acid cycle.

25.28 Adipose tissue is located under the skin and in the abdominal cavity and is used for storage and mobilization of triacylglycerols.

25.30 β Oxidation occurs in the mitochondrial matrix of cells.

25.32 The activated fatty acid must be transported from the cytosol into the mitochondrial matrix.

25.34 The sequence is a spiral because the same reaction series is repeated on a two-carbon-shortened fatty acid until the original acid is consumed. In a cycle, the product of the final step is a reactant in the first step.

25.36 In the previous problem, we calculated that each cycle of β oxidation produced 14 ATP. Since the last acetyl-SCoA doesn't undergo β oxidation, 4 fewer ATP are produced from that cycle. Two ATP are also used for activation, and when they are subtracted, we arrive at the formula:

ATP produced per fatty acid = $14n - 6$, where n = the number of acetyl-SCoA produced

For a 10-carbon acid, $n = 5$; thus, the energy content of $CH_3(CH_2)_8COOH$ (capric acid) is a maximum of 64 ATP per mole. For a 14-carbon acid, $n = 7$ and the energy content is a maximum of 92 ATP.

Least energy/mole ⟶ *Greatest energy/mole*

Molecule	Glucose	Sucrose	$CH_3(CH_2)_8COOH$	$CH_3(CH_2)_{12}COOH$
ATP content/mole	32 ATP	64 ATP	64 ATP	92 ATP

25.38

CH3CCH2CSCoA
HSCoA
Acetyl-SCoA
transferase
2 CH3CSCoA

25.40 Three cycles of β oxidation catabolize caprylic acid (a C_8 acid), and 6 cycles of β oxidation catabolize myristic acid (a C_{14} acid).

Fatty Acid Anabolism

25.42 Since β oxidation is an energetically favorable reaction, its exact reverse is energetically unfavorable and thus doesn't occur.

25.44 Fatty acids have an even number of carbons because they are synthesized from a starting material (acetyl-SCoA) that has an even number of carbons.

25.46 Each cycle of lipogenesis uses two NADPH molecules. For the synthesis of palmitic acid, which requires 7 cycles of lipogenesis, 14 molecules of NADPH are needed.

Applications

25.48 Atherosclerosis is the formation of deposits composed of cholesterol and other lipid-containing materials in the arteries of the brain and heart.

25.50 A cholesterol/HDL ratio of 3.5 is ideal, a ratio of 4.5 indicates an average risk, and a ratio of 5.5 shows a high risk.

25.52 A deficiency in leptin, a polypeptide hormone, may cause people to overeat and store the excess calories as fat.

25.54 Important functions of the liver include

(a) Synthesis of glycogen, glucose, triacylglycerols, fatty acids, cholesterol, bile acids, plasma proteins, and blood clotting factors.
(b) Catabolism of glucose, fatty acids, and amino acids.
(c) Storage of glycogen, lipids, amino acids, iron, and fat-soluble vitamins.
(d) Inactivation of toxic substances.

General Questions and Problems

25.56 An excess of carbohydrates produces an excess of acetyl-SCoA. If more acetyl-SCoA is produced than is needed in the respiratory chain, it is used to synthesize fatty acids, which are used to produce the triglycerides that are deposited in adipose tissue. Once carbohydrates have been catabolized to acetyl-SCoA, it is not possible to resynthesize them, because animals don't have enzymes to synthesize carbohydrates from acetyl-SCoA.

25.58 Acetone, acetoacetate and 3-hydroxybutyrate are ketone bodies, which are produced when blood sugar is low and the body metabolizes fats. If more acetyl-SCoA is produced than can enter the citric acid cycle, it is converted to ketone bodies, in the process known as ketogenesis, to be used as an alternate energy source. Ketone bodies are so named because they either contain the ketone functional group or are directly derived from ketones.

25.60 In uncontrolled diabetes, ketone bodies are produced faster than they can be used. The odor of acetone, a volatile ketone body, appears on the breath.

25.62 Consider a carbohydrate and a fatty acid with similar molar masses. Glucose (molar mass = 180 g) yields a maximum of 32 ATP/mole; $CH_3(CH_2)_8COOH$ (molar mass = 172 g) yields a maximum of 64 ATP/mole (Problem 25.33). Thus, the energy yield per mole from a fat is about twice the yield from a sugar. There are two principal reasons for this difference. (1) A carbohydrate has fewer carbons than a fatty acid of similar molar mass and thus produces fewer moles of acetyl-SCoA per mole of carbohydrate. (2) Only 2/3 of a carbohydrate's carbons are used to form acetyl-SCoA; the other carbons are released as CO_2 in the transformation pyruvate —> acetyl-SCoA.

25.64 The body synthesizes cholesterol when no cholesterol is present in the diet. Thus, eliminating exogenous sources of cholesterol won't eliminate cholesterol in the bloodstream. A certain amount of cholesterol is essential for membrane function and as the starting material for synthesis of steroid hormones.

25.66

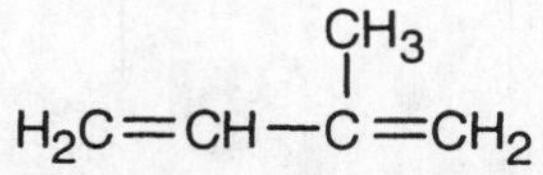

2-Methyl-1,3-butadiene

Since cholesterol contains 27 carbon atoms, at least 6 molecules of 2-methyl-1,3-butadiene are needed for its synthesis.

Self-Test for Chapter 25

Multiple Choice

1. ATP is ultimately produced in all of the following steps of fatty acid catabolism except (a) fatty acid activation (b) introduction of a double bond into a fatty acid (c) oxidation of an alcohol to a ketone (d) entry of acetyl-SCoA into the citric acid cycle

2. An excess of ketone bodies in the blood is known as (a) ketosis (b) ketonuria (c) ketoacidosis (d) ketonemia

3. The reactants for TAG synthesis are (a) glycerol and fatty acids (b) glycerol 3-phosphate and fatty acids (c) glyceraldehyde 3-phosphate and fatty acyl-SCoA (d) glycerol and fatty acyl-SCoA

4. Production of ketone bodies occurs in (a) the liver (b) adipose tissue (c) muscle (d) all of the above

5. Which of the following statements about lipogenesis is false? (a) Synthesis occurs two carbons at a time. (b) Formation of acyl-SACP intermediates requires ATP. (c) The coenzyme NADPH is needed. (d) Lipogenesis occurs when acetyl-SCoA is in abundance.

6. Chylomicrons transport all of the following except (a) acylglycerols (b) small-chain fatty acids (c) phospholipids (d) cholesterol

7. Fatty acids from storage in adipose tissue are transported (a) by chylomicrons (b) by VLDL (c) by serum albumin (d) free in the bloodstream

8. Acetyl-SCoA is the starting material for synthesis of all of the following except (a) steroids (b) fatty acids (c) ketone bodies (d) glycerol

9. β Oxidation of $CH_3(CH_2)_8COOH$ produces a maximum of how many ATPs? (a) 78 (b) 72 (c) 64 (d) 60

10. When glucose is in good supply, the body (a) synthesizes ketone bodies from acetyl-SCoA (b) hydrolyzes TAGs from adipocytes (c) breaks down fatty acids via β-oxidation (d) synthesizes TAGs for storage

Sentence Completion

1. One ______ and one ______ are needed for each β oxidation cycle.
2. Bile acids solubilize lipids by forming ______.
3. Triacylglycerols are stored in _______.
4. TAG synthesis begins with the conversion of glycerol to ______ ______.
5. An alternate name for β oxidation is the___ - ____ _____.
6. The first step in β oxidation involves introduction of a _______ _______.
7. _______ is the presence of ketone bodies in the urine.
8. _______ is a coenzyme for fatty-acid biosynthesis.
9. _______ is a ketone body containing a hydroxyl group.
10. Chylomicrons are transported in the ______ _____ and in the bloodstream.
11. TAGs that are released from storage are said to be ______.
12. All fatty acids are synthesized from ______.

True or False

1. Bile acids are steroids.
2. TAGs are hydrolyzed by pancreatic lipases to glycerol and fatty acids.
3. Activation of fatty acids for fatty-acid oxidation requires two phosphates to be cleaved.
4. A chylomicron is a type of lipoprotein.
5. Chylomicrons carry fatty acid-SCoA across the mitochondrial membrane.
6. A fatty acid with n carbons requires $n/2 - 1$ cycles of β-oxidation for complete breakdown.
7. TAGs are synthesized from glycerol and fatty acyl-SCoAs.
8. HDL transports cholesterol to tissues, where it can accumulate.
9. A fatty acid with a molecular weight similar to that of glucose yields more ATPs per molecule than glucose.
10. Fatty acid synthesis occurs in mitochondria.
11. The terminal —CH_3 group of a fatty acid comes from malonyl-SCoA.
12. Most naturally-occurring fatty acids have an even number of carbon atoms.

Match the entry on the left with its partner on the right.

1. Chylomicron	(a) Lipoprotein rich in cholesterol
2. Lipogenesis	(b) Protein that carries fatty acids in the bloodstream
3. LDL	(c) Solubilizes fats
4. Acetone	(d) Hydrolyzes TAG in adipose tissue
5. Malonyl-SCoA	(e) Lipoprotein that aids in lipid transport of fats in the diet
6. Fatty-acid spiral	(f) Lipoprotein rich in protein
7. Micelle	(g) Starting material in lipogenesis
8. Lipoprotein lipase	(h) Acidic ketone body
9. HDL	(i) Fatty-acid biosynthesis
10. Albumin	(j) Breakdown of fatty acids into acetyl-SCoA
11. Bile	(k) Formed from bile and lipids
12. Acetoacetate	(l) Nonacidic ketone body

Chapter 26 – Nucleic Acids and Protein Synthesis

Chapter Outline

I. Nucleic acids (Sections 26.1–26.4).
  A. Introduction (Section 26.1).
    1. When a cell isn't dividing, its nucleus consists of chromatin, a tangle of fibers composed of protein and DNA.
    2. Just before dividing, the DNA is duplicated.
    3. During division, chromatin organizes itself into chromosomes, each of which is a huge DNA molecule.
    4. The chromosomes are made up of genes, individual segments of DNA that contain instructions for synthesizing a single protein.
    5. The human body has 23 pairs of chromosomes.
  B. Composition of nucleic acids (Section 26.2).
    1. Nucleic acids are polymers of nucleotides.
       DNA and RNA are the two types of nucleic acids.
    2. Nucleotides consist of
      a. A heterocyclic base.
        i. The bases for DNA are the purines adenine and guanine, and the pyrimidines cytosine and thymine.
        ii. For RNA, uracil replaces thymine.
      b. A pentose.
        i. For DNA, the pentose is D-ribose.
        ii. For RNA, the pentose is D-2-deoxyribose.
        ii. The pentose is connected to the base by a β-*N*-glycosidic bond to the anomeric carbon.
      c. A phosphate group.
         The phosphate group is attached at C5 of the pentose.
    3. The combination of sugar + base is known as a nucleoside.
      a. Nucleosides are named by replacing the *-ine* of the base name by *-osine* for purines and *-idine* for pyrimidines.
      b. If the pentose is 2-deoxyribose, the prefix *deoxy-* is added to the name.
      c. To indicate position, numbers without primes are used for bases, and numbers with primes are used for the pentose.
      d. Nucleosides have important biochemical functions other than as components of nucleic acids.
    4. Nucleotides.
      a. Nucleotides are named by adding "5'-monophosphate" to the nucleoside name.
      b. Nucleotides can form di- and triphosphates.
         ATP plays an important role in biochemical energetics.
  C. The structure of nucleic acid chains (Section 26.3).
    1. Nucleotides are joined by phosphate ester bonds between the 5' phosphate and the 3' —OH group of the sugar of the next nucleotide.
    2. Vast numbers of nucleotides can be connected by these bonds to form immense polynucleotides.
    3. The structure and function of nucleic acids depends on the sequence of nucleotides.
    4. The sequence is described by starting at the 5' end and identifying the bases by one-letter abbreviations.

D. Base-pairing in DNA (Section 26.4).
  1. In DNA, two polynucleotide strands coil around each other in a double helix.
    a. The sugar–phosphate backbone is on the outside.
    b. The bases are inside.
  2. The two strands run in opposite directions.
  3. The two strands are held together by hydrogen bonding between bases.
    a. A and T form two hydrogen bonds to each other.
    b. C and G form three hydrogen bonds to each other.
  4. The two strands are complementary.
    a. A and T always occur in DNA in the same percentage.
    b. C and G always occur in DNA in the same percentage.

II. The function of nucleic acids (Sections 26.5–26.10).
A. The central dogma of molecular genetics (Section 26.5).
  1. The function of DNA is to store genetic information.
  2. The function of RNA is to read and decode DNA and use the information to synthesize proteins.
  3. Nucleic acids take part in three major processes.
    a. Replication is the process in which DNA makes a copy of itself.
    b. Transcription is the process in which RNA reads the genetic message.
    c. Translation is the process in which the genetic message is used to make proteins.
B. Replication of DNA (Section 26.6).
  1. Mechanism of replication.
    a. The double helix partially unwinds, with the assistance of helicase enzymes. Unwinding occurs simultaneously at many locations.
    b. Bases line up and form hydrogen bonds with their complements.
    c. DNA polymerase catalyzes bond formation between the 5' phosphate group on the arriving nucleotide and the 3' —OH of the old strand.
  2. Two identical new copies of the double helix are formed.
  3. Because strand growth occurs in one direction (5' —> 3'), only one strand of DNA is synthesized continuously (the leading strand).
    a. The other strand (the lagging strand) is synthesized in segments, beginning at the replication fork.
    b. DNA ligase attaches the segments of the lagging strand.
  4. The copying of DNA requires several hours, involves many replication forks, and proceeds virtually without error.
C. RNA (Section 26.7).
  1. Structure of RNA.
    a. RNA resembles DNA but has the following differences;
      i. The pentose is ribose.
      ii. Uracil replaces thymine.
    b. RNA chains are shorter than DNA chains.
    c. RNA chains may be single-stranded or double-stranded.
  2. Types of RNA.
    a. Ribosomal RNA has a molecular weight of 5 x 10^6 amu and occurs in ribosomes, which are the site of protein synthesis.
    b. Messenger RNA reads DNA and carries the message to the ribosomes.
    c. Transfer RNA delivers amino acids to the growing protein chain.
D. Transcription (Section 26.8).
  1. mRNA is synthesized by transcription of DNA.
    a. RNA polymerase recognizes a control segment of DNA that precedes the nucleotides to be transcribed.
    b. A small section of DNA unwinds.
    c. Complementary bases are attached.

   d. Transcription stops when RNA polymerase recognizes a "stop" nucleotide sequence.
   e. All RNA is synthesized in the same way, although we will focus on mRNA in this description.
2. Only one DNA strand is transcribed — the template strand.
   a. The other strand is the information strand.
   b. mRNA is a copy of the information strand (with U replacing T).
3. Not all genes are continuous strands of DNA.
   a. The coding sections of DNA (exons) are interrupted by noncoding sections (introns).
   b. In the final mRNA, the intron sections are cut out.
4. Each mRNA controls the synthesis of one protein.

E. Translation (Sections 26.9–26.10).
1. The genetic code (Section 26.9).
   a. A sequence of three mRNA bases codes for a specific amino acid.
   b. The codes are written in the 5' —> 3' direction.
   c. Each amino acid is represented by one or more codes.
2. Transfer RNA (Section 26.10).
   a. The message carried by mRNA is decoded by tRNA.
   b. Each amino acid is transported by its own tRNA to the ribosome.
   c. Amino acids are bonded to tRNA by an ester bond between the —COOH group of an amino acid and C3' of ribose at the end of the tRNA.
   d. Each tRNA has an anticodon that corresponds to a codon sequence on mRNA.
3. Protein synthesis.
   a. Initiation.
      i. The first AUG codon on the 5' end of mRNA is a "start" codon (which also codes for methionine).
      ii. When the Met tRNA comes together with the mRNA codon and occupies one of the two binding sites in the ribosome, elongation can start.
      iii. If Met isn't the first amino acid in the protein, it is removed after protein synthesis.
   b. Elongation.
      i. A tRNA with an anticodon complementary to the second mRNA codon occupies the second binding site.
      ii. An enzyme in the ribosome catalyzes peptide bond formation and breaks the bond between the first amino acid and its tRNA.
      iii. This tRNA leaves the ribosome.
      iv. The ribosome shifts one position along the mRNA chain (translocation).
      v. The second site is free to accept the next tRNA.
      vi. A single mRNA can be read by many ribosomes.
   c. Termination.
      i. A "stop" codon signals the end of translation.
      ii. An enzyme called "releasing factor" frees the polypeptide chain from the last tRNA, and the mRNA is released from the ribosome.

Solutions to Chapter 26 Problems

26.1

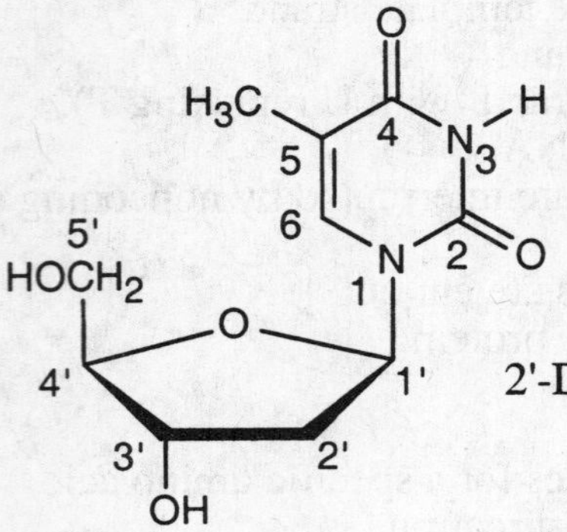
H3C
H
O
4
N3
5
6
N
2
O
5'
HOCH2
1
O
4'
1'
3'
2'
OH

2'-Deoxythymidine

26.2 D-Ribose has one more oxygen atom than 2-deoxy-D-ribose. This added oxygen allows D-ribose to form an extra hydrogen bond.

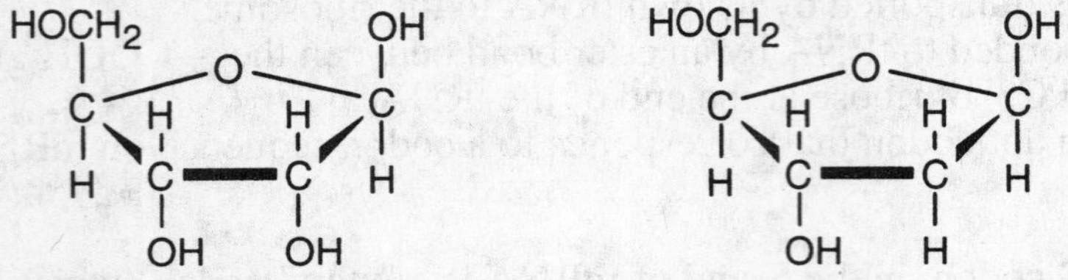
HOCH2
OH
O
C
H
H
C
H
C
C
H
OH
OH

β-D-Ribose
($C_5H_{10}O_5$)

β-2-Deoxy-D-ribose
($C_5H_{10}O_4$)

26.3

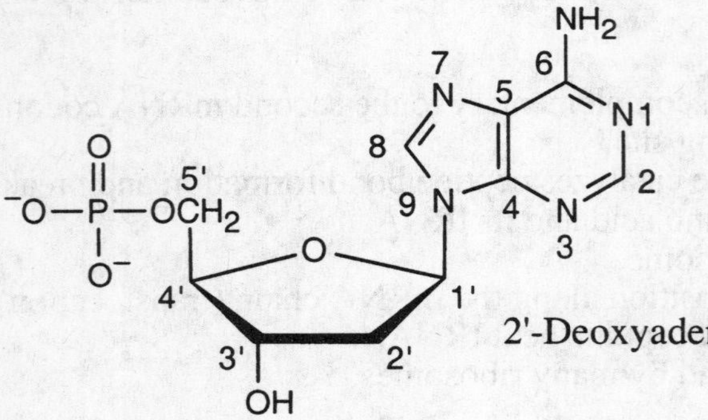
NH2
7
6
N
5
N1
8
2
9
N
4
N
3
O
5'
⁻O–P–OCH2
O⁻
O
4'
1'
3'
2'
OH

2'-Deoxyadenosine 5'-monophosphate

26.4

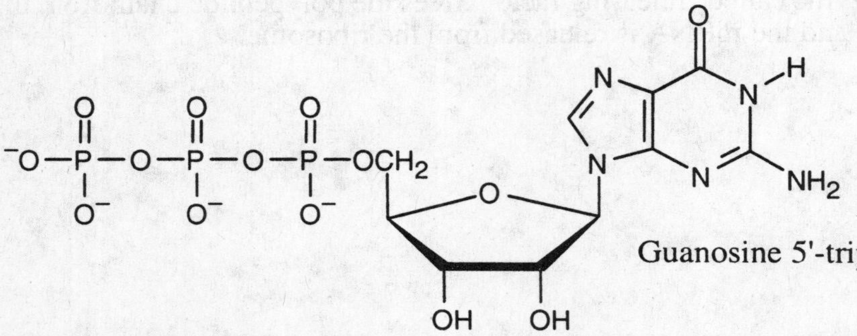
O
N
N
H
N
N
NH2
⁻O–P–O–P–O–P–OCH2
O⁻
O⁻
O⁻
O
OH
OH

Guanosine 5'-triphosphate (GTP)

26.5 dCMP — 2'-Deoxycytidine 5'-monophosphate
CMP — Cytidine 5'-monophosphate
UDP — Uridine 5'-diphosphate
AMP — Adenosine 5'-monophosphate
ATP — Adenosine 5'-triphosphate

26.6 C-G-A-U-A = cytosine-guanine-adenine-uracil-adenine. The pentanucleotide comes from RNA because it contains uracil.

26.7

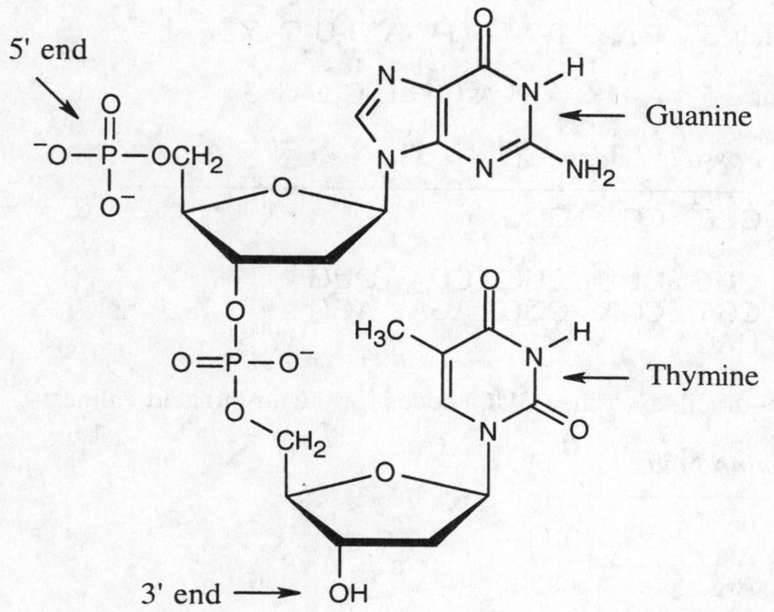
5' end
Guanine
Thymine
3' end

26.8 (a) Original strand: 5' G-C-C-T-A-G-T 3'
Complement: 3' C-G-G-A-T-C-A 5'

(b) Original strand: 5' A-A-T-G-G-C-T-C-A 3'
Complement: 3' T-T-A-C-C-G-A-G-T 5'

26.9

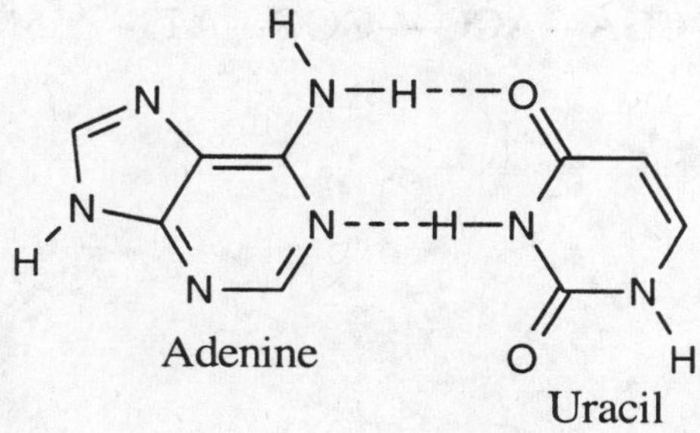
Adenine
Uracil

26.10 The phosphate groups cause the DNA molecule to be negatively charged.

26.11 (a) A longer strand of DNA has a higher "melting temperature" because larger molecules have greater numbers of hydrogen bonds.
(b) A strand of DNA containing a higher percentage of C/G base pairs has a higher "melting temperature." A C/G base pair has three hydrogen bonds, whereas an A/T pair has only two hydrogen bonds. A DNA strand with a higher percent of C/G base pairs has more hydrogen bonds, and more heat is required to separate the two strands.

26.12 (a) DNA template strand: 5' C-A-T–A–C-T-G-G-A-C-A-C 3'
: : : : : : : : : : : :
mRNA complement: 3' G-U-A-U-G-A-C-C-U-G-U-G 5'

(b) DNA template strand: 3' T-A-G-T-A-T–G-C-A-G-G-C 5'
: : : : : : : : : : : :
mRNA complement 5' A-U-C-A-U-A-C-G-U-C-C-G 3'

26.13

Amino Acid	*Possible Codons* (5' –> 3')					
(a) Ala	GCU	GCC	GCA	GCG		
(b) Trp	UGG					
(c) Leu	UUA	UUG	CUU	CUC	CUA	CUG
(d) Arg	CGU	CGC	CGA	CGG	AGA	AGG
(e) Tyr	UAU	UAC				

26.14 The sequence guanine–uracil–cytosine (GUC) codes for the amino acid valine.

26.15

Codon	*Amino Acid*
(a) AUU	Ile
(b) GCG	Ala
(c) CGA	Arg
(d) AAC	Asn

26.16 Three mRNA base triplets code for isoleucine: AUU, AUC, AUA. Six possible mRNA strands could code for this tripeptide if different codons were used for each Ile.
5' AUUAUCAUA 3'   5' AUCAUUAUA 3'   5' AUAAUCAUU 3'
5' AUUAUAAUC 3'   5' AUCAUAAUU 3'   5' AUAAUUAUC 3'

26.17 – 26.18

mRNA sequence:	5'	CUU—AUG—GCU—UGG—CCC—UAA						3'
Amino-acid sequence:		Leu—Met—Ala—Trp—Pro—Stop						
tRNA anticodons:	3'	GAA	UAC	CGA	ACC	GGG	AUU	5'
DNA template sequence:	3'	GAA—TAC—CGA—ACC—GGG—ATT						5'

Understanding Key Concepts

26.19

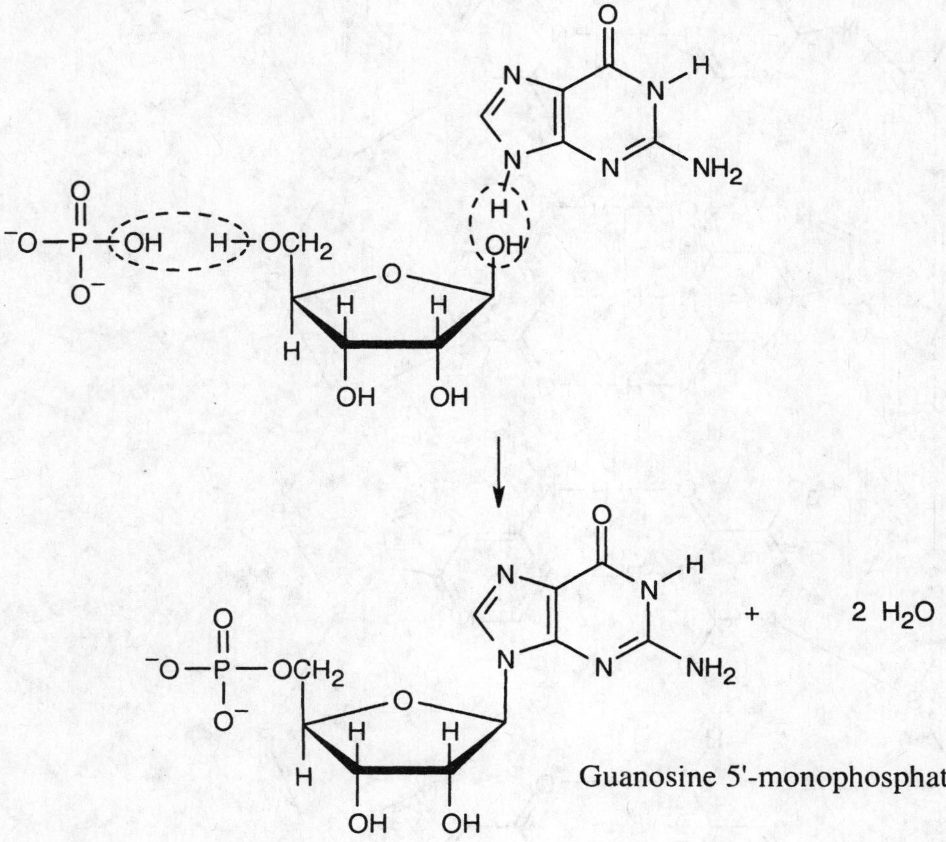

Guanosine 5'-monophosphate

26.20

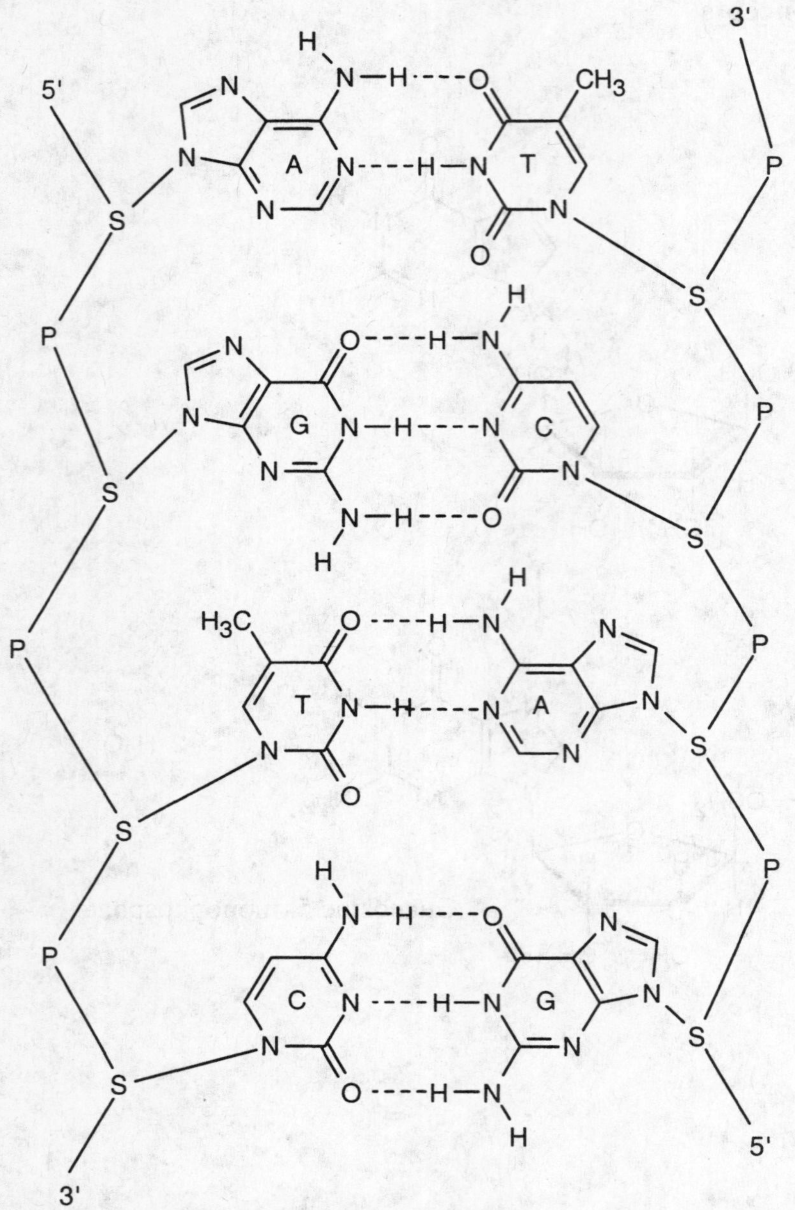
5'
3'
A
T
G
C
T
A
C
G
CH3
H3C
S
P
3'
5'

The sequence of the left chain: 5' –A–G–T–C– 3'.
The sequence of the right chain: 3' –G–A–C–T– 5'.

26.21

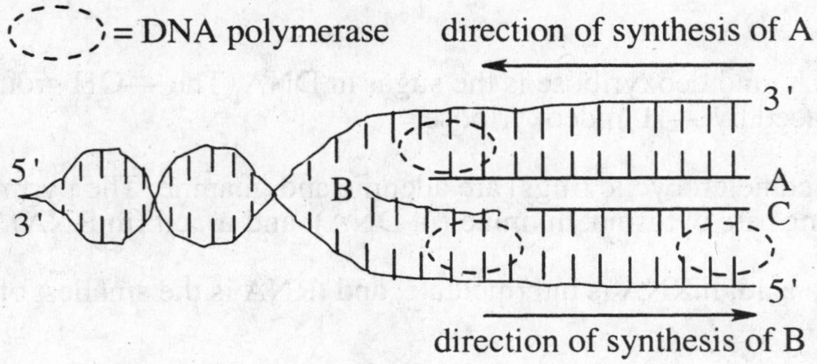
= DNA polymerase
direction of synthesis of A
3'
5'
3'
B
A
C
5'
direction of synthesis of B

Segments B and C are joined by the action of a DNA ligase enzyme.

26.22 The sugar–phosphate backbone is found on the exterior of the DNA double helix. Since the phosphate groups are negatively charged, histone proteins should have a large number of positively charged amino acids, such as lysine, arginine, and histidine, on their surfaces.

26.23

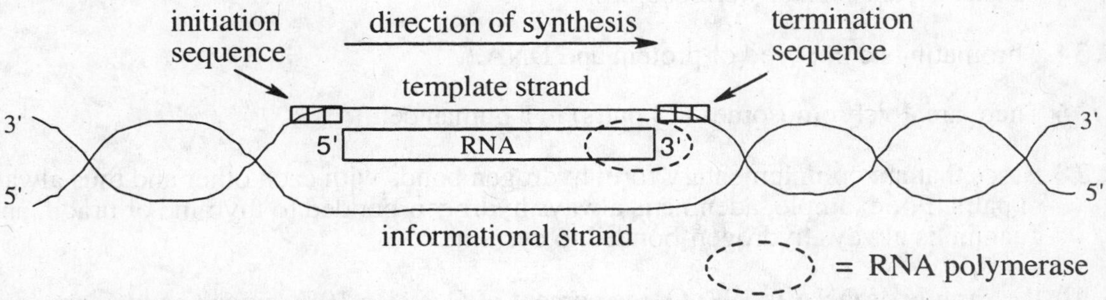
initiation sequence
direction of synthesis
termination sequence
template strand
3'
5'
5'
RNA
3'
3'
5'
informational strand
= RNA polymerase

The nucleotides adenosine 5'-monophosphate, cytidine 5'-monophosphate, guanosine 5'-monophosphate, and uridine 5'-monophosphate are used to synthesize messenger RNA.

26.24 Each amino acid has more than one mRNA codon.
Codons for Gln: CAA, CAG
Codons for His: CAC, CAU
Codons for Pro: CCC, CCU, CCA, CCG
Codons for Gly: GGG, GGU, GGA, GGC
Using the first codon listed:

(a) 5' C A A | C A C | C C C | G G G 3' mRNA

(b) 3' G T T | G T G | G G G | C C C 5' DNA template strand

(c) 5' C A A | C A C | C C C | G G G 3' DNA informational strand

The upper strand of DNA is the template for the synthesis of mRNA, and its sequence of bases is the complement of the sequence of bases that make up the pro-TRH gene (with T replacing U). The lower strand is the informational strand.

(d) To find the number of DNA sequences, multiply the numbers of different codons for each amino acid.
2 x 2 x 4 x 4 = 64 possible DNA sequences code for the first four amino acids in pro-TRH.

Structure and Function of Nucleic Acids

26.26 Ribose is the sugar in RNA, and deoxyribose is the sugar in DNA. The —OH group at carbon 2 of ribose is replaced by —H in deoxyribose.

26.28 The purine bases (two fused heterocyclic rings) are adenine and guanine. The pyrimidine bases (one heterocyclic ring) are cytosine, thymine (in DNA), and uracil (in RNA).

26.30 DNA is the largest nucleic acid, mRNA is intermediate, and tRNA is the smallest of the three nucleic acids.

26.32 *Similarities:* Replication, transcription and translation are all polymerizations in which a nucleic acid is used as a template for the synthesis of another biopolymer. In all of these processes, hydrogen bonding is used to bring the subunits into the correct position for bond formation and to determine the order of assembly.
Differences: In replication, DNA makes a copy of itself. In transcription, DNA is used as a template for the synthesis of mRNA. In translation, mRNA is used as a template for the synthesis of proteins. Replication and transcription take place in the nucleus of cells, and translation takes place in ribosomes.

26.34 Chromatin is composed of protein and DNA.

26.36 There are 46 chromosomes (23 pairs) in a human cell.

26.38 Bases that are complementary form hydrogen bonds with each other and thus always occur in pairs. For example, adenine is always hydrogen-bonded to thymine or uracil, and guanine is always hydrogen-bonded to cytosine.

26.40 If a sample of DNA is 19% G, the percent of C is also 19%, since G and C are complementary. The sample contains 31% A and 31% T, because A and T are also complementary.

26.42 Polynucleotides are written from 5' to 3'.

26.44

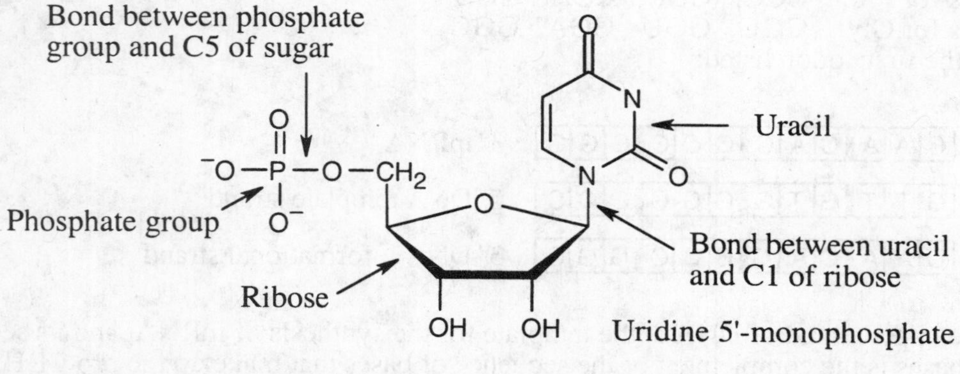
Bond between phosphate group and C5 of sugar
O
$^{-}O-P-O-CH_2$
O^{-}
Phosphate group
O
N
Uracil
N
O
O
Bond between uracil and C1 of ribose
Ribose
OH
OH
Uridine 5'-monophosphate

A phosphate ester bond is formed between the phosphate group and the sugar. Water is removed in the formation of both the sugar–phosphate linkage and the sugar–base linkage.

26.46

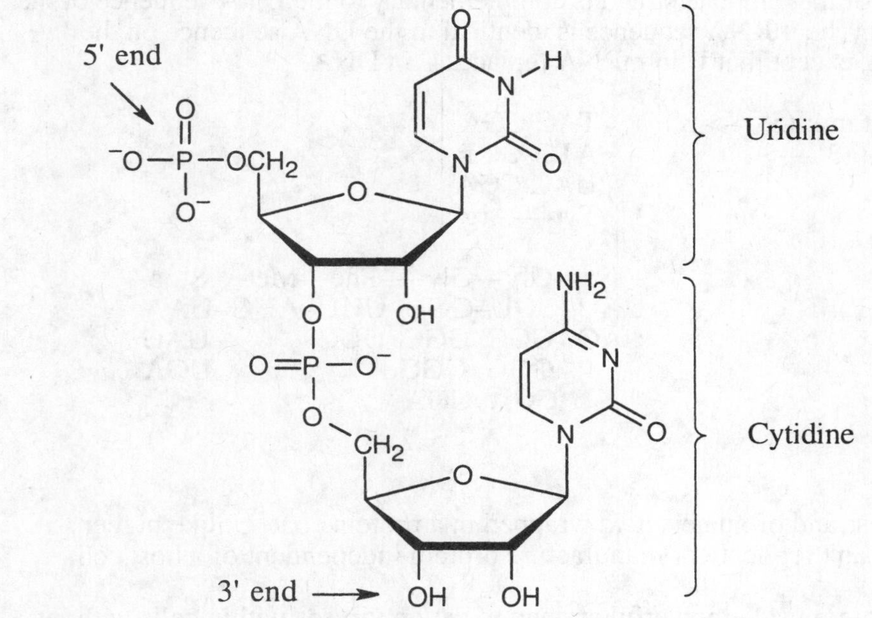
5' end
Uridine
Cytidine
3' end

Nucleic Acids and Heredity

26.48 Transcribed RNA is complementary to the template strand of DNA.

26.50 To say that DNA replication is semiconservative means that each of the two new copies of DNA has a strand of DNA that was the original template and one strand that is newly synthesized.

26.52 An anticodon is a sequence of three nucleotides that is complementary to a sequence on a codon. The anticodon occurs on tRNA and matches the codon sequence on mRNA when it brings the correct amino acid into position for protein synthesis.

26.54 The tRNAs for each amino acid differ in their anticodon sequences.

26.56

Amino Acid	Codons (5' –> 3')	
(a) Gln	CAA	CAG
(b) Lys	AAA	AAG
(c) Met	AUG	

26.58

Codon (5' —> 3')	*Amino Acid*	*tRNA Anticodon* (3' —> 5')
(a) ACU	Thr	UGA
(b) GGA	Gly	CCU
(c) CUU	Leu	GAA

26.60, 26.62
The DNA sequence of the template strand is complementary to the DNA sequence of the informational strand. The mRNA sequence is identical to the DNA sequence on the informational strand, except that U in mRNA replaces T in DNA.

Informational strand: (5' —> 3')	TAC-CGA
Template strand: (3' —> 5')	ATG-GCT
mRNA: (5' —> 3')	UAC-CGA
Dipeptide:	Tyr—Arg

26.64 Metenkephalin:

	Tyr	Gly	Gly	Phe	Met	Stop
mRNA (5' —> 3'):	UAU–	GGU–	GGU–	UUU–	AUG–	UAA
	UAC	GGC	GGC	UUC		UAG
		GGG	GGG			UGA
		GGA	GGA			

Applications

26.66 Viruses consist of a strand of nucleic acid wrapped in a protein coat. Unlike higher organisms, viruses can't replicate or manufacture protein independent of a host cell.

26.68 To be effective, a drug must be powerful enough to act on viruses within cells without damaging the cells and their genetic material. Also, drugs quickly lose their effectiveness against AIDS because of the high mutation rate of the AIDS virus.

26.70 In early 2006, a vaccine was developed against the H5N1 virus. There are concerns, however, that there may be as many as four strains of the virus, and it is not known if the vaccine is effective against all of them. Fortunately, there is no known human-to-human spread of the virus.

General Questions and Problems

26.72 To code for preproinsulin, 81 x 3 = 243 bases are needed to code for the protein's 81 amino acids. In addition, a three-base "start" codon and a three-base "stop" codon are needed, for a total of 249 bases .

26.74 If a protein doesn't have methionine as its first amino acid, the methionine is removed after protein synthesis is complete.

Self-Test for Chapter 26

Multiple Choice

1. The name for a nucleoside formed from cytidine and 2'-deoxyribose is
(a) deoxycytidine 5'-monophosphate (b) 2'-deoxycytidine (c) 2'-deoxycytosine
(d) 2'-deoxycytosine 5'-monophosphate

2. Adenine and thymine are complementary because
(a) they are both purines. (b) they are both pyrimidines. (c) they both occur in DNA.
(d) they form two hydrogen bonds to each other.

3. If the base sequence CAC-TTA-GGT appears on the informational strand of DNA, which sequence occurs in mRNA?
(a) CAC-TTA-GGT (b) CAC-UUA-GGU (c) GTG-AAT-CCA (d) GUG-AAU-CCA

4. Which statement about the RNA base sequence CGG-AAA-GUU is true?
(a) It codes for a basic tripeptide. (b) It contains a "stop" codon. (c) Changing the third codon from GUU to GUC changes the amino acids in the tripeptide. (d) The 5' end is on the right, and the 3' end is on the left.

5. Which of the following completes the initiation phase of protein synthesis?
(a) the small subunit of a ribosome (b) the large subunit of a ribosome (c) mRNA (d) tRNA

6. The process by which the genetic message contained in DNA is read is called
(a) replication (b) transcription (c) translation (d) translocation

7. Which of the following heterocyclic bases contains a methyl group?
(a) guanine (b) cytosine (c) thymine (d) uracil

8. An enzyme involved in translation is
(a) DNA polymerase (b) restriction endonuclease (c) RNA polymerase (d) releasing factor

9. Which of the following statements about DNA replication is untrue?
(a) Replication is semiconservative. (b) Each DNA strand has many replication forks.
(c) DNA ligase catalyzes bond formation between each arriving nucleotide.
(d) Replication proceeds in the 5'—>3' direction.

10. Which heterocyclic base contains only carbon, hydrogen, and nitrogen?
(a) adenine (b) guanine (c) cytosine (d) thymine

Sentence Completion

1. _____ is the process by which an identical copy of DNA is made.

2. The two strands of DNA have base sequences that are _____.

3. When a cell is not actively dividing, its nucleus is occupied by ______.

4. Another name for an RNA virus is a _______.

5. An _____ is a segment of a gene that does not code for protein synthesis.

6. tRNA binds to an amino acid by an _____ linkage.

7. A ______ consists of a heterocyclic amine base bonded to an aldopentose.

8. An enzyme called a _____ _____ frees the polypeptide chain from the last tRNA during protein synthesis.

9. The point of replication of a DNA chain is called the _________ _____.

10. The sugar _____ has an —H instead of an —OH at its 2' position.

11. The _____ - _____ model describes DNA as two polynucleotide strands coiled about each other in a double helix.

12. The enzyme _____ _____ catalyzes the bonding of nucleotides to form new strands of DNA.

True or False

1. There are a total of 64 codons for the 20 amino acids.

2. The amount of adenine in an organism's DNA is equal to the amount of guanine.

3. In transcription, mRNA is a copy of the informational strand of DNA.

4. An amino acid codon occurs on tRNA.

5. The codon AUG initiates protein synthesis.

6. Synthetase enzymes catalyze the formation of ester bonds between amino acids and their tRNAs.

7. The individual units of RNA and DNA are called nucleotides.

8. The two strands of the DNA double helix run in the same direction.

9. Transcription is the process by which the genetic message is decoded and used to make proteins.

10. Most human DNA contains genetic instructions.

11. Each amino acid is specified by more than one codon.

12. The correct name for the RNA nucleotide containing G is guanidine 5'-monophosphate.

Match each entry on the left with its partner on the right.

1. 5' end	(a) Enzyme used in replication
2. A-C-G	(b) Cysteine codon
3. U-G-C	(c) Forms three hydrogen bonds
4. Adenine	(d) Coded for by six codons
5. DNA ligase	(e) RNA containing both exons and introns
6. 3' end	(f) "Stop" codon
7. Leu	(g) Purine
8. Cytosine	(h) Enzyme used in transcription
9. hnRNA	(i) —OH group
10. Uracil	(j) Cysteine anticodon
11. U-G-A	(k) Pyrimidine
12. RNA polymerase	(l) Phosphate group

Chapter 27 – Genomics

Chapter Outline

I. Mapping the human genome (Section 27.1).
   Two research groups have collectively decoded 99% of the human genome.
   1. The Human Genome Project.
      a. The Human Genome Project is made up of 20 international not-for-profit groups.
      b. The technique:
         i. For each chromosome, a genetic map is developed; the map shows the location of markers determined by inheritance.
         ii. A map of finer resolution (physical map) shows markers determined by other methods.
         iii. The chromosome is cut into large segments, and the resulting clones are organized into an overlapping sequence.
         iv. Each clone is fragmented into hundreds of pieces, which are labelled and separated by electrophoresis.
         v. The sequences are assembled into a nucleotide map.
   2. Celera.
      a. Celera is a for-profit research group.
      b. The technique:
         i. The entire genome is broken into fragments, without identifying their origin.
         ii. The fragments are copied many times, sequenced and separated.
         iii. The sequences are reassembled, using a supercomputer.

II. Characteristics of chromosomes (Sections 27.2–27.3).
   A. Chromosome structure (Section 27.2).
   1. Telomeres.
      a. Telomeres are long series of repeating DNA that are found at the ends of each chromosome.
      b. Telomeres protect the ends of chromosomes from accidents.
      c. Telomeres also prevent the ends of chromosomes from pairing with other DNA.
      d. The enzyme telomerase catalyzes the addition of telomeres to DNA.
         Telomerase is more active in young cells than in older cells.
   2. Centromeres.
      a. Centromeres are constrictions that determine the shapes of chromosomes during cell division.
      b. Centromeres contain large repetitive base sequences.
   3. Other noncoding DNA.
      Not all of the functions of noncoding DNA are known.
         i. Some segments are regulatory.
         ii. Other proposed functions: accommodation of DNA folding, evolutionary roles.
   4. Genes.
      The coding sections of a gene (exons) are interspersed with noncoding introns.
   B. Mutations and polymorphisms (Section 27.3).
   1. Mutations.
      a. An error in mRNA transcription is not serious.

b. An error in DNA replication is a mutation and is passed on each time DNA replicates.
   i. Substances that cause mutations are mutagens.
   ii. Each time mRNA is transcribed, the resulting protein will have an error.
   iii. The consequences of a mutation range from insignificant to lethal.
c. If the error occurs in a somatic cell, cancer may result.
d. If the error occurs in a germ cell, a genetic defect may be passed on to the offspring.

2. Polymorphisms.
   a. Polymorphisms are variations in nucleotide sequences that are common within a given population.
   b. Replacement of one nucleotide by another in the same location is a single-nucleotide polymorphism (SNP).
      i. SNPs are responsible for most of the variation among human beings.
      ii. SNPs are responsible for many genetic diseases.
      iii. A catalog of SNPs has been developed; it now has 1.4 million SNPs.
      iv. This catalog has been used to identify SNPs responsible for abnormalities.

III. Recombinant DNA and genomics (Section 27.4–27.5).

A. Recombinant DNA technology is used to cut a specific gene out of one organism and insert it into the DNA of another organism (Section 27.4).
   1. The second organism is usually a bacterium.
   2. Bacterial DNA is contained in plasmids, which are easy to isolate.

B. Technique of recombinant DNA.
   1. The plasmid is cleaved by a restriction endonuclease.
      a. There are more than 200 restriction endonucleases.
      b. Cleavage occurs at a specific site in a base sequence.
      c. Each DNA strand is left with a few unpaired bases, called "sticky ends."
   2. The gene to be inserted is also cleaved by the same endonucleases and thus has complementary sticky ends.
   3. The gene and the plasmid are mixed in the presence of a DNA ligase enzyme and the gene is inserted into the plasmid.
   4. The plasmid can be reinserted into a bacterial cell, and the bacteria, which multiply rapidly, manufacture the protein.

C. Uses of recombinant DNA technology — genomics (Section 27.5).
   1. Agriculture.
      Transgenic plants and animals have been bred; their DNA includes single genes that code for desirable traits.
   2. Medicine.
      a. Gene therapy might cure inherited diseases by replacing a disease-causing gene with a healthy copy of that gene.
      b. A personal genomic survey might be helpful in drug and therapeutic choices.
      c. DNA chip screening can be used to detect polymorphisms associated with diseases and drug responses.

Solutions to Chapter 27 Problems

27.1 uuiioouoppagfdtttrr**once**trtrnnnaedigop**upon**sldjflsjfxxxbvgf**a**qqqeu**time**abrrxoknuw (once upon a time)

27.2 Look back to Table 26.4 and note that UGU codes for cysteine, and UGG codes for tryptophan. In the synthesized protein, a tryptophan would replace a cysteine. Since cysteine forms disulfide bridges, the protein's three-dimensional structure would most likely be disrupted and its function might be affected.

27.3 The complementary DNA strand is drawn by pairing the bases and by reversing the labels of the two ends of the strands. The restriction enzyme cleaves the complementary strand at the same location.

5' –A– // –G–A–T–C–T– 3'
3' –T–C–T–A–G– // –A– 5'

27.4 To be sticky, base sequences must be complementary. Draw the complement of the first sequence. If the complement you draw is identical to the second sequence, the two sequences are sticky.
(a) The pairs are sticky.
(b), (c) the pairs aren't sticky.

27.5 (a) The field of *comparative genomics* deals with the identification of genes that perform identical functions in mice and humans.
(b) A person working in *genetic engineering* might be involved with creating a variety of wheat that is not harmed by a herbicide that kills weeds that interfere with wheat crops.
(c) *Pharmacogenetics* is used for screening a individual's genome to choose the most appropriate pain-killing medication for that person.
(d) *Bioinformatics* is the computer analysis of base-sequence information from groups of people with and without a certain disease to discover where the disease-causing polymorphism lies.

Understanding Key Concepts

27.6 (1) A genetic map, which shows the location of markers one million nucleotides apart, is created. (2) Next comes a physical map, which refines the distance between markers to 100,000 base pairs. (3) The chromosome is cleaved into large segments of overlapping clones. (4) The clones are fragmented into 500 base pieces, which are sequenced.

27.7 The variations in DNA sequences occupy only a small part of the genome; the rest is identical among humans. A diverse group of individuals contributed DNA to the project.

27.8 *Telomeres* protect the chromosome from mutations, prevent DNA from bonding to other DNA, and are believed to play a role in human aging. *Centromeres* form the constrictions that determine the shapes of chromosomes during cell division. *Promoter sequences* determine which genes will be replicated. *Introns* are noncoding segments that are interspersed with gene-encoding exons and whose function is unknown.

27.9 Both mutations and polymorphisms are variations in base sequences. A mutation is an error in a base sequence that is transferred during DNA replication, occurs in a very small number of individuals, and is caused by a random error or a mutagen. A polymorphism is a variation in DNA sequence that is common within a given population.

27.10 Recombinant DNA contains two or more DNA segments that do not occur together in nature. The DNA that codes for a specific human protein can be incorporated into a bacterial plasmid using recombinant DNA technology. The plasmid is then reinserted into a bacterial cell, where its protein-synthesizing machinery makes the desired protein.

27.11 Major benefits of genomics include creation of disease-resistant and nutrient-rich crops, gene therapy to cure or prevent genetic diseases, and genetic screening that leads to more effective health care. Major negative outcomes are associated with the misuse of an individual's genetic information, and with prediction of a genetic disease for which there is no cure.

The Human Genome Map

27.12 Celera broke the genome into many unidentified fragments. The fragments were multiplied and cut into 500 base pieces, which were sequenced. A supercomputer was used to determine the order of the bases.

27.14 Approximately 50% of the human genome is composed of repeat sequences.

27.16 (a) About 200 genes are identical to bacterial genes.
(b) A single gene may produce several proteins.

27.18 The clones used in DNA mapping are multiple identical copies of DNA segments from a single individual. Clone samples large enough for experimental manipulation are essential for mapping.

Chromosomes, Mutations, and Polymorphisms

27.20 The youngest cells have long telomeric sequences of DNA, and the telomeres shorten as cells age. Thus, cell age can be predicted by telomere length.

27.22 The centromere is the constriction that determines the shape of a chromosome during cell division. It is composed of noncoding and repetitive DNA.

27.24 A silent mutation is a single base change that specifies the same amino acid.

27.26 Some mutations result from random and spontaneous events. Other mutations are caused by exposure to a mutagen.

27.28 An SNP can result in the change in identity of an amino acid inserted into a protein at a particular location in a polypeptide chain. The effect of an SNP depends on the function of the protein and the nature of the SNP. Most of the variations between individual human beings are due to SNPs.

27.30 Analysis of an individual's DNA for SNPs would allow a physician to predict the age at which inherited diseases might become active, their severity, and the response of the individual to various types of treatment.

27.32 A change in the nature of an amino acid's side chain determines whether an amino acid will create a major or a minor alteration in the protein's shape. Similar side chains have a lesser effect than very different side chains.

27.34

	Normal Codon	*Codes For:*	*Mutated Codon*	*Codes For:*
(a)	GUC	Val	GCC	Ala
(b)	CCC	Pro	CAC	His

In (a), the mutated mRNA codes for an amino acid (Ala) that is somewhat similar to the normal amino acid (Val), and the effect of the mutation may be small. In (b) the mutated mRNA codes for an amino acid that is basic, whereas the normal amino acid is proline, a bulky, neutral amino acid. The second mutation is more serious because the mutation changes the type of amino acid in the protein and would probably affect the shape and function of the protein.

Recombinant DNA

27.36 Proteins can be produced in greater quantity than otherwise possible.

27.38 Sticky ends are unpaired bases on each end of the cleaved DNA. Recombinant DNA is formed when the sticky ends of the DNA of interest and of the DNA of the plasmid have complementary base pairs and can be joined by a DNA ligase. If the sticky ends are not complementary, the DNA segments can't be joined.

27.40 Write out the sticky sequence for the first of the two base sequences. If the sticky sequence agrees with the second sequence shown, the two sequences are sticky.
(a) The sequence TTAGC is sticky with AATCG, not AAACG. Thus, the two sequences shown aren't sticky.
(b) CGTACG isn't sticky with GTACGT.

Genomics

27.42 Proteomics is the study of the complete set of proteins coded for by a genome or synthesized by a given type of cell. It might provide information about the role of a protein in both healthy and diseased cells.

27.44 Corn and soybeans have been genetically altered and improved to provide disease and herbicide resistance.

27.46 A DNA chip could be used to match a patient's DNA fragments with polymorphic sequences linked to known genetic disorders, in order to diagnose inherited diseases.

Applications

27.48 Many anonymous individuals were the DNA donors for these projects.

27.50 The five steps of DNA fingerprinting:

(1) A sample of DNA is digested with a restriction endonuclease.
(2) The resulting fragments are separated by size using gel electrophoresis.
(3) The DNA fragments are transferred to a nylon membrane.
(4) The DNA blot is treated with a radioactive DNA probe, which binds to the sticky ends of the DNA fragments.
(5) The radioactive RFLPs can be identified by exposing an X-ray film to the blot.

It is important to standardize DNA fingerprinting techniques because all samples must be analyzed under the same conditions in order to be compared.

26.52 A polymerase chain reaction is used to produce a large number of copies of a specific DNA chain.

General Questions and Problems

27.54 A monogenic disease is caused by the variation in just one gene.

27.56 TATGACT is sticky with ATACTGA.

27.58 A hereditary disease is caused by a mutation in the DNA of a germ cell and is passed from parent to offspring. The mutation affects the amino-acid sequence of an important protein and causes a change in the biological activity of the protein.

Self-Test for Chapter 27

Multiple choice:

1. A field of study that deals with the use of computers to manage and interpret genetic information is
(a) genetic engineering (b) proteomics (c) bioinformatics (d) gene therapy

2. Approximately how many genes are in the human genome?
(a) 3.1 billion (b) 1.4 million (c) 100,000 (d) 20,000

3. Which of the following is not a characteristic of a telomere?
(a) It has a repeating series of nucleotides. (b) Each chromosome has one telomere. (c) The nucleotide groups of telomeres are noncoding. (d) A telomere protects the end of a chromosome from accidental damage.

4. Which of the following mutations is least likely to cause genetic damage?
(a) AUC to AUA (b) AUC to AUG (c) GUU to GGU (d) CAA to CGA

5. Which of the following mutations is most likely to cause genetic damage?
(a) AUC to AUA (b) AUC to AUG (c) GUU to GGU (d) CAA to CGA

6. All of the following are composed of noncoding DNA except
(a) telomere (b) centromere (c) promoter sequence (d) exon

7. Which of the following is not a characteristic of plasmids?
(a) They are easy to isolate. (b) They replicate in the same way as human DNA does.
(c) They are circular. (d) Each cell has one plasmid.

8. A hereditary disease caused by a defect in hemoglobin is
(a) cystic fibrosis (b) sickle-cell anemia (c) Tay–Sachs disease (d) albinism

9. In which type of map are marker locations determined by inheritance patterns?
(a) clone map (b) physical map (c) chromosome (d) genetic map

10. DNA fingerprinting uses all of the following except
(a) a radioactive DNA probe (b) restriction endonuclease (c) a fluorescent marker (d) gel electrophoresis

Sentence Completion

1. Groups of unpaired bases at the end of a DNA chain treated with a restriction endonuclease are known as ______ ______.

2. Repeat sequences in noncoding DNA are often referred to as ______ DNA.

3. In recombinant DNA technology, plasmids are cut open with a ________ ________.

4. The heat-stable enzyme used in the polymerase chain reaction is ________.

5. The ELSI program of the National Human Genome Research Institute deals with ______.

6. Mutations may be caused by exposure to ______ ______ or to chemicals called ______.

7. An _____ is a segment of a gene that does not code for protein synthesis.

8. The replacement of one nucleotide by another in the same location along the polynucleotide chain is known as a _____-______ ________.

9. The field of _____ is directed to the study of the complete set of proteins coded by a genome or synthesized within a given type of cell.

10. A ______ is a constriction that determines the shape of a chromosome during cell division.

11. A point mutation that doesn't change the amino acid incorporated into a protein is a _____ mutation.

12. The film result of DNA fingerprinting is an ________.

True or False

1. In a frameshift mutation, the number of inserted or deleted nucleotides is not a multiple of 3.

2. "SNP" stands for single-nucleoside polymorphism.

3. The DNA used for the Human Genome Project came from a single donor.

4. By reorganization of exons during mRNA synthesis, a gene can produce several different proteins.

5. A person working in the field of pharmacogenomics is likely to work at a company that manufactures drugs.

6. Mapping of each chromosome starts at one end and works to the other end.

7. Telomeres consist of a long series of repeats of the nucleotide sequence TTAGGG.

8. The nucleotide sequences -GAACT- and -CTGGA- are "sticky."

9. The mutation of GAU to GAG is a nonsense mutation.

10. A mutation in RNA causes little damage.

11. Telomerase is responsible for removing telomeres from DNA.

12. Human insulin can be manufactured by recombinant DNA technology.

Match each entry on the left with its partner on the right.

1. Silent mutation	a. UUG —> UAG
2. Exon	b. UUA —> CUA
3. Human Genome Project	c. Shows little telomerase activity
4. Mature somatic cell	d. Addition or loss of a nucleotide
5. Missense mutation	e. Occurs in a very small number of individuals
6. Plasmid	f. Noncoding DNA
7. Mutation	g. Uses a series of "maps" for genome mapping
8. Nonsense mutation	h. Occurs in at least 1% of population
9. Celera	i. Coding DNA
10. SNP	j. GCU —> GGU
11. Intron	k. "Shotgun" approach to DNA mapping
12. Frameshift mutation	l. Bacterial DNA

Chapter 28 – Protein and Amino Acid Metabolism

Chapter Outline

I. Introduction to protein and amino acid metabolism (Sections 28.1–28.2).
  A. Protein digestion (Section 28.1).
    1. Proteins are denatured in the stomach.
    2. In the stomach, the enzyme pepsin hydrolyzes proteins to polypeptides.
    3. In the intestine, other enzymes hydrolyze the polypeptides to amino acids.
    4. Amino acids cross the cell membrane of the intestine and are absorbed directly into the bloodstream.
      Active transport is required for amino acids to cross the intestinal lining.
  B. Overview of amino acid metabolism (Section 28.2).
    1. The amino acid pool is the collection of all free amino acids in the body.
      The amino acid pool is the source of amino acids for protein synthesis and of nitrogen for the synthesis of nitrogen-containing biomolecules.
    2. Amino acid catabolism occurs in two steps:
      a. Removal of nitrogen, which can be
        i. Used for synthesis of nitrogen-containing biomolecules.
        ii. Excreted as urea.
      b. Entry of the remaining carbon atoms into metabolic pathways.
        i. Citric acid cycle.
        ii. Gluconeogenesis.
        iii. Ketogenesis.
        iv. Lipogenesis.

II. Amino acid catabolism (Sections 28.3–28.5).
  A. Removal of the amino group (Section 28.3).
    1. Transamination.
      a. In transamination, the amino group of an amino acid and the keto group of an α-keto acid change places.
      b. Transaminase enzymes are usually specific for α-ketoglutarate as the amino group acceptor.
      c. Transamination reactions are equilibria that regulate amino acid concentration.
    2. Deamination.
      a. If the glutamate from transamination is in excess, the $—NH_3^+$ group can be removed and excreted and α-ketoglutarate regenerated.
      b. This reaction is known as oxidative deamination.
      c. Either NAD^+ or $NADP^+$ is required.
      d. The reverse reaction, reductive amination, occurs in biosynthesis.
  B. The urea cycle (Section 28.4).
    1. Because ammonia is toxic, the human body converts it to urea in order to excrete it.
    2. The reactions of the urea cycle take place in the liver.
    3. Ammonia is first converted to carbamoyl phosphate.
      $NH_4^+ + HCO_3^- + 2\ ATP \longrightarrow$ carbamoyl phosphate $+ 2\ ADP + HOPO_3^{2-} + H_2O$.
    4. Steps of the cycle:
      a. Step 1: Carbamoyl phosphate + ornithine —> citrulline + $HOPO_3^{2-}$.
      b. Step 2: Citrulline + aspartate + ATP —> argininosuccinate + AMP + $P_2O_7^{4-}$.
      c. Step 3: Argininosuccinate —> fumarate + arginine.
      d. Step 4: Arginine + H_2O —> urea + ornithine.

5. Results of the cycle:
   a. Urea is eliminated.
      The urea carbon comes from bicarbonate, the nitrogen comes from aspartate, and the other nitrogen comes from ammonia.
   b. Four phosphate bonds are broken.
   c. Fumarate, a citric acid cycle intermediate, is produced.
      Fumarate is converted to oxaloacetate, which undergoes transamination to yield aspartate, which reenters the cycle. (Fumarate can also enter gluconeogenesis.)

C. Fate of the carbon atoms (Section 28.5).
   1. All amino acid carbon skeletons are either citric acid cycle intermediates or fatty acid metabolism intermediates.
   2. Glucogenic amino acids.
      a. Amino acids that are converted to pyruvate or enter the citric acid cycle as α-ketoglutarate, succinyl-SCoA, fumarate, or oxaloacetate are glucogenic.
      b. These amino acids can be converted to glucose.
   3. Ketogenic amino acids.
      a. Amino acids that are converted to acetyl-SCoA or acetoacetyl-SCoA are known as ketogenic amino acids.
      b. These amino acids can enter either ketogenesis to form ketone bodies or fatty acid biosynthesis.
   4. Some amino acids are both glucogenic and ketogenic.

III. Biosynthesis of nonessential amino acids (Section 28.6).
   A. The human body can synthesize 11 of the 20 common amino acids.
   B. All 11 amino acids derive their amino group from glutamate.
   C. Pyruvate, oxaloacetate, α-ketoglutarate, and 3-phosphoglycerate are the precursors of all nonessential amino acids.
   D. Tyrosine is formed from phenylalanine.
      An inability of the body to perform this conversion is the metabolic error in phenylketonuria.

Solutions to Chapter 28 Problems

28.1 (a) False. The amino acid pool is the collection of free amino acids in the body. (b) True (c) True. (d) False. (e) False. Glycine isn't essential because it can be synthesized in the human body.

28.2 The first reaction is catalyzed by an oxidoreductase (hydroxylase), and the second step is catalyzed by a lyase (decarboxylase).

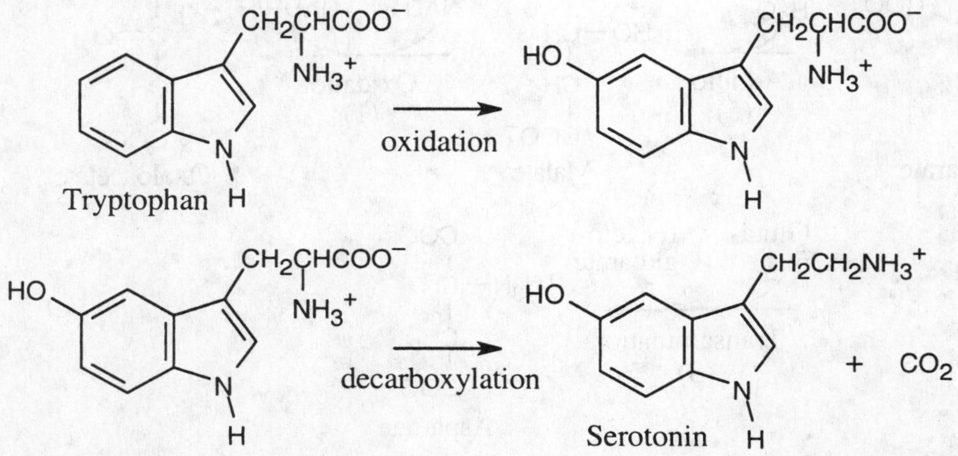

CH2CHCOO⁻
NH3⁺
N
H
Tryptophan
oxidation
HO
decarboxylation
CH2CH2NH3⁺
+ CO2
Serotonin

28.3

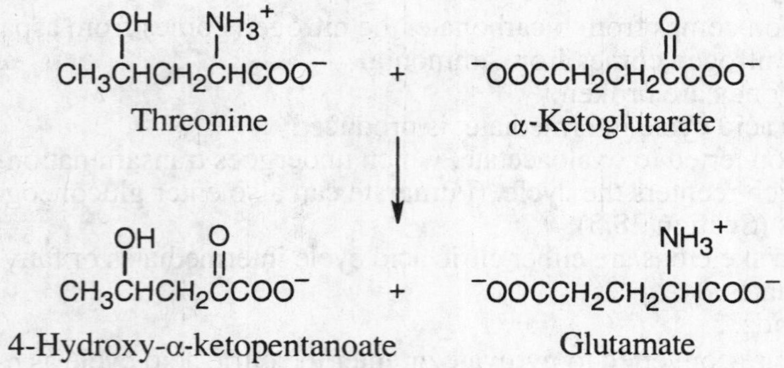
CH3CHCH2CHCOO−
OH NH3+
Threonine
−OOCCH2CH2CCOO−
α-Ketoglutarate
CH3CHCH2CCOO−
4-Hydroxy-α-ketopentanoate
−OOCCH2CH2CHCOO−
Glutamate

28.4

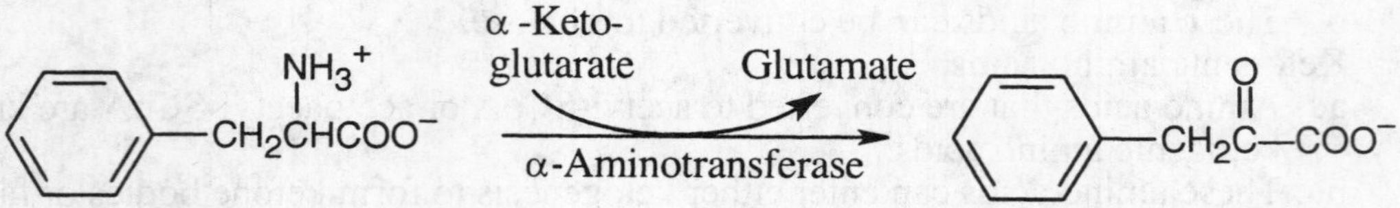
α -Keto-
glutarate
Glutamate
CH2CHCOO−
CH2C—COO−
α-Aminotransferase

28.5 The conversion of alanine to pyruvate can be identified as an oxidation by noting the reduction of the coenzymes NAD^+ or $NADP^+$.

28.6 The three branched-chain amino acids are valine, leucine, and isoleucine.

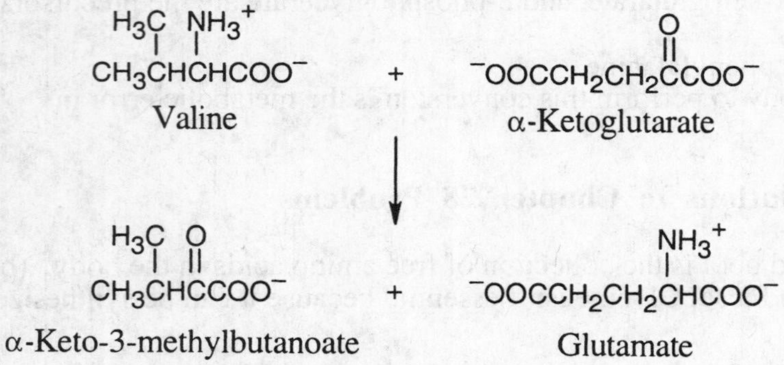
CH3CHCHCOO−
Valine
−OOCCH2CH2CCOO−
α-Ketoglutarate
CH3CHCCOO−
α-Keto-3-methylbutanoate
−OOCCH2CH2CHCOO−
Glutamate

28.7

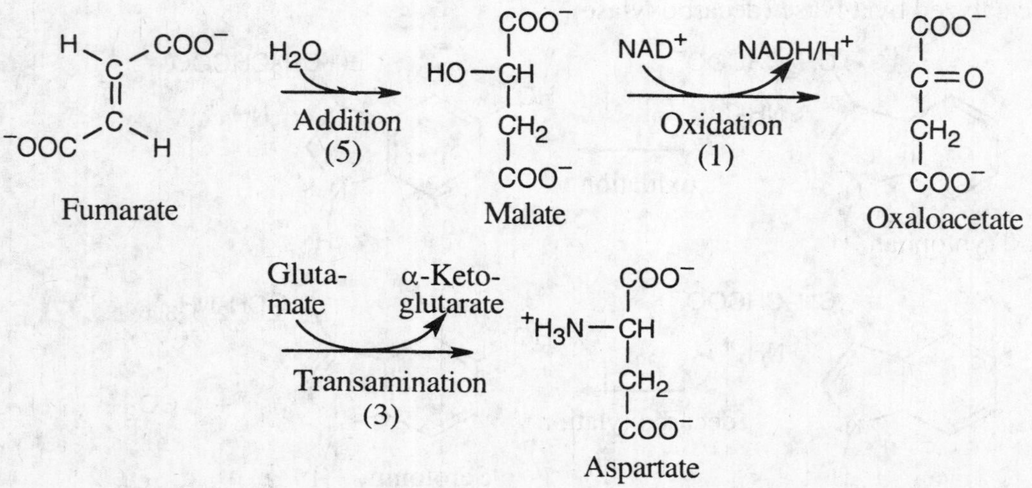
Fumarate
H2O
Addition
(5)
Malate
NAD+
NADH/H+
Oxidation
(1)
Oxaloacetate
Gluta-
mate
α-Keto-
glutarate
Transamination
(3)
Aspartate

28.8

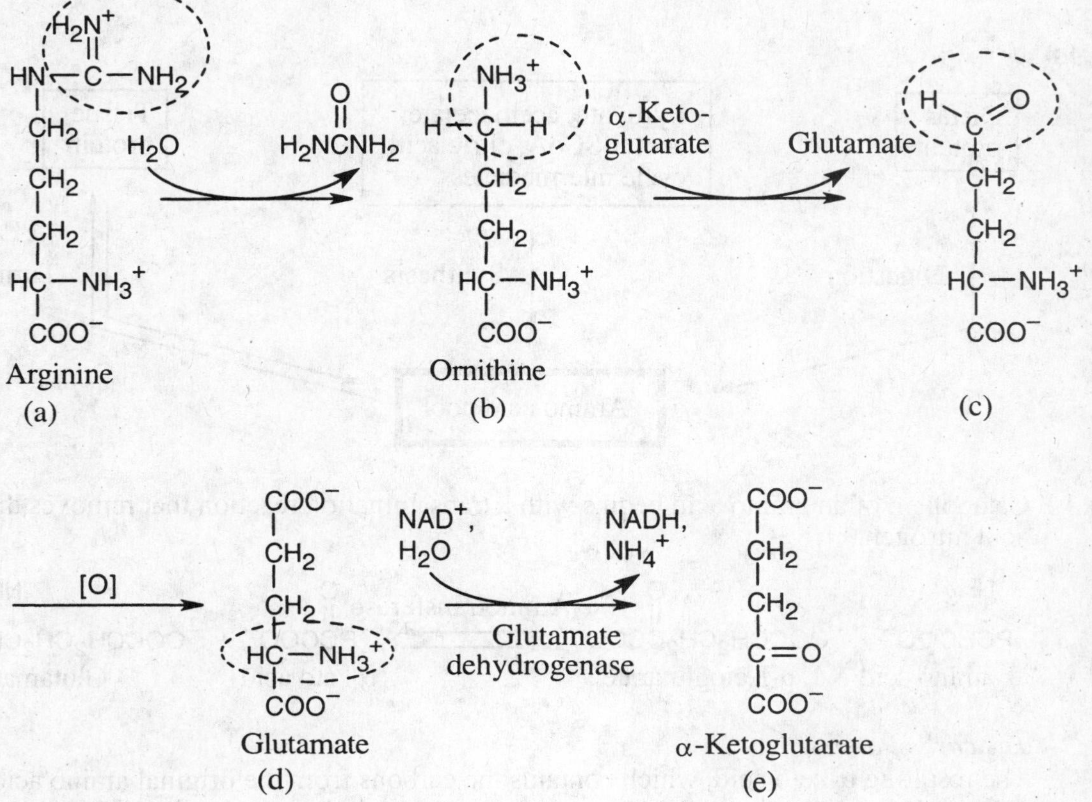
H2O
H2NCNH2
α-Keto-
glutarate
Glutamate
Arginine
(a)
Ornithine
(b)
(c)
[O]
NAD+,
H2O
NADH,
NH4+
Glutamate
dehydrogenase
Glutamate
(d)
α-Ketoglutarate
(e)

28.9

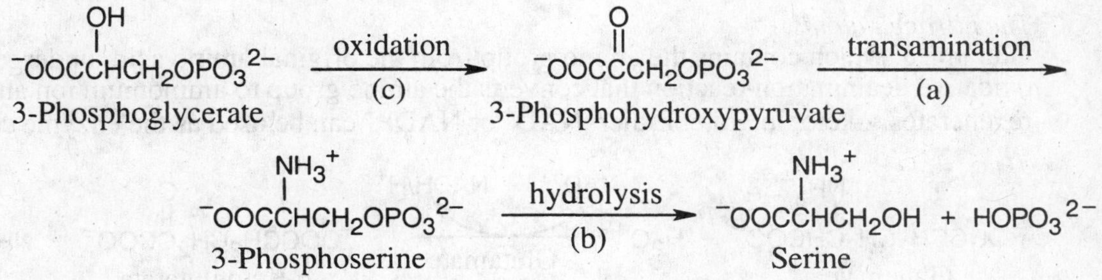
oxidation
(c)
3-Phosphoglycerate
3-Phosphohydroxypyruvate
transamination
(a)
hydrolysis
(b)
3-Phosphoserine
Serine

Understanding Key Concepts

28.10

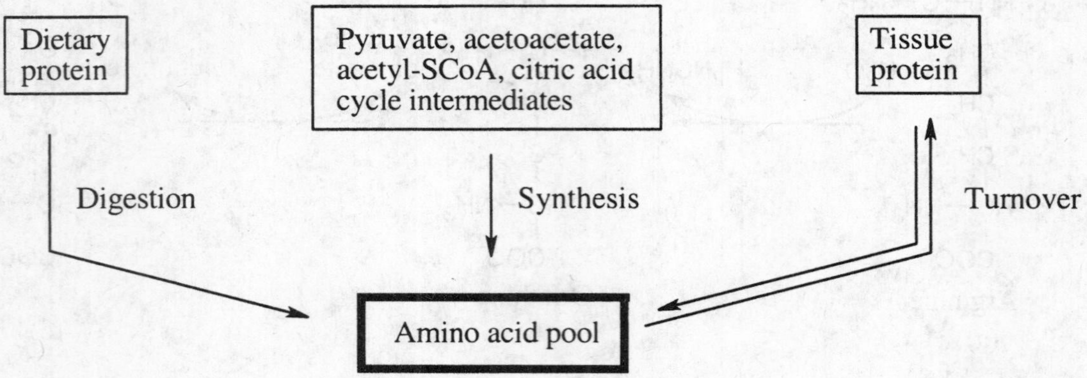
Dietary protein
Pyruvate, acetoacetate, acetyl-SCoA, citric acid cycle intermediates
Tissue protein
Digestion
Synthesis
Turnover
Amino acid pool

28.11 Catabolism of an amino acid begins with a transamination reaction that removes the amino acid nitrogen.

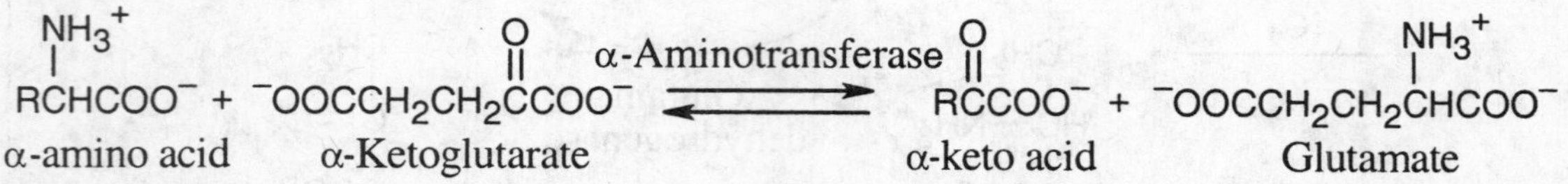
α-Aminotransferase
α-amino acid
α-Ketoglutarate
α-keto acid
Glutamate

The carbon atoms:
The resulting α-keto acid, which contains the carbons from the original amino acid, undergoes reactions that convert it to a common metabolic intermediate. This intermediate may be a citric acid cycle intermediate, pyruvate, acetyl-SCoA, or acetoacetyl-SCoA.

The nitrogen atoms:
Glutamate, which contains the amino group from the original amino acid, undergoes an oxidative deamination reaction that converts the amino group to ammonium ion and that regenerates α-ketoglutarate. Either NAD^+ or $NADP^+$ can be used as the enzyme cofactor.

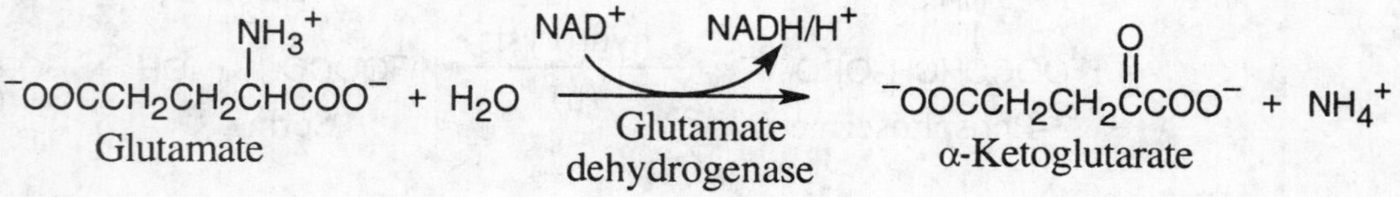
NAD+
NADH/H+
H2O
Glutamate
Glutamate dehydrogenase
α-Ketoglutarate
NH4+

Ammonium ion enters the urea cycle, where it is transformed to urea and is excreted.

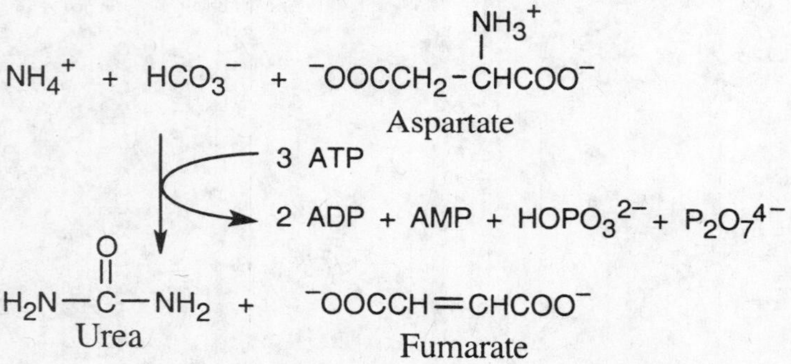
NH4+ + HCO3− +
Aspartate
3 ATP
2 ADP + AMP + HOPO3 2− + P2O7 4−
Urea
Fumarate

28.12

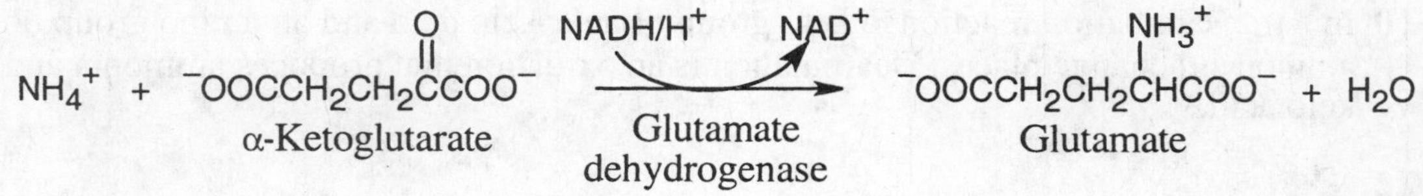

$$NH_4^+ + {}^-OOCCH_2CH_2CCOO^- \xrightarrow[\substack{\text{Glutamate} \\ \text{dehydrogenase}}]{\text{NADH/H}^+ \quad \text{NAD}^+} {}^-OOCCH_2CH_2CHCOO^- + H_2O$$

α-Ketoglutarate   Glutamate

NADPH/H$^+$ can also be used as an enzyme cofactor.

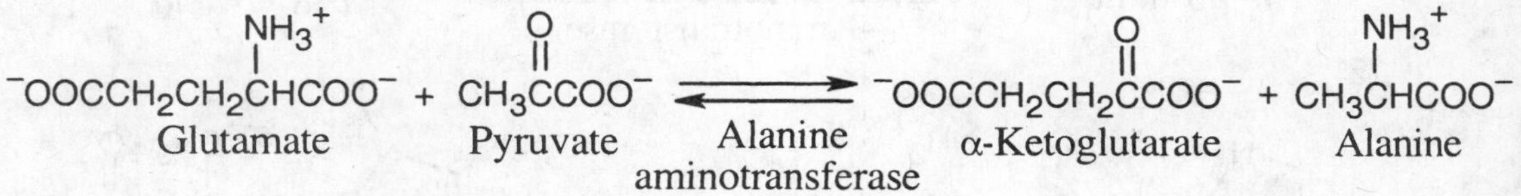

$${}^-OOCCH_2CH_2CHCOO^- + CH_3CCOO^- \underset{\substack{\text{Alanine} \\ \text{aminotransferase}}}{\rightleftarrows} {}^-OOCCH_2CH_2CCOO^- + CH_3CHCOO^-$$

Glutamate   Pyruvate   α-Ketoglutarate   Alanine

The enzymes for both reactions can catalyze reaction in both directions. The product is the amino acid alanine.

28.13 The carbon atoms from ketogenic amino acids can be converted to ketone bodies or to acetyl-SCoA. The carbon atoms from glucogenic amino acids can be converted to compounds that can enter gluconeogenesis and can form glucose, which can enter glycolysis and also yield acetyl-SCoA.

28.14 An essential nutrient can't be synthesized by the body and must be provided in the diet. For example, all amino acids are "essential" in the sense that all of them are necessary for protein synthesis. The body can synthesize half of them from non-amino acid precursors; these are described as "nonessential." The other amino acids must be part of the diet.

28.15 It is important for ornithine transcarbamoylase to have a high activity in order to remove NH$_4^+$ from the body quickly. It is also important that arginase activity be high in order to release urea for excretion by the kidneys and to provide the ornithine needed to react with carbamoyl phosphate. If arginase activity were low, hyperammonemia might result.

Amino Acid Pool

28.16 The body's amino acid pool, which is the collection of free amino acids that result from diet or tissue breakdown, occurs throughout the body.

28.18 Pyruvate and 3-phosphoglycerate are glycolytic precursors of amino acids.

Amino Acid Catabolism

28.20 In a transamination reaction, a keto group of an α-keto acid and an amino group of an α-amino acid change places. Deamination is an oxidation that produces ammonia and an α-keto acid.

28.22

Amino Acid

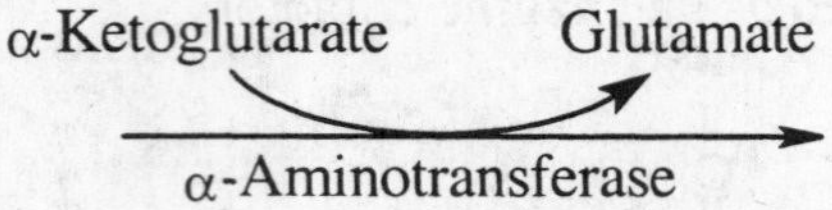
α-Ketoglutarate
Glutamate
α-Aminotransferase

α-Keto acid

(a)

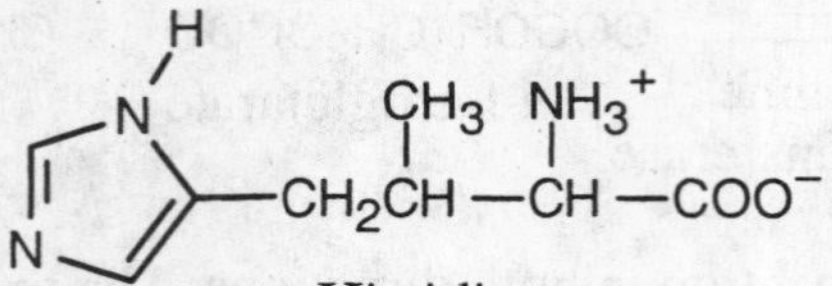

Histidine

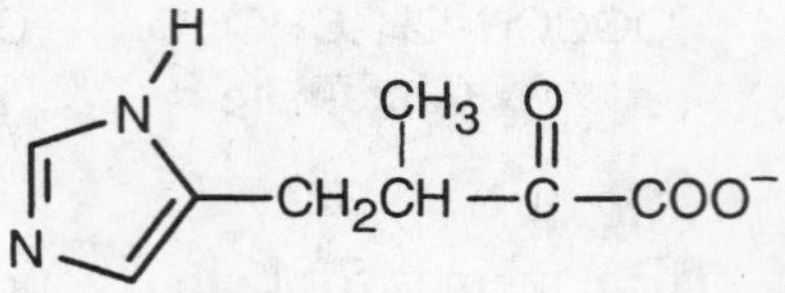

(b)

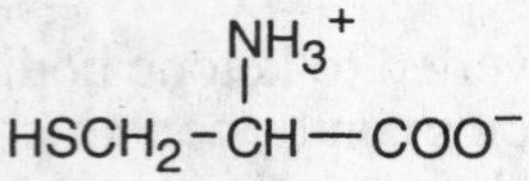

Cysteine

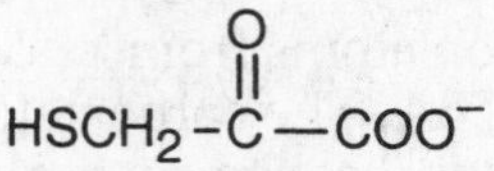

28.24 In an oxidative deamination reaction, an $—NH_3^+$ group of an amino acid (usually glutamate) is replaced by a carbonyl oxygen, and ammonium ion is eliminated.

28.26

Amino Acid *α-Keto acid*

(a)

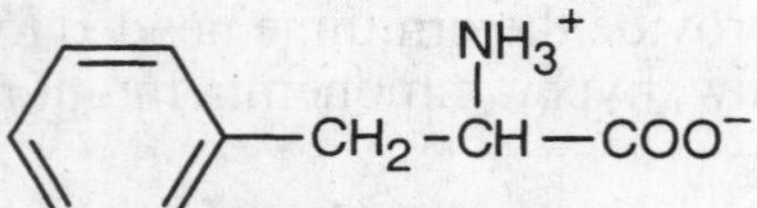

Phenylalanine

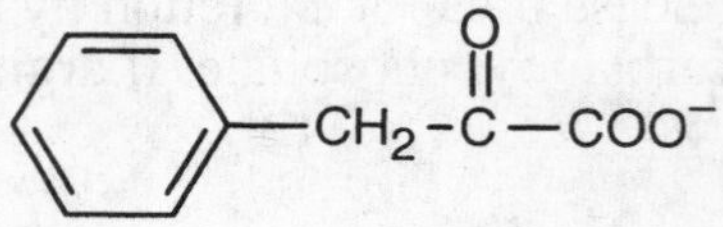

(b)

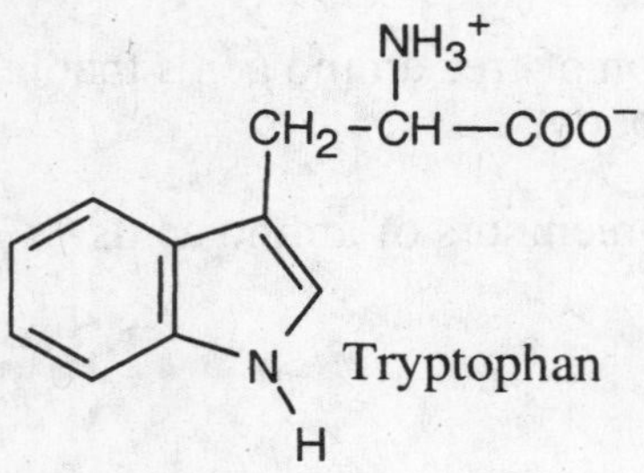

Tryptophan

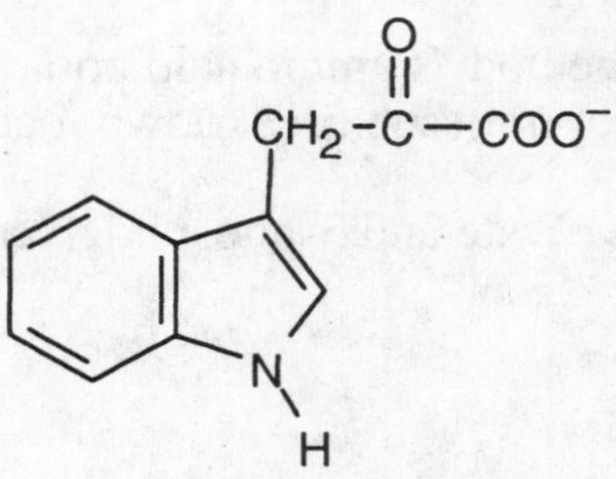

28.28 A ketogenic amino acid is catabolized to acetoacetyl-SCoA or acetyl-SCoA, which can be used either in the synthesis of ketone bodies or in fatty acid biosynthesis.

The Urea Cycle

28.30 Ammonia is toxic and must be eliminated as nontoxic urea, which is water-soluble.

28.32 *One nitrogen* comes from carbamoyl phosphate, which is synthesized from ammonium ion produced from oxidative deamination.
One nitrogen comes from aspartate.

Amino Acid Biosynthesis

28.34 Nonessential amino acids can be synthesized in one to three steps by most organisms. Plants and microorganisms synthesize essential amino acids in many more steps.

28.36 Amino acids are synthesized from non-nitrogen metabolites by transamination reactions with glutamate, which is itself synthesized from α-ketoglutarate and ammonium ion by reductive amination, the reverse of oxidative deamination.

28.38 Phenylketonuria (PKU) is caused by a genetic inability to convert phenylalanine to tyrosine, leading to the accumulation of phenylalanine and its metabolites in the body. PKU causes mental retardation if not detected early in life. Treatment consists of a diet restricted in phenylalanine.

28.40 All biomolecules that contain nitrogen acquire it from amino acids. These include (b) nitric oxide, (c) collagen, and (d) epinephrine.

Applications

28.42

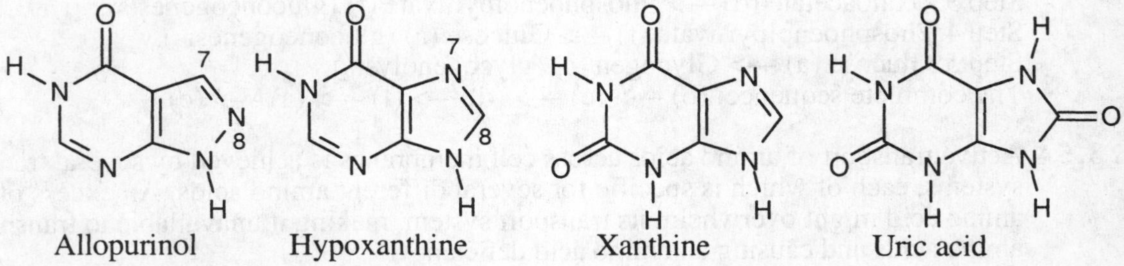
Allopurinol
Hypoxanthine
Xanthine
Uric acid

Allopurinol is identical to hypoxanthine in all but one respect: The nitrogen at position 7 of the hypoxanthine ring is at position 8 of the allopurinol ring. Just as hypoxanthine can be oxidized to xanthine, allopurinol can be oxidized to a compound similar to xanthine (alloxanthine). The product of allopurinol oxidation, however, is an inhibitor of the enzyme that converts xanthine to uric acid. Instead of producing uric acid, purine catabolism ends with the formation of the more soluble hypoxanthine and xanthine, which can be easily excreted.

Oxidation of xanthine to uric acid occurs at position 8 of the purine ring system. In allopurinol, this site is occupied by nitrogen.

28.44 A deficiency of tryptophan, "nature's Prozac," may lead to serotonin deficiency syndrome, which causes behavioral and emotional problems.

General Questions and Problems

28.46

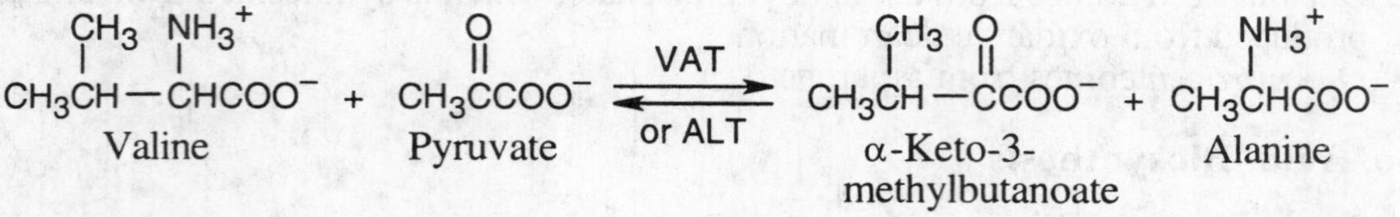

Valine + Pyruvate ⇌ α-Keto-3-methylbutanoate + Alanine (VAT or ALT)

The enzyme that catalyzes the transamination is either valine aminotransferase or alanine aminotransferase.

28.48 An amino acid can be both glucogenic and ketogenic. After catabolism, certain amino acids yield products that can enter the citric acid cycle and other products that can be intermediates of fatty acid metabolism.

28.50 Tissue is dynamic because its components are constantly being broken down and reformed. Dynamic relationships are common in protein and amino acid metabolism, where proteins are digested and resynthesized, and where amino acids are converted to other amino acids and to carbohydrate intermediates.

28.52 The basic scheme of the conversion of glutamate to glycogen is deamination —> gluconeogenesis —> glycogenesis.

Step 1: Glutamate (b) —> α-Ketoglutarate (e) (deamination or transamination).
Step 2: α-Ketoglutarate (e) —> Oxaloacetate (d) (citric acid cycle).
Step 3: Oxaloacetate (d) —> Phosphoenolpyruvate (f) (gluconeogenesis).
Step 4: Phosphoenolpyruvate (f) —> Glucose (a) (gluconeogenesis).
Step 5: Glucose (a) —> Glycogen (c) (glycogenolysis).
The complete sequence: (b) —> (e) —> (d) —> (f) —> (a) —> (c).

28.54 Active transport of amino acids across cell membranes is achieved by several transport systems, each of which is specific for several different amino acids. An excess of one amino acid might overwhelm its transport system, making it unavailable to transport other amino acids and causing an amino acid deficiency.

28.56 The nitrogen may be converted to urea and excreted in the urine, or it may be used in the synthesis of a new nitrogen-containing compound.

Self-Test for Chapter 28

Multiple Choice

1. Which of the following amino acids is strictly ketogenic?
(a) proline (b) threonine (c) leucine (d) isoleucine

2. The product of transamination of valine is
(a) α-keto-3-methylbutanoic acid (b) α-ketobutanoic acid (c) α-keto-4-methylpentanoic acid (d) α-ketopentanoic acid

3. The amino acid proline is probably synthesized by cyclization of
(a) arginine (b) glutamate (c) leucine (d) threonine

4. The urea cycle takes place in the
(a) muscles (b) kidneys (c) bloodstream (d) liver

5. Which of the following proteases is necessary for the activation of other proteases?
(a) pepsin (b) chymotrypsin (c) carboxypeptidase (d) trypsin

6. How many grams of protein tissue are broken down in an adult body per day?
(a) none (b) 50 g (c) 300 g (d) 1000 g

7. Ornithine is
(a) a urea cycle intermediate (b) an amino acid (c) an acceptor of a carbamoyl group (d) all three

8. Which of the following nitrogen-containing compounds is used to treat gout?
(a) hypoxanthine (b) xanthine (c) allopurinol (d) uric acid

9. Which of the following isn't a precursor in nonessential amino acid biosynthesis?
(a) fumarate (b) pyruvate (c) α-ketoglutarate (d) 3-phosphoglycerate

10. Glucogenic amino acids enter gluconeogenesis via
(a) acetyl-SCoA (b) oxaloacetate (c) α-ketoglutarate (d) fumarate

Sentence Completion

1. In the transamination reaction of alanine and α-ketoglutarate, _____ and _____ are formed.

2. _______ is a primary metabolic source of sulfur.

3. Ketogenic amino acids are catabolized to ________ or _____ _____.

4. The first step in the urea cycle is the formation of ______ ______ from ammonia, CO_2, and ATP.

5. A ______ is an enzyme that carries out peptide hydrolysis.

6. The amino acid serine enters the citric acid cycle as ______.

7. _________ is the key reaction in amino acid anabolism.

8. The essential amino acid ______ is part of the urea cycle.

9. PKU is a metabolic error in converting ______ to _____.

10. The pain of gout is caused by an inflammatory response to _____ ______ in tissues.

11. Liver damage is associated with a high level of the enzyme ______.

12. The carbon in urea comes from ______.

True or False

1. 3-Phosphoglycerate is a precursor in the synthesis of nonessential amino acids.

2. Protein digestion starts in the mouth.

3. All ketogenic amino acids except lysine and isoleucine are also glucogenic amino acids.

4. Essential amino acids can neither be synthesized nor catabolized in the human body.

5. Some organisms can excrete nitrogen as ammonia without undergoing any harm.

6. Amino acid catabolism occurs in the intestinal lining.

7. Some intermediates in the urea cycle also occur in the citric acid cycle.

8. The urea cycle is an endergonic process.

9. Both nitrogens of urea come from ammonium ion.

10. Proline is a nonessential amino acid.

11. Each amino acid is associated with its own transaminase enzyme.

12. Oxidative deamination is the reverse of reductive amination.

Match each entry on the left with its partner on the right.

1. Oxidative deamination	(a) Hydrolyzes proteins in the small intestine
2. Ornithine	(b) Process for synthesizing glutamate from α-ketoglutarate and NH_4^+
3. α-Ketoglutarate	(c) Ketogenic amino acid
4. Serine	(d) End product of purine catabolism
5. Trypsin	(e) Process that transfers an amino group from an amino acid to α-ketoglutarate
6. Reductive amination	(f) Nonessential amino acid
7. Leucine	(g) Intermediate in the urea cycle
8. Phenylketonuria	(h) Process that regenerates α-ketoglutarate from glutamate
9. Pepsin	(i) Glucogenic amino acid
10. Uric acid	(j) Intermediate in both the citric acid cycle and in amino acid metabolism
11. Transamination	(k) Hydrolyzes proteins in the stomach
12. Threonine	(l) Metabolic disease

Chapter 29 – Body Fluids

Chapter Outline

I. Water (Sections 29.1–29.2).
  A. Body water and its solutes (Section 29.1).
    1. Types of body fluids.
      a. Intracellular fluid is within cells.
      b. Extracellular fluid is outside of cells.
        i. Blood plasma
        ii. Interstitial fluid, which fills the spaces between cells.
    2. Components of body fluids.
      a. Electrolytes (inorganic ions).
      b. Gases — O_2 and CO_2.
      c. Small organic molecules.
      d. Ionized biomolecules.
      e. All body fluids have the same osmolarity, even if they differ in composition.
    3. Movement of body fluids.
      a. Blood travels through peripheral tissues in capillaries.
        i. At the arterial end, blood pressure is higher and pushes solutes into interstitial fluid.
        ii. At the venous end, blood pressure is lower, and solutes reenter blood plasma.
        iii. Blood plasma and interstitial fluid have similar composition.
      b. Lymph capillaries collect excess interstitial fluid and other molecules too large to pass through capillary walls; this combination is called lymph.
        i. Lymph can't return to surrounding tissue.
        ii. Lymph enters the blood stream at the thoracic duct.
      c. Solutes in interstitial and intracellular fluid are exchanged by crossing cell membranes.
        Often, active transport is needed to maintain concentration differences.
  B. Maintenance of fluid balance (Section 29.2).
    1. Fluid balance is controlled by hormones.
    2. Receptors in the hypothalamus monitor concentration of blood solutes.
    3. If the concentration of solutes is too high, secretion of antidiuretic hormone increases.
      a. In SIADH, too much hormone keeps kidneys from excreting enough water.
      b. In *diabetes insipidus*, excessive amounts of dilute urine are excreted.

II. Blood (Sections 29.3–29.6).
  A. Components of blood (Section 29.3).
    1. Whole blood contains:
      a. Plasma.
      b. Blood cells.
    2. Blood serum is the fluid portion that remains after blood has clotted.
  B. Functions of blood.
    1. Transport.
    2. Regulation: redistribution of heat and solutes, and buffering of tissues.
    3. Defense.
      a. Immune response.
      b. Clotting.
  C. Immune response (Section 29.4).
    1. A foreign invader (antigen) is a substance that the body does not recognize as part of itself.

2. The body responds to antigens in three ways.
   a. Inflammatory responses (nonspecific).
      i. Inflammation produces swelling, warmth, and pain.
      ii. The chemical messenger histamine is released at the site of injury.
      iii. Histamine dilates capillaries and increases blood flow to the injured area, allowing clotting factors and white blood cells to pass.
      iv. Bacteria are destroyed by phagocytes (white blood cells), which can also initiate specific immune responses.
      v. Inflammation disappears when infectious agents have been removed.
   b. Cell-mediated immune response (specific).
      i. The cell-mediated immune response is under the control of T lymphocytes.
      ii. The cell-mediated immune response guards against abnormal cells due to bacteria, viruses or cancer.
      iii. When a T cell recognizes an invader, it produces killer T cells (that destroy the invader), helper T cells (that enhance defenses), and memory T cells (that remain on guard).
   c. Antibody-mediated immune response (specific).
      i. The antibody-mediated immune response is under the control of B lymphocytes (with the assistance of T lymphocytes).
      ii. A B cell is activated when it binds to an antigen and encounters a helper T cell.
      iii. The B cells divide to produce plasma cells, which form non-cell-bound antibodies called immunoglobulins.
      iv. The antibodies find their antigens and inactivate them by one of several methods.
      v. Memory cells produce more antibodies if the same antigen reappears.
      vi. The body contains thousands of different immunoglobulins, and many have been identified.

D. Blood clotting (Section 29.5).
   1. A blood clot consists of blood cells trapped in a mesh of the protein fibrin. The process of clot formation requires many steps.
   2. The body's mechanism for halting blood loss is called hemostasis.
      a. The first event is constriction of blood vessels and formation of a plug of platelets.
      b. Then, blood clotting occurs by either of two pathways.
         i. In the intrinsic pathway, blood makes contact with the negatively charged surface of collagen.
         ii. In the extrinsic pathway, damaged tissue releases a glycoprotein called tissue factor.
      c. In either pathway, several zymogen clotting factors are released.
      d. After several steps, the enzyme thrombin catalyzes the formation of insoluble fibrin, which forms the clot.
   3. After the injury has healed, the clot is broken down by hydrolysis of its peptide bonds.

E. Red blood cells and blood gases (Section 29.6).
   1. The purpose of red blood cells (erythrocytes) is to transport blood gases.
   2. Hemoglobin is responsible for transporting O_2 and CO_2. Hemoglobin consists of four protein chains and four heme molecules.
   3. Oxygen transport.
      a. Oxygen is transported via bonding with Fe^{2+} through an unshared electron pair.
      b. The percent of heme molecules that carry oxygen is the percent saturation.
      c. The binding curve is s-shaped.
         i. The uptake of the first molecule of oxygen is more difficult than the uptake of the remaining molecules.
         ii. The release of the first O_2 is more difficult than the release of the other three.

4. CO_2 transport.
   a. CO_2 can be transported in three ways.
      i. Dissolved (about 7%).
      ii. Bonded to Hb.
      iii. As HCO_3^- in solution.
   b. Carbonic anhydrase in erythrocytes catalyzes the formation of HCO_3^- from CO_2.
   c. The HCO_3^- can be transported in blood to the lungs, where it is exhaled as CO_2.
   d. Electrolyte balance in erythrocytes is maintained by entry of one Cl^- for every HCO_3^- removed.
   e. Excess acidity is controlled by binding of H^+ to hemoglobin, with release of O_2.
5. The effects of changes in the oxygen saturation curve with changing pCO_2 and $[H^+]$ are illustrated in Figure 29.12.
6. Acidosis and alkalosis result from disruption of the body's mechanism for maintaining pH and by imbalances in CO_2 metabolism.

III. Urine (Sections 29.7–29.8).
  A. The kidney and urine formation (Section 29.7).
    1. The kidney is composed of nephrons.
    2. Blood enters the nephrons at the glomerulus, where filtration occurs.
       Plasma and smaller solutes are filtered into the surrounding fluid.
    3. Reabsorption recaptures water and smaller solutes.
    4. In secretion, some solutes are excreted in higher concentration than occurs in the filtrate.
    5. Some substances move by passive diffusion; others move by active transport.
    6. Hormones influence urine composition.
  B. Urine composition and function (Section 29.8).
    1. Composition of urine.
       a. The components of urine are mainly electrolytes and nitrogen-containing wastes.
       b. The concentration of these substances varies with water intake, temperature, exercise and state of health.
    2. Acid–base balance.
       a. Of the 50–100 mEq of H^+ produced in metabolism, very little appears in the urine.
       b. H^+ is produced from CO_2 in the reaction:
          $CO_2 + H_2O \longrightarrow H^+ + HCO_3^-$
       c. The resulting H^+ combines with either NH_3 or HPO_4^{2-} and is excreted.
       d. H^+ also combines with HCO_3^- in urine filtrate to produce CO_2, which enters the bloodstream.
    3. Fluid and Na^+ balance.
       a. The amount of H_2O reabsorbed depends on
          i. The osmolarity of the fluid passing through the kidney.
          ii. Antidiuretic hormone-controlled membrane permeability.
          iii. The amount of Na^+ reabsorbed.
       b. Reabsorption of Na^+ is under the control of aldosterone.

Solutions to Chapter 29 Problems

29.1 When chloride concentrations are low, the reaction should proceed farther to the right, according to Le Châtelier's principle. When chloride concentrations are high, the reaction proceeds to the left. In order to move passively into a cell, a molecule cannot be charged because a cell membrane is non-polar. Therefore, the form of cisplatin shown on the left enters the cell more readily. Once inside, the equilibrium shifts to the right and forms the charged version of cisplatin, which does not cross back through the cell membrane.

29.2 (a) interstitial fluid — (iii) fluid that fills spaces between cells
(b) whole blood — (ii) fluid, solutes and cells that together flow through veins and arteries
(c) blood serum — (iv) fluid that remains after clotting agents are removed from plasma
(d) intracellular fluid — (v) fluid within cells
(e) blood plasma — (i) fluid that remains when blood cells are removed

29.3 (a) The value of pH goes down because of the formation of carbonic acid from dissolved CO_2, which increases $[H_3O]^+$ and thus increases acidity.
(b) A blood gas analysis measures $[O_2]$, $[CO_2]$, and pH.

29.4 (a) Emphysema is a cause of *respiratory acidosis*. In pneumonia, the lungs have difficulty exhaling CO_2, and increased blood acidity results.
(b) Failure of the kidneys to excrete H_3O^+ results in *metabolic acidosis.*
(c) Overdose of an antacid leads to overneutralization of H_3O^+, which raises pH and leads to *metabolic alkalosis*.
(d) A panic attack causes hyperventilation, which removes CO_2 from the body, raising pH and resulting in *respiratory alkalosis.*
(e) Congestive heart failure is a cause of *respiratory alkalosis.*

Understanding Key Concepts

29.5 (a) The body fluid found inside cells is called intracellular fluid.
(b) The body fluid found outside cells is called extracellular fluid.
(c) Blood plasma and interstitial fluid are the major body fluids found outside of cells.
(d) K^+, Mg^{2+}, and HPO_4^{2-} are the major electrolytes found inside cells.
(e) The major electrolytes found outside cells are Na^+ and Cl^-.

29.6

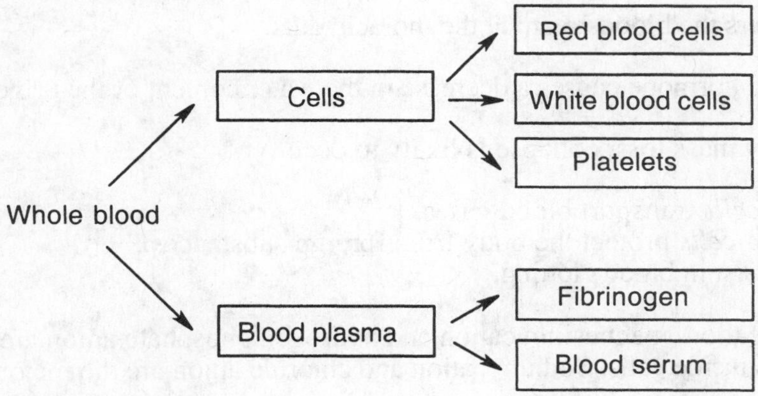
Whole blood
Cells
Red blood cells
White blood cells
Platelets
Blood plasma
Fibrinogen
Blood serum

29.7 (a) Blood carries O_2 from lungs to tissues.
(b) Blood carries CO_2 (dissolved and as HCO_3^-) from the tissues to the lungs.
(c) Blood transports nutrients from the digestive system to the tissues.
(d) Blood carries waste products from the tissues to the site of excretion.
(e) Blood transports hormones from endocrine glands to their site of binding.
(f) Blood transports defensive agents such as white blood cells (to destroy foreign material) and platelets (to prevent blood loss).

29.8 Symptoms of inflammation include swelling, redness, warmth, and pain.

29.9 Histamine, produced by the enzymatic decarboxylation of histidine, causes the symptoms of inflammation by dilating capillaries, causing an increased blood flow that reddens and warms the skin. Pain and swelling occur when blood-clotting factors and defensive proteins enter the intercellular space.

29.10 *Cell-mediated immune response,* which is under the control of T cells, arises when abnormal cells, bacteria or viruses enter cells. The invading cells are killed by T cells that destroy the invader.
Antibody-mediated immune response, which is under the control of B cells, assisted by T cells, occurs when antigenic substances enter cells. When an antigen is recognized, B cells divide to produce plasma cells, which form antibodies to the antigen. These antibodies form an antibody–antigen complex that inactivates the antigen.

29.11 Excess hydrogen ions are excreted by reaction with NH_3 or HPO_4^{2-}. H^+ ions also combine with bicarbonate, producing CO_2 that returns to the bloodstream and is again converted to bicarbonate.

Body Fluids

29.12 The three principal body fluids are intracellular fluid (64%), extracellular fluid (8%), and interstitial fluid (25%).

29.14 Substances not soluble in blood, such as lipids, are transported by blood proteins.

29.16 Blood pressure in arterial capillaries is higher than interstitial fluid pressure, and blood pressure in venous capillaries is lower than interstitial fluid pressure.

29.18 Lymph enters the bloodstream at the thoracic duct.

29.20 Antidiuretic hormone causes a decrease in the water content of the urine.

21.22 At 7% body mass loss, collapse is likely to occur.

29.24 *Red blood cells* transport blood gases.
White blood cells protect the body from foreign substances..
Platelets assist in blood clotting.

29.26 Potassium cation, magnesium cation and hydrogen phosphate anion are the major electrolytes inside cells. Sodium cation and chloride anion are the major electrolytes outside of cells.

29.28 Antihistamines block attachment of the neurotransmitter histamine to its receptors.

29.30 Immunoglobulins are the plasma proteins involved in the antibody-mediated immune response.

29.32 When a T cell recognizes an antigen on the surface of an invader, three kinds of T cells are produced. *Killer* T cells destroy the invader, *helper* T cells enhance defenses against the invader, and *memory* T cells can produce new killer T cells if the invader reappears.

29.34 Memory cells, which are produced from B cells, can quickly produce more plasma cells if the same antigen appears in the future. Memory cells "remember" the antigen and are capable of producing antibodies to it for a long time.

29.36 Vitamin K and calcium ion are needed for blood clotting.

29.38 Blood-clotting enzymes are released as zymogens in order to avoid undesirable clotting in noninjured tissues.

29.40 Hemoglobin iron must be in the +2 oxidation state in order to bind with oxygen.

29.42 When the partial pressure of oxygen drops below 10 mm Hg, hemoglobin is unsaturated. When the partial pressure of oxygen is greater than 100 mm Hg, hemoglobin is completely saturated. Between these pressures, hemoglobin is partially saturated.

29.44 CO_2 can be transported as a dissolved gas, as bicarbonate ion, or as bonded to hemoglobin.

29.46 CO_2 in the blood raises $[H^+]$ in two types of reactions:

(1) Reaction of CO_2 with nonionized —NH_2 groups of hemoglobin amino acids produces H^+.

$$Hb{-}NH_2 + CO_2 \longrightarrow Hb{-}NHCOO^- + H^+$$

(2) Carbonic anhydrase catalyzes the reaction of CO_2 with H_2O, producing bicarbonate and H^+.

$$CO_2 + H_2O \xrightleftharpoons{\text{Carbonic anhydrase}} HCO_3^- + H^+$$

29.48 A blood serum pH of 7.25 indicates a condition of acidosis.

29.50 Acidosis due to congestive heart failure is considered to be respiratory acidosis because it is caused by a failure to efficiently remove CO_2 from the blood.

29.52

$$H^+ + HCO_3^- \rightleftharpoons CO_2 + H_2O$$

$$H^+ + HPO_4^{2-} \rightleftharpoons H_2PO_4^-$$

Applications

29.54 In an asymmetric transport system, substances can either be transported into a cell or be transported out of a cell, but not both. For example, there exists a system for transport of glycine out of brain cells, but no system exists for transport of glycine into brain cells.

29.56 A medicinal chemist might want to breach the blood–brain barrier to deliver medication to the brain to cure an illness such as brain cancer.

29.58 A change in enzyme level in body fluids may indicate organ damage. An automatic analyzer can reproducibly measure the rate of an enzyme-catalyzed reaction to detect the presence of elevated or reduced levels of enzymes.

General Questions and Problems

29.60 Ethanol is soluble in blood because it is a small, polar molecule.

29.62 When the concentration of sodium in the blood is high, the secretion of antidiuretic hormone (ADH) increases. ADH causes the water content of the urine to decrease, and causes the amount of water retained by the body to increase, causing swelling.

29.64 Active transport is necessary when a cell needs a substance that has a higher concentration inside the cell than outside, or when a cell needs to secrete a substance that has a higher concentration outside the cell than inside.

29.66 *Homeostasis* is the maintenance of a constant internal environment in the body. *Hemostasis* is the body's mechanism for preventing blood loss and could be considered a part of homeostasis.

Self-Test for Chapter 29

Multiple Choice

1. Which oxygen is taken up by heme with the most difficulty?
(a) the first oxygen (b) the second oxygen (c) the last oxygen (d) All bind with equal ease.

2. Cardiac arrest may result in
(a) metabolic alkalosis (b) metabolic acidosis (c) respiratory alkalosis (d) respiratory acidosis

3. Cell-mediated immune response guards against all of the following except
(a) cancer cells (b) transplanted organs (c) allergens (d) bacteria

4. Potassium ion is most abundant in
(a) interstitial fluid (b) intracellular fluid (c) plasma (d) extracellular fluid

5. All of the following are involved in blood clotting except
(a) tissue factor (b) zymogens (c) thrombin (d) memory cells

6. Which of the following disorders is not an autoimmune disease?
(a) hemophilia (b) arthritis (c) lupus erythematosus (d) diabetes mellitus

7. The amount of water reabsorbed in kidney tubules depends on
(a) the amount of sodium reabsorbed (b) control of membrane permeability by antidiuretic hormone (c) aldosterone (d) all three

8. Blood is at its lowest percent saturation with oxygen in
(a) peripheral tissue (b) muscles (c) veins (d) arteries

9. All of the following decrease the oxygen affinity of hemoglobin except
(a) increased $[H^+]$ (b) increased $[O_2]$ (c) increased $[CO_2]$ (d) increased temperature

10. B cells divide to produce all of the following except
(a) memory cells (b) antibodies (c) phagocytes (d) plasma cells

Sentence Completion

1. The percentage of heme molecules that carry oxygen is dependent on the _____ _____ of O_2.

2. Antigens can be small molecules known as ______.

3. In the process of blood clotting, ______ are activated to give active clotting factors.

4. Inorganic ions are the major contributors to the ______ of body fluids.

5. Histamine is synthesized from ______.

6. ______ ion and vitamin ____ assist in blood clotting.

7. In ______ ______, substances move from regions of low concentration to regions of high concentration.

8. The three functions of blood are ______, ______, and ______.

9. Bacteria at the site of inflammation are attacked by ______.

10. Arthritis and allergies are known as ______ diseases.

11. ______ is caused by the absence of one or more clotting factors.

12. Fibrin molecules are bound into fibers by crosslinks between the side chains of the amino acids ______ and ______.

True or False

1. The walls of lymph capillaries are constricted so that lymph can't return to surrounding tissues.

2. Homeostasis is the body's mechanism for halting blood loss.

3. O_2, H^+, and CO_2 all bond to heme.

4. Secreted H^+ is eliminated in the urine as NH_4^+ or $H_2PO_4^-$.

5. When the partial pressure of CO_2 increases, the percent saturation of hemoglobin decreases.

6. Allergies and asthma are caused by an underproduction of immunoglobulin E.

7. Blood plasma is the fluid remaining after blood has completely clotted.

8. Blood clotting begins with the release of tissue factor from injured tissue.

9. Reabsorption is the movement of solutes and water out of the kidney.

10. The metabolism of food contributes to one's water intake.

11. Lymphocytes surround and destroy bacteria.

12. Caffeine causes increased output of urine.

Match each entry on the left with its partner on the right.

1. B cells	(a) Foreign substance
2. Active transport	(b) Enzyme that catalyzes the formation of histamine
3. Fibrin	(c) Movement of solute against a concentration gradient
4. Carbonic anhydrase	(d) White blood cells involved in antibody-directed immune response
5. Erythrocytes	(e) Controls reabsorption of Na^+
6. T cells	(f) Blood protein responsible for clotting
7. Antigen	(g) Enzyme that catalyzes reaction between H_2O and CO_2
8. Histidine decarboxylase	(h) Movement of water in response to a concentration difference
9. Osmosis	(i) White blood cells involved in cell-directed immune response
10. Antidiuretic hormone	(j) Red blood cells
11. Antibody	(k) Protein molecule that identifies a foreign substance
12. Aldosterone	(l) Causes a decrease in the water content of urine

Answers to Self Tests

Chapter One

Multiple choice: 1. b 2. d 3. b 4. d 5. a 6. a 7. c 8. b
Sentence completion: 1. nonmetallic 2. physical 3. Bi 4. condenses 5. mass and volume 6. liquid 7. pure substance 8. chemical formulas 9. malleable 10. carbon, hydrogen, oxygen and nitrogen
True/false: 1. T 2. T 3. T 4. F (physical methods) 5. F (seven atoms) 6. T 7. F (Ag) 8. T 9. F (a gas) 10. T

Chapter Two

Number questions: 1. (a) micrometer (b) deciliter (c) megagram (d) liter (e) nanogram 2. (a) kL (b) pg (c) cm (d) hL 3. (a) 5 (b) 2 (c) 1 (d) exact (e) 3, 4, 5 or 6 4. (a) 7.03×10^{-5} g; 3 sig. fig. (b) $1.371\,00 \times 10^{5}$ m; 4, 5,or 6 sig. fig. (c) 1.1×10^{-2} L; 2 sig. fig. (d) $1.837\,100\,8 \times 10^{7}$ mm; 8 sig. fig. 5. (a) 8.07×10^{2} L (b) 4.77×10^{6} people (c) 1.27×10^{-3} g (d) 1.04×10^{4} µm 6. (a) 0.564 lb (b) 0.417 m (c) 7.6 L (d) 85.4 in. (e) 95°F (f) 25°C (g) 5.92 fl oz (h) 6.17×10^{-3} oz 7. 31 cal 8. 217 g
Multiple choice: 1. b 2. d 3. b 4. a 5. c 6. d 7. b 8. c 9. c 10. a
Sentence completion : 1. kilogram, meter, cubic meter, Kelvin 2. number, unit 3. specific heat 4. nano- 5. 3 6. 1 lb/454 g 7. calorie, joule 8. factor-label 9. Specific gravity 10. Celsius, Kelvin
True/false: 1. F (specific gravity is unitless) 2. T 3. F (three sig. fig.) 4. F (0.9464 L/1 qt.) 5. T 6. F 7. F 8. T 9. F 10. T
Matching: 1. e 2. j 3. g 4. i 5. h 6. l 7. f 8. k 9. c 10. a 11. d 12. b

Chapter Three

Multiple choice: 1. c 2. b 3. a 4. c 5. d 6. d 7. a 8. b 9. d 10. d 11. a 12. b
Sentence completion: 1. *p* 2. dalton 3. protons, neutrons 4. atomic number 5. shells 6. group 7. 13 8. subatomic particles 9. isotopes 10. 18 11. quantized
True/false: 1. T 2. F (5.486×10^{-4} amu) 3. F 4. T 5. F (atomic number indicates only protons) 6. F (They're less reactive.) 7. F (in the same group) 8. T 9. T 10. F (Subshells can contain 2,6,10 ·· electrons.) 11. T 12. F
Matching: 1. h 2. e 3. k 4. a 5. j 6. l 7. c 8. b 9. i 10. d 11. g 12. f

Chapter Four

Multiple choice: 1. d 2. a 3. d 4. c 5. a 6. b 7. b 8. d 9. b 10. d
Sentence completion: 1. Ionization energy 2. potassium phosphate 3. 2 4. polyatomic 5. simplest 6. 8 7. base 8. Hydroxyapatite 9. crystalline 10. 4A or 5A
True/false: 1. F (It forms only Zn^{2+}.) 2. T 3. F (energy needed to form an ion) 4. T 5. F (ions formed may be H^{+}, $H_2PO_4^{-}$, and HPO_4^{2-}.) 6. F (Solutions of ions conduct electricity.) 7. F 8. T 9. T 10. F (group 8A) 11. T 12. F
Matching: 1. e 2. l 3. k 4. a 5. h 6. j 7. i 8. b 9. f 10 g 11. d 12. c

Chapter Five

Multiple choice: 1. c 2. d 3. b 4. c 5. a 6. a 7. d 8. b 9. d 10. a
Sentence completion: 1. electronegative 2. biomolecule 3. covalent 4. C≡C, C≡N 5. diatomic 6. planar trigonal 7. *d* 8. triple 9. Binary 10. organic 11. condensed
True/false: 1. T 2. T 3. F 4. F (valence electrons) 5. F (It's planar.) 6. F (covalent compounds) 7. T 8. F 9. F (Some bent molecules have bond angles that are approx. 109.5°.) 10. T 11. T
Matching: 1. h (or c) 2. j 3. f 4. a 5. k 6. i 7. e 8. c 9. b 10. g 11. d 12. l

Chapter Six

Multiple choice: 1. a 2. a 3. c 4. b 5. d 6. c 7. c 8. b 9. a 10. d
Sentence completion: 1. coefficients 2. precipitate 3. spectator 4. aqueous 5. molar mass 6. percent yield 7. reactants 8. +3 9. reducing 10. neutralization
True/false: 1. F (It has the same number of atoms.) 2. T 3. T 4. F 5. T 6. F (Molar mass is the conversion factor.) 7. F 8. F (The mole ratio is 1/2.) 9. T 10. T
Matching: 1. h 2. f 3. k 4. a 5. i 6. c 7. j 8. b 9. g 10. l 11. d 12. e

Chapter Seven

Multiple choice: 1. c 2. b 3. d 4. d 5. b 6. a 7. c 8. a 9. d 10. d
Sentence completion: 1. 1 2. conservation of energy 3. catalyst 4. reversible 5. endothermic 6. equilibrium-constant expression 7. temperature, pressure, catalyst 8. metabolism 9. Reaction rate 10. collide
True/false: 1. F (produced) 2. F (At equilibrium, the ratio of concentrations is constant.) 3. T 4. T 5. F (The size of E_{act} and ΔH are unrelated.) 6. F (not always true for biochemical reactions) 7. T 8. F (Catalysts lower the height of the energy barrier.) 9. F (At equilibrium, the rate of the forward reaction equals the rate of the reverse reaction.) 10. T
Matching: 1. c 2. j 3. l 4. i 5. a 6. k 7. b 8. f 9. d 10. e 11. g 12. h

Chapter Eight

Multiple choice: 1. b 2. c 3. d 4. a 5. d 6. c 7. a 8. b 9. c 10. d
Sentence completion: 1. pressure, volume 2. definite, indefinite 3. Dalton's 4. standard temperature and pressure 5. Avogadro's 6. equilibrium 7. atmosphere, Pascal, mm Hg, pounds per square inch 8. heat of fusion 9. number of atoms, volume 10. temperature 11. change of state 12. volatile
True/false: 1. T 2. F (Only ideal gases have similar physical behavior.) 3. T 4. F (Doubling pressure halves the volume.) 5. T 6. F (only true in crystals) 7. F (273 K) 8. T 9. F (higher) 10. F (Vapor pressure doesn't depend on quantity of liquid.) 11. F (viscosity)
Matching: 1. g 2. e 3. k 4. f 5. h 6. a 7. j 8. l 9. b 10. d 11. c 12. i

Chapter Nine

Multiple choice: 1. b 2. d 3. a 4. b 5. c 6. d 7. c 8. c 9. a 10. b
Sentence completion: 1. miscible 2. equivalent 3. volumetric flask 4. solubility, partial pressure 5. isotonic 6. hygroscopic 7. $M_1 \times V_1 = M_2 \times V_2$. 8. colloid 9. solvent, small solute molecules 10. saturated 11. glucose 12. lower
True/false: 1. F (solvent) 2. T 3. F (A quantity of the second liquid is added to make 100 mL of solution.) 4. F 5. T 6. F (Weight/weight percent is rarely used.) 7. T 8. F (Effect of temperature is unpredictable.) 9. T (It also differs with respect to particle size.) 10. F (hemolysis) 11. F (raise) 12. T
Matching: 1. h 2. f 3. d 4. j 5. a 6. k 7. b 8. i 9. g 10. l 11. e 12. c

Chapter Ten

Multiple choice: 1. b 2. a 3. c 4. d 5. c 6. c 7. b 8. a 9. b 10. d
Sentence completion: 1. equivalent 2. red 3. diprotic 4. strong 5. Dissociation 6. OH^- ions 7. Neutralization 8. pH 9. 30.0 mL 10. conjugate 11. carbonate/bicarbonate 12. amphoteric
True/false: 1. F (60 mL of 0.1 M NaOH) 2. T 3. F (H_2SO_4 is a strong acid.) 4. F 5. F 6. T 7. T 8. F (According to this definition, an acid donates H^+.) 9. F (Ammonia yields ammonium ion, plus the anion of the acid.) 10. T 11. F 12. T
Matching: 1. d 2. e 3. g 4. l 5. a 6. b 7. i 8. j 9. c 10. f 11. k 12. h

Chapter Eleven

Multiple choice: 1. c 2. d 3. c 4. a 5. c 6. d 7. a 8. d 9. b 10. c
Sentence completion: 1. transmutation 2. Gamma radiation 3. tracer 4. background 5. nucleons 6. ^{14}C 7. curie 8. nuclear fission 9. film badges 10. body imaging 11. nuclear fusion 12. critical mass
True/false: 1. F (3/4 will have decayed after 24 days.) 2. T 3. T 4. F (Becquerel) 5. T 6. F 7. F (Atomic number increases by 1.) 8. F (Hazards are due to emissions of radiation.) 9. F (The rem is more common.) 10. T 11. F (Most are synthetic.) 12. F
Matching: 1. f 2. i 3. l 4. k 5. c 6. j 7. d 8. h 9. b 10. a 11. e 12. g

Chapter Twelve

Multiple choice: 1. a 2. c 3. d 4. c 5. b 6. d 7. c 8. a 9. c 10. a
Sentence completion: 1. paraffins 2. triple 3. oxygen 4. distillation 5. condensed structure 6. quaternary 7. lower 8. ring 9. IUPAC 10. isomers 11. Combustion 12. higher
True/false: 1. F (They have different molecular formulas.) 2. T 3. F (It's puckered.) 4. F (3-Methylhexane) 5. T 6. T 7. F (It's polar covalent.) 8. T 9. T 10. F (Reactivity depends on the nature of the functional groups.) 11. T 12. F
Matching: 1. i 2. j 3. f 4. l 5. h 6. c 7. a 8. k 9. e 10. b 11. g 12. d

Chapter Thirteen

Multiple choice: 1. d 2. b 3. a 4. c 5. a 6. c 7. c 8. c 9. d 10. d
Sentence completion: 1. 2-heptyne 2. hydrogenation 3. *para* 4. more, fewer 5. hydration 6. catalyst 7. carbocation 8. unsaturated 9. Toluene 10. substitution 11. Polycyclic aromatic compounds 12. thermal cracking
True/false: 1. F 2. T 3. T 4. F (2-bromobutane) 5. F (Halogenation is the reaction of X_2 with an alkene, where X is a halogen.) 6. T 7. F 8. F (Hydration requires a strong acid as a catalyst.) 9. T 10. F 11. F 12. T
Matching: 1. e 2. k 3. i 4. j 5. b 6. l 7. d 8. c 9. a 10. f 11. g 12. h

Chapter Fourteen

Multiple choice: 1. c 2. b 3. b 4. a 5. d 6. d 7. a 8. b 9. c 10. d
Sentence completion: 1. wood alcohol 2. glycols 3. phenols 4. alkene 5. thiols 6. $KMnO_4$ or $K_2Cr_2O_7$ 7. lower 8. BHT 9. greater 10. free radical 11. peroxide 12. CFC
True/false: 1. T 2. F (A ketone is formed from the oxidation of a secondary alcohol.) 3. T 4. F (carbolic acid) 5. T 6. T 7. F (Ethyl chloride is an anesthetic.) 8. F (two hydrogen atoms) 9. T 10. T 11. F 12. T
Matching: 1. j 2. g 3. f 4. h 5. l 6. b 7. e 8. a 9. k 10. d 11. i 12. c

Chapter Fifteen

Multiple choice: 1. c 2. a 3. d 4. c 5. c 6. a 7. b 8. d 9. a 10. b
Sentence completion: 1. *amino-* 2. quaternary 3. DNA 4. Toxicology 5. heterocycle 6. Alkaloids 7. hydrogen bonding 8. ammonium 9. free radical 10. nonaromatic amines
True/false: 1. T 2. T 3. F (They're lower boiling.) 4. T 5. F 6. T 7. F (It's synthetic.) 8. T 9. F (NO lowers blood pressure.) 10. F (*N*-Methylbutylamine)
Matching: 1. d 2. l 3. h 4. i 5. a 6. j 7. b 8. k 9. f 10. g 11. e 12. c

Chapter Sixteen

Multiple choice: 1. c 2. b 3. a 4. d 5. c 6. b 7. b 8. a 9. d 10. b
Sentence completion: 1. carbonyl 2. silver 3. Hydrolysis 4. positive, negative 5. Acetone 6. Acetaldehyde 7. more 8. reduction 9. disinfectant or preservative 10. hemiacetal 11. Benedict's 12. Acetone
True/False: 1. F (a hemiacetal link) 2. T 3. F (Ketones don't undergo Tollens' reaction.) 4. F ($NaBH_4$ is used for reduction.) 5. F 6. F (Both aldehydes and ketones form acetals.) 7. T 8. T 9. F (NADH) 10. T 11. T 12. T
Matching: 1. e 2. i 3. d (or l) 4. a 5. h 6. j 7. k 8. b 9. l 10. f 11. g 12. c

Chapter Seventeen

Multiple choice: 1. d 2. c 3. a 4. d 5. b 6. d 7. b 8. a 9. d 10. a
Sentence completion: 1. carbonyl group substitution 2. polyamide 3. carboxylate salt 4. esterification 5. attracts 6. -oic acid 7. propyl propanoate 8. esters 9. Phosphorylation 10. fats 11. hydrolysis or saponification 12. propanedioic acid
True/false: 1. T 2. F (basic hydrolysis) 3. F (Amides are nonbasic.) 4. T 5. F (The products are acetate ion and ethanol.) 6. F (*N*,*N*-dimethylformamide) 7. F 8. T 9. T 10. F (Esterification is acid-catalyzed.) 11. F (It's an acid anhydride.) 12. T
Matching: 1. j 2. f 3. k 4. b 5. i 6. d 7. a 8. e 9. l 10. h 11. c 12. g

Chapter Eighteen

Multiple choice: 1. a 2. d 3. c 4. b 5. b 6. a 7. d 8. b 9. c 10. d
Sentence completion : 1. 5.0-6.3 2. enantiomers 3. zwitterions 4. backbone 5. loop 6. glycoprotein 7. Tertiary 8. β-sheet 9. polar 10. sulfur 11. polypeptide 12. Hydrophobic
True/false: 1. F (Glycine is achiral.) 2. T 3. F (Denaturation disrupts all structural elements except primary structure.) 4. F (They're different.) 5. T 6. F 7. T 8. T 9. T 10. F (Fibrous proteins are insoluble.) 11. T 12. T
Matching: 1. e 2. g 3. j 4. a 5. b 6. k 7. c 8. l 9. f 10. h 11. d 12. i

Chapter Nineteen

Multiple choice: 1. c 2. a 3. c 4. d 5. b 6. b 7. d 8. c 9. b 10. d
Sentence completion: 1. isomerase 2. Isoenzymes 3. K 4. induced-fit 5. noncompetitive 6. denature 7. turnover number 8. phosphoryl 9. proximity 10. 10^9 11. allosteric 12. zymogen
True/false: 1. T 2. F 3. F 4. F (a dehydrase) 5. F (Enzyme-substrate interactions are noncovalent.) 6. F (Minerals, not vitamins, are inorganic ions.) 7. T 8. F (Retinol, retinal, retinoic acid are all active forms of vitamin A.) 9. T 10. T 11. F (Reaction rate increases.) 12. T
Matching: 1. c 2. h 3. i 4. g 5. k 6. j 7. b 8. a 9. d 10. f 11. e 12. l

Chapter Twenty

Multiple choice: 1. a 2. c 3. b 4. c 5. d 6. a 7. d 8. a 9. d 10. d
Sentence Completion: 1. Anaphylaxis 2. adrenal 3. vesicles 4. Histamine 5. cholinergic 6. progesterone 7. enkephalin 8. ethnobotanist 9. synaptic cleft 10. dopamine 11. thyroxine 12. phosphodiesterase
True/false: 1. F (Thyroxine can cross the cell membrane.) 2. F (It blocks reuptake.) 3. T 4. T 5. F (presynaptic neurons) 6. T 7. F (It increases blood pressure and heart rate.) 8. F (It's a symptom of iodine deficiency.) 9. T 10. T
Matching: 1. e 2. h 3. k 4. b 5. g 6. a 7. d 8. j 9. f 10. l 11. c 12. i

Chapter Twenty-one

Multiple choice: 1. b 2. c 3. a 4. c 5. a 6. d 7. b 8. c 9. b 10. d
Sentence completion: 1. Eukaryotic 2. metabolic pathway or linear sequence 3. ADP and phosphate 4. unfavorable 5. Krebs cycle, tricarboxylic acid cycle 6. succinyl-SCoA, CO_2 7. NAD^+ 8. one (plus 4 reduced coenzymes) 9. Cytoplasm 10. Catalase 11. succinate dehydrogenase 12. Basal metabolism
True/false: 1. T 2. F (Only eukaryotic cells are found in higher organisms.) 3. F (Anabolism is the synthesis of complicated molecules from simpler molecules.) 4. F 5. T 6. T 7. F ($FADH_2$ donates electrons to coenzyme Q.) 8. T 9. F (decrease in order) 10. F (ATP can be formed in the citric acid cycle) 11. F (a phosphate anhydride) 12. T
Matching: 1. d 2. j 3. f 4. a 5. l 6. k 7. e 8. c 9. b 10. g 11. i 12. h

Chapter Twenty-two

Multiple choice: 1. a 2. d 3. c 4. c 5. d 6. d 7. d 8. c 9. b 10. b
Sentence completion: 1. chiral 2. amylases 3. enantiomers 4. cyclic hemiacetal 5. fructose 6. amylose, amylopectin 7. glycoside 8. Glycogen 9. aldohexose 10. achiral 11. diastereomer 12. Glycoproteins
True/false: 1. T 2. T 3. F (The hydroxyl group on the chiral carbon farthest from the carbonyl group is on the left.) 4. F (α, not β) 5. T 6. F (Crystalline glucose is the α-anomer.) 7. F (Sucrose contains only an acetal bond.) 8. T 9. F (An acetal resembles an ether.) 10. F (Maltose is composed of two glucose molecules.) 11. F (The relationship between the rotations of diastereomers is not predictable.) 12. T
Matching: 1. e 2. l 3. j 4. h 5. i 6. k 7. b 8. a 9. d 10. g 11. c 12. f

Chapter Twenty-three

Multiple choice: 1. c 2. c 3. b 4. d 5. a 6. b 7. d 8. c 9. d 10. a
Sentence completion: 1. Embden-Meyerhof 2. 6 3. Pyruvate dehydrogenase complex 4. Insulin 5. glucose 1-phosphate 6. 1-5 7. diabetes mellitus 8. GTP, ATP 9. CO_2 10. glucose 6-phosphate isomerase 11. glucagon 12. Hypoglycemia
True/false: 1. F (It produces NADPH.) 2. T 3. F 4. F 5. T 6. F (Glycolysis occurs in the cytosol.) 7. F (The yield of ATP was formerly considered to be 38 ATP/1 mol glucose. The new estimate is 30-32 ATP/ 1 mol glucose.) 8. F (glycogen) 9. F (Fermentation occurs only in yeasts.) 10. T (but one results from isomerization of dihydroxyacetone phosphate) 11. T 12. F (It produces two ATPs.)
Matching: 1. l 2. k 3. i 4. j 5. c 6. h 7. d 8. a 9. f 10. g 11. b 12. e

Chapter Twenty-four

Multiple choice: 1. d 2. c 3. a 4. a 5. d 6. d 7. c 8. b 9. a 10. b
Sentence completion: 1. glycoside 2. Soap 3. hydrophilic, hydrophobic 4. Glycolipids, cholesterol, glycoproteins 5. fluid-mosaic 6. tetracyclic 7. arachidonic 8. micelles 9. Sphingomyelins 10. lipid bilayer 11. Eicosanoids 12. Integral
True/false: 1. T 2. F 3. F (They contain an amide group.) 4. T 5. T 6. F (They form a micelle.) 7. F (Cholesterol is a steroid component of cell membranes.) 8. F (The major difference is in the quantity of unsaturated fatty acids they contain.) 9. F (Cerebrosides are components of nerve cell membranes in the brain.) 10. T 11. T 12. F (In facilitated diffusion, solutes are transported across cell membranes by proteins, but no energy investment is required.)
Matching: 1. l 2. h 3. e 4. f 5. a 6. j 7. k 8. b 9. d 10. g 11. i 12. c

Chapter Twenty-five

Multiple choice: 1. a 2. d 3. c 4. a 5. b 6. b 7. c 8. d 9. c 10. d
Sentence completion: 1. NAD^+, FAD 2. micelles 3. adipocytes 4. dihydroxyacetone phosphate 5. fatty-acid spiral 6. double bond 7. Ketonuria 8. NADPH 9. 3–Hydroxybutyrate 10. lymphatic system 11. mobilized 12. acetyl-SCoA
True/false: 1. T 2. F (The products are mainly mono- and diacylglycerols.) 3. T 4. T 5. F 6. T 7. F (Dihydroxyacetone phosphate, not glycerol) 8. F (LDL transports cholesterol.) 9. T 10. F (It occurs in the cytosol.) 11. F (It comes from acetyl–SCoA.) 12. T.
Matching: 1. e 2. i 3. a 4. l 5. g 6. j 7. k 8. d 9. f 10. b 11. c 12. h

Chapter Twenty-six

Multiple choice: 1. c 2. d 3. b 4. a 5. b 6. b 7. c 8. d 9. c 10. a
Sentence completion: 1. Replication 2. complementary 3. chromatin 4. retrovirus 5. intron 6. ester 7. nucleoside 8. releasing factor 9. replication fork 10. 2'-deoxyribose 11. Watson-Crick 12. DNA polymerase
True/false: 1. F (61 codons code for the 20 amino acids; the other three are "stop" codons.) 2. F (The amount of adenine equals the amount of thymine.) 3. T 4. F (An anticodon occurs on tRNA.) 5. T 6. T 7. T 8. F (They run in opposite directions.) 9. F (translation) 10. F (Most DNA consists of introns.) 11. F (Two have only one codon.) 12. F (guanosine 5'-monophosphate)
Matching; 1. l 2. j 3. b 4. g 5. a 6. i 7. d 8. c 9. e 10. k 11. f 12. h

Chapter Twenty-seven

Multiple choice: 1. c 2. d 3. b 4. a 5. d 6. d 7. d 8. b 9. c 10. b
Sentence completion: 1. “sticky” ends 2. ‘junk” 3. restriction endonuclease 4. Taq polymerase 5. bioethics 6. ionizing radiation, mutagens 7. intron 8. single nucleotide polymorphism 9. proteomics 10. centromere 11. silent 12. autoradiogram
True/false: 1. T 2. F (nucleotide) 3. F (from several people) 4. T 5. T 6. F (starts from base-base sequences at known locations) 7.T 8.F 9. F (missense) 10.T 11. F (adding) 12. T
Matching: 1. b 2. i 3. g 4. c 5. j 6. l 7. e 8. a 9. k 10. h 11. f 12. d

Chapter Twenty-eight

Multiple choice: 1. c 2. a 3. b 4. d 5. a 6. c 7. d 8. c 9. a 10. b
Sentence completion: 1. pyruvate, glutamate 2. Methionine 3. acetyl-SCoA, acetoacetyl–SCoA 4. carbamoyl phosphate 5. protease 6. pyruvate 7. Transamination 8. arginine 9. phenylalanine, tyrosine 10. urate crystals 11. ALT 12. bicarbonate
True/false: 1. T 2. F (It starts in the stomach.) 3. F (lysine and leucine) 4. F (The human body can catabolize essential amino acids.) 5. T 6. F (Catabolism occurs in the liver and in the cytosol.) 7. T 8. T 9. F (One is from aspartate; the other is from ammonium ion.) 10. T 11. F (Some transaminases have several amino acid donors.) 12. T
Matching: 1. h 2. g 3. j 4. f 5. a 6. b 7. c 8. l 9. k 10. d 11. e 12. i

Chapter Twenty-nine

Multiple choice: 1. a 2. d 3. c 4. b 5. d 6. a 7. d 8. b 9. b 10. c
Sentence completion: 1. partial pressure 2. haptens 3. zymogens 4. osmolarity 5. histidine 6. calcium, K 7. active transport 8. transport, regulation, defense 9. phagocytes 10. autoimmune 11. Hemophilia 12. lysine, glutamine
True/false: 1. F (constructed) 2. F (hemostasis) 3. F (CO_2 bonds to hemoglobin) 4. T 5. T 6. F (overproduction) 7. F (blood serum) 8. T 9. F (tubule) 10. T 11. F (phagocytes) 12. T
Matching: 1. d 2. c 3. f 4. g 5. j 6. i 7. a 8. b 9. h 10. l 11. k 12. e

Y0-BDI-800

LITHGOW REGIONAL LIBRARY
[redacted]4762

111126

JAPAN STYLE

JAPAN STYLE

LITHGOW REGIONAL LIBRARY
DON 9.8.99
NF 709.52 JAP
301064762.

Essays by Mitsukuni Yoshida, J. V. Earle, Masaru Katzumie, Jean-Pierre Lehmann Art direction by Ikko Tanaka

Published by Kodansha International Ltd., Tokyo and New York in collaboration with The Japan Foundation and the Victoria and Albert Museum

Produced by Kodansha International Ltd.
with the assistance of a grant from the
Commemorative Association for the Japan
World Exposition.

Copyright © 1980 by The Japan Foundation,
Park Building, 3 Kioi-cho, Chiyoda-ku,
Tokyo 102.

Published by Kodansha International Ltd.,
17-14 Otowa 1-chome, Bunkyo-ku, Tokyo 112,
in collaboration with The Japan Foundation,
Park Building, 3 Kioi-cho, Chiyoda-ku,
Tokyo 102.

All rights reserved.
Printed in Japan.

First edition, 1980
First paperback edition, 1990

ISBN 0-87011-963-X
LCC 79-66243
ISBN 4-7700-1463-5 (in Japan)

CONTENTS

Essays — 6

Japan — 33

Materials — 45

Elegance — 61

Simplicity — 77

Compactness — 91

Graphism — 107

Vitality — 125

Today — 139

Captions — 149

Japan Style—Yesterday, Today and Tomorrow

Masaru Katzumie

I must admit that when our British friends suggested the title of this exhibition should be "Japan Style", we had certain reservations about accepting the phrase as it stood. Supposing we could climb aboard a time machine and travel back to nineteenth century Japan, we would probably find, it is true, that the words "Japan Style" aptly described the life being lived then; again, if we were to climb aboard the famous Bullet Train and travel from Tokyo (the modern capital) to Kyoto (the former capital, with a proud history going back more than a millennium), I think we would realise that the life of the latter city still had a certain unity and harmony, which justified the use of the same expression.

I know, however, that if I were to speak of modern Kyoto, a city with a population of over one million, as being no more than a cultural relic, I should probably incur the wrath of the inhabitants. Nevertheless, the weight of history and the force of tradition have given the streets of the city an undeniably unified and harmonious atmosphere. Even though Kyoto has yielded to Tokyo the role of political and financial capital, there remains, underlying the complex psychology of her citizens, a certain pride in the fact that, when it comes to traditional life and culture, their city is still at the centre of things.

Everywhere in Japan there may be found old castle-towns, which retain something of the flavour of days gone by (although not in such perfect form as Kyoto itself), and some years ago the Japan National Railways ran a publicity campaign with the English title "Discover Japan" in an effort to get tourists of the younger generation to visit these little Kyotos. As a result, every holiday large charabancs disgorged crowds of young people who strolled around the ancient streets of such towns in brightly coloured T-shirts and jeans. So essential has it become for us to draw attention to the fact that the fine old traditions and cultural patterns of Japan are being lost or destroyed that we have to make deliberate use of the English word "discover" in appealing to the young people who will shape the future of our country. And yet the "Japanese things" in which our foreign friends show most interest almost all pertain to that fine old tradition. Woodblock prints, *shōji* (translucent sliding paper screens), *noren* (decorative curtains), *monshō* (heraldic crests), *tatami* matting, *bonsai* trees, *kimono*, *kabuki* theatre, *sumō* wrestling—all of them developed in the Edo period (1615–1868), and we have done no more than inherit them in an already perfected state and repeat and perpetuate them without alteration.

Japan in the Edo period occupied a peculiar position in the general history of the world: just when the countries of Europe and America were embracing mercantilism and plunging headlong into the industrial revolution, the Tokugawa government was virtually cutting Japan off from the outside world by a conscious policy of national isolation. Apart from maintaining commercial relations with Chinese and Dutch merchants via the single port of Nagasaki, to which the foreigners were confined, the authorities allowed no external trade of any kind. By way of compensation they pursued a domestic policy of strengthening the feudal system and encouraging cultural unity and in so doing they managed to keep the country at peace for more than 250 years.

At the end of the seventeenth century the city of Edo (the old name for Tokyo) already had a million inhabitants, and it is not often realised that the government was forced to adopt a number of measures to stem the drift of population away from the provinces towards this large city. It is estimated that there were about thirty million people in Japan at the time; on the one hand the government introduced measures to prevent any further increase, and on the other hand it encouraged the stepping up of food production to meet the needs of the existing population. James Clavell's best-selling historical novel *Shogun* performed an eminently useful task in drawing the world's attention to this important and hitherto hidden chapter in Japanese history.

But the new government that overthrew the Tokugawa regime in 1868 (the year of the so-called Meiji Restoration) decided to reverse the existing policy of national isolation and encourage population increase and contacts with the outside world. The radical approach of the Meiji government, which aimed to establish a modern state by introducing science and technology from advanced Western nations, is reflected in the contemporary slogan *bummei kaika* ("civilisation and enlightenment"), while another phrase fashionable at the time, *jōtō hakurai* ("high-class imports"), is a vivid illustration of the susceptibility of ordinary people to the novel goods that were being imported from the industrialised countries of Europe and America. But the traditional life and culture referred to above, which had grown to maturity and refinement over the previous 250 years, were not so powerless nor so lacking in practical value as to be easily swept away by this new tide of "civilisation and enlightenment" and "high-class imports". The result was a kind of dichotomy —a dichotomy by which, for the past hundred years, we have been in a state of perpetual oscillation between the opposed phenomena of tradition and progress, Japanese and Western.

Such oppositions have of course been experienced in the West as well, but there the choice has been between the maintenance or rejection of traditions based on a continuous and homogeneous historical process. This guarantee of historical continuity does not exist in Japan, and so the opposition between modernism and traditionalism has tended to be equated with two quite different historical experiences, that of the West and that of Japan. The resulting, peculiarly Japanese, brand of dualism has invaded every aspect of our life, from clothes, food and houses to art and culture in general. We make distinctions between Japanese rooms and Western rooms, Japanese clothes and Western clothes, Japanese food and Western food.

We Japanese have grown quite used to this kind of dualism and as a rule we are quite unconscious of these distinctions, but it seems that they can raise problems for foreign visitors to Japan. For example, because of the quite obvious difference between modern Japanese-style painting (*Nihonga*) and modern Japanese Western-style painting (*Yōga*), it has become customary to display the two types in separate rooms when exhibitions are set up. But it was not until some German friends raised the matter that I noticed our failure to make such a distinction in the case of sculpture.

In spite of this kind of inconsistency and vagueness, which may in any case be a specially Japanese trait, it is an undeniable fact that there does exist a dualistic tendency to make distinctions between the Western and the Japanese aspects of our lives. Since the Meiji period (1868–1912) we have been through all manner of trials and errors in our efforts to overcome this kind of dualism and achieve a unified cultural pattern, but so far none of our experiments has been entirely successful. In fact the position we have reached after a century of struggle seems to be more a kind of resourceful eclecticism, which admits the existence of the dualism I have described and makes best use of Japanese or Western things according to time and circumstance. This sensitive realisation and practical acceptance of the situation may be seen as an eloquent expression of the positive outlook of the Japanese people: they turn eclecticism to their advantage and use it as a means of adding variety and enjoyment to their lives.

To give a well-known example, a commuter who wears a convenient Western-style suit at the office during the day relaxes in a Japanese *yukata* (light cotton *kimono*) when he gets home in the evening. In the same way, girls who normally prefer to wear Western-style clothes choose to put on splendid *kimono*s for weddings and other formal occasions. The sight of young women, who up until the day before were in hippy-style clothes, gathering all dressed in formal *kimono*s for a coming-of-age ceremony is a modern spectacle on a par with the traditional folk festivals of old. Before the war, middle-class households preferred to live in one-family houses, which included, as a status symbol, at least one room in Western style complete with piano and sofa. Post-war apartment blocks are, generally speaking, in Western style, but the planners of such buildings have always to bear in mind the fondness of the people who will live in them for rooms floored in Japanese style with *tatami* straw matting.

To turn to our eating habits, it seems that the heterogeneous nature of modern Japanese food is such that it is not possible to make an analysis in terms of "native" and "foreign". In Tokyo there are countless restaurants, serving dishes from throughout the world, and every one of them seems to be doing good business. One never hears of a restaurant going bankrupt. If an article recommending one of these places appears in a mass-circulation newspaper, you can be sure that it will be packed from then on. These are simple proofs of the fact that the snobbishness of the Japanese people is by no means confined to art and music alone.

Some years ago an able ceramic designer by the name of Masahiro Mori decided he would try to design a "national tableware", but he has since come to realise that this task is far more difficult than he originally expected it to be. In response to the advice and suggestions of various consultants, Mori has continued to add new items to his set of tableware until now there are more than two hundred different pieces, but he has still not finished. He has held exhibitions of work in which he divided the tableware into three groups—breakfast, lunch and dinner. In fact, there are quite a few Japanese who eat a Western-style breakfast, a lunch consisting of Japanese snacks, and an evening meal that is a combination of Japanese and Western food.

Perhaps the most obvious instance of the Japanese tendency to dualism is the Japanese writing system. More than a thousand years ago we imported the ideographic script (called *kanji* in Japanese) from China and from it we developed two separate sets of syllabic symbols called *hiragana* and *katakana*. Nowadays we use all three systems in conjunction, according to context. All three scripts are written vertically and the columns arranged from right to left, but since the Meiji period we have adopted Arabic numerals and Roman script as well, and when these are used it is necessary to make a choice between writing horizontally or vertically. Probably the first attempts at writing pure Japanese horizontally were inspired by the notes taken by Japanese learning English or French or by bank and company ledgers that made use of Arabic numerals. But even when a decision has been made to write Japanese horizontally, there remains another choice—whether to write from right to left or from left to right. Traditionally, when large signs (for example, the framed notices put up at the entrances to Buddhist temples) were written horizontally, they were written from right to left. To begin with, placards and street signs followed the same practice, but inconsistencies occurred when Roman and Japanese script were used together—for instance, in signs giving the names of railway stations—since the Japanese read from right to left and the Roman script from left to right; such inconsistencies often gave rise to argument and debate. It was not until after the last war that we finally decided on a consistent policy of writing from left to right in such situations. This problem even has a fundamental effect on the binding of books, for whether a magazine or book should open from right to left (Western style) or from left to right depends on whether the writing inside is vertical or horizontal and whether the lines are arranged from right to left or from left to right. Except in publications where illustrations have most importance and there is not much text, it is rare to find the Western style of binding from right to left in use. It is worth noting that even ephemeral, unbound publications of Western origin such as newspapers open in the traditional way, though people do not notice the fact because newspapers are not bound. This can be seen as yet another instance of Japanese dualism.

Japan's great newspapers are read all over the country, and there are several with a circulation of more than five million; consequently their influence on the population is enormous. But although these great newspapers are basically printed vertically, special headlines, passages involving many Arabic numerals and pages giving details of radio and T.V. programmes are written horizontally, while the advertisements are a veritable jungle of Roman and Japanese, vertical and horizontal. I have wondered for a long time why on earth this dualism is allowed. It is partly due, of course, to the positive outlook of the Japanese people, but it is also true that we have behind us a thousand years and more of indigenous culture: the hundred years or so that have elapsed since the Meiji Restoration are nowhere near long enough for us to absorb a civilisation imported from the West. Furthermore, our writing system has one distinct advantage, which should not be overlooked: Japanese script is usually arranged in a grid layout, which takes the uniformly square shape of the Chinese-derived *kanji* as its basic unit, and this layout permits free interchange between vertical and horizontal writing. It is not possible at present to be certain if this will prove to be much of an advantage in the long run, but, for the time being, the acceptance of a mixed writing system has a powerful effect on our modern culture in general.

The *Kojiki* ("Record of Ancient Matters"), which holds a position in Japanese culture analogous to that of the Norse sagas or the Old Testament in the West, describes the creation of the universe in terms of a giant jellyfish. I sometimes wonder whether modern Japan, these four small islands holding a population of more than a hundred million, may not itself be rather like a giant jellyfish, drifting helplessly on the sea of civilisation. Will we ever achieve a culture unified and homogeneous enough to justify us calling it "Japan Style"? All we can do for the moment is to ask our British friends to look at Japan as it is.

Of course we Japanese have not been idle in our efforts to establish a "Japan Style". I remember how at one time we argued furiously among ourselves about the comparative merits of "Japanese Modern" and "Japonica". The debate was sparked off by an article by Rose Slivka in the American magazine *Craft Horizons* (July – August 1956, special issue on Japan, Finland and Italy), in which she expressed the view that "to America . . . has come the old from Japan, the new from Finland and a combination of the old and the new from Italy". I cannot remember who it was who gave Mrs. Slivka her material, but it must be admitted that when we feel that we are playing to an international audience, we Japanese tend to be too self-conscious about Japan, and as a result when we send material to be displayed at international exhibitions we continue *ad nauseam* to choose objects executed in traditional Japanese techniques, which can easily be recognised as "Japanese" in style. If you ask me, this is essentially an expression of the same attitude as is manifested in the calculated exoticism of souvenir-shop "Japonica". We are still searching for a "Japanese modern style"; although this style is still incomplete and imperfect in many ways, it is my sincere wish that our friends in the international community will acknowledge the validity of our efforts.

I should like to recount in this connection a most interesting anecdote concerning Walter Gropius and Yūsaku Kamekura. Kamekura was more strongly influenced than any other Japanese graphic designer by the Bauhaus movement, and he is famous for the functionalist style of his work; yet when Gropius happened to visit Japan and see a logo designed by Kamekura, he (Gropius) asked if its shape did not derive from some Japanese folk implement. I would not be surprised if Kamekura was a little upset by this totally unexpected enquiry. Be that as it may, the lesson of this story, in my view, is that a logo that Kamekura designed with no consciousness of his Japanese background should appear in Gropius's eyes to have something Japanese about it.

Even the so-called pictograms, whose use I have been striving to encourage since the 1964 Tokyo Olympics and which have recently begun to receive international support, were not conceived with the traditional Japanese heraldic crests (*monshō*) particularly in mind. In fact it was because of my previous experience of the serious language barriers existing in the international community that I resolved to become an advocate of the use of these pictograms. I was motivated by a sincere desire to make it just a little easier for the people who assembled for the 1964 Olympics and 1970 Osaka Expo to overcome the language barriers; if I was conscious of any particular background inspiration at the time, it was not the tradition of the Japanese *monshō* but the Isotypes (International System of Typographic Picture Education) of Otto Neurath in the 1930s or the 1949 United Nations Geneva Protocol on International Communication Signs.

I should like to believe that when we conceive a design in an international context but unconsciously adopt a Japanese approach, the result is something worthy of the description "Japan Style". For the time being, however, we have no choice but to go through an arduous and repetitious process of selection and rejection in our pursuit of this goal. All the same, I should like to conclude by saying how very grateful we are to our British friends for their great kindness in giving us a valuable opportunity to indulge in this rigorous self-analysis.

Why Japan?

J. V. Earle

It may well be asked why a museum in London should devote a major exhibition to modern Japanese craft and design and, more particularly, why that exhibition should attempt not only to display modern Japanese artefacts as beautiful objects in their own right but also to convey to the visitor some idea of the visual context in which they are made and used.

The first and probably the most important reason for holding the exhibition at all is that we (and that "we" could mean "we Europeans" as much as "we British") know remarkably little about Japan in spite of its very obvious importance in the modern world. Dr. Lehmann has written, elsewhere in this catalogue, of Western stereotypes of Japanese thought and behaviour, but since this exhibition is, inevitably, devoted primarily to the "look" of modern Japan, it is as well to mention here a widespread *visual* stereotype, which this exhibition aims to dispel, namely that Japan is an undifferentiated megalopolitan hell of jam-packed commuter trains and office buildings, pollution, coin-operated oxygen machines and roof-top golf-courses. In such a stereotype, Japan is seen as somehow vaguely "American", "Westernised" or "international" and entirely devoid of any visual merits or any features that are characteristically Japanese, apart from a few carefully preserved ancient monuments or objects in museum showcases.

In connection with the "Japanese" features whose absence is deplored by subscribers to this stereotype, there are two other widely held misconceptions that should be described. When attempting to analyse the Japanese artistic tradition in a very general way, art historians often speak of two broad stylistic tendencies, the one colourful, decorative, exuberant and inventive, the other monochrome, linear, refined and austere. This is a useful distinction in its way, but it is remarkable how many people with a passing interest in Japanese art imagine one of the characterisations to be true to the almost complete exclusion of the other. In Britain the most popular representative of the first tendency is the colour woodblock print, while books devoted to the tea ceremony and its architecture, Nō drama, rock gardens and flower arrangement have encouraged belief in the refined, austere stereotype. Neither tendency could survive, of course, in the machine- and commerce-dominated stereotype of modern Japan; such a Japan would be too drab for the life and colour typified by woodblock prints, while traditional austerity and restraint would be drowned in a sea of commercialism. This exhibition aims to demonstrate not only that these two stylistic currents are by no means mutually exclusive, but also that both are very much alive and well in modern Japan.

A second reason for the attempt to convey something of the totality of modern Japanese life (inevitably, this means mostly city life) lies in the opportunities it gives us to make comparisons with our own society. These comparisons are basically of two kinds. It is interesting and instructive on the one hand to see what the Japanese have made of those features of Western material culture that they have borrowed, and on the other hand to identify the aspects of their life today that are purely Japanese in origin. The merchant and artisan classes that came to prominence during the Edo period (1615–1868) developed a distinctive way of life, combining elements from many diverse native traditions, whose visual manifestations were extraordinarily lively and attractive. Since Japan managed to avoid any foreign conquest or occupation during the early stages of contact with Western industrial nations, a surprisingly large number of the characteristic features of this merchant society have survived to the present day. Modern Japan, in fact, is a unique example of the way in which a sophisticated traditional urban culture has adopted Western methods to take on and outstrip the West in terms of trade, industry and the like and yet, to a remarkable degree, has retained its distinctive character. As such, it is in some ways an "alternative" late twentieth century culture. By studying it, we in the West may well discover new and refreshing ways of making and using everyday objects and solving some of the problems that seem increasingly to beset most industrialised nations.

On my first visit to Japan some years ago, since I work in a museum and specialise in traditional Japanese art, I was naturally very keen to see as much as I could in my limited time of Japan's artistic heritage—the temples of Kyoto with their sculptures and gardens, the narrative scrolls of the Kamakura period, the ink paintings of the Muromachi period, the decorative screens of the Momoyama, and the finest possible examples of all the great craft traditions. The longer I stayed there, however, the more I found that my attention was taken up just as much by the beauty of those aspects of Japan's past that survive, albeit often in somewhat altered form, in modern daily life. For example, like every visitor to Japan I was especially struck by the marked attention to visual appearance with which food is served in every Japanese restaurant with any pretensions to quality. The wide range of bowls, boxes, cups, plates and dishes made from many different materials and decorated in many different styles and yet carefully selected to present a harmonious whole, and the meticulous preparation and presentation of the food itself can make eating in Japan as much an aesthetic as a gastronomic experience. Again, even the most unobservant visitor to Japan cannot fail to notice the widespread survival of traditional techniques and concepts of interior design. Although such a visitor, assuming him to be on a business trip, will stay in a hotel in (almost) pure Western style, the very first time he is entertained (as he surely will be) he will very likely find himself in a restaurant floored with *tatami* straw matting and with sliding paper screens instead of doors and perhaps featuring a *tokonoma* alcove. These two instances of the survival of traditional elements are rather superficial, but in fact most private houses and a great many apartment blocks have Japanese-style rooms, and although the notion that the Japanese like to make the most everyday things beautiful is a cliché, it is nevertheless a cliché with a firm foundation in fact. In the presentation of food, this fact takes its most striking and immediate form.

I mentioned above that some Japanese ways of doing things might suggest solutions to contemporary problems. The plain and almost furnitureless *tatami* and *tokonoma* style of interior design was largely due to the ascetic, spartan tastes of the warrior classes, and although its combination of beauty and convenience has been a great influence on modern architecture, the possibilities that it offers for sparing use of dwindling natural resources have, it seems, not yet been fully exploited. The traditional manner of serving food described above provides similar possibilities for making a pleasure of frugality.

When the visitor ventures out into the shopping streets of Tokyo, he is certain to be struck by the overwhelming bombardment of graphic material that greets his eye wherever he looks. Styles and scripts are many, from elegantly calligraphic characters on wooden notice-boards in temples, which may turn out to mean "No Smoking", to amusing transmogrifications of English, chosen more for *chic* than for literal meaning, if any. The latter are added to practically every commercial advertisement: AT SPRING PLACE; *fashion joyful*; *interior wide space*; and, in large letters atop a department store, MY CITY. Bold use of the Japanese scripts was an important feature of Edo culture, but the wider range of scripts available today (three indigenous systems plus every possible style of Roman script and Arabic numerals) together with the techniques of colour-printing have spurred the modern Japanese on to even greater inventiveness and originality. Although we in the West have to make do with a smaller number of symbols, there is no reason why we should not learn more than we have done to date from the extravagant vitality of modern Japanese graphics.

When we look at Japanese industrial products that are truly "international" in style (electrical goods, cameras, cars, motorcycles and the like), it may seem difficult to account for their excellence in terms of the lasting influence of traditional concepts. However, even if we leave aside such factors as social organisation and attitudes to work, which are beyond the scope of this essay, there are in fact a number of tendencies in traditional design that continue to influence the appearance of modern, factory-produced goods. Of these tendencies, the most prominent is perhaps the decorative use of functional attributes. Utilitarian objects that are "decorated" in the normal sense of the word (that is to say, the decoration itself makes no contribution to the object's function) abound in Japan and are well represented in Western collections, but we are perhaps not quite so familiar with those objects whose beauty lies in their functional simplicity. The *tatami* straw matting mentioned above and the sliding translucent paper screens (*shōji*) that do the job of windows are examples in the sphere of architecture and interior design. In fact *tatami* (which measure six feet by three feet) were originally used as beds, but the beauty of the patterns made by their black tape edgings when two or more were combined led, eventually, to rooms being entirely floored in *tatami*, a practice that combines great comfort with considerable aesthetic appeal. Two instances of this decorative exploitation of materials, the paper lampshade (derived from the traditional lantern) and the bamboo blind (which was already in use in Japan during the twelfth century), now enjoy widespread popularity in the West; other examples in the exhibition include knives and chopping boards, craftsmen's tools and *geta* (wooden clogs), and the same principle can be seen at work in a great many of the craft items displayed.

There are two features of traditional architecture that testify to the fact that this use of functionalism is by no means always something inevitable, unintentional or unselfconscious. In the framework of a building, the horizontal bracing member called *nageshi* is often far larger that its practical purpose alone would justify and is designed to look like a solid beam when in reality it is made up of planks. The *nageshi* is almost always exposed to view on both sides of the wall and, in fact, while appearing functional, is often included in a building merely for the aesthetic value of the patterns it creates by its intersections with columns and corners. Similarly, in the construction of roofs, elaborate precautions are often taken, in designing the ends of the eaves, to make the roof as a whole appear thicker or thinner than it actually is. Sometimes extra roofing material is added at the edge, sometimes non-functional rafters are put in to hide the real ones. This ability to make use of or tinker with functional elements continues to be of great value in the design of industrial products, for example in deciding the size and distribution of knobs, buttons and switches in the controls of a pocket calculator or amplifier, or in emphasising or playing down the structural members in the construction of a chair, camera or motorcycle.

The pursuit of adaptability and convenience is another traditional tendency that appears to fit in very well with the practice of industrial design. Adaptability is a key concept in traditional domestic architecture: rooms do not have specific functions as they do in the West and they may be separated off or combined simply by inserting or removing sliding screens. Other traditional domestic articles, for example the light *futon* (quilt), which is laid out at night for sleeping and put away during the day, seem to have come into being in response to a liking for objects that are uncluttering and easy to use. Perhaps it is not too far-fetched to see in the *yatate* (ink and brush in a portable case) the same principle as inspires the design of a radio, calculator and clock as a single unit which fits easily into the pocket or, to take a recent and already celebrated example, the combined traditional abacus (*soroban*) and modern calculator.

Closely related to this penchant for functional simplicity and adaptability is the traditional respect for the inherent beauty of materials. Although it is a far cry from the glazes of tea-ceremony pottery, the brilliant clarity of Japanese porcelain, the grain in the wood of house floors, walls and ceilings or the subtle textures of lacquer to the modern uses of glass, metal and plastic, the Japanese preference for beautifying the surface of an object not by decorating it but by bringing out its natural qualities can be and has been applied successfully to industrial products.

Some visitors to Japan (and to this exhibition) will perhaps be struck not so much by the excellence of industrial design (which is already well known abroad) as by the vitality of the world of the crafts. The styles and schools are many, the polemics are fiercely argued, and craft objects, at every level of quality, are far more widely available than they are in Britain. The example of ceramics vividly illustrates the range: there are potters perpetuating the style of the old tea-ceremony kilns, with varying degrees of departure from classical types; there are members of the *mingei* (folkcraft) movement, of whom the most famous was Shōji Hamada, as well as a few remaining practitioners of crafts in the popular tradition; there are experimenters with Chinese styles and techniques, designer craftsmen attempting to devise international styles combining Japanese and foreign shapes, and avant-garde artist-potters producing everything from vessels loosely based on traditional types to abstract, modernistic ceramic sculptures. The differing levels of quality, from individually crafted masterpieces to mass-produced utensils are, for the uninitiated outsider, bafflingly difficult to disentangle, and the range of materials used is, by comparison with the West, very wide. Although there are cases of considerable hardship—largely a part of the past now—especially in certain purely traditional fields, most craftsmen manage to make a living, helped by associations that hold annual exhibitions and enterprising private craft and department store galleries. Some eventually attain government recognition and receive titles such as "Living National Treasure". It is hoped that the present exhibition, by giving some idea of the breadth and vitality of this side of modern Japanese culture, will provide British craftsmen with ideas, challenges and inspiration.

I have attempted above to give some examples of the survival of traditional ideas of design and to illustrate the ways in which these ideas have been adapted to the demands of modern industrialised society. Japan is not alone in having experienced these processes of survival and adaptation, but she is, to date, the only fully industrialised non-Western nation. This exhibition, by illustrating some of the uses that Japan has made of her splendid and distinctive traditions, may perhaps encourage Western designers and craftsmen to turn to Japan as a source of new ideas and as a yardstick against which to measure the successes and shortcomings of the industrialised West.

Japanese Aesthetic Ideals

Mitsukuni Yoshida

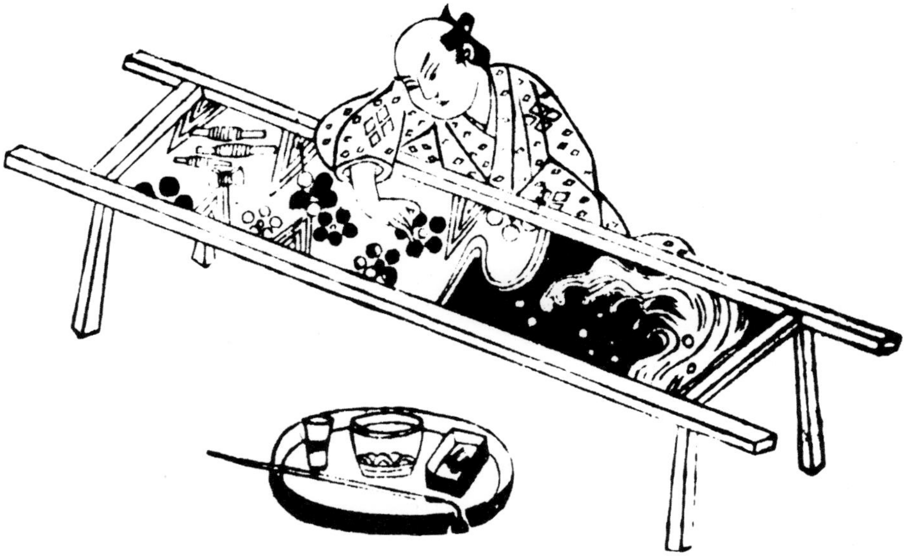

The Earl of Elgin's Mission, which visited Japan in 1858 to negotiate and sign a Treaty of Peace, Friendship and Commerce with Britain, was escorted by a flagship commanded by Captain Sherard Osborn, C.B., and in 1861, after he had completed his tour of duty and returned home, Osborn published a short work with the title *Japanese Fragments* in which he reproduced six landscapes by the famous print artist Andō Hiroshige. Osborn clearly had a high opinion of the print artists of Japan, of whose work he wrote: "these native illustrations, procured in the city of Yedo [modern Tokyo] itself . . . will bring before us in vivid relief the scenery, the towns and villages, the highways and byways of that strange land—the costumes, tastes, and, I might almost say, the feelings of the people—so skilful are Japanese artists in the Hogarth-like talent of transferring to their sketches the characteristics of passing scenes"; and in a comment on one of the prints he reproduces he refers to the artist as "our embryo Turner". For Osborn, the products of the Japanese artisan were filled with refinement and delicacy of feeling: even when gold and silver are liberally used, he says, the effect is not "monstrous, heavy [or] overladen with ornament", but he goes on to imply that the Japanese seemed to him to have taken a conscious decision to avoid investing their artistic productions with anything approaching greatness or grandeur.

The Japanese section of the Great International Exhibition held in London in 1862 (the first occasion of its kind at which Japanese arts and crafts were displayed) was made up of objects collected by Sir Rutherford Alcock, at that time her Majesty's Minister at Edo (Tokyo). Soon after his arrival in Japan, Alcock came to realise that Japanese aesthetic expression and artistic methods were founded on principles quite different from those that prevailed in Europe, and on his return home he made his experiences and observations the basis for a book called *Art and Art Industries in Japan*, published in 1878, in which he made a comparison between the arts and crafts of Europe since classical times and the products of the widely differing aesthetic system of Japan. In his view Japanese arts and crafts, even cheap goods on sale in ordinary shops, were given their special character by perfection of workmanship, variety of form, novelty of design, beauty and grace.

In its constant search for variety of form, Japanese design had developed its own peculiar form of symmetry, which did not depend, as in Europe, on precise geometrical values. For example, the Japanese preferred to use a diagonal, rather than a centrally placed horizontal or vertical line when dividing a rectangle symmetrically. In other cases, they would seek to achieve a balance based on inner meaning rather than shape: in a pair of folding screens, the left-hand screen might represent autumn by a maple tree and the right-hand screen, spring, by a cherry tree. To Japanese eyes, such a composition seems symmetrical and well balanced, in spite of the fact that cherry trees and maples are not at all symmetrical as shapes. Alcock also discovered that the technique of perspective was known in Japan as well as in Europe, and he speculated that it had been brought there around the sixteenth century as a result of missionary influence, either directly by the Jesuits who visited Japan at the time or indirectly by way of China. Modern scholarship has confirmed the correctness of Alcock's surmise; perspective is nowadays generally held to have been introduced from China.

Alcock also devotes some space to an account of the pottery, enamels, ivory, wood-carving and lacquerware of Japan and examines the characteristically Japanese aesthetic consciousness common to work in all these different media. He asserts that "the pictorial side of art is in a comparatively undeveloped state among the Japanese", but he goes on to say that "power of expression, combined with simplicity of treatment, is a characteristic of Japanese Art". Elsewhere he observes that there is inherent in this expressive power an "intense sympathy with Nature", and in spite of his statement about "the pictorial side of Art", he admits that the Japanese "have great dormant pictorial powers".

The Japanese seemed to him, both in major works of art and in those of lesser importance, to have sought to develop their modes of expression to a state of "mechanical perfection", and other qualities of the work of the Japanese craftsman that he noted included a ceaseless and passionate devotion to variety and to natural beauty. In his view, this love of nature's variety took a form in Japanese art quite unlike that which had characterised the art of Europe since classical times. In the Western tradition, artistic creation sprang from the mind and consisted in the production of works possessing a physical, plastic beauty, while Japanese artistic creativity had been channelled in very different ways. Art objects in Japan, he said, were made with a certain emotional quality about them, which brought enjoyment to the lives of ordinary people and evoked in them a sympathetic response to the beauties of nature.

The "Japonisme" which was fashionable in Europe at the time he wrote came in for some harsh criticism from Alcock. He felt that any attempt to copy Japanese artefacts, which were based on special non-European aesthetic considerations, was doomed to failure. What was worse, at a time when Japan was undergoing rapid industrialisation, "English taste was killing Japanese Art", and Alcock foresaw that the current decline in quality of Japanese goods would be a serious problem in the future. This was regrettable, because Japanese arts and crafts, in spite of the very individual position that they held in world culture, had a certain universality about them, which was attributable to the profoundly human standpoint from which they were made. There is much that we can still agree with in Sir Rutherford Alcock's observations on the arts and crafts of Japan, even though he set them down in writing more than a century ago. In particular, the Japanese people's distinctive sense of symmetry and pursuit of perfection in workmanship, both of which he noticed, even today form an important part of the mental attitudes that dominate all of modern Japan's industries.

Naturally Alcock was fully aware that Japan's culture had come into being under strong Chinese influence. He believed, however, that this influence had come to an end some five hundred years before, after which Japan had begun to pursue an independent line of development. In actual fact Chinese influences had been even stronger during those five centuries. If we take the case of colour, for example, we find that even today the "five colours" of traditional Chinese origin—blue, red, yellow, white and black—are held in high regard. In China these five colours corresponded to the "five elements" of wood, fire, earth, metal and water, which were traditionally believed to be the constituents of the physical world. In Japan, as well, chromatic culture developed on the basis of these five hues. In time, the Japanese discovered the beauty of the intermediate shades that lie between the five colours; they arrived, too, at an understanding of the aesthetic value of the harmonious mixture that results when they are combined with one another. This high regard for colour harmony made an important contribution to the emergence of a feeling for elegance and grace. For the most part it was the ladies of the Heian period (794–1185) court who were the first to discover and develop an appreciation of the beauty of these blended colours, but they soon came to influence the aesthetic attitudes of the male court aristocracy. As a result, even the Japanese warriors' suits of armour were constructed with gorgeously coloured silk threads and leather. At first it was the culture of the Heian court that was most strongly characterised by this feeling for elegance and grace, but in time the courtiers' example led to the widespread diffusion throughout Japanese society of a sensitivity to those qualities.

The motifs used to express this feeling for elegance were always drawn from the natural world, especially the plant kingdom. The climate of Japan is characterised by clear seasonal variations, and because of its never-ending changes nature is seen by the Japanese not as an immutable constant but as a perpetual process of transformation. For this reason, when they speak of the beauty of nature, they are not praising the beauty of its permanence; its aesthetic quality is considered to lie in the fact that its face is forever changing as the seasons go by.

As Alcock implied, the Japanese depiction of this ever-changing natural world is dominated by a pictorial quality, a quality that has sometimes been given the name "graphism". But this "graphism" is in no way a form of realism. In Europe, as well, there are many designs in the applied arts that have a pictorial quality. One example is the tapestries that decorated European courts, but since these tapestries always depict some biblical story, classical myth or mediaeval romance, they are strongly realistic in feeling. Japanese designs, by contrast, are characterized above all by their symbolic qualities. A design incorporating irises growing in profusion by a flowing river immediately conjures up in the Japanese mind the gentle world of the court aristocracy of the Heian period, and the juxtaposition of pines and a single *koto* (Japanese harp) evokes similar mental associations. The romances and the lyrics of the eleventh and twelfth centuries were well known among the Japanese educated classes, just as the mediaeval romances and poems were in Europe. A scene from such a story allowed Japanese viewers to place themselves in the situation implied by the design and indulge freely in pleasant fantasies undistracted by any realistic qualities of the picture. It sometimes seems that such pictures are solely concerned with the external beauty of nature, but even a design that seems to be nothing more than an abstract pattern based on elements drawn from the natural world often holds concealed within itself subtle suggestions of some fable or lyric verse.

Japanese artists made skilful use of this graphic symbolism as a means by which to instil a feeling of human life into scenes taken from nature. But, paradoxically, in achieving this effect, they often try to do without human artifice, relying as much as possible on the latent strength of nature herself, as Alcock and Osborn and other early observers of Japan realised. The pre-industrial crafts make extensive use of natural substances, and the Japanese craftsman in conceiving and executing a product gives full consideration to the special properties of his materials, on which he relies for much of his artistic effect.

An example of this is the use of bamboo, which spread from South-East Asia to China and Japan. The tough and flexible qualities of this material are well known; in China the sight of a flourishing and vigorous grove of bamboo inspired the development of a philosophical attitude that stresses the importance of the individual and makes its aim the internal cultivation and perfection of the self. Such ideas have been influential in Japan as well. Another extraordinary characteristic of bamboo—the fact that a young bamboo plant can grow as much as one metre in a single night—has given the plant mysterious, almost magical associations.

Because of its many and varied properties, bamboo has been put to a number of different uses. Sometimes its quality of flexibility is utilised, at other times it is used in situations where its mysterious properties and its legendary associations are stressed. For example, in that famous indoor cultural activity, the tea ceremony, many articles made from bamboo are used, and the mystery associated with the material makes a definite contribution to the inner meaning of the proceedings. It was in the tea ceremony that bamboo flower holders, either in basket or cylindrical form, were first used. The latter are often no more than a simple chopped-off piece of stalk. Such simplicity, as Alcock discovered more than a century ago, is an important element of Japanese design. The concentration of perfect workmanship in a simple object is a design principle that has influenced many Japanese craftsmen and become on occasion something of an article of faith. However, simplicity cannot be successful unless it is supported by perfection of craftsmanship; complexity, on the other hand, has on occasion served in attempts to cover up imperfection.

This love of simplicity is closely connected with the idea of modularity, by which a desired shape is achieved by the combination of simpler unit forms. As everyone knows, the tea ceremony is conducted within the confined space of a teahouse (*chashitsu*). But since the size and shape of this space is regulated by the use of *tatami* mats of fixed size for flooring, people find it convenient to use the module afforded by the *tatami* as a guide by which to systematise their physical actions. Furthermore, the size and positioning of every tea utensil is decided after due consideration of the available space, which is itself, of course, fixed by the *tatami* module. It is natural for human beings, surrounded in this way by standardised space and standardised objects, to standardise their own movements.

This tendency to arrange objects in a standardised way in narrow spaces explains the Japanese liking for compactness, in the sense both of many elements skilfully arranged in a limited space and of sparseness, the lack of anything extraneous. In the *chashitsu*, a simple human activity involving fire and water is dramatised by being compressed into a very confined area. In fact, it is not only the drinking of tea that is dramatised in a full tea ceremony, for a complete ceremony involves a formal meal accompanied by *saké* (rice wine).

The love of compactness has even had an effect on literature. The short poetic form known as the *haiku*, which consists of a mere seventeen syllables, has been in existence for five hundred years, and yet even today *haiku* poets and *haiku* clubs can be found in large numbers in every corner of Japan. Another poetic form, the *waka*, made up of thirty-one syllables, dates back more than twelve hundred years, but there are still a surprisingly large number of people who write *waka* and, as with *haiku*, there are specialist groups. More surprising still, most of these poets are amateurs, devoting themselves to the task of achieving a rich expression of the human condition and the beauties of nature within the limited confines of concise poetic forms. The Japanese admire this kind of concision of form and compactness of meaning because they feel that, like simplicity, it derives its aesthetic merit from the fact that it cannot be fully achieved without perfect execution. The reader should take special note of the extensive popularity of these old poetic forms among ordinary people, for it is a proof of the continuing and widespread survival of a feeling for beauty among the Japanese population at large. As Alcock and his contemporaries found, Japanese craftsmen, as well as serving the very narrow circle of court and aristocracy, also tried to make the lives of the masses more enjoyable. The belief that it is not enough to create objects of perfect workmanship for the court and aristocracy alone has survived unchanged into the production system of modern industrialised Japanese society. Perfection and durability were the aims of workmanship in old Japan, and constant devotion to work for its own sake is necessary for these aims to be achieved. Labour is not simply a painful activity; it is a means of testing the level of perfection of our own abilities by creating objects of perfect workmanship. For this reason the tools that help a man in his work and that extend the range of what he can do are often personified and regarded as having life and suffering death in the same way as a man. The date on which a tool was first used is often recorded in writing on its surface—this is the day the tool came to life. And when the tool has been in use for a long time and is no longer serviceable, it is ceremonially buried.

The Japanese people's innate feeling for beauty and the high importance they attach to work are characteristics that have continued virtually unchanged from the pre-industrial to the industrial age, and many of the industrialised products of modern Japan possess these age-old virtues in modern form.

Since so many traditional Japanese goods were made with the popular market in mind, one often finds in their designs a certain exaggerated humour, as many foreign observers have pointed out in recent times. Even tiny objects such as *netsuke* can be powerfully expressive and filled with unexpected or even grotesque humour, and the elegance that we have taken as a key aspect of the Japanese conception of beauty often contains within it a grain of humour, for this is something that runs through the whole of Japanese and, for that matter, Western culture. Even the most glorious life will end in darkness and death; holiness and profanity, splendour and gloom form the dual basis of man's culture. In spite of its sometimes idiosyncratic manifestations, Japan's culture, like any other, draws its essential vitality from the universally dualistic phenomenon of human existence.

Madame Butterfly in a Rabbit-Hutch: Western Perceptions and Stereotypes of the Japanese

Jean-Pierre Lehmann

In the narrative of his extraordinary travels and adventures Marco Polo occasionally referred to an island country lying to the east of China which he called *Jipangu*. He may, therefore, be at least partly responsible for the fact that we call that country Japan (or le Japon, il Giappone, el Japón, etc.). In Japanese it is either Nippon or Nihon, the choice being somewhat dependent on the individual or on the national mood: Nippon is rather masculine and connotes an attitude of assertiveness, defiance or belligerency, while Nihon is somewhat more gentle, more feminine and thus perhaps more accommodating. The West first heard about Japan from China, and the Chinese reading of the two characters for Nippon is Jih-pen.

Marco Polo, however, never visited Japan, and indeed it took almost another three centuries before the first Western foot stepped on Japanese soil. It was in the mid-sixteenth century that Iberian missionaries and traders arrived, to be followed within a few decades by their enemies, the Dutch and the English. This turbulent and exciting period of Japanese history is the subject matter of James Clavell's best-selling novel *Shogun*, with Will Adams, the first Englishman in Japan, as the hero. In the course of the first few decades of the seventeenth century, however, all foreigners came to be banned from Japan, with only two exceptions: Chinese merchants were granted access to the port of Nagasaki and the Dutch obtained permission to maintain a small trading post in the islet of Deshima.

Although some information regarding Japan filtered out to the Western world, generally she remained hidden behind a seemingly impenetrable veil of secrecy. The American Commodore Perry's "opening" of Japan's doors in 1854, however, heralded the advent of a new age. Japan's contact with the outside world was renewed, but this time on a much more intensive and international scale.

In the last thirteen decades many things have happened in the relations between

Japan and Western countries; many books have been written, many dreams have been born, in some cases fulfilled, and some tragic nightmares have been endured. All of these have provided ample material for the creation of Western images and stereotypes of the Japanese.

In one nation's perception of another—especially when the nations are as distant from each other as Europe and Japan—an element of fantasy may at times creep in. Perhaps the most prominent feature of the Western image of Japan in the latter part of the nineteenth century was the belief that the country was inhabited by the most exquisite females on earth. In itself that is not necessarily complete fantasy; but when the poet Alfred Noyes, in a poem entitled "A Japanese Love Song", enthused about a Japanese maiden in these words—

Though the great skies are dark,
And your small feet are white,
Though your wide eyes are blue (*sic*),
And the closed poppies red ...

—his imagination had obviously got the better of him as to the shape and colour of his idol's eyes.

Generally, however, stereotypes are based on real experiences, even if these experiences belong to the past and no longer necessarily apply to contemporary reality. Indeed the past is probably more influential than the present. Because of the last war, the fact that the Japanese may still be perceived by at least some Westerners as "the enemy"—even though the battleground may now be economic rather than military—is something which by and large has to be accepted and which only time will heal. An illustration of this can perhaps be suggested by the probability that even Westerners who have never been to Japan, and never evinced the slightest interest in her, are nevertheless likely to know at least two Japanese words, one of which is *kamikaze* (the other is *geisha*).

Even the more hostile impulsive reaction towards the Japanese is not always lacking in humorous side-effects or consequences. At least for those generations born before 1945 there will probably always remain a feeling, extending from conviction to suspicion, that basically the Japanese are cruel. Now as everyone knows (talk of stereotypes!) what the British people love above all else are their dogs. In 1969 a British journalist returning from Japan published a piece in a national newspaper alleging that the Japanese were cruel to dogs. An outcry ensued and there were loud protestations that henceforth all exports of British dogs to Japan (the trade deficit was not in 1969 what it is today) should be banned. This British outrage was reported in the Japanese press with the result that there followed what must have been one of the oddest demonstrations in the history of the world: the solemn, awe-inspiring British Embassy, situated opposite the Imperial Palace, was besieged by a mass of human and canine marchers, the former vociferously protesting that they were not cruel to their dogs, while the latter bow-wowed agreement in chorus.

One might briefly pause here to consider some of the features of stereotyping which emerge from this incident. "Cruelty" is generally a relative and subjective phenomenon. Thus, by English standards it is true that the Japanese are "cruel" to their dogs; they tend to keep them confined in small enclosures or tied by a rope. By Japanese standards, however, we are "cruel" to our children; Japanese children are not spanked, rarely scolded, they tend to be breast-fed until a more advanced age, they will generally sleep with, or in very close proximity to, their parents and they will not be left in the care of a babysitter while the parents go out to paint the town red. The differences are diminishing with time: the Japanese are less "cruel" to their dogs than they were, we are less "cruel" to our children than we were (with Dr. Spock, depending on one's viewpoint, either to thank or to blame). Still, from our perspective we might be tempted to say that the Japanese "indulge" their children, while a Japanese might feel that the British "indulge" their dogs: hence the Japanese remark that whereas Japan is a paradise for children, England is a paradise for dogs. It is also clear that there is always an element of hypocrisy lurking in a stereotype's background. While on the subject of animals, for example, one might mention that the Japanese do not engage in blood-sports, nor is shooting a popular form of leisure.

So far as the contemporary scene is concerned, stereotypes are usually founded on some aspect of reality, though with the result that a single aspect can become distorted, exaggerated, either embellished or sullied. When the anthropologist Ruth Benedict was commissioned by the U.S. government in 1944 to carry out research on Japanese society, one of the things which most interested her was that Japan appeared to be a nation of such amazing contrasts. For any positive assertion, the converse seemed equally true: the Japanese are the most gentle people, they can also be the most hideously brutal; they are the most hospitable people to foreigners, they are also the most xenophobic. She entitled her work *The Chrysanthemum and the Sword*, thereby hoping to convey the stark contrasts which she felt coexist within the same society.

Equally great contrasts can be found in Western stereotypes of Japan. Perhaps one might suggest that this arises from the fact that whereas some have chosen to completely ignore the chrysanthemum and concentrate their attention entirely on the sword (today more likely to be the *soroban*—abacus—or perhaps the miniature pocket calculator), others forget the sword and extol the chrysanthemum. The Japanese, it is said, are undoubtedly the most materialistic people on earth, whatever spiritual values they once had have now been completely washed away by the tide of time, prosperity and greed; the name of the country is "Japan, Inc.", its inhabitants are "economic animals" and the national religion is "GNPism". The Japanese (runs the contrary view) are the most ascetic race in the world; it is they who perform the tea ceremony (*cha-no-yu*), who are incomparable in the art of flower arrangement (*ikebana*), who have fashioned the most sublime rock gardens, and, in view of the current craze for Zen, they are clearly a meditative, spiritually rich people who know how to escape from the tawdry mess of contemporary reality.

Japan is one of the very few countries of the non-Western world which was not colonised; so far as early Western attitudes towards the country are concerned, however, they could perhaps be described as quasi-colonial. But, of all the country's treasures, what the Western imagination sought to possess above all was the Japanese female; no women from foreign lands captivated the hearts and minds of Western males so much as the ladies from Japan. A word entered the English vocabulary, the *musmee* (from the Japanese word *musume* meaning daughter or young woman), which was supposed to convey all the charm, the grace, the delicacy, the exoticism, the beauty, and the availability, of Japanese girls; the word has disappeared from the English language, but *une mousmé* is still current in French, today perhaps equivalent to (and as respectful as) the use of the word "bird" in referring to a young woman.

Western novels, poems, operettas, etc. in which figure a romance between a Japanese girl and a Western man abound, the most famous being Pierre Loti's *Madame Chrysanthème*, which was the inspiration for Giacomo Puccini's *Madama Butterfly*. Although by the first decade or so of this century, at least in quantitative terms, the output of literary and other works on this theme abated, the genre nevertheless remained. There were, for example, the works of Frank Ashton-Gwatkin (with the nom de plume John Paris) and the exceedingly funny, though tragically ending, *L'Honorable Partie de Campagne* (*The Honourable Picnic*) by Roger Poidatz; Poidatz chose as his pseudonym Thomas Raucat, homonymous as it is with the Japanese *tomarō-ka*, which can be interpreted as "Shall we stop here for the night?". Not surprisingly the thirties and forties brought a halt to this particular industry, though immediately after the war there appeared Richard Mason's moving novel *The Wind Cannot Read*, shortly followed by James Michener's *Sayonara*. In the decades since the war the theme has continued in a number of (generally mediocre) works, the latest (1976), to my knowledge, being John Drew's *Seven Nights in Japan*, which was made into a film starring Michael York and Hidemi Aoki.

There have been a few instances in which the roles are reversed, namely Japanese male and Western female, perhaps the most widely known being Alain Resnais' film *Hiroshima Mon Amour*; these, however, are rare. So far as the more general use of the theme is concerned, however, and irrespective of the creators' intentions, all these works have, to varying degrees, contributed to several Western images of Japan. Certainly they have cast Japan in a romantically exotic glow. They have also provided a feminine picture of the country and its inhabitants; indeed, it has been alleged that one of the reasons why the czar's court did not take seriously Japan's threat to go to war in 1904 was that the only knowledge they had of the country was derived from reading *Madame Chrysanthème*. Be that as it may, at least some of these works have also tended to give the impression that the morals of Japanese women are loose. In the Victorian age this belief was also encouraged by descriptions of certain Japanese customs, notably that of mixed bathing. The stereotype of Japan as the permissive society *par excellence* is perhaps less prominent today than it was for several decades; nevertheless, I cannot be the only person who, upon returning from Japan, has been invariably asked at some stage or another, "what about the geisha, then?", with the inevitable accompanying nudge in the ribs.

Patterns and perceptions of moral behaviour vary significantly in both time and space; the question of Japanese sexual mores is, therefore, far too complex to be treated adequately in just a few sentences. Generally, the comments made about the relativity and subjectivity (and hypocrisy) of "cruelty" would equally apply to "morality". Images, by definition, are caricatures. The torch of promiscuity—in terms of reputation, not necessarily in terms of reality—passed from the Japanese, to be held for a long time by the French, whereas now it would appear to be firmly in the grasp of the Swedes. But the exotic appeal of Japanese girls, so deeply ensconced in Western literature and folklore, will no doubt endure. Here, however, it might only be fair to warn aspiring Pinkertons with illusions of easy conquests that they may be in for a bit of a disappointment. As to Western perceptions of the *geisha*, the orthodox interpretation was that she was a prostitute; orthodoxy inevitably gives way to revisionism, with the result that some of the writing on the subject today would lead one to believe that *geisha* are Sisters of Mercy. The truth, as often happens in such cases, lies somewhere in between the two extremes.

Regarding other features of Japan's development during the last century or so, it is not surprising that the West has reacted with considerable perplexity. As Japan became industrialised and a formidable military power, she seemed to be defying the rules of the game—rules invented by the West, but which seemed on the evidence to be appropriate. Europeans were the conquerors, the Asians the conquered; Europeans produced manufactured goods, Asians raw materials; Europeans, imbued with the puritanical protestant ethic, were successful entrepreneurs, Asians were backward, decadent and unduly given to the pleasures of the senses. Then came the Japanese! In 1905, to the astonishment, and in some cases panic, of the West, Japan defeated Russia in a major war. By the time of the 1914–18 war the Japanese were competing in hitherto exclusively Western markets in the sale of manufactured goods, while the vessels of their merchant marine plied the oceans of the world. In due course the names of such mammoth concerns as Mitsui, Mitsubishi, Sumitomo became familiar. Today a typical European family is likely to drive a Honda car, watch a Sony colour television set, play a Yamaha piano, and so forth. (The English author, Lewis Bush, recounted how on one occasion he went to visit one of the first Suzuki-method schools of violin playing in Kent; taking a five-year-old pupil aside he asked him, "Do you like Mr. Suzuki's violins?", to which the little boy quickly replied, "Oh yes, and when I grow up I shall buy one of his motorcycles".)

Well, how did all this happen? Why Japan successfully modernised is due to a multiplicity of factors which need not detain us here; but certainly one of the more common Western instant explanations has been that the country underwent a thorough process of occidentalisation. Quite a number of Western visitors to Japan from the Victorian age onwards fall into a category which one might classify as the "conservationists"; they strongly felt that the country should conserve what they perceived to be the essence of Japan, and should not sacrifice it at the altar of vulgar Western material progress. For example, Kipling, visiting Japan in 1889, was completely taken by the charm and beauty of the country, but at the same time he expressed considerable anxiety about the damaging effects of European and American influences; he wrote, "It would pay us to put the whole Empire in a glass case and mark it *Hors Concours*, Exhibit A". The alleged metamorphosis from Oriental to Occidental has led a number of Western observers of Japan, such as the Dutch novelist Louis Couperus in the early part of this century and more recently James Kirkup in his last book, *Heaven, Hell and Harakiri*, to accuse Japan of having lost her soul. Thus the view of Japan as thoroughly westernised serves two purposes: it explains why an Asian nation could beat the West at its own game, and at the same time consoles the anti-Japanese lobby because of the clear implications to be drawn from this story of a latter-day Esau who sold his birthright for a pottage of GNP.

Japan is an industrialised society and industrialisation tends to make equals of us all, at least so far as external appearances are concerned. That the nation has changed over the decades is an indisputable and inevitable fact, that a degree of westernisation has taken place is true, that the result of all this is that Japan should no longer be situated culturally in the Far East, but in the Far West, is rubbish. It has been a characteristic of Japanese civilisation and a measure of its genius over the last millennium-and-a-half to import certain products, ideas, techniques, fashions from outside and to adapt these to the indigenous milieu. The Japanese have retained their soul, their personality, their individuality, although these have ineluctably evolved as external circumstances have changed.

Another Western stereotype of the Japanese is that they are a nation of sheep, in the sense that the Japanese islands are inhabited not by so many individuals, but by one enormous collective flock. We tend to exaggerate this trait, as the Japanese are equally naive in perceiving Western countries as being populated by nothing but robust individualists. We are far less individualistic, while the Japanese are less collectivistic than is often made out. Nevertheless, owing to both cultural and demographic factors, there is a difference, and it is true that generally speaking there is less manifestation of individualism in Japan than in the West.

This can sometimes make the importing of certain Western products hazardous. A Japanese friend of mine told me a story in order to illustrate the group impulse of his compatriots. At a time when the Japanese phoenix was rising from the ashes, when the deprivations of the war and the immediate postwar period began disappearing and a degree of prosperity appeared, as had previously happened in the 1870s, a mania for foreign things gripped the nation. The Bardot hairstyle was popular with girls as the Presley "duck-tail" was with young men. In the general scramble for introducing sundry facets of Western civilisation to the Japanese, one promoter had the genial idea of staging a bullfight in Tokyo. The huge Kōrakuen stadium was chosen as the venue and months beforehand tickets for this affair had been sold out; in the meantime, matadors, picadors, banderilleros, horses, and, of course, the bulls were being shipped from Spain. On the appointed day the crowds filed into the stadium and took their seats; the event began, as is the custom, with the trumpets blaring *pasa dobles* while the matadors strutted across the arena. The parade over, the matadors took up their position, the first bull was set loose. But nothing much happened. The bull was dissolutely roaming about, while the spectators watched the proceedings in complete silence; it began to look as if the affair would end up as a flop. Then a voice came over the loudspeaker explaining to the aspiring *aficionados* that in Spain, in order to encourage both bull and matador, it is the custom to shout "olé". The consequence of this elucidation was that at regular intervals of six-and-a-half minutes fifty thousand people shouted in unison, "oré" (the Japanese language having no "l", they tend to substitute it with the "r"), with the result that both matador and bull were in grave danger of dying from heart seizure, rather than the former being pierced by a vengeful horn or the latter dispatched by a skilful *estocada*.

What about "workaholism"? A number of years ago the Italian writer Fosco Maraini was taking a Japanese friend of his, in Europe for the first time, around Rome. They reached the Vatican and entered the Sistine chapel. Maraini began explaining to his friend the story of Genesis as together they followed the details of Michelangelo's frescoes; as they reached the bit about Eve, the apple and the banishment from the Garden of Eden, he added to his attentive partner, "and so, as punishment Adam and Eve were forced to work". The countenance of the Japanese suddenly changed dramatically and in the most startled manner he cried out, "What? Work is punishment?". As Fosco Maraini subsequently pointed out, there is nothing in the traditional Japanese religions or philosophies—whether the indigenous Shinto or the centuries-old imported Buddhism and Confucianism—which sets out work as punishment; on the contrary it is perceived as a reward.

There are certainly cultural phenomena which help to explain why the Japanese, if not necessarily addicted to work, are less allergic to it than we are. There are also other reasons. One is that Japan is very poor in natural resources and hence dependent on the maximum use of human resources. Another reason has to do with their living environment; it is a fact that in many cases the working-place is more comfortable, or at least less cramped, than the dwelling-place.

Is it true then that they live in "rabbit-hutches"? The short answer is yes—but they call them "mansions". The craze for Western things has extended to the language, but the adopted Western word may not necessarily have the same meaning, or convey the same sense, as its original. A hypothetical Mr. Tanaka will give as his address "Blue Hill Mansion", but the building may be grey, located in the flattest section of town and the quarters he and his family occupy may be limited to two small rooms, plus kitchen and bathroom.

Two fairly obvious points should be made. Firstly, Japan has a population of some 115 millions living in a country whose total land mass is only about two-thirds that of France, but more than 80 percent of which is mountainous and uninhabitable. Secondly, although modern building techniques have been perfected to a considerable extent, it is nevertheless the case that Japan cannot build too high because of frequent earthquakes. It follows that there is not much space for living accommodation, vertically or horizontally. Perhaps a general observation can be made which, I hope, may help to put the question of the "living environment" into perspective. Japan, it must not be forgotten, has only recently become an urban society. The transition from an agrarian rural economy to a predominantly industrial urban setting was accompanied, as elsewhere, by some wanton destruction and rapid, sordid construction. This was particularly true of roughly the two decades which followed the war; it cannot be denied that during this period the appearance of Japanese cities was one of fairly unadulterated squalor. But just as Japan has not lost her soul, she has not lost her ascetic sense of beauty. Today new forms in architecture, design and urbanisation are being sought and not without a considerable degree of success. In more recent years the urban landscape has undoubtedly and markedly changed for the better; Japanese cities are becoming more attractive and comfortable places to live in.

Of course a great deal of improvement remains to be carried out, and the problem of living conditions should, and probably will, become a matter of national priority. In the meantime, however, there has been a trend over the last few years, generally referred to as *mai-hōmu-shugi* (my-home-ism). The *mai* (my) here denotes an attachment to private property and the private domain, a reaction against the self-sacrificing collectivist ethic, but one which some Japanese decry as evidence of selfishness rather than individualism. It could perhaps be described as the Japanese variant of "cultivating one's own garden". The *mai-hōmu-shugisha* (my-home-ists) advocate disintoxication from "workaholism" and a concentration of efforts on improving the quality of the individual's own environment. This is a phenomenon to be found primarily among the younger generations of the middle class; whether it is the wave of the Japanese future and what its consequences are likely to be is impossible to say.

Western stereotypes of the Japanese should be seen in terms of a moving mosaic; it moves along the passage of time, though not necessarily at the same pace. There are bright flashes in some places, dark patches in others. How far have Western perceptions penetrated the reality? This is an impossible question to answer, but a few considerations should be borne in mind. The veil we mentioned earlier has been lifted—gently or otherwise—not torn asunder. Partly because of this, the constant *leitmotiv* of the stereotype mosaic has been that the Japanese are inscrutable. Often, and for good measure, to this alleged trait of inscrutability will be added those of secretiveness, humourlessness, suspicion of foreigners and inhospitability. Many Europeans, including myself, have found that this is simply not the case; on the contrary, there is hospitality, a great sense of fun, generosity and warmth, the likes of which can seldom be encountered anywhere else.

Nonetheless, one can understand why this impression should arise in the

Western consciousness of Japan. One must not underestimate the rather formidable linguistic and cultural barriers. This, it might be countered, is surely the case with other non-European societies. Perhaps, but Japan remains, for the time being, the only non-Western fully-fledged industrial power, having indeed, as suggested earlier, beaten the West at its own game. To the possible frustration arising from the difficulties in overcoming these barriers there is also, it would seem, a fairly strong element of jealousy and resentment. From that viewpoint, it is clear that being told that the Japanese are "workaholics living in rabbit-hutches" has a rather soothing effect. How the Japanese may respond to these epithets is clearly not the major preoccupation. In cases such as these, not only is there wild exaggeration, there is also an obvious lack of tact and sensitivity.

So far as inscrutability is concerned, however, the Japanese themselves cannot be entirely exonerated. In order to illustrate the point we wish to make here, let us briefly return to Fosco Maraini. Maraini explained the frescoes of the Sistine chapel to his Japanese visitor; he did not, however, assume that the latter would be incapable of understanding. The obverse would not necessarily be the case. The Westerner visiting, say, the famous garden of the Ryōan-ji in Kyoto will, as likely as not, be told by his Japanese host that he cannot "really understand". The Japanese in Britain who speaks English fluently may be looked upon with some admiration, while the Westerner speaking fluent Japanese may be regarded in Japan in a manner approximating to the sudden apparition of the yeti. All of this is comprehensible to a certain degree. Reasonably fluent Japanese speakers of European languages are not that rare, while fairly fluent Western speakers of Japanese are—though not quite as rare as the yeti. In the Western consciousness of its own culture there is an assumption of universality (born, perhaps, of arrogance) which simply does not exist in Japan. The same is true of food. The Japanese will tend to be amazed at a European who says he actually likes *sashimi* (raw fish), while an Englishman will serve his hapless Japanese guest boiled mutton with mint sauce without a moment's hesitation. Clearly there are differences. The ideal prescription, surely, is for Westerners to make greater efforts in overcoming the barriers, while the Japanese on their side might strain a bit more in attempting to lower them.

Let us attempt to see what the perspective might be from the bridge spanning the Japan-West gulf. When glancing at the West and assessing attitudes towards Japan, one tends to find that these oscillate between affable condescension and mistrustful disdain. The insulting manner in which they are often expressed reveals a high degree of insensitivity. When attention is focussed on the Japanese, they seem to react with occasional hyper-sensitivity. Stereotypes are quite simply a fact of life; one should not over-react to injurious remarks, especially when, as is often the case, they are uttered in ignorance. Also, perhaps the Japanese sometimes forget that stereotyping and insensitivity are by no means a monopoly of the West; they too are guilty of perceiving others in terms of (not always flattering) stereotypes. Surely, what is rather desperately needed is far greater maturity on both sides.

Japan is very far away from the West. This is hardly a statement of revolutionary novelty. It needs, however, to be emphasised. Although Japan has retained her indigenous culture, at the same time it is clear that we have also a great deal in common. We should know each other far better than we do. Unfortunately, however, Japan is not only far away in terms of distance, but also in terms of expense. No Sir Freddie Laker has yet appeared to work miracles. So long as Japan remains difficult of access, it will probably be the case that misconstrued stereotypes will continue to influence Western perceptions of the country and its inhabitants. In the meantime, however, one can express the hope that exhibitions, such as the present one, may help to dispel some of the misunderstanding, and arouse greater interest, curiosity and appreciation for this remarkable society. Japan is enchanting, she is also perplexing, indeed at times exceedingly frustrating, to the point of being infuriating; but, in whatever guise she may appear, and in whatever mood we may approach her, she always remains supremely fascinating.

JAPAN

御祈
帳
金

MATERIALS

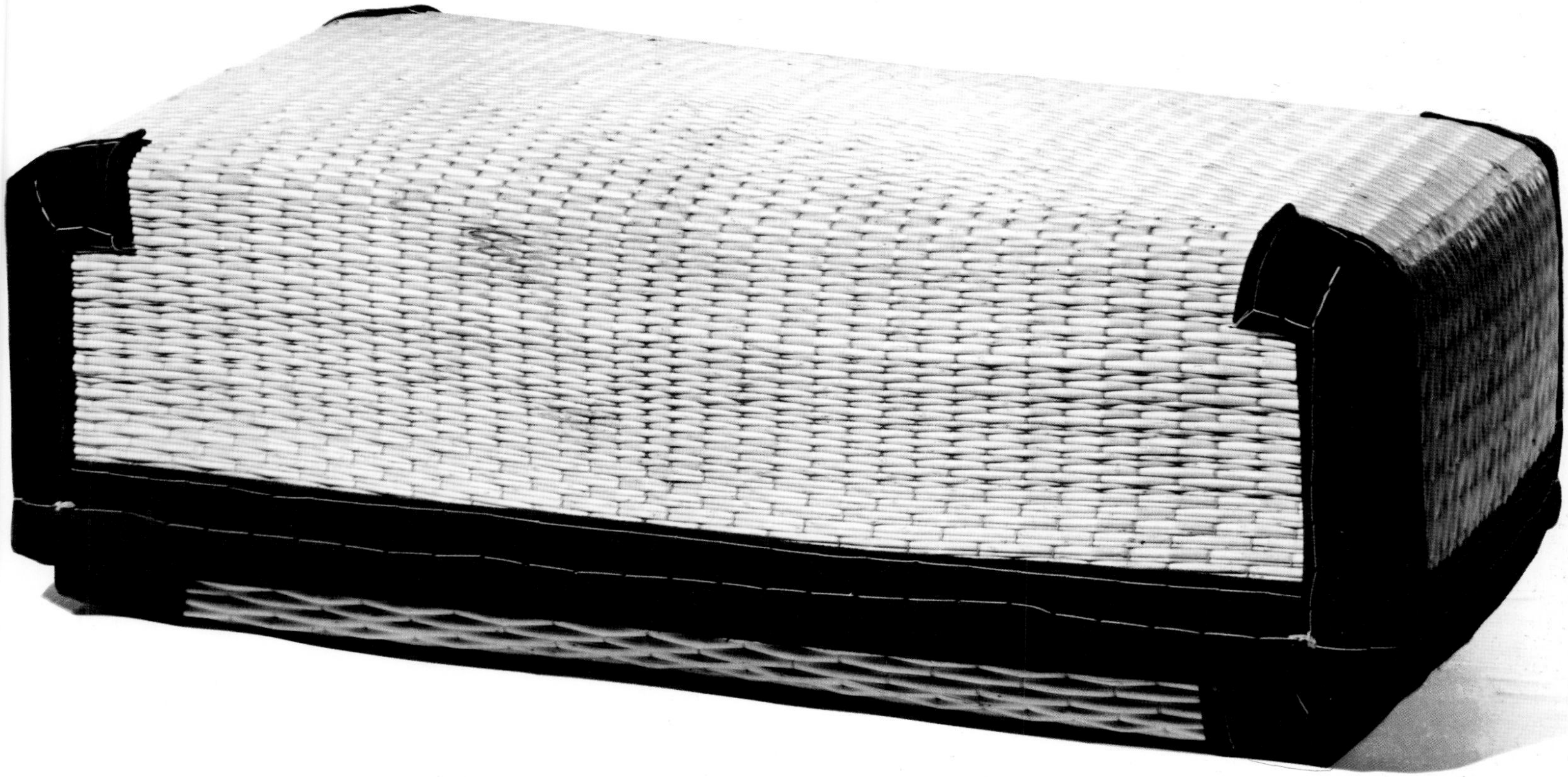

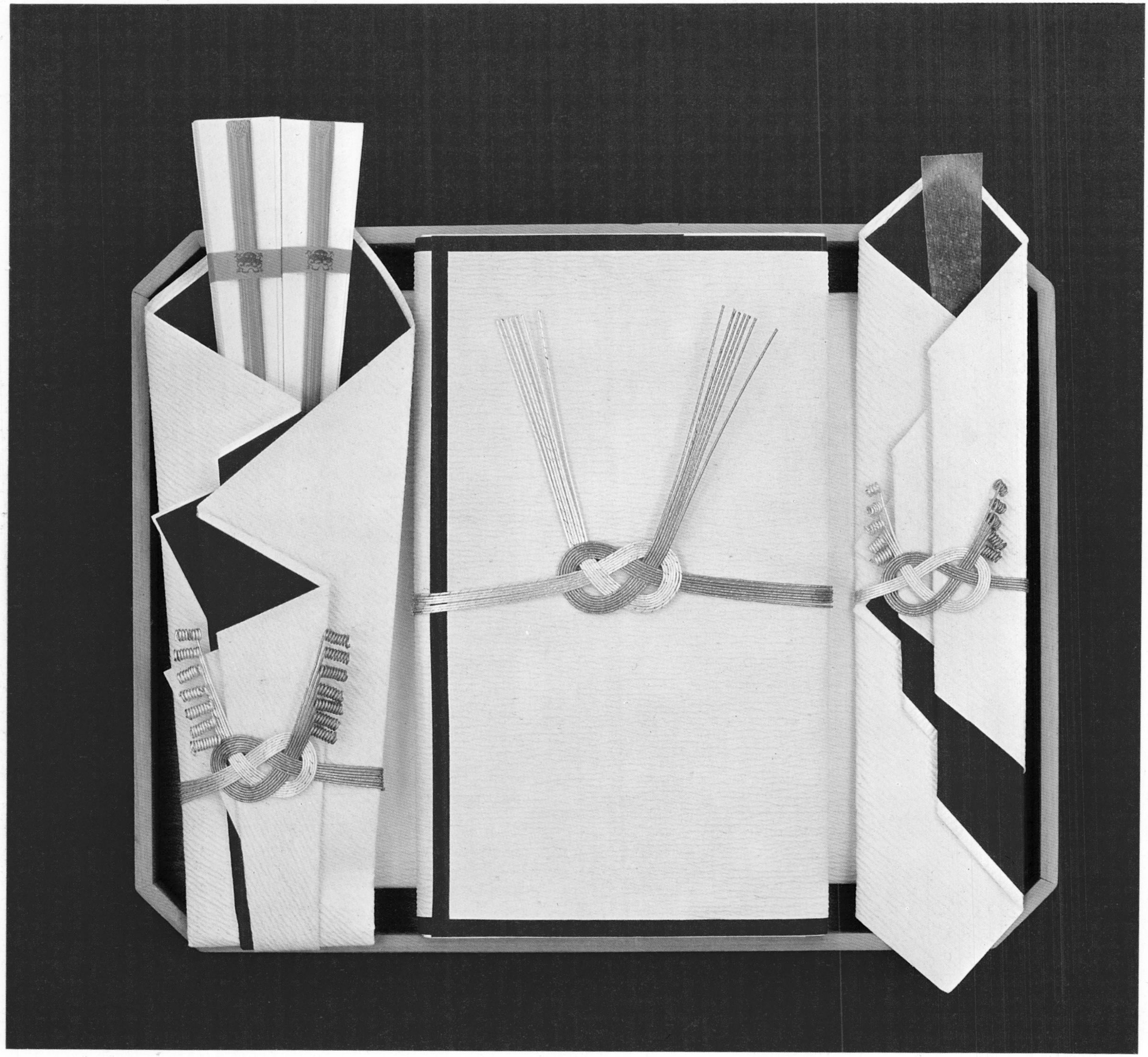

ELEGANCE

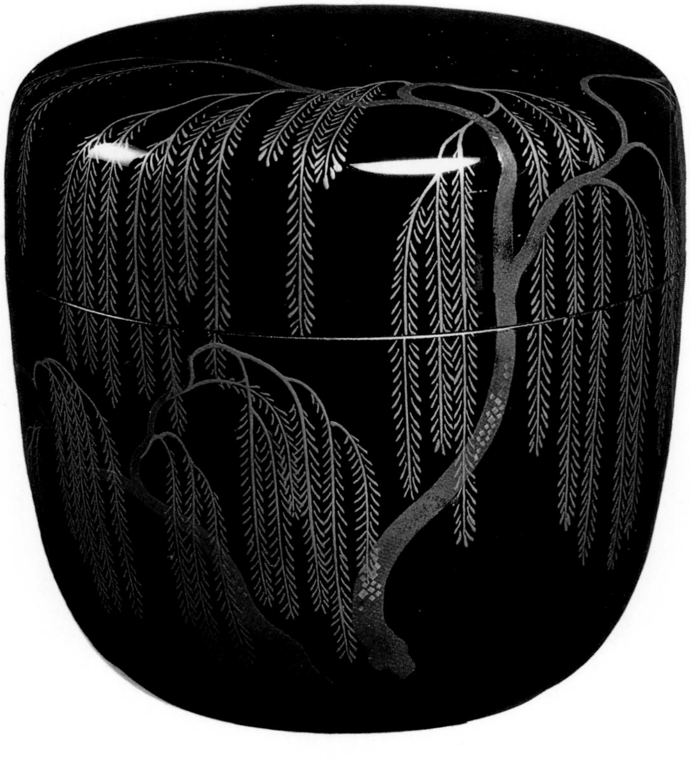

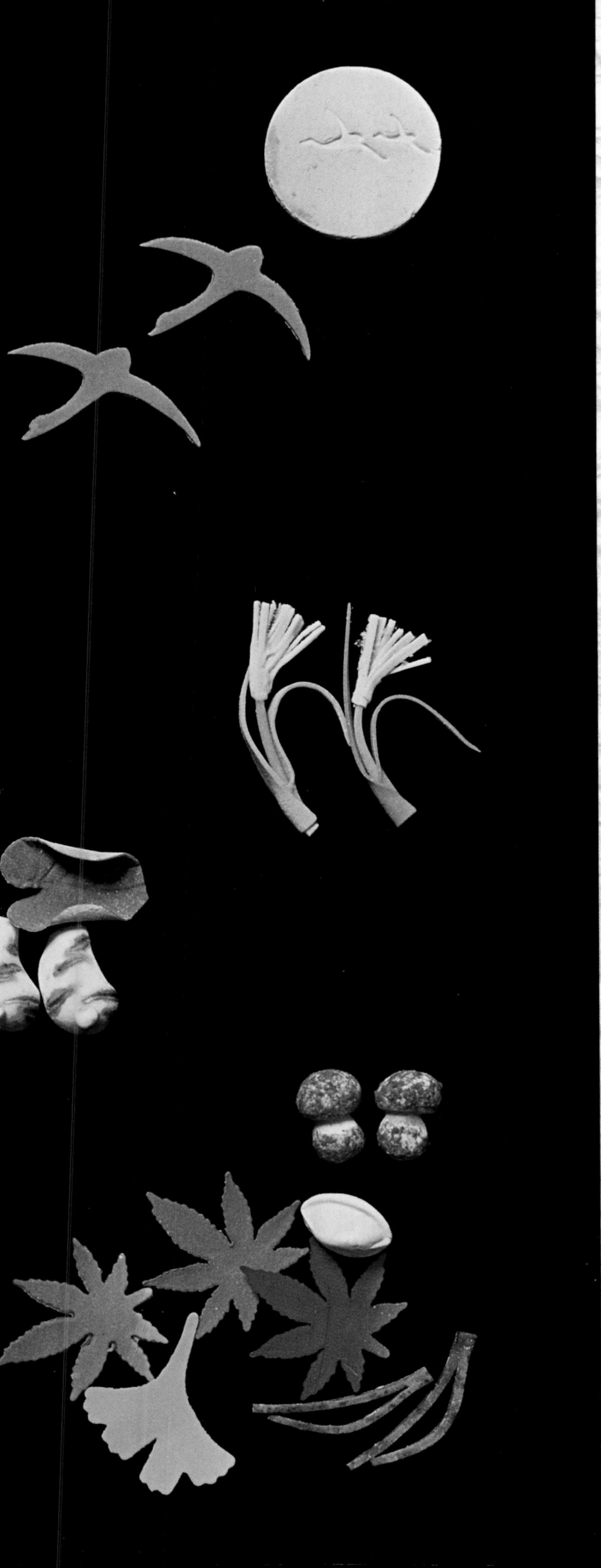

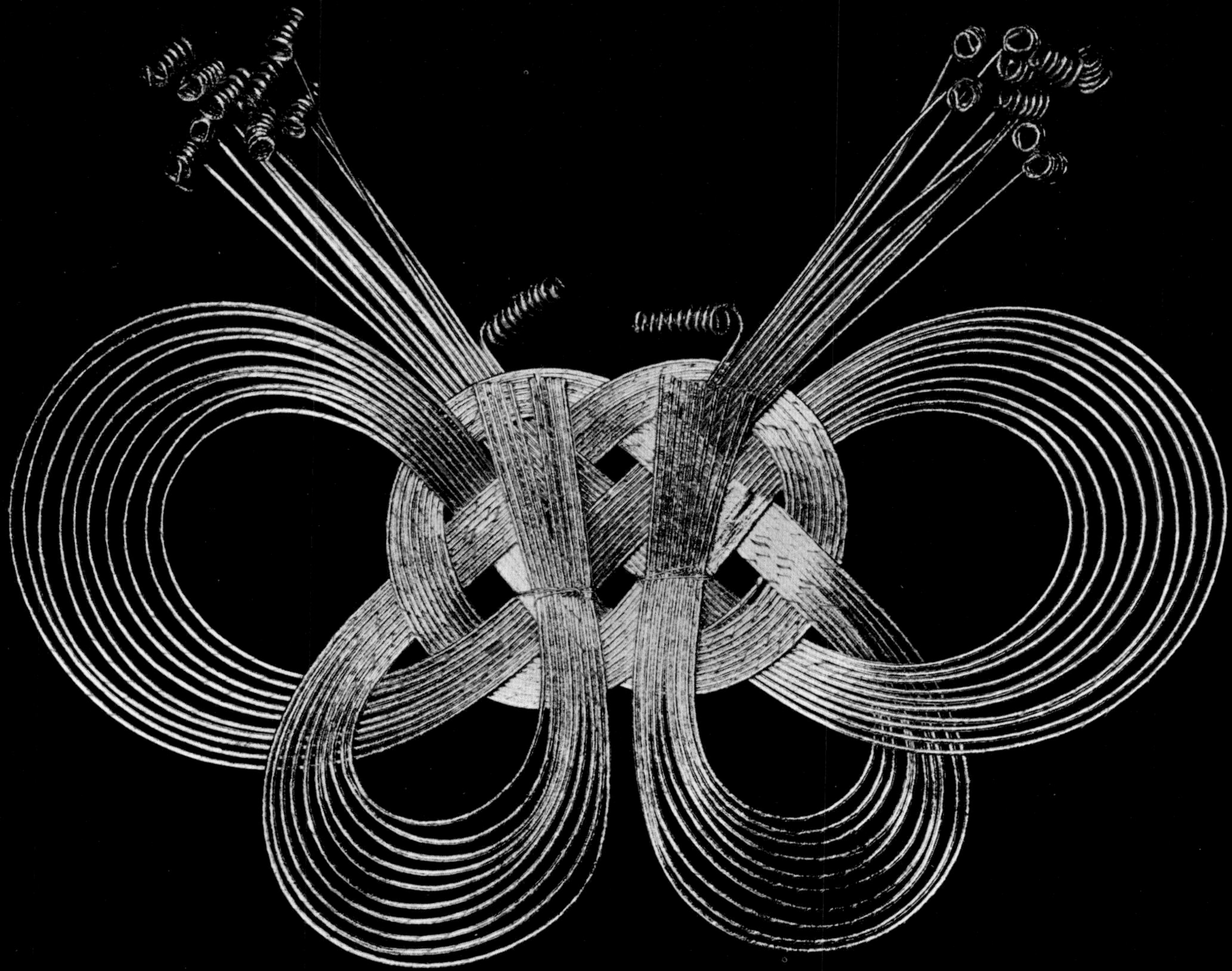

74

SIMPLICITY

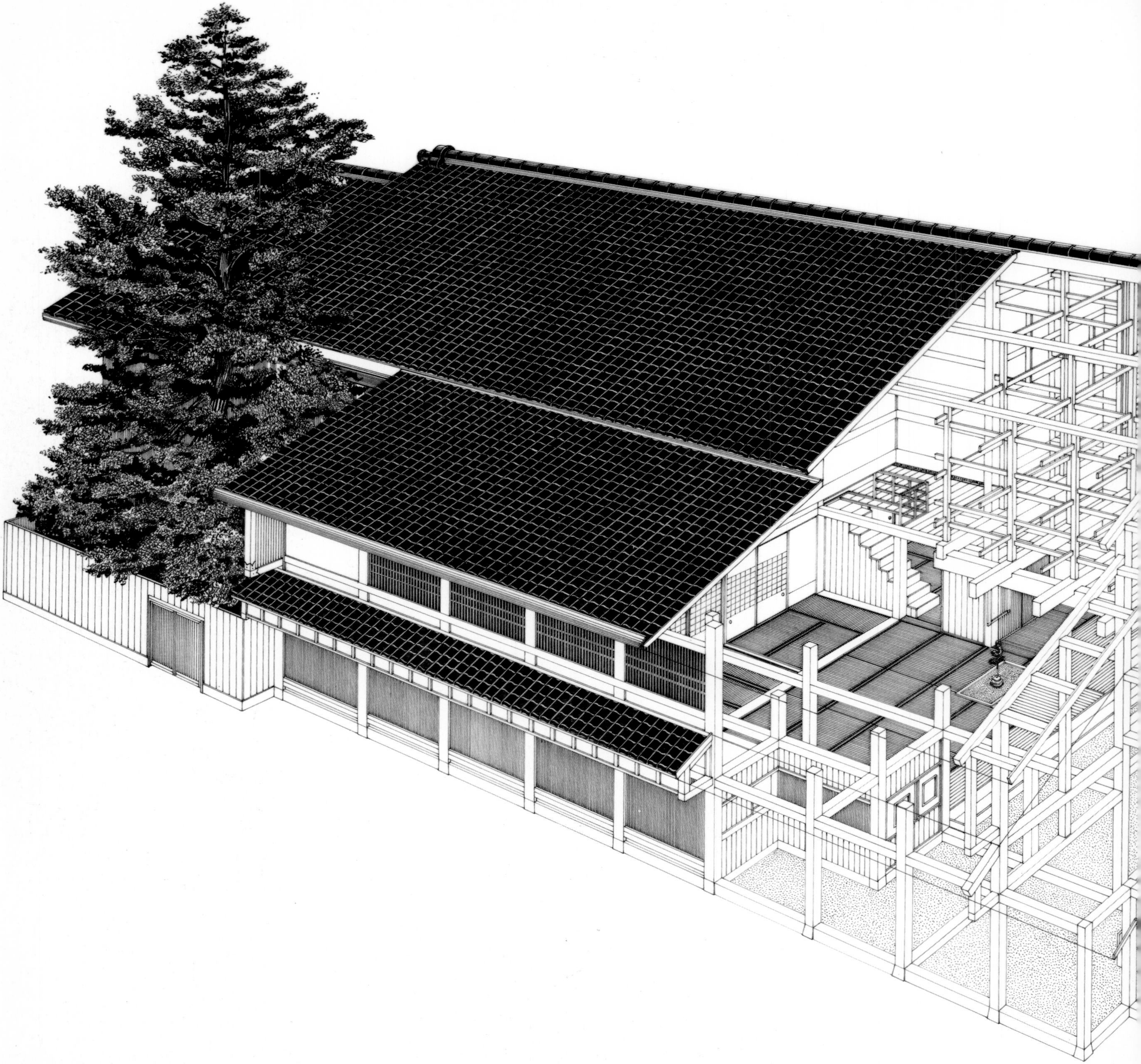

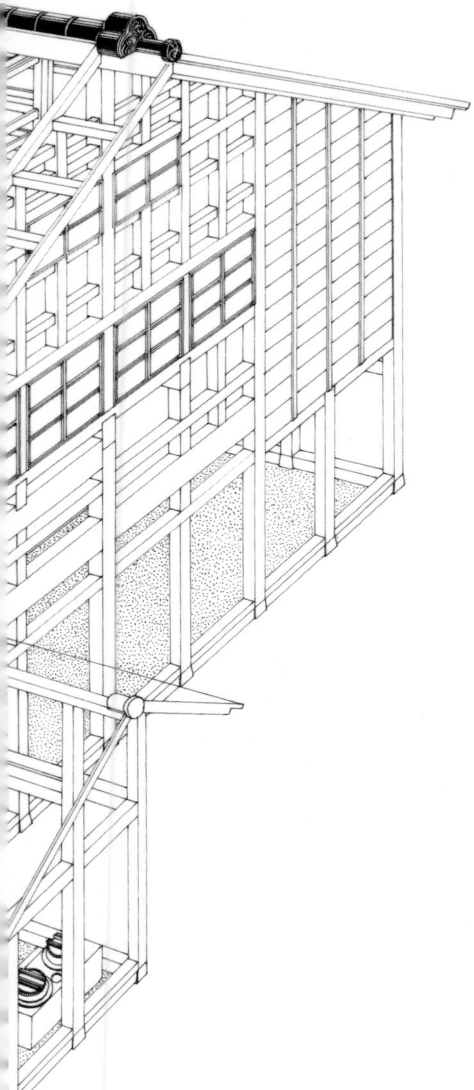

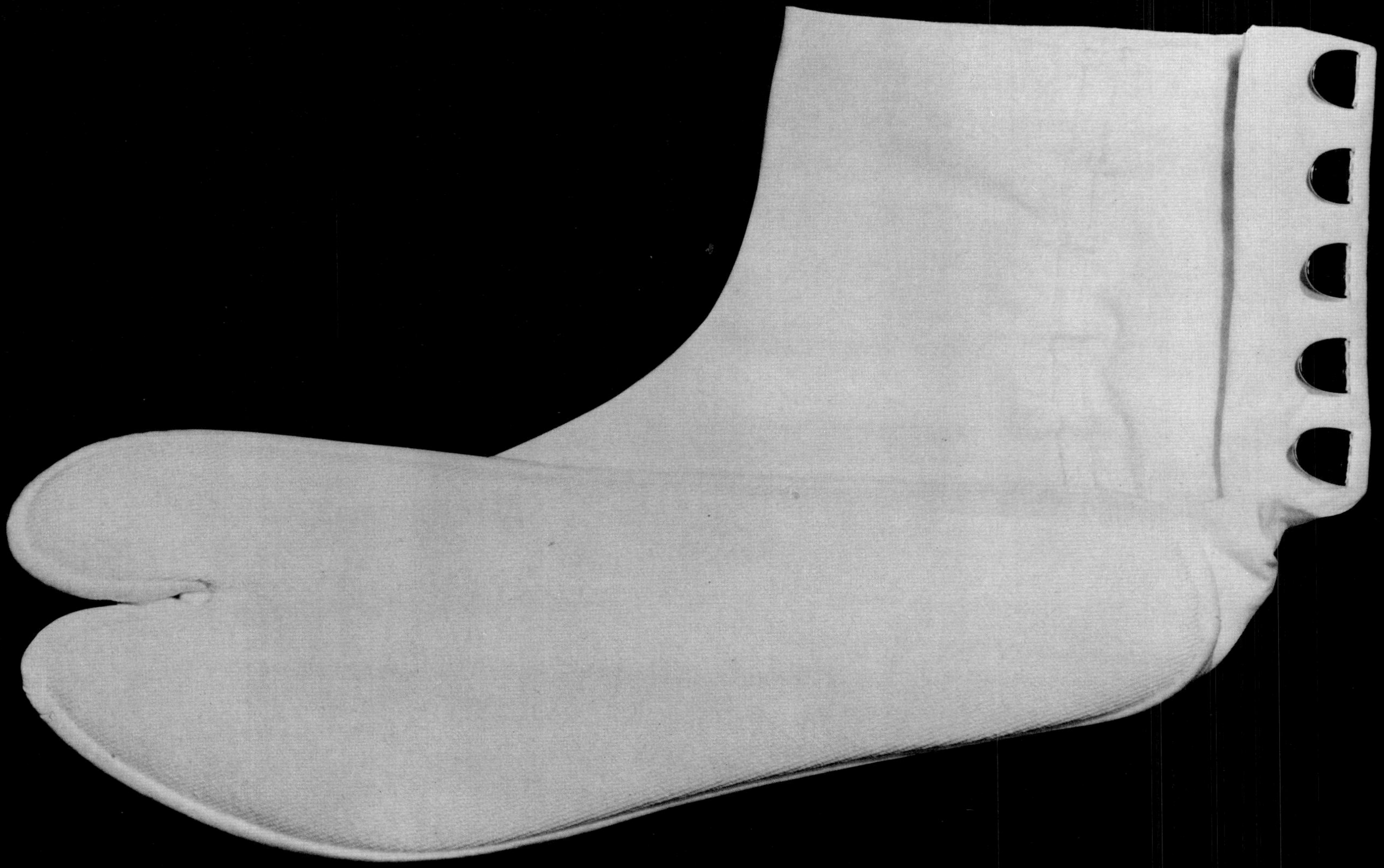

正久
正久
正久

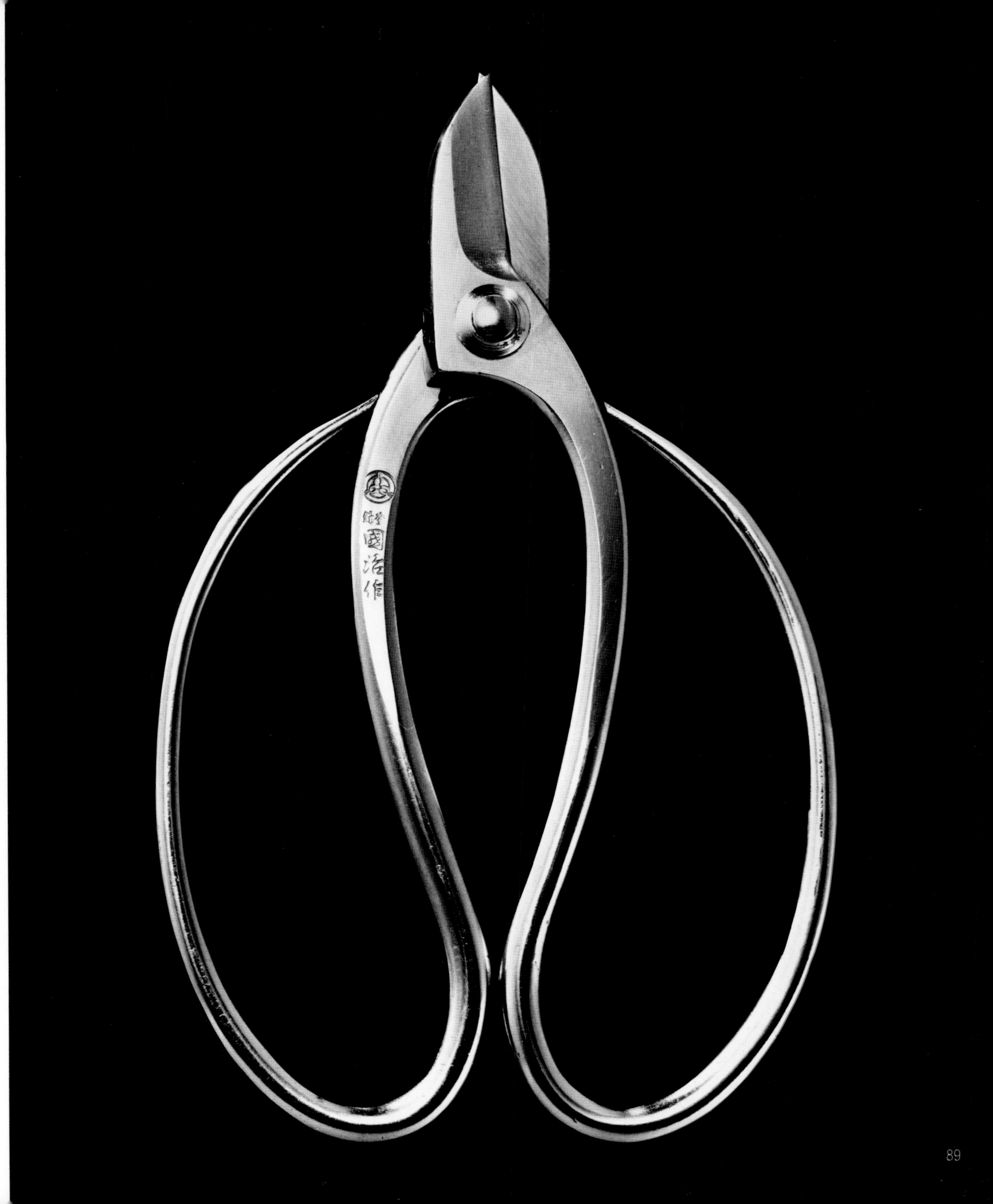

COMPACTNESS

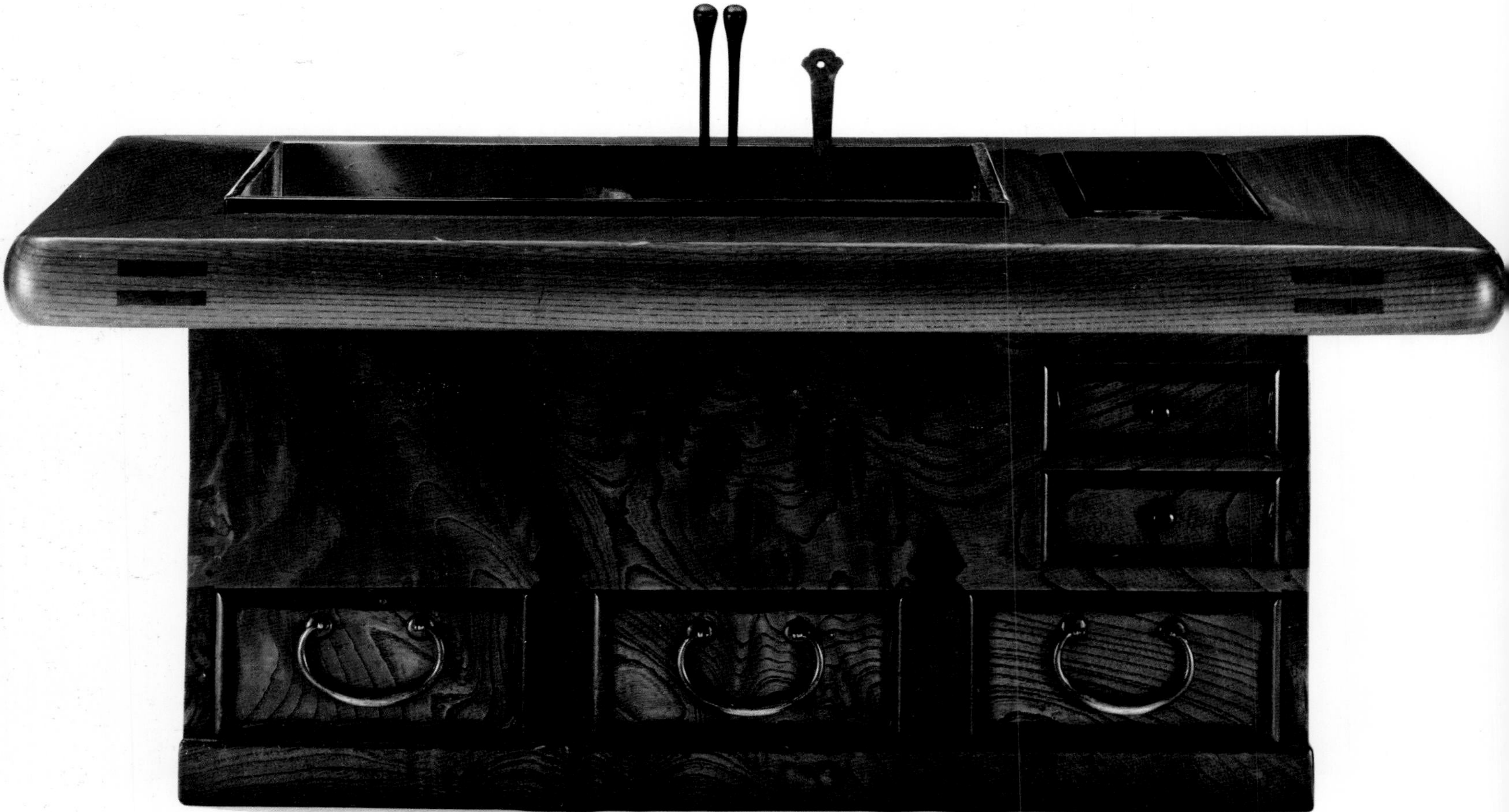

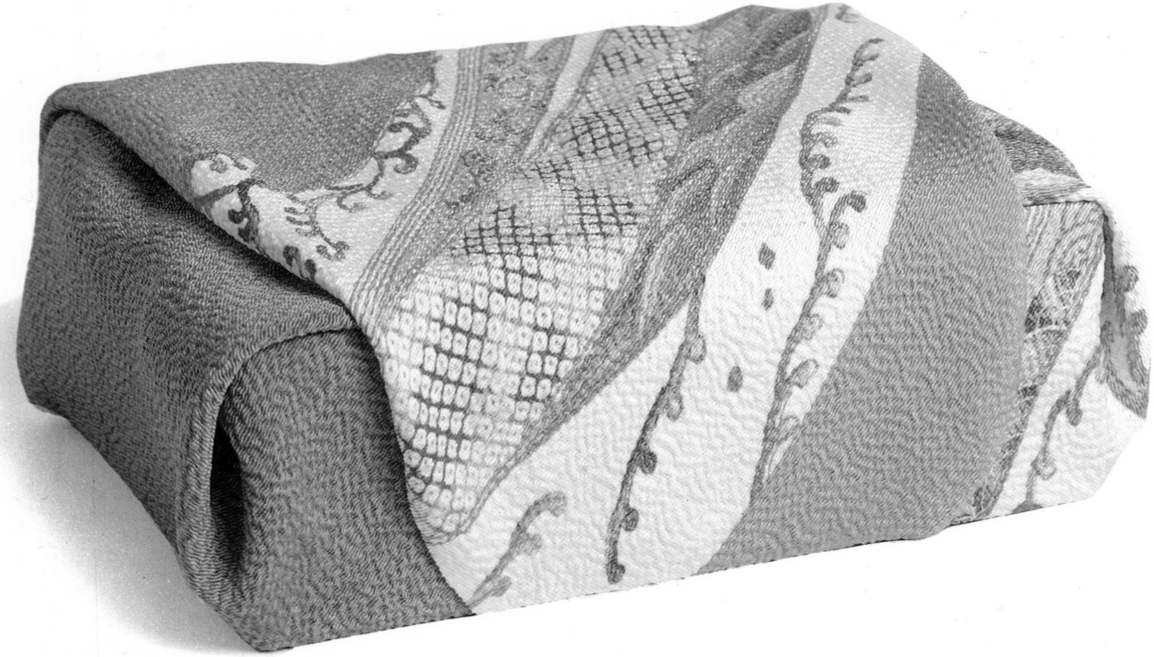

SONY
REC
REVIEW
CUE
STOP/EJECT
OFF
POWER
TV/RADIO
RADIO
REC/BATT/TUNE
MIC
TV TUNE
SONY
CONTRAST
TV
SELECTOR
VHF
LOW HIGH UHF
SOLID STATE
JACKAL 300
TV-FM/AM RADIO
CASSETTE CORDER
VOLUME
MAX
MIN
TONE
HIGH
LOW
AFC/LIGHT
ON
OFF
RADIO
BAND
FM
AM
RADIO
TUNE
MHz
kHz
FM
AM
EARPHONE
MIC

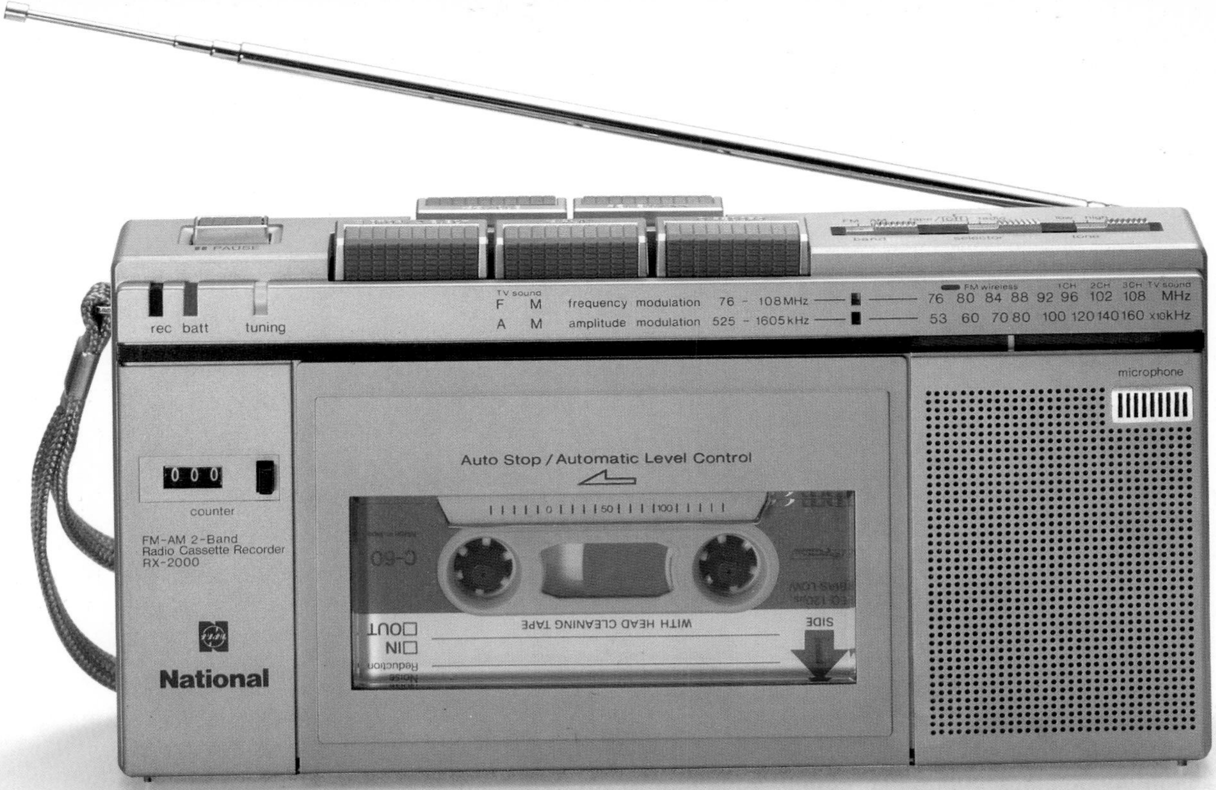
rec
batt
tuning
frequency modulation 76 - 108 MHz
amplitude modulation 525 - 1605 kHz
microphone
Auto Stop / Automatic Level Control
counter
FM-AM 2-Band
Radio Cassette Recorder
RX-2000
National

ALPHA
LETTER
FIGURE
SHIFT
SHARP
ELSI MATE EL-8160

Canon

GRAPHISM

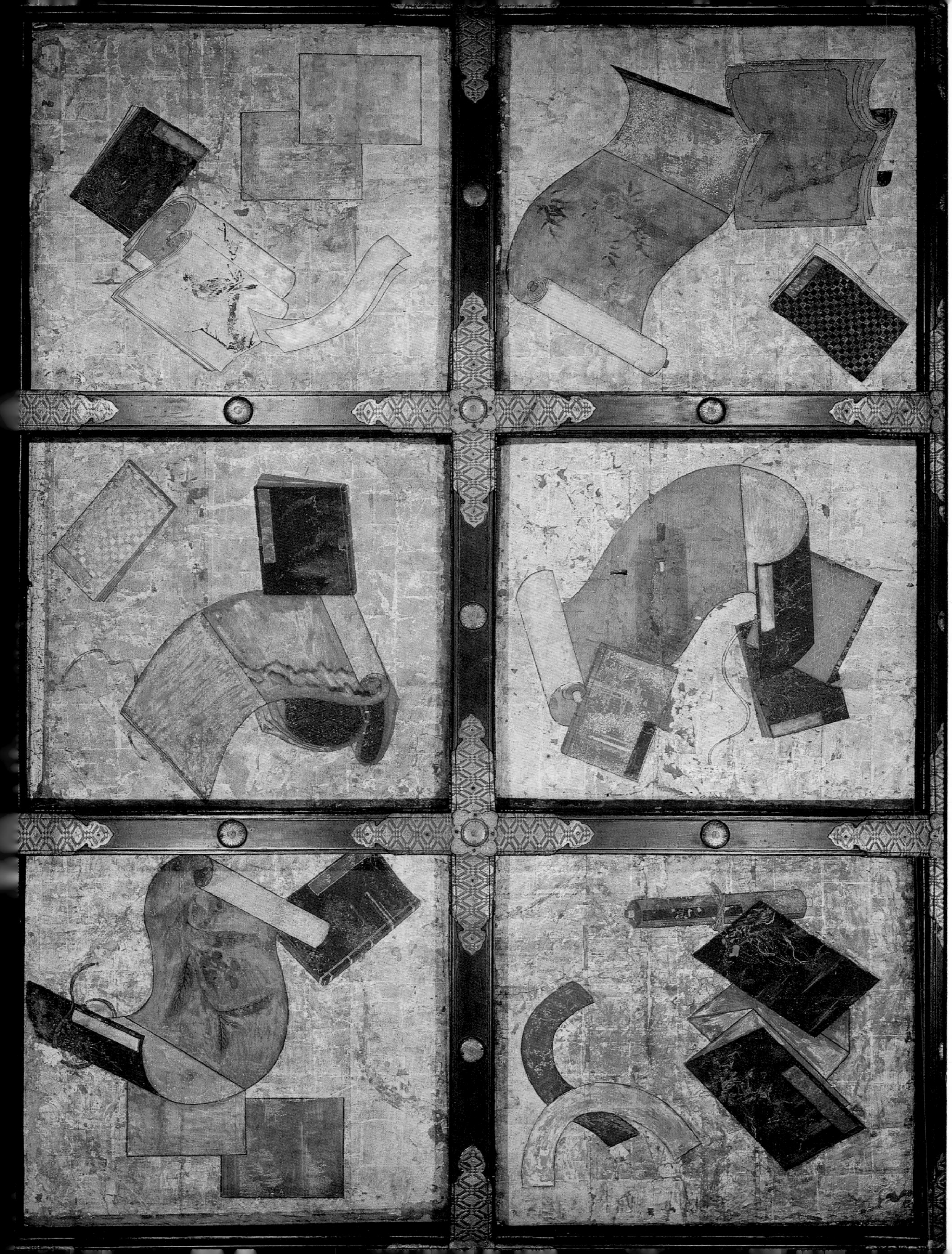

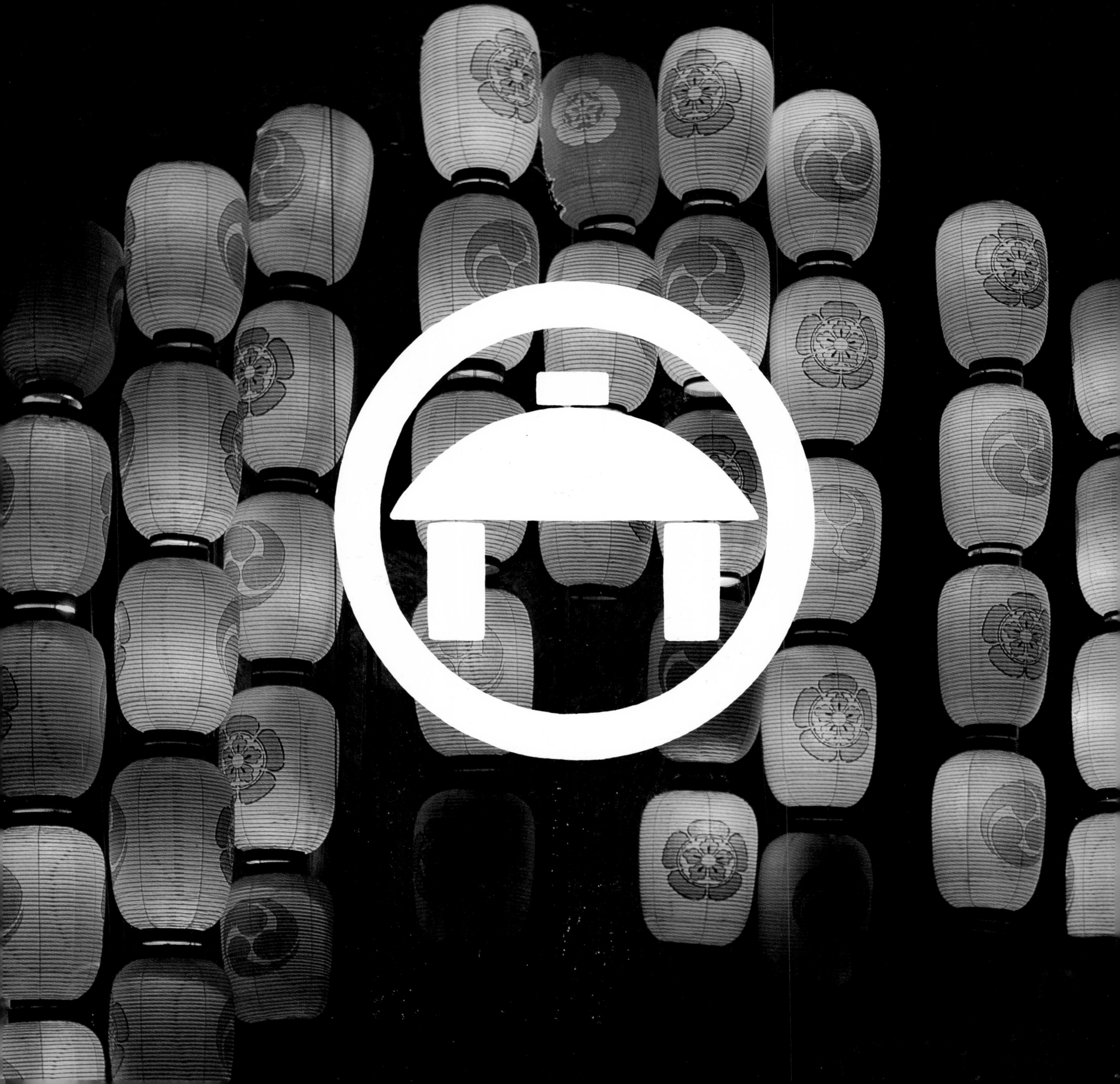

芸術院会員
中村歌右衛門

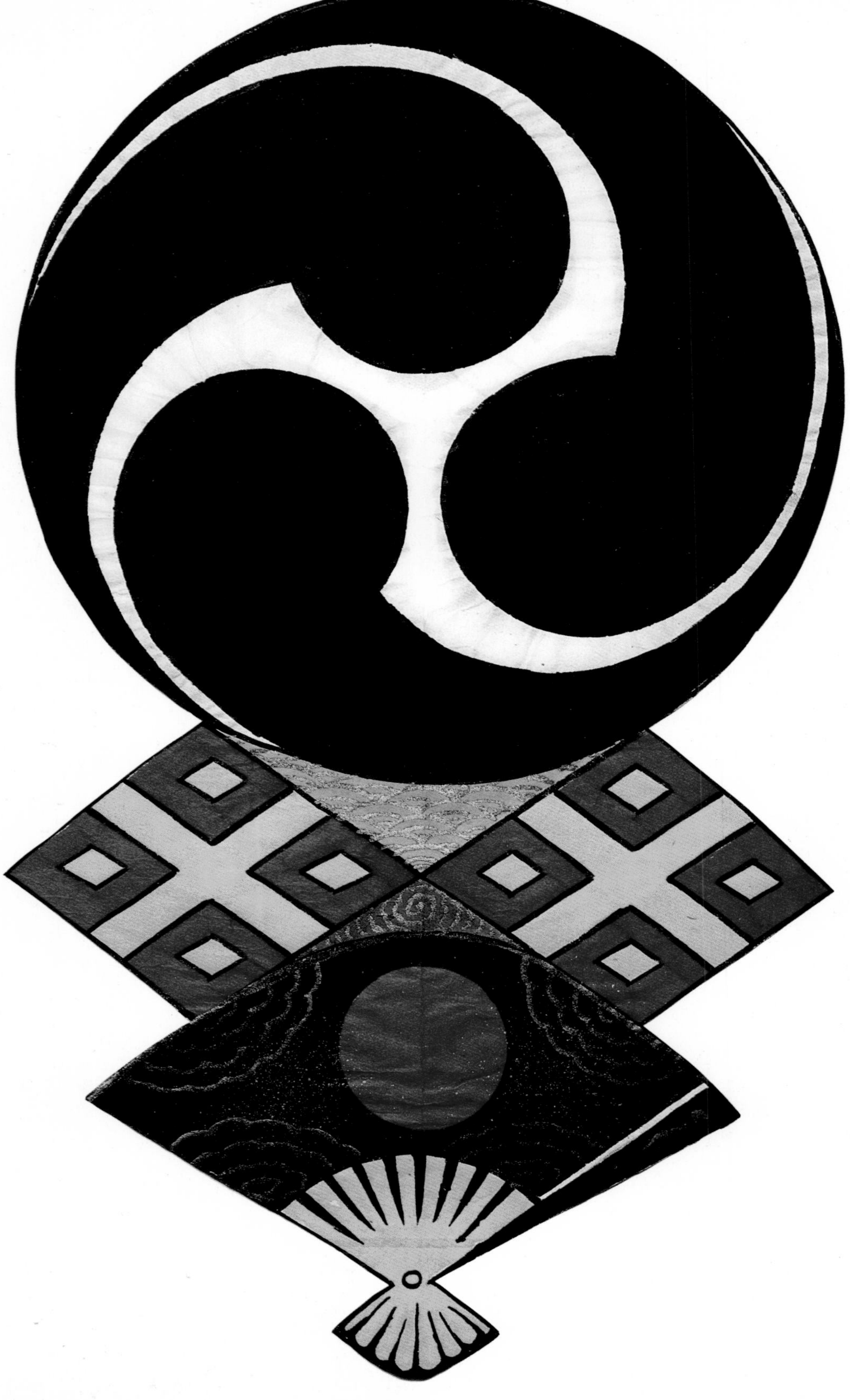

田無線電機商会

郎

任天堂

小錦八十吉
白真弓
小柳常吉
横綱

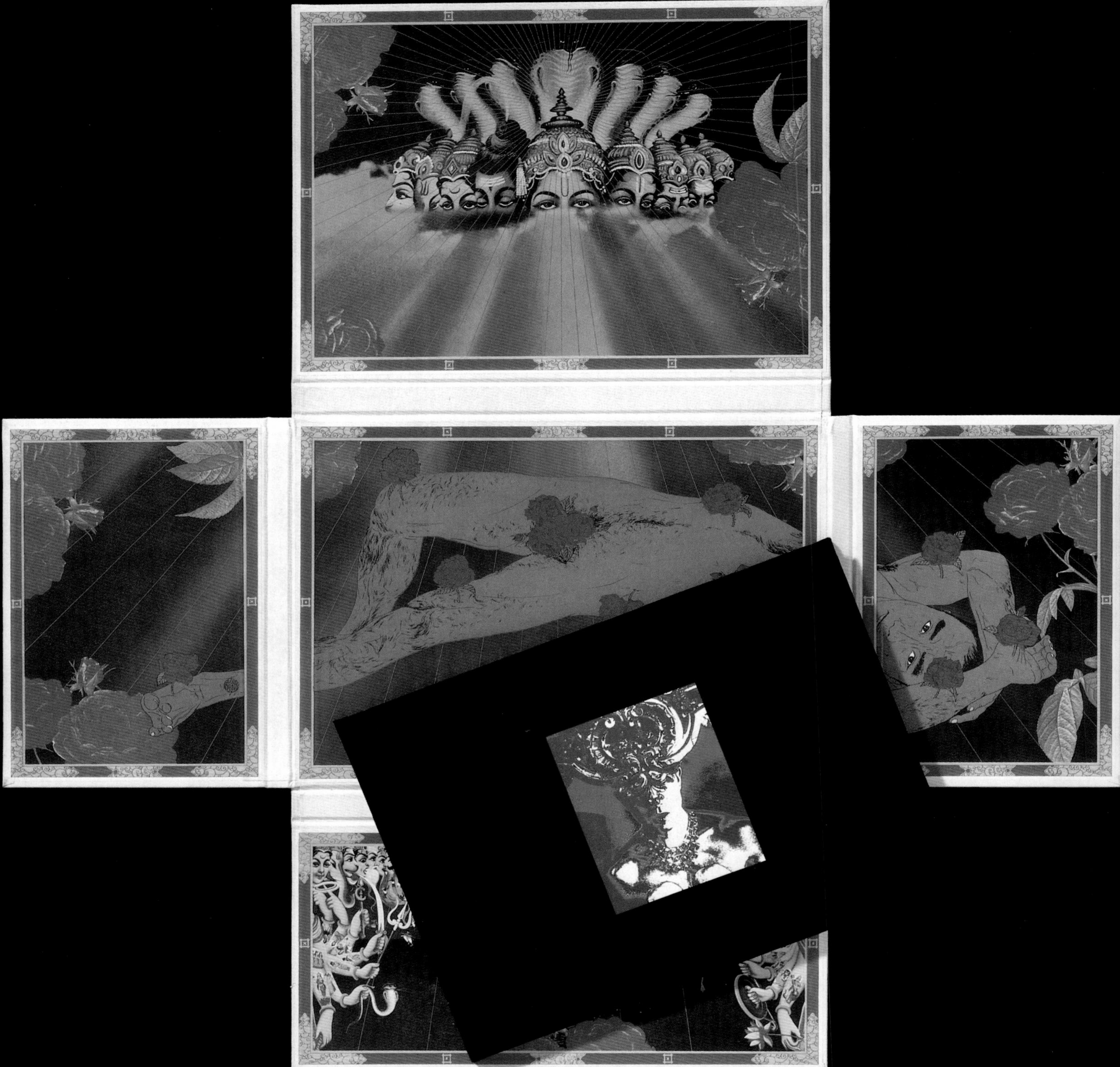

京
劇

上方芸の会
西武劇場プロデュース公演
ご案内 小沢昭一 永六輔
茂山千之丞
吉村雄輝
桂 米朝
西武劇場

mano-dharma -concert
電子の波動と即興音楽
小杉武久
マノ・ダルマ・コンサート
思念の道
虚空の理法
風
光
映像
音

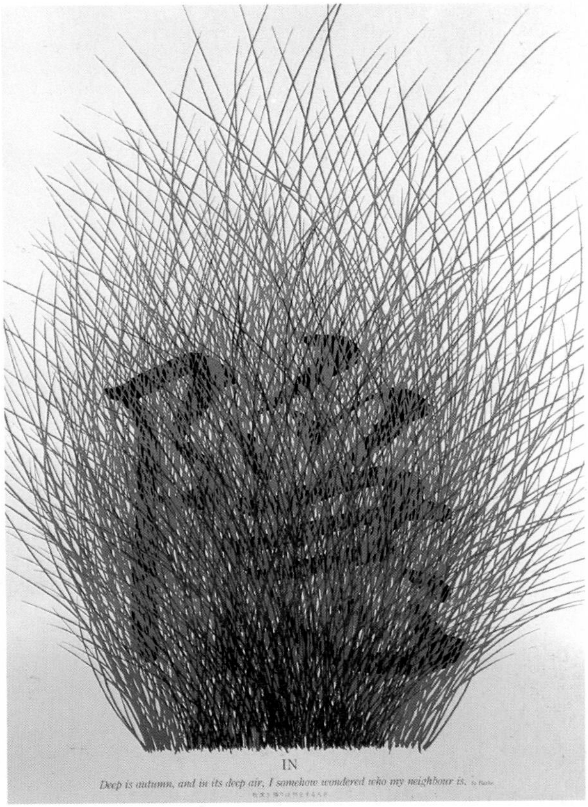

IN
Deep is autumn, and in its deep air, I somehow wondered who my neighbour is.

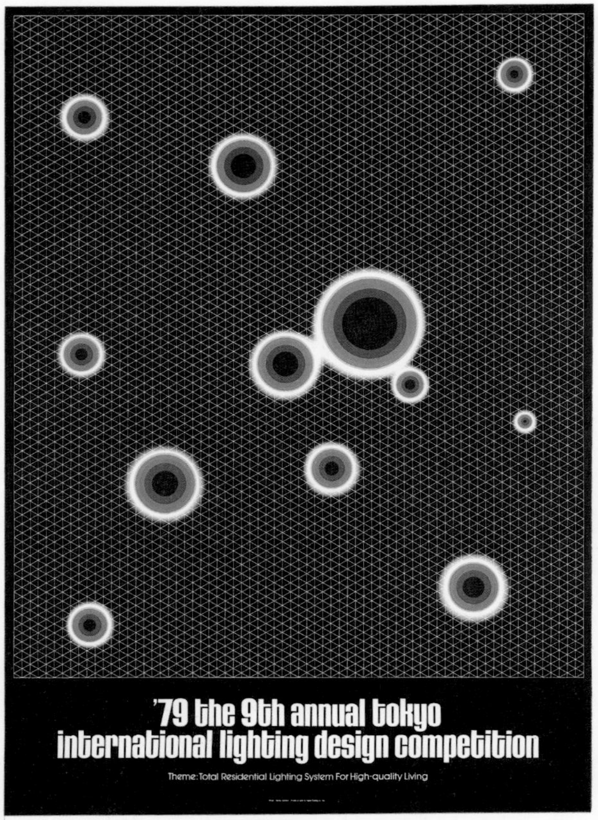
'79 the 9th annual tokyo
international lighting design competition
Theme: Total Residential Lighting System For High-quality Living

ほのかな香りほど悩ましい。資生堂練香水[舞]
2,500円

JIDC 3rd
第3回日本インダストリアルデザイン会議
3rd Japan Industrial Design Conference
1977年デザイン振興月間協賛事業
サブテーマ・共生をもとめて
1977年11月17日[木]・18日[金]
場所——東京平河町日本海運倶楽部
balance

GLOBAL EYE '78
3月3日(金)—3月8日(水) 会場 銀座松屋8階催場 主催 日本デザインコミッティー
7 NEW DESIGN POWERS・ニューデザインパワー7

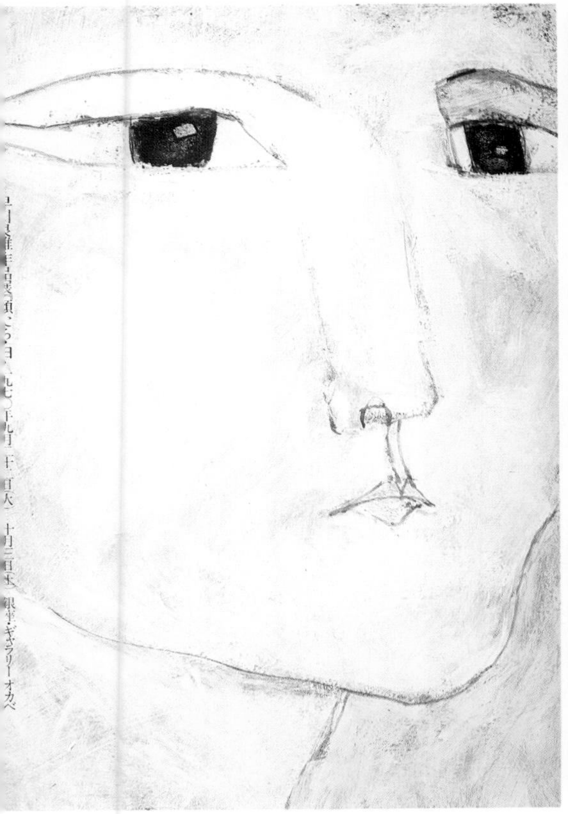

浅草夜楽「仁丹塔奇譚」

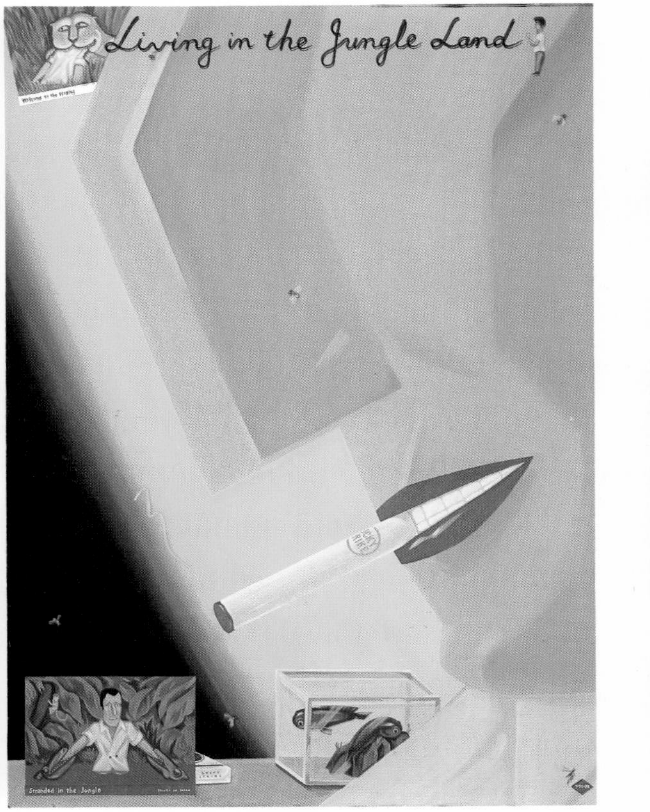
Living in the Jungle Land
Stranded in the Jungle

THE GINZA
SHISEIDO BOUTIQUE
ほんとに猫はよく眠る。
ネ・コラージュ
1977年11月4日[金]～13日[日]・水曜日定休
銀座7丁目角・資生堂ザ・ギンザ5階ホール
Né Collage 山城隆一個展

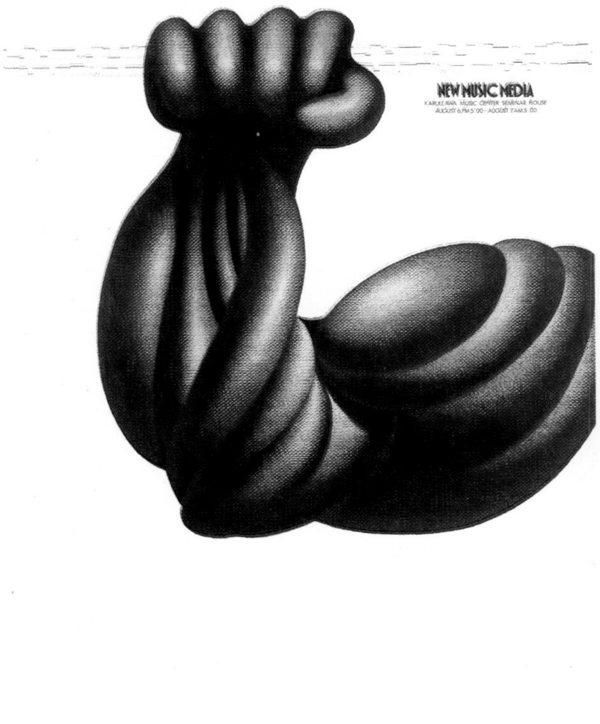
NEW MUSIC MEDIA
KARUIZAWA MUSIC CENTER SEMINAR HOUSE
AUGUST 6,PM 5:00—AUGUST 7,AM 5:00

HAVE YOU HIT HIM?
MANNS WINES

VITALITY

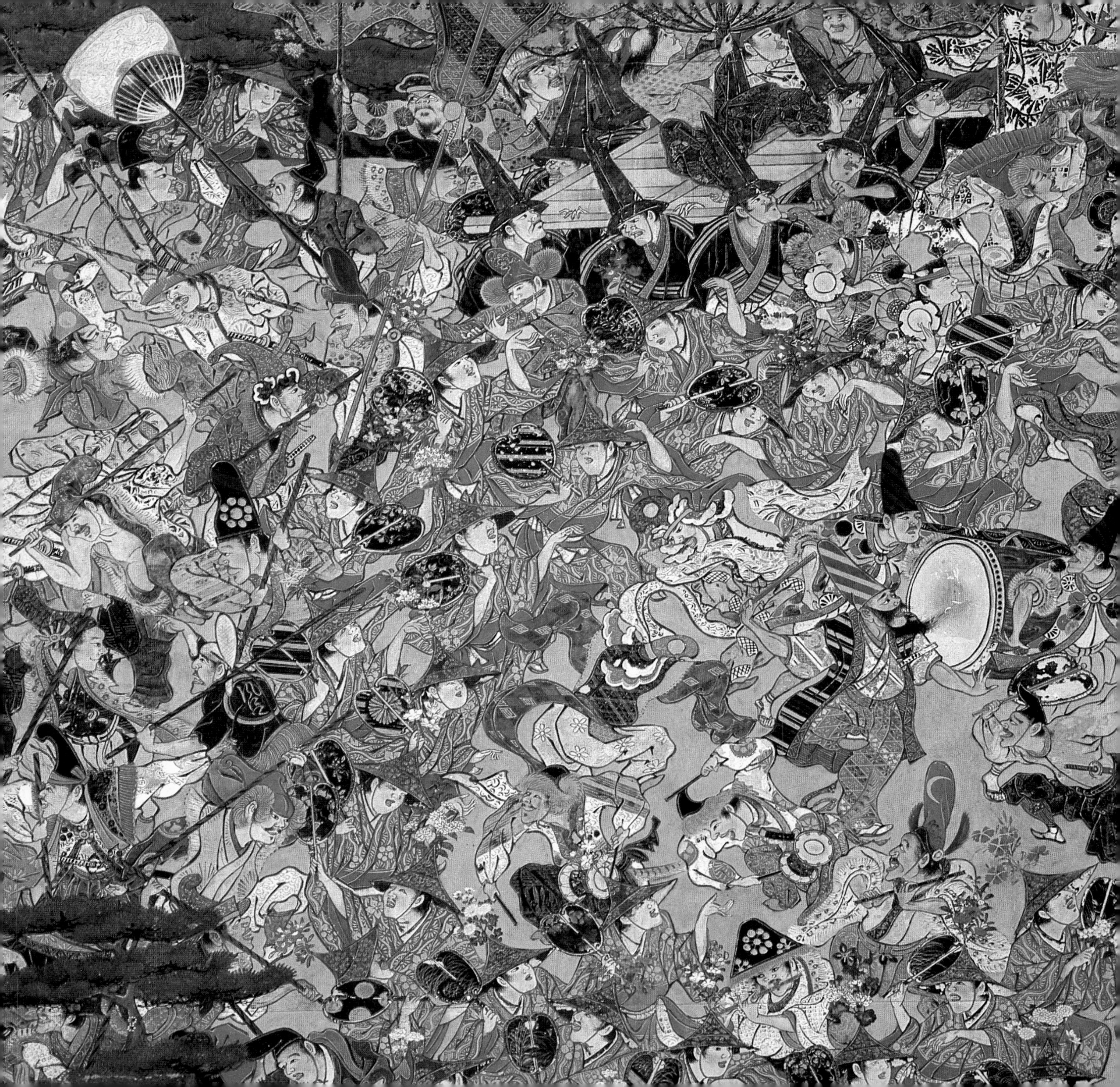

ブラック
L·Q
佳江
天狗
椿
ポパイ
MIZUTANI
レイスポット
ジュリアス
シーザー
明治チーズサロン
SUNTORY BRICK
PHILIPPE
銀座会
銀座ピアースビル
銀座
渡邊ビル
優
檜
阿凡
ちこ
三田

IDOL
DS
Vanguard
IDOL

サービス
¥300
住宅新報
勝馬
公共住宅
女郎くも
昭和大相撲史
HUSTLER
JACKER
POPEYE
SAISON
女性セブン
週刊小説
婦人公論
エコノミスト
小説新潮
ダイヤモンド
月刊小説
サンケイ
特選中古車
OARトップ
現代
近代麻雀
スーパーコミック
週刊平凡
微笑
週刊現代
ヤングレディ

狼
YATABE
YATABE RS
PEATER

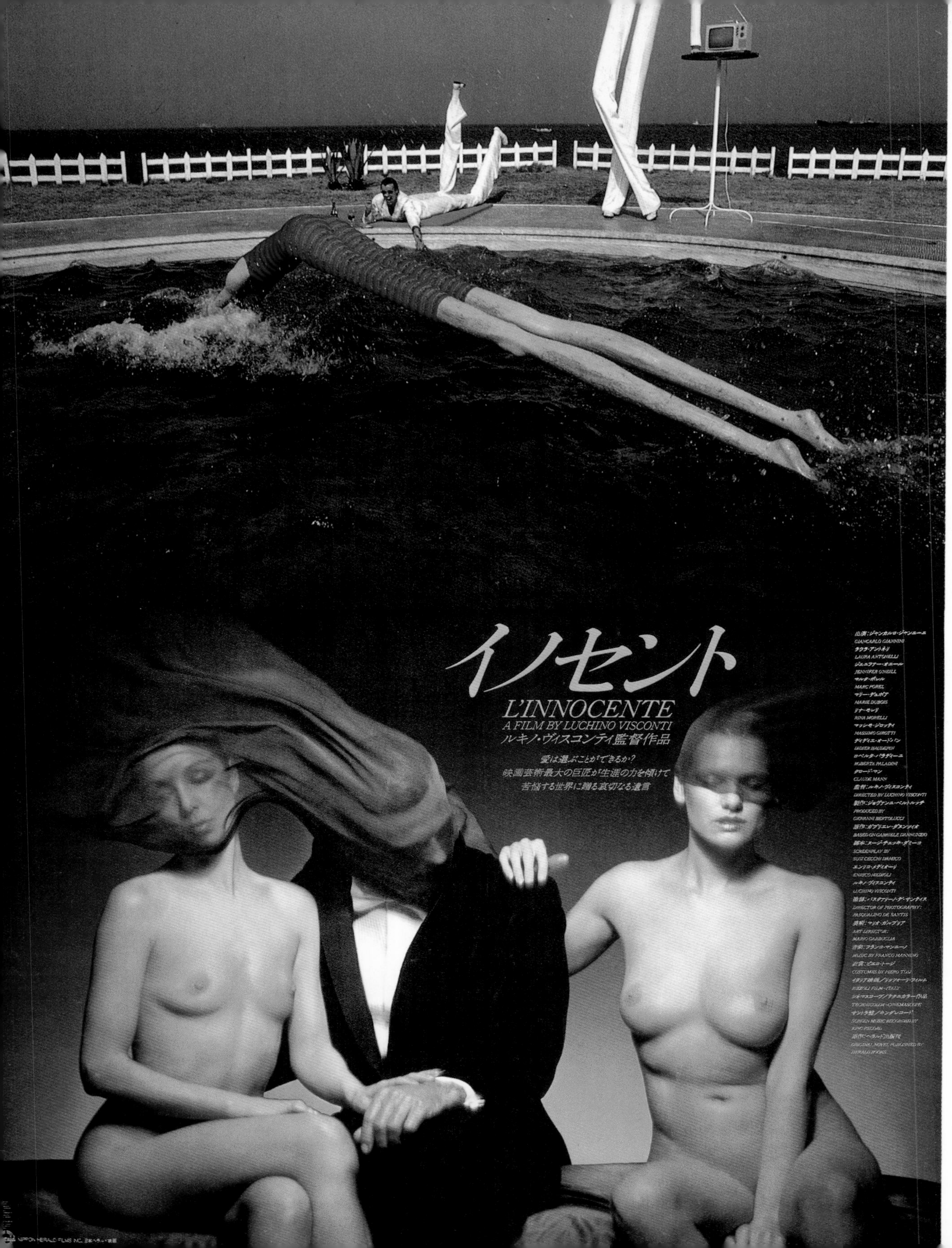
イノセント
L'INNOCENTE
A FILM BY LUCHINO VISCONTI
ルキノ・ヴィスコンティ監督作品
愛は選ぶことができるか？
映画芸術最大の巨匠が生涯の力を傾けて
苦悩する世界に贈る哀切なる遺言
出演：ジャンカルロ・ジャンニーニ
GIANCARLO GIANNINI
ラウラ・アントネリ
LAURA ANTONELLI
ジェニファー・オニール
JENNIFER O'NEILL
マルク・ポレル
MARC POREL
マリー・デュボア
MARIE DUBOIS
リナ・モレリ
RINA MORELLI
マッシモ・ジロッティ
MASSIMO GIROTTI
ディディエ・オードパン
DIDIER HAUDEPIN
ロベルタ・パラディーニ
ROBERTA PALADINI
クロード・マン
CLAUDE MANN
監督：ルキノ・ヴィスコンティ
DIRECTED BY LUCHINO VISCONTI
製作：ジョヴァンニ・ベルトルッチ
PRODUCED BY
GIOVANNI BERTOLUCCI
原作：ガブリエレ・ダヌンツィオ
BASED ON GABRIELE D'ANNUNZIO
脚本：スーゾ・チェッキ・ダミーコ
SCREENPLAY BY
SUSI CECCHI D'AMICO
エンリコ・メディオーリ
ENRICO MEDIOLI
ルキノ・ヴィスコンティ
LUCHINO VISCONTI
撮影：パスクァリーノ・デ・サンティス
DIRECTOR OF PHOTOGRAPHY:
PASQUALINO DE SANTIS
美術：マリオ・ガルブリア
ART DIRECTOR:
MARIO GARBUGLIA
音楽：フランコ・マンニーノ
MUSIC BY FRANCO MANNINO
衣裳：ピエロ・トージ
COSTUMES BY PIERO TOSI
イタリア映画／リッツォーリ・フィルム
RIZZOLI FILM - ITALY
シネマスコープ／テクニカラー作品
TECHNICOLOR - CINEMASCOPE
サントラ盤／キングレコード
SCREEN MUSIC RECORDED BY
KING RECORD
原作：ヘラルド出版刊
ORIGINAL NOVEL PUBLISHED BY
HERALD BOOKS
NIPPON HERALD FILMS INC.

HITACHI 新キドスカープ
Victor 純白カラー SONY プラストリニ

TODAY

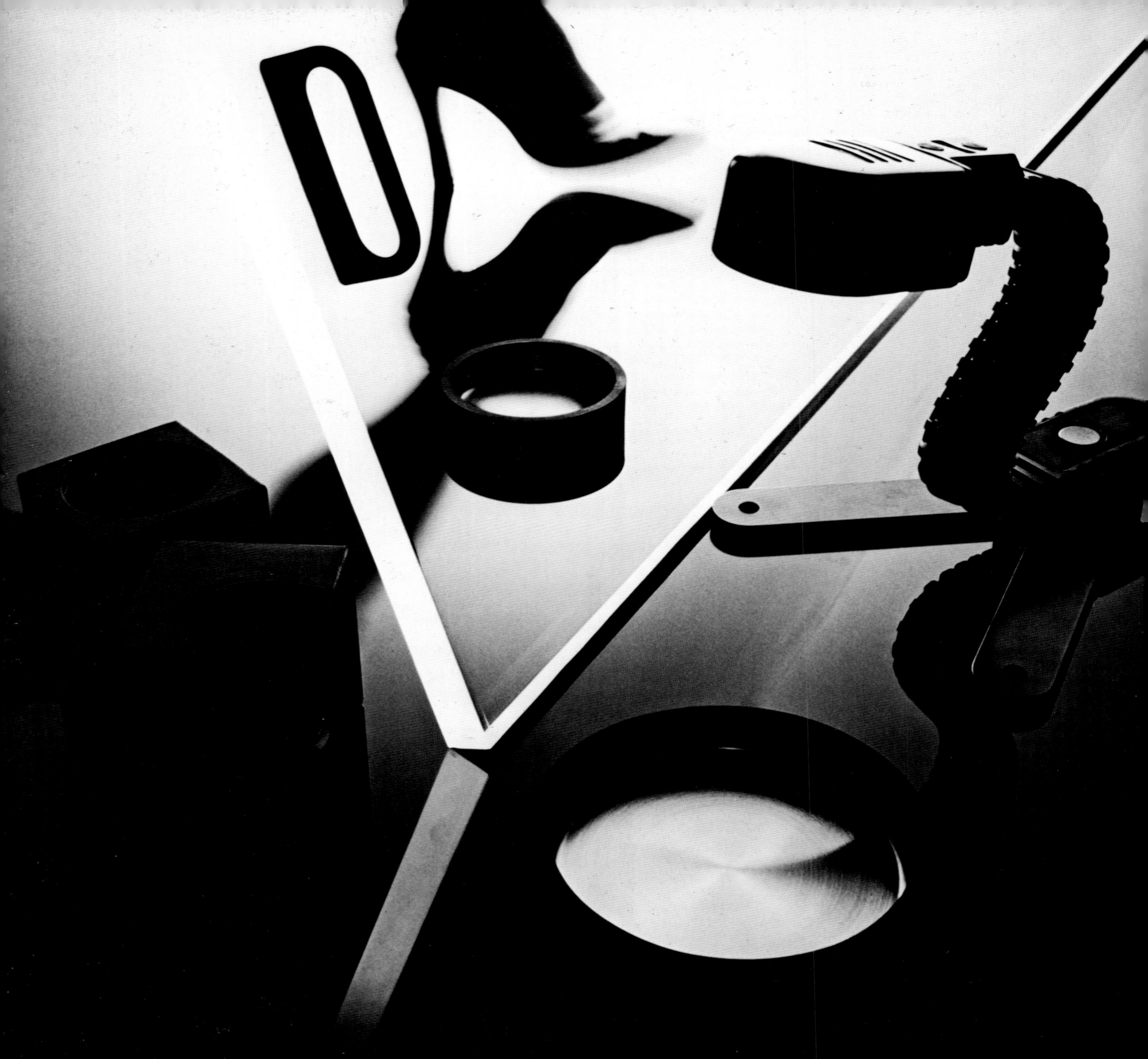

Captions

Cover. *Kumade*, decorative ''rake'' bought at the Otori Festival to ensure financial success for the coming year. Costume by Issey Miyake. (photo: Bishin Jūmonji).

pp. 34–35. Morning on the Japan Sea coast. (photo: Takeji Iwamiya)

pp. 36–37. *Ukiyo-e* print by Andō Hiroshige (1797–1858), ''Suhara'', the fortieth station, from ''The Sixty-nine Stations on the Kisokaidō''. Travellers seek shelter and bearers scurry from a sudden squall.

p. 38. Two beliefs—Buddhism and Shinto—exist together in Japan. On New Year's Eve, Buddhist temple bells ring out; on New Year's Day, people visit Shinto shrines.

The *shimenawa* of the Izumo Grand Shrine, Shimane Prefecture. Such straw *shimenawa* mark off the most sacred parts of shrines. (photo: Yasuhiro Ishimoto)

p. 39. Hana-e ritual at Yakushi-ji temple, Nara. This ritual combines worship of the Buddha with a welcome to spring. (photo: Ken Domon)

p. 40. Cherry blossoms, the symbol of spring, at Kyoto's Tenryū-ji temple. (photo: Takeji Iwamiya)

p. 41. Autumn maples at Kongōrin-ji temple, Shiga Prefecture. (photo: Naomi Maki)

p. 42. Girls in kimono at a graduation party. Nowadays such bright attire is worn only on formal, celebratory occasions. (photo: Gorō Iwaoka)

p. 43. The naked festival held in winter at Kōnomiya shrine, Aichi Prefecture. Cold and bare bodies in energetic competition purge the year's evil from the men of this parish. (photo: Yoshimasa Watanabe)

p. 44. *Okame* mask. The *okame* figure is a complex of feminine beauty, humour, sex and folk religion. (photo: Takeji Iwamiya)

p. 46. Earthenware pot (*yukihira*) for making rice gruel. (photo: Takeji Iwamiya)

p. 47. Potter at work. (photo: Kidō Ushio)

p. 48. Rain cape (*mino*). Such capes made from reeds, rushes, grasses and straw were used by farmers, fishermen and mountain people. (photo: Takeji Iwamiya)

p. 49. Willow basketwork trunk. (photo: Takeji Iwamiya)

p. 50. Bamboo basket. Bamboo was one of the most important materials for making containers for everyday use. (photo: Yōichi Yamazaki)

p. 51. Bamboo fencing on top of a stone wall, Daitoku-ji temple, Kyoto. (photo: Takeji Iwamiya)

p. 52. Cedars cover the slopes of the hills north of Kyoto. The trunks are trimmed to prevent the formation of knots in the wood. (photo: Takeji Iwamiya)

p. 53. Wooden container for cooked rice. (photo: Takeji Iwamiya)

p. 54. Lacquer tray and service setting. (photo: Takeji Iwamiya)

p. 55. Applying gold decoration on lacquer, Aizu, Fukushima Prefecture. (photo: Hidekichi Kanekawa)

p. 56. Iron kettle for boiling water, from the Nambu area, Iwate Prefecture. (photo: Yōichi Yamazaki)

p. 57. Stone basin in the form of an old coin, Ryōan-ji temple, Kyoto. (photo: Takeji Iwamiya)

p. 58. Indigo-dyed cotton in *e-gasuri* technique (threads dyed prior to weaving). (photo: Kidō Ushio)

p. 59. Washing the resist paste from dyed silk textiles, Kanazawa, Ishikawa Prefecture. (photo: Kidō Ushio)

p. 60. Paper-cord decorations (*mizuhiki*) and envelopes used for formal gifts. (photo: Takeji Iwamiya)

p. 62. Lacquer inkstone box, gold decoration and inlay, by Ogata Kōrin (1658–1716), entitled ''Yatsuhashi''. The motifs on the box are drawn from an episode in the *Tales of Ise*, a 10th-century romance. (collection: Tokyo National Museum)

p. 63. Fan-painting, showing a scene from *The Tale of Genji*, 17th century.

pp. 64–65 top. Lacquer bowls with designs of pine (winter) and plum (spring). (photo: Kidō Ushio)

pp. 64–65 bottom. Lacquer tea-caddies with designs of willow (summer) and pampas grass, bush-clover and chrysanthemum (autumn). (photo: Kidō Ushio)

p. 66. Nō drama dance fan *(chūkei)*. (photo: Ikkō Narahara)

p. 67. Calligraphy from the original manuscript of *The Thirty-six Poetic Geniuses* (ca. 11th century). (collection: Nishi Hongan-ji temple, Kyoto)

p. 68. The autumn full moon is the time for the moon-viewing ritual. (photo: Takashi Hatakeyama)

p. 69. Sword-guards (*tsuba*). (photos: Tsuneo Suzuki)

pp. 70–71. Dried sweets (*higashi*), whose shapes and decoration symbolize the four seasons. (photo: Taku Aramasa)

p. 71. Sweets (*namagashi*) in the form of cherry blossom (spring) and ginkgo leaf (autumn). (photo: Takashi Hatakeyama)

p. 72. Bamboo screen, Kitamura residence, Kyoto. (photo: Yukio Futagawa)

p. 73. Paper-cord decoration (*mizuhiki*) in butterfly form. See also p. 60. (photo: Takeji Iwamiya)

p. 74. *Yūzen* textile—tie-dyed and hand-painted silk. (photo: Takeji Iwamiya)

p. 75. Evening dress by Hanae Mori. (photo: HIRO)

P. 76. Wall lantern, Kyoto. (photo: Ikko Tanaka)

pp. 78–79. A town house in Kanazawa, Ishikawa Prefecture, showing the standardised unit of construction (*ken*—about six feet). (illustration: Noritsugu Oda)

p. 79 right. Kurahama-sō, a town house in Bōnotsu, Kagoshima Prefecture. (photo: Kishin Shinoyama)

p. 80. Modular construction of Japanese rooms with *tatami* mats and *fusuma* (sliding paper doors), Nagatomi residence, near Himeji, Hyōgo Prefecture. (photo: Yasuhiro Ishimoto)

p. 81. *Shōji*—sliding paper screens. (photo: Yasuhiro Ishimoto)

p. 82. Detail of *tatami* floor mats. (photo: Yukio Futagawa)

p. 83. "Akari"—lighting fixtures designed by Isamu Noguchi. (photo: Yasuhiro Ishimoto)

p. 84. Ivory *shamisen* (stringed instrument) plectrum. (photo: Yasuhiro Ishimoto)

p. 85. Boxwood combs used for the traditional women's coiffure. (photo: Yasuhiro Ishimoto)

p. 86. These "socks" *(tabi)* are a part of the traditional Japanese wardrobe. (photo: Takeji Iwamiya)

p. 87. Wooden clogs (*geta*). (photo: Takeji Iwamiya)

p. 88. Kitchen knives: from left, *sashimi* (raw fish) slicer, vegetable knife, *sashimi* slicer, fish knife. (photo: Yasuhiro Ishimoto)

p. 89. Gardener's secateurs. (photo: Yasuhiro Ishimoto)

p. 90. Garden, Daisen-in, Daitoku-ji temple, Kyoto. (photo: Yasuhiro Ishimoto)

p. 92. Lacquer lunch-boxes, mid-19th century. (photo: Naomi Maki; collection: Meiji Shrine, Tokyo)

p. 93. Meal prepared for tiered food-box. (photo: Naomi Maki)

p. 94. Individual servings of buckwheat noodles in tiered containers. (photo: Yasuhiro Ishimoto)

p. 95. Straw wrapping for eggs.

p. 96. The decoration of a Japanese room is confined to a few objects in the *tokonoma* alcove. (photo: Takeshi Nishikawa)

p. 97. The ambience of a large temple is captured in this gold-and-black lacquer household Buddhist altar. Height about six feet.

p. 98. Long brazier *(nagahibachi)* with drawers. The panel on the top right covers a recess used for warming *sake*. (photo: Takeji Iwamiya)

p. 99. Staircase chest (*kaidan-dansu*) in a town house. (photo: Kidō Ushio)

p. 100. Carrying-cloths *(furoshiki)*. (photo: Takeji Iwamiya)

p. 101. Clothing chest, paulownia wood (*kiri*), 19th century. (photo: Keizō Kaneko; collection: Furniture Museum, Tokyo)

p. 102. "49 Drawers", chest designed by Shirō Kuramata. (photo: Takayuki Ogawa)

p. 103. Mobile kitchen unit designed by Masanori Umeda.

p. 104. Sony "Jackal"—T.V.-radio-cassette tape recorder combination.

p. 105 top. National AM-FM radio-cassette tape recorder combination.

p. 105 bottom. Sharp Elsi Mate EL-8160 pocket calculator. This model displays letters of the alphabet as well as numbers.

p. 106. Interior of a Canon A-1 camera.

p. 108. Pictorial decoration in architecture: detail of the coffered ceiling of Nishi Hongan-ji temple, Kyoto.

p. 109. Old Kutani dish (17th century), phoenix design, diameter 13 1/4 inches. (photo: Ken Domon)

p. 110. *Kabuki* costume. The bold square crest of the Danjūrō line of *kabuki* actors marks the costume for *Shibaraku*, one of the "Eighteen Famous Plays" associated with Danjūrō VII (1791–1859). (photo: Chiaki Yoshida)

p. 111. Fisherman's festival coat. (collection: Shirahama Maritime Museum)

p. 112. Gion festival lanterns with crests. A traditional heraldic crest is superimposed on the photograph. (photo: Takeji Iwamiya)

p. 113. *Kabuki* theatre wooden name-posters for the *kaomise* (coming-together) performance of famous actors held in December at Kyoto's Minami-za Theatre. (photo: Takeji Iwamiya)

p. 114. Kite from Yokosuka, Shizuoka Prefecture. (photo: Takeji Iwamiya)

p. 115. Banners and flags on fishing boats usually announce an abundant catch but also celebrate the launching of a new boat. (photo: Takeji Iwamiya)

p. 116. Tattoo, an *ukiyo-e* print by Toyohara Kunichika (1835 – 1900) showing a scene from a *kabuki* play. (photo: Yutaka Seki; collection: Mitsuaki Ōwada)

p. 117. Costume by Issey Miyake with print by Tadanori Yokoo. (photo: Noriaki Yokosuka)

p. 118. *Hanafuda* playing cards decorated with motifs of the four seasons. (photo: Takeji Iwamiya)

p. 119. Stylised "aprons" worn by *sumō* wrestlers on certain ceremonial occasions. *Ukiyo-e sumō* prints by various artists. (collection: Shigeo Tomimura)

p. 120. Book and case design by Tadanori Yokoo.

p. 121. Posters.

(top left) Kōhei Sugiura. Peking Opera announcement.
(top right) Ikko Tanaka. Theatrical performance series.
(bottom left) Kiyoshi Awazu. Mano-Dharma-Concert.
(bottom right) Gan Hosoya. Morisawa Photosetting Company.

p. 122. Posters.
(top left) Yūsaku Kamekura. 9th Annual Tokyo International Lighting Design Competition.
(top right) Makoto Nakamura. Shiseidō perfume.
(bottom left) Mitsuo Katsui. 3rd Japan Industrial Design Conference.
(bottom right) Kazumasa Nagai. Seven New Design Powers.

p. 123. Posters.
(top left) Yoshio Hayakawa. "Faces in White" (announcement of his own exhibition).
(top centre) K^2 (Keisuke Nagatomo and Seitarō Kuroda). Theatre poster.
(top right) Yōsuke Kawamura. "Living in the Jungle Land".
(bottom left) Ryūichi Yamashiro. "Né Collage" (announcement of his own exhibition).
(bottom centre) Takahisa Kamijō. New Music Media concert.
(bottom right) Harumi Yamaguchi. Mann's Wines.

p. 124. Textile design by Hiroshi Awatsuji. (photo: Mitsumasa Fujitsuka)

p. 126. Screen-painting of a festival commemorating the warlord Toyotomi Hideyoshi, early 17th century. (collection: Tokugawa Reimeikai Foundation)

p. 127. The hero mounts an immense fire-breathing toad and displays his magic power. Scene from the *kabuki* play *Tenjiku Tokubei Ikoku Banashi*. (photo: Keizō Kaneko)

p. 128. Plastic toy masks, mainly of popular television cartoon figures, are seen at every festival. (photo: Taishi Hirokawa)

p. 129. Papier-mâché Daruma dolls. One eye is painted in when a wish is made, the other when the wish is fulfilled. (photo: Kidō Ushio)

p. 130. Bicycles parked near a suburban commuter train station. (photo: Haruo Tomiyama)

p. 131. Restaurants advertise their menus by displaying realistic plastic food models. (photo: Haruo Tomiyama)

p. 132. Illuminated signs bombard the senses in Japan's cities. (photo: Haruo Tomiyama)

p. 133. For the bored player of *pachinko*, Japan's version of pinball, some *pachinko* parlours installed mini-televisions in the centre of the machines. (photo: Taishi Hirokawa)

p. 134. Weekly magazines are the most widely read publications besides newspapers; the number of such weeklies is always on the increase. (photo: Haruo Tomiyama)

p. 135. Comic books have come to capture the time and money of a large part of the Japanese population. (cartoonist: Satoshi Ikezawa)

p. 136 top. Magazine advertisement for a black-and-white television set.
Art directors: Masaharu Higashizawa,
Yōzō Nakamori
Photography: Bishin Jūmonji

p. 136 bottom. Poster for the film *L'Innocente*.
Art director: Eiko Ishioka
Photography: Kazumi Kurigami

p. 137. Photograph from a fashion magazine.
Art director: Katsumi Asaba
Photography: Eiichirō Sakata

p. 138. Display of television sets for sale. (photo: Haruo Tomiyama)

p. 140. Moving sculpture by Takamichi Itō. (photo: Yoshio Shiratori)

p. 141. "Solaris Drawers", chest designed by Shirō Kuramata. (photo: Mitsumasa Fujitsuka)

p. 142. Butterfly stool designed by Sōri Yanagi.

p. 143. "Saturno", lighting fixture designed by Kazuo Motozawa. (photo: Mitsumasa Fujitsuka)

p. 144. "Cobra", rubber desk lamp designed by Masayuki Kurokawa. (photo: Shinichirō Shishido)

p. 145. Porcelain water-pitcher and ice-bucket designed by Masahiro Mori.

p. 146. Porcelain vase designed by Makoto Komatsu. (photo: Mitsumasa Fujitsuka)

p. 147. "Edge Lamp", lighting fixture designed by Minami Tada. (photo: Shigeyoshi Nobori)

p. 148. "Bird Tree", wooden toy designed by Shigeo Fukuda.

Photo Credits:
p. 63. Kōrinsha Publishing Co.
p. 70. Bunka Publishing Bureau
p. 80. Kajima Institute Publishing Co.
p. 95. John Weatherhill, Inc.
p. 97. Wakabayashi Butsugu Seisakujo
p. 104. Sony Corporation
p. 105. Matsushita Electric Industrial Co.
p. 105. Sharp Corporation
p. 106. Canon Inc.
p. 110. Shochiku Co.
p. 135. Shūeisha Publishing Co.
p. 137. Fashion News

Note: Names of all pre-modern Japanese are given in Japanese order, surname first; those of all modern Japanese, in Western order.

Catalogue design:——Ken'ichi Samura
Editorial supervision:–Ikko Tanaka Design Studio
Kayoko Takagi
J. V. Earle
Machiko Moriyasu
Translation:———J. V. Earle